John Carey is Merton Professor of English at Oxford University. He is a distinguished critic, reviewer and broadcaster, and the author of many acclaimed books, including *The Intellectuals and the Masses* and, most recently, *Pure Pleasure: A Guide to the Twentieth Century's most Enjoyable Books*. He is also the editor of *The Faber Book of Science* and *The Faber Book of Utopias*.

Praise for *The Faber Book of Science*:

'This excellent anthology of science writing captures the flavour of modern science through many illustrious epochs . . . Carey's collection crystallises the essence of great science – the awe of discovery, the emotions stirred by breakthroughs and the intellectual brilliance of those who have shaped our understanding of the world.' *The Times*

'Everything an anthology should be; it is entertaining, stimulating and occasionally startling. Carey's reading is prodigious, and even the more familiar of his choices are illuminated by commentaries that crackle with literary and indeed scientific insights.' *Nature*

Praise for *The Faber Book of Utopias*:

'An excellent book . . . John Carey has gathered together a vast range of texts from Ancient Egypt to modern California, the authors of which, in different ways, attempt to describe a better world than our own.' *Alain de Botton, Daily Telegraph*

'John Carey shimmers Jeeves-like – courteous, unflappable and discreet – through the most lurid and improbable of imaginary worlds. This is a fascinating anthology.' *Sunday Telegraph*

Praise for *The Intellectuals and the Masses*:

'A brilliant new study . . . There are many thrilling moments in John Carey's excoriating study of intellectual snobbery.' Laura Cumming, *Literary Review*

'This polemic against highbrows can the more easily be swallowed, indeed savoured, because it was written by a highbrow . . . Carey is acknowledged to wield one of the sharpest, most entertaining pens in town.' Ian Hamilton, *London Review of Books*

also by John Carey

THE VIOLENT EFFIGY: A STUDY OF
DICKENS' IMAGINATION

THACKERAY: PRODIGAL GENIUS

JOHN DONNE: LIFE, MIND AND ART

WILLIAM GOLDING, THE MAN AND HIS BOOKS (ED.)

ORIGINAL COPY

THE INTELLECTUALS AND THE MASSES

THE FABER BOOK OF SCIENCE (ED.)

THE FABER BOOK OF UTOPIAS (ED.)

PURE PLEASURE: A GUIDE TO THE TWENTIETH
CENTURY'S MOST ENJOYABLE BOOKS

The Faber Book of Reportage

EDITED BY

John Carey

faber and faber

First published in 1987
by Faber and Faber Limited
3 Queen Square London WC1N 3AU
First paperback edition published in 1988
This paperback edition first published in 2003

Phototypeset by Wilmaset Ltd, Wirral
Printed in the UK by CPI Group (UK) Ltd, Croydon, CR0 4YY

A CIP record for this book
is available from the British Library

ISBN 978-0-571-14163-0

Contents

Introduction

Before editing a book of reportage you need to decide what reportage is, and how you tell the good from the bad. I decided early on that for my purposes reportage must be written by an eye witness, and I have stuck to this most of the time, though occasionally I have let in a piece that is not eye witness itself but based on eye-witness accounts. An example is William of Newburgh's story about two green children who landed on earth out of some other dimension in the middle of the twelfth century. This, like other exceptions to the eye-witness rule, seemed too good to miss, and must surely be based on facts of some sort, however garbled.

One advantage of insisting on eye-witness evidence is that it makes for authenticity. All knowledge of the past which is not just supposition derives ultimately from people who can say 'I was there', as the assortment of chance bystanders, travellers, warriors, murderers, victims, and professional reporters I assemble here can. Another advantage is stylistic. Eye-witness accounts have the feel of truth because they are quick, subjective and incomplete, unlike 'objective' or reconstructed history, which is laborious but dead.

For the sake of sharp focus I also decided to prefer accounts of happenings that could be dated exactly — day, month, year. Sometimes in the earlier and less time-conscious eras this requirement had to be waived. Even in later periods I have let in the odd piece which — like W. H. Hudson's memories of a Norfolk-coast holiday — is vague as to date but precise in other ways. However, the general rule about dating holds. The reporter is a private eye working in a public area, and the subject of his report must not be inward or fanciful, but pinned verifiably to the clockface of world time.

That does not mean reportage has to be about 'important' happenings. I had to choose, at the start, between a principle of selection that would put a premium on subject matter (is this event of major historical interest?), and one that would be concerned primarily with the qualities of writing and observation displayed. I chose the second, on the grounds that nothing is important – or unimportant – except as it is perceived.

Of course, a lot of the pieces selected are nevertheless about big historical events, because those are the kind people feel incited to record if they are around when they occur. But – to give an instance of the other kind – one of the pieces I should have defended most stubbornly if anyone had suggested leaving it out is Joe Ackerley's diary entry about going rabbiting with a small boy one afternoon. Obviously this is trivial in a sense. But because it tells how one young male began to be acclimatized to killing, it is also momentous – the loss of innocence observed through Ackerley's fastidious lens – and it is germane to all the massacres and atrocities this book logs.

Some definitions of reportage insist it should have been written in the heat of the moment, reflecting the rush and compression and ignorance of what is going to happen next that all reporters have to put up with. There are plenty of these on-the-spot pieces in this collection, and some gain power from the spot they are on – like Samuel Wilkeson's Gettysburg despatch, penned beside the dead body of his son. But to include only instant-response stories seemed too cramping. Rushed reportage can carry the tang of crisis, but it can also be just rushed. So I have drawn as well on autobiographies and travel books, often written long after the event; and when reporters like Richard Harding Davis or Webb Miller have left two accounts of an incident, one in newspaper columns, the other in their memoirs, I have sometimes chosen the later, more worked-at version.

What makes good reportage good? We get some help in answering this from Stendhal's account, in *La Chartreuse de Parme*, of Fabrizio's experiences at Waterloo. Fabrizio is an innocent. He has never been in a battle before. The chaos bewilders him, and since he has no idea what he is supposed to be doing, he simply goes through the same motions as those around him, his mind filled meanwhile with romantic imaginings about Marshal Ney, whom he catches sight of riding by with his escort:

> Suddenly they all moved off at full gallop. A few minutes later Fabrizio saw, twenty paces ahead of him, a piece of tilled land that was being ploughed up in a singular fashion. The

bottoms of the furrows were full of water, and the very damp soil that formed the ridges of these furrows was flying about in little black lumps flung three or four feet into the air. Fabrizio noted this curious effect as he was passing; then his mind turned to dreaming of the Marshal and his glory. He heard a sharp cry close by him; it was two hussars falling struck by shot; and when he looked round at them they were already twenty paces behind the escort.

'Ah! so I am under fire at last,' he said to himself. 'I have seen the firing!' he repeated with a sense of satisfaction. 'Now I am a real soldier.' At that moment the escort began to go at a tearing pace, and our hero realized that it was shot from the guns that was making the earth fly up all around him.

Stendhal here manages to avoid the usual relations between language and reality. He shows us what Fabrizio actually sees (little black lumps flying in the air), and only afterwards supplies the coded linguistic formula for it ('I am under fire') so that both we and Fabrizio are rather surprised to find that is what was happening. By this means he reminds us how removed from the actual such linguistic formulae are. Fabrizio repeats the formula to himself with satisfaction, because it is language's way of ascribing merit to what he has been through. But it is also language's way of receiving it into the huge collection of known quantities and dead experiences, rubbed smooth and featureless by persistent use, which makes up most everyday discourse.

The power of language to confront us with the vivid, the frightening or the unaccustomed is equalled only by its opposite – the power of language to muffle any such alarms. Either power is available for language-users, but bad reportage opts firmly for the second. Anyone compiling an anthology of this kind will have to trudge through, for example, hundreds of pages of battle accounts filled with sentences like 'Our horse inflicted severe punishment on the enemy's right flank' or 'Four brigade did tremendous execution with the bayonet' – circumlocutions that, with their bizarre use of singulars for plurals, and their scrupulous exclusion of any mention of killing, are designed to neutralize and conceal experiences the writers felt were too terrible or too unseemly or too prejudicial to the future of good order and military discipline to record directly. Such euphemisms illustrate one major function of language, which is to keep reality at bay.

A distinguishing feature of good reportage is that it combats this inevitable and planned retreat of language from the real. However good it is, good reportage cannot, of course, get beyond language, because it is language itself. It is an axiom of modern critical theory that there are no accessible 'realities', only texts that relate to one another intertextually. But even if he believes this, the good reporter must do everything in his power to counteract it, struggling to isolate the singularities that will make his account real for his readers – not just something written, but something seen.

This book is (and is meant to be) full of unusual or indecorous or incidental images that imprint themselves scaldingly on the mind's eye: the ambassador peering down the front of Queen Elizabeth I's dress and noting the wrinkles; Joe Louis's nostrils like a double-barrelled shotgun; Mata Hari drawing on her filmy stockings on the morning of her execution; the Tamil looter at the fall of Kuala Lumpur upending a carton of snowy Slazenger tennis balls; Richard Hillary closing one eye to see his lips like motor tyres; the men at Gallipoli crying because they were dirty; the unsheathed steel at Balaclava like 'the turn of a shoal of mackerel'; the assassin Booth catching his boot-heel in the drapery round Lincoln's box; Pliny watching people with cushions on their heads against the ash from the volcano; Mary, Queen of Scots, suddenly aged in death, with her pet dog cowering among her skirts and her head held on by one recalcitrant piece of gristle; the starving Irish with their mouths green from their diet of grass.

It is history these accounts offer, but history deprived of generalizations. The writers are strangers to omniscience. The varnish of interpretation has been removed so we can see people clearly, as they originally were – gazing incredulously at what was, for that moment, the newest thing that had ever happened to them.

To achieve this effect the good reporter's report must be individual. It must restore to his experience the uniqueness it rightly possesses – and which worn-out language tries to rob it of. Nietzsche argued that language was originally developed to shield mankind from the inconceivable welter of pre-linguistic reality in which everything – every tree, stone and breath of wind – was unique. To simplify this mind-jamming variety, language supplied category words – stone, tree, wind – which allowed man to generalize. Though this brought gains, it also entailed losses, because the individuality each creature actually possesses is now hidden beneath the grey blanket of words.

The good reporter must resist this, and resist language's – and reportage's – daily slide into sameness. The results of the slide are portrayed in Michael Frayn's *The Tin Men*. Frayn's novel describes a research institute where a computer is being programmed to produce daily newspapers which will have all the variety and news-sense of the genuine article, but will bear no relation to events that have actually happened. The computer's programmers have organized mass surveys to discover what news stories people like best, how often they want them to recur, and which details they would like included. Should there be an air-crash story every month, or more frequently? Is it preferred, or not, that children's toys should be found lying pathetically among the wreckage? If a murder is reported, should the victim be, preferably, a small girl, an old lady, or an illegitimately pregnant young woman, and should the corpse be naked or clad in underclothes? When the computer has collected and analysed these reader requirements, it will be able to turn out popular daily papers indefinitely without the preliminary bother and expense of actually gathering any news.

Frayn's satire highlights the reporter's difficulty. Massive accumulations of standardized language and hackneyed story-lines lie in wait, ready to leap from his fingers to the typing paper. In a sense this is any writer's problem, but it is worse for the reporter, because he must stay true to the real, yet constantly defamiliarize it. He must see it, and tell it, as if for the first time.

This raises another difficulty. The good reporter must cultivate the innocent eye, but he must not be innocent. What innocence would be like at reporting, we can judge from Tolstoy's description, in *War and Peace*, of Natasha's reaction when, for the first time in her life, she is taken to an opera, and feels ashamed to be present at anything so absurd:

> Smooth boards formed the centre of the stage, at the side stood painted canvases representing trees, and in the background was a cloth stretched over boards. In the middle of the stage sat some girls in red bodices and white petticoats. One extremely fat girl in a white silk dress was sitting apart on a low bench, to the back of which a piece of green cardboard

was glued. They were all singing something. When they had finished their chorus the girl in white advanced towards the prompter's box, and a man with stout legs encased in silk tights, a plume in his cap and a dagger at his waist, went up to her and began to sing and wave his arms about.

The good reporter must have something of Natasha's devastating literalism, and must see, like her, what is there, not what is meant to be. But her account would obviously not do as an opera review. She is ignorant, and the reporter cannot be. It is his job to know. He must be Experience simulating Innocence – as Tolstoy was when he put together Natasha's mind.

Why do we need reportage? It is clear we do, for hundreds of thousands of words of it are produced daily to glut the world's appetite. Yet this is a comparatively recent development, made possible only by technology and mass literacy. The crucial innovations were the education acts of the late nineteenth century, and the electric telegraph, which was first used by American reporters during the Civil War. When they came to Europe to cover the Franco-Prussian war, they telegraphed battle stories to their papers back home, and British popular papers quickly followed suit.

In September 1870 William Howard Russell, the veteran reporter of the Crimea, travelled in person from the battlefield of Sedan to Printing House Square, writing all night, to get his dramatic story of the slaughter ready for *The Times*. But other London papers, using the telegraph, had printed news of the German victory two days earlier. In the years that followed, the results of this advance were consumed by the new mass readership in ever increasing quantities. Between 1880 and 1900, the number of newspapers doubled.

Arguably the advent of mass communications represents the greatest change in human consciousness that has taken place in recorded history. The development, within a few decades, from a situation where most of the inhabitants of the globe would have no day-to-day knowledge of or curiosity about how most of the others were faring, to a situation where the ordinary person's mental space is filled (and must be refilled daily or hourly, unless a feeling of disorientation is to ensue) with accurate reports about the doings of complete strangers, represents a revolution in mental activity which is incalculable in its effects.

To early-modern man the current situation would have been

incomprehensible. Ben Jonson's play *The Staple of News* (acted around 1626) turns on the self-evident absurdity of news-gathering as an activity. History has not supported Jonson's judgement. It is hard for communication-age man to imagine what pre-communication-age man found to think about. But if we ask what took the place of reportage in the ages before it was made available to its millions of consumers, the likeliest answer seems to be religion.

Not, of course, that we should assume pre-communication-age man was deeply religious, in the main. There is plenty of evidence to suggest he was not. But religion was the permanent backdrop to his existence, as reportage is for his modern counterpart. Reportage supplies modern man with a constant and reassuring sense of events going on beyond his immediate horizon (reassuring even, or particularly, when the events themselves are terrible, since they then contrast more comfortingly with the reader's supposed safety). Reportage provides modern man, too, with a release from his trivial routines, and a habitual daily illusion of communication with a reality greater than himself. In all these ways religion suggests itself as the likeliest substitute pre-modern man could have found for reportage, at any rate in the West.

When we view reportage as the natural successor to religion, it helps us to understand why it should be so profoundly taken up with the subject of death. Death, in its various forms of murder, massacre, accident, natural catastrophe, warfare, and so on, is the subject to which reportage naturally gravitates, and one difficulty, in compiling an anthology of this kind, is to stop it becoming just a string of slaughters. Religion has traditionally been mankind's answer to death, allowing him to believe in various kinds of permanency which make his own extinction more tolerable, or even banish his fear of it altogether. The Christian belief in personal immortality is an obvious and extreme example of this. Reportage, taking religion's place, endlessly feeds its reader with accounts of the deaths of other people, and therefore places him continually in the position of a survivor – one who has escaped the violent and terrible ends which, it graphically apprises him, others have come to. In this way reportage, like religion, gives the individual a comforting sense of his own immortality.

If reportage performs these various functions it clearly has a social value comparable to that which religion once had. Its 'cultural' value, on the other hand, has generally been considered negligible – with certain favoured exceptions such as Mark Twain's *The Innocents Abroad*, which are allowed to be literature because their authors also wrote respectable literary books. The question of whether reportage is 'literature' is not in itself interesting or even meaningful. 'Literature', we now realize, is not an objectively ascertainable category to which certain works naturally belong, but rather a term used by institutions and establishments and other culture-controlling groups to dignify those texts to which, for whatever reasons, they wish to attach value. The question worth asking therefore is not whether reportage is literature, but why intellectuals and literary institutions have generally been so keen to deny it that status.

Resentment of the masses, who are regarded as reportage's audience, is plainly a factor in the development of this prejudice. The terms used to express it are often social in their implications. 'High' culture is distinguished from the 'vulgarity' said to characterize reportage. But the disparagement of reportage also reflects a wish to promote the imaginary above the real. Works of imagination are, it is maintained, inherently superior, and have a spiritual value absent from 'journalism'. The creative artist is in touch with truths higher than the actual, which give him exclusive entry into the soul of man.

Such convictions seem to represent a residue of magical thinking. The recourse to images of ascent which their adherents manifest, the emphasis on purity, the recoil from earthly contamination, and the tendency towards a belief in inspiration, all belong to the traditional ambience of priesthoods and mystery cults. Those who hold such views about literature are likely, also, to resent critical attempts to relate authors' works to their lives. The biographical approach, it is argued, debases literature by tying it to mere reality: we should release texts from their authors, and contemplate them pure and disembodied, or at any rate only in the company of other equally pure and disembodied texts.

The superstitions that lie behind such dictates are interesting as primitive cultural vestiges, but it would be wrong to grant them serious attention as arguments. The advantages of reportage over imaginative literature, are, on the other hand, clear. Imaginative literature habitually depends for its effect on a 'willing suspension of disbelief' in audience or reader, and this necessarily entails an element of game or collusion or self-deception. Reportage, by contrast, lays claim directly to the power of the real, which imaginative literature can approach only through make-believe.

It would be foolish, of course, to belittle imaginative literature on this score. The fact that it is not real – that its griefs, loves and deaths are all a pretence, is one reason why it can sustain us. It is a dream from which we can awake when we wish, and so it gives us, among the obstinate urgencies of real life, a precious illusion of freedom. It allows us to use for pleasure passions and sympathies (anger, fear, pity, etc.), which in normal circumstances would arise only in situations of pain or distress. In this way it frees and extends our emotional life. It seems probable that much – or most – reportage is read as if it were fiction by a majority of its readers. Its panics and disasters do not affect them as real, but as belonging to a shadow world distinct from their own concerns, and without their pressing actuality. Because of this, reportage has been able to take the place of imaginative literature in the lives of most people. They read newspapers rather than books, and newspapers which might just as well be fictional, as Frayn's are.

However enjoyable this is, it represents, of course, a flight from the real, as does imaginative literature, and good reportage is designed to make that flight impossible. It exiles us from fiction into the sharp terrain of truth. All the great realistic novelists of the nineteenth century – Balzac, Dickens, Tolstoy, Zola – drew on the techniques of reportage, and even built eye-witness accounts and newspaper stories into their fictions, so as to give them heightened realism. But the goal they struggled towards always lay beyond their reach. They could produce, at best, only imitation reportage, lacking the absolutely vital ingredient of reportage which is the simple fact that the reader knows all this actually happened.

When we read (to choose the most glaring example) accounts of the Holocaust by survivors and onlookers, some of which I have included in this book, we cannot comfort ourselves (as we can when distressed by accounts of suffering in realistic novels) by reminding ourselves that they are, after all, just stories. The facts presented demand our recognition, and require us to respond, though we do not know how to. We read the details – the Jews by the mass grave waiting to be shot; the father comforting his son and pointing to the sky; the grandmother amusing the baby – and we are possessed by our own inadequacy, by a ridiculous desire to help, by pity which is unappeasable and useless.

Or not quite useless, perhaps. For at this level (so one would like to hope) reportage may change its readers, may educate their sympathies, may extend – in both directions – their ideas about what it is to be a human being, may limit their capacity for the inhuman. These gains have traditionally been claimed for imaginative literature. But since reportage, unlike literature, lifts the screen from reality, its lessons are – and ought to be – more telling; and since it reaches millions untouched by literature, it has an incalculably greater potential.

Over the last four years I have regularly pestered friends and acquaintances and any likely stranger with whom I managed to get into conversation for suggestions as to what might be included in this book. I hope they will accept a general but heartfelt thank you for their patience and help. I must, though, single out Craig Raine for special thanks, since the book was originally his idea, and he has been invaluable at every stage since then.

JOHN CAREY
Oxford
January 1987

Thucydides

The Athens plague has not been identified with any known disease. It had some of the symptoms of typhus fever.

The disease began, it is said, in Ethiopia beyond Egypt, and then descended into Egypt and Libya and spread over the greater part of the King's territory. Then it suddenly fell upon the city of Athens, and attacked first the inhabitants of the Peiraeus . . . I shall describe its actual course, explaining the symptoms, from the study of which a person should be best able, having knowledge of it beforehand, to recognize it if it should ever break out again. For I had the disease myself and saw others sick of it.

That year, as was agreed by all, happened to be unusually free from disease so far as regards the other maladies; but if anyone was already ill of any disease all terminated in this. In other cases from no obvious cause, but suddenly and while in good health, men were seized first with intense heat of the head, and redness and inflammation of the eyes, and the parts inside the mouth, both the throat and the tongue, immediately became blood-red and exhaled an unnatural and fetid breath. In the next stage sneezing and hoarseness came on, and in a short time the disorder descended to the chest, attended by severe coughing. And when it settled in the stomach, that was upset, and vomits of bile of every kind named by physicians ensued, these also attended by great distress; and in most cases ineffectual retching followed producing violent convulsions, which sometimes abated directly, sometimes not until long afterwards. Externally, the body was not so very warm to the touch; it was not pale, but reddish, livid, and breaking out in small blisters and ulcers. But internally it was consumed by such a heat that the patients could not bear to have on them the lightest coverings or linen sheets, but wanted to be quite uncovered and would have liked best to throw themselves into cold water – indeed many of those who were not looked after did throw themselves into cisterns – so tormented were they by thirst which could not be quenched; and it was all the same whether they drank much or little.

They were also beset by restlessness and sleeplessness which never abated. And the body was not wasted while the disease was at its height, but resisted surprisingly the ravages of the disease, so that when the patients died, as most of them did on the seventh or ninth day from the internal heat, they still had some strength left; or, if they passed the crisis, the disease went down into the bowels, producing there a violent ulceration, and at the same time an acute diarrhoea set in, so that in this later stage most of them perished through weakness caused by it. For the malady, starting from the head where it was first seated, passed down until it spread through the whole body, and if one got over the worst, it seized upon the extremities at last and left its marks there; for it attacked the privates and fingers and toes, and many escaped with the loss of these, though some lost their eyes also. In some cases the sufferer was attacked immediately after recovery by loss of memory, which extended to every object alike, so that they failed to recognize either themselves or their friends . . . And the most dreadful thing about the whole malady was not only the despondency of the victims, when they once became aware that they were sick, for their minds straightway yielded to despair and they gave themselves up for lost instead of resisting, but also the fact that they became infected by nursing one another and died like sheep . . .

But in addition to the trouble under which they already laboured, the Athenians suffered further hardship owing to the crowding into the city of the people from the country districts; and this affected the new arrivals especially. For since no houses were available for them and they had to live in huts that were stifling in the hot season, they perished in wild disorder. Bodies of dying men lay one upon another, and half-dead people rolled about in the streets and, in their longing for water, near all the fountains. The temples, too, in which they had quartered themselves were full of the corpses of those who had died in them; for the calamity which weighed upon them was so overpowering that men, not knowing what was to become of them, became careless of all law, sacred as well as profane. And the customs which they had hitherto observed regarding burial were all thrown into confusion, and they buried their dead each one as he could. And many resorted to shameless modes of burial because so many members of their households had already died that they lacked the proper funeral materials. Resorting to other people's pyres, some, anticipating those who had raised them, would put on their own dead and kindle the fire; others would throw the body they were carrying upon one which was already burning and go away.

The Greeks March to the Sea, 401 BC

Xenophon

After the defeat of the Persian, Cyrus, whom he had been assisting, Xenophon led his army of Greek mercenaries up the Tigris valley and through the wilds of Kurdistan to the Black Sea, in an epic retreat.

The third day's march was a hard one, with a north wind blowing into their faces, cutting into absolutely everything like a knife and freezing people stiff. One of the soothsayers then proposed making a sacrifice to the wind and his suggestion was carried out. It was agreed by all that there was then a distinct falling off in the violence of the wind. The snow was six feet deep and many of the animals and the slaves perished in it, as did about thirty of the soldiers. They kept their fires going all night, as there was plenty of wood in the place where they camped, though those who came up late got no wood. The ones who had arrived before and had lit the fires would not let the late-comers approach their fire unless they gave them a share of their corn or any other foodstuff they had. So each shared with the other party what he had. When the fires were made, great pits were formed reaching down to the ground as the snow melted. This gave one a chance of measuring the depth of the snow . . .

Soldiers who had lost the use of their eyes through snow-blindness or whose toes had dropped off from frostbite were left behind. It was a relief to the eyes against snow-blindness if one held something black in front of the eyes while marching; and it was a help to the feet if one kept on the move and never stopped still, and took off one's shoes at night. If one slept with one's shoes on, the straps sank into the flesh and the soles of the shoes froze to the feet. This was the more likely to happen since, when their old shoes were worn out, they had made themselves shoes of undressed leather from the skins of oxen that had just been flayed . . .

It seemed safe for the troops to take up their quarters in the villages. Chirisophus stayed where he was, and the other officers drew lots for the villages which were in sight, and each went with his men to the one he got.

On this occasion Polycrates, an Athenian captain, asked leave to go on independently and, taking with him the men who were

quickest on their feet, ran to the village which had been allotted to
Xenophon and surprised all the villagers, with their headman,
inside the walls, together with seventeen colts which were kept
there for tribute to the King, and the headman's daughter, who
had been married only nine days ago. Her husband had gone out
to hunt hares and was not captured in the village.

The houses here were built underground; the entrances were
like wells, but they broadened out lower down. There were
tunnels dug in the ground for the animals, while the men went
down by ladder. Inside the houses there were goats, sheep, cows
and poultry with their young. All these animals were fed on food
that was kept inside the houses. There was also wheat, barley,
beans and barley wine in great bowls. The actual grains of barley
floated on top of the bowls, level with the brim, and in the bowls
there were reeds of various sizes and without joints in them. When
one was thirsty, one was meant to take a reed and suck the wine
into one's mouth. It was a very strong wine, unless one mixed it
with water, and, when one got used to it, it was a very pleasant
drink.

Xenophon invited the chief of the village to have supper with
him, and told him to be of good heart, as he was not going to be
deprived of his children, and that, if he showed himself capable of
doing the army a good turn until they reached another tribe, they
would restock his house with provisions when they went away.
He promised to co-operate and, to show his good intentions, told
them of where some wine was buried. So for that night all the
soldiers were quartered in the villages and slept there with all sorts
of food around them, setting a guard over the head-man of the
village and keeping a watchful eye on his children too.

On the next day Xenophon visited Chirisophus and took the
head-man with him. Whenever he went past a village he turned
into it to see those who were quartered there. Everywhere he
found them feasting and merry-making, and they would invariably
refuse to let him go before they had given him something for
breakfast. In every single case they would have on the same table
lamb, kid, pork, veal and chicken, and a number of loaves, both
wheat and barley. When anyone wanted, as a gesture of friendship, to drink to a friend's health, he would drag him to a huge
bowl, over which he would have to lean, sucking up the drink like
an ox. They invited the head-man too to take what he liked, but

he refused their invitations, only, if he caught sight of any of his relatives, he would take them along with him.

When they came to Chirisophus, they found his men also feasting, with wreaths of hay round their heads, and with Armenian boys in native dress waiting on them. They showed the boys what to do by signs, as though they were deaf mutes. After greeting each other, Chirisophus and Xenophon together interrogated the head-man through the interpreter who spoke Persian, and asked him what country this was. He replied that it was Armenia. Then they asked him for whom the horses were being kept, and he said that they were a tribute paid to the King. The next country, he said, was the land of the Chalybes, and he told them the way there.

Xenophon then went away and took the head-man back to his own people. He gave him back the horse (rather an old one) which he had taken, and told him to fatten it up and sacrifice it. This was because he had heard that it was sacred to the Sun and he was afraid that it might die, as the journey had done it no good. He took some of the colts himself, and gave one colt to each of the generals and captains. The horses in this part of the world were smaller than the Persian horses, but much more finely bred. The head-man told the Greeks to tie small bags round the feet of the horses and baggage animals whenever they made them go through snow, as, without these bags, they sank in up to their bellies . . .

Then came a seven days' march of a hundred and fifty miles through the country of the Chalybes. These were the most warlike of all the tribes on their way, and they fought with the Greeks at close quarters. They had body armour of linen, reaching down to the groin, and instead of skirts to their armour they wore thick twisted cords. They also wore greaves and helmets, and carried on their belts a knife of about the size of the Spartan dagger. With these knives they cut the throats of those whom they managed to overpower, and then would cut off their heads and carry them as they marched, singing and dancing whenever their enemies were likely to see them. They also carried a spear with one point, about twenty feet long. They used to stay inside their settlements, and then, when the Greeks had gone past, they would follow behind and were always ready for a fight. They had their houses in fortified positions, and had brought all their provisions inside the fortifications. Consequently the Greeks could take nothing from them, but lived on the supplies which they had seized from the Taochi.

The Greeks arrived next at the river Harpasus which was four hundred feet across. Then they marched through the territory of the Scytheni, a four days' march of sixty miles over level ground until they came to some villages, where they stayed for three days and renewed their stocks of provisions. Then a four days' march of sixty miles brought them to a large, prosperous and inhabited city, which was called Gymnias. The governor of the country sent the Greeks a guide from this city, with the idea that he should lead them through country which was at war with his own people. When the guide arrived, he said that in five days he would lead them to a place from which they could see the sea; and he said he was ready to be put to death if he failed to do so. So he led the way, and, when they had crossed the border into his enemies' country, he urged them to burn and lay waste the land, thus making it clear that it was for this purpose that he had come to them, and not because of any goodwill to the Greeks.

They came to the mountain on the fifth day, the name of the mountain being Thekes. When the men in front reached the summit and caught sight of the sea there was great shouting. Xenophon and the rearguard heard it and thought that there were some more enemies attacking in the front, since there were natives of the country they had ravaged following them up behind, and the rearguard had killed some of them and made prisoners of others in an ambush, and captured about twenty raw ox-hide shields, with the hair on. However, when the shouting got louder and drew nearer, and those who were constantly going forward started running towards the men in front who kept on shouting, and the more there were of them the more shouting there was, it looked then as though this was something of considerable importance. So Xenophon mounted his horse and, taking Lycus and the cavalry with him, rode forward to give support, and, quite soon, they heard the soldiers shouting out, 'The sea! The sea!' and passing the word down the column. Then certainly they all began to run, the rearguard and all, and drove on the baggage animals and the horses at full speed; and when they had all got to the top, the soldiers, with tears in their eyes, embraced each other and their generals and captains. In a moment, at somebody or other's suggestion, they collected stones and made a great pile of them. On top they put a lot of raw ox-hides and staves and shields which they had captured. The guide himself cut the shields into pieces and urged the others to do so too. Afterwards the Greeks sent the guide back and gave him as presents from the common store a horse, and a silver cup and a Persian robe and ten darics. What he particularly wanted was the rings which the soldiers had and he got a number of these from them. He pointed out to them a village where they could camp, and showed them the road by which they had to go to the country of the Macrones. It was then evening and he went away, travelling by night.

The Death of Socrates, 399 BC

Plato

Socrates had been condemned to death for 'corruption of the young' and 'neglect of the gods'. He remained in prison for a month after sentence until the sacred ship had returned from Delos: during its absence no execution could take place. Xanthippe was Socrates' wife: he had three sons by her. Plato was not an eye-witness of the death, but was in close touch with those who were.

I will try to tell you everything from the beginning. On the previous days I and the others had always been in the habit of visiting Socrates. We used to meet at daybreak in the court where the trial took place, for it was near the prison; and every day we used to wait about, talking with each other, until the prison was opened, for it was not opened early; and when it was opened, we went in to Socrates and passed most of the day with him. On that day we came together earlier; for the day before, when we left the prison in the evening we heard that the ship had arrived from Delos. So we agreed to come to the usual place as early in the morning as possible. And we came, and the gaoler who usually answered the door came out and told us to wait and not go in until he told us. 'For', he said, 'the eleven are releasing Socrates from his fetters and giving directions how he is to die today.' So after a little delay he came and told us to go in. We went in then and found Socrates just released from his fetters and Xanthippe – you know her – with his little son in her arms, sitting beside him. Now when Xanthippe saw us, she cried out and said the kind of thing that women always do say: 'Oh Socrates, this is the last time now that your friends will speak to you or you to them.' And Socrates glanced at Crito and said, 'Crito, let somebody take her home.' And some of Crito's people took her away wailing and beating her breast. But Socrates sat up on his couch and bent his leg and rubbed it with his hand, and while he was rubbing it, he said, 'What a strange thing, my friends, that seems to be which men call pleasure! How wonderfully it is related to that which seems to be its opposite, pain, in that they will not both come to a man at the same time, and yet if he pursues the one and captures it, he is generally obliged to take the other also, as if the two were joined together in one head. And I think', he said, 'if Aesop had thought of them, he would have made a fable telling how they were at war and god wished to reconcile them, and when he could not do that, he fastened their heads together, and for that reason, when one of them comes to anyone, the other follows after. Just so it seems that in my case, after pain was in my leg on account of the fetter, pleasure appears to have come following after.'

When he had finished speaking, Crito said, 'Well, Socrates, do you wish to leave any directions with us about your children or anything else – anything we can do to serve you?'

'What I always say, Crito,' he replied, 'nothing new. If you take care of yourselves you will serve me and mine and yourselves, whatever you do, even if you make no promises now; but if you neglect yourselves and are not willing to live following step by step, as it were, in the path marked out by our present and past discussions, you will accomplish nothing, no matter how much or how eagerly you promise at present.'

'We will certainly try hard to do as you say,' he replied. 'But how shall we bury you?'

'However you please,' he replied, 'if you can catch me and I do not get away from you.' And he laughed gently, and looking towards us, said, 'I cannot persuade Crito, my friends, that the Socrates who is now conversing and arranging the details of his argument is really I; he thinks I am the one whom he will presently see as a corpse, and he asks how to bury me. And though I have been saying at great length that after I drink the poison I shall no longer be with you, but shall go away to the joys of the blessed you know of, he seems to think that was idle talk uttered to encourage you and myself. So,' he said, 'give security for me to Crito, the opposite of that which he gave the judges at my trial; for he gave security that I would remain, but you must give security that I shall not remain when I die, but shall go away, so that Crito may bear it more easily, and may not be troubled when he sees my body being burned or buried, or think I am undergoing terrible treatment, and may not say at the funeral that he is laying out Socrates, or following him to the grave, or burying him. For, dear Crito, you may be sure that such wrong words are not only undesirable in themselves, but they infect the soul with evil. No, you must be of good courage, and say that you bury my body – and bury it as you think best and as seems to you most fitting.'

When he had said this, he got up and went into another room to bathe; Crito followed him, but he told us to wait. So we waited, talking over with each other and discussing the discourse we had heard, and then speaking of the great misfortune that had befallen us, for we felt that he was like a father to us and that when bereft of him we should pass the rest of our lives as orphans. And when he had bathed and his children had been brought to him – for he had two little sons and one big one – and the women of the family had come, he talked with them in Crito's presence and gave them such directions as he wished; then he told the women to go away, and he came to us. And it was now nearly sunset; for he had spent a long time within. And he came and sat down fresh from the bath. After that not much was said, and the servant of the eleven came and stood beside him and said 'Socrates, I shall not find fault with you, as I do with others, for being angry and cursing me, when at the behest of the authorities, I tell them to drink the poison. No, I have found you in all this time in every way the noblest and gentlest and best man who has ever come here, and now I know your anger is directed against others, not against me, for you know who are to blame. Now, for you know the message I came to bring you, farewell and try to bear what you must as easily as you can.' And he burst into tears and turned and went away. And Socrates looked up at him and said, 'Fare you well, too; I will do as you say.' And then he said to us, 'How charming the man is! Ever since I have been here he has been coming to see me and talking with me from time to time, and has been the best of men, and now how nobly he weeps for me! But come, Crito, let us obey him, and let someone bring the poison, if it is ready; and if not, let the man prepare it.' And Crito said, 'But I think, Socrates, the sun is still upon the mountains and has not yet set; and I know that others have taken the poison very late, after the order has come to them, and in the meantime have eaten and drunk and some of them enjoyed the society of those whom they loved. Do not hurry; for there is still time.'

And Socrates said, 'Crito, those whom you mention are right in doing as they do, for they think they gain by it; and I shall be right in not doing as they do; for I think I should gain nothing by taking the poison a little later. I should only make myself ridiculous in my own eyes if I clung to life and spared it, when there is no more profit in it. Come,' he said, 'do as I ask and do not refuse.'

Thereupon Crito nodded to the boy who was standing near. The boy went out and stayed a long time, then came back with the man who was to administer the poison, which he brought with him in a cup ready for use. And when Socrates saw him, he said, 'Well, my good man, you know about these things; what must I do?' 'Nothing,' he replied, 'except drink the poison and walk about till your legs feel heavy; then lie down, and the poison will take effect of itself.'

At the same time he held out the cup to Socrates. He took it, and very gently, Echecrates, without trembling or changing colour or expression, but looking up at the man with wide open eyes, as was his custom, said, 'What do you say about pouring a libation to some deity from this cup? May I, or not?' 'Socrates,' said he, 'we prepare only as much as we think is enough.' 'I understand,' said Socrates; 'but I may and must pray to the gods that my departure hence be a fortunate one; so I offer this prayer, and may it be granted.' With these words he raised the cup to his lips and very cheerfully and quietly drained it. Up to that time most of us had been able to restrain our tears fairly well, but when we watched him drinking and saw that he had drunk the poison, we could do so no longer, but in spite of myself my tears rolled down in floods, so that I wrapped my face in my cloak and wept for myself; for it was not for him that I wept, but for my own misfortune in being deprived of such a friend. Crito had got up and gone away even before I did, because he could not restrain his tears. But Apollodorus, who had been weeping all the time before, then wailed aloud in his grief and made us all break down, except Socrates himself. But he said, 'What conduct is this, you strange men! I sent the women away chiefly for this very reason, that they might not behave in this absurd way; for I have heard that it is best to die in silence. Keep quiet and be brave.' Then we were ashamed and controlled our tears. He walked about and, when he said his legs were heavy, lay down on his back, for such was the advice of the attendant. The man who had administered the poison laid his hands on him and after a while examined his feet and legs, then pinched his foot hard and asked if he felt it. He said 'No'; then after that, his thighs; and passing upwards in this way he showed us that he was growing cold and rigid. And again he touched him and said that when it reached his heart, he would be gone. The chill had now reached the region about the groin, and uncovering his face, which had been covered, he said – and these were his last words – 'Crito, we owe a cock to Aesculapius. Pay it and do not neglect it.' 'That', said Crito, 'shall be done; but see if you have anything else to say.' To this question he made no reply, but after a little while he moved; the attendant uncovered him; his eyes were fixed. And Crito when he saw it, closed his mouth and eyes.

Such was the end, Echecrates, of our friend, who was, as we may say, of all those of his time whom we have known, the best and wisest and most righteous man.

Caesar Invades Britain, 55 BC

Julius Caesar

The Romans were faced with very grave difficulties. The size of the ships made it impossible to run them aground except in fairly deep water; and the soldiers, unfamiliar with the ground, with their hands full, and weighed down by the heavy burden of their arms, had at the same time to jump down from the ships, get a footing in the waves, and fight the enemy, who, standing on dry land or advancing only a short way into the water, fought with all their limbs unencumbered and on perfectly familiar ground, boldly hurling javelins and galloping their horses, which were trained to this kind of work. These perils frightened our soldiers, who were quite unaccustomed to battles of this kind, with the result that they did not show the same alacrity and enthusiasm as they usually did in battles on dry land.

Seeing this, Caesar ordered the warships – which were swifter and easier to handle than the transports, and likely to impress the natives more by their unfamiliar appearance – to be removed a short distance from the others, and then to be rowed hard and run ashore on the enemy's right flank, from which position slings, bows, and artillery could be used by men on deck to drive them back. This manoeuvre was highly successful. Scared by the strange shape of the warships, the motion of the oars, and the unfamiliar machines, the natives halted and then retreated a little. But as the Romans still hesitated, chiefly on account of the depth of the water, the man who carried the eagle of the tenth legion, after praying to the gods that his action might bring good luck to the legion, cried in a loud voice, 'Jump down, comrades, unless you want to surrender our eagle to the enemy; I, at any rate, mean to do my duty to my country and my general.' With these words he leapt out of the ship and advanced towards the enemy with the eagle in his hands. At this the soldiers, exhorting each other not to submit to such a disgrace, jumped with one accord from the ship, and the men from the next ships, when they saw them, followed them and advanced against the enemy.

Rome Burns, AD 64

Tacitus

Nero now tried to make it appear that Rome was his favourite abode. He gave feasts in public places as if the whole city were his own home. But the most prodigal and notorious banquet was given by Tigellinus. To avoid repetitious accounts of extravagance, I shall describe it, as a model of its kind. The entertainment took place on a raft constructed on Marcus Agrippa's lake. It was towed about by other vessels, with gold and ivory fittings. Their rowers were degenerates, assorted according to age and vice. Tigellinus had also collected birds and animals from remote countries, and even the products of the ocean. On the quays were brothels stocked with high-ranking ladies. Opposite them could be seen naked prostitutes, indecently posturing and gesturing.

At nightfall the woods and houses nearby echoed with singing and blazed with lights. Nero was already corrupted by every lust, natural and unnatural. But he now refuted any surmises that no further degradation was possible for him. For a few days later he went through a formal wedding ceremony with one of the perverted gang called Pythagoras. The emperor, in the presence of witnesses, put on the bridal veil. Dowry, marriage bed, wedding torches, all were there. Indeed everything was public which even in a natural union is veiled by night.

Disaster followed. Whether it was accidental or caused by a criminal act on the part of the emperor is uncertain – both versions have supporters. Now started the most terrible and destructive fire which Rome had ever experienced. It began in the Circus, where it adjoins the Palatine and Caelian hills. Breaking out in shops selling inflammable goods, and fanned by the wind, the conflagration instantly grew and swept the whole length of the Circus. There were no walled mansions or temples, or any other obstructions, which could arrest it. First, the fire swept violently over the level spaces. Then it climbed the hills – but returned to ravage the lower ground again. It outstripped every counter-measure. The ancient city's narrow winding streets and irregular blocks encouraged its progress.

Terrified, shrieking women, helpless old and young, people intent on their own safety, people unselfishly supporting invalids or waiting for them, fugitives and lingerers alike – all heightened the confusion. When people looked back, menacing flames sprang up before them or outflanked them. When they escaped to a neighbouring quarter, the fire followed – even districts believed remote proved to be involved. Finally, with no idea where or what to flee, they crowded on to the country roads, or lay in the fields. Some who had lost everything – even their food for the day – could have escaped, but preferred to die. So did others, who had failed to rescue their loved ones. Nobody dared fight the flames. Attempts to do so were prevented by menacing gangs. Torches, too, were openly thrown in, by men crying that they acted under orders. Perhaps they had received orders. Or they may just have wanted to plunder unhampered.

Nero was at Antium. He returned to the city only when the fire was approaching the mansion he had built to link the Gardens of Maecenas to the Palatine. The flames could not be prevented from overwhelming the whole of the Palatine, including his palace. Nevertheless, for the relief of the homeless, fugitive masses he threw open the Field of Mars, including Agrippa's public buildings, and even his own Gardens. Nero also constructed emergency accommodation for the destitute multitude. Food was brought from Ostia and neighbouring towns, and the price of corn was cut to less than ¼ sesterce a pound. Yet these measures, for all their popular character, earned no gratitude. For a rumour had spread that, while the city was burning, Nero had gone on his private stage and, comparing modern calamities with ancient, had sung of the destruction of Troy.

By the sixth day enormous demolitions had confronted the raging flames with bare ground and open sky, and the fire was finally stamped out at the foot of the Esquiline Hill. But before panic had subsided, or hope revived, flames broke out again in the more open regions of the city. Here there were fewer casualties; but the destruction of temples and pleasure arcades was even worse. This new conflagration caused additional ill-feeling because it started on Tigellinus' estate in the Aemilian district. For people believed that Nero was ambitious to found a new city to be called after himself.

Of Rome's fourteen districts only four remained intact. Three were levelled to the ground. The other seven were reduced to a few scorched and mangled ruins.

The Siege of Jerusalem, AD 70

Josephus

Jerusalem fell, after siege, to a Roman army under Titus. Josephus was a Jew who had gone over to the Romans.

Throughout the city people were dying of hunger in large numbers, and enduring indescribable sufferings. In every house the merest hint of food sparked violence, and close relatives fell to blows, snatching from one another the pitiful supports of life. No respect was paid even to the dying; the ruffians [anti-Roman zealots] searched them, in case they were concealing food somewhere in their clothes, or just pretending to be near to death. Gaping with hunger, like mad dogs, lawless gangs went staggering and reeling through the streets, battering upon the doors like drunkards, and so bewildered that they broke into the same house two or three times in an hour. Need drove the starving to gnaw at anything. Refuse which even animals would reject was collected and turned into food. In the end they were eating belts and shoes, and the leather stripped off their shields. Tufts of withered grass were devoured, and sold in little bundles for four drachmas.

But why dwell on the commonplace rubbish which the starving were driven to feed upon, given that what I have to recount is an act unparalleled in the history of either the Greeks or the barbarians, and as horrible to relate as it is incredible to hear? For my part I should gladly have omitted this tragedy, lest I should be suspected of a monstrous fabrication. But there were many witnesses of it among my contemporaries; and besides, I should do poor service to my country if I were to suppress the agonies she went through.

Among the residents of the region beyond Jordan was a woman called Mary, daughter of Eleazar, of the village of Bethezuba (the name means 'House of Hyssop'). She was well off, and of good family, and had fled to Jerusalem with her relatives, where she became involved in the siege. Most of the property she had packed up and brought with her from Peraea had been plundered by the tyrants [Simon and John, leaders of the Jewish war-effort], and the rest of her treasure, together with such food as she had been able to procure, was being carried off by their henchmen in their daily raids. In her bitter resentment the poor woman cursed and abused these extortioners, and this incensed them against her. However, no one put her to death either from exasperation or pity. She grew weary of trying to find food for her kinsfolk. In any case, it was by now impossible to get any, wherever you tried. Famine gnawed at her vitals, and the fire of rage was even fiercer than famine. So, driven by fury and want, she committed a crime against nature. Seizing her child, an infant at the breast, she cried, 'My poor baby, why should I keep you alive in this world of war and famine? Even if we live till the Romans come, they will make slaves of us; and anyway, hunger will get us before slavery does; and the rebels are crueller than both. Come, be food for me, and an avenging fury to the rebels, and a tale of horror to the world to complete the monstrous agony of the Jews.' With these words she killed her son, roasted the body, swallowed half of it, and stored the rest in a safe place. But the rebels were on to her at once, smelling roast meat, and threatening to kill her instantly if she did not produce it. She assured them she had saved them a share, and revealed the remains of her child. Seized with horror and stupefaction, they stood paralysed at the sight. But she said, 'This is my own child, and my own handiwork. Eat, for I have eaten already. Do not show yourselves weaker than a woman, or more pitiful than a mother. But if you have pious scruples, and shrink from human sacrifice, then what I have eaten can count as your share, and I will eat what is left as well.' At that they slunk away, trembling, not daring to eat, though they were reluctant to yield even this food to the mother. The whole city soon rang with the abomination. When people heard of it, they shuddered, as though they had done it themselves.

The Eruption of Vesuvius, 24 August, AD 79

Pliny the Younger

It was this eruption that destroyed and buried the towns of Pompeii and Herculaneum.

My uncle was stationed at Misenum, in active command of the fleet. On 24 August, in the early afternoon, my mother drew his attention to a cloud of unusual size and appearance. He had been out in the sun, had taken a cold bath, and lunched while lying down, and was then working at his books. He called for his shoes and climbed up to a place which would give him the best view of the phenomenon. It was not clear at that distance from which mountain the cloud was rising (it was afterwards known to be Vesuvius); its general appearance can best be expressed as being like an umbrella pine, for it rose to a great height on a sort of trunk and then split off into branches, I imagine because it was thrust upwards by the first blast and then left unsupported as the pressure subsided, or else it was borne down by its own weight so that it spread out and gradually dispersed. In places it looked white, elsewhere blotched and dirty, according to the amount of soil and ashes it carried with it. My uncle's scholarly acumen saw at once that it was important enough for a closer inspection, and he ordered a boat to be made ready, telling me I could come with him if I wished. I replied that I preferred to go on with my studies, and as it happened he had himself given me some writing to do.

As he was leaving the house he was handed a message from Rectina, wife of Tascus whose house was at the foot of the mountain, so that escape was impossible except by boat. She was terrified by the danger threatening her and implored him to rescue her from her fate. He changed his plans, and what he had begun in a spirit of inquiry he completed as a hero. He gave orders for the warships to be launched and went on board himself with the intention of bringing help to many more people besides Rectina, for this lovely stretch of coast was thickly populated. He hurried to the place which everyone else was hastily leaving, steering his course straight for the danger zone. He was entirely fearless, describing each new movement and phase of the portent to be noted down exactly as he observed them. Ashes were already falling, hotter and thicker as the ships drew near, followed by bits of pumice and blackened stones, charred and cracked by the flames: then suddenly they were in shallow water, and the shore was blocked by the debris from the mountain. For a moment my uncle wondered whether to turn back, but when the helmsman advised this he refused, telling him that Fortune stood by the courageous and they must make for Pomponianus at Stabiae. He was cut off there by the breadth of the bay (for the shore gradually curves round a basin filled by the sea) so that he was not as yet in danger, though it was clear that this would come nearer as it spread. Pomponianus had therefore already put his belongings on board ship, intending to escape if the contrary wind fell. This wind was of course full in my uncle's favour, and he was able to bring his ship in. He embraced his terrified friend, cheered and encouraged him, and thinking he could calm his fears by showing his own composure, gave orders that he was to be carried to the bathroom. After his bath he lay down and dined; he was quite cheerful, or at any rate he pretended he was, which was no less courageous.

Meanwhile on Mount Vesuvius broad sheets of fire and leaping flames blazed at several points, their bright glare emphasized by the darkness of night. My uncle tried to allay the fears of his companions by repeatedly declaring that these were nothing but bonfires left by the peasants in their terror, or else empty houses on fire in the districts they had abandoned. Then he went to rest and certainly slept, for as he was a stout man his breathing was rather loud and heavy and could be heard by people coming and going outside his door. By this time the courtyard giving access to his room was full of ashes mixed with pumice stones, so that its level had risen, and if he had stayed in the room any longer he would never have got out. He was wakened, came out and joined Pomponianus and the rest of the household who had sat up all night. They debated whether to stay indoors or take their chance in the open, for the buildings were now shaking with violent shocks, and seemed to be swaying to and fro as if they were torn from their foundations. Outside, on the other hand, there was the danger of falling pumice stones, even though these were light and porous; however, after comparing the risks they chose the latter. In my uncle's case one reason outweighed the other, but for the others it was a choice of fears. As a protection against falling objects they put pillows on their heads tied down with cloths.

Elsewhere there was daylight by this time, but they were still in darkness, blacker and denser than any ordinary night, which they relieved by lighting torches and various kinds of lamp. My uncle decided to go down to the shore and investigate on the spot the possibility of any escape by sea, but he found the waves still wild and dangerous. A sheet was spread on the ground for him to lie down, and he repeatedly asked for cold water to drink. Then the flames and smell of sulphur which gave warning of the approaching fire drove the others to take flight and roused him to stand up. He stood leaning on two slaves and then suddenly collapsed, I imagine because the dense fumes choked his breathing by blocking his windpipe which was constitutionally weak and narrow and often inflamed. When daylight returned on the 26th – two days after the last day he had seen – his body was found intact and uninjured, still fully clothed and looking more like sleep than death.

Meanwhile my mother and I were at Misenum ... After my uncle's departure I spent the rest of the day with my books, as this was my reason for staying behind. Then I took a bath, dined, and then dozed fitfully for a while. For several days past there had been earth tremors which were not particularly alarming because they are frequent in Campania: but that night the shocks were so violent that everything felt as if it were not only shaken but overturned. My mother hurried into my room and found me already getting up to wake her if she were still asleep. We sat down in the forecourt of the house, between the buildings and the sea close by. I don't know whether I should call this courage or folly on my part (I was only seventeen at the time) but I called for a volume of Livy and went on reading as if I had nothing else to do. I even went on with the extracts I had been making. Up came a friend of my uncle's who had just come from Spain to join him. When he saw us sitting there and me actually reading, he scolded us both – me for my foolhardiness and my mother for allowing it. Nevertheless, I remained absorbed in my book.

By now it was dawn, but the light was still dim and faint. The buildings round us were already tottering, and the open space we were in was too small for us not to be in real and imminent danger if the house collapsed. This finally decided us to leave the town. We were followed by a panic-stricken mob of people wanting to act on someone else's decision in preference to their own (a point in which fear looks like prudence), who hurried us on our way by pressing hard behind in a dense crowd. Once beyond the buildings we stopped, and there we had some extraordinary experiences which thoroughly alarmed us. The carriages we had ordered to be brought out began to run in different directions though the ground was quite level, and would not remain stationary even when wedged with stones. We also saw the sea sucked away and apparently forced back by the earthquake: at any rate it receded from the shore so that quantities of sea creatures were left stranded on dry sand. On the landward side a fearful black cloud was rent by forked and quivering bursts of flame, and parted to reveal great tongues of fire, like flashes of lightning magnified in size.

At this point my uncle's friend from Spain spoke up still more urgently, 'If your brother, if your uncle is still alive, he will want you both to be saved; if he is dead, he would want you to survive him – why put off your escape?' We replied that we would not think of considering our own safety as long as we were uncertain of his. Without waiting any longer, our friend rushed off and hurried out of danger as fast as he could.

Soon afterwards the cloud sank down to earth and covered the sea; it had already blotted out Capri and hidden the promontory of Misenum from sight. Then my mother implored, entreated and commanded me to escape as best I could – a young man might escape, whereas she was old and slow and could die in peace as long as she had not been the cause of my death too. I refused to save myself without her, and grasping her hand forced her to quicken her pace. She gave in reluctantly, blaming herself for delaying me. Ashes were already falling, not as yet very thickly. I looked round: a dense black cloud was coming up behind us, spreading over the earth like a flood. 'Let us leave the road while we can still see,' I said, 'or we shall be knocked down and trampled underfoot in the dark by the crowd behind.' We had scarcely sat down to rest when darkness fell, not the dark of a moonless or cloudy night, but as if the lamp had been put out in a closed room. You could hear the shrieks of women, the wailing of infants, and the shouting of men; some were calling their parents, others their children or their wives, trying to recognize them by their voices. People bewailed their own fate or that of their relatives, and there were some who prayed for death in their terror of dying. Many besought the aid of the gods, but still more imagined there were no gods left, and that the universe was plunged into eternal darkness for evermore. There were people, too, who added to the real perils by inventing fictitious dangers: some reported that part of Misenum had collapsed or another part was on fire, and though their tales were false they found others to believe them. A gleam of light returned, but we took this to be a warning of the approaching flames rather than daylight. However, the flames remained some distance off; then darkness came on once more and ashes began to fall again, this time in heavy showers. We rose from time to time and shook them off, otherwise we should have been buried and crushed beneath their weight. I could boast that not a groan or cry of fear escaped me in these perils, but I admit that I derived some poor consolation in my mortal lot from the belief that the whole world was dying with me and I with it.

At last the darkness thinned and dispersed like smoke or cloud; then there was genuine daylight, and the sun actually shone out, but yellowish as it is during an eclipse. We were terrified to see everything changed, buried deep in ashes like snowdrifts. We returned to Misenum where we attended to our physical needs as best we could, and then spent an anxious night alternating between hope and fear. Fear predominated, for the earthquakes went on, and several hysterical individuals made their own and other people's calamities seem ludicrous in comparison with their frightful predictions. But even then, in spite of the dangers we had been through and were still expecting, my mother and I had still no intention of leaving until we had news of my uncle.

Of course these details are not important enough for history, and you will read them without any idea of recording them; if they seem scarcely worth putting in a letter, you have only yourself to blame for asking for them.

The Deification of the Emperor Septimius Severus,
AD 211

Herodian

Septimius Severus had died in Britain. Herodian was a Greek historian living in Rome at the time.

Before doing anything else Caracalla and Geta completed the funeral honours of their father.

It is the Roman custom to give divine status to those of their emperors who die with heirs to succeed them. This ceremony is called deification. Public mourning, with a mixture of festive and religious ritual, is proclaimed throughout the city, and the body of the dead man is buried in the normal way with a costly funeral. Then they make an exact wax replica of the man, which they put on a huge ivory bed, strewn with gold-threaded coverings, raised high up in the entrance to the palace. This image, deathly pale, rests there like a sick man. Either side of the bed is attended for most of the day, the whole Senate sitting on the left, dressed in black, while on the right are all the women who can claim special honours from the position of their husbands or fathers. Not one of these can be seen wearing gold or adorned with necklaces, but they are all dressed in plain white garments, giving the appearance of mourners.

This continues for seven days, during each of which doctors come and approach the bed, take a look at the supposed invalid and announce a daily deterioration in his condition. When at last the news is given that he is dead, the bed or bier is raised on the shoulders of the noblest members of the Equestrian Order and chosen young Senators, carried along the Sacred Way, and placed in the Forum Romanum, where the Roman magistrates usually lay down their office. Tiers of seats rise up on either side, and on one flank a chorus of children from the noblest and most respected families stands facing a body of women selected on merit. Each group sings hymns and songs of thanksgiving in honour of the dead emperor, composed in a solemn and mournful key.

After this the bier is raised and carried outside the city walls to the Campus Martius, where on the widest part of the plain a square structure is erected, looking like a house, made from only the largest timbers jointed together. The whole inside is filled with firewood, and the outside is covered with golden garments, ivory decorations and rich pictures. On top of this rests another structure, similar in design and finish but smaller, with doors and open panels. Third and fourth storeys, decreasing in size, are topped by a fifth, the smallest of all. The shape of the whole might be compared with a lighthouse at the entrance to a harbour which guides ships on safe courses at night by its light. (Such a lighthouse is commonly called a *Pharos*.) When the bier has been taken to the second storey and put inside, aromatic herbs and incense of every kind produced on earth, together with flowers, grasses and juices collected for their smell, are brought and poured in in heaps. Every nation and city, every person without distinction of rank or position competes in bringing these last gifts in honour of their emperor. When the pile of aromatic material is very high and the whole space filled, a mounted display is held around the structure. The whole Equestrian Order rides round, wheeling in well-disciplined circles in the Pyrrhic style. Chariots also circle in the same formations, the charioteers dressed in purple and carrying images with the masks of famous Roman generals and emperors.

The display over, the heir to the throne takes a brand and sets it to the building. All the spectators crowd in and add to the flame. Everything is very easily and readily consumed by the fire because of the mass of firewood and incense inside. From the highest and smallest storey, as from some battlement, an eagle is released and carried up into the sky with the flames. The Romans believe that this bird bears the soul of the emperor from earth to heaven. Thereafter the dead emperor is worshipped with the rest of the gods.

Dinner with Attila the Hun, *c.* AD 450

Priscus

Attila, the 'Scourge of God', became King of the Huns in AD 445.
Priscus went on an embassy to him on behalf of the Eastern
Empire.

Attila invited both parties of us to dine with him about three
o'clock that afternoon. We waited for the time of the invitation,
and then all of us, the envoys from the Western Romans as well,
presented ourselves in the doorway facing Attila. In accordance
with the national custom the cupbearers gave us a cup for us to
make our libations before we took our seats. When that had been
done and we had sipped the wine, we went to the chairs where we
would sit to have dinner. All the seats were ranged down either side
of the room, up against the walls. In the middle Attila was sitting on
a couch with a second couch behind him. Behind that a few steps
led up to his bed, which for decorative purposes was covered in
ornate drapes made of fine linen, like those which Greeks and
Romans prepare for marriage ceremonies. I think that the more
distinguished guests were on Attila's right, and the second rank on
his left, where we were with Berichos, a man of some renown
among the Scythians, who was sitting in front of us. Onegesios was
to the right of Attila's couch, and opposite him were two of the
king's sons on chairs. The eldest son was sitting on Attila's own
couch, right on the very edge, with his eyes fixed on the ground in
fear of his father.

When all were sitting properly in order, a cupbearer came to
offer Attila an ivy-wood bowl of wine, which he took and drank a
toast to the man first in order of precedence. The man thus
honoured rose to his feet and it was not right for him to sit down
again until Attila had drunk some or all of the wine and had handed
the goblet back to the attendant. The guests, taking their own cups,
then honoured him in the same way, sipping the wine after making
the toast. One attendant went round to each man in strict order
after Attila's personal cupbearer had gone out. When the second
guest and then all the others in their turn had been honoured, Attila
greeted us in like fashion in our order of seating.

After everyone had been toasted, the cupbearers left, and a table was put in front of Attila and other tables for groups of three or four men each. This enabled each guest to help himself to the things put on the table without leaving his proper seat. Attila's servant entered first with plates full of meat, and those waiting on all the others put bread and cooked food on the tables. A lavish meal, served on silver trenchers, was prepared for us and the other barbarians, but Attila just had some meat on a wooden platter, for this was one aspect of his self-discipline. For instance, gold or silver cups were presented to the other diners, but his own goblet was made of wood. His clothes, too, were simple, and no trouble was taken except to have them clean. The sword that hung by his side, the clasps of his barbarian shoes and the bridle of his horse were all free from gold, precious stones or other valuable decorations affected by the other Scythians. When the food in the first plates was finished we all got up, and no one, once on his feet, returned to his seat until he had, in the same order as before, drunk the full cup of wine that he was handed, with a toast for Attila's health. After this honour had been paid him, we sat down again and second plates were put on each table with other food on them. This also finished, everyone rose once more, drank another toast and resumed his seat.

As twilight came on torches were lit, and two barbarians entered before Attila to sing some songs they had composed, telling of his victories and his valour in war. The guests paid close attention to them, and some were delighted with the songs, others excited at being reminded of the wars, but others broke down and wept if their bodies were weakened by age and their warrior spirits forced to remain inactive. After the songs a Scythian entered, a crazy fellow who told a lot of strange and completely false stories, not a word of truth in them, which made everyone laugh. Following him came the Moor, Zerkon, totally disorganized in appearance, clothes, voice and words. By mixing up the languages of the Italians with those of the Huns and Goths, he fascinated everyone and made them break out into uncontrollable laughter, all that is except Attila. He remained impassive, without any change of expression, and neither by word or gesture did he seem to share in the merriment except that when his youngest son, Ernas, came in and stood by him, he drew the boy towards him and looked at him with gentle eyes. I was surprised that he paid no attention to his other sons, and only had time for this one. But the barbarian at my side, who understood Italian and what I had said about the boy, warned me not to speak up, and said that the seers had told Attila that his family would be banished but would be restored by this son. After spending most of the night at the party, we left, having no wish to pursue the drinking any further.

A Viking Funeral, AD 922

Performed by Scandinavian Merchants on the Volga; Observed by an Envoy from the Caliph of Baghdad

Ibn Fadlan

I was told that the least of what they do for their chiefs when they die, is to consume them with fire. When I was finally informed of the death of one of their magnates, I sought to witness what befell. First they laid him in his grave – over which a roof was erected – for the space of ten days, until they had completed the cutting and sewing of his clothes. In the case of a poor man, however, they merely build for him a boat, in which they place him, and consume it with fire. At the death of a rich man, they bring together his goods, and divide them into three parts. The first of these is for his family; the second is expended for the garments they make; and with the third they purchase strong drink, against the day when the girl resigns herself to death, and is burned with her master. To the use of wine they abandon themselves in mad fashion, drinking it day and night; and not seldom does one die with the cup in his hand.

When one of their chiefs dies, his family asks his girls and pages, 'Which one of you will die with him?' Then one of them answers, 'I.' From the time that he utters this word, he is no longer free: should he wish to draw back, he is not permitted. For the most part, however, it is the girls that offer themselves. So, when the man of whom I spoke had died, they asked his girls, 'Who will die with him?' One of them answered, 'I.' She was then committed to two girls, who were to keep watch over her, accompany her wherever she went, and even, on occasion, wash her feet. The people now began to occupy themselves with the dead man – to cut out the clothes for him, and to prepare whatever else was needful. During the whole of this period, the girl gave herself over to drinking and singing, and was cheerful and gay.

When the day was now come that the dead man and the girl were to be committed to the flames, I went to the river in which his ship lay, but found that it had already been drawn ashore. Four corner-blocks of birch and other woods had been placed in position for it, while around were stationed large wooden figures in the semblance of human beings. Thereupon the ship was brought up, and placed on the timbers above-mentioned. In the meantime the people began to walk to and fro, uttering words which I did not understand. The dead man, meanwhile, lay at a distance in his grave, from which they had not yet removed him. Next they brought a couch, placed it in the ship, and covered it with Greek cloth of gold, wadded and quilted, with pillows of the same material. There came an old crone, whom they call the angel of death, and spread the articles mentioned on the couch. It was she who attended to the sewing of the garments, and to all the equipment; it was she, also, who was to slay the girl. I saw her; she was dark, thick-set, with a lowering countenance.

When they came to the grave, they removed the earth from the wooden roof, set the latter aside, and drew out the dead man in the loose wrapper in which he had died. Then I saw that he had turned quite black, by reason of the coldness of that country. Near him in the grave they had placed strong drink, fruits, and a lute; and these they now took out. Except for his colour, the dead man had not changed. They now clothed him in drawers, leggings, boots, and a *kurtak* and *chaftan* of cloth of gold, with golden buttons, placing on his head a cap made of cloth of gold, trimmed with sable. Then they carried him into a tent placed in the ship, seated him on the wadded and quilted covering, supported him with the pillows, and, bringing strong drink, fruits, and basil, placed them all beside him. Then they brought a dog, which they cut in two, and threw into the ship; laid all his weapons beside him; and led up two horses, which they chased until they were dripping with sweat, whereupon they cut them in pieces with their swords, and threw the flesh into the ship. Two oxen were then brought forward, cut in pieces, and flung into the ship. Finally they brought a cock and a hen, killed them, and threw them in also.

The girl who had devoted herself to death meanwhile walked to and fro, entering one after another of the tents which they had there. The occupant of each tent lay with her, saying, 'Tell your master, "I [the man] did this only for love of you." '

When it was now Friday afternoon, they led the girl to an object which they had constructed, and which looked like the framework of a door. She then placed her feet on the extended hands of the men, was raised up above the framework, and uttered something in her language, whereupon they let her down. Then again they raised her, and she did as at first. Once more they let her down, and then lifted her a third time, while she did as at the previous times. They then handed her a hen, whose head she cut off and threw away; but the hen itself they cast into the ship. I inquired of the interpreter what it was that she had done. He replied: 'The first time she said, "Lo, I see here my father and mother"; the second time, "Lo, now I see all my deceased relatives sitting"; the third time, "Lo, there is my master, who is sitting in Paradise. Paradise is so beautiful, so green. With him are his men and boys. He calls me, so bring me to him." ' Then they led her away to the ship.

Here she took off her two bracelets, and gave them to the old woman who was called the angel of death, and who was to murder her. She also drew off her two anklets, and passed them to the two serving-maids, who were the daughters of the so-called angel of death. Then they lifted her into the ship, but did not yet admit her to the tent. Now men came up with shields and staves, and handed her a cup of strong drink. This she took, sang over it, and emptied it. 'With this,' so the interpreter told me, 'she is taking leave of those who are dear to her.' Then another cup was handed her, which she also took, and began a lengthy song. The crone admonished her to drain the cup without lingering, and to enter the tent where her master lay. By this time, as it seemed to me, the girl had become dazed; she made as though she would enter the tent, and had brought her head forward between the tent and the ship, when the hag seized her by the head, and dragged her in. At this moment the men began to beat upon their shields with the staves, in order to drown the noise of her outcries, which might have terrified the other girls, and deterred them from seeking death with their masters in the future. Then six men followed into the tent, and each and every one had carnal companionship with her. Then they laid her down by her master's side, while two of the men seized her by the feet, and two by the hands. The old woman known as the angel of death now knotted a rope around her neck, and handed the ends to two of the men to pull. Then with a broad-bladed dagger she smote her between the ribs, and drew the blade forth, while the two men strangled her with the rope till she died.

The next of kin to the dead man now drew near, and, taking a piece of wood, lighted it, and walked backwards towards the ship, holding the stick in one hand, with the other placed upon his buttocks (he being naked), until the wood which had been piled under the ship was ignited. Then the others came up with staves and firewood, each one carrying a stick already lighted at the upper end, and threw it all on the pyre. The pile was soon aflame, then the ship, finally the tent, the man, and the girl, and everything else in the ship. A terrible storm began to blow up, and this intensified the flames, and gave wings to the blaze.

The Green Children, c. 1150

William of Newburgh

Nor does it seem right to pass over an unheard-of prodigy, which, as is well known, took place in England during the reign of King Stephen. Though it is asserted by many, yet I have long been in doubt concerning the matter, and deemed it ridiculous to give credit to a circumstance supported on no rational foundation, or at least one of a very mysterious character; yet, at length I was so overwhelmed by the weight of so many and such competent witnesses, that I have been compelled to believe, and wonder over a matter, which I was unable to comprehend, or unravel, by any powers of intellect.

In East Anglia there is a village, distant, as it is said, four or five miles from the noble monastery of the blessed king and martyr, Edmund; near this place are seen some very ancient cavities, called 'Wolfpittes', that is, in English, 'Pits for wolves', and which give their name to the adjacent village [Wulpet]. During harvest, while the reapers were employed in gathering in the produce of the fields, two children, a boy and a girl, completely green in their persons, and clad in garments of a strange colour, and unknown materials, emerged from these excavations. While wandering through the fields in astonishment, they were seized by the reapers, and conducted to the village, and many persons coming to see so novel a sight, they were kept some days without food. But, when they were nearly exhausted with hunger, and yet could relish no species of support which was offered to them, it happened, that some beans were brought in from the field, which they immediately seized with avidity, and examined the stalk for the pulse, but not finding it in the hollow of the stalk, they wept bitterly. Upon this, one of the bystanders, taking the beans from the pods, offered them to the children, who seized them directly, and ate them with pleasure. By this food they were supported for many months, until they learned the use of bread. At length, by degrees, they changed their original colour, through the natural effect of our food, and became like ourselves, and also learned our language. It seemed fitting to certain discreet persons that they should receive the sacrament of baptism, which was administered accordingly. The boy, who appeared to be the younger, surviving the baptism but a little time, died prematurely; his sister, however, continued in good health, and differed not in the least from the women of our own country. Afterwards, as it is reported, she was married at Lynne, and was living a few years since, at least, so they say. Moreover, after they had acquired our language, on being asked who and whence they were, they are said to have replied, 'We are inhabitants of the land of St Martin, who is regarded with peculiar veneration in the country which gave us birth.' Being further asked where that land was, and how they came thence hither, they answered, 'We are ignorant of both those circumstances; we only remember this, that on a certain day, when we were feeding our father's flocks in the fields, we heard a great sound, such as we are now accustomed to hear at St Edmund's, when the bells are chiming; and whilst listening to the sound in admiration, we became on a sudden, as it were, entranced, and found ourselves among you in the fields where you were reaping.' Being questioned whether in that land they believed in Christ, or whether the sun arose, they replied that the country was Christian, and possessed churches; but said they, 'The sun does not rise upon our countrymen; our land is little cheered by its beams; we are contented with that twilight, which, among you, precedes the sunrise, or follows the sunset. Moreover, a certain luminous country is seen, not far distant from ours, and divided from it by a very considerable river.' These, and many other matters, too numerous to particularize, they are said to have recounted to curious inquirers. Let every one say as he pleases, and reason on such matters according to his abilities; I feel no regret at having recorded an event so prodigious and miraculous.

The Murder of Thomas Becket, 29 December 1170
In Canterbury Cathedral, on the Orders of Henry II

Edward Grim

Therefore the said persons, no knights but miserable wretches, as soon as they landed summoned the King's officials, whom the archbishop had excommunicated, and by lyingly declaring that they were acting by the King's orders and in his name they got together a band of followers. They then collected in a body, ready for any impious deed, and on the fifth day after the Nativity of Christ, that is on the day after the festival of the Holy Innocents, gathered together against the innocent. The hour of dinner being over, the saint had departed with some of his household from the crowd into an inner room, to transact some business, leaving a crowd waiting in the hall outside. The four knights with one attendant entered. They were received with respect as the servants of the King and well known; and those who had waited on the Archbishop being now themselves at dinner invited them to table. They scorned the food, thirsting rather for blood. By their order the Archbishop was informed that four men had arrived who wished to speak with him from the King. He consented and they entered. They sat for a long time in silence and did not salute the Archbishop or speak to him. Nor did the man of wise counsel salute them immediately they came in, that according to the Scripture, 'By thy words thou shalt be justified', he might discover their intentions from their questions. After a while, however, he turned to them, and carefully scanning the face of each one he greeted them in a friendly manner, but the wretches, who had made a treaty with death, answered his greeting with curses, and ironically prayed that God might help him. At this speech of bitterness and malice the man of God coloured deeply, now seeing that they had come for his hurt. Whereupon Fitzurse, who seemed to be the chief and the most eager for crime among them, breathing fury, broke out in these words, 'We have somewhat to say to thee by the King's command: say if thou wilt that we tell it here before all.' But the Archbishop knew what they were going to say, and replied, 'These things should not be spoken in private or in the chamber, but in public.' Now these wretches so burned for the slaughter of the Archbishop that if the doorkeeper had not called back the clerks – for the Archbishop had ordered them all to go out – they would have killed him, as they afterwards confessed, with the shaft of his cross which stood by. When those who had gone out returned, he, who had before thus reviled the Archbishop, said, 'The King, when peace was made between you and all disputes were ended, sent you back free to your own see, as you demanded: but you on the other hand adding insult to your former injuries have broken the peace and wrought evil in yourself against your lord' . . .

'Now,' said these butchers, 'this is the King's command that you depart with all your men from the kingdom, and the land which lies under his sway: for from this day can there be no peace with you, or any of yours, for you have broken the peace.' Then said he, 'Let your threats cease and your wranglings be stilled. I trust in the King of heaven, who for His own suffered on the Cross: for from this day no one shall see the sea between me and my church. I came not to fly; here he who wants me shall find me. And it befitteth not the King so to command; sufficient are the insults which I and mine have received from the King's servants, without further threats' . . .

Confounded at these words the knights sprang up, for they could bear his firmness no longer, and coming close to him they said, 'We declare to you that you have spoken in peril of your head.' 'Do you come to kill me?' he answered. 'I have committed my cause to the Judge of all; wherefore I am not moved by threats, nor are your swords more ready to strike than is my soul for martyrdom. Seek him who flees from you; me you will find foot to foot in the battle of the Lord.' As they went out with tumult and insults, he who was fitly surnamed Ursus [a bear], called out in brutal sort, 'In the King's name we order you, both clerk and monk, that ye take and hold that man, lest he escape by flight ere the King have full justice on his body.' As they went out with these words, the man of God followed them to the door and exclaimed, 'Here, here shall ye find me'; putting his hand over his neck as though showing the place where they were to strike.

He returned then to the place where he had sat before, and

consoled his clerks, and exhorted them not to fear; and, as it seemed to us who were present, waited as unperturbed – though him alone did they seek to slay – as though they had come to invite him to a bridal. Ere long back came the butchers with swords and axes and falchions and other weapons fit for the crime which their minds were set on. When they found the doors barred and they were not opened to their knocking, they turned aside by a private way through the orchard to a wooden partition which they cut and hacked till they broke it down. At this terrible noise were the servants and clerks horribly affrighted, and, like sheep before the wolf, dispersed hither and thither. Those who remained called out that he should flee to the church, but he did not forget his promise not to flee from his murderers through fear of death, and refused to go . . . But when he would not be persuaded by arguments or prayer to take refuge in the church the monks caught hold of him in spite of his resistance, and pulled, dragged, and pushed him, not heeding his clamours to be let go, and brought him to the church.

But the door, through which was the way into the monk's cloister, had been carefully secured some days before, and as the tormentors were now at hand, it seemed to take away all hope of escape; but one of them, running forward, caught hold of the lock, and, to the surprise of all, unfastened it with as much ease as if it had been glued to the door.

When the monks had entered the church, already the four knights followed behind with rapid strides. With them was a certain subdeacon, armed with malice like their own, Hugh, fitly surnamed for his wickedness Mauclerc, who showed no reverence for God or the saints, as the result showed. When the holy Archbishop entered the church, the monks stopped vespers which they had begun and ran to him, glorifying God that they saw their father, whom they had heard was dead, alive and safe. They hastened, by bolting the doors of the church, to protect their shepherd from the slaughter. But the champion, turning to them, ordered the church doors to be thrown open, saying, 'It is not meet to make a fortress of the house of prayer, the church of Christ: though it be not shut up it is able to protect its own; and we shall triumph over the enemy rather in suffering than in fighting, for we came to suffer, not to resist.' And straightway they entered the house of peace and reconciliation with swords sacrilegiously drawn, causing horror to the beholders by their very looks and the clanging of their arms.

All who were present were in tumult and fright, for those who had been singing vespers now ran hither to the dreadful sight.

[As he descended the steps towards the door, John of Salisbury and his other clerks, save Robert the canon and William Fitz-Stephen, and Edward Grim, who was newly come to him, sought shelter, some at the altars, some in hiding places, and left him. And, indeed, if he had wished, the Archbishop might easily have saved himself by flight, for both time and place gave occasion. It was evening, a very long night at hand, and the crypt was near wherein are many dark recesses. There was also a door, nearby which a winding stair led to the lofts and roof of the church. But none of these ways would he take.[1]]

Inspired by fury the knights called out, 'Where is Thomas Becket, traitor to the King and realm?' As he answered not they cried out the more furiously, 'Where is the Archbishop?' At this, intrepid and fearless, as it is written, 'The just, like a bold lion, shall be without fear,' he descended from the stair where he had been dragged by the monks in fear of the knights, and in a clear voice answered, 'I am here, no traitor to the King, but a priest. Why do ye seek me?' And whereas he had already said that he feared them not, he added, 'So I am ready to suffer in His name, Who redeemed me by His Blood: be it far from me to flee from your swords, or to depart from justice.' Having thus said, he turned to the right, under a pillar, having on one side the altar of the blessed Mother of God and ever Virgin Mary, on the other that of St Benedict the Confessor: by whose example and prayers, having crucified the world with its lusts, he bore all that the murderer could do with such constancy of soul as if he had been no longer in the flesh. The murderers followed him; 'Absolve', they cried, 'and restore to communion those whom you have excommunicated, and restore their powers to those whom you have suspended.' He answered, 'There has been no satisfaction, and I will not absolve them.' 'Then you shall die,' they cried, 'and receive what you deserve.' 'I am ready,' he replied, 'to die for my Lord, that in my blood the Church may obtain liberty and peace. But in the name of Almighty God, I forbid you to hurt my people whether clerk or lay.' Thus piously and thoughtfully, did the noble martyr provide that no one near him should be hurt or the innocent be brought to death, whereby his glory should be dimmed

[1]The paragraph within square brackets is from William FitzStephen.

as he hastened to Christ. Thus did it become the martyr-knight to follow in the footsteps of his Captain and Saviour Who when the wicked sought Him said, 'If ye seek Me, let these go their way.' Then they laid sacrilegious hands on him, pulling and dragging him that they might kill him outside the church, or carry him away a prisoner, as they afterwards confessed. But when he could not be forced away from the pillar, one of them pressed on him and clung to him more closely. Him he pushed off calling him 'pander', and saying, 'Touch me not, Reginald; you owe me fealty and subjection; you and your accomplices act like madmen.' The knight, fired with terrible rage at this severe repulse, waved his sword over the sacred head. 'No faith', he cried, 'nor subjection do I owe you against my fealty to my lord the King.' Then the unconquered martyr seeing the hour at hand which should put an end to this miserable life and give him straightway the crown of immortality promised by the Lord, inclined his neck as one who prays and joining his hands he lifted them up, and commended his cause and that of the Church to God, to St Mary, and to the blessed martyr Denys. Scarce had he said the words than the wicked knight, fearing lest he should be rescued by the people and escape alive, leapt upon him suddenly and wounded this lamb who was sacrificed to God on the head, cutting off the top of the crown which the sacred unction of the chrism had dedicated to God; and by the same blow he wounded the arm of him who tells this. For he, when the others, both monks and clerks, fled, stuck close to the sainted Archbishop and held him in his arms till the one he interposed was almost severed. Behold the simplicity of the dove, the wisdom of the serpent, in the martyr who opposed his body to those who struck that he might preserve his head, that is his soul and the Church, unharmed, nor would he use any forethought against those who destroyed the body whereby he might escape. O worthy shepherd, who gave himself so boldly to the wolves that his flock might not be torn. Because he had rejected the world, the world in wishing to crush him unknowingly exalted him. Then he received a second blow on the head but still stood firm. At the third blow he fell on his knees and elbows, offering himself a living victim, and saying in a low voice, 'For the Name of Jesus and the protection of the Church I am ready to embrace death.' Then the third knight inflicted a terrible wound as he lay, by which the sword was broken against the pavement, and the crown which was large was separated from the head; so that the blood white with the brain and the brain red with blood, dyed the surface of the virgin mother church with the life and death of the confessor and martyr in the colours of the lily and the rose. The fourth knight prevented any from interfering so that the others might freely perpetrate the murder. As to the fifth, no knight but that clerk who had entered with the knights, that a fifth blow might not be wanting to the martyr who was in other things like to Christ, he put his foot on the neck of the holy priest and precious martyr, and, horrible to say, scattered his brains and blood over the pavement, calling out to the others, 'Let us away, knights; he will rise no more.'

Richard I Massacres Prisoners after Taking Acre, 2–20 August 1191

A Saracen View of the Crusades

Behâ-ed-Din

The same day Hossâm ad-Din Ibn Barîc, an interpreter working with the English, issued from Acre accompanied by two officers of the King of England [Richard I]. He brought news that the King of France had set out for Tyre, and that they had come to talk over the matter of a possible exchange of prisoners and to see the true cross of the Crucifixion if it were still in the Mussulman camp, or to ascertain if it really had been sent to Baghdad. The True Cross was shown to them, and on beholding it they showed the profoundest reverence, throwing themselves on the ground till they were covered with dust, and humbling themselves in token of devotion. These envoys told us that the European princes had accepted the Sultan's [Saladin's] proposition, viz., to deliver all that was specified in the treaty by three instalments at intervals of a month. The Sultan then sent an envoy to Tyre with rich presents, quantities of perfumes, and fine raiment – all of which were for the King of the French.

In the morning of the tenth day of Rajab, [3 August] Ibn Barîc and his comrades returned to the King of England while the Sultan went off with his bodyguard and his closest friends to the hill that abuts on Shefa'Amr . . . Envoys did not cease to pass from one side to the other in the hope of laying the foundation of a firm peace.

These negotiations continued till our men had procured the money and the number of prisoners that they were to deliver to the Christians at the end of the first period in accordance with the treaty. The first instalment was to consist of the Holy Cross, 100,000 dinars and 1,600 prisoners. Trustworthy men sent by the Christians to conduct the examination found it all complete saving only the prisoners who had been demanded by name, all of whom had not yet been gathered together. And thus the negotiations continued to drag on till the end of the first term. On this day, the 18th of Rajab [11 August], the enemy sent demanding what was due.

The Sultan replied as follows: 'Choose one of two things. Either send us back our comrades and receive the payment fixed for this term, in which case we will give hostages to ensure the full execution of all that is left. Or accept what we are going to send you today, and in your turn give us hostages to keep until those of our comrades whom you hold prisoners are restored.' To this the envoys made answer: 'Not so. Send us what is due for this term and in return we will give our solemn oath that your people shall be restored you.'

This proposition the Sultan rejected, knowing full well that if he were to deliver the money, the Cross, and the prisoners, while our men were still kept captive by the Christians, he would have no security against treachery on the part of the enemy, and this would be a great disaster to Islam.

Then the King of England, seeing all the delays interposed by the Sultan to the execution of the treaty, acted perfidiously as regards his Mussulman prisoners. On their yielding the town of Acre he had engaged to grant them life, adding that if the Sultan carried out the bargain he would give them freedom and suffer them to carry off their children and wives; if the Sultan did not fulfil his engagements they were to be made slaves. Now the King broke his promises to them and made open display of what he had till now kept hidden in his heart, by carrying out what he had intended to do after he had received the money and the Christian prisoners. It is thus that people in his nation ultimately admitted.

In the afternoon of Tuesday, 27 Rajab [20 August], about four o'clock, he came out on horseback with all the Christian army, knights, footmen, Turcopoles [light-armed soldiers of the Order of St John of Jerusalem] and advanced to the pits at the foot of the hill of Al 'Ayâdîyeh, to which place he had already sent on his tents.

The Christians, on reaching the middle of the plain that stretches between this hill and that of Keisân, close to which place the Sultan's advanced guard had drawn back, ordered all the Mussulman prisoners, whose martyrdom God had decreed for this day, to be brought before him. They numbered more than three thousand and were all bound with ropes. The Christians then flung themselves upon them all at once and massacred them with sword and lance in cold blood. Our advanced guard had already told the Sultan of the enemy's movements and he sent it some reinforcements, but only after the massacre. The Mussulmans, seeing what was being done to the prisoners, rushed against the Christians and in the combat, which lasted till nightfall, several were slain and wounded on either side. On the morrow morning our people gathered at the spot and found the Mussulmans stretched out upon the ground as martyrs for the faith. They even recognized some of the dead, and the sight was a great affliction to them. The enemy had only spared the prisoners of note and such as were strong enough to work.

The motives of this massacre are differently told; according to some, the captives were slain by way of reprisal for the death of those Christians whom the Mussulmans had slain. Others again say that the King of England, on deciding to attempt the conquest of Ascalon, thought it unwise to leave so many prisoners in the town after his departure. God alone knows what the real reason was.

Kublai Khan's Park, c. 1275

Marco Polo

Kublai Khan (1216–1294) was the Mongol emperor who completed the conquest of China. Marco Polo spent several years in his service.

In this city [Shang-tu] Kublai Khan built a huge palace of marble and other ornamental stones. Its halls and chambers are all gilded, and the whole building is marvellously embellished and richly adorned. At one end it extends into the middle of the city; at the other it abuts on the city wall. At this end another wall, running out from the city wall in the direction opposite to the palace, encloses and encircles fully sixteen miles of parkland well watered with springs and streams and diversified with lawns. Into this park there is no entry except by way of the palace. Here the Great Khan keeps game animals of all sorts, such as hart, stag, and roebuck, to provide food for the gerfalcons and other falcons which he has here in mew. The gerfalcons alone amount to more than 200. Once a week he comes in person to inspect them in the mew. Often, too, he enters the park with a leopard on the crupper of his horse; when he feels inclined, he lets it go and thus catches a hart or stag or roebuck to give to the gerfalcons that he keeps in mew. And this he does for recreation and sport.

In the midst of this enclosed park, where there is a beautiful grove, the Great Khan has built another large palace, constructed entirely of canes, but with the interior all gilt and decorated with beasts and birds of very skilful workmanship. It is reared on gilt and varnished pillars, on each of which stands a dragon, entwining the pillar with his tail and supporting the roof on his outstretched limbs. The roof is also made of canes, so well varnished that it is quite waterproof . . . And the Great Khan has had it so designed that it can be moved whenever he fancies; for it is held in place by more than 200 cords of silk.

Mishaps in Childhood, 1301–37

Calendar of Coroner's Rolls

Playing in the Street, 1301

On Tuesday the Feast of St Philip and James [4 May] a certain Hugh Picard was riding a white horse after the hour of vespers, when Petronilla, daughter of William de Wyntonia, aged three years, was playing in the street; and the horse, being strong, quickly carried Hugh against his will over Petronilla so that it struck her on her right side with its right forefoot. Petronilla lingered until the next day, when she died, at the hour of vespers, from the blow. Being asked who were present, the jurors know only of those mentioned. The corpse viewed, the right side of which appeared blue and badly bruised, and no other hurt. The horse valued at a mark, for which Richard de Caumpes, the sheriff, will answer. Hugh fled and has no chattels; he afterwards surrendered to John de Boreford, sheriff.

A Game on the Way to School, 1301

On Tuesday [19 July], Richard, son of John le Mazon, who was eight years old, was walking immediately after dinner across London Bridge to school. For fun, he tried to hang by his hands from a beam on the side of the bridge, but his hands giving way, he fell into the water and was drowned. Being asked who were present, the jurors say a great multitude of passers-by, whose names they know not, but they suspect no one of the death except mischance.

Playing on the Timber Pile, 1322

On the Sunday before the Feast of St Dunstan, Robert, son of John de St Botulph, a boy seven years old, Richard, son of John de Chesthunt, and two other boys whose names are unknown were playing on certain pieces of timber in the lane called 'Kyrounelane' in the ward of Vintry, and one piece fell on Robert and broke his right leg. In course of time Johanna his mother arrived and rolled the timber off him and carried him to the shop, where he lingered until the Friday before the Feast of St Margaret, when he died at the hour of prime, of the broken leg and of no other felony; nor do the jurors suspect anyone of the death, but only the accident and the fracture.

A Boy Thief, 1324

On Monday [in April, 1324] at the hour of vespers John, son of William de Burgh, a boy five years old, was in the house of Richard le Latthere and had taken a parcel of wool and placed it in his cap. Emma, the wife of Richard, chastising him, struck him with her right hand under his left ear so that he cried. On hearing this, Isabella, his mother, raised the hue and carried him thence. He lingered until the hour of curfew of the same day, when he died of the blow and not of any felony. Emma forthwith fled, but where she went or who received her the jurors knew not. Afterwards she surrendered herself to the prison at Newgate.

A Lost Ball, 1337

On Tuesday in Pentecost week John, son of William atte Noke, chandler, got out of a window in the rent of John de Wynton, plumber, to recover a ball lost in a gutter at play. He slipped and fell, and so injured himself that he died on the Saturday following, of the fall.

The Battle of Crécy, 26 September 1346

Sir John Froissart

Crécy was fought when Edward III, having ravaged Normandy, was retreating towards the coast, pursued by the French under Philip VI. The Prince of Wales mentioned is Edward, the Black Prince, Edward III's eldest son.

That night the King of France entertained at supper, in Abbeville, all the princes and chief lords of his army. There was much conversation relative to the war; and after supper the King entreated them always to remain in friendship with each other; 'to be friends without jealousy, and courteous without pride'. All the French forces had not yet arrived, for the King was still expecting the Earl of Savoy, who ought to have been there with a thousand lances, as he had well paid for them at Troyes in Champaign, three months in advance. That same evening the King of England also gave a supper to his earls and barons, and when it was over he withdrew into his oratory, where falling on his knees before the altar, he prayed to God that if he should combat his enemies on the morrow, he might come off with honour. About midnight he retired to rest, and rising early the next day, he and the Prince of Wales heard mass and communicated. The great part of his army did the same. After mass the King ordered his men to arm themselves and assemble on the ground which he had before fixed upon.

There was a large park near a wood, on the rear of the army, which King Edward enclosed, and in it placed all his baggage, wagons and horses; for his men-at-arms and archers were to fight on foot. He afterwards ordered, through his constable and his two marshals, that the army should be divided into three battalions. In the first, he placed the young Prince of Wales, and with him the Earls of Warwick and Oxford, Sir Godfrey de Harcourt, the Lord Reginald Cobham, Lord Thomas Holland, Lord Stafford, Lord Mauley, the Lord Delaware, Sir John Chandos, Lord Bartholomew

Burghersh, Lord Robert Neville, Lord Thomas Clifford, the Lord Bouchier, the Lord Latimer, and many other knights and squires whom I cannot name. There might be, in this first division, about 800 men-at-arms, 2000 archers, and 1000 Welshmen; all of whom advanced in regular order to their ground, each lord under his banner and pennon, and in the centre of his men. In the second battalion were the Earl of Northampton, the Earl of Arundel, the Lords Ross, Willoughby, Basset, Saint Albans, Sir Lewis Tufton, Lord Multon, the Lord Lascels, and many others, amounting in the whole to about 800 men-at-arms, and 1200 archers. The third battalion was commanded by the King in person, and was composed of about 700 men-at-arms, and 2000 archers. The King was mounted on a small palfrey, having a white wand in his hand, and attended by his two marshals. In this manner he rode at a foot's pace through all the ranks, encouraging the army and entreating that they would guard his honour and defend his right; so sweetly and with such a cheerful countenance did he speak, that all who had been before dispirited, were directly comforted by hearing him. By the time he had thus visited all the battalions it was nearly ten o'clock: he then retired to his own division, having ordered the men to regale themselves, after which all returned to their own battalions, according to the marshal's orders, and seated themselves on the ground, placing their helmets and bows before them, in order that they might be the fresher when their enemies should arrive.

That same Saturday the King of France also rose betimes, heard mass in the monastery of St Peter's in Abbeville, where he lodged; and having ordered his army to do the same, left that town after sunrise. When he had marched about two leagues from Abbeville and was approaching the enemy, he was advised to form his army in order of battle, and to let those on foot march forward that they might not be trampled on by the horses. This being done, he sent off four knights, the Lord Moyne, of Bastleberg, the Lord of Noyers, the Lord of Beaujeu, and the Lord of Aubigny, who rode so near to the English, that they could clearly distinguish their position. The English plainly perceived that these knights came to reconnoitre; however, they took no notice of it, but suffered them to return unmolested.

When the King of France saw them coming back, he halted his army, and the knights pushing through the crowds came near to the

King, who said to them, 'My lords, what news?' Neither chose to speak first – at last the King addressed himself personally to the Lord Moyne, who said, 'Sir, I will speak since it pleases you to order me, but under correction of my companions. We have advanced far enough to reconnoitre your enemies. Know, then, that they are drawn up in three battalions, and are waiting for you. I would advise for my part (submitting, however, to your better counsel) that you halt your army here and quarter them for the night; for before the rear shall come up, and the army be properly drawn up, it will be very late, and your men will be tired and in disorder, whilst they will find your enemies fresh and properly arrayed. On the morrow you may draw up your army more at your ease, and may at leisure reconnoitre on what part it will be most advantageous to begin the attack, for be assured they will wait for you.' The King commanded that it should so be done; and the two marshals rode, one to the front and the other to the rear, crying out, 'Halt banners, in the name of God and St Denis.' Those that were in front, halted; but those that were behind said they would not halt until they were as forward as the front. When the front perceived the rear pressing on, they pushed forward; and as neither the King nor the marshals could stop them, they marched on without any order until they came in sight of their enemies. As soon as the foremost rank saw the English they fell back at once in great disorder, which alarmed those in the rear, who thought they had been fighting. All the roads between Abbeville and Crécy were covered with common people, who, when they were come within three leagues of their enemies, drew their swords, bawling out, 'Kill, kill'; and with them were many lords eager to make a show of their courage.

There is no man, unless he had been present, that can imagine or describe truly the confusion of that day, especially the bad management and disorder of the French, whose troops were out of number. What I know, and shall relate in this book, I have learned chiefly from the English, and from those attached to Sir John of Hainault, who was always near the person of the King of France. The English, who, as I have said, were drawn up in three divisions, and seated on the ground, on seeing their enemies advance, rose up undauntedly and fell into their ranks. The Prince's battalion, whose archers were formed in the manner of a portcullis, and the men-at-arms in the rear, was the first to do so. The Earls of Northampton and Arundel, who commanded the second division, posted themselves in good order on the Prince's wing to assist him if necessary.

You must know that the French troops did not advance in any regular order, and that as soon as their King came in sight of the English his blood began to boil, and he cried out to his marshals, 'Order the Genoese forward and begin the battle in the name of God and St Denis.' There were about 15,000 Genoese crossbow men; but they were quite fatigued, having marched on foot that day six leagues, completely armed and carrying their crossbows, and accordingly they told the Constable they were not in a condition to do any great thing in battle. The Earl of Alençon hearing this, said, 'This is what one gets by employing such scoundrels, who fall off when there is any need for them.' During this time a heavy rain fell, accompanied by thunder and a very terrible eclipse of the sun; and, before this rain, a great flight of crows hovered in the air over all the battalions, making a loud noise; shortly afterwards it cleared up, and the sun shone very bright; but the French had it in their faces, and the English on their backs. When the Genoese were somewhat in order they approached the English and set up a loud shout, in order to frighten them; but the English remained quite quiet and did not seem to attend to it. They then set up a second shout, and advanced a little forward; the English never moved. Still they hooted a third time, advancing with their crossbows presented, and began to shoot. The English archers then advanced one step forward, and shot their arrows with such force and quickness, that it seemed as if it snowed. When the Genoese felt these arrows, which pierced through their armour, some of them cut the strings of their crossbows, others flung them to the ground, and all turned about and retreated quite discomfited.

The French had a large body of men-at-arms on horseback to support the Genoese, and the King, seeing them thus fall back, cried out, 'Kill me those scoundrels, for they stop up our road without any reason.' The English continued shooting, and some of their arrows falling among the horsemen, drove them upon the Genoese, so that they were in such confusion, they could never rally again.

In the English army there were some Cornish and Welsh men on foot, who had armed themselves with large knives, these advancing through the ranks of the men-at-arms and archers, who made way for them, came upon the French when they were in this danger, and falling upon earls, barons, knights, and squires, slew many, at which the King of England was exasperated. The valiant King of Bohemia was slain there; he was called Charles of Luxembourg, for he was the son of the gallant king and emperor, Henry of Luxembourg, and, having heard the order for the battle, he inquired where his son the Lord Charles was; his attendants answered that they did not know, but believed he was fighting. Upon this, he said to them, 'Gentlemen, you are all my people, my friends, and brethren at arms this day; therefore, as I am blind, I request of you to lead me so far into the engagement that I may strike one stroke with my sword.' The knights consented, and in order that they might not lose him in the crowd, fastened all the reins of their horses together, placing the King at their head that he might gratify his wish, and in this manner advanced towards the enemy. The Lord Charles of Bohemia, who already signed his name as King of Germany, and bore the arms, had come in good order to the engagement; but when he perceived that it was likely to turn out against the French he departed. The King, his father, rode in among the enemy, and he and his companions fought most valiantly; however, they advanced so far that they were all slain, and on the morrow they were found on the ground with all their horses tied together.

The Earl of Alençon advanced in regular order upon the English, to fight with them, as did the Earl of Flanders in another part. These two lords with their detachments, coasting, as it were, the archers, came to the Prince's battalion, where they fought valiantly for a length of time. The King of France was eager to march to the place where he saw their banners displayed, but there was a hedge of archers before him: he had that day made a present of a handsome black horse to Sir John of Hainault, who had mounted on it a knight of his, called Sir John de Fusselles, who bore his banner; the horse ran off with the knight and forced his way through the English army, and when about to return, stumbled and fell into a ditch and severely wounded him; he did not, however, experience any other inconvenience than from his horse, for the English did not quit their ranks that day to make prisoners: his page alighted and raised him up, but the French knight did not return the way he came, as he would have found it difficult from the crowd. This battle, which was fought on Saturday, between La Broyes and Crécy, was murderous and cruel; and many gallant deeds of arms were performed that were never known: towards evening, many knights and squires of the French had lost their masters, and wandering up and down the plain, attacked the English in small parties; but they were soon destroyed, for the English had determined that day to give no quarter, nor hear of ransom from anyone.

Early in the day some French, Germans, and Savoyards had broken through the archers of the Prince's battalion, and had engaged with the men-at-arms; upon this the second battalion came to his aid, and it was time they did so, for otherwise he would have been hard pressed. The first division, seeing the danger they were in, sent a knight off in great haste to the King of England, who was posted upon an eminence near a windmill. On the knight's arrival he said, 'Sir, the Earl of Warwick, the Lord Stafford, the Lord Reginald Cobham, and the others who are about your son, are vigorously attacked by the French, and they entreat that you will come to their assistance with your battalion, for if numbers should increase against him, they fear he will have too much to do.' The King replied, 'Is my son dead, unhorsed, or so badly wounded that he cannot support himself?' 'Nothing of the sort, thank God,' rejoined the knight, 'but he is in so hot an engagement that he has great need of your help.' The King answered, 'Now, Sir Thomas, return to those that sent you, and tell them from me not to send again for me this day, nor expect that I shall come, let what will happen, as long as my son has life; and say that I command them to let the boy win his spurs, for I am determined, if it please God, that all the glory of this day shall be given to him, and to those into whose care I have entrusted him.' The knights returned to his lords and related the King's answer, which mightily encouraged them, and made them repent they had ever sent such a message.

It is a certain fact, that Sir Godfrey de Harcourt, who was in the prince's battalion, having been told by some of the English that they had seen the banner of his brother engaged in the battle against him, was exceedingly anxious to save him; but he was too late, for he was left dead on the field, and so was the Earl of Aumarle, his nephew. On the other hand, the Earls of Alençon and Flanders were fighting lustily under their banners with their own people; but they could not resist the force of the English, and were there slain, as well as many other knights and squires, who were attending on, or accompanying them.

The Earl of Blois, nephew to the King of France, and the Duke of

Lorraine, his brother-in-law, with their troops, made a gallant defence; but they were surrounded by a troop of English and Welsh, and slain in spite of their prowess. The Earl of St Pol, and the Earl of Auxerre, were also killed, as well as many others. Late after vespers, the King of France had not more about him than sixty men, every one included. Sir John of Hainault, who was of the number, had once remounted the King, for his horse had been killed under him by an arrow: and seeing the state he was in, he said, 'Sir, retreat whilst you have an opportunity, and do not expose yourself so simply; if you have lost this battle, another time you will be the conqueror.' After he had said this he took the bridle of the King's horse and led him off by force, for he had before entreated him to retire. The king rode on until he came to the castle of La Broyes, where he found the gates shut, for it was very dark: he ordered the Governor of it to be summoned, who, after some delay, came upon the battlements, and asked who it was that called at such an hour. The King answered, 'Open, open, Governor, it is the fortune of France.' The Governor hearing the King's voice immediately descended, opened the gate, and let down the bridge; the King and his company entered the castle, but he had with him only five barons: Sir John of Hainault, the Lord Charles of Montmorency, the Lord of Beaujeu, the Lord of Aubigny, and the Lord of Montfort. It was not his intention, however, to bury himself in such a place as this, but having taken some refreshments, he set out again with his attendants about midnight, and rode on under the direction of guides, who were well acquainted with the country, until about daybreak he came to Amiens, where he halted. This Saturday the English never quitted their ranks in pursuit of anyone, but remained on the field guarding their position and defending themselves against all who attacked them. The battle ended at the hour of vespers, when the King of England embraced his son and said to him, 'Sweet son, God give you perseverance: you are my son; for most loyally have you acquitted yourself; you are worthy to be a sovereign.' The Prince bowed very low, giving all honour to the King, his father. The English during the night made frequent thanksgivings to the Lord for the happy issue of the day; and with them there was no rioting, for the King had expressly forbidden all riot or noise.

On the following day, which was Sunday, there were a few encounters with the French troops; however, they could not withstand the English, and soon either retreated or were put to the sword. When Edward was assured that there was no appearance of the French collecting another army, he sent to have the number and rank of the dead examined. This business was entrusted to Lord Reginald Cobham and Lord Stafford, assisted by three heralds to examine the arms, and two secretaries to write down the names. They passed the whole day upon the field of battle, and made a very circumstantial account of all they saw: according to their report it appeared that 80 banners, the bodies of 11 princes, 1200 knights, and about 30,000 common men were found dead on the field.

The Black Death, 1348

Henry Knighton

It is estimated that the Black Death killed a quarter of the population of Europe, or 25m people. There is controversy about the nature of the disease: it may have been bubonic plague.

In this year there was a general mortality among men throughout the world. It began first in India, and then appeared in Tharsis, then among the Saracens, and at last among the Christians and Jews, so that in the space of one year, namely, from Easter to Easter, 8000 legions of men, according to widely prevalent rumours in the Court of Rome, died in those remote regions, besides Christians. The King of Tharsis, seeing such a sudden and unheard-of mortality among his people, set out with a great multitude of nobles, intending to seek out the Pope at Avignon and have himself baptized as a Christian, believing the vengeance of God to have overtaken his people because of their sinful disbelief. But when he had travelled twenty days he heard along the road that the plague had invaded the ranks of the Christians as well as other nations, and therefore he turned about to go back to his own country. But the Christians, following the Tharsians, attacked them from the rear and slew 2000 of them . . .

The dreadful pestilence penetrated the sea coast by Southampton and came to Bristol, and there almost the whole population of the town perished, as if it had been seized by sudden death; for few kept their beds more than two or three days, or even half a day.

Then this cruel death spread everywhere around, following the course of the sun. And there died at Leicester in the small parish of St Leonard more than 380 persons, in the parish of Holy Cross, 400; in the parish of St Margaret's, Leicester, 700; and so in every parish, a great multitude. Then the Bishop of London sent word throughout his whole diocese giving general power to each and every priest, regular as well as secular, to hear confessions and to give absolution to all persons with full episcopal authority, except only in case of debt. In this case, the debtor was to pay the debt, if he was able, while he lived, or others were to fulfil his obligations from his property after his death. Likewise the Pope granted full remission of all sins to anyone receiving absolution when in danger of death, and granted that this power should last until Easter next following, and that everyone might choose whatever confessor he pleased.

In the same year there was a great murrain of sheep everywhere in the kingdom, so that in one place in a single pasture more than 5000 sheep died; and they putrefied so that neither bird nor beast would touch them. Everything was low in price because of the fear of death, for very few people took any care of riches or property of any kind. A man could have a horse that had been worth 40s for half a mark [6s 8d], a fat ox for 4s, a cow for 12d, a heifer for 6d, a fat wether for 4d, a sheep for 3d, a lamb for 2d, a large pig for 5d; a stone of wool [24 lbs] was worth 9d. Sheep and cattle ran at large through the fields and among the crops, and there was none to drive them off or herd them; for lack of care they perished in ditches and hedges in incalculable numbers throughout all districts, and none knew what to do. For there was no memory of death so stern and cruel since the time of Vortigern, King of the Britons, in whose day, as Bede testifies, the living did not suffice to bury the dead.

In the following autumn a reaper was not to be had for a lower wage than 8d, with his meals; a mower for not less than 10d, with meals. Wherefore many crops wasted in the fields for lack of harvesters. But in the year of the pestilence, as has been said above, there was so great an abundance of every kind of grain that almost no one cared for it.

The Scots, hearing of the dreadful plague among the English, suspected that it had come about through the vengeance of God, and, according to the common report, they were accustomed to swear 'be the foul deth of Engelond'. Believing that the wrath of

God had befallen the English, they assembed in Selkirk forest with the intention of invading the kingdom, when the fierce mortality overtook them, and in a short time about 5000 perished. As the rest, the strong and the feeble, were preparing to return to their own country, they were followed and attacked by the English, who slew countless numbers of them.

Master Thomas of Bradwardine was consecrated by the Pope Archbishop of Canterbury, and when he returned to England he came to London, but within two days was dead . . .

Meanwhile the King sent proclamation into all the counties that reapers and other labourers should not take more then they had been accustomed to take, under the penalty appointed by statute. But the labourers were so lifted up and obstinate that they would not listen to the King's command, but if anyone wished to have them he had to give them what they wanted, and either lose his fruit and crops, or satisfy the lofty and covetous wishes of the workmen. And when it was known to the King that they had not observed his command, and had given greater wages to the labourers, he levied heavy fines upon abbots, priors, knights, greater and lesser, and other great folk and small folk of the realm, of some 100s, of some 40s, of some 20s, from each according to what he could give. And afterwards the King had many labourers arrested, and sent them to prison; many withdrew themselves and went into the forests and woods; and those who were taken were heavily fined. Their ringleaders were made to swear that they would not take daily wages beyond the ancient custom, and then were freed from prison. And in like manner was done with the other craftsmen in the boroughs and villages . . . After the aforesaid pestilence, many buildings, great and small, fell into ruins in every city, borough, and village for lack of inhabitants, likewise many villages and hamlets became desolate, not a house being left in them, all having died who dwelt there; and it was probable that many such villages would never be inhabited.

Women Ape Men, 1348

Henry Knighton

In these days a rumour and a great complaint arose among the people that when tournaments were held, in every place a company of ladies appeared, somewhat like performers in interludes, in the diverse and marvellous dress of a man, to the number sometimes of about forty, sometimes fifty, ladies from the more handsome and the more beautiful, but not the better sort, of the entire kingdom; in divided tunics, that is, one part of one kind and the other of another kind, with small hoods and liripipes flying about the head in the manner of cords, and well encircled with silver or gold, even having across their stomachs, below the middle, knives which they vulgarly called daggers placed in pouches from above. Thus they came, on excellent chargers or other horses splendidly adorned, to the place of the tournament. And in such manner they spent and wasted their riches and injured their bodies with abuses and ludicrous wantonness that the common voice of the people exclaimed. Thus, they neither respected God nor blushed on account of the modest outcries of the people, having freed themselves from the restraint of matrimonial chastity . . . But God against these as against all others appeared with a marvellous remedy, putting their frivolity to rout, for at the places and times designed for this vanity, he defeated them with heavy rainstorms, thunder, and the flash of lightning, and with the fury of diverse extraordinary tempests.

The Capture of Guines, January 1352

Geoffrey le Baker of Swinbrook

Calais had fallen to the English under Edward III in 1347.

About the beginning of January, the Frenchmen being occupied in repairing the walls of Guines town, which had been destroyed by the Englishmen, some men of arms at Calais, understanding what they were doing, planned how they might overthrow the work in this way. There was an archer named John Dancaster in prison in the castle of Guines, who, not having money to pay his ransom, was freed on condition that he should work there among the Frenchmen. This fellow chanced to lie with a laundress, a strumpet, and learned from her where, beyond the principal ditch, from the bottom of the ditch there was a wall two feet broad stretching from the ramparts across to the edge of the ditch so that, being covered with water, it could not be seen, yet not so submerged but that a man walking along the top of it would not be wet past the knees. It was made for the use of fishers, and therefore in the middle there was a two-foot gap. The archer (his harlot shewing it to him) measured the height of the wall with a thread.

After he had learned these things, one day, slipping down from the wall, he crossed the ditch by that hidden wall, and, lying hid in the marsh till evening, came in the night near to Calais, where, waiting for daylight, he went into the town . . . Here he told those who were greedy for prey and were eager to scale the castle, how they could enter it. They had ladders made to the length which the archer told them. Thirty men, plotting together, clothed themselves in black armour without any brightness, went to the castle by the guiding of the said John Dancaster, and, climbing the wall with their ladders, they slew the watchmen and threw them down headlong beside the wall. After this, in the hall, they slew many whom they found unarmed, playing chess and hazard. They then broke into the chambers and turrets upon the ladies and knights that lay there asleep, and so became masters of all that was within. Shutting all the prisoners into a strong chamber and taking away all their armour, they released the Englishmen that had been taken the year before and kept there in prison, and, after they had relieved them well with meat and drink, they made them guardians over those who had had them in custody; and so they won all the fortresses of the castle . . .

The Earl of Guines came to the castle and demanded of those within, as at other times, in whose name they kept it. As they constantly affirmed that they kept it in the name of John Dancaster, he asked whether the same John were the King of England's liegeman or would obey him, and when the said John answered that he did not know what messengers had been in England, the Earl offered for the castle, besides all the treasure found in it, many thousands of crowns, or possessions for exchange, and a perpetual peace with the King of France. To this the defenders replied that, before taking that castle, they had been Englishmen by nation, but by their demerits banished for the peace of the King of England; wherefore the place which they thus held they would willingly sell or exchange, but to none sooner than to their natural King of England, to whom they said they would sell their castle to obtain their peace; but if he would not buy it, then they would sell it to the King of France or to whosoever would give most for it. The Earl being thus shifted off, the King of England bought it, indeed, and so had that place which he greatly desired.

False Mutes, October 1380

City of London Letter-books

On the 24th day of October, in the 4th year of Richard II, John Warde, of the County of York, and Richard Lynham, of the County of Somerset, two impostors, were brought to the Hall of the Guildhall of London, before John Hadlee, Mayor, the Aldermen, and the Sheriffs, and questioned for that, whereas they were stout enough to work for their food and raiment, and had their tongues to talk with, they, the same John Warde and Richard Lynham, did there pretend that they were mutes, and had been deprived of their tongues; and went about in divers places of the city aforesaid, carrying in their hands two ell measures, an iron hook and pincers, and a piece of leather, in shape like part of a tongue, edged with silver, and with writing around it, to this effect – THIS IS THE TONGUE OF JOHN WARDE – with which instruments, and by means of divers signs, they gave many persons to understand that they were traders, in token whereof they carried the said ell measures; and that they had been plundered by robbers of their goods; and that their tongues had also been drawn out with the said hook, and then cut off with the pincers; they making a horrible noise, like unto a roaring, and opening their mouths; where it seemed to all who examined the same, that their tongues had been cut off: to the defrauding of other poor and infirm persons, and in manifest deceit of the whole of the people.

Wherefore, they were asked how they would acquit themselves thereof; upon which, they acknowledged that they had done all the

things above imputed to them. And as it appeared to the Court that
of their evil intent and falsity they had done the things aforesaid,
and in deceit of all the people; and to the end that other persons
might beware of such and the like evil intent, falsity, and deceit, it
was awarded that they should be put upon the pillory on three
different days, each time for one hour in the day; namely, on the
Wednesday, Friday, and Saturday, before the Feast of St Simon and
St Jude [28 October]; the said instruments being hung about their
necks each day. And precept was given to the Sheriffs to do
execution of the judgment aforesaid, and to have proclamation
there made each day, as to the cause thereof; which punishment
being completed, they were instructed to have them taken back to
the Gaol of Newgate, there to remain until orders should be given
for their release.

The Peasants' Revolt, May–June 1381

Sir John Froissart

*Among the causes of the Peasants' Revolt was the unpopularity of
the Statute of Labourers (1351), which fixed maximum wages
during the labour shortage following the Black Death. At the time
of the Revolt Richard II was fourteen.*

In order that this disastrous rebellion may serve as an example to
mankind, I will speak of all that was done from the information I
had at the time. It is customary in England, as well as in several
other countries, for the nobility to have great privileges over the
commonalty; that is to say, the lower orders are bound by law to
plough the lands of the gentry, to harvest their grain, to carry it
home to the barn, to thrash and winnow it; they are also bound to
harvest and carry home the hay. All these services the prelates and
gentlemen exact of their inferiors; and in the counties of Kent,
Essex, Sussex, and Bedford, these services are more oppressive than
in other parts of the kingdom. In consequence of this the evil
disposed in these districts began to murmur, saying, that in the
beginning of the world there were no slaves, and that no one ought
to be treated as such, unless he had committed treason against his
lord, as Lucifer had done against God; but they had done no such

thing, for they were neither angels nor spirits, but men formed after the same likeness as these lords who treated them as beasts. This they would bear no longer; they were determined to be free, and if they laboured or did any work, they would be paid for it. A crazy priest in the county of Kent, called John Ball, who for his absurd preaching had thrice been confined in prison by the Archbishop of Canterbury, was greatly instrumental in exciting these rebellious ideas. Every Sunday after mass, as the people were coming out of church, this John Ball was accustomed to assemble a crowd around him in the marketplace and preach to them. On such occasions he would say, 'My good friends, matters cannot go on well in England until all things shall be in common; when there shall be neither vassals nor lords; when the lords shall be no more masters than ourselves. How ill they behave to us! for what reason do they thus hold us in bondage? Are we not all descended from the same parents, Adam and Eve? And what can they show, or what reason can they give, why they should be more masters than ourselves? They are clothed in velvet and rich stuffs, ornamented with ermine and other furs, while we are forced to wear poor clothing. They have wines, spices, and fine bread, while we have only rye and the refuse of the straw; and when we drink, it must be water. They have handsome seats and manors, while we must brave the wind and rain in our labours in the field; and it is by our labour they have wherewith to support their pomp. We are called slaves, and if we do not perform our service we are beaten, and we have no sovereign to whom we can complain or who would be willing to hear us. Let us go to the King and remonstrate with him; he is young, and from him we may obtain a favourable answer, and if not we must ourselves seek to amend our condition.' With such language as this did John Ball harangue the people of his village every Sunday after mass. The Archbishop, on being informed of it, had him arrested and imprisoned for two or three months by way of punishment; but the moment he was out of prison, he returned to his former course. Many in the city of London envious of the rich and noble, having heard of John Ball's preaching, said among themselves that the country was badly governed, and that the nobility had seized upon all the gold and silver. These wicked Londoners, therefore, began to assemble in parties, and to show signs of rebellion; they also invited all those who held like opinions in the adjoining counties to come to London; telling them that they would find the town open to them and the commonalty of the same way of thinking as themselves, and that they would so press the King, that there should no longer be a slave in England.

By this means the men of Kent, Essex, Sussex, Bedford, and the adjoining counties, in number about 60,000, were brought to London, under command of Wat Tyler, Jack Straw, and John Ball. This Wat Tyler, who was chief of the three, had been a tiler of houses – a bad man and a great enemy to the nobility. When these wicked people first began their disturbances, all London, with the exception of those who favoured them, was much alarmed. The Mayor and rich citizens assembled in council and debated whether they should shut the gate and refuse to admit them; however, upon mature reflection they determined not to do so, as they might run the risk of having the suburbs burned. The gates of the city were therefore thrown open, and the rabble entered and lodged as they pleased. True it is that full two-thirds of these people knew neither what they wanted, nor for what purpose they had come together; they followed one another like sheep. In this manner did many of these poor fellows walk to London from distances of one hundred, or sixty leagues, but the greater part came from the counties I have mentioned, and all on their arrival demanded to see the King. The country gentlemen, the knights and squires, began to be much alarmed when they saw the people thus assembling, and indeed they had sufficient reason to be so, for far less causes have excited fear. As the Kentish rebels were on their road towards London, the Princess of Wales, the king's mother, was returning from a pilgrimage to Canterbury; and when they saw her the scoundrels attacked her car and caused the good lady much alarm; but God preserved her from violence, and she came the whole journey from Canterbury to London without venturing to make any stoppage. On her arrival in London, King Richard was at the Tower; thither then the Princess went immediately, and found the King, attended by the Earl of Salisbury, the Archbishop of Canterbury, Sir Robert de Namur, and several others, who had kept near his person from suspicion of the rebels. King Richard well knew that this rebellion was in agitation long before it broke out, and it was a matter of astonishment to every one that he attempted to apply no remedy.

In order that gentlemen and others may take example and learn to correct such wicked rebels, I will most amply detail how the whole business was conducted. On the Monday preceding the feast of the Holy Sacrament in the year 1381, these people sallied forth from their homes to come to London, intending, as they said, to remonstrate with the King, and to demand their freedom. At Canterbury, they met John Ball, Wat Tyler, and Jack Straw. On entering this city they were well feasted by the inhabitants, who were all of the same way of thinking as themselves; and having held a council there, resolved to proceed on their march to London. They also sent emissaries across the Thames into Essex, Suffolk, and Bedford, to press the people of these parts to do the same, in order that the city might be quite surrounded. It was the intention of the leaders of this rabble, that all the different parties should be collected on the feast of the Holy Sacrament on the day following. At Canterbury the rebels entered the church of St Thomas, where they did much damage; they also pillaged the apartments of the Archbishop, saying as they were carrying off the different articles, 'The Chancellor of England has had this piece of furniture very cheap; he must now give us an account of his revenues, and of the large sums which he has levied since the coronation of the King.' After this they plundered the abbey of St Vincent, and then leaving Canterbury took the road towards Rochester. As they passed they collected people from the villages right and left, and on they went like a tempest, destroying all the houses belonging to attorneys, king's proctors, and the Archbishop, which came in their way. At Rochester they met with the same welcome as at Canterbury, for all the people were anxious to join them. Here they went at once to the castle, and seizing a knight by name Sir John de Newtoun, who was constable of the castle and captain of the town, told him that he must accompany them as their commander-in-chief and do whatever they wished. The knight endeavoured to excuse himself; but they met his excuses by saying, 'Sir John, if you refuse you are a dead man.' Upon which, finding that the outrageous mob were ready to kill him, he was constrained to comply with their request.

In other counties of England the rebels acted in a similar manner, and several great lords and knights, such as the Lord Manley, Sir Stephen Hales, and Sir Thomas Cossington, were compelled to march with them ... When the rebels had done all they wanted at Rochester, they left that city and came to Dartford, continuing to destroy all the houses of lawyers and proctors on the right and left of the road; from Dartford they came to Blackheath, where they took up their quarters, saying, that they were armed for the King and commons of England. When the principal citizens of London found that the rebels were quartered so near them, they caused the gates of London Bridge to be closed, and placed guards there, by order of Sir William Walworth, Mayor of London; notwithstanding there were in the city more than 30,000 who favoured the insurgents. Information that the gates of London Bridge had been closed against them soon reached Blackheath, whereupon the rebels sent a knight to speak with the King and to tell him that what they were doing was for his service; for the kingdom had now for many years been wretchedly governed, to the great dishonour of the realm and to the oppression of the lower orders of the people, by his uncles, by the clergy, and more especially by the Archbishop of Canterbury, his chancellor, from whom they were determined to have an account of his ministry. The knight who was appointed to this service would willingly have excused himself, but he did not dare to do it; so advancing to the Thames opposite the Tower, he took a boat and crossed over. The King and those who were with him in the Tower were in the greatest possible suspense and most anxious to receive some intelligence when the knight's arrival was announced, who was immediately conducted into the royal presence. With the King at this time were the Princess his mother, his two natural brothers, the Earl of Kent and Sir John Holland, the Earls of Salisbury, Warwick, and Suffolk, the Archbishop of Canterbury, the great Prior of the Templars, Sir Robert de Namur, the Mayor of London, and several of the principal citizens. Immediately upon entering the apartment the knight cast himself on his knees before the king, saying, 'My much redoubted lord, do not be displeased with me for the message which I am about to deliver to you; for, my dear lord, I have been compelled to come hither.' 'By no means, sir knight,' said the King. 'Tell us what you are charged with, we hold you excused.' 'My most redoubted lord, the commons of this realm have sent me to entreat you to come to Blackheath and speak with them. They wish to have no one but yourself: and you need not fear for your person, as they will not do you the least harm; they always have respected you as their king, and will continue to do so; but they desire to tell you many things which they say it is necessary you should hear: with these, however, they have not empowered me to make you acquainted. Have the goodness, dear lord, to give me such an answer as may satisfy them, and that they may be convinced that I have really been in your presence; for they have my children as hostages for my return, and if I go not back they will assuredly put them to death.' To this the King merely replied, 'You shall have my answer speedily'; and when the knight had withdrawn, he desired his council to consider what was to be done; after some consultation, the King was advised to send word to the insurgents, that if on Thursday they would come down to the river Thames, he would without fail speak with them. The knight on receiving this answer was well satisfied, and taking leave of the King and his barons, returned to Blackheath, where upwards of 60,000 men were assembled. He told them from the King, that if they would send their leaders the next morning to the Thames, the King would come and hear what they had to say. The answer was deemed satisfactory; and the rebels passed the night as well as they could, but you must know that one-fourth of them were without provisions.

On Corpus Christi day King Richard heard mass in the Tower of London, after which he entered his barge, attended by the Earls of Salisbury, Warwick, and Suffolk, and some other knights, and rowed down the Thames towards Rotherhithe, a royal manor, where upwards of 10,000 of the insurgents had assembled. As soon as the mob perceived the royal barge approaching, they began shouting and crying as if all the spirits of the nether world had been in the company. With them, also, was the knight whom they had sent to the Tower to the King; for if the King had not come, they determined to have him cut to pieces, as they had threatened him.

When the King and his lords saw this crowd of people, and the wildness of their manner, the boldest of the party felt alarm, and the King was advised not to land, but to have his barge rowed up and down the river. 'What do you wish for?' he demanded of the multitude; 'I am come hither to hear what you have to say.' Those near him cried out, 'We wish you to land, and then we will tell you what our wants are.' Upon this the Earl of Salisbury cried out, 'Gentlemen, you are not properly dressed, nor are you in a fit condition for a king to talk with.' Nothing more was said on either side, for the King was prevailed upon at once to return to the Tower. The people seeing this were in a great passion, and returned to Blackheath to inform their companions how the King had served them; upon hearing which, they all cried out, 'Let us instantly march to London.' Accordingly they set out at once, and on the road thither destroyed all the houses of lawyers and courtiers, and all the monasteries they met with. In the suburbs of London, which are very handsome and extensive, they pulled down many fine houses: they demolished also the King's prison, called the Marshalsea, and set at liberty all who were confined in it; moreover, they threatened the Londoners at the entrance of the bridge for having shut the gates of it, declaring that they would take the city by storm, and afterwards burn and destroy it.

With regard to the common people of London, numbers entertained these rebellious opinions, and on assembling at the bridge asked of the guards, 'Why will you refuse admittance to these honest men? They are our friends, and what they are doing is for our good.' So urgent were they, that it was found necessary to open the gates, when crowds rushed in and took possession of those shops which seemed best stocked with provisions; indeed, wherever they went, meat and drink were placed before them, and nothing was refused in the hope of appeasing them. Their leaders, John Ball, Jack Straw, and Wat Tyler, then marched through London, attended by more than 20,000 men, to the palace of the Savoy, which is a handsome building belonging to the Duke of Lancaster, situated on the banks of the Thames on the road to Westminster: here they immediately killed the porters, pushed into the house, and set it on fire. Not content with this outrage, they went to the house of the Knight-hospitalers of Rhodes, dedicated to St John of Mount Carmel, which they burned, together with their church and hospital.

After this they paraded the streets, and killed every Fleming they could find, whether in house, church, or hospital; they broke open several houses of the Lombards, taking whatever money they could lay their hands upon. They murdered a rich citizen, by name Richard Lyon, to whom Wat Tyler had formerly been servant in France, but having once beaten him, the varlet had never forgotten it; and when he had carried his men to his house, he ordered his head to be cut off, placed upon a pike, and carried through the streets of London. Thus did these wicked people act, and on this Thursday they did much damage to the city of London. Towards evening they fixed their quarters in a square, called St Catherine's, before the Tower, declaring that they would not depart until they had obtained from the King everything they wanted – until the Chancellor of England had accounted to them, and shown how the great sums which were raised had been expended. Considering the mischief which the mob had already done, you may easily imagine how miserable, at this time, was the situation of the King and those who were with him. In the evening, he and his barons, together with Sir William Walworth, and some of the principal citizens, held a council in the Tower, when it was proposed to arm themselves and fall by night upon these wretches while they were drunk and asleep, for they might have been killed like so many fleas, as not one of them in twenty had arms: and the citizens were very capable of doing this, for they had secretly received into their house their friends and servants properly prepared for action. Sir Robert Knolles remained in his house guarding it, with more than six score companions completely armed, who could have sallied forth at a minute's notice. Sir Perducas d'Albret was also in London at this period, and would of course have been of great service, so that altogether they could have mustered upwards of 8000 men well armed. However, nothing was done; they were really too much afraid of the commonalty; and the King's advisers, the Earl of Salisbury and others, said to him, 'Sir, if you can appease them by fair words, it will be so much the better; for, should we begin what we cannot go through, it will be all over with us and our heirs, and England will be a desert.' This council was followed, and the Mayor ordered to make no stir; who obeyed, as in reason he ought. On Friday morning the rebels, who lodged in the square of St Catherine's, before the Tower, began to make themselves ready. They shouted much and said, that if the King would not come out to them, they would attack the Tower, storm it, and slay all who were within. The King, alarmed at these menaces, resolved to speak with the rabble; he therefore sent orders for them to retire to a handsome meadow at Mile End, where, in the summertime, people go to amuse themselves, at the same time signifying that he would meet them there and grant their demands. Proclamation to this effect was made in the King's name, and thither, accordingly, the commonalty of the different villages began to march; many, however, did not care to go, but stayed behind in London, being more desirous of the riches of the nobles and the plunder of the city. Indeed, covetousness and the desire of plunder was the principal cause of these disturbances, as the rebels showed very plainly. When the gates of the Tower were thrown open, and the King, attended by his two brothers and other nobles, had passed through,

Wat Tyler, Jack Straw, and John Ball, with upwards of 400 others, rushed in by force, and running from chamber to chamber, found the Archbishop of Canterbury, by name Simon, a valiant and wise man, whom the rascals seized and beheaded. The Prior of St John's suffered the same fate, and likewise a Franciscan friar, a doctor of physic, who was attached to the Duke of Lancaster, also a sergeant-at-arms whose name was John Laige.

The heads of these four persons the rebels fixed on long spikes and had them carried before them through the streets of London; and when they had made sufficient mockery of them, they caused them to be placed on London Bridge, as if they had been traitors to their king and country. The scoundrels then entered the apartment of the Princess and cut her bed to pieces, which so terrified her that she fainted, and in this condition was carried by her servants and ladies to the riverside, when she was put into a covered boat and conveyed to a house called the Wardrobe, where she continued for a day and night in a very precarious state. While the King was on his way to Mile End, his two brothers, the Earl of Kent and Sir John Holland, stole away from his company, not daring to show themselves to the populace. The King himself, however, showed great courage, and on his arrival at the appointed spot instantly advanced into the midst of the assembled multitude, saying in a most pleasing manner, 'My good people, I am your king and your lord, what is it you want? What do you wish to say to me?' Those who heard him made answer, 'We wish you to make us free for ever. We wish to be no longer called slaves, nor held in bondage.' The King replied, 'I grant your wish; now therefore return to your homes, and let two or three from each village be left behind, to whom I will order letters to be given with my seal, fully granting every demand you have made: and in order that you may be the more satisfied, I will direct that my banners be sent to every stewardship, castlewick, and corporation.'

These words greatly appeased the more moderate of the multitude, who said, 'It is well: we wish for nothing more.' The King, however, added yet further, 'You, my good people of Kent, shall have one of my banners; and you also of Essex, Sussex, Bedford, Suffolk, Cambridge, Stafford, and Lincoln, shall each have one; I pardon you all for what you have hitherto done, but you must follow my banners and now return home on the terms I have mentioned,' which they unanimously consented to do. Thus did this great assembly break up. The king instantly employed upwards of thirty secretaries, who drew up the letters as fast as they could, and when they were sealed and delivered to them, the people departed to their own counties. The principal mischief, however, remained behind: I mean Wat Tyler, Jack Straw, and John Ball, who declared, that though the people were satisfied, they were by no means so, and with them were about 30,000, also of the same mind. These all continued in the city without any wish to receive the letters or the King's seal, but did all they could to throw the town into such confusion, that the lords and rich citizens might be murdered and their houses pillaged and destroyed. The Londoners suspected this, and kept themselves at home, well armed and prepared to defend their property.

After he had appeased the people at Mile End Green, King Richard went to the Wardrobe, in order that he might console the Princess, who was in the greatest possible alarm. But I must not omit to relate an adventure which happened to these clowns before Norwich and to their leader, William Lister, who was from the county of Stafford. At the same time that a party of these wicked people in London burned the palace of the Savoy, the church and house of St John's, and the hospital of the Templars, there were collected numerous bodies of men from Lincolnshire, Norfolk, and Suffolk, who, according to the orders they had received, were marching towards London. On their road they stopped near Norwich, and forced everyone whom they met to join them.

The reason of their stopping near Norwich was, that the governor of the town was a knight, by name Sir Robert Salle, who was not by birth a gentleman; but who, because of his ability and courage, had been created a knight by King Edward: he was, moreover, one of the handsomest and strongest men in England. Lister and his companions took it into their heads that they would make this man their commander. They, therefore, sent orders to him to come out into the fields to speak with them, declaring, in case he refused, that they would attack and burn the city. The knight, considering it was much better for him to go to them than that they should commit such outrages, mounted his horse and went out of the town alone to hear what they had to say. On his approach they showed every mark of respect, and courteously entreated him to dismount and talk with them. He did dismount, and in so doing committed a great folly, for immediately the mob surrounded him, and at first conversed in a friendly way, saying, 'Robert, you are a knight and a man of great weight in this country, renowned for your valour; yet, notwithstanding all this, we know who you are; you are not a gentleman, but the son of a poor mason, such as ourselves. Come with us, therefore, as our commander, and we will make you so great a man that one-quarter of England shall be under your control.'

The knight, on hearing them speak thus, was exceedingly enraged, and, eyeing them with angry looks, said, 'Begone, scoundrels and false traitors, would you have me desert my natural lord for such a company of knaves as you are? Would you have me dishonour myself? I would rather have you all hanged, for that must be your end.' On saying this, he attempted to mount his horse; but his foot slipping from the stirrup, the animal took fright, and the mob upon this cried out, 'Put him to death.' Upon hearing which, Sir Robert let go his horse, and drawing a handsome Bordeaux sword, began to skirmish, and soon cleared the crowd from about him in an admirable manner. Many attempted to close with him; but each stroke he gave cut off heads, arms, feet, or legs so that the boldest became afraid to approach him. The wretches were 40,000 in number, and he killed twelve of them and wounded many before they overpowered him, which at last they did with their missiles; and as soon as he was down, they cut off his arms and legs and rent his body piecemeal. Such was the pitiable end of Sir Robert Salle.

On Saturday morning the King left the Wardrobe and went to Westminster, when he and his lords heard mass in the abbey. In this church there is a statue of Our Lady, in which the kings of England have much faith. To this on the present occasion King Richard and his nobles paid their devotions and made their offerings; they then rode in company along the causeway to London; but when they had proceeded a short distance, King Richard, with a few attendants, turned up a road on the left to go away from the city.

This day all the rabble again assembled under Wat Tyler, Jack Straw, and John Ball, at a place called Smithfield, where every Friday the horsemarket is kept. There were present about 20,000, and many more were in the city, breakfasting, and drinking Rhenish wine and Malmsey Madeira in the taverns and in the houses of the Lombards, without paying for anything; and happy was he who could give them good cheer to satisfy them. Those who collected in Smithfield had with them the King's banner, which had been given to them the preceding evening; and the wretches, notwithstanding this, wanted to pillage the city, their leaders saying, that hitherto they had done nothing. 'The pardon which the King has granted will be of no use to us; but if we be of the same mind, we shall pillage this rich and powerful town of London before those from Essex, Suffolk, Cambridge, Bedford, Warwick, Reading, Lancashire, Arundel, Guildford, Coventry, Lynne, Lincoln, York and Durham shall arrive; for they are on their road, and we know for certain that Vaquier and Lister will conduct them hither. Let us, then, be beforehand in plundering the wealth of the city; for if we wait for their arrival, they will wrest it from us.' To this opinion all had agreed, when the King, attended by sixty horses, appeared in sight; he was at the time not thinking of the rabble, but had intended to continue his ride, without coming into London; however, when he arrived before the Abbey of St Bartholomew, which is in Smithfield, and saw the crowd of people, he stopped, saying that he would ascertain what they wanted, and endeavour to appease them. Wat Tyler, seeing the King and his party, said to his men, 'Here is the King, I will go and speak with him; do you not stir until I give you a signal.' He then made a motion with his hand, and added, 'When you shall see me make this signal, then step forward, and kill everyone except the King; but hurt him not, for he is young, and we can do what we please with him; carrying him with us through England, we shall be lords of the whole country, without any opposition.' On saying which he spurred his horse and galloped up to the King, whom he approached so near that his horse's head touched the crupper of the King's horse.

His first words were these: 'King, dost thou see all these men here?' 'Yes,' replied the King; 'why dost thou ask?' 'Because they are all under my command, and have sworn by their faith and loyalty to do whatsoever I shall order.' 'Very well,' said the King; 'I have no objection to it.' Tyler, who was only desirous of a riot, made answer: 'And thou thinkest, King, that these people, and as many more in the city, also under my command, ought to depart without having thy letters? No, indeed, we will carry them with us.' 'Why,' replied the King, 'it has been so ordered, and the letters will be delivered out one after another; but, friend, return to thy companions, and tell them to depart from London; be peaceable and careful of yourselves; for it is our determination that you shall all have the letters by towns and villages according to our agreement.' As the King finished speaking, Wat Tyler, casting his eyes round, spied a squire attached to the King's person bearing a sword. This squire Tyler mortally hated, and on seeing him cried out, 'What hast thou there? Give me thy dagger.' 'I will not,' said the squire; 'why should I give it thee?' The King upon this said, 'Give it to him; give it to him'; which the squire did, though much against his will. When Tyler took the dagger, he began to play with it in his hand, and again addressing the squire, said, 'Give me that sword.' 'I will not,' replied the squire, 'for it is the King's sword, and thou being but a mechanic art not worthy to bear it; and if only thou and I were together, thou wouldst not have dared to say what thou hast, for a heap of gold as large as this church.' 'By my troth,' answered Tyler, 'I will not eat this day before I have thy head.' At these words the Mayor of London, with about twelve men, rode forward, armed under their robes, and seeing Tyler's manner of behaving, said 'Scoundrel, how dare you to behave thus in the King's presence?' The King, also enraged at the fellow's impudence, said to the Mayor, 'Lay hands on him.' Whilst King Richard was giving this order, Tyler still kept up the conversation, saying to the Mayor, 'What have you to do with it; does what I have said concern you?' 'It does,' replied the Mayor, who found himself supported by the King, and then added, 'I will not live a day unless you pay for your insolence.' Upon saying which he drew a kind of scimitar, and struck Tyler such a blow on the head as felled him to his horse's feet. As soon as the rebel was down, he was surrounded on all sides, in order that his own men might not see him; and one of the King's squires, by name John Standwich, immediately leaped from his horse, and drawing his sword, thrust it into his belly, so that he died.

When the rebels found that their leader was dead, they drew up in a sort of battle array, each man having his bow bent before him. The King at this time certainly hazarded much, though it turned out most fortunately for him; for as soon as Tyler was on the ground, he left his attendants, giving orders that no one should follow him, and riding up to the rebels, who were advancing to revenge their leader's death, said, 'Gentlemen, what are you about? You shall have me for your captain: I am your King, remain peaceable.' The greater part, on hearing these words, were quite ashamed, and those among them who were inclined for peace began to slip away; the riotous ones, however, kept their ground. The King returned to his lords, and consulted with them what next should be done. Their advice was to make for the fields; but the Mayor said that to retreat would be of no avail. 'It is quite proper to act as we have done; and I reckon we shall very soon receive assistance from our good friends in London.'

While things were in this state, several persons ran to London, crying out, 'They are killing the King and our Mayor'; upon which alarm, all those of the King's party sallied out towards Smithfield, in number about seven or eight thousand. Among the first came Sir Robert Knolles and Sir Perducas d'Albret, well attended; then several aldermen, with upwards of 600 men-at-arms, and a powerful man of the city, by name Nicholas Bramber, the king's draper, bringing with him a large force on foot. These all drew up opposite to the rebels, who had with them the King's banner, and showed as if they intended to maintain their ground by offering combat.

The King created at this time three knights: Sir William Walworth, Sir John Standwich, and Sir Nicholas Bramber. As soon as Sir Robert Knolles arrived at Smithfield, his advice was immediately to fall upon the insurgents, and slay them; but King Richard would not consent to this. 'You shall first go to them,' he said, 'and demand my banner; we shall then see how they will behave; for I am determined to have this by fair means or foul.' The new knights were accordingly sent forward, and on approaching the rebels made signs to them not to shoot, as they wished to speak with them; and when within hearing said, 'Now attend; the King orders you to send back his banners; and if you do so, we trust he will have mercy upon you.' The banners, upon this, were given up directly, and brought to the King. It was then ordered, under pain of death, that all those who had obtained the King's letters should deliver them up. Some did so, but not all; and the King on receiving them had them torn in pieces in their presence. You must know that from the time the King's banners were surrendered, these fellows kept no order; but the greater part, throwing their bows upon the ground, took to their heels and returned to London. Sir Robert Knolles was very angry that the rebels were not attacked at once and all slain; however, the King would not consent to it, saying, that he would have ample revenge without doing so.

When the rabble had dispersed, the King and his lords, to their great joy, returned in good array to London, whence the King immediately took the road to the Wardrobe, to visit the Princess his mother, who had remained there two days and two nights under the greatest apprehension. On seeing her son, the good lady was much rejoiced, and said, 'Ah, ah, fair son, what pain and anguish have I not suffered for you this day!' 'Madam,' replied the King, 'I am well assured of that; but now rejoice, and thank God, for it behoves us to praise him, as I have this day regained my inheritance – the kingdom of England, which I had lost.'

This whole day the King passed with his mother, and a proclamation was made through all the streets, that every person who was not an inhabitant of London, and who had not resided there for a whole year, should instantly depart; for if any of a contrary description were found in the city on Sunday morning at sunrise, they would be arrested as traitors to the King, and have their heads cut off. This proclamation no one dared to infringe, but all instantly departed to their homes quite discomfited.

John Ball and Jack Straw were found hidden in an old ruin, where they had secreted themselves, thinking to steal away when things were quiet; but this they were prevented doing, for their own men betrayed them. With this capture the King and his barons were much pleased, and had their heads cut off, as was that of Tyler's, and fixed on London Bridge, in the room of those whom these wretches themselves had placed there.

News of this total defeat of the rebels in London was sent throughout the neighbouring counties, in order that all those who were on their way to London might hear of it; and as soon as they did so, they instantly returned to their homes, without daring to advance farther.

The Battle of Agincourt, 25 October 1415

A French Knight's Account

Jehan de Wavrin

At Agincourt Henry V's exhausted army was attacked by large French forces under the Constable Charles I d'Albret. About 6000 of the French were killed.

Next day the King of England, having left his night quarters, rode on in the usual manner, always taking the direct way towards Calais; and it was the 24th day of October, the eve of St Crispin; but he had scarcely turned out when his scouts reported that they had seen the French in large bodies guarding his road, and they were informed that they were to lodge at Rousseauville and Agincourt in order to fight him on the morrow, to which the King replied that it was well.

King Henry, then being apprised of this, and because the passage of the river at Blangy, in Ternois, was long and narrow, before crossing it, made six noblemen of his vanguard divest themselves of their coats of mail and cross first to see whether the passage had no guard. They found it had none, and that there was no opposition; so the whole English army crossed with great expedition. When they had got over, and regained the road, they had gone but a little way when they perceived before them the French in great force; wherefore King Henry made all his men dismount, and put them in good order of battle, expecting to be fought on this day. And all the English were engaged in devotional exercises, praying our Lord God that he would be their help; and there they remained till sunset. Similarly the French, who could well discern the battle array of the English, expecting to fight them, put themselves in good order, put on their coats of mail, displayed banners and pennons, and made several new knights. Among those who received the order of knighthood was Philip Count of Nevers, by Marshal Boucicault, with a great number of other noble esquires; and there near Agincourt gathered all the French in a single body.

When the King of England saw that it was already late, he made all his army draw towards Maisoncelles, which was near; but before he lay down he gave liberty to the prisoners, nobles, and others, who were at that time with his army, they promising him that if the victory turned on his side they would all return to him and to their masters if they were living, but if it fell to him to lose the battle, he for ever freed them from fealty and ransom. After the prisoners were thus liberated, the King of England lodged in the said town of Maisoncelles, so near his enemies that the foremost of his vanguard saw them quite plainly, and heard them call each other by name, and make a great noise; but as for the English, never did people make less noise, for hardly did one hear them utter a word, or speak together.

When the French saw that the King of England had lodged himself at Maisoncelles, and that they would not be fought that day, it was commanded on behalf of the King of France and his Constable that each one should sleep in the place where he was. Then you might have seen banners and pennons furled round the lances, and coats of mail put off, mules and trunks unpacked, and each of the lords sending their servants and harbingers into the neighbouring villages to seek for straw or litter to put under them, that they might sleep in the same place where they were, which was much beaten down by the trampling of the horses. And almost all the night it ceased not to rain, and there continued a great noise of pages, grooms, and all kinds of people; such that, as it is said, the English could hear them plainly, but those on their side were not heard; for during this night all that could find a priest confessed themselves; the men-at-arms tightened their armour, sharpening their aguilettes, and doing whatever was their business; the archers looked to their bows and cords, and whatever was necessary for them. Then when it came to be early morning, the King of England began to hear his masses; for it was his custom to hear three every day, one after the other; and he had on every piece of his armour, except his head gear; but after the masses were said he had brought to him his helmet, which was very rich, and had a handsome crown of gold around it like an imperial crown; then when he was fully equipped, he mounted a small grey horse, without spurs, and without causing any trumpet or other instrument to sound, he quietly drew his battalion from its night quarters, and there on a fine field of young corn arranged his troops; and, to guard his baggage and that of his men, he appointed a gentleman with ten lances, and twenty archers, besides pages, who were of noble birth, and some sick, who could be no help. He formed all his men into a single body, as closely massed as he could, his men-at-arms in the middle, and all his banners pretty near each other. At each side of the men-at-arms were the archers; and there might be in all about 10,000 good fighting men; and to speak of the banners of the King of England there were five about his own person, that is to say, the banner of the Trinity, the banner of Our Lady, the banner of St George, the banner of St Edward, and the banner of his own arms. Afterwards were the following banners, viz., of the Duke of Gloucester, the Duke of York, the Earl of March, the Earl of Huntingdon, the Earl of Oxford, the Earl of Kent, the Lords de Ros, Cornwall, and several others.

These things being arranged, the King went along the ranks to see if nothing was wanting to the work of his army; and, in passing, he made fine speeches everywhere, exhorting and begging them to do well; saying that he had come into France to recover his rightful heritage, and that he had good and just cause for so doing; saying further that they could fight safely and with free heart in this quarrel, and that they should remember that they were born of the realm of England where they had been brought up, and where their fathers, mothers, wives, and children were living; wherefore it became them to exert themselves, that they might return thither with great joy and approval. And he showed them besides how his predecessors, kings of England, had gained many splendid victories over the French, and caused them marvellous discomfiture; and he begged that this day each one would assist in protecting his person and the crown of England, with the honour of the kingdom. And further he told them and explained how the French were boasting that they would cut off three fingers of the right hand of all the archers that should be taken prisoners to the end that neither man nor horse should ever again be killed with their arrows. Such exhortations and many others, which cannot all be written, the King of England addressed to his men.

Now we shall tell of the condition of the French, who, as it has been said, lay down on the Thursday evening on the field between Agincourt and Tramecourt, in which place on the morning of next day they made their preparations and arrangements for fighting the King of England and his force that day; for, on the Thursday, they had chosen that spot where they bivouacked in order to fight the English there, if they tried to pass it, as this was their direct way to go to Calais. And to the royal banner of the Constable all the great lords of the gathering gladly joined their own; namely, marshals, admirals, and other royal officers; and this night the French made great fires round the banner under which they were to fight. And the French were at least 50,000, with a great number of wagons, baggage, artillery, and all appurtenances suitable to the case. They had few musical instruments, and during this night one hardly heard a single horse neigh throughout the host.

I, the author of this work, know the truth about this, for I was in this assemblage on the French side.

Then on the morning of the next day, that is to say, Friday, St Crispin's day, the 25th of October 1415, the Constable and all the other officers of the King of France, the Dukes of Orleans, Bourbon, Bar, and Alençon, the Counts of Eu, Richemont, Vendôme, Marle, Vaudemont, Blaumont, Salines, Grampré, Roussy, Dampmartin, and generally all the other nobles and warriors armed themselves and issued from their bivouac; and then it was ordered by the Constable and marshals of the King of France that three battalions should be formed . . .

When the battalions of the French were thus formed, it was grand to see them; and as far as one could judge by the eye, they were in number fully six times as many as the English. And when this was done the French sat down by companies around their banners, waiting the approach of the English, and making their peace with one another; and then were laid aside many old aversions conceived long ago; some kissed and embraced each other, which it was affecting to witness; so that all quarrels and discords which they had had in time past were changed to great and perfect love. And there were some who breakfasted on what they had. And these Frenchmen remained thus till nine or ten o'clock in the morning, feeling quite assured that, considering their great force, the English could not escape them; however, there were at least some of the wisest who greatly feared a fight with them in open battle. Among the arrangements made on the part of the French, as I have since heard related by eminent knights, it happened that, under the banner of the Lord of Croy, eighteen gentlemen banded themselves together of their own choice, and swore that when the two parties should come to meet they would strive with all their might to get so near the King of England that they would beat down the crown from his head, or they would die, as they did; but before this they got so near the said King that one of them with the lance which he held struck him such a blow on his helmet that he knocked off one of the ornaments of his crown. But not long afterwards it only remained that the eighteen gentlemen were all dead and cut to pieces; which was a great pity; for if every one of the French had been willing thus to exert himself, it is to be believed that their affairs would have gone better on this day. And the leaders of these gentlemen were Louvelet de Massinguehem and Garnot de Bornouille . . .

The French had arranged their battalions between two small thickets, one lying close to Agincourt, and the other to Tramecourt. The place was narrow, and very advantageous for the English, and, on the contrary, very ruinous for the French, for the said French had been all night on horseback, and it rained, and the pages, grooms, and others, in leading about the horses, had broken up the ground, which was so soft that the horses could with difficulty step out of the soil. And also the said French were so loaded with armour that they could not support themselves or move forward. In the first place they were armed with long coats of steel, reaching to the knees or lower, and very heavy, over the leg harness, and besides plate armour also most of them had hooded helmets; wherefore this weight of armour, with the softness of the wet ground, as has been said, kept them as if immovable, so that they could raise their clubs only with great difficulty, and with all these mischiefs there was this, that most of them were troubled with hunger and want of sleep. There was a marvellous number of banners, and it was ordered that some of them should be furled. Also it was settled among the said French that every one should shorten his lance, in order that they might be stiffer when it came to fighting at close quarters. They had archers and cross-bowmen enough, but they would not let them shoot, for the plain was so narrow that there was no room except for the men-at-arms.

Now let us return to the English. After the parley between the two armies was finished and the delegates had returned, each to their own people, the King of England, who had appointed a knight called Sir Thomas Erpingham to place his archers in front in two wings, trusted entirely to him, and Sir Thomas, to do his part, exhorted every one to do well in the name of the King, begging them to fight vigorously against the French in order to secure and save their own lives. And thus the knight, who rode with two others only in front of the battalion, seeing that the hour was come, for all things were well arranged, threw up a baton which he held in his hand, saying 'Nestrocq' ['Now strike'] which was the signal for attack; then dismounted and joined the King, who was also on foot in the midst of his men, with his banner before him. Then the English, seeing this signal, began suddenly to march, uttering a very loud cry, which greatly surprised the French. And when the English saw that the French did not approach them, they marched dashingly towards them in very fine order, and again raised a loud cry as they stopped to take breath.

Then the English archers, who, as I have said, were in the wings, saw that they were near enough, and began to send their arrows on the French with great vigour. The said archers were for the most part in their doublets, without armour, their stockings rolled up to their knees, and having hatchets and battle-axes or great swords hanging at their girdles; some were bare-footed and bare-headed, others had caps of boiled leather, and others of osier, covered with harpoy or leather.

Then the French, seeing the English come towards them in this fashion, placed themselves in order, everyone under his banner, their helmets on their heads. The Constable, the Marshal, the admirals, and the other princes earnestly exhorted their men to fight the English well and bravely; and when it came to the approach the trumpets and clarions resounded everywhere; but the French began to hold down their heads, especially those who had no bucklers, for the impetuosity of the English arrows, which fell so heavily that no one durst uncover or look up. Thus they went forward a little, then made a little retreat, but before they could come to close quarters, many of the French were disabled and wounded by the arrows; and when they came quite up to the English, they were, as has been said, so closely pressed one against another that none of them could lift their arms to strike their enemies, except some that were in front, and these fiercely pricked with the lances which they had shortened to be more stiff, and to get nearer their enemies.

The French had formed a plan which I will describe, that is to say, the Constable and Marshal had chosen ten or twelve hundred men-at-arms, of whom one party was to go by the Agincourt side and the other on that of Tramecourt, to break the two wings of the English archers; but when it came to close quarters there were but six score left of the band of Sir Clugnet de Brabant, who had the charge of the undertaking on the Tramecourt side. Sir William de Saveuse, a very brave knight, took the Agincourt side, with about three hundred lances; and with two others only he advanced before the rest, who all followed, and struck into these English archers, who had their stakes fixed in front of them, but these had little hold in such soft ground. So the said Sir William and his two companions pressed on boldly; but their horses stumbled among the stakes, and they were speedily slain by the archers, which was a great pity. And most of the rest, through fear, gave way and fell back into their vanguard, to whom they were a great hindrance; and they opened their ranks in several places, and made them fall back and lose their footing in some land newly sown; for their horses had been so wounded by the arrows that the men could no longer manage them. Thus, by these principally and by this adventure, the vanguard of the French was thrown into disorder, and men-at-arms without number began to fall; and their horses feeling the arrows coming upon them took to flight before the enemy, and following their example many of the French turned and fled. Soon afterwards the English archers, seeing the vanguard thus shaken, issued from behind their stockade, threw away their bows and quivers, then took their swords, hatchets, mallets, axes, falcon-beaks and other weapons, and, pushing into the places where they saw these breaches, struck down and killed these Frenchmen without mercy, and never ceased to kill till the said vanguard which had fought little or not at all was completely overwhelmed, and these went on striking right and left till they came upon the second battalion, which was behind the advance guard, and there the King personally threw himself into the fight with his men-at-arms. And there came suddenly Duke Anthony of Brabant, who had been summoned by the King of France, and had so hastened for fear of being late, that his people could not follow him, for he would not wait for them, but took a banner from his trumpeters, made a hole in the middle of it, and dressed himself as if in armour; but he was soon killed by the English. Then was renewed the struggle and great slaughter of the French, who offered little defence; for, because of their cavalry above mentioned, their order of battle was broken; and then the English got among them more and more, breaking up the two first battalions in many places, beating down and slaying cruelly and without mercy; but some rose again by the help of their grooms, who led them out to the mêlée; for the English, who were intent on killing and making prisoners, pursued nobody.

And then all the rearguard, being still on horseback, and seeing the condition of the first two battalions turned and fled, except some of the chiefs and leaders of these routed ones. And it is to be told that while the battalion was in rout, the English had taken some good French prisoners.

And there came tidings to the King of England that the French were attacking his people at the rear, and that they had already taken his sumpters and other baggage, which enterprise was conducted by an esquire named Robert de Bornouille, with whom were Rifflart de Plamasse, Yzembart d'Agincourt, and some other men-at-arms, accompanied by about six hundred peasants, who carried off the said baggage and many horses of the English while their keepers were occupied in the fight, about which robbery the King was greatly troubled, nevertheless he ceased not to pursue his victory, and his people took many good prisoners, by whom they expected all to become rich, and they took from them nothing but their head armour.

At the hour when the English feared the least there befell them a perilous adventure, for a great gathering of the rearguard and centre division of the French, in which were many Bretons, Gascons, and Poitevins, rallied with some standards and ensigns, and returned in good order, and marched vigorously against the conquerors of the field. When the King of England perceived them coming thus he caused it to be published that every one that had a prisoner should immediately kill him, which those who had any were unwilling to do, for they expected to get great ransoms for them. But when the King was informed of this he appointed a gentleman with two hundred archers whom he commanded to go through the host and kill all the prisoners, whoever they might be. This esquire, without delay or objection, fulfilled the command of his sovereign lord, which was a most pitiable thing, for in cold blood all the nobility of France was beheaded and inhumanly cut to pieces, and all through this accursed company, a sorry set compared with the noble captive chivalry, who when they saw that the English were ready to receive them, all immediately turned and fled, each to save his own life. Many of the cavalry escaped; but of those on foot there were many among the dead.

When the King of England saw that he was master of the field and had got the better of his enemies he humbly thanked the Giver of victory, and he had good cause, for of his people there died on the spot only about sixteen hundred men of all ranks, among whom was the Duke of York, his great-uncle, about whom he was very sorry. Then the King collected on that place some of those most intimate with him, and inquired the name of a castle which he perceived to be the nearest; and they said, 'Agincourt.' 'It is right then,' said he, 'that this our victory should for ever bear the name of Agincourt, for every battle ought to be named after the fortress nearest to the place where it was fought.'

When the King of England and his army had been there a good while, waiting on the field, and guarding the honour of the victory more than four hours, and no one whatever, French or other, appeared to do them injury, seeing that it rained and evening was drawing on, he returned to his quarters at Maisoncelles. And the English archers busied themselves in turning over the dead, under whom they found some good prisoners still alive, of whom the Duke of Orleans was one; and they carried the armour of the dead by horse loads to their quarters. And they found on the field the Duke of York and the Earl of Oxford, whom they carried into their camp; and the French did little injury to the said English, except in the matter of these two.

When evening came the King of England, being informed that there was so much baggage accumulated at the lodging places, caused it to be proclaimed everywhere with sound of trumpet that no one should load himself with more armour than was necessary for his own body, because they were not yet wholly out of danger from the King of France. And this night the corpses of the two English princes, that is to say, the Duke of York and the Earl of Oxford, were boiled, in order to separate the bones and carry them to England; and this being done, the King further ordered that all the armour that was over and above what his people were wearing, with all the dead bodies on their side, should be carried into a barn or house, and there burned altogether; and it was done according to the King's command.

Next day, which was Saturday, the King of England and his whole army turned out from Maisoncelles, and passed through the scene of slaughter, where they killed all the French that they found still living, except some that they took prisoners; and King Henry stood there, looking on the pitiable condition of those dead bodies, which were quite naked, for during the night they had been stripped as well by the English as by the peasantry.

Norwegian Fisherfolk, 1432

Observations of a Venetian Traveller

Cristoforo Fioravanti

Cristoforo Fioravanti was shipwrecked on the coast of Norway in 1432 and, with another survivor, Nicolò de Michiel, wrote an account of his adventures.

In this Iland there are twelve little Houses, with about one hundred and twentie persons, for the most part Fishermen, and they are by nature indued with understanding to know how to make Boates, Buckets, Tunnes, Baskets, Nets of all sorts, and every other thing necessarie for their use and trade. And they are very curteous one toward another and serviceable, desirous to please rather for love, than for hope of any gift or good turne to bee done them againe. Fishes called Stock-fish, in all their payments and bartering, are used in stead of coyned money, and they are all as it were of one bignesse and measure, of the which every yeere they drie an infinite number in the winde: and in the time of May fraight themselves with them, carrying them through the Realmes of Denmarke, that is to say, Sweden, Denmarke, and Norway, being all Subject to the King of Dacia: where they barter and exchange the said Fish, for Leather, Cloathes, Iron, Pulse and other things, whereof they have scarcitie . . .

The Inhabitants of this place both young and old, are of so great simplicitie of heart, and obedient to the Commandement of God, that they neither understand, know, nor imagine in any wise, what Fornication, or Adulterie may bee: but use Marriage according to Gods Commandement. And to give you a true proofe hereof I Christophoro say, that we were in the house of our foresaid Host, and slept in one and the same Cottage, where hee also and his Wife slept, and successively in one Bed neere adjoyning, were their Daughters and Sonnes of ripe age together, neere to the which Beds we also slept, almost close adjoyning to them: so that when they went to sleepe, or when they arose, or when they stripped themselves naked, and wee in like manner, we indifferently saw one another, and yet with this puritie, as if wee had beene little children. But I will tell you more, that for two dayes together, our said Host, with his elder Sonnes arose to goe a fishing, even at the time of the most delightfull houre of sleepe, leaving his Wife and Daughters in the Bed, with that securitie and puritie, as if he had properly left them in the armes and embracements of the Mother, not returning to his home in lesse time than the space of eight houres . . .

There at the beginning of May we saw great varietie and alteration. First, their women use to goe unto the Bathes, which are very neere and commodious, as well for puritie, as for the custome they observe, which they hold agreeable unto Nature: they use to come forth of their houses starke naked, as they came out of their Mothers wombe, going without any regard to their way, carrying only in their right hand an heape of grasse, in manner of a broome, as they say, to rub the sweat from their backe, and the left hand they hold upon their hip, spreading it as it were for a shadow to cover their hinder parts, that they should not much appeare: where having twice seene them, we passed away by them, as easily as their owne people, the Countrey was so cold, and the continuall seeing of them, that it caused us to make no account thereof. On the contrary part, these very women were seene on the Sunday to enter into the Church in long and comely Garments. And that they might not by any meanes be seene in the face, they weare on their head a thing like a compleat Morion with a Gorget, which hath an hole to see through at the end, like the hole of a Pipe, through the which they behold within that, no further off from their eyes than the hole is long, so that they seeme to have it in their mouthes to pipe: and worse then that, they can neither see nor speake, unlesse they turne themselves a yard or more, from the hearer. I thought good to note these two extreame varieties, as worthy to bee understood.

The New World, January–February 1502
Amerigo Vespucci Reports on South America

Amerigo Vespucci

On his second voyage to the New World Vespucci reached the coast of Brazil and sailed as far south as the Rio de la Plata, which he was the first European to discover.

This land is very pleasing, full of an infinite number of very tall trees which never lose their leaves and throughout the year are fragrant with the sweetest aromas and yield an endless supply of fruits, many of which are good to taste and conducive to bodily health. The fields produce many herbs and flowers and most delicious and wholesome roots. Sometimes I was so wonder-struck by the fragrant smells of the herbs and flowers and the savour of the fruits and the roots that I fancied myself near the Terrestrial Paradise. What shall we say of the multitude of birds and their plumes and colours and singing and their numbers and their beauty? I am unwilling to enlarge upon this description, because I doubt if I would be believed.

What should I tell of the multitude of wild animals, the abundance of pumas, of panthers, of wild cats, not like those of Spain, but of the antipodes; of so many wolves, red deer, monkeys, and felines, marmosets of many kinds, and many large snakes? We saw so many other animals that I believe so many species could not have entered Noah's ark. We saw many wild hogs, wild goats, stags and does, hares, and rabbits, but of domestic animals, not one.

Let us come to rational animals. We found the whole land inhabited by people entirely naked, the men like the women without any covering of their shame. Their bodies are very agile and well proportioned, of light colour, with long hair, and little or no beard. I strove a great deal to understand their conduct and customs. For twenty-seven days I ate and slept among them, and what I learned about them is as follows.

Having no laws and no religious faith, they live according to nature. They understand nothing of the immortality of the soul. There is no possession of private property among them, for everything is in common. They have no boundaries of kingdom or province. They have no king, nor do they obey anyone. Each one is his own master. There is no administration of justice, which is unnecessary to them, because in their code no one rules. They live in communal dwellings, built in the fashion of very large cabins. For people who have no iron or indeed any metal, one can call their cabins truly miraculous houses. For I have seen habitations which are two hundred and twenty paces long and thirty wide, ingeniously fabricated; and in one of these houses dwelt five or six hundred persons. They sleep in nets woven out of cotton, going to bed in mid-air with no other coverture. They eat squatting upon the ground. Their food is very good: an endless quantity of fish; a great abundance of sour cherries, shrimps, oysters, lobsters, crabs and many other products of the sea. The meat which they eat most usually is what one may call human flesh *à la mode*. When they can get it, they eat other meat, of animals or birds, but they do not lay hold of many, for they have no dogs, and the country is a very thick jungle full of ferocious wild beasts. For this reason they are not wont to penetrate the jungle except in large parties.

The men have a custom of piercing their lips and cheeks and setting in these perforations ornaments of bone or stone; and do not suppose them small ones. Most of them have at least three holes, and some seven, and some nine, in which they set ornaments of green and white alabaster, half a palm in length and as thick as a Catalonian plum. This pagan custom is beyond description. They say they do this to make themselves look more fierce. In short, it is a brutal business.

Their marriages are not with one woman only, but they mate with whom they desire and without much ceremony. I know a man who had ten women. He was jealous of them, and if it happened that one of them was guilty, he punished her and sent her away. They are a very procreative people. They do not have heirs, because they do not have private property. When their children, that is, the females, are of age to procreate, the first who seduces one has to act as her father in place of the nearest relative. After they are thus violated, they marry.

Their women do not make any ceremony over childbirth, as do ours, but they eat all kinds of food, and wash themselves up to the very time of delivery, and scarcely feel any pain in parturition.

They are a people of great longevity, for according to their way of attributing issue, they had known many men who had four generations of descendants. They do not know how to compute time in days, months, and years, but reckon time by lunar months. When they wished to demonstrate something involving time, they did it by placing pebbles, one for each lunar month. I found a man of advanced age who indicated to me with pebbles that he had seen seventeen hundred lunar months, which I judged to be a hundred and thirty-two years, counting thirteen moons to the year.

They are also a warlike people and very cruel to their own kind. All their weapons and the blows they strike are, as Petrarch says, 'committed to the wind', for they use bows and arrows, darts, and stones. They use no shields for the body, but go into battle naked.

They have no discipline in the conduct of their wars, except that they do what their old men advise. When they fight, they slaughter mercilessly. Those who remain on the field bury all the dead of their own side, but cut up and eat the bodies of their enemies. Those whom they seize as prisoners, they take for slaves to their habitations. If women sleep with a male prisoner and he is virile, they marry him with their daughters. At certain times, when a diabolical frenzy comes over them, they invite their kindred and the whole tribe, and they set before them a mother with all the children she has, and with certain ceremonies they kill them with arrow shots and eat them. They do the same thing to the above-mentioned slaves and to the children born of them. This is assuredly so, for we found in their houses human flesh hung up to smoke, and much of it. We purchased from them ten creatures, male as well as female, which they were deliberating upon for the sacrifice, or better to say, the crime. Much as we reproved them, I do not know that they amended themselves. That which made me the more astonished at their wars and cruelty was that I could not understand from them why they made war upon each other, considering that they held no private property or sovereignty of empire and kingdoms and did not know any such thing as lust for possession, that is, pillaging or a desire to rule, which appear to me to be the causes of wars and of every disorderly act. When we requested them to state the cause, they did not know how to give any other cause than that this curse upon them began in ancient times and they sought to avenge the deaths of their forefathers.

A Salamander, 1505

Benvenuto Cellini

When I was about five years old my father happened to be in a basement chamber of our house, where they had been washing, and where a good fire of oak logs was still burning; he had a viol in his hand, and was playing and singing alone beside the fire. The weather was very cold. Happening to look into the fire, he spied in the middle of those most burning flames a little creature like a lizard, which was sporting in the core of the intensest coals.

Becoming instantly aware of what the thing was, he had my sister and me called, and pointing it out to us children, gave me a great box on the ears, which caused me to howl and weep with all my might. Then he pacified me good-humouredly, and spoke as follows: 'My dear little boy, I am not striking you for any wrong that you have done, but only to make you remember that that lizard which you see in the fire is a salamander, a creature which has never been seen before by any one of whom we have credible information.' So saying, he kissed me and gave me some pieces of money.

Spanish Atrocities in the West Indies, *c.* 1513–20

Bartolomé de Las Casas

Las Casas, who became a Dominican missionary, was the first European to expose the oppression of the native races of Latin America. He had himself taken apart in the conquest of Cuba, 1513.

The Spaniards with their Horses, their Speares and Lances, began to commit murders, and strange crueltics: they entred into Townes, Borowes, and Villages, sparing neither children nor old men, neither women with childe, neither them that lay in, but that they ripped their bellies, and cut them in peeces, as if they had beene opening of Lambes shut up in their fold. They laid wagers with such as with one thrust of a sword would paunch or bowell a man in the middest, or with one blow of a sword would most readily and most deliverly cut off his head, or that would best pierce his entrals at one stroake. They tooke the little soules by the heeles, ramping them from the mothers dugges, and crushed their heads against the clifts. Others they cast into the Rivers laughing and mocking, and when they tumbled into the water, they said, now shift for thy selfe such a ones corpes. They put others, together with their mothers, and all that they met, to the edge of the sword. They made certaine Gibbets long and low, in such sort, that the feete of the hanged on, touched in a manner the ground, every one enough for thirteene, in honour and worship of our Saviour and his twelve Apostles (as they used to speake) and setting to fire, burned them all quicke that were fastened. Unto all others, whom they used to take and reserve alive, cutting off their two hands as neere as might be, and so letting them hang, they said; Get you with these Letters, to carry tydings to those which are fled by the Mountaines. They murdered commonly the Lords and Nobility on this fashion: They made certaine grates of pearches laid on pickforkes, and made a little fire underneath, to the intent, that by little and little yelling and despairing in these torments, they might give up the Ghost.

One time I saw foure or five of the principall Lords roasted and broyled upon these gredirons. Also I thinke that there were two or three of these gredirons, garnished with the like furniture, and for that they cryed out pittiously, which thing troubled the Captaine that he could not then sleepe: he commanded to strangle them. The Sergeant, which was worse than the Hangman that burned them (I know his name and friends in Sivil) would not have them strangled, but himselfe putting Bullets in their mouthes, to the end that they should not cry, put to the fire, untill they were softly roasted after his desire. I have seene all the aforesaid things and others infinite. And forasmuch as all the people which could flee, hid themselves in the Mountaines, and mounted on the tops of them, fled from the men so without all manhood, emptie of all pitie, behaving them as savage beasts, the slaughterers and deadly enemies of mankinde: they taught their Hounds, fierce Dogs, to teare them in peeces at the first view, and in the space that one may say a Credo, assailed and devoured an Indian as if it had beene a Swine. These Dogges wrought great destructions and slaughters. And forasmuch as sometimes, although seldome, when the Indians put to death some Spaniards upon good right and Law of due Justice: they made a Lawe betweene them, that for one Spaniard they had to slay an hundred Indians . . .

One time the Indians came to meete us, and to receive us with victuals, and delicate cheere, and with all entertainment ten leagues off a great Citie, and being come at the place, they presented us with a great quantity of fish, and of bread, and other meate, together with all that they could doe for us to the uttermost. See incontinent the Divell, which put himselfe into the Spaniards, to put them all to the edge of the sword in my presence, without any cause whatsoever, more than three thousand soules, which were set before us, men, women, and children. I saw there so great cruelties, that never any man living either have or shall see the like.

Another time, but a few dayes after the premisses, I sent

messengers unto all the Lords of the Province of Havana, assuring them, that they should not neede to feare (for they had heard of my credit) and that without withdrawing themselves, they should come to receive us, and that there should be done unto them no displeasure: for all the Countrie was afraid, by reason of the mischiefes and murderings passed, and this did I by the advice of the Captaine himselfe. After that we were come into the Province, one and twenty Lords and Caciques came to receive us, whom the Captaine apprehended incontinently, breaking the safe conduct which I had made them, and intending the day next following to burne them alive, saying that it was expedient so to doe, for that otherwise those Lords one day, would doe us a shrewd turne. I found my selfe in a great deale of trouble to save them from the fire; howbeit in the end they escaped.

After that the Indians of this Iland [Cuba] were thus brought into bondage and calamitie, like unto those of the Ile of Hispaniola, and that they saw that they died and perished all without remedy: some of them began to flye into the Mountaines, others quite desperate hanged themselves, and there hung together husbands with their wives, hanging with them their little children. And through the crueltie of one only Spaniard, which was a great tyrant, and one whom I know, there hung themselves more then two hundred Indians: and in this fashion died an infinite of people.

There was in this Ile an officer of the Kings, to whom they gave for his share three hundred Indians, of whom at the end of three moneths there died by him in the travell of the Mines, two hundred and sixty: in such sort, that there remained now but thirty, which was the tenth part. Afterwards they gave him as many more, and more, and those also hee made havocke of in like manner, and still as many as they gave him, so many he slew, until he died himselfe, and that the Divell carried him away.

In three or foure moneths (my selfe being present) there died more then sixe thousand children, by reason that they had plucked away from them their fathers and mothers, which they sent into the Mines.

The Performing Ass, Cairo, 1516

John Leo

Born in Granada, John Leo was brought up in Morocco and travelled widely in North Africa as a young man.

The Suburbe, called Beb Elloch, being distant from the Walles of Cairo about the space of a mile, and containing almost three thousand Families, is inhabited by Merchants and Artizans of divers sorts. Upon a certaine large place of this Suburbe standeth a great Palace, and a stately Colledge, built by a certaine Mammaluck, called Jazbach, being Counsellor unto the Soldan of those times; and the place it selfe is called after his name, Jazbachia. Hither, after Mahumetan Sermons & devotions, the common people of Cairo, together with the Bawds and Harlots, doe usually resort; and many Stage-Players also, and such as teach Camels, Asses, and Dogs, to dance; which dancing is a thing very delightfull to behold, and especially that of the Asse: who having frisked and danced a while, his Master comes unto him, and tells him with a loud voyce, That the Soldan being about to build some great Palace, must use all the Asses of Cairo to carry Morter, Stones, and other necessary provision. Then the Asse falling presently to the ground, and lying with his heeles upward, maketh his belly to swell, and closeth his eyes as if he were starke dead. In the meane while his Master lamenting the misfortune of the Asse unto the standers by, earnestly craveth their friendly assistance and liberalitie to buy him a new Asse. And having gathered of each one as much money as hee can get; You are much deceived my Masters (quoth he) that thinke mine Asse to be dead: for the hungry Jade knowing his Masters necessity, hath wrought this sleight, to the end hee might get some money to buy him Provender. Then turning about to the Asse, hee commandeth him with all speed to arise: but the Asse lyeth starke still, though hee command and beate him never so much: whereupon, turning againe to the people; Bee it knowne (quoth hee) unto you all, that the Soldan hath published an Edict or Proclamation, that to morrow next all the people shall goe forth of the Citie to behold a Triumph, and that all the honourable and beautifull Ladies and Gentlewomen shall ride upon the most comely Asses, and shall give them Oates to eate, and Christall water of Nilus to drinke. Which words being scarce ended, the Asse suddenly starteth from the ground, prancing and leaping for joy: then his Master prosecuting still his narration; But (saith he) the Warden of our streete hath borrowed this goodly Asse of mine for his deformed and old Wife to ride upon. At these words the Asse, as though he were indued with humaine reason, coucheth his eares, and limpeth with one of his legges, as if it were quite out of joynt. Then saith his Master; What, sir Jade, are you so in love with faire women? The Asse nodding his head seemeth to say, yea. Come on therefore Sirra (quoth his Master) and let us see among all these pretty Damosels, which pleaseth your fancie best. Whereupon the Asse going about the company, and espying some woman more comely and beautifull then the rest, walketh directly unto her and toucheth her with his head: and then the beholders laugh and crie out amaine: Loe, the Asses Paramour, the Paramour of the Asse. Whereupon, the fellow that shewed all this sport leaping upon the backe of his Asse rideth to some other place.

Human Sacrifice among the Aztecs, *c.* 1520

José de Acosta

The author of this account was a Jesuit missionary in Peru and Mexico. He wrote a catechism in local Indian languages, which was the first book printed in Peru.

In truth the Mexicans did not sacrifice any to their Idols, but Captives, and the ordinary warres they made, was onely to have Captives for their Sacrifices: and therefore when they did fight, they laboured to take their enemies alive, and not to kill them, to enjoy their Sacrifices . . . The manner they used in these Sacrifices, was, they assembled within the Palissadoe of dead mens Sculles such as should be sacrificed, using a certayne Ceremony at the foot of the Palissadoe, placing a great guard about them. Presently there stept forth a Priest, attyred with a short Surplice full of tassels beneath, who came from the top of the Temple with an Idoll made of Paste of Wheate and Mays mingled with Honey, which had the eyes made of the graines of greene glasse, and the teeth of the graines of Mays, he descended the steps of the Temple with all the speed he could, and mounted on a great stone planted upon a high Terrasse in the midst of the Court. This stone was called Quauxicalli, which is to say, the stone of Eagle, whereon he mounted by a little Ladder, which was in the fore-part of the Terrasse, and descended by another staire on the other side, still imbracing his Idoll. Then did he mount to the place where those were that should be sacrificed, shewing this Idoll to every one in particular, saying unto them; this is your God. And having ended his shew, he descended by the other side of the staires, and all such as should dye, went in procession unto the place where they should bee sacrificed, where they found the Ministers ready for that Office. The ordinary manner of sacrificing was, to open the stomake of him that was sacrificed, and having pulled out his heart halfe alive, they tumbled the man downe the staires of the Temple, which were all imbrewed and defiled with bloud: And to make it the more plaine, sixe Sacrificers being appointed to this dignitie, came into the place of Sacrifice, foure to hold the hands and feet of him that should be sacrificed, the fift to hold his head, and the sixt to open his stomake, and to pull out the heart of the sacrificed. They called them Chachalmua, which in our Tongue is as much, as the Ministers of holy things. It was a high dignitie and much esteemed amongst them, wherein they did inherit and succeed as in a Fee-simple. The Minister who had the Office to kill, which was the sixt amongst them, was esteemed and honoured as the Sovereigne Priest and Bishop, whose name was different, according to the difference of times and Solemnities. Their habits were likewise divers when they came forth to the Sacrifice, according to the diversitie of times. The name of their chiefe dignitie was Papa and Topilzin, their Habite and Robe was a red Curtayne after the Dalmatike fashion, with tassels below, a Crowne of rich Feathers, greene, white, and yellow upon his head, and at his eares like pendants of Gold, wherein were set greene stones, and under the lip upon the middest of the beard he had a Peece like unto a small Canon of an azured stone. These Sacrificers came with their faces and hands coloured with a shining blacke. The other five had their haire much curled, and tyed up with Laces of Leather, bound about the middest of the head: upon their forehead they carried small Roundelets of Paper painted with divers colours, and they were attyred in a Dalmatike Robe of white, wrought with blacke. With this attyre they represented the very figure of the Devill, so as it did strike feare and terrour into all the people, to see them come forth with so horrible a representation. The Sovereigne Priest carried a great Knife in his hand, of a large and sharpe flint: another Priest carried a coller of wood wrought in forme of a Snake: All six put themselves in order, joyning to this Pyramidall stone, whereof I have spoken, being directly against the doore of the Chappell of their Idoll. This stone was so pointed, as the man which was to be sacrificed, being laid thereon, upon his backe, did bend in such sort, as letting the Knife but fall upon his stomack it opened very easily in the middest. When the Sacrificers were thus in order, they drew forth such as had beene taken in warre, which were to bee sacrificed at that Feast, and being accompanied with a guard of men all naked, they caused them to mount up these large staires in ranke, to the place where the Ministers were prepared: and as every one of them came in their order, the six Sacrificers tooke the Prisoner, one by one foote, another by the other, and one by one hand, another by the other, casting on his backe upon this pointed stone, where the fift of these Ministers put the coller of wood about his necke, and the High Priest opened his stomack with the Knife, with a strange dexteritie and nimblenesse, pulling out his heart with his hands, the which hee shewed smoking unto the Sunne, to whom hee did offer this heate and fume of the heart, and presently he turned towards the Idoll and did cast the heart at the face, then did they cast away the body of the sacrificed, tumbling it downe the staires of the Temple, the stone being set so neere the staires, as there were not two foote space betwixt the stone and the first step, so as with one spurne with their foote, they cast the bodie from the top to the bottome. In this sort one after one they did sacrifice all those that were appointed. Being thus slaine, and their bodies cast downe, their Masters, or such as had taken them, went to take them up, carried them away; then having divided them amongst them, they did eate them, celebrating their Feast and Solemnitie. There were ever fortie or fiftie at the least thus sacrificed, for that they had men very expert in taking them. The neighbour Nations did the like, imitating the Mexicans in the Customes and Ceremonies of the Service of their Gods.

The Incas' Golden Garden, *c.* 1530

Garcilaso de la Vega

The author of this account, was the illegitimate son of an Inca princess and a Spanish labourer. He was born in Cuzco, the Inca capital of Peru, in 1539.

This Garden was in the Incas time a Garden of Silver and Gold, as they had in the Kings houses, where they had many sorts of Hearbes, Flowers, Plants, Trees, Beasts great and small, wilde, tame, Snakes, Lizards, Snailes, Butterflies, small and great Birds, each set in their place. They had Maiz, Quinva, Pulse, Fruit-trees with the fruite on them all of Gold and Silver, resembling the naturall. They had also in the house heapes of wood, all counterfeit of Gold and Silver, as they had in the house royall: likewise they had great statues of men and women, and children, and many Pirva or Trosses for corne, every day inventing new fashions of greater Majestie, using yearely on the Sunnes chiefe festivities to present him so much Silver and Gold wrought into counterfeit formes. All the Vessell (which was infinite) for the Temples service, Pots, Pans, Tubs, Hogsheads, was of Gold and Silver, even to the Spades, and Pickaxes for the Garden. Like to this Temple of Cozco were others in many Provinces of that Kingdome, in which every Curaca indevoured according to his power to have such riches of Gold and Silver.

The Progress of the English Reformation, 1537–8

Cromwell's Agents' Report

John London, Roger Townshend, Richard Layton, Geoffrey Chamber

Thomas Cromwell, Henry VIII's Lord Privy Seal, was largely responsible for establishing the Reformation in England.

In my most humble manner I have me commended unto your good lordship, ascertaining the same that I have pulled down the image of Our Lady at Caversham, whereunto was great pilgrimage. The image is plated over with silver, and I have put it in a chest fast locked and nailed up, and by the next barge that cometh from Reading to London it shall be brought to your lordship. I have also pulled down the place she stood in, with all other ceremonies, as lights, shrowds, crosses, and images of wax hanging about the chapel, and have defaced the same thoroughly in eschewing of any further resort thither. This chapel did belong to Notley Abbey, and there always was a canon of that monastery which was called the Warden of Caversham, and he sung in this chapel and had the offerings for his living. He was accustomed to show many pretty relics, among the which were (as he made report) the holy dagger that killed King Henry, and the holy knife that killed St Edward. All these with many other, with the coats of this image, her cap and hair, my servants shall bring unto your lordship this week, with the surrender of the friars under their convent seal, and their seal also. I have sent the canon home again to Notley, and have made fast the doors of the chapel, which is thoroughly well covered with lead, and if it be your lordship's pleasure I shall see it made sure to the King's grace's use. And if it be not so ordered, the chapel standeth so wildly that the lead will be stolen by night, as I was served at the Friars. For as soon as I had taken the Friars' surrender, the multitude of the poverty of the town resorted thither, and all things that might be had they stole away, insomuch that they had conveyed the very clappers of the bells. And saving that Mr Fachell, which made me great cheer at his house, and the Mayor did assist me, they would have made no little spoil . . . At Caversham is a proper lodging where the canon lay, with a fair garden and an orchard, meet to be bestowed upon some friend of your lordship's in these parts . . .

Please it your good lordship to be advertised that there was a poor woman of Wells, beside Walsingham, that imagined a false tale of a miracle to be done by the image of Our Lady that was at Walsingham, since the same was brought from thence to London. And upon the trial thereof, by my examination from one person to another, to the number of six persons, and at last came to hear that she was the reporter thereof, and to be the very author of the same, as far forth as my conscience and perceiving could lead me, I committed her therefore to the ward of the constable at Walsingham. The next day after, being market day, there I caused her to be set in stocks in the morning, and about 9.00 of the clock when the said market was fullest of people, with a paper set about her head, written with these words upon the same A REPORTER OF FALSE TALES, was set in a cart and so carried about the market stead and other streets in the town, staying in divers places where most people assembled, young people and boys of the town casting snowballs at her. This done and executed, was brought to the stocks again, and there set till the market was ended. This was her penance; for I knew no law otherwise to punish her but by discretion, trusting it shall be a warning to other light persons in such wise to order themself. Howbeit, I cannot perceive but the said image is not yet out of some of their heads, I thought it convenient to advertise your lordship of the truth of this matter . . .

The Abbot of Langdon passeth all other that ever I knew in profound bawdry; the drunkennest knave living. All his canons be even as he is, not one spark of virtue amongst them; arrant bawdy knaves every man. The Abbot caused his chaplain to take an whore, and instigate him to it, brought her up into his own chapter, took one of his feather-beds off his own bed, and made his chaplain's bed in the inner chamber, within him, and there caused him to go to bed with his whore that the Abbot had provided for him. To rehearse you the whole story, it were long and too abominable to hear. The house is in utter decay and will shortly fall down. You must needs depose him and suddenly sequestrate the fruits, and take an inventory of the goods. You can do no less of justice . . .

My singular good lord, my duty remembered unto your lordship, this shall be to advertise the same that upon the defacing of the late monastery of Boxley, and plucking down the images of the same, I found in the image of the Rood called the Rood of Grace, the which heretofore hath been had in great veneration of the people, certain engines and old wire, with old rotten sticks in the back of the same, that did cause the eyes of the same to move and stare in the head thereof, like unto a living thing; and also the nether lip in like wise to move as though it should speak, which, so famed, was not a little strange to me and other that was present at the plucking down of the same, whereupon the abbot, hearing this bruit, did thither resort, whom to my little wit and cunning, with other of the old monks, I did examine of their knowledge of the premises; who do declare themselves to be ignorant of the same.

With the Spaniards in Paraguay, 1537–40

Hulderike Schnirdel

Schnirdel, a native of Antwerp, joined Pedro de Mendoza's expedition to South America in 1535. He was present at the founding of Buenos Aires in 1536 and, as related here, at the founding of Asunción in 1537 by Mendoza's Lieutenant-Governor, Juan de Ayolas.

These people of Carios inhabit a large Countrie, extending it selfe three hundred leagues in length, and breadth: they are men of a short stature, and thicke, and more able to indure worke and labour than the rest. The men have a little hole in their lippes, and yellow Christall therein (which in their language they call Parabol) of two spannes long, and of the thicknesse of a quill or reede. The men and women both in this Countrie, goe all naked, as they were created of God. Amongst these Indians the Father sels the Daughter, the Husband the wife. Sometimes also the Brother doth either sell or change the Sister. They value a Woman at a Shirt, a Knife, a Hatchet, or some other thing of this kinde. These Carios also eate mans flesh, if they can get it. For when they take any in the warres, whether they be men or women, young or old, they fatten them, no otherwise then wee doe Hogges. But they keepe a woman some yeeres, if she be yong, and of a commendable beautie, but if in the meane time, she apply not her selfe to all their desires, they kill, and eate her, making a solemne banquet, as marriages are wont to be celebrated with us. But they keepe an old woman, till she dye of her owne accord. These Carios undertake longer journies than any of these Nations upon the River of Plate. They are couragious and fierce in battaile, and their Villages and Townes are situate upon the River Parana, on an high and mounting land.

The Citie of these people (which the Inhabitants call Lampere) was compassed with a double bulwarke cunningly made of timber, as with a hedge or inclosure, every trench being of the bredth and thicknesse of a man, and one bulwarke or trench was twelve paces distant from the other. The trenches being digged a fathome deepe into the earth, were so high above the ground, as a man might reach with the length of a Sword. They had also Pits and Caves fifteene paces distant from the walls cast up the height of three men, in the middest whereof pikes were stucke, yet not appearing above ground, as sharpe pointed as a Pinne. They made these Pits so covered with straw, putting twigs and branches therein, with a little earth strowed betweene, that we Christians pursuing them, or being readie to assault their Towne, might fall into them. But they cast these pits for themselves, and at length they fell into them: for when our Generall John Eyollas, gathering all his Souldiers together, who were not above three hundred (for they left sixtie to guard the Brigantines) ordering and ranging the companies, went against their Citie Lampere, they understanding before of our comming, making a stand a Musket shot off with their armie of foure thousand men, furnished with Bowe and Arrowes after their manner, commanded that we should be told, that they would provide us victuall, and other necessaries, desiring us to goe backe and returne unto our Ships, that so departing as soone as we could, we might peaceably returne to our companions. But it was neither good for our Generall, nor our selves, that we should consent to their request: for this Nation and Countrie, by reason of the plenty of victuall, was also most fit, and commodious for us, especially when in foure whole yeares past, we had not seene a morsell of bread, living onely with fish and flesh, and oftentimes also in great penurie.

These Carios therefore taking their Bowe and Arrowes, entertained and saluted us therewith. But as yet, wee had no minde to hurt them, but commanded to signifie unto them, that they should be quiet, and we would become their friends. But they would not be so contented, for they had not yet tried our Gunnes and Swords. When therefore we came somewhat neerer unto them, wee discharged our brasse Peeces against them. Which when they heard, and saw that so many men fell downe dead, and when neither Bullets, nor Arrowes appeared, but holes onely were seene in their bodies, they wondred with astonishment, and horribly terrified, tooke their flight in troopes, overthrowing one another like Dogs: and while with great celeritie they hasten to shelter themselves in their Towne, more then three hundred men, in that amased feare, fell into the foresaid pits, which themselves had digged.

Afterward comming to their Citie, we assaulted it, they couragiously defending themselves, till the third day. But when they could defend themselves no longer, and were much afraid of their wives and children, which they had with them in the Towne, they earnestly entreated our favour and mercie, promising, that they would doe any thing for us, and for our sakes, at our pleasure, so that wee would spare their lives. In this stirre sixteene of our men were slaine. They brought also to our Generall Eyolas, sixe women, among which the eldest was but eighteene yeeres old, they presented also sixe Stags, and another wilde beast, entreating us to stay with them. They gave two women to the Souldiers, to serve them for Laundresses and other services. They also provided us victuals, and other necessaries for foode. And so peace was concluded betweene them and us.

These things being so done, the Carios were compelled to build us a great House, of stone, timber, and earth, that the Christians might have a place of refuge, if hereafter they moved any sedition against them wherein they might be safe, and might defend themselves against injurie. Wee tooke this Village or Citie of theirs by assault the yeere of Christ 1537, in the feast of the Assumption and gave it that name [Asunción]. And here wee abode two moneths. These Carios are fiftie leagues distant from the Aygais, and from the Iland of Bona Speranza, which the Tiembus inhabite about three hundred thirtie and foure leagues.

Making therefore a league with these Carios, they promised, that they would aide us, when we went to the warres, and if we were to undertake any service against the Aygais, they would send eighteene thousand men with us. When our Generall had thus determined, taking three hundred Spaniards, with these Carios, going downe the River of Parabol, with the streame, wee marched thirtie leagues by land, till we came to the place, where the said Aygais dwelt: we slue them both old and young, in the old place where wee left them, unawares in their houses, while they yet slept, early in the morning betweene three and foure of the clocke (for the Carios had diligently searched out all) oppressing them even to the death; for the Carios have this custome that being conquerers in warre, they kill all without any commiseration or pitie.

After this, taking away five hundred Canoas or Boates, we burnt all the Villages to the which we came, doing much hurt besides. After one moneth past, some of the people of Aygais came unto us, who being absent farre from home, were not present at this fight, and craving pardon, yeelded themselves into our hands . . .

The ninth day after our departure from them, we came to the Scherves. This Nation is very populous, yet they are not true and naturall, among whom the King himselfe hath an house. But these

Scherves maintaine a Priest expert in the Mysteries of Religion, and have a ring of wood hanging at their eares. These men also weare a blue Christall in their lips, of the shape and bignesse of Dice, they are painted with a blue colour from the paps to the privities, with that excellency that I thinke a Painter is not to be found in all Germany, which could performe the like so finely and artificially. They goe naked, and are beautifull after their manner.

We stayed therefore one day with these Scherves, and after going fourteene leagues forward in three dayes journey, at length wee came to the place where their King dwelleth, from the which the Inhabitants are called Scherves. His Country containeth only foure leagues in length. Yet hath he a Village situate upon the River of Parabol. Therefore leaving our ships heere, we committed the custodie thereof to twelve Spaniards, that returning wee might use them for our defence. Wee also intreated the Scherves dwelling there, that in the meane space they would friendly converse with the Christians, and intreate them courteously, which also they did; with necessaries for our journey, passing over the River Parobol, wee arrived at that place, where the seate and house of the King was. Who, when we were almost yet a league from him, commeth forth to meete us guarded with more then 12,000 men in a Champion plaine, yet friendly and peaceably. The path wherein they marched, was eight paces broad, strewed with flowres and grasse on every side, and made so cleane, that not so much as any little stone, stick, or straw appeared. The King had also with him his Musicians, whose Instruments were like our crooked Trumpets, which wee call Schalmes. Hee gave commandement also, that they should hunt Stags and other wilde beasts on both sides of the way which hee went, so that they tooke about thirtie Stags and twentie Estridges or Jandu, which spectacle was very pleasant to behold. When we were entred into the Village, he alwaies appointed one lodging for two Christians. But our Captaine together with his Servants or followers was brought into the Kings Palace.

He is wont to have Musicke at the Table, and at his meate, whensoever he pleaseth. For then they play upon the Flutes or Pipes, men leading the dances and skipping with most beautifull women, which dances and skippings seemed so strange unto us, that looking upon them, wee had almost forgot our selves. In the rest the Scherves are like those people of whom wee spoke before. The women make them gownes or upper garments of thinne

Cotton, almost like our clothes which are some part silke, which we call Arras or Burschet. They weave in these divers shapes of Stags, Estridges and Indian sheepe, according as every of them is more skilfull in the art of weaving.

In these garments they sleepe, if the Aire happen to be somewhat cold, or putting them under them they sit upon them, or use them at their pleasure for other services. These women are very faire and venerous . . .

In performing this Journey we spent a yeere and an halfe, doing nothing else, but making continuall warre. And in this Journey we had brought into our subjection about twelve thousand men, women, and children, who were compelled to serve us as bond-slaves: as I for mine owne person did possesse about fiftie men, women, and children.

The Execution of Archbishop Cranmer, 21 March 1556

Related by a Bystander

Cranmer, the first Protestant Archbishop of Canterbury, was convicted of heresy under the Catholic Mary I. In prison he was induced to write an abject recantation of Protestantism, but he confounded his enemies by publicly disavowing his recantation before he died.

But that I know for our great friendships, and long continued love, you look even of duty that I should signify to you of the truth of such things as here chanceth among us; I would not at this time have written to you the unfortunate end, and doubtful tragedy, of Thomas Cranmer late bishop of Canterbury: because I little pleasure take in beholding of such heavy sights. And, when they are once overpassed, I like not to rehearse them again; being but a renewing of my woe, and doubling my grief. For although his former life, and wretched end, deserves a greater misery, (if any greater might have chanced than chanced unto him), yet, setting aside his offences to God and his country, and beholding the man without his faults, I think there was none that pitied not his case, and bewailed not his fortune, and feared not his own chance, to see so noble a prelate, so grave a counsellor, of so long continued honour, after so many dignities, in his old years to be deprived of his estate, adjudged to die, and in so painful a death to end his life. I have no delight to increase it. Alas, it is too much of itself, that ever so heavy a case should betide to man, and man to deserve it.

But to come to the matter: on Saturday last, being 21 of March, was his day appointed to die. And because the morning was much rainy, the sermon appointed by Mr Dr Cole to be made at the stake, was made in St Mary's church: whither Dr Cranmer was brought by the mayor and aldermen, and my lord Williams: with whom came divers gentlemen of the shire, sir T. A. Bridges, sir John Browne, and others. Where was prepared, over against the pulpit, an high place for him, that all the people might see him. And, when he had ascended it, he kneeled him down and prayed, weeping tenderly: which moved a great number to tears, that had conceived an assured hope of his conversion and repentance . . .

When praying was done, he stood up, and, having leave to speak, said, 'Good people, I had intended indeed to desire you to pray for me; which because Mr Doctor hath desired, and you have done already, I thank you most heartily for it. And now will I pray for myself, as I could best devise for mine own comfort, and say the prayer, word for word, as I have here written it.' And he read it standing: and after kneeled down, and said the Lord's Prayer; and all the people on their knees devoutly praying with him . . .

And then rising, he said, 'Every man desireth, good people, at the time of their deaths, to give some good exhortation, that other may remember after their deaths, and be the better thereby. So I beseech God grant me grace, that I may speak something, at this my departing, whereby God may be glorified, and you edified . . .

'And now I come to the great thing that troubleth my conscience more than any other thing that ever I said or did in my life: and that is, the setting abroad of writings contrary to the truth. Which here now I renounce and refuse, as things written with my hand, contrary to the truth which I thought in my heart, and written for fear of death, and to save my life, if it might be: and that is, all such bills, which I have written or signed with mine own hand since my degradation: wherein I have written many things untrue. And forasmuch as my hand offended in writing contrary to my heart, therefore my hand shall first be punished: for if I may come to the fire, it shall be first burned. And as for the pope, I refuse him, as Christ's enemy and antichrist, with all his false doctrine.'

And here, being admonished of his recantation and dissembling, he said, 'Alas, my lord, I have been a man that all my life loved plainness, and never dissembled till now against the truth; which I am most sorry for it.' He added hereunto, that, for the sacrament, he believed as he had taught in his book against the bishop of Winchester. And here he was suffered to speak no more . . .

Then was he carried away; and a great number, that did run to see him go so wickedly to his death, ran after him, exhorting him, while time was, to remember himself. And one Friar John, a godly and well learned man, all the way travelled with him to reduce him. But it would not be. What they said in particular I cannot tell, but the effect appeared in the end: for at the stake he professed, that he died in all such opinions as he had taught, and oft repented him of his recantation.

Coming to the stake with a cheerful countenance and willing mind, he put off his garments with haste, and stood upright in his shirt: and a bachelor of divinity, named Elye, of Brazen-nose college, laboured to convert him to his former recantation, with the two Spanish friars. And when the friars saw his constancy, they said in Latin one to another 'Let us go from him: we ought not to be nigh him: for the devil is with him.' But the bachelor in divinity was more earnest with him: unto whom he answered, that, as concerning his recantation, he repented it right sore, because he knew it was against the truth; with other words more. Whereby the Lord Williams cried, 'Make short, make short.' Then the bishop took certain of his friends by the hand. But the bachelor of divinity refused to take him by the hand, and blamed all others that so did, and said, he was sorry that ever he came in his company. And yet again he required him to agree to his former recantation. And the bishop answered, (shewing his hand), 'This was the hand that wrote it, and therefore shall it suffer first punishment.'

Fire being now put to him, he stretched out his right hand, and thrust it into the flame, and held it there a good space, before the fire came to any other part of his body; where his hand was seen of every man sensibly burning, crying with a loud voice, 'This hand hath offended.' As soon as the fire got up, he was very soon dead, never stirring or crying all the while.

His patience in the torment, his courage in dying, if it had been taken either for the glory of God, the wealth of his country, or the testimony of truth, as it was for a pernicious error, and subversion of true religion, I could worthily have commended the example, and matched it with the fame of any father of ancient time: but, seeing that not the death, but cause and quarrel thereof, commendeth the sufferer, I cannot but much dispraise his obstinate stubbornness and sturdiness in dying, and specially in so evil a cause. Surely his death much grieved every man; but not after one sort. Some pitied to see his body so tormented with the fire raging upon the silly carcass, that counted not of the folly. Other that passed not much of the body, lamented to see him spill his soul, wretchedly, without redemption, to be plagued for ever. His friends sorrowed for love; his enemies for pity: strangers for a common kind of humanity, whereby we are bound one to another. Thus I have enforced myself, for your sake, to discourse this heavy narration, contrary to my mind: and, being more than half weary, I make a short end, wishing you a quieter life, with less honour; and easier death, with more praise.

Prisoners of the Inquisition, 1568–75

Adventures of English Sailors in Mexico

Miles Phillips

John Hawkins made two successful slave-trading voyages to the Caribbean, but disaster struck his third voyage (1568) and he was forced to abandon some of his company, as this survivor recounts. Phillips eventually got back to England in 1583.

The morrow after [25th September], the storm being ceased, and the weather fair; we weighed and set sail: being many men in number, and but small store of victuals to suffice us for any long time: by means whereof we were in despair and fear, that we should perish through famine, so that some were in mind to yield themselves to the mercy of the Spaniards, others to the savages or infidels.

And wandering thus certain days in these unknown seas, hunger constrained us to eat hides, cats and dogs, mice, rats, parrots and monkeys: to be short, our hunger was so great, that we thought it savoury and sweet, whatever we could get to eat.

And on the 8th of October, we came to land again in the bottom of the Bay of Mexico, where we hoped to have found some inhabitants, that we might have had some relief of victuals, and a place where to repair our ship, which was so greatly bruised that we were scarce able, with our weary arms, to keep forth the water.

Being thus oppressed with famine on the one side, and danger of drowning on the other; not knowing where to find relief, we began to be in wonderful despair, and we were of many minds. Amongst whom there were a great many that did desire our General [Sir John Hawkins] to set them on land; making their choice rather to submit themselves to the mercy of the savages or infidels than longer to hazard themselves at sea: where they very well saw that, if they should all remain together, if they perished not by drowning, yet hunger would enforce them, in the end, to eat one another. To which request, our General did very willingly agree, considering with himself that it was necessary for him to lessen his number; both for the safety of himself and the rest.

And thereupon being resolved to set half his people on shore, that he had then left alive; it was a world to see how suddenly men's minds were altered! For they which, a little before, desired to be set on land, were now of another mind, and requested rather to stay.

By means whereof, our General was enforced, for the more contentation of all men's minds, and to take away all occasions of offence, to take this order. First, he made choice of such persons of service and account as were needful to stay: and that being done, of those who were willing to go, he appointed such as he thought might best be spared. And presently appointed that, by the boat, they should set on shore: our General promising us, that, the next year, he would either come himself, or else send to fetch us home.

Here again, it would have caused any stony heart to have relented, to have heard the pitiful moan that many did make; and how loath they were to depart. The weather was then somewhat stormy and tempestuous, and therefore we were to pass with great danger; yet notwithstanding there was no remedy but we that were appointed to go away, must of necessity do so.

Howbeit, those that went in the first boat were safely set ashore; but of them which went in the second boat, of which number I myself was one, the seas wrought so high that we could not attain to the shore: and therefore we were constrained through the cruel dealing of John Hampton, Captain of the *Minion*, John Sanders,

Boatswain of the *Jesus*, and Thomas Pollard, his Mate, to leap out of the boat into the main sea, having more than a mile to the shore; and so to shift for ourselves, and either to sink or swim. And of those that were so, as it were, thrown out, and compelled to leap into the sea, there were two drowned, which were of Captain Bland's men.

In the evening of the same day, it being Friday, the 8th of October 1568, when we were all come ashore, we found fresh water; whereof some of our men drank so much that they had almost cast themselves away, for we could scarce get life in them for the space of two or three hours after. Some others were so cruelly swollen, what with the drinking in of the salt water, and what with the eating of the fruit, which is called capule, having a stone in it much like an almond, which we found on land, they were all in very ill case. So that we were, in a manner, all of us, both feeble, faint, and weak.

The next morning, it being Saturday, the 9th of October, we thought it best to travel along by the sea coast, to seek out some place of habitation; whether they were Christians or savages, we were indifferent, so that we might have wherewithal to sustain our hungry bodies.

So departing from a hill, where we had rested all night, not having any dry thread about us: for those that were not wet, being thrown into the sea, were thoroughly wet with rain; for it rained cruelly all the night.

As we went from the hill, and were come into the plain, we were greatly troubled to pass, for the grass and woods that grew there higher than any man. On the left hand, we had the sea; and upon the right hand, great woods: so that, of necessity, we must needs pass, on our way westward, through those marshes.

Going thus, suddenly, we were assaulted by the Indians, a warlike kind of people; which are, in a manner as cannibals, although they do not feed upon men's flesh as cannibals do. These people are called Chichemics; and they use to wear their hair long, even down to their knees. They do also colour their faces green, yellow, red, and blue; which maketh them to seem very ugly and terrible to behold.

These people do keep wars against the Spaniards; of whom they have been oftentimes very cruelly handled: for with the Spaniards there is no mercy.

They perceiving us, at our first coming on land, supposed us to have been their enemies, the bordering Spaniards; and having by their forerunners descried what number we were, and how feeble and weak, without armour or weapon, they suddenly (according to their accustomed manner when they encounter with any people in warlike sort) raised a terrible and huge cry; and so came running fiercely upon us, shooting off their arrows as thick as hail.

Unto whose mercy, we were constrained to yield, not having amongst us any kind of armour: nor yet weapon, saving one caliver and two old rusty swords, whereby to make any resistance or to save ourselves. Which when they perceived that we sought not any other than favour and mercy at their hands, and that we are not their enemies, the Spaniards; they had compassion on us, and came and caused us all to sit down. And when they had a while surveyed and taken a perfect view of us, they came to all such as had any coloured clothes amongst us, and those they did strip stark naked, and took their clothes away with them; but they that were apparelled in black, they did not meddle withal. And so went their ways, and left us, without doing us any further hurt: only in the first brunt, they killed eight of our men.

At their departure, they perceiving in what weak case we were, pointed us with their hands, which way we should go to come to a town of the Spaniards (which, as we afterwards perceived, was not past ten leagues from thence), using these words, 'Tampeco! tampeco Christiano! tampeco Christiano!', which is as much, we think, as to say in English, 'Go that way, and you shall find the Christians!' The weapons that they use, are no others but bows and arrows; and their aim is so good that they very seldom miss to hit anything that they shoot at.

Shortly after they had left us stript, as aforesaid, we thought it best to divide ourselves into two companies. So being separated, half of us went under the leading of Anthony Goddard (who is a man alive, and dwelleth at this instant in the town of Plymouth), whom before, we chose to be Captain over us all: and those which went under his leading (of which number, I, Miles Phillips, was one), travelled westward, that way which the Indians with their hands had before pointed us to go.

The other half went, under the leading of one John Hooper whom they did choose for their Captain (and with the company that went with him, David Ingram was one), and they took their way, and travelled northward. And shortly after, within the space of two days, they were again encountered with the savage people: and their Captain, Hooper, and two more of their company were slain.

Then, again, they divided themselves. Some held on their way still northward: and some others, knowing that we were gone westward, sought to meet with us again; as, in truth, there was about the number of 25 or 26 of them that met with us, in the space of four days again.

Then we began to reckon among ourselves, how many we were that were set on shore: and we found the number to be 114: whereof two were drowned in the sea, and eight slain at the first encounter; so that there remained 104, of which 25 went westward with us, and 52 to the north with Hooper and Ingram. And as Ingram since hath often told me, there were not past three of their company slain; and there were but 26 of them that came again to us. So that of the company that went northward, there is yet lacking, and not certainly heard of, to the number of 23 men: and verily I do think that there are some of them yet alive, and married in the said country, at Sibola; as hereafter I purpose, God willing! to discourse of more particularly, with the reason and causes that make me so to think of them, that were lacking; which were David Ingram, Twide, Browne and sundry others whose names we could not remember.

Being thus met again together, we travelled on still westward, sometimes through such thick woods that we were enforced to break away, with cudgels, the brambles and bushes from tearing our naked bodies. Some other times, we should travel through the plains in such high grass that we could scarce see one another. And as we passed, in some places, we should have our men slain, and fall down suddenly; being sticken by the Indians, which stood behind trees and bushes, in secret places, and so killed our men as they went by: for we went scatteringly in seeking of fruits to relieve ourselves.

We were also, oftentimes, greatly annoyed with a kind of fly, which in the Indian tongue is called, *tequani*, and the Spaniards call them *musketas* [mosquitoes].

There are also in the said country, a number of other flies, but none so noisome as these *tequanies* be. You shall hardly see them, they be so small; for they are scarce so big as a gnat. They will suck one's blood marvellously, and if you kill them, while they are sucking, they are so venomous that the place will swell extremely even as one that is stung with a wasp or bee: but if you let them suck their fill and to go away of themselves, they do you no other hurt, but leave behind them a red spot somewhat bigger than a flea-biting. At first, we were terribly troubled with these kind of flies, not knowing their qualities: and resistance we could make none against them, being naked. As for cold, we feared not any: the country there is always so warm.

And as we travelled thus, for the space of ten or twelve days, our Captain did oftentimes cause certain to go to the tops of high trees to see if they could descry any town or place of inhabitants; but they could not perceive any.

Using often the same order, to climb up into high trees, at the length, they descried a great river that fell from the north-west into the main sea; and presently after, we heard a harquebuss shot off, which did greatly encourage us, for thereby we knew that we were near to some Christians, and did therefore hope shortly to find some succour and comfort.

Within the space of one hour after, as we travelled, we heard a cock crow: which was no small joy to us.

So we came to the north side of the river of Panuco; where the Spaniards have certain *salinas* [salt pans]: at which place it was that the harquebuss was shot off, which we heard before. To which place, we went not directly; but missing thereof, we left it about a bow shot upon our left hand.

Of this river, we drank very greedily; for we had not met with any water, in six days before.

As we were here by the river, resting ourselves, and longing to come to the place where the cock did crow, and where the harquebuss was shot off; we perceived many Spaniards upon the other side of the river, riding up and down on horseback: and they perceiving us, did suppose that we had been of the Indians their bordering enemies, the Chichemics. The river was not past half a bow shot over.

Presently, one of the Spaniards took an Indian boat called a canoe; and so came over, being rowed by two Indians. Having taken the view of us, he did presently row over back again to the Spaniards: who, without any delay, made out about the number of twenty horsemen; and embarking themselves in the canoes, they led their horses by the reins, swimming over after them. Being come over, to that side of the river where we were, they saddled their horses; and being mounted upon them, with their lances charged, they came very fiercely, running at us.

Our Captain, Anthony Goddard, seeing them come in that order, did persuade us to submit and yield ourselves unto them; for being naked as we were at this time, without weapon, we could not make any resistance: whose bidding we obeyed.

Upon the yielding of ourselves, they perceived us to be Christians; and did call for more canoes, and carried us over by four and four in a boat. Being come on the other side, they understanding by our Captain how long we had been without meat, imparted between two and two, a loaf of bread made of that country wheat which the Spaniards call maize, of the bigness of one of our halfpenny loaves; which bread is named in the Indian tongue, *clashacally*.

This bread was very sweet and pleasant unto us, for we had not eaten anything in a long time before: and what is it that hunger doth not make to have a savoury and a delicate taste?

Having thus imparted the bread amongst us, those which were men, they sent afore to the town; having also many Indians, inhabitants of that place, to guard them. They which were young, as boys; and some such also as were feeble, they took up upon their horses behind them. And so carried us to the town, where they dwelt; which was very near a mile distant from the place where we came over.

This town [Tampico] is well situated, and well replenished with all kinds of fruits, as oranges, lemons, pomegranates, apricots, and peaches, and sundry others: and is inhabited with a number of tame Indians or Mexicans; and had in it, also, at that time, about the number of 200 Spaniards (men, women, and children), besides Negroes.

Of the *salinas*, which lie upon the west side of the river, more than a mile distant from thence, they make a great profit. For salt is an excellent good merchandise there. The Indians do buy much thereof, and carry it up into the country and there sell it to their own people, doubling the price.

When we were all come to the town, the Governor there shewed himself very severe unto us, and threatened to hang us all. Then he demanded, 'What money we had?' which, in truth, was very little: for the Indians had, in a manner, taken all from us; and of that which was left, the Spaniards, which brought us over, took away a good part also. Howbeit, the Governor here had from Anthony Goddard a chain of gold, which was given unto him at Cartagena, by the Governor there; and from others, he had some small store of money. So that we accounted that among us all, he had the number of 500 pesos besides the chain of gold.

Having thus satisfied himself, when he had taken all that we had; he caused us to be put into a little house, much like a hogsty, where we were almost smothered.

Before we were thus shut up in that little cot, they gave us some of the country wheat, called maize, sodden: which they feed their hogs withal. But many of our men, which had been hurt by the Indians at our first coming on land, whose wounds were very sore and grievous, desired to have the help of their Surgeons to cure their wounds. The Governor, and most of them, all answered that 'We should have none other surgeon but the hangman; which should sufficiently heal us of all our griefs.'

Thus reviling us, and calling us, 'English dogs!' and 'Lutheran heretics!' we remained the space of three days in this miserable state, not knowing what should become of us; waiting every hour to be bereaved of our lives.

Upon the fourth day, after our coming thither, and there remaining in a perplexity; looking every hour when we should suffer death: there came a great number of Indians and Spaniards, weaponed, to fetch us out of the house. And amongst them, we espied one that brought a great many of new halters: at the sight whereof, we were greatly amazed, and made no other account but that we should presently have suffered death; and so, crying and calling on God for mercy and forgiveness of our sins, we prepared ourselves, making us ready to die.

Yet in the end, as the sequel shewed, their meaning was not so. For when we were come out of the house, with those halters, they bound our arms behind us; and so coupling us two and two together, they commanded us to march on through the town, and so alongst the country, from place to place, towards the city of Mexico; which is distant from Panuco [Tampico], west-and-by-south, the space of threescore leagues: having only but two Spaniards to conduct us; they being accompanied with a great number of Indians, warding, on each side, with bows and arrows, lest we should escape from them.

Travelling in this order, upon the second day, at night, we came unto a town, which the Indians call Nohele; and the Spaniards call it Santa Maria. In which town there is a House of White Friars; which did very courteously use us, and gave us hot meat, as mutton and broth; and garments also to cover ourselves withal, made of white baize. We fed very greedily of the meat, and of the Indian fruit called *Nochole*, which fruit is long and small, much like in fashion to a little cucumber. Our greedy feeding caused us to fall sick of hot burning agues.

And here at this place, one Thomas Baker one of our men, died of a hurt; for had been before shot in the throat with an arrow, at the first encounter.

The next morrow, about ten of the clock, we departed from thence, bound two and two together, and guarded as before. And so travelled on our way towards Mexico, till we came to a town within forty leagues of Mexico, named Mesticlan; where is a House of Black Friars; and in this town there are about the number of 300 Spaniards, men, women, and children. The Friars sent us meat from the House ready dressed; and the Friars, and men and women, used us very courteously, and gave us some shirts and other such things as we lacked. Here our men were very sick of their agues; and with the eating of another fruit, called in the Indian tongue, *guiaccos*.

The next morning, we departed from thence, with our two Spaniards, and Indian guard; as aforesaid.

Of these two Spaniards, the one was an aged man, who, all the way, did very courteously intreat us; and would carefully go before to provide for us, both meat and things necessary, to the uttermost of his power. The other was a young man, who, all the way, travelled with us, and never departed from us; who was a very cruel caitiff. He carried a javelin in his hand; and sometimes when our men, with very feebleness and faintness, were not able to go as fast as he required them; he would take his javelin in both his hands, and strike them with the same, between the neck and the shoulders so violently that he would strike them down: then would he cry, and say, 'Marches! marches Ingleses perros! Lutheranos; enemicos de Dios!', which is as much as to say in English, 'March! march on, you English dogs! Lutherans! enemies to God!'

And the next day, we came to a town called Pachuca. There are two places of that name, as this Town of Pachuca; and the Mines of Pachuca, which are mines of silver, and are about six leagues distant from this town of Pachuca, towards the north-west.

Here, at this town, the good old man, our governor, suffered us to stay two days and two nights, having compassion of our sick and weak men: full sore against the mind of the young man, his companion.

From thence, we took our journey, and travelled four or five days, by little villages, and *stantias* which are farms or dairy houses of the Spaniards; and ever, as we had need, the good old man would still provide us sufficiently of meats, fruits, and water to sustain us.

At the end of which five days, we came to a town within five leagues of Mexico, which is called Quoglilican; where we also stayed one whole day and two nights; where was a fair House of Grey Friars; howbeit, we saw none of them.

Here we were told by the Spaniards in the town, that we were not past fifteen English miles from thence to Mexico; whereof we were all very joyful and glad: hoping that when we came thither, we should either be relieved and set free out of bonds, or else be quickly despatched out of our lives. For seeing ourselves thus carried bound from place to place, although some used us courteously, yet could we never joy nor be merry till we might perceive ourselves set free from that bondage, either by death or otherwise.

The next morning, we departed from thence, on our journey towards Mexico; and so travelled till we came within two leagues of it. Where there was built by the Spaniards a very fair church, called Our Lady's Church; in which, there is an image of Our Lady, of silver and gilt, being as high and as large as a tall woman; in which church, and before this image, there are as many lamps of silver, as there be days in the year; which, upon high days, are all lighted.

Whensoever any Spaniards pass by this church, although they be on horseback, they will alight, and come into the church, and kneel before this image, and pray to our Lady to defend them from all evil; so that, whether he be horseman or footman, he will not pass by, but first go into the church, and pray as aforesaid; which if they do not, they think and believe that they shall never prosper. Which image, they call in the Spanish tongue, *Nostra Señora de Guadaloupe*.

At this place, there are certain cold baths, which arise, springing up as though the water did seethe. The water whereof is somewhat brackish in taste, but very good for any that have any sore or wound, to wash themselves therewith. For, as they say, it healeth many. And every year, upon our Lady's Day, the people use to repair thither to offer, and to pray in the church before the image: and they say that Our Lady of Guadaloupe doth work a number of miracles. About this church, there is not any town inhabited by Spaniards; but certain Indians do dwell there, in houses of their own country building.

Here, we were met with a great number of Spaniards on horseback, which came from Mexico to see us, both gentlemen and men of occupations; and they came as people to see a wonder. We were still called upon to march on; and so, about four of the clock in the afternoon of the said day, we entered into the city of Mexico, by the way or street called *La Calla de Santa Catharina*: and we stayed not in any place till we came to the House or Palace of the Viceroy, Don Martin de Henriquez, which standeth in the midst of the city, hard by the Market Place, called *La Plaza dell Marquess*.

We had not stayed any long time at the place, but there was brought us by the Spaniards from the Market Place, great store of meat sufficient to have satisfied five times so many as we were. Some also gave us hats, and some gave us money. In which place, we stayed for the space of two hours.

From thence, we were conveyed by water in large canoes to an Hospital, where certain of our men were lodged, which were taken before, at the fight at San Juan de Ulua. We should have gone to Our Lady's Hospital; but there were there also so many of our men taken before, at that fight, that there was no room for us.

After our coming thither, many of the company that came with me from Panuco died, within the space of fourteen days. Soon after which time, we were taken forth from that place, and put together in Our Lady's Hospital; in which place, we were courteously used, and oftentimes visited by virtuous gentlemen and gentlewomen of the city: who brought us divers things to comfort us withal, as succets [sweetmeats], marmalades, and such other things; and would also many times give us many things, and that very liberally.

In which Hospital, we remained for the space of six months, until we were all whole and sound of body.

Then we were appointed by the Viceroy, to be carried into the town of Tescuco, which is distant from Mexico, south-west, eight leagues. In which town, there are certain Houses of Correction and

Punishment, for ill people called *obraches*; like to Bridewell here in London. Into which place, divers Indians were sold for slaves; some for ten years and some for twelve.

It was no small grief unto us, when we understood that we should be carried thither; and to be used as slaves. We had rather be put to death.

Howbeit, there was no remedy; but we were carried to the Prison of Tescuco: where we were not put to any labour; but were very straitly kept, and almost famished. Yet, by the good providence of our merciful God, we happened to meet there, with one Robert Sweeting, who was the son of an English man born of a Spanish woman. This man could speak very good English; and by his means we were helped very much with victuals from the Indians, as muttons, hens, and bread. And if we had not been so relieved, we had surely perished. And yet all the provision that we had got that way was but slender. And continuing thus straitly kept in prison there, for the space of two months; at the length, we agreed amongst ourselves to break forth of prison, come of it what would. For we were minded rather to suffer death, than to live longer in that miserable state.

And so having escaped out of prison, we knew not what way to fly for the safety of ourselves. The night was dark, and it rained terribly: and not having any guide, we went we knew not whither.

In the morning, at the appearing of the day, we perceived ourselves to be come hard to the city of Mexico; which is 24 English miles from Tescuco.

The day being come, we were espied by the Spaniards, and pursued, and taken: and brought before the Viceroy and the Head Justices, who threatened to hang us, for breaking the King's prison.

Yet, in the end, they sent us into a garden belonging to the Viceroy; and coming thither, we found there our English gentlemen, which were delivered as hostages when our General was betrayed at San Juan de Ulua, as is aforesaid. And with them also, we found Robert Barret, the Master of the *Jesus*.

In which place, we remained, labouring and doing such things as we were commanded, for the space of four months; having but two sheep a day allowed to suffice us all, being very nearly a hundred men; and for bread, we had every man, two loaves a day, of the quantity of one halfpenny loaf.

At the end of which four months, they having removed our

Gentlemen hostages and the Master of the *Jesus* to a prison in the Viceroy's own house; he did cause it to be proclaimed, that what gentleman Spaniard soever was willing, or would have any Englishman to serve him, and be bound to keep him forthcoming, to appear before the Justices within one month after notice given; that he should repair to the said garden, and there take his choice: which Proclamation was no sooner made, but the gentlemen came and repaired to the garden amain: so that happy was he, that could soonest get one of us.

The Gentlemen that took us for their servants or slaves did new apparel us throughout; with whom we abode, doing such service as they appointed us unto, which was, for the most part, to attend upon them at the table, and to be as their chamberlains, and to wait upon them, when they went abroad, which they greatly accounted of. For in that country, no Spaniard will serve another; but they are, all of them, attended and served by Indians, weekly; and by Negroes, which be their slaves, during their life.

In this sort, we remained, and served in the said city of Mexico and thereabouts, for the space of a year and somewhat longer . . .

Now after that six years were fully expired since our first coming into the Indies, in which time, we had been imprisoned and served in the said country, as is before truly declared: in the year of our Lord 1574, the Inquisition began to be established in the Indies; very much against the minds of many of the Spaniards themselves. For never until this time, since their first conquering and planting in the Indies, were they subject to that bloody and cruel Inquisition.

The Chief Inquisitor was named Don Pedro Moya de Contreres, and Juan de Bouilla, his companion; and Juan Sanchis, the Fiscal; and Pedro de la Rios, the Secretary.

They being come and settled, and placed in a very fair house near unto the White Friars (considering with themselves that they must make an entrance and beginning of that their most detestable Inquisition here in Mexico, to the terror of the whole country) thought it best to call us that were Englishmen first in question. We were sent for, and sought out in all places of the country, and Proclamation made, upon pain of losing of goods and excommunication, that no man should hide or keep secret any Englishman or any part of his goods.

By means whereof, we were all soon apprehended in all places, and all our goods seized and taken for the Inquisitors' use. And so, from all parts of the country, we were conveyed and sent as prisoners to the city of Mexico; and there committed to prison, in sundry dark dungeons, where we could not see but by candle light; and were never past two together in one place: so that we saw not one another, neither could one of us tell what was become of another.

Thus we remained close imprisoned for the space of a year and a half, and others for some less time: for they came to prison ever as they were apprehended.

During which time of our imprisonment, at the first beginning, we were often called before the Inquisitors alone; and there severely examined of our faith; and commanded to say the *Pater noster*, the *Ave Maria*, and the *Creed* in Latin: which, God knoweth! a great number of us could not say otherwise than in the English tongue. And having the said Robert Sweeting, who was our friend at Tescuco always present with them for an interpreter, he made report for us, that in our own country speech, we could say them perfectly, although not word for word as they were in the Latin.

Then did they proceed to demand of us, upon our oaths, 'What we did believe of the Sacrament?' and 'Whether there did remain any bread or wine, after the words of consecration, Yea or No?' and 'Whether we did not believe that the Host of bread which the priest did hold up over his head, and the wine that was in the chalice, was the very true and perfect body and blood of our Saviour Christ, Yea or No?'

To which, if we answered not 'Yea!' then there was no way but death.

Then they would demand of us, 'What did we remember of ourselves, what opinions we had held or been taught to hold contrary to the same, whiles we were in England?'

So we, for the safety of our lives, were constrained to say that, 'We never did believe, nor had been taught otherwise than as before we had said.'

Then would they charge us that 'We did not tell them the truth. That they knew to the contrary, and therefore we should call ourselves to remembrance, and make them a better answer at the next time, or else we should be racked, and made to confess the truth whether we would or not!'

And so coming again before them, the next time, we were still demanded of 'our belief whiles we were in England, and how we

had been taught'; and also what we thought, or did know of such of
our own company as they did name unto us. So that we could never
be free from such demands.

And, at other times, they would promise us that if we would tell
them truth, then should we have favour and be set at liberty;
although we very well knew their fair speeches were but means to
intrap us, to the hazard and loss of our lives.

Howbeit, God so mercifully wrought for us, by a secret means
that we had, that we kept us still to our first answer; and would still
say that 'we had told the truth unto them; and knew no more by
ourselves, nor any other of our fellows than as we had declared;
and that for our sins and offences in England, against God, and Our
Lady, and any of His blessed Saints; we were right heartily sorry for
the same, and did cry God, mercy!' And besought the Inquisitors,
'For God's sake, considering that we came unto those countries by
force of weather, and against our wills; and that we had never, in
all our lives, either spoken or done anything contrary to their laws;
that therefore they would have mercy upon us!' Yet all this would
not serve.

About the space of three months before [i.e., in January 1575]
they proceeded to their severe judgment, we were all racked; and
some enforced to utter against themselves, which afterwards cost
them their lives.

And having thus got, from our own mouths, sufficient for them
to proceed in judgment against us; they caused a large scaffold to be
made in the midst of the Market Place in Mexico, right over against
the Head Church: and fourteen or fifteen days before the day of
their judgment, with the sound of trumpet and the noise of their
attabalies (which are a kind of drums) they did assemble the people
in all parts of the city; before whom it was then solemnly
proclaimed that 'whosoever would, upon such a day, repair to the
Market Place, they should hear the sentence of the Holy Inquisition
against the English heretics, Lutherans; and also see the same put in
execution'.

Which being done, and the time approaching of this cruel
judgment; the night before, they came to the prison where we were,
with certain Officers of that Holy Hellish House, bringing with
them certain fools' coats, which they had prepared for us, being
called in their language, *San Benitos*, which coats were made of
yellow cotton, and red crosses upon them both before and behind.

They were so busied in putting on their coats about us, and in bringing us out into a large yard, and placing and pointing us in what order we should go to the scaffold or place of judgment upon the morrow, that they did not once suffer us to sleep all that night long.

The next morning being come, there was given to every one of us, for our breakfast, a cup of wine and a slice of bread fried in honey; and so about eight of the clock in the morning, we set forth of the prison: every man alone, in his yellow coat, and a rope about his neck, and a great green wax candle in his hand unlighted; having a Spaniard appointed, to go upon either side of every one of us.

So marching in this order and manner towards the Scaffold in the Market Place, which was a bow shot distant or thereabouts, we found a great assembly of people all the way, and such a throng that certain of the Inquisitors' Office, on horseback, were constrained to make way.

So coming to the Scaffold, we went up by a pair of stairs, and found seats ready made, and prepared for us to sit down on, every man in the order as he should be called to receive his judgment.

We being thus set down as we were appointed: presently the Inquisitors came up another pair of stairs; and the Viceroy and all the Chief Justices with them.

When they were set down under the Cloth of Estate, and placed according to their degrees and calling; then came up also a great number of Friars, White, Black, and Grey. They, being about the number of 300 persons, were set in the places appointed for them there.

There was there a solemn *Oyez!* made; and silence commanded.

And then presently began their severe and cruel judgment.

The first man that was called, was one Roger, the Chief Armourer of the *Jesus*: and he had judgment to have 300 stripes on horseback; and, after, was condemned to the galleys, as a slave, for ten years.

After him, were called John Gray, John Browne, John Rider, John Moon, James Collier, and one Thomas Browne. These were adjudged to have 200 stripes on horseback; and, after, to be committed to the galleys for the space of eight years.

Then was called John Keies, and was adjudged to have 100 stripes on horseback; and condemned to serve in the galleys for the space of six years.

Then were severally called, to the number of fifty-three; one after another: and every man had his several judgment. Some to have 200 stripes on horseback, and some 100; and condemned for slaves in the galleys, some for six years, some for eight, and some for ten.

And then was I, Miles Phillips, called; and was adjudged to serve in a Monastery for five years without any stripes; and to wear a fool's coat, or *San Benito*, during all that time.

Then were called John Story, Richard Williams, David Alexander, Robert Cooke, Paul Horsewell, and Thomas Hull. These six were condemned to serve in Monasteries without stripes; some for three years, and some for four, and to wear the *San Benito* during all the said time.

Which being done, and it now drawing towards night, George Rivelie, Peter Momfrie, and Cornelius the Irishman were called: and had their judgment to be burnt to ashes. And so were presently sent away to the place of execution in the Market Place, but a little from the Scaffold: where they were quickly burned and consumed.

And as for us that had received our judgment, being 68 in number; we were carried back that night to prison again.

And the next day, in the morning, being Good Friday, the year of our Lord 1575, we were all brought into a court of the Inquisitors' Palace; where we found a horse in a readiness for every one of our men which were condemned to have stripes, and to be committed to the galleys, which were in number 61.

So they being enforced to mount up on horseback, naked from the middle upwards, were carried to be shewed as a spectacle for all the people to behold throughout the chief and principal streets of the city; and had the number of stripes appointed to every one of them, most cruelly laid upon their naked bodies with long whips, by sundry men appointed to be the executioners thereof. And before our men there went a couple of Criers, which cried as they went, 'Behold these English dogs! Lutherans! enemies to God!' And all the way as they went, there were some of the Inquisitors themselves, and of the Familiars of that rakehell Order, that cried to the executioners, 'Strike! Lay on those English heretics! Lutherans! God's enemies!'

So this horrible spectacle being shewed round about the city; and they returned to the Inquisitor's House, with their backs all gore blood, and swollen with great bumps: they were then taken from their horses; and carried again to prison, where they remained until they were sent into Spain to the galleys, there to receive the rest of their martyrdom.

I, and the six others with me, which had judgment, and were condemned amongst the rest, to serve an apprenticeship in the Monasteries, were taken presently, and sent to certain Religious Houses appointed for the purpose.

The Sack of Antwerp by a Spanish Army, 4 November 1576

George Gascoigne

The so-called 'Spanish Fury' which laid Antwerp waste was an incident in the religious wars of the late sixteenth century. Gascoigne was an English poet and novelist.

I was lodged in the English House, and had not gone abroad that morning by reason of weighty business which I had in hand the same day. At dinner time [midday], the Merchantmen of my country, which came out of the town and dined in my chamber, told me, That a hot skirmish was begun in the Castle Yard, and that the fury thereof still increased, About the midst of dinner, news came, That the shot was so thick, as neither ground, houses, nor people could be discerned for the smoke thereof: and before dinner were fully ended, That the Spaniards were like to win the Trenches.

Whereat I stept from the table, and went hastily up into a high tower of the said English House: from whence I might discover fire in four or five places of the town towards the Castle Yard; and thereby I was well assured that the Spaniards indeed were entered within the Trenches.

So that I came down, and took my cloak and sword, to see the certainty thereof: and as I passed towards the Bourse I met many; but I overtook none. And those which I met were no townsmen, but soldiers; neither walked they as men which use traffic, but ran as men which are in fear.

Whereat, being somewhat grieved, and seeing the townsmen stand every man before his door with such weapons as they had; I demanded of one of them, What it meant?

Who answered me in these words, 'Hélas, Monsieur, il n'y a point d'ordre; et voilà la ruine de cette ville!' ['Alas, Sir, there is no order; and behold the ruin of this town!']

'Ayez courage, mon ami!' ['Have courage, my friend!'], quoth I; and so went onwards yet towards the Bourse: meeting all the way more and more which mended their pace.

At last, a Walloon trumpeter on horseback, who seemed to be but a boy of years, drew his sword, and laid about him, crying, 'Où est ce que vous enfuyez, canaille? Faisons tête, pour l'honneur de la patrie! [Where are you flying to, rascals? Make head, for the honour of our country!'] Wherewith fifty or threescore of them turned head, and went backwards towards the Bourse.

The which encouraged me, *par compagnie*, to proceed.

But alas, this comfort endured but a while. For by that time I came on the farther side of the Bourse, I might see a great troop coming in greater haste, with their heads as close together as a school of young fry or a flock of sheep; who met me, on the farther side of the Bourse, towards the Market Place: and, having their leaders foremost (for I knew them by their javelins, boar spears, and staves), bare me over backwards; and ran over my belly and my face, long time before I could recover on foot.

At last, when I was up, I looked on every side, and seeing them run so fast, began thus to bethink me, 'What, in God's name, do I here? which have no interest in this action; since they who came to defend this town are content to leave it at large, and shift for themselves.'

And whilst I stood thus musing, another flock of flyers came so fast that they bare me on my nose, and ran as many over my back, as erst had marched over my stomach. In fine, I got up like a tall fellow; and went with them for company: but their haste was such as I could never overtake them until I came at a broad cross street, which lieth between the English House and the said Bourse.

There I overtook some of them grovelling on the ground, and groaning for the last gasp; and some others which turned backwards to avoid the tickling of the Spanish Musquets [Musketeers]: who had gotten the ends of the said broad cross street, and flanked it both ways. And there I stayed a while till, hearing the shot increase and fearing to be surprised with such as might follow in tail of us; I gave adventure to pass through the said cross street: and, without vaunt be it spoken, passed through five hundred shots before I could recover the English House.

At my coming thither, I found many of the Merchants standing before the gate: whom I would not discomfort nor dismay but said,

That the Spaniards had once entered the town, and that I hoped they were gone back again.

Nevertheless I went to the Governor: and privily persuaded him to draw in the company; and to shut up the gates.

The which he consented unto: and desired me, because I was somewhat better acquainted with such matters than the Merchants, to take charge of the key.

I took it willingly, but before I could well shut and bar the gate, the Spaniards were now come forwards into the same street; and passing by the door, called to come in; bestowing five or six musquet shot at the gate, where I answered them; whereof one came very near my nose, and piercing through the gate, strake one of the Merchants on the head, without any great or dangerous hurt. But the heat of the pursuit was yet such, that they could not attend the spoil; but passed on in chase to the New Town, where they slew infinite numbers of people: and, by three of the clock, or before, returned victors; having slain, or put to flight, all their enemies.

And now, to keep promise and to speak without partiality, I must needs confess that it was the greatest victory, and the roundliest executed, that hath been seen, read, or heard of, in our age: and that it was a thing miraculous to consider how trenches of such a height should be entered, passed over, and won, both by footmen and horsemen.

For immediately after that the footmen were gotten in, the horsemen found means to follow: and being, many of them, Harquebussiers on horseback, did pass by their own footmen in the streets; and much hastened both the flight of the Walloons, and made the way opener unto speedy executioners.

But whosoever will therein most extoll the Spaniards for their valour and order, must therewith confess that it was the very ordinance of God for a just plague and scourge unto the town. For otherwise it passeth all men's capacity to conceive how it should be possible.

And yet the disorder and lack of foresight in the Walloons did great help to augment the Spanish glory and boast.

To conclude. The Count d'Oberstein was drowned in the New Town. The Marquis d'Havre and Champagney escaped out of the said New Town, and recovered the Prince of Orange's ships.

Only the young Count of Egmont was taken, fighting by St Michael's. Monsieur de Capres and Monsieur de Gogines were also taken. But I heard of none that fought stoutly, saving only the said Count of Egmont; whom the Colonel Verdugo, a Spaniard of an honourable compassion and good mind, did save: with great danger to himself in defending the Count.

In this conflict there were slain 600 Spaniards, or thereabouts. And on the Thursday next following [8 November], a view of the dead bodies in the town being taken, it was esteemed at 17,000 men, women, and children. A pitiful massacre, though God gave victory to the Spaniards.

And surely, as their valiance was to be much commended; so yet I can much discommend their barbarous cruelty in many respects. For methinks that as when God giveth abundance of wealth, the owner ought yet to have regard on whom he bestow it: even so, when God giveth a great and miraculous victory, the conquerors ought to have great regard unto their execution. And though some, which favour the Spanish faction, will alledge sundry reasons to the contrary: yet, when the blood is cold and the fury over, methinks that a true Christian heart should stand content with victory; and refrain to provoke God's wrath by shedding of innocent blood.

These things I rehearse the rather, because they neither spared Age nor Sex, Time nor Place, Person nor Country, Profession nor Religion, Young nor Old, Rich nor Poor, Strong nor Feeble: but, without any mercy, did tyrannously triumph, when there was neither man nor means to resist them.

For Age and Sex, Young and Old; they slew great numbers of young children; but many more women more than four score years of age.

For Time and Place; their fury was as great ten days after the victory, as at the time of their entry; and as great respect they had to the Church and Churchyard, for all their hypocritical boasting of the Catholic Religion, as the butcher had to his shambles or slaughter house.

For Person and Country, they spared neither friend nor foe, Portuguese nor Turk.

For Profession and Religion, the Jesuits must give their ready coin; and all other Religious Houses, both coin and plate: with all short ends that were good and portable.

The Rich was spoiled because he had; and the Poor were hanged because they had nothing. Neither Strength could prevail to make resistance, nor Weakness move pity for to refrain their horrible cruelty.

And this was not only done when the chase was hot; but, as I erst said, when the blood was cold; and they now victors without resistance.

I refrain to rehearse the heaps of dead carcasses which lay at every trench where they entered; the thickness whereof did in many places exceed the height of a man.

I forbear also to recount the huge numbers drowned in the New Town: where a man might behold as many sundry shapes and forms of man's motion at time of death as ever Michael Angelo did portray in his Tables of Doomsday.

I list not to reckon the infinite number of poor Almains [Germans], who lay burned in their armour. Some the entrails scorched out, and all the rest of the body free. Some their head and shoulders burnt off; so that you might look down into the bulk and breast, and there take an anatomy of the secrets of Nature. Some standing upon their waist; being burnt off by the thighs. And some no more but the very top of the brain taken off with fire; whiles the rest of the body did abide unspeakable torments.

I set not down the ugly and filthy polluting of every street with the gore and carcasses of horses; neither do I complain that the one lacked burial, and the other flaying, until the air, corrupted with their carion, infected all that yet remained alive in the town.

And why should I describe the particularity of every such annoyance as commonly happens both in camps and castles where martial feats are managed?

But I may not pass over with silence the wilful burning and destroying of the stately Town House, and all the muniments and records of the city: neither can I refrain to tell their shameful rapes and outrageous forces presented unto sundry honest dames and virgins.

It is also a ruthful remembrance, that a poor English Merchant, who was but a servant, having once redeemed his master's goods for 300 crowns, was yet hanged until he were half dead, because he had not 200 more to give them. And the halter being cut down, and he come to himself again; besought them on knees, with bitter tears, to give him leave to seek and try his credit and friends in the town, for the rest of their unreasonable demand. At his return, because he sped not, as indeed no money was then to be had, they hung him again outright: and afterwards, of exceeding courtesy, procured the Friars Minor to bury him.

To conclude. Of the 17,000 carcasses which were viewed on the Thursday: I think, in conscience, 5000, or few less, were massacred after their victory; because they had not ready money wherewith to ransom their goods at such prices as they pleased to set on them. At least, all the world will bear me witness, that ten days after, whosoever was but pointed at, and named to be a Walloon, was immediately massacred without further audience or trial.

For mine own part, it is well known that I did often escape very narrowly; because I was taken for a Walloon. And on Sunday, the 11th of this instant, which was the day before I gat out of the town, I saw three poor souls murdered in my presence, because they were pointed at to be Walloons: and it was well proved, immediately after, that one of them was a poor artificer, who had dwelt in the town eight years before, and never managed arms, but truly followed his occupation.

Furthermore, the seed of these and other barbarous facts brought forth this crop and fruit, That, within three days, Antwerp, which was one of the richest towns in Europe, had now no money nor treasure to be found therein, but only in the hands of murderers and strumpets. For every Don Diego must walk, jetting up and down the streets, with his harlot by him, in her chain and bracelets of gold. And the notable Bourse, which was wont to be a safe assembly for merchants and men of all honest trades, had now none other merchandise therein but as many dicing tables as might be placed round about it, all the day long.

The Arrest of the Catholic Priest Edmund Campion and his Associates, 17 July 1581

Report of a Government Agent

Edmund Campion, Jesuit Missionary to England, was hanged, drawn and quartered at Tyburn on 1 December 1581. He was beatified in 1886, as was William Filbie, mentioned at the end of this account, who was executed on 30 May 1582.

It happened that after the receipt of our Commission, we consulted between ourselves, What way were best to take first? For we were utterly ignorant where, or in what place, certainly to find out the said Campion, or his compeers. And our consultation was shortly determined: for the greatest part of our travail and dealings in this service did lie chiefly upon mine own determination, by reason of mine acquaintance and knowledge of divers of the like sect.

It then presently came to my remembrance of certain acquaintance which I once had with one Thomas Cooper a cook, who, in November [1578] was two years, served Master Thomas Roper of [Orpington in] Kent; where, at that time, I in like manner served: and both of us, about the same month, departed the said Master Roper his service; I into Essex, and the said Cooper to Lyford in Berkshire, to one Master Yate. From whence, within one half year after, I was advertised in Essex, that the said Cook was placed in service; and that the said Master Yate was a very earnest Papist, and one that gave great entertainment to any of that sect.

Which tale, being told me in Essex two years before we entered [on] this journey, by God's great goodness, came to my memory but even the day before we set forth. Hereof I informed the said David Jenkins, being my fellow in Commission, and told him it would be our best way to go thither first: for that it was not meant that we should go to any place but where indeed I either had acquaintance; or by some means possible in our journey, could get acquaintance. And told him we would dispose of our journey in such sort as we might come to the said Master Yate's upon the Sunday about eight of the clock in the morning: 'where,' said I, 'if we find the said Cook, and that there be any Mass to be said there that day, or any massing Priest in the house; the Cook, for old acquaintance and for that he supposeth me to be a Papist, will bring me to the sight thereof.'

And upon this determination, we set from London the 14th day of July last; and came to the said Master Yate's house, the 16th of the same month, being Sunday, about the hour aforesaid.

Where, without the gates of the same house, we espied one of the servants of the house, who most likely seemed, by reason of his lying aloof, to be as it were a Scout Watcher, that they within might accomplish their secret matters more safely.

I called the said servant, and inquired of him for the said Thomas Cooper the Cook.

Who answered, That he could not well tell, whether he were within or not.

I prayed him that he would friend me so much as to see; and told him my name.

The said servant did so, it seemed; for the Cook came forth presently unto us where we sat still upon horseback. And after a few such speeches, as betwixt friend and friend when they have been long asunder, were passed; still sitting upon our horses, I told him That I had longed to see him; and that I was then travelling into Derbyshire to see my friends, and came so far out of my way to see him. And said I, 'Now I have seen you, my mind is well satisfied; and so fare you well!'

'No,' saith he, 'that shall you not do before dinner.'

I made the matter very earnest to be gone; and he, more earnest and importune to stay me. But in truth I was as willing to stay as he to have me.

And so, perforce, there was no remedy but stay we must. And having lighted from horseback; and being by him brought into the house, and so into the buttery, and there caused to drink: presently after, the said Cook came and whispered with me, and asked, Whether my friend (meaning the said Jenkins) were within the Church or not? Therein meaning, Whether he were a Papist or no?

To which I answered, 'He was not; but yet,' said I, 'he is a very honest man, and one that wisheth well that way.'

Then said the Cook to me, 'Will you go up?' By which speech, I knew he would bring me to a Mass.

And I answered him and said, 'Yea, for God's sake, that let me do: for seeing I must needs tarry, let me take something with me that is good.'

And so we left Jenkins in the buttery; and I was brought by the Cook through the hall, the dining parlour, and two or three other odd rooms, and then into a fair large chamber: where there was, at the same instant, one Priest, called Satwell, saying Mass; two other Priests kneeling by, whereof one was Campion, and the other called Peters *alias* Collington; three Nuns, and 37 other people.

When Satwell had finished his Mass; then Campion he invested himself to say Mass, and so he did: and at the end thereof, made holy bread and delivered it to the people there, to every one some, together with holy water; whereof he gave me part also.

And then was there a chair set in the chamber something beneath the altar, wherein the said Campion did sit down; and there made a sermon very nigh an hour long: the effect of his text being, as I remember, 'That Christ wept over Jerusalem, &c.' And so applied the same to this our country of England for that the Pope his authority and doctrine did not so flourish here as the same Campion desired.

At the end of which sermon, I gat down unto the said Jenkins so soon as I could. For during the time that the Masses and the sermon were made, Jenkins remained still beneath in the buttery or hall; not knowing of any such matter until I gave him some intelligence what I had seen.

And so we departed, with as convenient expedition as we might, and came to one Master Fettiplace, a Justice of the Peace in the said country: whom we made privy of our doings therein; and required him that, according to the tenour of our Commission, he would take sufficient Power, and with us thither.

Whereupon the said Justice of Peace, within one quarter of an hour, put himself in a readiness, with forty or fifty men very well weaponed: who went, in great haste, together with the said Master Fettiplace and us, to the said Master Yate his house.

Where, at our coming upon the sudden, being about one of the clock in the afternoon of the same day, before we knocked at the gates which were then (as before they were continually accustomed to be) fast shut (the house being moated round about; within which moat was great store of fruit trees and other trees, with thick hedgerows: so that the danger for fear of losing of the said Campion and his associates was the more doubted); we beset the house with our men round about the moat in the best sort we could devise: and then knocked at the gates, and were presently heard and espied; but kept out by the space of half an hour.

In which time, as it seemeth, they had hidden Campion and the other two Priests in a very secret place within the said house; and had made reasonable purveyance for him as hereafter is mentioned: and then they let us into the house.

Where came presently to our sight, Mrs Yate, the good wife of the house; five Gentlemen, one Gentlewoman, and three Nuns: the Nuns being then disguised in Gentlewomen's apparel, not like unto that they heard Mass in. All which I well remembered to have seen, the same morning, at the Masses and Sermon aforesaid: yet every one of them a great while denied it. And especially the said Mistress Yate; who could not be content only to make a plain denial of the said Masses and the Priests: but, with great and horrible oaths, forsware the same, betaking herself to the Devil if any such there were; in such sort as, if I had not seen them with mine own eyes, I should have believed her.

But knowing certainly that these were but bare excuses, and that we should find the said Campion and his compeers if we made narrow search; I eftsoons put Master Fettiplace in remembrance of our Commission: and so he, myself, and the said Jenkins Her Majesty's Messenger, went to searching the house; where we found many secret corners.

Continuing the search, although with no small toil, in the orchards, hedges, and ditches, within the moat and divers other places; at the last found out Master Edward Yate, brother to the good man of the house, and two countrymen called Weblin and Mansfield, fast locked together in a pigeon house: but we could not find, at that time, Campion and the other two Priests whom we specially sought for.

It drew then something towards evening, and doubting lest we were not strong enough; we sent our Commission to one Master Foster, High Sheriff of Berkshire; and to one Master Wiseman, a Justice of Peace within the same County; for some further aid at their hands.

The said Master Wiseman came with very good speed unto us the same evening, with ten or twelve of his own men, very able men and well appointed: but the said Master Foster could not be found, as the messenger that went for him returned us answer.

And so the said house was beset the same night with at the least three score men well weaponed; who watched the same very diligently.

And the next day, being Monday, in the morning very early, came one Master Christopher Lydcot, a Justice of Peace of the same shire, with a great sort of his own men, all very well appointed: who, together with his men, shewed such earnest loyal and forward service in those affairs as was no small comfort and encouragement to all those which were present, and did bear true hearts and good wills to Her Majesty.

The same morning, began a fresh search for the said Priests; which continued with very great labour until about ten of the clock in the forenoon of the same day: but the said Priests could not be found, and every man almost persuaded that they were not there.

Yet still searching, although in effect clean void of any hope for finding of them, the said David Jenkins, by God's great goodness, espied a certain secret place, which he quickly found to be hollow; and with a pin of iron which he had in his hand much like unto a harrow tine, he forthwith did break a hole into the said place: where then presently he perceived the said Priests lying all close together upon a bed, of purpose there laid for them; where they had bread, meat, and drink sufficient to have relieved them three or four days together.

The said Jenkins then called very loudly, and said, 'I have found the traitors!'; and presently company enough was with him: who there saw the said Priests, when there was no remedy for them but *nolens volens*, courteously yielded themselves.

Shortly after came one Master Reade, another Justice of the Peace of the said shire, to be assistant in these affairs.

Of all which matters, news was immediately carried in great haste to the Lords of the Privy Council: who gave further Commission that the said Priests and certain others their associates should be brought to the Court under the conduction of myself and the said Jenkins; with commandment to the Sheriff to deliver us sufficient aid forth of his shire, for the safe bringing up of the said people.

After the rumour and noise for the finding out of the said Campion, Satwell, and Peters *alias* Collington, was in the said house something assuaged; and that the sight of them was to the people there no great novelty: then was the said High Sheriff sent for once again; who all that while had not been seen in this service. But then came, and received into his charge the said Priests and certain others from that day until Thursday following.

The fourth Priest which was by us brought up to the Tower, whose name is William Filbie, was not taken with the said Campion and the rest in the said house: but was apprehended and taken in our watch by chance, in coming to the said house to speak with the said Peters, as he said; and thereupon delivered likewise in charge to the Sheriff, with the rest.

Upon Thursday, the 20th day of July last, we set forwards from the said Master Yate his house towards the Court, with our said charge; being assisted by the said Master Lydcot and Master Wiseman, and a great sort of their men; who never left us until we came to the Tower of London. There were besides, that guarded us thither, 50 or 60 Horsemen; very able men and well appointed: which we received by the said Sheriff his appointment.

We went that day to Henley upon Thames, where we lodged that night.

And about midnight we were put into great fear by reason of a very great cry and noise that the said Filbie made in his sleep; which wakened the most that were that night in the house, and that in such sort that every man almost thought that some of the prisoners had been broken from us and escaped; although there was in and about the same house a very strong watch appointed and charged for the same. The aforesaid Master Lydcot was the first that came unto them: and when the matter was examined, it was found no more but that the said Filbie was in a dream; and, as he said, he verily thought one to be a ripping down his body and taking out his bowels.

Some London Criminals, 1581

The Recorder of London Reports to Lord Burghley

William Fleetwood

Upon Wednesday last a French merchant, in a bag sealed, delivered to a carrier's wife of Norwich £40 to be carried to Norwich. She secretly conveyed the money to a house a good way off from the inn, and within half a quarter of an hour the French merchant came again to see his money packed up. But the woman denied that ever she received any one penny, with such horrible protestations as I never heard before. Mr Secretary Walsingham wrote me his letters for the aid of the Frenchman, and, after great search made, the money was found and restored. She not knowing of the same, I examined her in my study privately, but by no means she would confess the same, but did bequeath herself to the Devil, both body and soul, if she had the money or ever saw it. And this was her craft, that she then had not the money, and indeed she said the truth, for it was either at her friend's, where she left it, or else delivered. And then I, perceiving her fewte [drift], I asked her whether the French merchant did not bring her a bag sealed full of metal that was weighty, were it either plats, coin, counters or such like. 'Then', quoth she, 'I will answer no further.' And then I used my Lord Mayor's advice, and bestowed her in Bridewell, where the

Masters and I saw her punished. And being well whipped, she said that the Devil stood at her elbow in my study, and willed her to deny it. But so soon as she was upon the Cross to be punished, he gave her over. And thus, my singular good Lord, I end this tragical part of this wicked woman . . .

Mr Nowell of the Court hath lately been here in London. He caused his man to give a blow unto a carman. His man hath stricken the carman with the pummel of his sword, and therewith hath broken his skull, and killed him. Mr Nowell and his man are like to be indicted, whereof I am sure to be much troubled, what with letters and his friends, and what by other means, as in the very like case heretofore I have been, even with the same man. Here are sundry young gentlemen that use the Court, that most commonly term themselves 'gentlemen'. When any of these have done anything amiss, and are complained of, or arrested for debt, they then run unto me, and no other excuse or answer can they make but say, 'I am a Gentleman, and being a Gentleman I am not thus to be used at a slave and a cullion's hands.' I know not what other parley Mr Nowell can plead; but this I say, the fact is foul. God send him good deliverance. I think in my conscience that he maketh no reckoning of the matter . . .

Upon Friday last we sat at the Justice Hall at Newgate from 7.00 in the morning until 7.00 at night . . . Amongst our travails, this one matter tumbled out by the way, that one Wotton, a gentleman born, and sometime a merchantman of good credit, who falling by time into decay kept an alehouse at Smart's Quay, near Billingsgate, and after, for some misdemeanour being put down, he reared up a new trade of life, and in the same house he procured all the cutpurses about this city to repair to his said house. There was a schoolhouse set up to learn young boys, to cut purses. There were hung up two devices, the one was a pocket, the other was a purse. The pocket had in it certain counters, and was hung about with hawks' bells, and over the top did hang a little sacring bell [i.e. the bell rung at the elevation of the host]; and he that could take out a counter without any noise, was allowed to be a 'public foister', and he that could take a piece of silver out of the purse without the noise of any of the bells, he was adjudged 'a judicial nipper'. *Nota*: that a 'foister' is a pickpocket, and a 'nipper' is termed a pickpurse, or a cutpurse.

John Eldred

The ruin identified by popular tradition as the Tower of Babel was that of the temple of Marduk, which had a tower built in seven stages.

The Euphrates at Bir is about the breath of the Thames at Lambeth; and, in some places narrower, in some broader, it runneth very swiftly, almost as fast as the river Trent. It hath divers sorts of fish in it; but all are scaled, and some are as big as salmon, like barbel.

We landed at Felugia, the 28th of June, where we made our abode for seven days, for lack of camels to carry our goods to Babylon. The heat, at that time of the year, is such in those parts, that men are loath to let their camels travel. This Felugia is a village of some hundred houses, and a place appointed for the discharging of such goods as come down the river. The inhabitants are Arabs. Not finding camels here: we were constrained to unlade our goods, and hired a hundred asses to carry our English merchandise only to New Babylon over a short desert; in crossing whereof we spent eighteen hours, travelling by night and part of the morning, to avoid the great heat.

In this place which we crossed over, stood the old mighty city of Babylon, many old ruins whereof are easily to be seen by daylight: which I, John Eldred, have often beheld at my good leisure: having made three voyages between the new city of Babylon and Aleppo, over this desert.

Here also are yet standing the ruins of the old Tower of Babel, which, being upon a plain ground, seemeth afar off very great; but the nearer you come to it, the lesser and lesser it appeareth. Sundry times I have gone thither to see it, and found the remnants yet standing, above a quarter of a mile in compass, and almost as high as the stone work of Paul's steeple in London; but it showeth much bigger. The bricks remaining of this most ancient monument be half a yard thick, and three-quarters of a yard long; being dried in the sun only: and between every course of bricks, there lieth a course of mats, made of canes, which remain sound and not perished, as though they had been laid within one year.

The city of New Babylon joineth upon the aforesaid small desert where the old city was; and the river Tigris runneth close under the wall: so they may, if they will, open a sluice, and let the water of the same run round about the town. It is above two English miles in compass; and the inhabitants generally speak three languages, to wit, the Persian, Arabian, and Turkish tongues. The people are of the Spaniards' complexion: and the women generally wear in one of the gristles of their noses, a ring like a wedding ring, but somewhat greater, with a pearl and a Turkish stone set therein; and this they do, be they ever so poor.

Natural Childbirth in India, 1583

John Huyghen Van Linschoten

Linschoten, a native of Haarlem, went to Goa with the Portuguese East India fleet in 1583.

The Canariins and Corumbiins are the Countrimen, and such as deale with Tilling the Land, Fishing and such like labours. These are the most contemptible, and the miserablest people of all India, and live very poorely, maintaining themselves with little meat. They dwell in little straw Houses, the doores whereof are so low, that men must creepe in and out, their houshold-stuffe is a Mat upon the ground to sleepe upon, and a Pit or hole in the ground to beat their Rice in, with a Pot or two to seeth it in, and so they live and gaine so much as it is a wonder. For commonly their Houses are full of small Children, which crall and creepe about all naked, untill they are seven or eight yeares old, and then they cover their privie members. When the women are readie to travell with Child, they are commonly delivered when they are all alone; and their Husbands in the fields, as it fortuned upon a time, as I and some other of my friends went to walke in the fields, and into the Villages where the Canariins dwell, and having thirst, I went to one of the Canariins houses to aske some water, therewith to refresh us, and because I was very thirstie, I stooped downe and thrust my head in at the doore, asking for some water, where I espied a Woman alone within the house, tying her cloth fast about her middle, and before her having a woodden Trough (by the Portugals called Gamello) full of water, where shee stood and washed a Child, whereof as then she had newly beene delivered without any helpe: which having washt, she laid it Naked on the ground upon a great Indian Figge leafe, and desired me to stay and she would presently give me water. When I understood by her that she had as then newly beene delivered of that Child without any helpe, I had no desire to drinke of her water, but went unto another to aske water, and perceived the same woman not long after going about her house, as if there had beene no such matter, and the Children are brought up in that manner cleane naked, nothing done unto them, but onely washed and made cleane in a little cold water, and doe in that sort prosper and come up as well as man would wish, or as any Child within these Countries can doe with all the tending they have, and live many times untill they be a hundreth yeares old, without any Head-ach, or Tooth-ach, or losing any of their Teeth.

Shipwreck off Mozambique, August 1585

John Huyghen Van Linschoten

In the month of May 1586, letters were brought to the Viceroy and Archbishop at Goa, from the Captain of Soffala and Mozambique, to certify them of the casting away of the admiral [flagship] *San Jago*, that set out of Portugal, the year before, anno 1585.

She was cast away in this manner. The ship having come, with a good speedy wind and weather, from the Cape of Good Hope to Mozambique: they had passed, as they thought, all dangers; so that they needed not to fear anything. Yet it is good for the Master and others to be careful and keep good watch, and not to stand too much upon their own cunning and conceits, as these did; which was the principal cause of their casting away.

Between the Island of St Lawrence and the firm land, in 22½° S., there are certain shallows called the 'India', ninety miles from the Mozambique. Those shallows are mostly of clear coral of black, white, and green colours, which is very dangerous. Therefore it is good reason they should shun them; and surely the Pilots ought to have great care, especially such as are in the Indian ships, because the whole ship and safety thereof lieth in their hands and is only ruled by them; and that, by express commandment from the King, so that no man may contrary them.

They being thus between the lands, and by all the sailors' judgements hard by the 'Shoals of India', the Pilot took the height of the sun, and made his account that they were past the Shallows; commanding the Master to make all the sail he could, and freely to sail to Mozambique, without any let or stay. And although there were divers sailors in the ship, that likewise had their 'cards', some to learn, others for their pleasure; as divers officers, the Master, and the Chief Boatswain, that said it was better to keep aloof, specially by night, and that it would be good to hold good watch because they found that they had not, as then, passed the Shallows: yet the Pilot said the contrary, and would needs show that he only had skill and power to command; as commonly the Portuguese, by pride, do cast themselves away; because they will follow no man's counsel, and be under no man's subjection, specially when they have authority. As it happened to this Pilot, that would hear no man speak, nor take any counsel but his own; and therefore commanded that they should do, as he appointed them.

Whereupon, they hoisted all their sails, and sailed in that sort till it was midnight, both with a good wind and fair weather; but the moon not shining, they fell full upon the Shallows, being of clear white coral, and so sharp that, with the force of wind and water that drave the ship upon them, it cut the ship in two pieces as if it had been sawn in sunder: so that the keel and two orlops [i.e. decks] lay still upon the ground, and the upper part, being driven somewhat further, at the last, stuck fast; the mast being also broken.

Wherewith, you might have heard so great a cry that all the air did sound therewith: for that in the ship, being admiral, there were at the least five hundred persons: among the which were thirty women, with many Jesuits and friars. So that, as then, there was nothing else to be done, but every man to shrift, bidding each other farewell, and asking of all men forgiveness; with weeping and crying, as it may well be thought.

The Admiral, called Fernando de Mendoza, the Master, the Pilot, and ten or twelve more, presently entered into the small boat, keeping it with naked rapiers, that no more should enter, saying they 'would go and see if there were any dry place in the Shallows; whereon they might work to make a boat of the pieces of the broken ship, therein to sail unto the shore, and so to save their lives'. Wherewith, they put them that were behind in some small comfort; but not much. But when they had rowed about, and finding no dry place, they durst not return again unto the ship: lest the boat should have been overladen and so drowned; and in the ship, they looked for no help. Wherefore, in fine, they concluded to row to land; having about twelve boxes of marmalade, with a pipe of wine and some biscuit, which, in haste, they had thrown into the boat; which they dealt among them, as need required. So commending themselves to God, they rowed forwards towards the coast; and after they had been seventeen days upon the sea, with great hunger, thirst, and labour, they fell on the land: where they saved themselves.

The rest that stayed in the ship, seeing the boat came not again; it may well be thought what case they were in. At the last, one side of the upper part of the ship, between both the upper orlops, where the great boat lay, burst out; and the boat being half burst, began to come forth: but, because there was small hope to be had, and few of them had little will to prove masteries, no man laid hand thereon, but every man sate looking one upon another. At the last, an Italian, called Cyprian Grimoaldo, rose up, and taking courage unto him, said, 'Why are we thus abashed? Let us seek to help ourselves, and see if there be any remedy to save our lives!' Wherewith presently, he leaped into the boat, with an instrument in his hand, and began to make it clean; whereat some others began to take courage, and to help him as well as they could, with such things as first came to their hands. So that in the end, there leaped, at the least, fourscore and ten persons into it, and many hung by the hands upon the boat swimming after it, among the which were some women: but because they would not sink the boat, they were forced to cut off the fingers, hands, and arms of such as held thereon, and let them fall into the sea; and they threw many overboard, being such as had not wherewith to defend themselves.

Which done, they set forward, committing themselves to God; with the greatest cry and pitifullest noise that ever was heard, as though heaven and earth had gone together: when they took their leave of such as stayed in the ship. In which manner, having rowed certain days, and having but small store of victuals; for that they were so many in the boat that it was ready to sink, it being likewise very leaky and not able to hold out. In the end, they agreed among themselves to chose a captain, to whom they would obey and do as he commanded: and among the rest, they chose a gentleman, a Mestizo [half-caste] of India; and swore to obey him. He presently commanded to throw some of them overboard, such as, at that time, had least means or strength to help themselves. Among the which, there was a carpenter that had, not long before, helped to dress the boat: who seeing that the lot fell upon him, desired them to give him a piece of marmalade and a cup of wine; which when they had done, he willingly suffered himself to be thrown overboard in the sea, and so was drowned.

There was another of those, that in Portugal are called New Christians. He being allotted to be cast overboard in the sea, had a younger brother in the same boat, that suddenly rose up and desired the Captain that he would pardon and make free his brother, and let him supply his place, saying, 'My brother is older, and of better knowledge in the world than I, and therefore more fit to live in the world, and to help my sisters and friends in their need: so that I had rather die for him, than to live without him.' At which request, they let the elder brother loose, and threw the younger at his own request into the sea; who swam at the least six hours after the boat. And although they held up their hands with naked rapiers willing him that he should not once come to touch the boat: yet laying hold thereon, and having his hand half cut in two, he would not let go; so that in the end, they were constrained to take him in again. Both the which brethren, I knew, and have been in company with them.

In this misery and pain, they were twenty days at sea; and in the end got to land: where they found the Admiral and those that were in the other boat.

Such as stayed in the ship, some took boards, deals, and other pieces of wood; and bound them together, which the Portuguese call jangadas [rafts]; every man what they could catch, all hoping to save their lives: but of all those, there came but two men safe to shore.

They that had before landed out of the boats, having escaped that danger, fell into another; for they had no sooner set foot on shore, but they were spoiled by the inhabitants of that country, called Kaffirs, of all their clothes: whereby they endured great hunger and misery, with many other mischiefs, which it would be over tedious to rehearse. In the end, they came unto a place where they found a

Factor of the Captains of Soffala and Mozambique, and he helped them as he might; and made means to send them unto Mozambique: and from thence, they went into India; where I knew many of them, and have often spoken with them.

Of those that were come safe to shore, some of them died before they got to Mozambique. So that in all, there were about sixty persons that saved themselves. All the rest were drowned or smothered in the ship; and there was never other news of the ship than as you have heard.

A London Merchant in Cairo, 1586

John Sanderson

The eight and twentieth of Aprill, 1586, I went to see the Pyramides and Momia, being of three Gentlemen of Germanie entreated to accompanie them. The next day wee returned. These Pyramides (one of the seven Wonders) are divers, but especially two of a like bignesse, at the bottome each a thousand paces about; one of them open, that in wee went with Waxe-candles lighted, and up to the top, where standeth in a square roome, a Tombe hewed out of blacke Marble or Jet, wherein they report, that Pharo should have beene buried, which pursued the Children of Israel: it is above a mans length and uncovered: I saw the Jet Coffin. The roofe of the said Pyramides is of five stones, five and twenty foot long and five broad, each stone: the stones on each side are of admirable greatnesse, and impossible to thinke how they were carried up so high. It is also marvelous in the foundations, which are upon mightie Pillars, they are well called one of the seven Wonders. There is likewise a huge Figure of a Head of stone, standing upright to the necke out of the ground.

The Momia, which is some five or six miles beyond, are thousands of imbalmed bodies; which were buried thousands of yeeres past in a sandy Cave; at which there seemeth to have bin some Citie in times past: we were let downe by ropes, as into a Well, with Waxe-candles burning in our hands, and so walked upon the bodies of all sorts and sizes, great and small, and some imbalmed in little earthen Pots, which never had forme: these are set at the feet of the greater bodies: they gave no noysome smell at all, but are like Pitch, being broken; for I broke of all the parts of the bodies to see how the flesh was turned to drugge, and brought home divers heads, hands, armes, and feet, for a shew: wee brought also 600 pounds for the Turkie Companie in Pieces: and brought into England in the Hercules: together with a whole body: they are lapped in above an hundred double of cloth, which rotting and pilling off, you may see the skin, flesh, fingers and nayles firme, altered blacke. One little hand I brought into England, to shew; and presented it my brother, who gave the same to a Doctor in Oxford.

The three and twentieth of September, the Emir Hagge, which is the Captaine of the Caravan, goeth out of Cairo towards Mecca, with very great shew; all the Citie comming out to see him and the rich covering which is carried with great pompe, to cover the Sepulchre of Mahumet their Prophet; all or most of the Rogues of Cairo (which they call Saints) attending it out with great devotion, and some goe with it to Medina; and they are the holiest men of all, who have beene twice or thrice there.

One grave old man, who had a long grey beard, I saw led with great ceremonie at that time out of the Citie, who had but one eye: and I likewise did see the same man return backe againe with the aforesaid Emire, and had left his other eye there, having had it pluckt out, after he had seene their Prophets Sepulchre, because he would see no more sinne. Many of the Turkes and Moores Women, and other, came about him, to bid him welcome, rejoycing of his return to Cairo; and they who had kissed his hand, arme, or garment, thought themselves very happy.

The Execution of Mary Queen of Scots, 8 February 1586

Robert Wynkfielde

Her prayers being ended, the executioners, kneeling, desired her Grace to forgive them her death: who answered, 'I forgive you with all my heart, for now, I hope, you shall make an end of all my troubles.' Then they, with her two women, helping her up, began to disrobe her of her apparel: then she, laying her crucifix upon the stool, one of the executioners took from her neck the *Agnus Dei*, which she, laying hands off it, gave to one of her women, and told the executioner he should be answered money for it. Then she suffered them, with her two women, to disrobe her of her chain of pomander beads and all other her apparel most willingly, and with joy rather than sorrow, helped to make unready herself, putting on a pair of sleeves with her own hands which they had pulled off, and that with some haste, as if she had longed to be gone.

All this time they were pulling off her apparel, she never changed her countenance, but with smiling cheer she uttered these words, 'that she never had such grooms to make her unready, and that she never put off her clothes before such a company'.

Then she, being stripped of all her apparel saving her petticoat and kirtle, her two women beholding her made great lamentation, and crying and crossing themselves prayed in Latin. She, turning herself to them, embracing them, said these words in French, 'Ne crie vous, j'ay promé pour vous', and so crossing and kissing them, bad them pray for her and rejoice and not weep, for that now they should see an end of all their mistress's troubles.

Then she, with a smiling countenance, turning to her men servants, as Melvin and the rest, standing upon a bench nigh the scaffold, who sometime weeping, sometime crying out aloud, and continually crossing themselves, prayed in Latin, crossing them with her hand bade them farewell, and wishing them to pray for her even until the last hour.

This done, one of the women having a *Corpus Christi* cloth lapped up three-corner-ways, kissing it, put it over the Queen of Scots' face, and pinned it fast to the caule of her head. Then the two women departed from her, and she kneeling down upon the cushion most resolutely, and without any token or fear of death, she spake aloud this Psalm in Latin, *In Te Domine confido, non confundar in eternam*, etc. Then, groping for the block, she laid down her head, putting her chin over the block with both her hands, which, holding there still, had been cut off had they not been espied. Then lying upon the block most quietly, and stretching out her arms cried, *In manus tuas, Domine*, etc., three or four times. Then she, lying very still upon the block, one of the executioners holding her slightly with one of his hands, she endured two strokes of the other executioner with an axe, she making very small noise or none at all, and not stirring any part of her from the place where she lay: and so the executioner cut off her head, saving one little gristle, which being cut asunder, he lift up her head to the view of all the assembly and bade *God save the Queen*. Then, her dress of lawn falling from off her head, it appeared as grey as one of threescore and ten years old, polled very short, her face in a moment being so much altered from the form she had when she was alive, as few could remember her by her dead face. Her lips stirred up and down a quarter of an hour after her head was cut off.

Then Mr Dean [Dr Fletcher, Dean of Peterborough] said with a loud voice, 'So perish all the Queen's enemies', and afterwards the Earl of Kent came to the dead body, and standing over it, with a loud voice said, 'Such end of all the Queen's and the Gospel's enemies.'

Then one of the executioners, pulling off her garters, espied her little dog which was crept under her clothes, which could not be gotten forth but by force, yet afterward would not depart from the dead corpse, but came and lay between her head and her shoulders, which being imbrued with her blood was carried away and washed, as all things else were that had any blood was either burned or washed clean, and the executioners sent away with money for their fees, not having any one thing that belonged unto her. And so, every man being commanded out of the hall, except the sheriff and his men, she was carried by them up into a great chamber lying ready for the surgeons to embalm her.

The Seasons in Russia, 1589

Giles Fletcher

Fletcher, a poet, went on a special embassy to Russia in 1588.

The whole Countrey differeth very much from it selfe, by reason of the yeere: so that a man would marvaile to see the great alteration and difference betwixt the Winter and the Summer in Russia. The whole Countrey in the Winter lyeth under Snow, which falleth continually, and is sometimes of a yard or two thicke, but greater towards the North. The Rivers and other waters are all frozen up, a yard or more thicke, how swift or broad soever they bee: and this continueth commonly five Moneths, viz. from the beginning of

November, till towards the end of March, what time the Snow beginneth to melt. So that it would breed a frost in a man to looke abroad at that time, and see the winter face of that Countrey. The sharpenesse of the ayre you may judge of by this: for the water dropped downe or cast up into the ayre, congealeth into Ice before it come to the ground. In the extremitie of Winter, if you hold a Pewter dish or pot in your hand, or any other metall (except in some chamber where their warme Stoves bee) your fingers will freeze fast unto it, and draw off the skinne at the parting. When you passe out of a warme roome into a cold, you shall sensibly feele your breath to waxe starke, and even stifeling with the cold, as you draw it in and out. Divers not onely that travell abroad, but in the very Markets, and streets of their Townes, are mortally pinched and killed withall: so that you shall see many drop downe in the Streets, many Travellers brought into the Townes sitting dead and stiffe in their Sleds. Divers lose their Noses, the tippes of their Eares, and the balls of their Cheekes, their Toes, Feete, &c. Many times (when the winter is very hard and extreame) the Beares and Wolves issue by troupes out of the woods driven by hunger, and enter the Villages, tearing and ravening all they can finde: so that the Inhabitants are faine to flee for safeguard of their lives. And yet in the Summer time you shall see such a new hew and face of a Countrey, the Woods (for the most part which are all of Firre and Birch) so fresh and so sweet, the Pastures and Meadowes so greene and well growne (and that upon the sudden), such varietie of Flowers, such noyse of Birds (specially of Nightingales, that seeme to be more loud and of a more variable note than in other Countries), that a man shall not lightly travell in a more pleasant Countrey.

And this fresh and speedy growth of the Spring there, seemeth to proceed from the benefit of the Snow: which all the Winter time being spred over the whole Countrey as a white robe, and keeping it warme from the rigour of the Frost, in the Spring time (when the Sunne waxeth warme, and dissolveth it into water) doth so throughly drench and soake the ground, that is somewhat of a sleight and sandie mold, and then shineth so hotly upon it againe, that it draweth the Hearbs and Plants forth in great plentie and varietie, in a very short time.

The Last Fight of the *Revenge*, 13 September 1591

John Huyghen Van Linschoten

The Revenge *had been Drake's flagship against the Armada in 1588.*

The 25th of August, the Spanish King's Armada, coming out of Ferrol, arrived at Terceira, being in all thirty ships, Biscayens, Portuguese, and Spaniards; and ten Dutch Fly-boats that were arrested in Lisbon to serve the King: besides other small vessels, *pataxos* that came to serve as messengers from place to place, and to discover the seas.

The 13th of September, the said Armada arrived at the island of Corvo, where the Englishmen, with about sixteen ships, then lay, staying for the Spanish [West Indian] fleet; whereof some, or the most part were come, and there the English were in good hopes to have taken them.

But when they perceived the King's Army to be strong: the Admiral, being the Lord Thomas Howard, commanded his fleet not to fall upon them; nor any of them once to separate their ships from him, unless he gave commission so to do.

Notwithstanding, the Vice-Admiral, Sir Richard Grenville, being in the ship called the *Revenge*, went into the Spanish fleet and shot among them, doing them great hurt; and thinking the rest of the company would have followed: which they did not, but left him there and sailed away. The cause why, could not be known. Which the Spaniards perceiving, with seven or eight ships they boarded her: but she withstood them all, fighting with them, at the least, twelve hours together: and sank two of them, one being a new Double Fly-boat, of 1200 tons; the other, a Biscayen. But, in the end, by reason of the number that came upon her, she was taken; to their great loss: for they had lost in fighting and by drowning, above four hundred men. Of the Englishmen, there were slain about a hundred; Sir Richard Grenville himself being wounded in the brain, whereof he died.

He was borne into the ship called the *San Paulo*, wherein was the Admiral of the fleet, Don Alonso de Bassan. There, his wounds were dressed by the Spanish surgeons; but Don Alonso himself would neither see him, nor speak with him. All the rest of the

Captains and gentlemen went to visit him, and to comfort him in his hard fortune; wondering at his courage and stout heart, for he showed not any sign of faintness, nor changing of colour: but feeling the hour of death to approach, he spake these words in Spanish, and said, Here die I, Richard Grenville, with a joyful and quiet mind, for I have ended my life as a true soldier ought to do, that hath fought for his country, Queen, religion, and honour: whereby my soul most joyfully departeth out of this body; and shall leave behind it, an everlasting fame of a valiant and true soldier, that hath done his duty, as he was bound to do.'

When he had finished these, or such like words, he gave up the ghost, with great and stout courage; and no man could perceive any true sign of heaviness in him.

This Sir Richard Grenville was a great and rich gentleman in England, and had great yearly revenues, of his own inheritance: but he was a man very unquiet in his mind, and greatly affected to war, inasmuch, as of his own private motion, he offered his services to the Queen. He had performed many valiant acts, and was greatly feared in these islands, and known of every man: but of nature very severe, so that his own people hated him for his fierceness, and spake very hardly of him.

For when they first entered into the Fleet or Armada, they had their great sail in a readiness, and might, possibly enough, have sailed away; for it was one of the best ships for sailing in England. The Master perceiving that the other ships had left them, and followed not after; commanded the great sail to be cut, that they might make away: but Sir Richard Grenville threatened both him and all the rest that were in the ship, that if any man laid hand upon it, he would cause him to be hanged. So by that occasion, they were compelled to fight; and, in the end, were taken.

He was of so hard a complexion that, as he continued among the Spanish Captains, while they were at dinner or supper with him, he would carouse three or four glasses of wine; and, in a bravery, take the glasses between his teeth, and crush them in pieces, and swallow them down, so that oftentimes the blood ran out of his mouth, without any harm at all to him: and this was told me, by divers credible persons that, many times, stood and beheld him.

Trapped in the Arctic Ice, 1596
Ordeal of Dutch Seamen

Gerrit de Veer

The leader of this expedition, the purpose of which was to discover a north-east passage to Asia, was the Dutch navigator Willem Barents. In June 1597 his ship was still trapped in the ice, and he and his party left in two open boats. Barents died a week later, but most of the others survived. In 1871 the house in which Barents had wintered was discovered, with many relics still intact.

The eleventh [of September] it was calme weather, and eight of us went on Land, every man armed, to see if that were true as our other three companions had said, that there lay Wood about the River, for that seeing we had so long wound and turned about, sometime in the Ice, and then againe got out, and thereby were compelled to alter our course, and at last saw that we could not get out of the Ice, but rather became faster, and could not loose our ship, as at other times we had done, as also that it began to be Winter, we tooke counsell together what we were best to doe, according to the time, that we might winter there, and attend such adventure as God would send us: and after we had debated upon the matter (to keepe and defend ourselves both from the cold, and wilde beasts) we determined to build a house upon the Land, to keepe us therein as well as wee could, and so to commit ourselves unto the tuition of God, and to that end we went further into the Land, to find out the convenientest place in our opinion, to raise our house upon, and yet we had not much stuffe to make it withall, in regard that there grew no trees, nor any other thing in that Countrey convenient to build it withall: but wee leaving no occasion unsought, as our men went abroad to view the Countrey, and to see what good fortune might happen unto us, at last we found an unexpected comfort in our need, which was, that we found certaine trees roots and all, (as our three companions had said before) which had beene driven upon the shoare, either from Tartaria, Muscovia, or elsewhere; for there was none growing upon that Land, wherewith (as if God had purposely sent them unto us) we were much comforted, being in good hope that God would shew us some further favour; for that Wood served us not onely to build our house, but also to burne, and serve us all the Winter long, otherwise without all doubt, we had died there miserably with extreme cold . . .

The sixe and twentieth, wee had a West wind and an open Sea, but our ship lay fast, wherewith we were not a little grieved, but it was Gods will, which we most patiently bare, and wee began to make up our house, part of our men fetched Wood to burne, the rest played the Carpenters: and were busie about the house, as then we were sixteene men in all, for our Carpenter was dead, and of our sixteene men there was still one or other sicke. The seven and twentieth, it blew hard North-east, and it froze so hard, that as we put a nayle into our mouthes (as when men worke Carpenters worke they use to doe) there would Ice hang thereon when we tooke it out againe, and make the bloud follow: the same day there came an old Beare and a young one towards us, as we were going to our house, being all together (for we durst not goe alone) which we thought to shoot at, but she ran away, at which time the Ice came forcibly driving in, and it was faire Sun-shine weather, but so extreme cold, that we could hardly worke, but extremity forced us thereunto.

The eight and twentieth, it was faire weather, and the Sunne shone, the Wind being West and very calme, the Sea as then being open, but our ship lay fast in the Ice and stirred not; the same day there came a Beare to the ship, but when she espyed us, she ranne away, and we made as much haste as wee could to build our House. The nine and twentieth in the morning, the Wind was West, and after-noone it blew Northerly, and then wee saw three Beares betweene us and the House, an old one and two young; but we notwithstanding drew our goods from the ship to the House, and so got before the Beares, and yet they followed us: nevertheless, we would not shun the way for them, but hollowed out as loud as we could, thinking that they wold have gone away, but they would not once goe out of their foot-path, but got before us, wherewith we and they that were at the house, made a great noyse, which made the Beares run away, and we were not a little glad thereof. The thirtieth the Wind was East, and East South-east, and all that night and the next day it snowed so fast, that our men could fetch no Wood, it lay so close and high one upon the other: then wee made a great fire without the House, therewith to thaw the ground, that so we might lay it about the House, that it might bee the closer; but it was all lost labour, for the Earth was so hard, and frozen so deepe into the ground, that wee could not thaw it, and it would have cost us too much Wood, and therefore wee were forced to leave off that labour.

The first of October, the Wind blew stiffe North-east, and afternoone it blew North, with a great storme and drift of Snow, whereby wee could hardly goe in the Wind, and a man could hardly draw his breath, the Snow drave so hard in our faces, at which time we could not see two ships length from us. The second before noone, the Sunne shone, and after noone it was cloudie againe, and it snew, but the weather was still, the Wind being North, and then South, and wee set up our House, and upon it wee placed a Maypole made of frozen Snow . . .

The thirteenth, the Wind was North and North-west, and it began againe to blow hard, and then three of us went aboord the ship, and laded a Sled with Beere, but when wee had laden it, thinking to goe to our House with it, suddenly there rose such a Wind, and so great a storme and cold, that wee were forced to goe into the ship againe, because wee were not able to stay without, and wee could not get the Beere into the ship againe, but were forced to let it stand without upon the Sled: being in the ship, wee indured extreame cold, because wee had but a few clothes in it.

The fourteenth, as wee came out of the ship, wee found the Barrell of Beere standing upon the Sled, but it was fast frozen at the heads, yet by reason of the great cold, the Beere that purged out, froze as hard upon the side of the Barrell as if it had bene glued thereon, and in that sort wee drew it to our House, and set the Barrell on end, and dranke it first up, but wee were forced to melt the Beere, for there was scant any unfrozen Beere in the Barrell, but in that thicke Yeast that was unfrozen lay the strength of the Beere, so that it was too strong to drinke alone, and that which was frozen tasted like water, and being melted we mixt one with the other, and so dranke it, but it had neither strength nor taste . . .

The seventh [of November] it was darke weather, and very still, the Winde West, at which time wee could hardly discerne the Day from the Night, specially because at that time our Clocke stood still, and by that meanes wee knew not when it was day, although it was day, and our men rose not out of their Cabins all that day; but onely to make water, and therefore they knew not whether the light they saw, was the light of the day or of the Moone; whereupon, they were of severall opinions, some saying, it was the light of the day, the others of the night: but as wee tooke good regard thereunto, wee found it to bee the light of the day about twelve of the clocke at noone . . .

The twentieth, it was faire still weather, the Wind Easterly, then wee washt our sheets, but it was so cold, that when wee had washt and wrung them, they presently froze so stiffe, that although wee layed them by a great fire, the side that lay next the fire thawed, but the other side was hard frozen, so that wee should sooner have torne them in sunder than have opened them, whereby wee were forced to put them into the seething water againe to thaw them, it was so exceeding cold . . .

The nine and twentieth, it was faire cleere weather, and a good Ayre: the Wind Northerly, and we found meanes to open our doore by shoveling away the Snow, whereby wee got one of our doores open, and going out, wee found all our Traps and Springes cleane covered over with Snow, which wee made cleane, and set them up againe to take Foxes: and that day wee tooke one, which as then served us not onely for meate, but of the skinnes wee made Caps to weare upon our heads, wherewith to keepe them warme from the extreame cold . . .

The first of December, it was foule weather with a South-west Wind, and great store of Snow, whereby we were once againe stopt up in the House, and by that meanes there was so great a smoake in the House, that we could hardly make fire, and so were forced to lye all day in our Cabins, but the Cooke was forced to make fire to dresse our meate . . .

The third, we had the like weather, at which time as we lay in our Cabins, wee might heare the Ice cracke in the Sea, and yet it was at the least halfe a mile from us, which made a huge noyse, and we were of opinion, that as then the great Hils of Ice which wee had seene in the Sea, in Summer-time, brake one from the other, and for that during those two or three dayes, because of the extreame smoake, we made not so much fire as we commonly used to doe, it froze so sore within the House, that the Wals and the Roofe thereof were frozen two fingers thick with Ice, and also in our Cabins where we lay all those three dayes, while wee could not goe out: by reason of the foule weather, we set up the Glasse of twelve houres, and when it was runne out, wee set it up againe, still watching it lest wee should misse our time. For the cold was so great, that our Clocke was frozen, and might not goe, although we hung more waight on it than before . . .

The seventh, it was still foule weather, and we had a great storme with a North-east Wind, which brought an extreame cold with it, at which time wee knew not what to doe, and while we sate consulting together, what were best for us to doe, one of our companions gave us counsell to burne some of the Sea-coales that we had brought out of the ship, which would cast a great heate and continue long, and so at Eevening we made a great fire thereof, which cast a great heat: at which time wee were very carefull to keepe it in: for that the heate beeing so great a comfort unto us, we tooke care how to make it continue long: whereupon wee agreed to stop up all the doores and the Chimney, thereby to keepe in the heate, and so went into our Cabins to sleepe, well comforted with the heate, and so lay a great while talking together; but at last we were taken with a great swounding and dazeling in our heads, yet some more than other some, which we first perceived by a sicke man, and therefore the lesse able to beare it, and found our selves to be very ill at ease, so that some of us that were strongest, start out of their Cabins, and first opened the Chimney, and then the doores, but he that opened the doore fell downe in a swound upon the Snow, which I hearing, as lying in my Cabin next to the doore, start up, and casting Vinegar in his face, recovered him againe, and so he rose up: and when the doores were open, we all recovered our healths againe, by reason of the cold Ayre, and so the cold which before had beene so great an Enemy unto us, was then the onely reliefe that wee had, otherwise without doubt, we had dyed in a sudden swound, after that the Master, when we were come to our selves againe, gave everyone of us a little Wine to comfort our hearts . . .

The eleventh, it was faire weather, and a cleere ayre but very cold, which hee that felt not would not beleeve, for our Shooes froze as hard as hornes upon our feete, and within they were white frozen, so that we could not weare our shooes, but were forced to make great Pattents, the upper part being Sheepe-skinnes, which we put on over three or foure payre of Sockes, and so went in them to keepe our feet warme . . .

The thirteenth, it was faire cleere weather, with an East winde: then we tooke another Foxe, and tooke great paines about preparing and dressing of our Springes, with no small trouble, for that if wee stayed too long without the doores, there arose blisters upon our Faces and our Eares . . .

The five and twentieth, being Christmasse day, it was foule weather, with a North-west winde, and yet though it was foule weather, we heard the Foxes runne over our House, wherewith some of our men sayd, it was an ill signe; and while we sate disputing why it should bee an ill signe, some of our men made answer, that it was an ill signe because wee could not take them, to put them into the Pot or roast them, for that had beene a very good signe for us.

The sixe and twentieth, it was foule weather, the winde North-west, and it was so cold that we could not warme us, although wee used all the meanes we could with great fires, good store of cloathes, and with hot stones and billets, layd upon our feete and upon our bodies, as we lay in our Cabbins; but notwithstanding all this, in the morning our Cabbins were frozen, which made us behold one the other with sad countenance, but yet wee comforted our selves againe as well as we could, that the Sunne was then as low as it could goe, and that it now began to come to us againe, and we found it to bee true: for that the Dayes beginning to lengthen, the Cold began to strengthen, but hope put us in good comfort, and eased our paine. The seven and twentieth, it was still foule weather, with a North-west wind, so that as then wee had not beene out in three dayes together, nor durst not thrust our heads out of doores, and within the house it was so extreame cold, that as we sate before a great Fire, and seemed to burne on the fore-side, we froze behind at our backes, and were all white as the Countrey-men use to bee, when they come in at the gates of the Towne in Holland with their Sleds, and have gone all night.

The eight and twentieth, it was still foule weather with a West wind, but about Eevening it began to cleere up, at which time one of our men made a hole open at one of our doores, and went out to see what newes abroad, but found it so hard weather that hee stayed not long, and told us that it had snowed so much, that the Snow lay higher than our house, and that if he had stayed out longer, his eares would undoubtedly have beene frozen off. The nine and twentieth, it was calme weather, and a pleasant ayre, the wind being Southward: that day, he, whose turne it was, opened the doore, and digged a hole through the Snow, where we went out of the house upon steps, as if it had beene out of a Celler, at least seven or eight steps high, each step a foote from the other, and then we made cleane our Springes for the Foxes, whereof for certaine dayes we had not taken any: and as we made them cleane, one of our men found a dead Foxe in one of them, that was frozen as hard as a stone, which he brought into the house, and thawed it before the fire, and after flaying it, some of our men eate it. The thirtieth, it was foule weather againe, with a storme out of the West, and great store of Snow, so that all the labour and paine that we had taken the day before to make steps to goe out of our house, and to clense our Springes, was all in vaine, for it was all covered over with Snow againe, higher than it was before. The one and thirtieth, it was still foule weather, with a storme out of the North-west, whereby we were so fast shut up into the house, as if wee had beene prisoners, and it was so extreame cold, that the fire almost cast no heate: for as we put our feet to the fire, we burnt our hose before we could feele the heate, so that we had worke enough to doe to patch our hose: and which is more, if we had not sooner smelt, than felt them, we should have burnt them ere we had knowne it . . .

The fifth [of January] it was somewhat still and calme weather: then wee digged our doore open againe, that we might goe out, and carrie out all the filth that had beene made, during the time of our being shut in the house; and made every thing handsome, and fetched in Wood which we cleft, and it was all our dayes worke to further ourselves as much as we could, fearing least we should be shut up againe: and as there were three doores in our portall, and for that our house lay covered over in Snow, wee tooke the middle doore thereof away, and digged a great hole in the snow, that lay without the house, like to a side of a vault, wherein we might goe to ease our selves, and cast other filth into it: and when we had taken paines all day, we remembered our selves that it was Twelfth Eeven, and then we prayed our Master that we might be merrie that night, and sayd, that we were content to spend some of the Wine that night which we had spared, and which was our share every second day, and whereof for certayne dayes wee had not drunke, and so that night we made merrie, and drunke to the three Kings, and therewith we had two pound of Meale, whereof wee made pancakes with Oyle, and every man a white Bisket, which we sopt in Wine, and so supposing that we were in our owne Countrey, and amongst our friends, it comforted us as well as if we had made a great banquet in our owne house: and we also made tickets, and our Gunner was King of Nova Zembla, which is at least two hundred miles long, and lyeth betweene two Seas.

The Jesuit is Tortured in the Tower, 14–15 April 1597

John Gerard

Gerard, a member of the Jesuit mission to England, escaped from the Tower in October 1597 by means of a rope suspended over Tower ditch.

On the third day the warder came to my room straight from his dinner. Looking sorry for himself, he said the Lords Commissioners had arrived with the Queen's Attorney-General and that I had to go down to them at once.

'I am ready,' I said, 'but just let me say an *Our Father* and *Hail Mary* downstairs.'

He let me go, and then we went off together to the Lieutenant's lodgings inside the walls of the Tower. Five men were there waiting for me, none of whom, except Wade, had examined me before. He was there to direct the charges against me.

The Attorney-General took out a sheet of paper and solemnly began to write out a form of juridical examination. They put no questions about individual Catholics – they were all about political matters – and I answered on the general lines I had always done before. I said that matters of state were forbidden to Jesuits and consequently I never had anything to do with them; if they wanted confirmation they had it. I had been in prison now three years and had been examined time and time again, and they had not produced a scrap of writing or a single trustworthy witness to show that I had taken part in any activities against the Government.

Then they asked me about the letters I had recently received from our Fathers abroad; and I realized for the first time why I had been removed to the Tower. I answered, 'If I have ever received any letters from abroad at any time, they have had nothing to do with politics. They were concerned merely with the financial assistance of Catholics living on the Continent.'

'Didn't you receive a packet a short time ago,' said Wade, 'and hand it over to so and so to give to Henry Garnet?'

'If I have received any such packet and forwarded it, I did what I was bound to do. But, I repeat, the only letters I have received or forwarded are those, as I have said, dealing with the despatch of money to religious and students on the Continent.'

'Very well,' they said, 'then tell us the name of the man you gave the letters to, and where he lives.'

'I don't know, and even if I did, I could not and would not tell you,' and I gave them the usual reasons for this answer.

'You say,' said the Attorney-General, 'you have no wish to obstruct the Government. Tell us, then, where Father Garnet is. He is an enemy of the state, and you are bound to report on all such men.'

'He isn't an enemy of the state,' I said. 'On the contrary, I am certain that if he were given the opportunity to lay down his life for his Queen and country, he would be glad of it. But I don't know where he lives, and if I did, I would not tell you.'

'Then we'll see to it that you tell us before we leave this place.'

'Please God, you won't,' I answered.

Then they produced a warrant for putting me to torture. They had it ready by them and handed it to me to read. (In this prison a special warrant is required for torture.)

I saw that the warrant was properly made out and signed, and then I answered, 'With God's help I shall never do anything that is unjust or act against my conscience or the Catholic faith. You have me in your power. You can do with me what God allows you to do – more you cannot do.'

Then they began to implore me not to force them to take steps they were loath to take. They said they would have to put me to the torture every day, as long as my life lasted, until I gave them the information they wanted.

'I trust in God's goodness,' I answered, 'that He will prevent me from ever committing a sin such as this – the sin of accusing innocent people. We are all in God's hands and therefore I have no fear of anything you can do to me.'

This was the sense of my answers, as far as I can recall them now.

We went to the torture room in a kind of solemn procession, the attendants walking ahead with lighted candles.

The chamber was underground and dark, particularly near the entrance. It was a vast place and every device and instrument of human torture was there. They pointed out some of them to me and said that I would try them all. Then they asked me again whether I would confess.

'I cannot,' I said.

I fell on my knees for a moment's prayer. Then they took me to a big upright pillar, one of the wooden posts which held the roof of this huge underground chamber. Driven in to the top of it were iron staples for supporting heavy weights. Then they put my wrists into iron gauntlets and ordered me to climb two or three wicker steps. My arms were then lifted up and an iron bar was passed through the rings of one gauntlet, then through the staple and rings of the second gauntlet. This done, they fastened the bar with a pin to prevent it slipping, and then, removing the wicker steps one by one from under my feet, they left me hanging by my hands and arms fastened above my head. The tips of my toes, however, still touched the ground, and they had to dig away the earth from under them. They had hung me up from the highest staple in the pillar and could not raise me any higher, without driving in another staple.

Hanging like this I began to pray. The gentlemen standing around asked me whether I was willing to confess now.

'I cannot and I will not,' I answered.

But I could hardly utter the words, such a gripping pain came over me. It was worst in my chest and belly, my hands and arms. All the blood in my body seemed to rush up into my arms and hands and I thought that blood was oozing out from the ends of my fingers and the pores of my skin. But it was only a sensation caused by my flesh swelling above the irons holding them. The pain was so intense that I thought I could not possibly endure it, and added to it, I had an interior temptation. Yet I did not feel any inclination or wish to give them the information they wanted. The Lord saw my weakness with the eyes of His mercy, and did not permit me to be tempted beyond my strength. With the temptation He sent me relief. Seeing my agony and the struggle going on in my mind, He gave me this most merciful thought: the utmost and worst they can do to you is to kill you, and you have often wanted to give your life for your Lord God. The Lord God sees all you are enduring – He can do all things. You are in God's keeping. With these thoughts, God in His infinite goodness and mercy gave me the grace of resignation, and, with a desire to die and a hope (I admit) that I would, I offered Him myself to do with me as He wished. From that moment the conflict in my soul ceased, and even the physical pain seemed much more bearable than before, though I am sure it must, in fact, have been greater with the growing strain and weariness of my body.

When the gentlemen present saw that I was not answering their questions, they went off to the Lieutenant's house, and stayed there. Every now and again they sent to find out how things were going with me.

Three or four robust men remained behind to watch and supervise the torture, and also my warder. He stayed, I think, out of kindness, for every few minutes he took a cloth and wiped the perspiration that ran in drops continuously down my face and whole body. That helped me a little, but he added to my sufferings when he started to talk. He went on and on, begging and imploring me to pity myself and tell the gentlemen what they wanted to know. And he urged so many human reasons for this that I thought that the devil instigated him to feign this affection or that my torturers had left him behind on purpose to trick me. But I felt all these suggestions of the enemy like blows in the distance: they did not seem to touch my soul or affect me in any way. More than once I interrupted him, 'Stop this talk, for heaven's sake. Do you think I'm going to throw my soul away to save my life? You exasperate me.'

But he went on. And several times the others joined in.

'You will be a cripple all your life if you live. And you are going to be tortured every day until you confess.'

But I prayed in a low voice as well as I could, calling on the names of Jesus and Mary.

Some time after one o'clock, I think, I fell into a faint. How long I was unconscious I don't know, but I don't think it was long, for the men held my body up or put the wicker steps under my feet until I came to. Then they heard me pray and immediately they let me down again. And they did this every time I fainted – eight or nine times that day – before it struck five.

After four or before five o'clock Wade returned. Coming to me he asked, 'Are you ready now to obey the Queen and her Council?'

I answered, 'You want me to do what is sinful. I will not do it.'

'All you have to say,' said Wade, 'is that you wish to speak to Cecil, Her Majesty's Secretary.'

'I have nothing to say to him,' I said, 'except what I have said to you already. If I asked to speak to him, people would be scandalized. They would think I had given way, that at last I was going to say something that I should not say.'

In a rage he suddenly turned his back on me and strode out of the room, shouting angrily in a loud voice, 'Then hang there until you rot off the pillar.'

He left. And I think all the Commissioners left the Tower then, for at five o'clock the Tower bell is rung, a signal for all to leave unless they want to have the gates locked on them. A little later they took me down. My legs and feet were not damaged, but it was a great effort to stand upright.

They led me back to my cell. On the way we met some prisoners who had the run of the Tower, and I turned to speak to my warder, intending them to overhear.

'What surprises me,' I said, 'is that the Commissioners want me to say where Father Garnet's house is. Surely they know it is a sin to betray an innocent man? I will never do it, even if I have to die.'

I said this to prevent them spreading a report, as they so often do, that I had confessed something. And I also wanted word to get round through these men that it was chiefly concerning Father Garnet that I had been questioned, so that he might get to hear and look to his own safety. I saw that the warder was not pleased at my talking in their hearing, but that made no difference to me.

When I reached my cell the man seemed really sorry for me. He laid a fire and brought me some food, as it was now nearly supper time. But I could eat only a little; and I lay down on my bed and rested quietly until the morning.

In the morning after the gates of the Tower were opened, my warder came up to say that Wade had arrived and that I had to go down and see him. I put on a cloak with wide sleeves – I could not get my swollen hands through the sleeves of my own gown – and I went down.

When I entered the Lieutenant's house, Wade said to me, 'I have been sent here in the name of the Queen and her Secretary, Cecil. They say they know for certain that Garnet meddles in politics and is a danger to the State. And this the Queen asserts on the word of a Sovereign and Cecil on his honour. Unless you choose to contradict them both, you must agree to hand him over.'

'They cannot be speaking from experience,' I answered, 'or from any reliable information; they don't know the man. I have lived with him and know him well, and I can say for certain that he is not that kind of man.'

'Come,' said Wade, 'why not admit the truth and answer our questions?'

'I cannot,' I said, 'and I will not.'

'It would be better for you if you did,' and saying this he called out to a gentleman waiting in the next room. He was a well-built man whom Wade called 'Master of Torture'. I knew such an officer existed, but I found out later that this was not the man. He was Master of the Artillery. Wade gave him this title to terrorize me.

'By order of the Queen and Council,' he addressed this gentleman, 'I hand this man over to you. You are to torture him twice today and twice every day until he confesses.'

The man took charge of me. Wade left. In the same way as before we went to the torture chamber.

The gauntlets were placed on the same part of my arms as last time. They would not fit anywhere else, because the flesh on either side had swollen into small mounds, leaving a furrow between; and the gauntlets could only be fastened in the furrow. I felt a very sharp pain when they were put on.

But God helped me and I gladly offered Him my hands and my heart. I was hung up in the same way as before, but now I felt a much severer pain in my hands but less in my chest and belly. Possibly this was because I had eaten nothing that morning.

I stayed like this and began to pray, sometimes aloud, sometimes to myself, and I put myself in the keeping of Our Lord Jesus and His blessed Mother. This time it was longer before I fainted, but when I did they found it so difficult to bring me round that they thought that I was dead, or certainly dying, and summoned the Lieutenant. I don't know how long he was there or how long I remained in a faint. But when I came to myself, I was no longer hanging but sitting on a bench with men supporting me on either side. There were many people about, and my teeth had been forced open with a nail or some iron instrument and hot water had been poured down my throat.

When the Lieutenant saw that I could speak he said, 'Don't you see how much better for you it would be if you submitted to the Queen instead of dying like this?'

God helped me and I was able to put more spirit into my answer than I had felt up to now.

'No, no I don't!' I said. 'I would prefer to die a thousand times rather than do as they suggest.'

'So you won't confess, then?'

'No, I won't,' I said. 'And I won't as long as there is breath left in my body.'

'Very well, then, we must hang you up again now, and a second time after dinner.'

He spoke as though he were sorry to have to carry out his orders.

'*Eamus in nomine Domini*,' I said. 'I have only one life, but if I had several I would sacrifice them all for the same cause.'

I struggled to my feet and tried to walk over to the pillar but I had to be helped. I was very weak now and if I had any spirit left in me it was given by God and given to me, although most unworthy, because I shared the fellowship of the Society.

I was hung up again. The pain was intense now, but I felt great consolation of soul, which seemed to me to come from a desire of death. Whether it arose from a true love of suffering for Christ, or from a selfish longing to be with Christ, God knows best. But I thought then that I was going to die. And my heart filled with great gladness as I abandoned myself to His will and keeping and condemned the will of men. Oh! that God would grant me the same spirit always, though I am sure that in His eyes it was far from a perfect spirit, for my life was to be longer than I then thought, and God gave me time to make it more perfect in His sight, since, it seems, I was not then ready.

Perhaps the Governor of the Tower realized he would gain nothing by torturing me any longer; perhaps it was his dinner hour or maybe he was moved with genuine pity for me; whatever the reason, he ordered me to be taken down. It seemed that I had been hanging only an hour in this second period today. Personally, I believe he was moved by compassion, for some time after my escape a gentleman of position told me that he had heard Sir Richard Berkeley, this same Lieutenant, say that he had freely resigned his office because he no longer wished to be an instrument in such torture of innocent men. At all events it is a fact that he did resign, and only three or four months after his appointment. His place was taken by another knight and it was under him that I escaped.

My warder brought me back to my room. His eyes seemed swollen with tears. He assured me that his wife, whom I had never seen, had wept and prayed for me all the time.

He brought me some food. I could eat little, and the little I did eat he had to cut up into small pieces. For many days after I could not hold a knife in my hands – that day I could not even move my fingers or help myself in the smallest way. He had to do everything for me. But in spite of this on orders from the authorities he took away my knife, scissors and razors. I thought they must be afraid that I would attempt suicide, but I later learned that they always do this in the Tower when a prisoner is under warrant for torture.

I expected to be taken again and tortured as they had threatened to do. But God knew the weakness of His soldier and gave him a short struggle lest he be defeated. To others stronger than me, to Father Walpole, Father Southwell and others, He offered a hard fight that they might conquer. These men 'in a brief time fulfilled a long space'; but I was clearly unworthy of their prize and was left to fulfil the length of my days, to make good my failings and wash with many tears a soul which I was not counted fit to wash – once and quickly – with my blood. It was God's good pleasure; and what is good in His sight, be it done.

A Private Audience with Elizabeth I, 8 December 1597
The French Ambassador Reports

André Hurault

On the 8th of December I did not think to be given an audience for that day and was resolved to make my complaint; but about one hour after noon there came a gentleman from the Queen who said to me that her Majesty was much grieved that she had not given me audience sooner, and that she prayed me to come to her that very hour. He brought me in a coach to take me down to the river where one of the barges awaited me, and we went thence to the gate of the Queen's palace. At our landing there came to seek me a gentleman who spoke very good Italian, called Monsieur Wotton, who told me that her Majesty sent word that I should be very welcome and that she was awaiting me. He had four or five other gentlemen with him. As he led me along he told me that the whole Court was well satisfied to see me, and that they knew well how greatly I loved their nation, and that in Italy I had done all that I could for them. I told him that I was very sorry that I had not done more; and that what had been done was by the command of the King, who wished me in all that concerned the Queen of England to busy myself as much as in his own affairs.

He led me across a chamber of moderate size wherein were the guards of the Queen, and thence into the Presence Chamber, as they call it, in which all present, even though the Queen be absent, remain uncovered. He then conducted me to a place on one side, where there was a cushion made ready for me. I waited there some time, and the Lord Chamberlain, who has the charge of the Queen's household (not as *maître d'hôtel*, but to arrange audiences and to escort those who demand them and especially ambassadors), came to seek me where I was seated. He led me along a passage somewhat dark, into a chamber that they call the Privy Chamber, at the head of which was the Queen seated in a low chair, by herself, and withdrawn from all the Lords and Ladies that were present, they being in one place and she in another. After I had made her my reverence at the entry of the chamber, she rose and came five or six paces towards me, almost into the middle of the chamber. I kissed the fringe of her robe and she embraced me with both hands. She looked at me kindly, and began to excuse herself that she had not sooner given me audience, saying that the day before she had been very ill with a gathering on the right side of her face, which I should never have thought seeing her eyes and face: but she did not remember ever to have been so ill before. She excused herself because I found her attired in her nightgown, and began to rebuke those of her Council who were present, saying, 'What will these gentlemen say' – speaking of those who accompanied me – 'to see me so attired? I am much disturbed that they should see me in this state.'

Then I answered her that there was no need to make excuse on my account, for that I had come to do her service and honour, and not to give her inconvenience. She replied that I gave her none, and that she saw me willingly. I told her that the King had commanded me to visit her and to kiss her hands on his behalf, and charged me to learn the news of her well-being and health, which (thanks be to God) I saw to be such as her servants and friends would desire; and which I prayed God might continue for long years, and in all prosperity and dignity. She stood up while I was speaking, but then she returned to her chair when she saw that I was only speaking of general matters. I drew nearer to her chair and began to deal with her in that wherewithal I had been charged; and because I was uncovered, from time to time she signed to me with her hand to be covered, which I did. Soon after she caused a stool to be brought, whereon I sat and began to talk to her.

She was strangely attired in a dress of silver cloth, white and crimson, or silver 'gauze', as they call it. This dress had slashed sleeves lined with red taffeta, and was girt about with other little sleeves that hung down to the ground, which she was for ever twisting and untwisting. She kept the front of her dress open, and one could see the whole of her bosom, and passing low, and often she would open the front of this robe with her hands as if she was too hot. The collar of the robe was very high, and the lining of the inner part all adorned with little pendants of rubies and pearls, very many, but quite small. She had also a chain of rubies and pearls about her neck. On her head she wore a garland of the same material and beneath it a great reddish-coloured wig, with a great number of spangles of gold and silver, and hanging down over her forehead some pearls, but of no great worth. On either side of her ears hung two great curls of hair, almost down to her shoulders and within the collar of her robe, spangled as the top of her head. Her bosom is somewhat wrinkled as well as one can see for the collar that she wears round her neck, but lower down her flesh is exceeding white and delicate, so far as one could see.

As for her face, it is and appears to be very aged. It is long and thin, and her teeth are very yellow and unequal, compared with what they were formerly, so they say, and on the left side less than on the right. Many of them are missing so that one cannot understand her easily when she speaks quickly. Her figure is fair and tall and graceful in whatever she does; so far as may be she keeps her dignity, yet humbly and graciously withal.

All the time she spoke she would often rise from her chair, and appear to be very impatient with what I was saying. She would complain that the fire was hurting her eyes, though there was a great screen before it and she six or seven feet away; yet did she give orders to have it extinguished, making them bring water to pour upon it. She told me that she was well pleased to stand up, and that she used to speak thus with the ambassadors who came to seek her, and used sometimes to tire them, of which they would on occasion complain. I begged her not to overtire herself in any way, and I rose when she did; and then she sat down again, and so did I. At my departure she rose and conducted me to that same place where she had come to receive me, and again began to say that she was grieved that all the gentlemen I had brought should see her in that condition, and she called to see them. They made their reverence before her, one after the other, and she embraced them all with great charm and smiling countenance.

English Merchants in Java, *c.* 1602
Problems with the Chinese

Edmund Scot

A Chinese born, but now turned Javan, who was our next neighbour, and kept a victualing house, and brewed Aracke, which is a kind of hot drinke, that is used in most of those parts of the world, in stead of Wine, had two Out-houses, where his guests did use to sit, and in the one hee used to brew, which joyned to our pales, on the South side of our house; but now he began another Trade, and became an Ingenor [miner], having got eight Fire-brands of hell more to him, onely of purpose to set our house a fire. These nine deepe workers digged a Well in one of these houses, from the bottome of which Well, they brought a Mine, quite under the foundation of our house: but when they came up to the Planckes of our Ware-house, they were at a stand, but before they could make this Mine, they were forced to dig a very deepe Well in their yard, to draw away the water which did abound in this Mine, and because we should mistrust nothing, they planted Tobacco, and many other hearbs, hard by that Well, and would every day be watering of them: Also, we might heare them boyling of water everie day, but because they were Brewers, and had many tubbs to wash and to fill, wee mistrusted nothing of that ensued. When they came to these Plancks afore-named, they durst not cut them, alwaies for some of us were walking over them, both night and day. After they had waited two moneths, and could never find opportunitie to cut the boords, they began to cast their Cerberous heads together how they should get in, but the Devill set them wrong to work, for if they had continued stil, until they had come

j

but crosse the ware-house opposite against them, they had found thirtie thousand Rials of eight buried in Jarres, for feare of fire, and also that roome was not boorded at all, so they might have come into the Ware-house, and had what they sought for. Well, one of these wicked consortship being a Smith, and brought up alwaies to worke in fire, told his fellowes he would worke out the plancks with fire, so that we should never heare nor see him: and upon the eight and twentieth of May, about ten of the clocke at night, they put to a Candle, and burnt a round hole through the boords. So soone as the fire came thorow, the Mats of our Packs tooke fire, which presently spread, and began to burne; all this while we knew nothing, nor could perceive nothing, by reason of the closenesse of the Ware-house, for all the windowes were plaistered up, for feare of fire over-head. After the first watch was out, wherein I was one my selfe, the second watch smelt a strong funcke of fire, for it was by that time much increased, but they knew not where it should be, and searched every roome and corner. One remembred a Rats hole at last, behind his Trunke, where he might plainly perceive the smoake to steame up out of the hole. Then presently he came into my Chamber, and told me our Cloath Ware-house was a fire, I hearing this word fire, although I was fast asleepe, yet it was no need to bid me rise, neither was I long a slipping on my clothes, but presently ran downe and opened the doores, whereat came out such a strong smoake, that had almost strangled us. This smoake, by reason it had no vent, was so thicke, that wee could not perceive where abouts the fire was, and at that time we had two great Jarres of Powder standing in the Ware-house, which caused us greatly to feare being blowne up; yet setting all feare aside, we plucked all things off that lay on them, which felt in our hands verie hot: The Powder we got out, and carried it into our backe-side, then we searched boldly for the fire and found it; we lighted Candles, but the thicknesse of the smoake put them out, then we tied twelve great Waxe-candles together, and lighted them all, which continued alight: we plucked out packes so fast as wee could, but by reason of the heat and smoake which choaked us, being so few as we were, could doe little good upon it: wherefore we let in the Chinois; then came in as well those that had done it, as others, hoping to get some spoile. When I saw that these damned Chinois would doe us little good, but rather harme, I was almost in dispaire, and having at that time a thousand pound in Gold, which I had received of Generall

Hymskerke for Pepper, in my Chest above staires, I ran up thinking to fetch it, and to throw it into a pond on our backe-side, but when I came to my Chamber doore, my mind altered, and I thought I would goe see once againe what might be done, and comming thorough our Hall, I chanced to cast mine eie into our dyning roome, which was right over the place where the fire was, where there were Chinois that had removed the Table, and were breaking up the Brickes of the Seeling; amongst which was our unkind neighbour, which was the principall Actor; I bid them leave and get them downe, the which they would not, untill I began to let flie amongst them: when I had driven them downe, I went downe after them, and desired some Merchants that stood by, with whom we had dealings, that they would urge the rest of the Chinois to help us plucke out packes, promising they should be well paid for their paines: it pleased God to put so much good in their minds, which I thinke, never had any before nor since, so that they fell to worke of all hands, and presently the roome was cleered, out of which came fiftie and odde packs, whereof sixteene were on a light fire. Thus by their help the fire was quenched, which they knew, and therefore would not worke any more, and the next day were paid for their worke, besides what they stole.

We wondered much how this fire should come, suspecting the Portugalls had hired Malayes to doe it. But a certaine Chines, a Bricklayer, which wrought at the Dutch house, in the morning, told a Flemming that had beene long in the Country, that certain Chinois had done it, which now were fled, and if we looked well in the roome, we should finde the manner how it was done. The Dutchman told an English Surgeon what he had heard, and willed him to come and tell us, and he himselfe, because he was perfect in the language, would go and inquire after them. The English Surgeon came to me, and desired me he might see the roome where the fire was, I presently called for a Candle, and shewed him the roome; he going to one corner, found a little round hole, which was burned thorough one plancke of the floore, whereat I put downe a long sticke which I had in my hand, but could feele no ground: then I called for an Axe, and as softly as we could, we wrinched up the plancke, where under was a way, that the greatest Chest or Packe in our house might have gone downe, which when I saw, as secretly as I could, I called three of our men, and went to the house from whence the Mine came, having our weapons. I set one in the doore, and charged him he should let none come out, whatsoever he were, and my selfe with the other two went in, where in one roome we found three men, there were two more in another roome, who hearing us, fled out at a backe doore, which we knew not of before we see them; those three, after two or three blowes given, we brought away, one was a dweller in the house, but the other two we could prove nothing against them: I laid them fast in Irons, and presently I sent Master Towerson to the Protector, to certifie him how the case stood, and to desire him they might be sought out, and have Justice done upon them, which he promised should be done, but was very slacke in performance.

The Dutch Merchants hearing we had taken some, and doubting the Chynois would rise against us, came very kindly with their weapons, and sware they would live and die in our quarrell: when we had laid out those goods that had received some water to ayre, then we examined this partie that dwelt in the house, who told us the names of sixe that were fled, but hee would not confesse that he knew any thing of it: also he said, the other two knew nothing of the matter, neither could he tell us, as hee said, whether the rest were fled. Then fearing him with an hot Iron, but not touching him, he confessed the whole manner of all, and that he did helpe; he said, those two out-houses were built for that purpose at the first, although they put them to other use, because we should not mistrust them: and more, that the myne was made two moneths before, in which time many nights before, they had been in the myne, striving to get into our house, but could not.

We tortured him, because when we had laid downe the yron, he denied all; but beeing tortured, made a second confession. The next morning I sent him to execution: as hee went out of our gates, the Javans (who doe much rejoyce when they see a Chynese goe to execution: as also the Chynois doe, when they see a Javan goe to his death) reviled him, but hee would answer againe, saying, The Englishmen were rich, and the Chynois were poore, therefore why should they not steale from the English if they could. The next day, the Admirall tooke another of them, and sent him to me, who knew there was but one way with him, and therefore resolved with himselfe not to confesse anything to us: he was found hid in a pryvie, and this was he that put the fire to our house; he was a Gold-smith, and confessed to the Admirall, he had clipped many Ryalls, and also coyned some counterfeit: some things he confessed to him concerning our matter, but not much, but he would tell us nothing. Wherefore because of his sullennesse, and that it was hee that fired us, I caused him to be burned under the nayles of his Thumbes, Fingers and Toes, with sharpe hot yrons, and the nayles to be torne off, and because he never blinshed at that, we thought that his hands and legs had been nummed with tying, wherefore we burned him in the hands, armes, shoulders, and necke, but all was one with him: then we burned him quite through the hands, and with rasphes of yron tore out the flesh and sinewes. After that I caused them to knock the edges of his shin-bones with hot searing yrons. Then I caused cold scrues of yron to be scrued into the bones of his armes, and suddenly to be snatched out: after that all the bones of his fingers and toes to be broken with pincers; yet for all this he never shed teare, no nor once turned his head aside, nor stirred hand nor foote; but when we demanded any question, he would put his tongue between his teeth, and strike his chin upon his knees to bite it off. When all the extremitie we could use was but in vaine, I caused him to be put fast in yrons againe, where the Amits or Ants, which doe greatly abound there, got into his wounds, and tormented him worse than we had done, as we might well see by his gesture. The Kings Officers desired me he might bee shot to death; I told them that was too good a death for such a villaine, and said more, That in our Countreys if a Gentleman, or a Souldior had committed a fact worthy of death, then he was shot to death, and yet he was befriended too, but they doe hold it to be the cruellest and basest death that is. Wherefore they being very importunate, in the evening we lead him into the fields, and made him fast to a stake: the first shot carried away a piece of his arme, bone and all; the next shot stroke him through the Breast up neere to the shoulder, then he holding downe his head, looked upon the wound: The third shot that was made, one of our men had cut a bullet in three parts, which stroke upon his Breast in a triangle, whereat he fell downe as low as the stake would give him leave; but between our Men and the Flemmings, they shot him almost all to pieces before they left him.

The Effects of Elizabethan Policy in Ireland, 1602

Fynes Moryson

Moryson was secretary to Sir Charles Blount, Elizabeth's Lord-Deputy in Ireland.

Now because I have often made mention formerly of our destroying the rebels' corn, and using all means to famish them, let me by two or three examples show the miserable state to which the rebels were thereby brought. Sir Arthur Chichester, Sir Richard Moryson, and the other commanders of the forces sent against Brian McArt, in their return homeward saw a most horrible spectacle of three children (whereof the eldest was not above ten years old) all eating and gnawing with their teeth the entrails of their dead mother, upon whose flesh they had fed twenty days past, and having eaten all from the feet upward to the bare bones, roasting it continually by a slow fire, were now come to the eating of her said entrails in the like sort roasted, yet not divided from the body, being as yet raw. Former mention hath been made in the Lord-Deputy's letters of carcasses scattered in many places, all dead of famine. And no doubt the famine was so great as the rebel soldiers taking all the common people had to feed upon, and hardly living thereupon (so as they besides fed not only upon hawks, kites, and unsavoury birds of prey, but on horseflesh, and other things unfit for man's feeding), the common sort of the rebels were driven to unspeakable extremities (beyond the record of most histories that ever I did read in that kind) the ample relating whereof were an infinite task, yet will I not pass it over without adding some few instances. Captain Trevor and many honest gentlemen lying in the Newry can witness that some old women of those parts used to make a fire in the fields, and divers little children driving out the cattle in the cold mornings, and coming thither to warm them, were by them surprised, killed and eaten, which at last was discovered by a great girl breaking from them by strength of her body, and Captain Trevor sending out soldiers to know the truth, they found the children's skulls and bones, and apprehended the old women, who were executed for the fact. The Captains of Carrickfergus and the adjacent garrisons of the northern parts can witness that, upon the making of peace and receiving the rebels to mercy, it was a common practice among the common sort of them (I mean such as were not swordmen) to thrust long needles into the horses of our English troops, and they dying thereupon, to be ready to tear out one another's throats for a share of them. And no spectacle was more frequent in the ditches of the towns, and specially in wasted countries, than to see multitudes of these poor people dead, with their mouths all coloured green by eating nettles, docks, and all things they could rend up above ground.

Newfoundland Mermaid, 1610

Richard Whitbourne

Now also I will not omit to relate something of a strange Creature that I first saw there in the yeere 1610, in a morning early as I was standing by the water side, in the Harbour of Saint Johns, which I espied verie swiftly to come swimming towards me, looking cheerefully, as it had beene a woman, by the Face, Eyes, Nose, Mouth, Chin, eares, Necke and Forehead: It seemed to be so beautifull, and in those parts so well proportioned, having round about upon the head, all blew strakes, resembling haire, downe to the Necke (but certainly it was haire) for I beheld it long, and another of my companie also, yet living, that was not then farre from me; and seeing the same comming so swiftly towards mee, I stepped backe, for it was come within the length of a long Pike. Which when this strange Creature saw that I went from it, it presently thereupon dived a little under water, and did swim to the place where before I landed; whereby I beheld the shoulders and backe downe to the middle, to be as square, white and smooth as the backe of a man, and from the middle to the hinder part, pointing in proportion like a broad hooked Arrow; how it was proportioned in the forepart from the necke and shoulders, I know not; but the same came shortly after unto a Boat, wherein one William Hawkridge, then my servant, was, that hath bin since a Captaine in a Ship to the East Indies, and is lately there imploied againe by Sir Thomas Smith, in the like Voyage; and the same Creature did put both his hands upon the side of the Boate, and did strive to come in to him and others then in the said Boate: whereat they were afraid; and one of them strooke it a full blow on the head; whereat it fell off from them: and afterwards it came to two other Boates in the Harbour; the men in them, for feare fled to land: This (I suppose) was a Mermaide.

Whirling Dervishes, 1613

Thomas Coryate

Coryate, one of the most intrepid early travellers, left this description, along with his other observations of Turkey, at Aleppo, before setting out on his last journey to India in September 1614.

There is a Colledge of Turkish Monkes in Galata, that are called Darvises, neere to one of their publike Buriall places, who every Tuesday and Friday (which is the Turkish Sabbath) doe performe the strangest exercise of Devotion that ever I saw or heard of. It was my chance to see it the ninth of Aprill, with some other Englishmen that went thither to observe the same, and therefore I will write a little of it according to mine owne experience. About halfe an houre after twelve of the clocke the same day, I entred a prettie faire roome, to which I passed through an outward Court, which roome was before almost full of Turkes that came thither to serve God in their superstitious kind, and had put off their Shooes (according to their wonted custome) and placed them upon Shelfes. Some parts of the walls of this roome were in the inside decked with Inscriptions and Poesies written in the Turkish language, one directly over the Interpreter or Expounder of the Law, and others heere and there, all tending to Religion. The middle part of the roome which is formed out square, is voyd, and reserved onely for the Religious men to sit in; but all the foure parts round about served for the Spectators to behold that which I will now expresse, which Spectators were as well Christians as Turkes. For hither the Turkes will suffer the Christians to have accesse, though not to their Mosquies. There are other inner roomes also somewhat neere this where Women sate apart by themselves, with their Maskes before their Faces. A little after I came into the roome the Darvises repayred into the middle voyd space, sitting Crosse-legged, bending their Bodies lowe towards the floore for Religion sake, even almost flat upon their Faces, and that by murmuring out certaine Religious tearmes: the whole companie of them were about two and fiftie. Their habits differing much from the other Turkes, first the covering of their Head was of a differing sort from the other, for they weare certaine gray Felts made in a forme not unlike the blockes of Hats that we use in England, some whereof about the lower end are covered with a little white Shash, likewise the Cloake or upper Vest of most of them was exceedingly patched, and mended with a great multitude of severall peeces, to which torne Gowne I thinke they attribute matter of Holinesse.

The whole company of them being now setled in their places, and holding their Turkish manuscript Bookes in their hands, a certaine Singing-man sitting apart in an upper roome began to sing certaine Hymnes, but with the most unpleasant and harsh notes that ever I heard, exceedingly differing from our Christian Church singing, for the yelling and disorderly squeaking of them did even grate mine eares. Whensoever hee pronounced the Name of Mahomet, all of them did cast downe their Heads to their knees. After hee had done, the Interpreter of the Law ascended into a Chaire, and read a certaine Turkish Booke for some halfe houre to the Assembly, which contayned the Mahometane Doctrine, but when hee named him they fell prostrate upon their Faces and kissed the ground. Almost a quarter of an houre before he had done, three Pipers sitting in the roome with the Singer, began to play upon certaine long Pipes not unlike Tabors, which yeelded a very ridiculous and foolish Musicke, and continued so very neere a quarter of an houre after the Clergie man had ended his Lecture: and with them there played another, that strucke with his hands a strange kind of Instrument made of Mettall, in the forme of a kind of Bason. Having played very neere a quarter of an houre, upon a sodaine they sounded much louder than ordinarie, whereupon some five and twentie of the two and fiftie Darvises, suddainly rose up bare-legged and bare-footed, and casting aside their upper Garment some of them having their brests all uncovered, they began by little and little to turne about the Interpreter of the Law turning gently in the middest of them all, afterward they redoubled their force and turned with such incredible swiftnesse, that I could not chuse but admire it. Amongst the rest, there was one little Boy of some twelve yeares of age, that turning in a corner of the roome strucke no small admiration in all the Spectators that were Strangers. This turning they kept for the space of one whole houre at the least: during which time, sometimes they turned exceeding swiftly, sometimes very gently. After they had halfe done, the Singer in the upper roome began to sing againe, at the pronunciation of some of whose words, the Darvises sodainly mumbled out certaine strange tearmes, with a most hideous kind of murmuring that did in a manner terrifie and astonish us that were meere strangers to these Ceremonies. This they did three or foure severall times with an acclamation of all the Turks that stood by. The forme of their Dauncing is as strange as the continuance of their swiftnesse, for sometimes they stretch out their Armes as farre as they can in length, sometimes they contract them in a lesser compasse, sometimes they hold them about their Heads, sometimes againe they performe certaine merry gestures, as if they were drawing a Bow and shooting forth an Arrow. Likewise some of them did continue turning during the whole time in one and the selfe same place, and others move forward from one corner to another. This exercise now driving to an end, one of the Darvises beginneth some Prayer in Arabicke, and continually turning about with the rest of the Company, pronounceth it with a very audible voyce, and his Prayer being ended there is an upshot of this ridiculous and Ethnike devotion for this time, after it had continued almost an houre and a halfe. The violence of their turning is so great, that I have heard some of them have fallen downe dead in the place, through the extremitie of their swift Circumgyration, and whosoever hee is that doth so, is esteemed for a Saint.

The Magnificence of the Great Mogul, November 1616 – September 1617

The English Ambassador Reports from Ajmir

Sir Thomas Roe

The dissolute Jahangir (1569–1627) was Mogul emperor of Delhi. His title means 'Conqueror of the World'.

The first of November, the King at noone sat out at the Durbar, where the Prince brought his Elephants about six hundred richly trapped and furnished, and his fellowes by estimation ten thousand Horse, many in cloth of gold, with heron top-feathers in their Turbants, all in gallantry; Himselfe in cloth of Silver imbroydered with great Pearle and shining in Diamonds like a Firmament. The King imbraced him and kissed him, and shewed much affection: at his departure he gave him a Sword, the Scabberd all of Gold set with stones, valued at an hundred thousand Rupias: a Dagger at forty thousand, an Elephant and two Horses with all the Furniture of Gold set with stones, and for a close one of the new Caroches (made in imitation, of that sent by his Majesty my Master [James I]) and commanded the English Coachman to drive him to his Tents, into which he ascended and sate in the middle, the sides open, his chiefest Nobles a foot walking by him to his Tents about foure mile. All the way he threw quarters of Rupias being followed with a multitude of people, he reached his hand to the Coachman, and put into his Hat about one hundred Rupias.

The second, the King removed to his Tents with his women, and all the Court about three mile. I went to attend him comming to the Pallace. I found him at the Farraco window, and went up on the Scaffold under him; which place not having seene before, I was glad of the occasion. On two Tressels stood two Eunuches with long Poles headed with Feathers, fanning him; hee gave many favours and received many Presents, what hee bestowed hee let downe by a Silke, rould on a turning Instrument; what was given him, a venerable fatte deformed olde Matrone, hung with Gymbals [rings] like an Image, pluckt up at a hole with such another Clue; at one side in a window were his two principall Wives, whose curiositie made them breake little holes in a grate of Reed that hung before it, to gaze on me. I saw first their fingers, and after laying their faces close, now one eye now another sometime I could discerne the full proportion, they were indifferently white, blacke haire smooth up, but if I had had no other light, their Diamonds and Pearles had sufficed to shew them: when I looked up they retyred and were so merry, that I supposed they laughed at me. Suddenly the King rose, and wee retyred to the Durbar, and sate on the Carpets attending his comming out: not long after he came and sate about half an houre, untill his Ladies at their doore were ascended their Elephants, which were about fifty, all most richly furnished, principally three with Turrets of Gold, grates of Gold-wyre every way to looke out, and Canopies over the cloath of Silver. Then the

King descended the staires with such an acclamation of Health to the King, as would have out-cryed Cannons. At the staires foote, where I met him, and shuffled to be next, one brought a mighty Carpe, another a dish of white stuffe like Starch, into which he put his finger, and touched the fish, and so rubbed it on his fore-head; a ceremony used presaging good fortune . . .

The first of September, was the Kings birth-day, and the solemnitie of his weighing, to which I went, and was carried into a very large and beautifull Garden, the square within all water, on the sides flowres and trees, in the midst a pinacle, where was prepared the scales, being hung in large tressels, and a crosse beame plated on with gold thinne: the scales of massie gold, the borders set with small stones, Rubies and Turkey, the chaines of gold large and massie, but strengthened with silke Cords. Here attended the Nobilitie all sitting about it on Carpets untill the King came; who at last appeared clothed, or rather loden with Diamonds, Rubies, Pearles, and other precious vanities, so great, so glorious! his Sword, Target, Throne to rest on correspondent; his head, necke, breast, armes, above the elbowes at the wrists, his fingers every one, with at least two or three rings; fettered with chaines, or dialled Diamonds; Rubies as great as Wall-nuts, some greater; and Pearles, such as mine eyes were amazed at. Suddenly he entered into the scales, sate like a woman on her legs, and there was put in against him, many bagges to fit his weight which were changed sixe times, and they say was silver, and that I understood his weight to be nine thousand Rupias, which was almost one thousand pound sterling: after with gold and jewels, and precious stones, but I saw none, it being in bagges might bee pebbles; then against cloth of Gold, Silke, Stuffes, Linnen, Spices, and all sorts of goods, but I must beleeve, for they were in fardles. Lastly, against Meale, Butter, Corne, which is said to be given to the Beniani, and all the rest of the Stuffe: but I saw it carefully carryed in, and none distributed. Onely the silver is reserved for the poore, and serves the ensuing yeere, the King using in the night to call for some before him, and with his owne hands in great familiaritie and humilitie to distribute that money. The scale he sate in by one side; he gazed on me, and turned me his stones and wealth, and smiled, but spake nothing, for my Interpreter could not bee admitted in. After he was weighed, he ascended his Throne, and had Basons of Nuts, Almonds, Fruits, Spices, of all sort made in thin silver, which hee cast about, and his great men scrambled prostrate upon their bellies, which seeing I did not, hee reached one bason almost full, and powred into my Cloke, his Noblemen were so bold as to put in their hands, so thicke, that they had left me none, if I had not put a remayner up. I heard he threw gold till I came in, but found it silver so thinne, that all I had at first being thousands of severall pieces had not weighed sixtie Rupias. I saved about twentie Rupias weight, yet a good dishfull, which I keepe to shew the ostentation, for by my proportion he could not that day cast away above one hundred pound sterling. At night he drinketh with all his Nobilitie in rich plate. I was invited to that, but told, I must not refuse to drinke, and their waters are fire. I was sicke and in a little fluxe of bloud, and durst not stay to venture my health.

The Great Mogul: His Cruelty, 1618

Edward Terry

For his cruelties, he put one of his women to a miserable death; one of his women he had formerly touched and kept company with, but now she was superannuated; for neither himself nor nobles (as they say) come near their wives or women after they exceed the age of thirty years. The fault of that woman was this, the Mogul upon a time found her and one of her eunuchs kissing one another, and for this very thing the King presently gave command that a round hole should be made in the earth, and that her body should be put in that hole, where she should stand with her head only above ground, and the earth to be put in again unto her close round about her, and so she might stand in the parching sun till the extreme hot beams thereof did kill her; in which torment she lived one whole day, and the night following, and almost till the next noon, crying out most lamentably, while she was able to speak, in her language, as the Shumanite's child did in his, 2 Kings 4, 'Ah my head, my head!', which horrid execution, or rather murder, was acted near our house; where the eunuch, by the command of the said King, was brought very near the place where this poor creature was thus buried alive, and there in his sight cut all to pieces.

The Murder of the Duke of Buckingham, 23 August 1620

Sir Dudley Carleton

Buckingham had been James I's favourite and was a close friend of his son, Charles I. Felton, the assassin, had been refused promotion by the Duke. He pleaded guilty to the murder and was hanged, 27 November 1620.

This day betwixt nine and ten of the clocke in the morning, the Duke of Buckingham, then coming out of a Parlor, into a Hall, to go to his coach and soe to the King (who was four miles off), having about him diverse Lords, Colonells, and Captains, & many of his own Servants, was by one Felton (once a Lieutenant of this our Army) slain at one blow, with a dagger knife. In his staggering he turn'd about, uttering onely this word, 'Villaine!' & never spake a word more, but presently plucking out the knife from himself, before he fell to the ground, he made towards the Traytor, two or three paces, and then fell against a Table although he were upheld by diverse that were neare him, that (through the villain's close carriage in the act) could not perceive him hurt at all, but guessed him to be suddenly oversway'd with some apoplexie, till they saw the blood come gushing from his mouth and the wound, soe fast, that life, and breath, at once left his begored body.

You may easily guess what outcries were then made, by us that were Commanders and Officers there present, when once we saw him thus dead in a moment, and slaine by an unknowne hand; for it seems that the Duke himself onely knew who it was that had murdered him, and by meanes of the confused presse at the instant about his person, wee neither did nor could. The Souldiers feare his losse will be their utter ruine, wherefore att that instant the house and court about it were full, every man present with the Dukes body, endeavouring a care of itt. In the meane time Felton pass'd the throng, which was confusedly great, not so much as mark'd or followed, in soe much that not knowing where, nor who he was that had done that fact, some came to keepe guard at the gates, and others went to the Ramports of the Towne; in all which time the villaine was standing in the kitchin of the same house, and after inquiry made by a multitude of captaines and gentlemen then pressing into the house and court, and crying out a maine 'Where is the villain? Where is the butcher?' he most audaciously and resolutely drawing forth his sword, came out and went amongst them, saying boldly, 'I am the Man, here I am'; upon which diverse drew upon him, with the intent to have dispatcht him; but Sir Thomas Morton, myself, and some others, us'd such means (though with much trouble and difficulty) that we drew him out of their hands, and by order of my Lord High Chamberlaine, wee had the charge of keeping him from any comming to him untill a guard of muskateers were brought, to convey him to the Governor's House, where wee were discharg'd.

My Lord High Chamberlaine and Mr Secretary Cooke that were then at the Governor's House, did there take his examination of which as yet there is nothing knowne, onely whilst he was in our custody I asked him several questions, to which he answer'd; viz. He sayd, he was a Protestant in Religion; he also express'd himself that he was partly discontented for want of eighty pounds pay which was due unto him; and for that he being Lieutenant of a company of foot, the company was given over his head unto another, and yett, he sayd, that that did not move him to this resolution, but that he reading the Remonstrance of the house of Parliament it came into his mind, that in committing the Act of killing the Duke, hee should do his Country great good service. And he sayd that to-morrow he was to be prayd for in London. I then asked him att what Church, and to what purpose; he told me at a Church by Fleet-Street-Conduit, and, as for a man much disconten-ted in mind. Now wee seeing things to fall from him in this manner, suffer'd him not to be further question'd, thinking it much fitter for the Lords to examine him, and to finde it out, and knowe from him whether he was encouraged and sett on by any to performe this wicked deed.

But to returne to the screeches made att the fatall blow given, the Duchesse of Buckingham and the Countesse of Anglesey came forth into a Gallery which look'd into a Hall where they might behold the blood of their dearest Lord gushing from him; ah, poor Ladies, such was their screechings, teares, and distractions, that I never in my Life heard the like before, and hope never to heare the like againe. His Majesties griefe for the losse of him, was express'd to be more than great, by the many teares hee shed for him, with which I will conclude this sad and untimely News.

Felton had sowed a writing in the crowne of his hatt, half within the lyning, to shew the cause why he putt this cruell act in excution;

thinking hee should have beene slaine in the place: and it was thus: 'If I bee slaine, let no man condemne me, but rather condemne himself; it is for our sinns that our harts are hardned, and become sencelesse, or else hee had not gone soe long unpunished. John Felton.' 'He is unworthy of the name of a Gentleman, or Soldier, in my opinion, that is afraid to sacrifice his life for the honor of God, his King and Country. John Felton.'

Landing in New England, November 1620

William Bradford

New England had been named by Captain John Smith, who explored its shores in 1614. The first permanent settlement was made at Plymouth, Massachusetts, in 1620 by the 'Pilgrim Fathers' aboard the Mayflower, *whose arrival is described here.*

About ten a clocke we came into a deepe Valley, full of brush, wood-gaile, and long grasse, through which wee found little paths or tracts, and there we saw a Deere, and found Springs of fresh Water, of which we were hartily glad, and sat us downe and drunke our first New England Water, with as much delight as ever we drunke drinke in all our lives.

When we had refreshed ourselves, we directed our course full South, that wee might come to the shoare, which within a short while after we did, and there made a fire, that they in the Ship might see where we were (as wee had direction) and so marched on towards this supposed River: and as we went in another Valley, we found a fine cleere Pond of fresh water, being about a Musket shot broad, and twice as long: there grew also many small Vines, and Fowle and Deere haunted there; there grew much Sasafras: from thence we went on and found much plain ground about fiftie Acres, fit for the Plow, and some signes where the Indians had formerly planted their Corne: after this, some thought it best for nearnesse of the River to goe downe and travaile on the Sea sands, by which meanes some of our men were tired, and lagged behinde, so we stayed and gathered them up, and strucke into the Land againe; where we found a little path to certaine heapes of Sand, one whereof was covered with old Mats, and had a wooden thing like a Morter whelmed on the top of it, and an earthen pot laid in a little hole at the end thereof; we musing what it might be, digged and found a Bowe, and as we thought, Arrowes, but they were rotten; We supposed there were many other things, but because we deemed them graves, we put in the Bow againe and made it up as it was, and left the rest untouched, because we thought it would be odious unto them to ransacke their Sepulchers. We went on further and found new stubble of which they had gotten Corne this yeare, and many Walnut trees full of Nuts, and great store of Strawberries, and some Vines; passing thus a field or two, which were not great, we came to another, which had also bin new gotten, and there wee found where an house had beene, and foure or five old Plankes laied together; also we found a great Kettle, which had beene some Ships kettle and brought out of Europe; there was also an heape of sand, made like the former, but it was newly done, wee might see how they had padled it with their hands, which we digged up, and in it we found a little old Basket full of faire Indian Corne, and digged further, and found a fine great new Basket full of very faire Corne of this yeare, with some sixe and thirty goodly eares of Corne, some yellow, and some red, and others mixt with blew, which was a very goodly sight: the Basket was round, and narrow at the top, it held about three or foure bushels, which was as much as two of us could lift up from the ground, and was very handsomely and cunningly made: But whilst we were busie about these things, we set our men Sentinell in a round ring, all but two or three which digged up the Corne. Wee were in suspense, what to doe with it, and the Kettle, and at length after much consultation, we concluded to take the Kettle, and as much of the Corne as wee could carry away with us: and when our Shallop came if we could finde any of the people, and came to parley with them, wee would give them the Kettle againe, and satisfie them for their Corne . . .

When wee had marched five or six miles into the Woods, and could find no signes of any people, wee returned againe another way, and as we came into the plaine ground, wee found a place like a grave, but it was much bigger and longer than any wee had yet seene. It was also covered with boords, so as wee mused what it should be, and resolved to dig it up; where we found, first a Mat, and under that a faire Bow, and there another Mat, and under that a Boord about three quarters long, finely carved and painted, with three Tynes, or broches on the top, like a Crown; also betweene the Mats we found Bowles, Trayes, Dishes, and such like Trinkets; at length wee came to a faire new Mat, and under that two Bundles, the one bigger, the other lesse, we opened the greater and found in it a great quantitie of fine and perfect Red Powder, and in it the bones and skull of a man. The skull had fine yellow haire still on it, and some of the flesh unconsumed; there was bound up with a Knife, a Packneedle, and two or three old Iron things. It was bound up in a Saylers Canvas Casacke, and a payre of Cloth Breeches; the Red Powder was a kind of Embaulment, and yeelded a strong, but not offensive smell; It was as fine as any Flower. We opened the lesse bundle like wise, and found of the same Powder in it, and the bones and head of a little childe, about the legges, and other parts of it was Bound strings, and Bracelets of fine white Beads; there was also by it a little Bow, about three quarters long, and some other odde knackes: we brought sundry of the pretiest things away with us, and covered the Corps up againe . . .

We went ranging up and downe till the Sunne began to draw low, and then we hasted out of the Woods, that we might come to our Shallop. By that time we had done, and our Shallop come to us it was within night, and we fed upon such victualls as we had, and betooke us to our rest after we had set out our watch. About midnight we heard a great and hideous cry, and our Sentinell called, 'Arme, Arme.' So we bestirred our selves and shot off a couple of Muskets and noise ceased: we concluded, that it was a company of Wolves & Foxes, for one told us he had heard such a noise in New-found-land. About five a clocke in the morning we began to be stirring . . . upon a sudden wee heard a great & strange cry which we knew to be the same voices, though they varied their notes; one of the company being abroad came running in, and cried, 'They are men, Indians, Indians'; and withall, their Arrowes came flying amongst us, our men ran out with all speed to recover their Armes . . . The cry of our enemies was dreadfull, especially, when our men ran out to recover their Armes, their note was after this manner, 'Woath woach ha ha hach woach': our men were no sooner come to their Armes, but the enemy was readie to assault them.

There was a lustie man, and no whit lesse valiant, who was thought to be their Captain, stood behind a Tree within halfe a Musket shot of us, and there let his Arrowes flie at us; hee stood three shots off a Musket, at length one tooke as he said full ayme at him, after which he gave an extraordinarie cry and away they went all, wee followed them about a quarter of a mile, but wee left sixe to keepe our Shallop, for wee were carefull of our businesse . . . We tooke up eighteene of their Arrowes, which wee had sent to England by Master Jones, some whereof were headed with brasse, others with Harts horne, and others with Eagles clawes; many more no doubt were shot, for these wee found were almost covered with leaves: yet by the speciall providence of God, none of them either hit or hurt us . . . On Munday we found a very good Harbour for our shipping, we marched also into the Land, and found divers corne Fields and little running Brookes, a place verie good for scituation, so we returned to our Ship againe with good newes to the rest of our people, which did much comfort their hearts.

Oliver Cromwell Writes to his Brother-in-Law after the Battle of Marston Moor, 2 July 1644

Oliver Cromwell

At Marston Moor the Northern army, the main hope of the Royalists in the Civil War, was destroyed, thanks to Cromwell's surprise tactics. He attacked late in the afternoon when the Royalist generals had strolled away to their coaches, and their troops were relaxing.

To my loving Brother, Colonel Valentine Walton: These
It's our duty to sympathize in all mercies; and to praise the Lord together in chastisements or trials, that so we may sorrow together.

Truly England and the Church of God hath had a great favour from the Lord, in this great victory given unto us, such as the like never was since this war began. It had all the evidences of an absolute victory obtained by the Lord's blessing upon the Godly Party principally. We never charged but we routed the enemy. The Left Wing, which I commanded, being our own horse, saving a few Scots in our rear, beat all the Prince's horse. God made them as stubble to our swords. We charged their regiments of foot with our horse, and routed all we charged. The particulars I cannot relate now; but I believe, of twenty thousand the Prince hath not four thousand left. Give glory, all the glory, to God.

Sir, God hath taken away your eldest son by a cannon-shot. It brake his leg. We were necessitated to have it cut off, whereof he died.

Sir, you know my own trials this way [Cromwell's own son had been killed shortly before]: but the Lord supported me with this, That the Lord took him into the happiness we all pant for and live for. There is your precious child full of glory, never to know sin or sorrow any more. He was a gallant young man, exceedingly gracious. God give you His comfort. Before his death he was so full of comfort that to Frank Russel and myself he could not express it, 'It was so great above his pain.' This he said to us. Indeed it was admirable. A little after, he said, One thing lay upon his spirit. I asked him, What that was? He told me it was, That God had not suffered him to be any more the executioner of His enemies. At his fall, his horse being killed with the bullet, and as I am informed three horses more, I am told he bid them, Open to the right and left, that he might see the rogues run. Truly he was exceedingly beloved in the Army, of all that knew him. But few knew him; for he was a precious young man, fit for God. You have cause to bless the Lord. He is a glorious Saint in Heaven; wherein you ought exceedingly to rejoice. Let this drink up your sorrow; seeing these are not feigned words to comfort you, but the thing is so real and undoubted a truth. You may do all things by the strength of Christ. Seek that, and you shall easily bear your trial. Let this public mercy to the Church of God make you to forget your private sorrow. The Lord be your strength: so prays

Your truly faithful and loving brother,
OLIVER CROMWELL

Circumcision: Rome, 16 January 1645

John Evelyn

I went to the Ghetto where the Jewes dwell, as in a suburbs by themselves; being invited by a Jew of my acquaintance to see a Circumcision: here I passed by the Piazza Judea (where their Serraglio begins) for being environd with walls, they are lock'd up every night: in this place remaines yet part of a stately fabric; which my Jew told me had been a Palace of theirs, for the Ambassador of their Nation in former times, when their Country was Subject to the Romans. There was a large Inscription on it, that I could not stay to reade.

Being lead through the Synagogue into a privat house, I found a world of people in a Chamber: by and by came an old man who prepar'd and layd in order divers Instruments brought by a little child of about 7 yeares old in a box. These the man layd in a silver bason: The knife was much like a short Razor to shut into the haft: Then they burnt some Insense in a Censor, which perfum'd the rome all the while the ceremony was doing: In the basin was also a little cap made of white paper like a Capuchins-hood, not bigger than my finger, also a paper of a red astringent powder, I suppose of bole: a small Instrument of Silver cleft in the midst, at one end to take up the prepuce withall, clowtes of fine linnen wrap'd up &c: These all in order the Women from out of another Chamber brought the Infant swadl'd, and deliver'd it to the Rabbie, who caried, and presented it before an Altar or Cuppord dress'd up, on which lay the 5 bookes of Moses, and the Commandments a little unrowled: Before this with profound reverence, and mumbling a few Words he waved the Child to and froo a while; then he delivered it to another Rabbie, who sate all this time upon a Table, he taking it in his hands put it betweene his thighs, whilest the other Jew unbound the blankets that were about it to come at the flesh: at this action all the company fell a singing of an hebrew hymn, and in as barbarous a tone, waving themselves to and fro, a ceremony they observe in all their devotions: The Infant now strip'd from the belly downewards, the Jew tooke the yard of the child and Chaf'd it within his fingers till it became a little stiff, then with the silver Instrument before describ'd (which was held to him in the basin) he tooke up as much of the Præputium as he could possibly gather, and so with the Razor, did rather Saw, than cutt it off; at which the miserable babe cry'd extreamely, whiles the rest continu'd their odd tone, rather like howling than singing: then the Rabby lifting the belly of the child to his face, and taking the yard all blody into his mouth he suck'd it a pretty while, having before taken a little Vinegar, all which together with the blood he spit out into a glasse of red wine of the Colour of french wine: This don he stripp'd downe the remainder of the fore-skin as farr and neere to the belly as he could, so as it appeared to be all raw, then he strew'd the read powder on it to stanch the bleeding and coverd it with the paper-hood, and upon all a Clowte, and so swath'd up the Child as before: All this while they continue their Psalme: Then two of the Women, and two men, viz., he who held the Child, and the Rabbin who Circumcis'd it (the rest I suppose were the Witnesses) dranke some of the Wine mingl'd with the Vinegar, blood and spittle: so ended the slovenly ceremony, and the Rabbin cryes out to me in the Italian tongue perceiving me to be a stranger: 'Ecco Signior mio, Un Miracolo di dio'; because the child had immediately left crying: The Jewes do all in Rome weare yellow hatts, and live onely upon brokage and Usury, very poore and despicable beyond what they are in other territories of Princes where they are permitted . . .

Suttee, *c.* 1650

Jean-Baptiste Tavernier

It is also an ancient custom among the idolaters of India that on a man dying his widow can never remarry; as soon, therefore, as he is dead she retires to weep for her husband, and some days afterwards her hair is shaved off, and she despoils herself of all the ornaments with which her person was adorned; she removes from her arms and legs the bracelets which her husband had given her, when espousing her, as a sign that she was to be submissive and bound to him, and she remains for the rest of her life without any consideration, and worse than a slave, in the place where previously she was mistress. This miserable condition causes her to detest life, and prefer to ascend a funeral pile to be consumed alive with the body of her deceased husband, rather than be regarded by all the world for the remainder of her days with opprobrium and infamy. Besides this the Brāhmans induce women to hope that by dying in this way, with their husbands, they will live again with them in some other world with more glory and more comfort than they have previously enjoyed. These are the two reasons which make these unhappy women resolve to burn themselves with the bodies of their husbands; to which it should be added that the priests encourage them with the hope that at the moment they are in the fire, before they yield up their souls, Rām will reveal wonderful things to them, and that after the soul has passed through several bodies it will attain to an exalted degree of glory for all eternity.

But it should be remarked that a woman cannot burn herself with the body of her husband without having received permission from the governor of the place where she dwells, and those governors who are Musalmāns, hold this dreadful custom of self-destruction in horror, and do not readily give permission. On the other hand, it is only childless widows who can be reproached for not having loved their husbands if they have not had courage to burn themselves after their death, and to whom this want of courage will be for the remainder of their lives a cause of reproach. For widows who have children are not permitted under any circumstances to burn themselves with the bodies of their husbands; and so far from custom obliging them, it is ordained that they shall live to watch over the education of their children. Those to whom the governors peremptorily refuse to grant permission to burn themselves pass the remainder of their lives in severe penances and in doing charitable deeds. There are some who frequent the great highways either to boil water with vegetables, and give it as a drink to passers-by, or to keep fire always ready to light the pipes of those who desire to smoke tobacco. There are others among them who make a vow to eat nothing but what they find undigested in the droppings of oxen, cows, and buffaloes, and do still more absurd things.

The governor, seeing that all remonstrances with women, who are urged to burn themselves even by their relatives and by the Brāhmans, fail to turn them from the damnable resolution which they have taken to die in so cruel a fashion, when his secretary indicates by a sign that he has received a bribe, at length allows them to do what they wish, and in a rage tells all the idolaters who accompany them that they may 'go to the devil'.

Immediately on permission being obtained, all kinds of music are heard, and with the sound of drums, flutes, and other instruments, all go to the house of the deceased, and thence, as I have said, accompany the body to the margin of a river or tank, where it is to be burned.

All the relatives and friends of the widow who desires to die after her husband congratulate her beforehand on the good fortune which she is about to acquire in the other world, and on the glory which all the members of the caste derive from her noble resolution. She dresses herself as for her wedding day, and is conducted in triumph to the place where she is to be burned. A great noise is made with instruments of music and the voices of the women who follow, singing hymns to the glory of the unhappy one who is about to die. The Brāhmans accompanying her exhort her to show resolution and courage, and many Europeans believe that in order to remove the fear of that death which man naturally abhors, she is given some kind of drink that takes away her senses and removes all apprehension which the preparations for her death might occasion. It is for the interest of the Brāhmans that these unhappy women maintain the resolution they have taken to burn themselves, for all the bracelets which they wear, both on arms and legs, with their ear-rings and rings, belong of right to the Brāhmans, who search for them in the ashes after the women are burned. According to the station and wealth of the women, the bracelets, ear-rings, and rings are either of gold or silver; the poorest wear them of copper and tin; but as for precious stones, they do not wear them at all when going to be burned.

I have seen women burned in three different ways, according to the customs of different countries. In the Kingdom of Gujarāt, and as far as Agra and Delhi, this is how it takes place: On the margin of a river or tank, a kind of small hut, about twelve feet square, is built of reeds and all kinds of faggots, with which some pots of oil and other drugs are placed in order to make it burn quickly. The woman is seated in a half-reclining position in the middle of the hut, her head reposes on a kind of pillow of wood, and she rests her back against a post, to which she is tied by her waist by one of the Brāhmans, for fear lest she should escape on feeling the flame. In this position she holds the dead body of her husband on her knees, chewing betel all the time; and after having been about half an hour in this condition, the Brāhman who has been by her side in the hut goes outside, and she calls out to the priests to apply the fire; this the Brāhmans, and the relatives and friends of the woman who are present immediately do, throwing into the fire some pots of oil, so that the woman may suffer less by being quickly consumed. After the bodies have been reduced to ashes, the Brāhmans take whatever is found in the way of melted gold, silver, tin, or copper, derived from the bracelets, ear-rings, and rings which the woman had on; this belongs to them by right, as I have said.

In the Kingdom of Bengal women are burned in another manner. A woman in that country must be very poor if she does not come with the body of her husband to the bank of the Ganges to wash it after he is dead, and to bathe herself before being burned. I have seen them come to the Ganges more than twenty days' journey, the bodies being by that time altogether putrid, and emitting an unbearable odour. There was one of them who came from the north, near the frontiers of the Kingdom of Bhutān, with the body of her husband which she had conveyed in a carriage, and travelled all the way on foot herself, without eating for fifteen or sixteen days, till she arrived at the Ganges, where after washing the body of her husband, which stank horribly, and bathing herself also, she had herself burned with him with a determination which surprised those who saw it. I was there at the time. As throughout the course of the Ganges, and also in all Bengal, there is but little fuel, these poor women send to beg for wood out of charity to burn themselves with the dead bodies of their husbands. A funeral pile is prepared for them, which is like a bed, with its pillow of small wood and reeds, in which pots of oil and other drugs are placed in order to consume the body quickly. The woman who intends to burn herself, preceded by drums, flutes, and hautboys, and adorned with her most beautiful jewels, comes dancing to the funeral pile, and ascending it she places herself, half-lying, half-seated. Then the body of her husband is laid across her, and all the relatives and friends bring her, one a letter, another a piece of cloth, this one flowers, that one pieces of silver or copper, asking her to give this from me to my mother, or to my brother, or to some relative or friend, whoever the dead person may be whom they have most loved while alive. When the woman sees that they bring her nothing more, she asks those present three times whether they have any more commissions for her, and if they do not reply she wraps all they have brought in a taffeta, which she places between her lap and the back of the body of her dead husband, calling upon the priests to apply fire to the funeral pile. This the Brāhmans and the relatives do simultaneously. There is, as I have remarked, but little wood in the Kingdom of Bengal; so as soon as these miserable women are dead and half burned, their bodies are thrown into the Ganges with those of their husbands, where they are eaten by the crocodiles.

I should not forget here an evil custom which is practised among the idolaters of the same Kingdom of Bengal. When a woman is delivered, and the infant, as often happens, is unwilling to take its mother's breast it is carried outside the village and placed in a cloth, which is tied by the four corners to the branches of a tree, and is thus left from morning to evening. In this way the poor infant is exposed to the crows, which torment it, and some have been found whose eyes have been torn out of their heads, which is the reason why many idolaters are seen in Bengal who have but one eye, and others who have both injured or altogether gone. In the evening the infant is taken to try whether it is willing to suckle during the following night, and should it happen that it still refuses the breast, it is taken back on the following day to the same place; this is done for three days in succession, after which, if the infant is unwilling to take the breast, in the belief that it is a demon, they cast it into the Ganges, or some other river or tank which is nearer at hand. In places where there are many monkeys these poor children are not so exposed to the attacks of crows, for this reason, that as soon as a monkey discovers a nest of these birds he climbs the tree, and throws the nest on one side and the eggs on the other. On the other hand, there are among the English, Dutch, and Portuguese charitable persons who, moved to compassion for the misfortune of these infants, remove them when they are thus exposed and hung in a tree and take care to have them brought up as I have once seen an example of at Hugly; this is done in the places near their factories.

Let us see now what is the practice along the coast of Coromandel when women are going to be burned with the bodies of their deceased husbands. A large hole of nine or ten feet deep, and twenty-five or thirty feet square, is dug, into which plenty of wood is thrown, with many drugs to make it burn quickly. When the hole is well heated, the body of the husband is placed on the edge, and then his wife comes dancing, and chewing betel, accompanied by all her relatives and friends, and with the sound of drums and cymbals. The woman then makes three turns round the hole, and at each time she embraces all her relatives and friends. When she completes the third turn the Brāhmans throw the body of the deceased into the fire, and the woman, with her back turned towards the hole, is pushed by the Brāhmans, and falls in backwards. Then all the relatives throw pots of oil and other drugs of that kind, as I have said is elsewhere done, so that the bodies may be the the sooner consumed. In the greater part of the same Coromandel coast the woman does not burn herself with the body of her deceased husband, but allows herself to be interred, while alive, with him in a hole which the Brāhmans dig in the ground, about one foot deeper than the height of the man or woman. They generally select a sandy spot, and when they have placed the man and woman in the hole, each of their friends fills a basket of sand, and throws it on the bodies until the hole is full and heaped over, half a foot higher than the ground, after which they jump and dance upon it till they are certain that the woman is smothered.

George Fox Visits Lichfield, 1651

George Fox

Fox, the author of this account, was founder of the Society of Friends (or Quakers).

Thus being set at liberty again, I went on, as before, in the work of the Lord; and as I was walking in a close with several Friends, I lifted up my head and espied three steeple-house spires, and they struck at my life. I asked them what place that was, and they said, Lichfield. Immediately the word of the Lord came to me that thither I must go. So, being come to the house we were going to, I bid Friends that were with me to walk into the house from me, saying nothing to them whither I was to go. As soon as they were gone I stepped away, and went by my eye over hedge and ditch till I came within a mile of Lichfield, where, in a great field, there were shepherds keeping their sheep. I was commanded by the Lord, of a sudden, to untie my shoes and put them off. I stood still for it was winter, and the word of the Lord was like a fire in me, so I put off my shoes and was commanded to give them to the shepherds, and was to charge them to let no one have them except they paid for them. The poor shepherds trembled and were astonished.

Then I walked on about a mile till I came into the town, and as soon as I was got within the town the word of the Lord came to me again, to cry, 'Woe unto the bloody city of Lichfield!' So I went up and down the streets, crying with a loud voice, 'Woe to the bloody city of Lichfield!' It being market-day, I went into the market-place, and to and fro in the several parts of it, and made stands, crying as before, 'Woe to the bloody city of Lichfield!' And no one laid hands on me; but as I went thus crying through the streets, there seemed to me to be a channel of blood running down the streets, and the market-place appeared like a pool of blood.

And so at last some Friends and friendly people came to me and said, 'Alack, George, where are thy shoes?' I told them it was no matter.

Now when I had declared what was upon me, and cleared myself, I came out of the town in peace; and returning to the shepherds, gave them some money, and took my shoes of them again. But the fire of the Lord was so in my feet, and all over me, that I did not matter to put on my shoes any more, and was at a stand whether I should or no, till I felt freedom from the Lord so to do; and as at last I came to a ditch and washed my feet, I put on my shoes again. After this a deep consideration came upon me, why, or for what reason, I should be sent to cry against that city, and call it the bloody city. For though the Parliament had the minster one while, and the King another, and much blood had been shed in the town during the wars between them, yet that could not be charged upon the town. But afterwards I came to understand that in the Emperor Dioclesian's time a thousand Christians were martyred in Lichfield, and so I must go in my stockings through the channel of their blood, and into the pool of their blood in the market-place, that I might raise up the memorial of the blood of those martyrs which had been shed above a thousand years before, and lay cold in their streets.

Religious Observances in Dunkirk, 1662

John Greenhalgh

Some of our English who had lived three or four years in Dunkirk told me that these monks do live mostly or merely upon alms; and I saw some mendicant friars go in the streets two together, with each a basket in his arms, and into shops and houses; and I noted how they, though as beggars, passed along, all people of all sorts take off their hats and showing great reverence towards them, as they do strictly observe towards all their religious. They told me that these friars do each day once cover their tables with a coarse but a clean cloth, and set on salt only, there expecting what their providers will bring them (which office they do by turns), of which be it more or less they make a dinner, and be it never so short they who beg the next day do not complain; their manner being not to ask but to stand silent, and to take what is given. But when it falls out, which sometimes though seldom doth, that they have had many short meals together, and too sore pinched, they have a bell on the top of a corner of their House, called the starving bell, which they (having first covered their empty table, setting on salt only, and setting their hall door wide open, and have out of modesty retired themselves into their cells out of sight) they ring out aloud, which being once heard abroad hath the same effect there that a fire bell being rung hath in a town with us; people running out into the streets and crying, 'Jesu, Maria, the starving bell, woe and alas for the holy men'; such an hubbub as though the judgment of Sodom were ready to fall upon the town, for their neglect of the holy men. So of the richer sort, the mistresses do in all haste send out each their maid, running one with a cheese, another with a loaf, another with a dish of butter, one carries half a great pasty, another runs with a standing piece of roast beef, etc., all which entering the monastery hall, they lay down upon the table, and get them out again; one monk peeping through a hole sees when the table is soundly furnished, then comes out and shuts the hall door of modesty, so as they who come after that go back again with their meat, saving both it and their credit; when all are gone the hungry friars, creeping out of their holes, do fall aboard . . .

In the top of the arched roof of the cathedral, which is very high, there is a cupulo or great round hole, as round and broad as a millstone. In that hole was first made a flash of fire lightning, as if the heaven opened there; there descended from thence a living milk-white dove, it was let down by a pulley with a small string, with its wings and tail extended and spread by two very small white sticks at back of them, to which the feathers were tied with white thread and could scarce be perceived. But I, standing very near, did discern it. And this done, the dove looking prettily about, as a dove will, descending by degrees, when it came near over the priest's head it stayed, hanging and hovering over them a good while, they still singing *Veni Sancte Spiritus*, etc., then it was drawn up by degrees into the cupulo out of sight. And after this out of the same great hole in the roof were thrown down as it were many cloven tongues of fire, which came down flaming over the priests' heads;

but they, instead of receiving them, opened to the right and left, and let those fall to the floor, so saving their shaven crowns. I perceived these were papers, besmeared with some sulphurous matter to make them blaze better. And at the coming down of these tongues there was a shout set up in the church, that the town rang again. Lastly, there was thrown down a shower of holy water, which fell in drops upon the people to sprinkle and hallow them. So ended the procession of all the foolish fopperies of the forenoon.

The Fire of London, 2 September 1666

Samuel Pepys

September 2 1666 Lords day. Some of our maids sitting up late last night to get things ready against our feast today, Jane called us up, about 3 in the morning, to tell us of a great fire they saw in the City. So I rose, and slipped on my nightgown and went to her window, and thought it to be on the back side of Markelane at the furthest; but being unused to such fires as fallowed, I thought it far enough off, and so went to bed again and to sleep. About 7 rose again to dress myself, and there looked out at the window and saw the fire not so much as it was, and further off. So to my closet to set things to rights after yesterday's cleaning. By and by Jane comes and tells me that she hears that above 300 houses have been burned down tonight by the fire we saw, and that it was now burning down all Fishstreet by London Bridge. So I made myself ready presently, and walked to the Tower and there got up upon one of the high places, Sir J. Robinsons little son going up with me; and there I did see the houses at that end of the bridge all on fire, and an infinite great fire on this and the other side the end of the bridge – which, among other people, did trouble me for poor little Michell and our Sarah on the Bridge. So down, with my heart full of trouble, to the Lieutenant of the Tower, who tells me that it begun this morning in the King's bakers house in Pudding-lane, and that it hath burned down St Magnes Church and most part of Fishstreete already. So I down to the water-side and there got a boat and through bridge, and there saw a lamentable fire. Poor Michells house, as far as the Old Swan, already burned that way and the fire running further, that in a very little time it got as far as the Stillyard while I was there. Everybody endeavouring to remove their goods, and flinging into the River or bringing them into lighters that lay off. Poor people staying in their houses as long as till the very fire touched them, and then running into boats or clambering from one pair of stair by the water-side to another. And among other things, the poor pigeons I perceive were loath to leave their houses, but hovered about the windows and balconies till they were some of them burned, their wings, and fell down.

Having stayed, and in an hour's time seen the fire rage every way, and nobody to my sight endeavouring to quench it, but to remove their goods and leave all to the fire; and having seen it get as far as the Steeleyard, and the wind mighty high and driving it into the city, and everything, after so long a drougth, proving combustible, even the very stones of churches, and among other things, the poor steeple by which pretty Mrs Horsley lives, and whereof my old school-fellow Elborough is parson, taken fire in the very top and there burned till it fall down – I to White-hall with a gentleman with me who desired to go off from the Tower to see the fire in my boat – to White-hall, and there up to the King's closet in the chapel, where people came about me and I did give them an account dismayed them all; and word was carried in to the King, so I was called for and did tell the King and Duke of York what I saw, and that unless his Majesty did command houses to be pulled down, nothing could stop the fire. They seemed much troubled, and the King commanded me to go to my Lord Mayor from him and command him to spare no houses but to pull down before the fire every way. The Duke of York bid me tell him that if he would have any more soldiers, he shall; and so did my Lord Arlington afterward, as a great secret. Here meeting with Captain Cocke, I in his coach, which he lent me, and Creed with me, to Pauls; and there walked along Watling-street as well as I could, every creature coming away loaden with goods to save – and here and there sick people carried away in beds. Extraordinary good goods carried in carts and on backs. At last met my Lord Mayor in Canning Streete, like a man spent, with a hankercher about his neck. To the King's message, he cried like a fainting woman, 'Lord, what can I do? I am spent. People will not obey me. I have been pulling down houses. But the fire overtakes us faster then we can do it.' That he needed no more soldiers; and that for himself, he must go and refresh himself, having been up all night. So he left me, and I him, and walked home – seeing people all almost distracted and no manner of means used to quench the fire. The houses too, so very thick thereabouts, and full of matter for burning, as pitch and tar, in Thames-street – and warehouses of oyle and wines and Brandy and other things. Here I saw Mr Isaccke Houblon, that handsome man – prettily dressed and dirty at his door at Dowgate, receiving some of his brothers things whose houses were on fire; and as he says, have been removed twice already, and he doubts (as it soon proved) that they must be in a little time removed from his house also – which was a sad consideration. And to see the churches all filling with goods, by people who themselfs should have been quietly there at this time . . .

As soon as dined, I and Moone away and walked through the City, the streets full of nothing but people and horses and carts loaden with goods, ready to run over one another, and removing goods from one burned house to another – they now removing out of Canning-street (which received goods in the morning) into Lumbard Streete and further; and among others, I now saw my little goldsmith Stokes receiving some friend's goods, whose house itself was burned the day after. We parted at Pauls, he home and I to Pauls-Wharf, where I had appointed a boat to attend me; and took in Mr Carcasse and his brother, whom I met in the street, and carried them below and above bridge, to and again, to see the fire, which was now got further, both below and above, and no likelihood of stopping it. Met with the King and Duke of York in their Barge, and with them to Queen-Hith and there called Sir Rd Browne to them. Their order was only to pull down houses apace, and so below bridge at the water-side; but little was or could be done, the fire coming upon them so fast. Good hopes there was of stopping it at the Three Cranes above, and at Buttolphs-Wharf below bridge, if care be used; but the wind carries it into the City, so as we know not by the water-side what it doth there. River full of lighters and boats taking in goods, and good goods swimming in the water; and only, I observed that hardly one lighter or boat in three that had the goods of a house in, but there was a pair of virginalls in it. Having seen as much as I could now, I away to White-hall by appointment, and there walked to St James's Park, and there met my wife and Creed and Wood and his wife and walked to my boat, and there upon the water again, and to the fire up and down, it still increasing and the wind great. So near the fire as we could for smoke; and all over the Thames, with one's face in the wind you were almost burned with a shower of Firedrops – this is very true – so as houses were burned by these drops and flakes of fire, three or four, nay five or six houses, one from another. When we could endure no more upon the water, we to a little alehouse on the Bankside over against the Three Cranes, and there stayed till it was dark almost and saw the fire grow; and as it grow darker, appeared more and more, and in Corners and upon steeples and between churches and houses, as far as we could see up the hill of the City, in a most horrid malicious bloody flame, not like a fine flame of an ordinary fire. Barbary and her husband away before us. We stayed till, it being darkish, we saw the fire as only one entire arch of fire from this to the other side the bridge, and in a bow up the hill, for an arch of above a mile long. It made me weep to see it. The churches, houses, and all on fire and flaming at once, and a horrid noise the flames made, and the cracking of houses at their ruine.

The Great Frost, January 1684

John Evelyn

January 24 1684. The frost still continuing more and more severe, the Thames before London was planted with boothes in formal streetes, as in a Citty, or Continual faire, all sorts of Trades and shops furnished, and full of Commodities, even to a Printing presse, where the People and Ladys tooke a fansy to have their names Printed and the day and yeare set downe, when printed on the Thames. This humour tooke so universaly, that 'twas estimated the Printer gained five pound a day, for printing a line onely, at six-pence a Name, besides what he gott by Ballads &c: Coaches now plied from Westminster to the Temple, and from severall other staires too and froo, as in the streetes; also on sleds, sliding with skeetes; There was likewise Bull-baiting, Horse and Coach races, Pupet-plays and interludes, Cookes and Tipling, and lewder places; so as it seem'd to be a bacchanalia, Triumph or Carnoval on the Water, whilst it was a severe Judgement upon the Land: the Trees not onely splitting as if lightning-strock, but Men and Cattell perishing in divers places, and the very seas so locked up with yce, that no vessells could stirr out, or come in: The fowle [fish] and birds, and all our exotique Plants & Greenes universaly perishing; many Parks of deere destroied, and all sorts of fuell so deare that there were greate Contributions to preserve the poore alive; nor was this severe weather much lesse intense in most parts of Europe even as far as Spaine, and the most southern tracts: London, by reason of the excessive coldnesse of the aire, hindring the ascent of the smoke, was so filld with the fuliginous steame of the Sea-Coale, that hardly could one see crosse the streete, and this filling the lungs with its grosse particles exceedingly obstructed the breast, so as one could scarce breath: There was no water to be had from the Pipes and Engines, nor could the Brewers, and divers other Tradesmen work, and every moment was full of disastrous accidents &c.

The English Love of Fighting, 1695

Misson de Valbourg

Anything that looks like fighting is delicious to an Englishman. If two little boys quarrel in the street the passengers stop, make a ring round them in a moment, and set them against one another that they may come to fisticuffs. When 'tis come to a fight, each pulls off his neckcloth and his waistcoat and gives them to hold to some of the standers-by. Then they begin to brandish their fists in the air. The blows are aimed all at the face. They kick one another's shins; they tug one another by the hair. He that has got the other down may give him one blow or two before he rises, but no more; and let the boy get up ever so often, the other is obliged to box him again as often as he requires it. During the fight the ring of bystanders encourage the combatants with great delight of heart, and never part them while they fight according to the rules. And these bystanders are not only boys, porters and rabble, but all sorts of men of fashion, some thrusting by the mob that they may see plain, others getting upon stalls; and all would hire places if scaffolds could be built in a moment. The father and mother of the boys let them fight on as well as the rest, and hearten him that gives ground or has the worst.

These combats are less frequent among men than children, but they are not rare. If a coachman has a dispute about his fare with a gentleman that has hired him, and the gentleman offers to fight him to decide the quarrel, the coachman consents with all his heart. The gentleman pulls off his sword, lays it in some shop, with his cane, gloves and cravat, and boxes in the manner that I have described above. If the coachman is soundly drubbed, which happens almost always, that goes for payment; but if he is the beater, the beatee must pay the money about which they quarrelled. I once saw the late Duke of Grafton at fisticuffs in the open street with such a fellow, whom he lammed most horribly. In France we punish such rascals with our cane, and sometimes with the flat of our sword; but in England this is never practised. They use neither sword nor stick against a man that is unarmed; and if any unfortunate stranger (for an Englishman would never take it into his head) should draw his sword upon one that had none, he'd have a hundred people upon him in a moment.

Conditions of Life aboard the French Galleys, 1703—4

John Bion

My being several campaigns Chaplain aboard one of the galleys, called *La Superbe*, gave me a sufficient opportunity of informing myself of the truth of the following Relation. But before I proceed to show the sufferings and misery the wretches in the galleys labour under, I shall give a short description of that vessel.

A Galley is a long flat one-decked vessel, though it hath two masts. Yet they generally make use of oars, because they are built so as not to be able to endure a rough sea: and therefore their sails for the most part are useless, unless in cruising, when they are out of sight of land; for then, for fear of being surprised by ill weather, they make the best of their way.

There are five slaves to every oar; one of them, a Turk; who being generally stronger than Christians, is set at the upper end, to work it with more strength.

There are in all 300 slaves; and 150 men, either Officers, soldiers, seamen, or servants.

There is at the stern of the galley, a chamber, shaped on the outside like a cradle, belonging to the Captain: and solely his, at night or in foul weather; but in the daytime, common to the Officers and Chaplain. All the rest of the crew (the Under Officers excepted, who retire to other convenient places) are exposed above deck, to the scorching heat of the sun by day, and the damps and inclemencies of the night. There is indeed a kind of a tent suspended by a cable from head to stern, that affords some little shelter: but the misfortune is, that this is only when they can best be without it, that is, in fair weather. For in the least wind or storm, it is taken down; the galley not being able to endure it for fear of oversetting.

The two winters (in *anno* 1703, and in 1704) we kept the coasts of Monaco, Nice, and Antibes; those poor creatures, after hard rowing, could not enjoy the usual benefit of the night, which puts an end to the fatigues and labours of the day: but were exposed to the winds, snow, hail, and all other inconveniences of that season. The only comfort they wished for, was the liberty of smoking: but that, on pain of the *bastinado*, the usual punishment of the place, is forbidden.

The vessel being but small for the number, the men consequently crowded, the continual sweat that streams down from their bodies whilst rowing, and the scanty allowance of linen; one may easily imagine, breed abundance of vermin. So that, in spite of all the care that can be taken, the galleys swarm with lice, &c.; which nestling in the plaits and laps of their clothes, relieve by night the executioners who beat and torment them by day.

Their whole yearly allowance for clothes is two shirts made of the coarsest canvas; and a little jerkin of red serge, slit on each side, up to their arm holes; the sleeves are also open, and come not down so low as their elbows. And every three years, a kind of a coarse frock; and a little cap to cover their heads, which they are obliged to keep close shaved, as a mark of infamy.

Instead of a bed, they are allowed, sick or well, only a board a foot and a half broad. And those who have the unfortunate honour of lying near the Officers, dare not presume, though tormented with vermin, to stir so much as a hand for their ease; for fear their chains should rattle, and awake any of them; which would draw on them a punishment more severe than the biting of those insects.

It is hard to give an exact description of the pains and labours the slaves undergo at sea, especially during a long campaign. The fatigue of tugging at the oar is extraordinary. They must rise to draw their stroke, and fall back again almost on their backs: insomuch that, in all seasons, through the continual and violent motion of their bodies, the sweat trickles down their harassed limbs.

And for fear they should fail, as they often do through faintness, there is a gang board, which runs through the middle of the ship, on which are constantly posted three *Comites*, an Officer somewhat like a Boatswain in Her Majesty's ships, who whenever they find or think that an oar does not keep touch with the rest, without ever examining whether it proceeds from weakness or laziness, they unmercifully exercise a tough wand on the man they suspect: which being long is often felt by two or three of his innocent neighbours, who being naked when they row, each blow imprints evident marks of the inhumanity of the executioner.

And that which adds to their misery, is that they are not allowed the least sign of discontent or complaint, that small and last comfort of the miserable! but must, on the contrary, endeavour with all their might, to exert the little vigour that remains, and try by their submission to pacify the rage of those relentless tigers; whose strokes are commonly ushered in, and followed by a volley of oaths and horrid imprecations.

No sooner are they arrived in any port, but their work, instead of being at an end, is increased; several laborious things previous to casting anchor being expected from them; which in a galley is harder than a ship. And as the *Comite*'s chief skill is seen in dexterously casting anchor, and that they think Blows are the life and soul of Work; nothing is heard for some time, but cries and lamentation: and as the poor slaves' arms are busy in the execution of his commands, his are as briskly exercised in lashing them.

To support their strength under all these hardships; during the campaign, every morning, at eight of the clock, they give each man his proportion of biscuit; of which indeed, they have enough, and pretty good. At ten, a porringer made of oil, with peas or beans often rotten, and commonly musty. I call it soup, according to their use; although it be nothing but a little hot water with about a dozen peas or beans floating on the top. And when on duty, a *pichone* of wine, a measure containing about two-thirds of an English pint, morning and evening.

When at anchor in any port, all who have any money are allowed to buy meat; and the Turk that commands the oar, and is not chained, is commonly the person employed for this purpose, as also to see it dressed in the Cook Room. But I have often seen the Captain's Cook, a brutal passionate man, take the poor men's pot, under pretence that it troubled him, and either break or throw it overboard: whilst the poor wretches were fainting for want of that little refreshment, without daring so much as to murmur or complain. This indeed is not usual, but where the Cook happens to be a villain: of which sort of men there are plenty in the galleys.

The Officer's table is well furnished both for plenty and delicacy: but this gives slaves only a more exquisite sense of their misery, and seems to brave their poverty and hunger.

We spent the Carnival of 1704 in the port of Monaco. Our Officers frequently treated the Prince of that place aboard the galley. Their entertainments were splendid. Music and all things that could promote Mirth were procured. But who can express the affliction of those poor creatures, who had only a prospect of pleasure, and whilst others revelled at their ease, were sinking under a load of chains, pinched with hunger in their stomachs, and nothing to support their dejected spirits.

Nay, and what is worse, they are forced to add to the pomp and honour done to Great Men, who visit their Officers: but in such a manner as moves the compassion of all who are not used to such dismal solemnities. When a Person of Quality comes on board, the *Comite* gives twice notice with his whistle. The first time they are all attentive; and the second, the slaves are obliged to *salute*, as they call it, three times: not with a cheerful Huzza as in an English Man-of-war; but by howling in a piteous tone making a lamentable complaining outcry.

When the badness of the weather hinders the galleys from putting to sea; such as have trades work in the galley. Such as have none learn to knit coarse stockings; the *Comite*, for whose profit they work, gives them yarn, and pays them about half the usual price; and this not in money, but some little victuals, or wine which they are obliged to take out of the Ship's Cellar (of which the *Comite* is the keeper), though it be generally bad, and dashed with water. For though they had as much gold as they could carry, they durst not, on pain of a *bastinado*, send for any wine from the shore.

The most moving spectacle of all is to see the poor souls that have no trade. They clean their comrades' clothes, and destroy the vermin that torment their neighbours: who in return, give them some small share of that scanty pittance they purchase by working.

One may imagine that such ill treatment, diet, and infection must needs occasion frequent sickness. In that case, the usage is thus:

There is in the hold, a close dark room. The air is admitted only by the scuttle two feet square; which is the only passage into it. At each end of the said room, there is a sort of a scaffold called *taular*; on which the sick are laid promiscuously, without beds or anything under them. When these are full, if there be any more, they are stretched all along the cables: as I saw in the year 1703, when being on the coast of Italy, in winter time, we had above threescore sick men.

In this horrid place, all kind of vermin rule with an arbitrary sway; gnawing the poor sick creatures without disturbance.

When the duties of my function called me in amongst them, to confess, advise, or administer some comfort; which was constantly twice a day: I was in an instant covered all over with them, it being impossible to preserve one's self from their swarms. The only way was to go down in a night gown, which I stript off when I came out, and by that means rid myself of them, by putting on my clothes.

But when I was in, methought I walked, in a literal sense, in the Shades of Death. I was obliged notwithstanding to make considerable stays in this gloomy mansion, to confess such who were ready to expire. And the whole space between the ceiling and the *taular* being but three feet; I was obliged to lie down, and stretch myself along their sides, to hear their confessions: and often, while I was confessing one, another expired just by my side.

The stench is most intolerable, insomuch as that there is no slave, though ever so weak, but will rather choose to tug at his oar, and expire under his chain, than to retire to this loathsome hospital . . .

I now proceed to show what sort of people are condemned there. There are in a galley, five several sorts of people, under the notion of slaves; besides seamen and soldiers: viz., Turks, such as are called *Faussoniers*, deserters, criminals, and Protestants.

The King buys the Turks to manage the stroke of the oar, as I have already shewn, and they are called *Vogueavants*; and they together with such as are on the seats called *banc du quartier*, *de la Conille*, and *les espalliers* have the same allowance with the soldiers. They are generally lusty strong men, and the least unfortunate of the whole crew. They are not chained; but only wear a ring on their foot, as a badge of slavery . . .

Those who are called *Faussoniers* [deceivers] are generally poor peasants, who are found to buy salt in such provinces where it is cheap, such as the country of Burgundy, or the country of Dombe. In France, what they call a pint of salt, weighing four pounds, costs 3s 6d.

There are some poor peasants and their whole families, who, for want of salt, eat no soup sometimes in a whole week; though it be their common nourishment. A man in that case, grieved to see his wife and children in a starving, languishing condition, ventures to go abroad, to buy salt in the Provinces where it is three parts in four cheaper. If discovered, he is certainly sent to the galleys. It is a very melancholy sight, to see a wife and children lament their father, whom they see ladened with chains and irrevocably lost; and that for no other crime but endeavouring to procure subsistence for those to whom he gave birth.

As for Deserters, their sentence runs during life. Formerly, they used to cut off their nose and ears: but because they stank, and commonly infected the whole crew, they only now give them a little slit.

Such as are condemned for Crimes are generally *filous* [pickpockets], sharpers, rooks or highwaymen. The most notorious villains are least daunted, and take heart soonest. They presently strike up a friendship with those of their own gang. They tell over their old rogueries, and boast of their crimes; and the greatest villain passes for the greatest hero. The Protestants are there purely because they chose rather to obey God than man; and were not willing to exchange their souls for the gain of the World.

The Battle of Schellenberg, 2 July 1704
A French Officer's account

M. de la Colonie

At Schellenberg, one of the battles in the War of the Spanish Succession, Marlborough attacked an entrenched hill defended by the Bavarians and French. Though successful, the attack cost 6000 men. Enemy casualties were 9000.

I made a point of impressing upon my men the necessity of attention to orders, and of prompt obedience in carrying out any manoeuvres during the action with courage and in good order. I assured them that herein lay our safety and, perhaps, victory.

I had scarcely finished speaking when the enemy's battery opened fire upon us, and raked us through and through. They concentrated their fire upon us, and with their first discharge carried off Count de la Bastide, the lieutenant of my own company with whom at the moment I was speaking, and twelve grenadiers, who fell side by side in the ranks, so that my coat was covered with brains and blood. So accurate was the fire that each discharge of the cannon stretched some of my men on the ground. I suffered agonies at seeing these brave fellows perish without a chance of defending themselves, but it was absolutely necessary that they should not move from their post.

This cannonade was but the prelude of the attack that the enemy were developing, and I looked upon the moment when they would fling themselves against one point or another in our entrenchments as so instant that I would allow no man even to bow his head before the storm, fearing that the regiment would find itself in disorder when the time came for us to make the rapid movement that would be demanded of us. At last the enemy's army began to move to the assault, and still it was necessary for me to suffer this sacrifice to avoid a still greater misfortune, though I had five officers and eighty grenadiers killed on the spot before we had fired a single shot.

So steep was the slope in front of us that as soon almost as the enemy's column began its advance it was lost in view, and it came into sight only two hundred paces from our entrenchments. I noticed that it kept as far as possible from the glacis of the town and close alongside of the wood, but I could not make out whether a portion might not also be marching within the latter with the purpose of attacking that part of our entrenchments facing it, and the uncertainty caused me to delay movement. There was nothing to lead me to suppose that the enemy had such an intimate knowledge of our defences as to guide them to one point in preference to another for their attack.

Had I been able to guess that the column was being led by that scoundrel of a corporal who had betrayed us, I should not have been in this dilemma, nor should I have thought it necessary to keep so many brave men exposed to the perils of the cannonade, but my doubts came to an end two hours after midday, for I caught sight of the tips of the Imperial standards, and no longer hesitated. I changed front as promptly as possible, in order to bring my grenadiers opposite the part of our position adjoining the wood, towards which I saw that the enemy was directing his advance.

The regiment now left a position awkward in the extreme on account of the cannon, but we soon found ourselves scarcely better off, for hardly had our men lined the little parapet when the enemy broke into the charge, and rushed at full speed, shouting at the top of their voices, to throw themselves into our entrenchments.

The rapidity of their movements, together with their loud yells, were truly alarming, and as soon as I heard them I ordered our drums to beat the 'charge' so as to drown them with their noise, lest they should have a bad effect upon our people. By this means I animated my grenadiers, and prevented them hearing the shouts of the enemy, which before now have produced a heedless panic.

The English infantry led this attack with the greatest intrepidity, right up to our parapet, but there they were opposed with a courage at least equal to their own. Rage, fury, and desperation were manifested by both sides, with the more obstinacy as the assailants and assailed were perhaps the bravest soldiers in the world. The little parapet which separated the two forces became the scene of the bloodiest struggle that could be conceived. Thirteen hundred grenadiers, of whom seven hundred belonged to the Elector's Guards, and six hundred who were left under my command, bore the brunt of the enemy's attack at the forefront of the Bavarian infantry.

It would be impossible to describe in words strong enough the details of the carnage that took place during this first attack, which lasted a good hour or more. We were all fighting hand to hand, hurling them back as they clutched at the parapet; men were slaying, or tearing at the muzzles of guns and the bayonets which pierced their entrails; crushing under their feet their own wounded comrades, and even gouging out their opponents' eyes with their nails, when the grip was so close that neither could make use of their weapons. I verily believe that it would have been quite impossible to find a more terrible representation of Hell itself than was shown in the savagery of both sides on this occasion.

At last the enemy, after losing more than eight thousand men in this first onslaught, were obliged to relax their hold, and they fell back for shelter to the dip in the slope, where we could not harm them. A sudden calm now reigned amongst us, our people were recovering their breath, and seemed more determined even than they were before the conflict. The ground around our parapet was covered with dead and dying, in heaps almost as high as our fascines, but our whole attention was fixed on the enemy and his movements; we noticed that the tops of his standards still showed at about the same place as that from which they had made their charge in the first instance, leaving little doubt but that they were reforming before returning to the assault. As soon as possible we set vigorously to work to render their approach more difficult for them than before, and by means of an increasing fire swept their line of advance with a torrent of bullets, accompanied by numberless grenades, of which we had several wagon loads in rear of our position. These, owing to the slope of the ground, fell right amongst the enemy's ranks, causing them great annoyance and doubtless added not a little to their hesitation in advancing the second time to the attack. They were so disheartened by the first attempt that their generals had the greatest difficulty in bringing them forward again, and indeed would never have succeeded in this, though they tried every other means, had they not dismounted and set an example by placing themselves at the head of the column, and leading them on foot.

Their devotion cost them dear, for General Stirum and many other generals and officers were killed. They once more, then, advanced to the assault, but with nothing like the success of their first effort, for not only did they lack energy in their attack, but after being vigorously repulsed, were pursued by us at the point of the bayonet for more than eighty paces beyond our entrenchments, which we finally re-entered unmolested.

After this second attempt many efforts were made by their generals, but they were never able to bring their men to the assault a third time . . .

But I noticed all at once an extraordinary movement on the part of our infantry, who were rising up and ceasing fire withal. I glanced around on all sides to see what had caused this behaviour, and then became aware of several lines of infantry in greyish white uniforms on our left flank. From lack of movement on their part, their dress and bearing, I verily believed that reinforcements had arrived for us, and anybody else would have believed the same. No information whatever had reached us of the enemy's success, or even that such a thing was the least likely, so in the error I laboured under I shouted to my men that they were Frenchman, and friends, and they at once resumed their former position behind the parapet.

Having, however, made a closer inspection, I discovered bunches of straw and leaves attached to their standards, badges the enemy are in the custom of wearing on the occasion of battle, and at that very moment was struck by a ball in the right lower jaw, which wounded and stupefied me to such an extent that I thought it was smashed. I probed my wound as quickly as possible with the tip of my finger, and finding the jaw itself entire, did not make much fuss about it; but the front of my jacket was so deluged with the blood which poured from it that several of our officers believed that I was dangerously hurt. I reassured them, however, and exhorted them to stand firmly with their men. I pointed out to them that so long as our infantry kept well together the danger was not so great, and that if they behaved in a resolute manner, the enemy, who were only keeping in touch with us without daring to attack us, would allow us to retire without so much as pursuing. In truth, to look at them it would seem that they hoped much more for our retreat than any chance of coming to blows with us. I at once, therefore, shouted as loudly as I could that no one was to quit the ranks, and then formed my men in column along the entrenchments facing the wood, fronting towards the opposite flank, which was the direction in which we should have to retire. Thus, whenever I wished to make a stand, I had but to turn my men about, and at any moment could resume the retirement instantaneously, which we thus carried out in good order. I kept this up until we had crossed the entrenchments on the other flank, and then we found ourselves free from attack. This retreat was not made, however, without loss, for the enemy, although they would not close with us when they saw our column formed for the retirement, fired volleys at close range into us, which did much damage.

My men had no sooner got clear of the entrenchments than they found that the slope was in their favour, and they fairly broke their ranks and took to flight, in order to reach the plain that lay before them before the enemy's cavalry could get upon their track. As each ran his hardest, intending to reform on the further side, they disappeared like a flash of lightning without ever looking back, and I, who was with the rearguard ready to make a stand if necessary against our opponents, had scarcely clambered over the entrenchments when I found myself left entirely alone on the height, prevented from running by my heavy boots.

I looked about on all sides for my drummer, whom I had warned to keep at hand with my horse, but he had evidently thought fit to look after himself, with the result that I found myself left solitary to the mercy of the enemy and my own sad thoughts, without the slightest idea as to my future fate. I cudgelled my brains in vain for some way out of my difficulty, but could think of nothing the least certain; the plain was too wide for me to traverse in my big boots at the necessary speed, and to crown my misfortunes, was covered with cornfields. So far the enemy's cavalry had not appeared on the plain, but there was every reason to believe that they would not long delay their coming; it would have been utter folly on my part to give them the chance of discovering me embarrassed as I was, for as long as I was hampered with my boots, a trooper would always find it an easy affair to catch me.

I noticed, however, that the Danube was not so very far away, and determined to make my way towards it at all risk, with the hope of finding some beaten track or place where there would be some chance of saving my life, as I saw it was now hopeless to think of getting my men together. As a matter of fact, I found a convenient path along the bank of the river, but this was not of much avail to me, for, owing to my efforts and struggles to reach it through several fields of standing corn, I was quite blown and exhausted and could only just crawl along at the slowest possible pace. On my way I met the wife of a Bavarian soldier, so distracted with weeping that she travelled no faster than I did. I made her drag off my boots, which fitted me so tightly about the legs that it was absolutely impossible for me to do this for myself. The poor woman took an immense time to effect this, and it seemed to me at least as if the operation would never come to an end. At last this was effected, and I turned over in my mind the best way to profit by my release, when, raising my head above the corn at the side of the road, I saw a number of the enemy's troopers scattered over the country, searching the fields for any of our people who might be hidden therein, with the intention, doubtless, of killing them for the sake of what plunder might be found upon them. At this cruel prospect all my hopes vanished, and the exultation I felt at my release from the boots died at the moment of its birth. My position was now more perilous than ever; nevertheless, I examined under the cover afforded by the corn the manoeuvres of these cavaliers to see if I could not find some way out of the difficulty. A notion came into my head which, if it could have been carried out, might have had a curious ending. It was that if one trooper only should approach me, and his comrades remained sufficiently distant, I should keep hidden and wait until he got near enough for me to kill him with a shot from my pistol, for I had two on my belt; I would then take his uniform, mount his horse, and make my escape in this disguise, a plan which would be favoured by the approaching darkness. But not seeing any chance of being able to carry out this idea, I thought of another, namely, to get into the river up to my chin in the water under the bushes on the bank, wait for nightfall and the return of the troopers to their camp, and then to escape in the dark. But there were more difficulties to contend with in risking this even than in the other case, and as a last resource it struck me I might save myself by crossing the river, for happily I knew how to swim, although the risk here was very great owing to the breadth and rapidity of the Danube. I hurriedly determined on this plan, as I now saw a number of troopers approaching ever nearer to my hiding place, who were refusing to give quarter to the unhappy wounded they found hidden in the corn, whom they ruthlessly despatched the more easily to despoil them. There was no reason to suppose that they were likely to show any more mercy to me, particularly as I was worth more in the shape of plunder than a private soldier, nor was there time to lose in making up my mind, so I then and there determined to swim the river. Before taking to the water I took the precaution of leaving on the bank my richly embroidered uniform, rather spoiled as it was by the events of the late action. I scattered in a similar manner my hat, wig, pistols, and sword, at one point and another, so that if the troopers came up before I had got well away, they would devote their attention to collecting these articles instead of looking in the water, and it turned out just as I thought. I kept on my stockings, vest, and breeches, simply buttoning the sleeves of the vest and tucking the pockets within my breeches for safety; this done, I threw myself upon the mercy of the stream. I had hardly got any distance when up came the troopers, who, as I had hoped, dismounted as quickly as they could to lay hands on the spoil lying before them; they even set to work to quarrel over it, for I distinctly heard them shouting and swearing in the most delightful manner. Others apparently got no share, and they amused themselves by saluting me with several musket shots, but the current of the river which carried me on my way soon put me out of their range. Finally, after a very long and hard swim, I was lucky enough to reach the other bank, in spite of the strength of the stream.

Robinson Crusoe Found, 2 February 1709

Woodes Rogers

Selkirk, prototype of Defoe's Robinson Crusoe, was a shoemaker's son who ran away to sea and joined a band of buccaneers. He was put ashore in September 1704 on the uninhabited Más a Tierra Island in the Juan Fernández cluster, 400 miles west of Valparaiso, Chile.

Our pinnace return'd from the shore, and brought abundance of craw-fish with a man cloth'd in goat-skins, who look'd wilder than the first owners of them. He had been on the island four years and four months, being left there by Captain Stradling in the *Cinque-Ports*. His name was Alexander Selkirk, a Scotchman, who had been Master of the *Cinque-Ports*, a ship that came here last with Captain Dampier, who told me that this was the best man in her; so I immediately agreed with him to be a mate on board our ship.

'Twas he that made the fire last night when he saw our ships, which he judg'd to be English. During his stay here he saw several ships pass by but only two came in to anchor. As he went to view them he found them to be Spanish and retired from 'em, upon which they shot at him. Had they been French, he would have submitted, but chose to risque dying alone on the Iland, rather than fall into the hands of the Spaniards in these parts, because he apprehended they would murder him, or make a slave of him in the mines; for he fear'd they would spare no stranger that might be capable of discovering the South Sea. The Spaniards had landed before he knew what they were, and they came so near him that he had much ado to escape: for they not only shot at him, but pursue'd him into the woods, where he climb'd to the top of a tree at the foot of which they made water, and kill'd several goats just by, but went off again without discovering him. He told us he was born at Largo in the county of Fife, Scotland, and was bred a sailor from his youth. The reason of his being left here was a difference betwixt him and his captain. . . . He had with him his clothes and bedding, with a firelock, some powder, bullets, and tobacco, a hatchet, a knife, a kettle, a Bible, some practical pieces, and his mathematical instruments and books.

He diverted and provided for himself as well as he could; but for the first eight months had much ado to bear up against melancholy, and the terror of being left alone in such a desolate place. He built two huts with piemento trees, cover'd them with long grass, and lin'd them with the skins of goats which he killed with his gun as he wanted, so long as his powder lasted, which was but a pound, and that being near spent, he got fire by rubbing two sticks of piemento wood together upon his knee. In the lesser hut, at some distance from the other, he dressed his victuals, and in the larger he slept, and employed himself in reading, singing Psalms, and praying, so that he said he was a better Christian while in this solitude, than ever he was before, or than he was afraid he should ever be again. At first he never eat anything till hunger constrain'd him, partly for grief, and partly for want of bread and salt; nor did he go to bed till he could watch no longer. The piemento wood, which burnt very clear, serv'd him both for firing and candle, and refresh'd him with its fragrant smell. He might have had fish enough, but could not eat 'em for want of salt, because they occasion'd a looseness; except Crawfish, which are there as large as lobsters and very good. These he sometimes boiled, and at other times broiled as he did his goats flesh, of which he made very good broth, for they are not so rank as ours; he kept an account of 500 that he kill'd while there, and caught as many more, which he marked on the ear and let go. When his powder fail'd he took them by speed of foot; for his way of living, and continual exercise of walking and running, clear'd him of all gross humours, so that he ran with wonderful swiftness thro the woods, and up the rocks and hills, as we perceiv'd when we employ'd him to catch goats for us. We had a bull dog which we sent with several of our nimblest runners to help him in catching goats; but he distanc'd and tir'd both the dog and the men, catch'd the goats and brought 'em to us on his back. He told us that his agility in pursuing a goat had once like to have cost him his life; he pursue'd it with so much eagerness that he catch'd hold of it on the brink of a precipice of which he was not aware, the bushes having hid it from him so that he fell with the goat down the said precipice a great height, and was so stun'd and bruised with the fall that he narrowly escap'd with his life, and when he came to his senses found the goat dead under him. He lay there about 24 hours and was scarce able to crawl to his hut which was about a mile distant, or to stir abroad again in ten days. He came at last to relish his meat well enough without salt or bread, and in the season had plenty of good turnips which had been sow'd there by Captain Dampier's men, and have now overspread some acres of ground. He had enough of good cabbage from the cabbage trees and season'd his meat with the fruit of the piemento trees, which is the same as the Jamaica pepper, and smells deliciously. He found there also a black pepper called *Maragita*, which was very good to expel wind, and against griping of the guts. He soon wore out all his shoes and clothes by running thro the woods; and at last, being forced to shift without them, his feet became so hard that he ran everywhere without annoyance, and it was some time before he could wear shoes after we found him. For not being used to any so long, his feet swelled when he came first to wear 'em again. After he had conquer'd his melancholy he diverted himself sometimes by cutting his name on the trees, and the time of his being left and continuance there. He was at first much pester'd with cats and rats, that had bred in great numbers from some of each species which had got ashore from ships that put in there to wood and water. The rats gnaw'd his feet and clothes while asleep, which oblige'd him to cherish the cats with his goats flesh; by which many of them became so tame that they would lie about him in hundreds, and soon deliver'd him from the rats.

He likewise tam'd some kids, and to divert himself would now and then sing and dance with them and his cats; so that by the care of Providence, and vigour of his youth, being now about 30 years old, he came at last to conquer all the inconveniences of his solitude and to be very easy. When his clothes wore out he made himself a coat and cap of goatskins, which he stitch'd together with little thongs of the same that he cut with his knife. He had no other needle but a nail, and when his knife was wore to the back, he made others as well as he could of some iron hoops that were left ashore, which he beat thin and ground upon stones. Having some linen cloth by him, he sow'd himself shirts with a nail and stitch'd 'em with the worsted of his old stockings, which he pull'd out on purpose. He had his last shirt on when we found him in the island.

At his first coming on board us, he had so much forgot his language for want of use, that we could scarce understand him, for he seemed to speak his words by halves. We offer'd him a dram, but he would not touch it, having drank nothing but water since his being there, and 'twas some time before he could relish our victuals. He could give us an account of no other product of the Island than what we have mentioned except small black plums, which are very good, but hard to come at, the trees which bear 'em growing on high mountains and rocks.

Bull-Baiting: London, 1710

Zacharias Conrad Von Uffenbach

Towards evening we drove to see the bull-baiting, which is held here nearly every Monday in two places. On the morning of the day the bull, or any other creature that is to be baited, is led round. It takes place in a large open space or courtyard, on two sides of which high benches have been made for the spectators. First a young ox or bull was led in and fastened by a long rope to an iron ring in the middle of the yard; then about thirty dogs, two or three at a time, were let loose on him, but he made short work of them, goring them and tossing them high in the air above the height of the first storey. Then amid shouts and yells the butchers to whom the dogs belonged sprang forward and caught their beasts right side up to break their fall. They had to keep fast hold of the dogs to hinder them from returning to the attack without barking. Several had such a grip of the bull's throat or ear that their mouths had to be forced open with poles. When the bull had stood it tolerably long, they brought out a small bear and tied him up in the same fashion. As soon as the dogs had at him, he stood up on his hind legs and gave some terrific buffets; but if one of them got at his skin, he rolled about in such a fashion that the dogs thought themselves lucky if they came out safe from beneath him. But the most diverting and worst of all was a common little ass, who was brought out saddled with an ape on his back. As soon as a couple of dogs had been let loose on him he broke into a prodigious gallop – for he was free, not having been tied up like the other beasts – and he stamped and bit all round himself. The ape began to scream most terribly for fear of falling off. If the dogs came too near him, he seized them with his mouth and twirled them round, shaking them so much that they howled prodigiously. Finally another bull appeared, on whom several crackers had been hung: when these were lit and several dogs let loose on him on a sudden, there was a monstrous hurly-burly. And thus was concluded this truly English sport, which vastly delights this nation but to me seemed nothing very special.

Turkish Bath: Adrianople, 1 April 1717

Lady Mary Wortley Montagu

The author was wife of the English ambassador to Turkey.

I went to the Bagnio about 10 a clock. It was already full of Women. It is built of Stone in the shape of a Dome with no Windows but in the Roofe, which gives Light enough. There was 5 of these domes joyn'd together, the outmost being less than the rest and serving only as a hall where the portress stood at the door. Ladys of Quality gennerally give this Woman the value of a crown or 10 shillings, and I did not forget that ceremony. The next room is a very large one, pav'd with Marble, and all round it rais'd 2 Sofas of marble, one above another. There were 4 fountains of cold Water in this room, falling first into marble Basins and then running on the floor in little channels made for that purpose, which carry'd the streams into the next room, something less than this, with the same sort of marble sofas, but so hot with steams of sulphur proceeding from the baths joyning to it, twas impossible to stay there with one's Cloths on. The 2 other domes were the hot baths, one of which had cocks of cold Water turning into it to temper it to what degree of warmth the bathers have a mind to.

I was in my travelling Habit, which is a rideing dress, and certainly appear'd very extrodinary to them, yet there was not one of 'em that shew'd the least surprize or impertinent Curiosity, but receiv'd me with all the obliging civillity possible. I know no European Court where the Ladys would have behav'd them selves in so polite a manner to a stranger.

I beleive in the whole there were 200 Women and yet none of those disdainfull smiles or satyric whispers that never fail in our assemblys when any body appears that is not dress'd exactly in fashion. They repeated over and over to me, *Uzelle, pek uzelle*, which is nothing but, Charming, very charming. The first sofas were cover'd with Cushions and rich Carpets, on which sat the Ladys, and on the 2nd their slaves behind 'em, but without any distinction of rank by their dress, all being in the state of nature, that is, in plain English, stark naked, without any Beauty or deffect conceal'd, yet there was not the least wanton smile or immodest Gesture amongst 'em. They Walk'd and mov'd with the same majestic Grace which Milton describes of our General Mother. There were many amongst them as exactly proportion'd as ever any Goddess was drawn by the pencil of Guido or Titian, and most of their skins shineingly white, only adorn'd by their Beautifull Hair divided into many tresses hanging on their shoulders, braided either with pearl or riband, perfectly representing the figures of the Graces. I was here convinc'd of the Truth of a Refflexion that I had often made, that if twas the fashion to go naked, the face would be hardly observ'd. I perceiv'd that the Ladys with the finest skins and most delicate shapes had the greatest share of my admiration, tho their faces were sometimes less beautifull than those of their companions. To tell you the truth, I had wickedness enough to wish secretly that Mr Gervase could have been there invisible. I fancy it would have very much improv'd his art to see so many fine Women naked in different postures, some in conversation, some working, others drinking Coffee or sherbert, and many negligently lying on their Cushions while their slaves (generally pritty Girls of 17 or 18) were employ'd in braiding their hair in several pritty manners. In short, tis the Women's coffee house, where all the news of the Town is told, Scandal invented, etc. They gennerally take this Diversion once a week, and stay there at least 4 or 5 hours without getting cold by immediate coming out of the hot bath into the cool room, which was very surprizing to me. The Lady that seem'd the most considerable amongst them entreated me to sit by her and would fain have undress'd me for the bath. I excus'd my selfe with some difficulty, they being all so earnest in perswading me. I was at last forc'd to open my skirt and shew them my stays, which satisfy'd 'em very well, for I saw they beleiv'd I was so lock'd up in that machine that it was not in my own power to open it, which contrivance they attributed to my Husband.

Albatross Shot, 1 October 1719

George Shelvocke

Coleridge's reading of this account provided him with the germ of The Ancient Mariner.

At 7 in the evening, as they were furling the main-sail, one William Camell cry'd out, that his hands and fingers were so benumb'd that he could not hold himself, but before those that were next to him could come to his assistance, he fell down and was drown'd.

The cold is certainly much more insupportable in these, than in the same Latitudes to the Northward, for, although we were pretty much advanced in the summer season, and had the days very long, yet we had continual squals of sleet, snow and rain, and the heavens were perpetually hid from us by gloomy dismal clouds. In short, one would think it impossible that any thing living could subsist in so rigid a climate; and, indeed, we all observed, that we had not had the sight of one fish of any kind, since we were come to the Southward of the streights of le Mair, nor one sea-bird, except a disconsolate black Albitross, who accompanied us for several days, hovering about us as if he had lost himself, till Hatley, (my second Captain) observing, in one of his melancholy fits, that this bird was always hovering near us, imagin'd, from his colour, that it might be some ill omen. That which, I suppose, induced him the more to encourage his superstition, was the continued series of contrary tempestuous winds, which had oppress'd us ever since we had got into this sea. But be that as it would, he, after some fruitless attempts, at length, shot the Albitross, not doubting (perhaps) that we should have a fair wind after it.

Solar Eclipse, 10 May 1724

William Stukeley

According to my promise, I send you what I observed of the solar eclipse, though I fear it will not be of any great use to you. I was not prepared with any instruments for measuring time, or the like, and proposed to myself only to watch all the appearances that Nature would present to the naked eye on so remarkable an occasion, and which generally are overlooked, or but grossly regarded. I chose for my station a place called Haradon hill, two miles eastward from Amsbury, and full east from the opening of Stonehenge avenue, to which it is as the point of view. Before me lay the vast plain where that celebrated work stands, and I knew that the eclipse would appear directly over it: beside, I had the advantage of a very extensive prospect every way, this being the highest hill hereabouts, and nearest the middle of the shadow. Full west of me, and beyond Stonehenge, is a pretty copped hill, like the top of a cone lifting itself above the horizon: this is Clay hill, near Warminster, twenty miles distant, and near the central line of darkness, which must come from thence; so that I could have notice enough before-hand of its approach. Abraham Sturgis and Stephen Ewens, both of this place and sensible men, were with me. Though it was very cloudy, yet now and then we had gleams of sun-shine, rather more than I could perceive at any other place around us. These two persons looking through smoaked glasses, while I was taking some bearings of the country with a circumferentor, both confidently affirmed the eclipse was begun; when by my watch I found it just half an hour after five: and accordingly from thence the progress of it was visible, and very often to the naked eye; the thin clouds doing the office of glasses. From the time of the sun's body being half covered, there was a very conspicuous circular *iris* round the sun, with perfect colours. On all sides we beheld the shepherds hurrying their flocks into fold, the darkness coming on; for they expected nothing less than a total eclipse, for an hour and a quarter.

When the sun looked very sharp, like a new moon, the sky was pretty clear in the spot: but soon after a thicker cloud covered it; at which time the *iris* vanished, the copped hill before mentioned grew very dark, together with the horizon on both sides, that is, to the north and south, and looked blue; just as it appears in the east at the declension of day: we had scarce time to tell then, when Salisbury steeple, six mile off southward, became very black; the copped hill quite lost, and a most gloomy night with full career came upon us. At this instant we lost sight of the sun, whose place among the clouds was hitherto sufficiently distinguishable, but now not the least trace of it to be found, no more than if really absent: then I saw by my watch, though with difficulty, and only by help of some light from the northern quarter, that it was six hours thirty-five minutes: just before this the whole compass of the heavens and earth looked of a lurid complexion, properly speaking, for it was black and blue; only on the earth upon the horizon the blue prevailed. There was likewise in the heavens among the clouds much green interspersed; so that the whole appearance was really very dreadful, and as symptoms of sickening nature.

Now I perceived us involved in total darkness, and palpable, as I may aptly call it: though it came quick, yet I was so intent that I could perceive its steps, and feel it as it were drop upon us, and fall on the right shoulder (we looking westward) like a great dark mantle, or coverlet of a bed, thrown over us, or like the drawing of a curtain on that side: and the horses we held in our hands were very sensible of it, and crowded close to us, startling with great surprise. As much as I could see of the men's faces that stood by me, had a horrible aspect. At this instant I looked around me, not without exclamations of admiration, and could discern colours in the heavens; but the earth had lost its blue, and was wholly black. For some time, among the clouds, there were visible streaks of rays, tending to the place of the sun as their centre; but immediately after, the whole appearance of the earth and sky was entirely black. Of all things I ever saw in my life, or can by imagination fancy, it was a sight the most tremendous.

Pantomimes and Gladiators, February 1728

A French Tourist in London

César de Saussure

The theatre at Lincoln's Inn Field is famous for its pantomimes, which follow the comedy. These entertainments are composed of two parts, serious and comical. The first is taken from a mythological fable; gods, goddesses, and heroes sing their parts; the decorations are very fine, and the machinery extraordinarily so. The second part, in which the actors are Harlequin, Columbine, Scaramouche, and Pierrot, is acted and not spoken, but the gestures and the machinery allow you to follow the intrigue easily, and it is generally very comical.

Mr Rich, the director of this theatre, spends a great deal of money on plays of this sort; two well-known ones are *The Rape of Europa* and *Orpheus in the Lower Regions*. In the former play a part of the theatre represents hell, in which are seated gods and goddesses; it rises gradually into the clouds; at the same instant out of the earth rises another stage. The scene represents a farmhouse, in front of which is a dunghill with an egg, the size of an ostrich's, on it. This egg, owing to the heat of the sun, grows gradually larger and larger; when it is of a very large size it cracks open, and a little Harlequin comes out of it. He is of the size of a child of three or four years old, and little by little attains a natural height. It is said Mr Rich spent more than £4,000 sterling on Orpheus. The serpent that kills Eurydice is of enormous size, and is covered all over with gold and green scales and with red spots; his eyes shine like fire, and he wriggles about the theatre with head upraised, making an awful but very natural hissing noise. The first night this pantomime was given the King was there, and I had the good fortune to be present. One of the two Grenadiers of the guard, who are posted at either side of the stage with their backs turned to the actors, noticed the serpent only when he was at his feet, and this reptile was so natural that the man dropped his musket, and drawing his sword made as though he would cut the monster in two. I do not know whether the soldier was really alarmed or whether he was acting, but if so it was admirably done, and the spectators laughed again and again. This piece is full of wonderful springs and clockwork machinery. When

Orpheus learns that his beloved is dead, he retires into the depth of the stage and plays on his lyre; presently out of the rocks appear little bushes; they gradually grow up into trees, so that the stage resembles a forest. On these trees flowers blossom, then fall off, and are replaced by different fruits, which you see grow and ripen. Wild beasts, lions, bears, tigers creep out of the forest attracted by Orpheus and his lyre. It is altogether the most surprising and charming spectacle you can imagine.

Mr Rich plays the part of Harlequin with great agility and address, and he is said to be the best actor of this part in Europe. In pantomimes most good dancers are French men and women from Paris. Ladies attend these plays in great numbers, and are always beautifully dressed.

I was sufficiently curious to wish to see the gladiators, and I will describe their manner of fighting.

The gladiators' stage is round, the spectators sit in galleries, and the spectacle generally commences by a fight with wicker staves by a few rogues. They do not spare each other, but are very skilful in giving great whacks on the head. When blood oozes from one of the combatants, a few coins are thrown to the victor. These games serve to pass the time till the spectators have arrived.

The day I went to see the gladiators fight I witnessed an extraordinary combat, two women being the champions. As soon as they appeared on the stage they made the spectators a profound reverence; they then saluted each other and engaged in a lively and amusing conversation. They boasted that they had a great amount of courage, strength, and intrepidity. One of them regretted she was not born a man, else she would have made her fortune by her powers; the other declared she beat her husband every morning to keep her hand in, etc. Both these women were very scantily clothed, and wore little bodices and very short petticoats of white linen. One of these amazons was a stout Irishwoman, strong and lithe to look at, the other was a small Englishwoman, full of fire and very agile. The first was decked with blue ribbons on the head, waist, and right arm; the second wore red ribbons. Their weapons were a sort of two-handed sword, three or three and a half feet in length; the guard was covered, and the blade was about three inches wide and not sharp – only about half a foot of it was, but then that part cut like a razor. The spectators made numerous bets, and some peers who were there some very large wagers. On either side of the two amazons a man stood by, holding a long staff, ready to separate them should blood flow. After a time the combat became very animated, and was conducted with force and vigour with the broad side of the weapons, for points there were none. The Irishwoman presently received a great cut across her forehead, and that put a stop to the first part of the combat. The Englishwoman's backers threw her shillings and half-crowns and applauded her. During this time the wounded woman's forehead was sewn up, this being done on the stage; a plaster was applied to it, and she drank a good big glass of spirits to revive her courage, and the fight began again, each combatant holding a dagger in her left hand to ward off the blows. The Irishwoman was wounded a second time, and her adversary again received coins and plaudits from her admirers. The wound was sewn up, and for the third time the battle recommenced, the women holding wicker shields as defensive weapons. This third combat was fought for some time without result, but the poor Irishwoman was destined to be the loser, for she received a long and deep wound all across her neck and throat. The surgeon sewed it up, but she was too badly hurt to fight any more, and it was time, for the combatants were dripping with perspiration, and the Irishwoman also with blood. A few coins were thrown to her to console her, but the victor made a good day's work out of the combat. Fortunately it is very rarely one hears of women gladiators.

The Princess of Wales is Delivered of a Daughter, 31 July 1737

Lord Hervey

Frederick Prince of Wales had married Augusta, daughter of Frederick II of Saxony, in 1736. The birth described here was of their first child, Augusta. Relations between the Prince and his father George II had been bad for a long time. After this episode he was banned from St James's Palace, and foreign ambassadors were requested not to visit him. Lord Hervey, the narrator, was vice-chamberlain in the royal household.

I am now come to a very extraordinary occurrence, in which I shall be very particular. It had been long talked of that the Prince intended the Princess should lie-in in London; and the King and Queen having resolved she should not, measures were concerting to prevent her doing so. It was at last resolved – that is, the King and Queen and Sir Robert Walpole had agreed – that the King should send a message to the Prince to tell His Royal Highness that he would have the Princess lie in at Hampton Court. Lord Hervey told the Queen and Princess Caroline that, notwithstanding this message, he would answer for it the Princess would not lie in where the King and Queen resided. The Queen asked him how he could imagine, as insolent as the Prince was, that he would venture to disobey the King's positive commands on this point. Lord Hervey said the Prince would pretend it was by chance; for as Dr Hollings and Mrs Cannons would be made to say that exercise was good for the Princess in her condition, she would be carried once or twice a week to Kew or London, and, whichever of these two places the Prince intended she should lie in at, he would make her, when she was within a month of her time, affect to be taken ill; and as nobody could disprove her having the pains she would complain of, the King and Queen could not take it in prudence upon them to say she should be removed; and there, of course, Her Royal Highness would bring forth. 'Well, if it is to be so,' replied the Queen, 'I cannot help it; but at her labour I positively will be, let her lie in where she will; for she cannot be brought to bed as quick as one can blow one's nose, and I will be sure it is her child. For my part, I do not see she is big; you all say you see it, and therefore I suppose it is so, and that I am blind.'

The Queen was every day pressing Sir Robert to have this message sent to the Prince, saying: 'Sir Robert, we shall be catched; he will remove her before he receives any orders for her lying in here, and will afterwards say that he talked so publicly of his intentions, he concluded if the King had not approved of them he should have heard something of it.' Sir Robert said, as the Princess did not reckon till the beginning of October, that it was full time enough; and in this manner, from day to day, this intended message was postponed, till it never went; for on Sunday, the 31st of July, the Princess was taken in the evening, after having dined in public that day with the King and Queen, so very ill, with all the symptoms of actual labour, that the Prince ordered a coach to be got ready that moment to carry her to London. Her pains came on so fast and so strong, that her water broke before they could get her out of the house. However, in this condition, M. Dunoyer, the dancing master, lugging her down stairs and along the passages by one arm, and Mr Bloodworth, one of the Prince's equerries, by the other, and the Prince in the rear, they, with much ado, got her into the coach; Lady Archibald Hamilton and Mr Townshend remonstrating strongly against this imprudent step, and the Princess begging, for God's sake, the Prince would let her stay in quiet where she was, for that her pains were so great she could not set one foot before the other, and was upon the rack when they moved her. But the Prince, with an obstinacy equal to his folly, and a folly equal to his barbarity, insisted on her going, crying, 'Courage! courage! ah, quelle sottise!' and telling her, with the encouragement of a toothdrawer, or the consolatory tenderness of an executioner, that it would be over in a minute. With these excitations, and in this manner, after enjoining all his servants not to say one word what was the matter, for fear the news of the Princess's circumstances should get to the other side of the house and their going should be prevented, he got her into the coach. There were in the coach, besides him and her, Lady Archibald Hamilton, and Mrs Clavering and Mrs Paine, two of the Princess's dressers; Vreid, his *valet de chambre*, who was a surgeon and man-midwife, was upon the coach-box; Mr Bloodworth, and two or three more, behind the coach; and thus loaded he ordered the coachman to drive full gallop to London. About ten this cargo arrived in town. Notwithstanding all the handkerchiefs that had been thrust one after another up Her Royal Highness's petticoats in the coach, her clothes were in such a condition with the filthy inundations which attend these circumstances that when the coach stopped at St James's the Prince ordered all the lights to be put out that people might not have the nasty ocular evidence which would otherwise have been exhibited to them of his folly and her distress. When they came to St James's, there was no one thing prepared for her reception. The midwife came in a few minutes; napkins, warming-pan, and all other necessary implements for this operation, were sought by different emissaries in different houses in the neighbourhood; and no sheets being to be come at, Her Royal Highness was put to bed between two table-cloths. At a quarter before eleven she was delivered of a little rat of a girl, about the bigness of a good large toothpick case, none of the Lords of the Council being present but my Lord President Wilmington, and my

Lord Godolphin, Privy Seal. To the first of these the Prince, at leaving Hampton Court, had despatched a messenger to bring him from his villa at Chiswick; and the last, living just by St James's, was sent for as soon as the Prince arrived in town. He sent also to the Lord Chancellor and the Archbishop; but the one was gone into the country, and the other came a quarter of an hour after the child was born.

In the meantime, this evening, at Hampton Court, the King played at commerce below stairs, the Queen above at quadrille, the Princess Emily at her commerce-table, and the Princess Caroline and Lord Hervey at cribbage, just as usual, and separated all at ten of the clock; and, what is incredible to relate, went to bed all at eleven, without hearing one single syllable of the Princess's being ill, or even of her not being in the house. At half an hour after one, which was above two hours after the Princess had been brought to bed, a courier arrived with the first news of her being in labour. When Mrs Titchburne, the Woman of the Bedchamber, came to wake the King and Queen, the Queen as soon as she came into the room asked what was the matter that occasioned their being waked up at so unusual an hour; and, as the most natural question, inquired if the house was on fire. When Mrs Titchburne said the Prince had sent to let Their Majesties know the Princess was in labour the Queen immediately cried: 'My God, my nightgown! I'll go to her this moment.' 'Your nightgown, Madam,' replied Titchburne, 'and your coaches too; the Princess is at St James's.' 'Are you mad,' interrupted the Queen, 'or are you asleep, my good Titchburne? You dream.' When Mrs Titchburne insisted on its being certainly true, the King flew into a violent passion, and, in German (as the Queen told me afterward), began to scold her, saying: 'You see, now, with all your wisdom, how they have outwitted you. This is all your fault. There is a false child will be put upon you, and how will you answer it to all your children?'

Crossing the Alps, November 1739

Thomas Gray

The Mr Walpole whose spaniel perished in this episode was Horace Walpole (1717–1797), Gray's travelling companion.

Turin, Nov. 7, 1739

I am this night arrived here, and have just set down to rest me after eight days tiresome journey: For the three first we had the same road we before past through to go to Geneva; the fourth we turned out of it, and for that day and the next travelled rather among than upon the Alps; the way commonly running through a deep valley by the side of the river Arc, which works itself a passage, with great difficulty and a mighty noise, among vast quantities of rocks, that have rolled down from the mountain tops. The winter was so far advanced, as in great measure to spoil the beauty of the prospect, however, there was still somewhat fine remaining amidst the savageness and horror of the place: The sixth we began to go up several of these mountains; and as we were passing one, met with an odd accident enough: Mr Walpole had a little fat black spaniel, that he was very fond of, which he sometimes used to set down, and let it run by the chaise side. We were at that time in a very rough road, not two yards broad at most; on one side was a great wood of pines, and on the other a vast precipice; it was noon-day, and the sun shone bright, when all of a sudden, from the wood-side, (which was as steep upwards, as the the other part was downwards) out rushed a great wolf, came close to the head of the horses, seized the dog by the throat, and rushed up the hill again with him in his mouth. This was done in less than a quarter of a minute; we all saw it, and yet the servants had not time to draw their pistols, or do any thing to save the dog. If he had not been there, and the creature had thought fit to lay hold of one of the horses; chaise, and we, and all must inevitably have tumbled above fifty fathoms perpendicular down the precipice. The seventh we came to Lanebourg, the last town in Savoy; it lies at the foot of the famous mount Cenis, which is so situated as to allow no room for any way but over the very top of it. Here the chaise was forced to be pulled to pieces, and the baggage and that to be carried by mules: We ourselves were wrapped up in our furs, and seated upon a sort of matted chair without legs, which is carried upon poles in the manner of a bier, and so begun to ascend by the help of eight men. It was six miles to the top, where a plain opens itself about as many more in breadth, covered perpetually with very deep snow, and in the midst of that a great lake of unfathomable depth, from whence a river takes its rise, and tumbles over monstrous rocks quite down the other side of the mountain. The descent is six miles more, but infinitely more steep than the going up; and here the men perfectly fly down with you, stepping from stone to stone with incredible swiftness in places where none but they could go three paces without falling. The immensity of the precipices, the roaring of the river and torrents that run into it, the huge crags covered with ice and snow, and the clouds below you and about you, are objects it is impossible to conceive without seeing them; and though we had heard many strange descriptions of the scene, none of them at all came up to it. We were but five hours in performing the whole, from which you may judge of the rapidity of the men's motion. We are now got into Piedmont, and stopped a little while at La Ferriere, a small village about three-quarters of the way down, but still among the clouds, where we began to hear a new language spoken round about us; at last we got quite down, went through the Pás de Suse, a narrow road among the Alps, defended by two fortresses, and lay at Bossolens: Next evening through a fine avenue of nine miles in length, as straight as a line, we arrived at this city.

Scurvy, 1741

Richard Walker

Soon after our passing Streights Le Maire, the scurvy began to make its appearance amongst us; and our long continuance at sea, the fatigue we underwent, and the various disappointments we met with, had occasioned its spreading of such a degree, that at the latter end of April there were but few on board, who were not in some degree afflicted with it, and in that month no less than forty-three died of it on board the *Centurion*. But though we thought that the distemper had then risen to an extraordinary height, and were willing to hope, that as we advanced to the northward its malignity would abate, yet we found, on the contrary, that in the month of May we lost near double that number: And as we did not get to land till the middle of June, the mortality went on increasing, and the disease extended itself so prodigiously, that after the loss of above two hundred men, we could not at last master more than six fore-mast men in a watch capable of duty.

This disease so frequently attending all long voyages, and, so particularly destructive to us, is surely the most singular and unaccountable of any that affects the human body. For its symptoms are inconstant and innumerable, and its progress and effects extremely irregular; for scarcely any two persons have the same complaints, and where there hath been found some conformity in the symptoms, the order of their appearance has been totally different. However, though it frequently puts on the form of many other diseases, and is therefore not to be described by any exclusive and infallible criterions; yet there are some symptoms which are more general than the rest, and therefore, occurring the oftnest, deserve a more particular enumeration. These common appearances are large discoloured spots dispersed over the whole surface of the body, swelled legs, putrid gums, and above all, an extraordinary lassitude of the whole body, especially after any exercise, however inconsiderable; and this lassitude at last degenerates into a proneness of swoon on the least exertion of strength, or even on the least motion.

This disease is likewise usually attended with a strange dejection of the spirits, and with shiverings, tremblings, and a disposition to be seized with the most dreadful terrors on the slightest accident. Indeed, it was most remarkable, in all our reiterated experience of this malady, that whatever discouraged our people, or at any time damped their hopes, never failed to add new vigour to the distemper; for it usually killed those who were in the last stages of it, and confined those to their hammocks, who were before capable of some kind of duty, so that it seemed as if alacrity of mind, and sanguine thoughts, were no contemptible preservatives from its fatal malignity.

But it is not easy to compleat the long roll of the various concomitants of this disease; for it often produced putrid fevers, pleurisies, the jaundice, and violent rheumatick pains, and sometimes it occasioned an obstinate costiveness, which was generally attended with a difficulty of breathing; and this was esteemed the most deadly of all the scorbutick symptoms: At other times the whole body, but more especially the legs, were subject to ulcers of the worst kind, attended with rotten bones, and such a luxuriancy of funguous flesh, as yielded to no remedy. But a most extraordinary circumstance, and what would be scarcely credible upon any single evidence, is, that the scars of wounds which had been for many years healed, were forced open again by this virulent distemper: Of this, there was a remarkable instance in one of the invalids on board the *Centurion*, who had been wounded above fifty years before at the battle of the Boyne; for though he was cured soon after, and had continued well for a great number of years past, yet on his being attacked by the scurvy, his wounds, in the progress of his disease, broke out afresh, and appeared as if they had never been healed: Nay, what is still more astonishing, the callous of a broken bone, which had been compleatly formed for a long time, was found to be hereby dissolved, and the fracture seemed as if it had never been consolidated. Indeed, the effects of this disease were in almost every instance wonderful; for many of our people, though confined to their hammocks, appeared to have no inconsiderable share of health, for they eat and drank heartily, were chearful, and talked with much seeming vigour, and with a loud strong tone of voice; and yet on their being the least moved, though it was only from one part of the ship to the other, and that in their hammocks, they have immediately expired; and others, who have confided in their seeming strength, and have resolved to get out of their hammocks, have died before they could well reach the deck; and it was no uncommon thing for those who were able to walk the deck, and to do some kind of duty, to drop down dead in an instant, on any endeavours to act with their utmost vigour, many of our people having perished in this manner during the course of this voyage.

John Wesley Preaches in Hull, 24 April 1752

John Wesley

Between five and six the coach called and took me to Mighton Car, about half a mile from the town. A huge multitude, rich and poor, horse and foot, with several coaches, were soon gathered together, to whom I cried with a loud voice and a composed spirit, 'What shall it profit a man, if he shall gain the whole world and lose his own soul?' Some thousands of the people seriously attended, but many behaved as if possessed by Moloch. Clods and stones flew about on every side, but they neither touched nor disturbed me. When I had finished my discourse, I went to take coach, but the coachman had driven clear away. We were at a loss, till a gentlewoman invited my wife and me to come into her coach. She brought some inconveniences on herself thereby; not only as there were nine of us in the coach, but also as the mob closely attended us, throwing in at the windows (which we did not think it prudent to shut) whatever came next to hand. But a large gentlewoman who sat in my lap screened me so that nothing came near me.

Kitten Overboard, 11 July 1754

Henry Fielding

A most tragical incident fell out this day at sea. While the ship was under sail, but making as will appear no great way, a kitten, one of four of the feline inhabitants of the cabin, fell from the window into the water: an alarm was immediately given to the captain, who was then upon deck, and received it with the utmost concern and many bitter oaths. He immediately gave orders to the steersman in favour of the poor thing, as he called it; the sails were instantly slackened, and all hands, as the phrase is, employed to recover the poor animal. I was, I own, extremely surprised at all this; less indeed at the captain's extreme tenderness than at his conceiving any possibility of success; for if puss had had nine thousand instead of nine lives, I concluded they had been all lost. The boatswain, however, had more sanguine hopes, for, having stripped himself of his jacket, breeches and shirt, he leaped boldly into the water, and to my great astonishment in a few minutes returned to the ship, bearing the motionless animal in his mouth. Nor was this, I observed, a matter of such great difficulty as it appeared to my ignorance, and possibly may seem to that of my fresh-water reader. The kitten was now exposed to air and sun on the deck, where its life, of which it retained no symptoms, was despaired of by all.

The captain's humanity, if I may so call it, did not so totally destroy his philosophy as to make him yield himself up to affliction on this melancholy occasion. Having felt his loss like a man, he resolved to show he could bear it like one; and, having declared he had rather have lost a cask of rum or brandy, betook himself to threshing at backgammon with the Portuguese friar, in which innocent amusement they had passed about two-thirds of their time.

But as I have, perhaps, a little too wantonly endeavoured to raise the tender passions of my readers in this narrative, I should think myself unpardonable if I concluded it without giving them the satisfaction of hearing that the kitten at last recovered, to the great joy of the good captain, but to the great disappointment of some of the sailors, who asserted that the drowning cat was the very surest way of raising a favourable wind; a supposition of which, though we have heard several plausible accounts, we will not presume to assign the true original reason.

The Black Hole of Calcutta, 21 June 1756

J. Z. Holwell

Calcutta, headquarters of the East India Company, was attacked in 1756 by the anti-British Suraj-ud-Dowlah. Prisoners were locked overnight in the military gaol of Fort William – the 'black hole'. A year later Clive defeated Suraj-ud-Dowlah at Plassey.

Figure to yourself, my friend, if possible, the situation of a hundred and forty-six wretches, exhausted by continual fatigue and action, crammed together in a cube of eighteen feet, in a close sultry night, in Bengal, shut up to the eastward and southward (the only quarters from whence air could reach us) by dead walls, and by a wall and door to the north, open only to the westward by two windows, strongly barred with iron, from which we could receive scarce any the least circulation of fresh air.

What must ensue, appeared to me in lively and dreadful colours, the instant I cast my eyes round and saw the size and situation of the room. Many unsuccessful attempts were made to force the door; for having nothing but our hands to work with, and the door opening inward, all endeavours were vain and fruitless . . .

We had been but few minutes confined before every one fell into a perspiration so profuse, you can form no idea of it. This brought on a raging thirst, which increased in proportion as the body was drained of its moisture.

Various expedients were thought of to give more room and air. To obtain the former, it was moved to put off their cloaths; this was approved as a happy motion, and in a few minutes I believe every man was stripped (myself, Mr Court, and the two young gentlemen by me excepted). For a little time they flattered themselves with having gained a mighty advantage; every hat was put in motion to produce a circulation of air, and Mr Baillie proposed that every man should sit down on his hams. This expedient was several times put in practice, and at each time many of the poor creatures, whose natural strength was less than that of others, or who had been more exhausted and could not immediately recover their legs, as others did when the word was given to rise, fell to rise no more; for they were instantly trod to death or suffocated. When the whole body sat down, they were so closely wedged together, that they were obliged to use many efforts before they could put themselves in motion to get up again.

Before nine o'clock every man's thirst grew intolerable, and respiration difficult. Efforts were made again to force the door, but in vain. Many insults were used to the guard to provoke them to fire in upon us. For my own part, I hitherto felt little pain or uneasiness, but what resulted from my anxiety for the sufferings of those within. By keeping my face between two of the bars, I obtained air enough to give my lungs easy play, though my perspiration was excessive, and thirst commencing. At this period, so strong a urinous volatile effluvia came from the prison, that I was not able to turn my head that way, for more than a few seconds at a time.

Now every body, excepting those situated in and near the windows, began to grow outrageous, and many delirious: *Water, water*, became the general cry. And the old Jemmautdaar before mentioned, taking pity on us, ordered the people to bring some skins of water. This was what I dreaded. I foresaw it would prove the ruin of the small chance left us, and essayed many times to speak to him privately to forbid its being brought; but the clamour was so loud, it became impossible. The water appeared. Words cannot paint to you the universal agitation and raving the sight of it threw us into. I flattered myself that some, by preserving an equal temper of mind, might out-live the night; but now the reflection, which gave me the greatest pain, was, that I saw no possibility of one escaping to tell the dismal tale.

Until the water came, I had myself not suffered much from thirst, which instantly grew excessive. We had no means of conveying it into the prison, but by hats forced through the bars; and thus myself and Messieurs Coles and Scott (notwithstanding the pains they suffered from their wounds) supplied them as fast as possible. But those who have experienced intense thirst, or are acquainted with the cause and nature of this appetite, will be sufficiently sensible it could receive no more than a momentary alleviation; the cause still subsisted. Though we brought full hats within the bars, there ensued such violent struggles, and frequent contests to get at it, that before it reached the lips of any one, there would be scarcely a small tea cup full left in them. These supplies, like sprinkling water on fire, only served to feed and raise the flame.

Oh! my dear Sir, how shall I give you a conception of what I felt at the cries and ravings of those in the remoter parts of the prison, who could not entertain a probable hope of obtaining a drop, yet could not divest themselves of expectation, however unavailing! and calling on me by the tender considerations of friendship and affection, and who knew they were really dear to me! Think, if possible, what my heart must have suffered at seeing and hearing their distress, without having it in my power to relieve them: for the confusion now became general and horrid. Several quitted the other window (the only chance they had for life) to force their way to the water, and the throng and press upon the window was beyond bearing; many forcing their passage from the further part of the room, pressed down those in their way, who had less strength, and trampled them to death.

From about nine to near eleven, I sustained this cruel scene and painful situation, still supplying them with water, though my legs were almost broke with the weight against them. By this time I myself was near pressed to death, and my two companions, with Mr William Parker (who had forced himself into the window) were really so . . .

For a great while they preserved a respect and regard to me, more than indeed I could well expect, our circumstances considered; but now all distinction was lost. My friend Baillie, Messrs Jenks, Revely, Law, Buchanan, Simpson, and several others, for whom I had a real esteem and affection, had for some time been dead at my feet: and were now trampled upon by every corporal or common soldier, who, by the help of more robust constitutions, had forced their way to the window, and held fast by the bars over me, till at last I became so pressed and wedged up, I was deprived of all motion.

Determined now to give every thing up, I called to them, and begged, as the last instance of their regard, they would remove the pressure upon me, and permit me to retire out of the window, to die in quiet. They gave way; and with much difficulty I forced a passage into the centre of the prison, where the throng was less by the many dead, (then I believe amounting to one-third) and the numbers who flocked to the windows; for by this time they had water also at the other window.

In the black hole there is a platform corresponding with that in the barrack: I travelled over the dead, and repaired to the further end of it, just opposite to the other window. Here my poor friend Mr Edward Eyre came staggering over the dead to me, and with his usual coolness and good-nature, asked me how I did? but fell and expired before I had time to make him a reply. I laid myself down on some of the dead behind me, on the platform; and, recommending myself to heaven, had the comfort of thinking my sufferings could have no long duration.

My thirst grew now insupportable, and the difficulty of breathing much increased; and I had not remained in this situation, I believe, ten minutes, when I was seized with a pain in my breast, and palpitation of heart, both to the most exquisite degree. These roused and obliged me to get up again; but still the pain, palpitation, thirst, and difficulty of breathing increased. I retained my senses notwithstanding; and had the grief to see death not so near me as I hoped; but could no longer bear the pains I suffered without attempting a relief, which I knew fresh air would and could only give me. I instantly determined to push for the window opposite to me; and by an effort of double the strength I had ever before possessed, gained the third rank at it, with one hand seized a bar, and by that means gained the second, though I think there were at least six or seven ranks between me and the window.

In a few moments the pain, palpitation, and difficulty of breathing ceased; but my thirst continued intolerable. I called aloud for *Water for God's sake*. I had been concluded dead; but as soon as they found me amongst them, they still had the respect and tenderness for me, to cry out, *Give him water, give him water!* nor would one of them at the window attempt to touch it until I had drank. But from the water I had no relief; my thirst was rather increased by it; so I determined to drink no more, but patiently wait the event; and kept my mouth moist from time to time by sucking the perspiration out of my shirt sleeves, and catching the drops as they fell, like heavy rain, from my head and face; you can hardly imagine how unhappy I was if any of them escaped my mouth.

I came into the prison without coat or waistcoat; the season was too hot to bear the former, and the latter tempted the avarice of one of the guards, who robbed me of it, when we were under the Veranda. Whilst I was at this second window, I was observed by one of my miserable companions on the right of me, in the expedient of allaying my thirst by sucking my shirt-sleeve. He took the hint, and robbed me from time to time of a considerable part of my store; though after I detected him, I had even the address to begin on that sleeve first, when I thought my reservoirs were sufficiently replenished; and our mouths and noses often met in the contest. This plunderer I found afterwards was a worthy young gentleman in the service, Mr Lushington, one of the few who escaped from death, and since paid me the compliment of assuring me, he believed he owed his life to the many comfortable draughts he had from my sleeves. Before I hit upon this happy expedient, I had in an ungovernable fit of thirst, attempted drinking my urine; but it was so intensely bitter, there was no enduring a second taste, whereas no Bristol water could be more soft or pleasant than what arose from perspiration . . .

Many to the right and left sunk with the violent pressure, and were soon suffocated; for now a steam arose from the living and the dead, which affected us in all its circumstances, as if we were forcibly held by our heads over a bowl of strong volatile spirit of hartshorn, until suffocated; nor could the effluvia of the one be distinguished from the other; and frequently, when I was forced by the load upon my head and shoulders, to hold my face down, I was obliged, near as I was to the window, instantly to raise it again, to escape suffocation . . .

When the day broke, and the gentlemen found that no intreaties could prevail to get the door opened, it occurred to one of them (I think to Mr Secretary Cooke) to make a search for me, in hopes I might have influence enough to gain a release from this scene of misery. Accordingly Messrs Lushington and Walcot undertook the search, and by my shirt discovered me under the dead upon the platform. They took me from thence, and imagining I had some signs of life, brought me towards the window I had first possession of.

But as life was equally dear to every man (and the stench arising from the dead bodies was grown so intolerable) no one would give up his station in or near the window: so they were obliged to carry me back again. But soon after Captain Mills, (now captain of the company's yacht) who was in possession of a seat in the window, had the humanity to offer to resign it. I was again brought by the same gentlemen and placed in the window.

At this juncture the suba [viceroy of Bengal], who had received an account of the havock death had made amongst us, sent one of his Jemmautdaars to enquire if the chief survived. They shewed me to him; told I had appearance of life remaining; and believed I might recover if the door was opened very soon. This answer being returned to the suba, an order came immediately for our release, it being then near six in the morning.

As the door opened inwards, and as the dead were piled up against it, and covered all the rest of the floor, it was impossible to open it by any efforts from without; it was therefore necessary that the dead should be removed by the few that were within, who were become so feeble, that the task, though it was the condition of life, was not performed without the utmost difficulty, and it was twenty minutes after the order came before the door could be opened.

About a quarter after six in the morning, the poor remains of 146 souls, being no more than three and twenty, came out of the black hole alive, but in a condition which made it very doubtful whether they would see the morning of the next day; among the living was Mrs Carey, but poor Leech was among the dead. The bodies were dragged out of the hole by the soldiers, and thrown promiscuously into the ditch of an unfinished ravelin, which was afterwards filled with earth.

The Burial of George II, 13 November 1760

Horace Walpole

Do you know I had the curiosity to go to the burying t'other night; I had never seen a royal funeral. Nay, I walked as a rag of quality, which I found would be, and so it was, the easiest way of seeing it. It is absolutely a noble sight. The Prince's Chamber hung with purple and a quantity of silver lamps, the coffin under a canopy of purple velvet, and six vast chandeliers of silver on high stands had a very good effect: the ambassador from Tripoli and his son were carried to see that chamber. The procession through a line of foot-guards, every seventh man bearing a torch, the horse-guards lining the outside, their officers with drawn sabres and crape sashes, on horseback, the drums muffled, the fifes, bells tolling and minute guns, all this was very solemn. But the charm was the entrance of the Abbey, where we were received by the Dean and chapter in rich copes, the choir and almsmen all bearing torches; the whole Abbey so illuminated, that one saw it to greater advantage than by day; the tombs, long aisles, and fretted roof all appearing distinctly, and with the happiest chiaroscuro. There wanted nothing but incense, and little chapels here and there with priests saying mass for the repose of the defunct – yet one could not complain of its not being Catholic enough. I had been in dread of being coupled with some boy of ten years old – but the heralds were not very accurate, and I walked with George Grenville, taller and older enough to keep me in countenance. When we came to the chapel of Henry VII all solemnity and decorum ceased – no order was observed, people sat or stood where they could or would, the yeomen of the guard were crying out for help, oppressed by the immense weight of the coffin, the Bishop read sadly, and blundered in the prayers, the fine chapter, *Man that is born of a woman*, was chanted not read, and the anthem, besides being unmeasurably tedious, would have served as well for a nuptial. The real serious part was the figure of the Duke of Cumberland, heightened by a thousand melancholy circumstances. He had a dark brown adonis [wig] and a cloak of black cloth with a train of five yards. Attending the funeral of a father, how little reason soever he had to love him, could not be pleasant. His leg extremely bad, yet forced to stand upon it near two hours, his face bloated and distorted with his late paralytic stroke, which has affected too one of his eyes, and placed over the mouth of the vault, into which in all probability he must himself so soon descend – think how unpleasant a situation! He bore it all with a firm and unaffected countenance. This grave scene was fully contrasted by the burlesque Duke of Newcastle – he fell into a fit of crying the moment he came into the chapel and flung himself back in a stall, the Archbishop hovering over him with a smelling bottle – but in two minutes his curiosity got the better of his hypocrisy and he ran about the chapel with his glass to spy who was or was not there, spying with one hand and mopping his eyes with t'other. Then returned the fear of catching cold, and the Duke of Cumberland, who was sinking with heat, felt himself weighed down, and turning round, found it was the Duke of Newcastle standing upon his train to avoid the chill of the marble. It was very theatric to look down into the vault, where the coffin lay, attended by mourners with lights. Clavering, the Groom of the Bedchamber, refused to sit up with the body, and was dismissed by the King's order.

The King of Ethiopia Expresses Displeasure, 23 December 1770

James Bruce

The explorer James Bruce, the author of this account, discovered the source of the Blue Nile. The King, who entertains Bruce at his capital Gondar, was Tekla Haimanot II.

It was the 23rd of December when we encamped on the Mogetch, just below Gondar. This behaviour was so conspicuous to the whole people, that no sooner were the tents pitched (it being about eleven o'clock), than they all stole home to Gondar in small parties without their dinner, and presently a report was spread, that the King and Ras Michael came determined to burn the town, and put the inhabitants all to the sword. This occasioned the utmost consternation, and caused many to fly to Fasil.

As for me, the King's behaviour shewed me plainly all was not right, and an accident in the way confirmed it. He had desired me to ride before him, and show him the horse I had got from Fasil, which was then in great beauty and order, which I had kept purposely for him. It happened that, crossing the deep bed of a brook, a plant of the kantuffa hung across it. I had upon my shoulders a white goat-skin, of which it did not take hold; but the King, who was dressed in the habit of peace, his long hair floating all around his face, wrapt up in his mantle, or thin cotton cloak, so that nothing but his eyes could be seen, was paying more attention to the horse than to the branch of kantuffa beside him; it took first hold of his hair, and the fold of the cloak that covered his head, then spread itself over his whole shoulder in such a manner, that, notwithstanding all the help that could be given him, and that I had, at first seeing it, cut the principal bough asunder with my knife, no remedy remained but he must throw off the upper garment, and appear in the under one, or waistcoat, with his head and face bare before all the spectators.

This is accounted great disgrace to a King, who always appears covered in public. However, he did not seem to be ruffled, nor was there anything particular in his countenance more than before, but with great composure, and in rather a low voice, he called twice, 'Who is the Shum of this district?' Unhappily he was not far off. A thin old man of sixty, and his son about thirty, came trotting, as their custom is, naked to their girdle, and stood before the King, who was, by this time, quite cloathed again. What had struck the old man's fancy, I know not, but he passed my horse laughing, and seemingly wonderfully content with himself. I could not help considering him as a type of mankind in general, never more confident and careless than when on the brink of destruction. The King asked if he was Shum of that place? he answered in the affirmative, and added, which was not asked of him, that the other was his son.

There is always near the King, when he marches, an officer called Kanitz Kitzera, the executioner of the camp; he has upon the tore of his saddle a quantity of thongs made of bull hide, rolled up very artificially; this is called the tarade. The King made a sign with his head, and another with his hand, without speaking; and two loops of the tarade were instantly thrown round the Shum and his son's neck, and they were both hoisted upon the same tree, the tarade cut, and the end made fast to a branch. They were both left hanging, but I thought so awkwardly, that they would not die for some minutes, and might surely have been saved had any one dared to cut them down; but fear had fallen upon every person who had not attended the King to Tigre.

Dr Johnson's Playfulness, 10 May 1773

James Boswell

He maintained the dignity and propriety of male succession, in opposition to the opinion of one of our friends [Bennet Langton] who had that day employed Mr Chambers to draw his will, devising his estate to his three sisters, in preference to a remote heir male. Johnson called them 'three *dowdies*', and said, with as high a spirit as the boldest Baron in the most perfect days of the feudal system, 'An ancient estate should always go to males. It is mighty foolish to let a stranger have it because he marries your daughter, and takes your name. As for an estate newly acquired by trade, you may give it, if you will, to the dog *Towser*, and let him keep his *own* name.'

I have known him at times exceedingly diverted at what seemed to others a very small sport. He now laughed immoderately, without any reason that we could perceive, at our friend's making his will; called him the *testator*, and added, 'I dare say, he thinks he has done a mighty thing. He won't stay till he gets home to his seat in the country, to produce this wonderful deed: he'll call up the landlord of the first inn on the road; and, after a suitable preface upon mortality and the uncertainty of life, will tell him that he should not delay making his will; and here, Sir, will he say, is my will, which I have just made, with the assistance of one of the ablest lawyers in the kingdom; and he will read it to him (laughing all the time). He believes he has made this will; but he did not make it: you, Chambers, made it for him. I trust you have had more conscience than to make him say, "being of sound understanding"; ha, ha, ha! I hope he has left me a legacy. I'd have his will turned into verse, like a ballad.'

In this playful manner did he run on, exulting in his own pleasantry, which certainly was not such as might be expected from the author of *The Rambler*, but which is here preserved, that my readers may be acquainted even with the slightest occasional characteristicks of so eminent a man.

Mr Chambers did not by any means relish this jocularity upon a matter of which *pars magna fuit* [he was no small part], and seemed impatient till he got rid of us. Johnson could not stop his merriment, but continued it all the way till we got without the Temple-gate. He then burst into such a fit of laughter, that he appeared to be almost in a convulsion; and, in order to support himself, laid hold of one of the posts at the side of the foot pavement, and sent forth peals so loud, that in the silence of the night his voice seemed to resound from Temple-bar to Fleet-ditch.

Christmas Day at New College, Oxford, 1773

James Woodforde

I dined in the Hall, and fourteen senior fellows with me. I invited the Warden to dine with us as is usual on this day, but his sister being here, could not. We had a very handsome dinner of my ordering, as I order dinner every day being Sub-Warden.

We had for dinner two fine cods boiled, with fried soles round them, and oyster sauce, a fine sirloin of beef roasted, some pease soup and an orange pudding, for the first course; for the second we had a lease of wild ducks roasted, a fore-quarter of lamb, and salad, and mince pies. We had a grace cup before the second course brought by the butler to the steward of the Hall who was Mr Adams a Senior Fellow, who got out of his place and came to my chair and then drank to me out of it, wishing me a merry Christmas. I then took it of him and drank, wishing him the same, and then it went round, three standing up all the time. From the high table the grace cup goes to the bachelors and scholars. After the second course there was a fine plum cake brought to the senior table as is usual on this day, which also goes to the bachelors after. After grace is said there is another grace cup to drink *omnibus Wickhamisis* [to all Wickhamists] which is drunk as the first, only the steward of hall does not attend the second grace cup. We dined at three o'clock and were an hour and a half at it. We all then went into the senior common room, where the Warden came to us and sat with us till prayers. The wine drunk by the senior fellows, domus pays for. Prayers this evening did not begin till 6 o'clock, at which I attended as did the Warden. I supped etc. in the Chequer. We had rabbits for supper roasted as is usual on this day. The Sub-Warden has one to himself; the bursars each one apiece; the senior fellows half a one each. The junior fellows a rabbit between three. N.B. Put on this day a new coat and waistcoat for the first time.

Garrick Plays Hamlet, September 1775

Georg Christoph Lichtenberg

David Garrick began his acting career with Richard III in 1741. His new naturalistic style earned him ecstatic public acclaim.

Now, my dear B., in case you should picture from what I have said a Garrick other than he is, you shall now see him through my eyes in a few scenes. Being so disposed, I will today take those from *Hamlet*, where the ghost appears to him . . .

Hamlet appears in a black dress, the only one in the whole court, alas! still worn for his poor father, who has been dead scarce a couple of months. Horatio and Marcellus, in uniform, are with him, and they are awaiting the ghost; Hamlet has folded his arms under his cloak and pulled his hat down over his eyes; it is a cold night and just twelve o'clock; the theatre is darkened, and the whole audience of some thousands are as quiet, and their faces as motionless, as though they were painted on the walls of the theatre; even from the farthest end of the playhouse one could hear a pin drop. Suddenly, as Hamlet moves towards the back of the stage slightly to the left and turns his back on the audience, Horatio starts, and saying: 'Look, my lord, it comes,' points to the right, where the ghost has already appeared and stands motionless, before anyone is aware of him. At these words Garrick turns sharply and at the same moment staggers back two or three paces with his knees giving way under him; his hat falls to the ground and both his arms, especially the left, are stretched out nearly to their full length, with the hands as high as his head, the right arm more bent and the hand lower, and the fingers apart; his mouth is open: thus he stands rooted to the spot, with legs apart, but no loss of dignity, supported by his friends, who are better acquainted with the apparition and fear lest he should collapse. His whole demeanour is so expressive of terror that it made my flesh creep even before he began to speak. The almost terror-struck silence of the audience, which preceded this appearance and filled one with a sense of insecurity, probably did much to enhance this effect. At last he speaks, not at the beginning, but at the end of a breath, with a trembling voice: 'Angels and ministers of grace defend us!' words which supply anything this scene may lack and make it one of the greatest and most terrible which will ever be played on any stage. The ghost beckons to him; I wish you could see him, with eyes fixed on the ghost, though he is speaking to his companions, freeing himself from their restraining hands, as they warn him not to follow and hold him back. But at length, when they have tried his patience too far, he turns his face towards them, tears himself with great violence from their grasp, and draws his sword on them with a swiftness that makes one shudder, saying: 'By Heaven! I'll make a ghost of him that lets me.' That is enough for them. Then he stands with his sword upon guard against the spectre, saying: 'Go on, I'll follow thee,' and the ghost goes off the stage. Hamlet still remains motionless, his sword held out so as to make him keep his distance, and at length, when the spectator can no longer see the ghost, he begins slowly to follow him, now standing still and then going on, with sword still upon guard, eyes fixed on the ghost, hair disordered, and out of breath, until he too is lost to sight. You can well imagine what loud applause accompanies this exit. It begins as soon as the ghost goes off the stage and lasts until Hamlet also disappears. What an amazing triumph it is.

The Gordon Riots, 8 June 1780

George Crabbe

Lord George Gordon (1751–1793) headed an anti-Catholic mob demanding repeal of the Catholic Relief Act. Nearly 500 people died in a week of rioting.

Yesterday, my own business being decided, I was at Westminster at about three o'clock in the afternoon, and saw the members go to the

House. The mob stopped many persons, but let all whom I saw pass, excepting Lord Sandwich, whom they treated roughly, broke his coach windows, cut his face, and turned him back. A guard of horse and foot were immediately sent for, who did no particular service, the mob increasing and defeating them.

I left Westminster when all the members, that were permitted, had entered the House and came home. In my way I met a resolute band of vile-looking fellows, ragged, dirty, and insolent, armed with clubs, going to join their companions. I since learned that there were eight or ten of these bodies in different parts of the City.

About seven o'clock in the evening I went out again. At Westminster the mob were few, and those quiet, and decent in appearance. I crossed St George's Fields, which were empty, and came home again by Blackfriars Bridge; and in going from thence to the Exchange, you pass the Old Bailey; and here it was that I saw the first scene of terror and riot ever presented to me. The new prison was a very large, strong, and beautiful building, having two wings, of which you can suppose the extent, when you consider their use; besides these, were the keeper's (Mr Akerman's) house, a strong intermediate work, and likewise other parts, of which I can give you no description. Akerman had in his custody four prisoners, taken in the riot; these the mob went to his house and demanded. He begged he might send to the sheriff, but this was not permitted. How he escaped, or where he is gone, I know not; but just at the time I speak of they set fire to his house, broke in, and threw every piece of furniture they could find into the street, firing them also in an instant. The engines came, but were only suffered to preserve the private houses near the prison.

As I was standing near the spot, there approached another body of men, I suppose 500, and Lord George Gordon in a coach, drawn by the mob towards Alderman Bull's, bowing as he passed along. He is a lively-looking young man in appearance, and nothing more, though just now the reigning hero.

By eight o'clock, Akerman's house was in flames. I went close to it, and never saw any thing so dreadful. The prison was, as I said, a remarkably strong building; but, determined to force it, they broke the gates with crows and other instruments, and climbed up the outside of the cell part, which joins the two great wings of the building, where the felons were confined; and I stood where I plainly saw their operations. They broke the roof, tore away the rafters, and having got ladders they descended. Not Orpheus himself had more courage or better luck; flames all around them, and a body of soldiers expected, they defied and laughed at all opposition.

The prisoners escaped. I stood and saw about twelve women and eight men ascend from their confinement to the open air, and they were conducted through the street in their chains. Three of these were to be hanged on Friday. You have no conception of the phrensy of the multitude. This being done, and Akerman's house now a mere shell of brickwork, they kept a store of flame there for other purposes. It became red-hot, and the doors and windows appeared like the entrance to so many volcanoes. With some difficulty they then fired the debtor's prison – broke the doors – and they, too, all made their escape.

Tired of the scene, I went home, and returned again at eleven o'clock at night. I met large bodies of horse and foot soldiers coming to guard the Bank, and some houses of Roman Catholics near it. Newgate was at this time open to all; anyone might get in, and, what was never the case before, anyone might get out. I did both; for the people were now chiefly lookers on. The mischief was done, and the doers of it gone to another part of the town.

But I must not omit what struck me most. About ten or twelve of the mob getting to the top of the debtors' prison, whilst it was burning, to halloo, they appeared rolled in black smoke mixed with sudden bursts of fire – like Milton's infernals, who were as familiar with flame as with each other. On comparing notes with my neighbours, I find I saw but a small part of the mischief. They say Lord Mansfield's house is now in flames.

Ranelagh, 12 June 1782

Carl Philipp Moritz

The pleasure gardens and Rotunda at Ranelagh in Chelsea were opened to the public in 1742 and closed in 1805.

Often as I had heard Ranelagh spoken of, I had yet formed only an imperfect idea of it. I supposed it to be a garden somewhat different from that of Vauxhall; but, in fact, I hardly knew what I thought of it. Yesterday evening I took a walk, in order to visit this famous place of amusement; but I missed my way and got to Chelsea; where I met a man with a wheelbarrow, who not only very civilly showed me the right road, but also conversed with me the whole of the distance, which we walked together. And finding, on inquiry, that I was a subject of the King of Prussia, he desired me, with much eagerness, to relate to him some anecdotes concerning that mighty monarch.

At length I arrived at Ranelagh; and having paid my half-crown, on entrance, I soon inquired for the garden door, and it was readily shown to me; when, to my infinite astonishment, I found myself in a poor, mean-looking, and ill-lighted garden, where I met but few people. I had not been here long before I was accosted by a young lady, who also was walking there, and who, without ceremony, offered me her arm, asking me why I walked thus solitarily? I now concluded, this could not possibly be the splendid, much-boasted Ranelagh; and so, seeing not far from me a number of people entering a door, I followed them, in hopes either to get out again, or to vary the scene.

But it is impossible to describe, or indeed to conceive, the effect it had on me, when, coming out of the gloom of the garden, I suddenly entered a round building, illuminated by many hundred lamps; the splendour and beauty of which surpassed everything of the kind I had ever seen before. Everything seemed here, to be round: above, there was a gallery, divided into boxes; and in one part of it an organ with a beautiful choir, from which issued both instrumental and vocal music. All around, under this gallery, are handsome painted boxes for those who wish to take refreshments: the floor was covered with mats; in the middle of which are four high black pillars; within which there are neat fire places for preparing tea, coffee, and punch: and all around also there are placed tables, set out with all kinds of refreshments. Within these four pillars, in a kind of magic rotundo, all the *beau-monde* of London move perpetually round and round.

I at first mixed with this immense concourse of people, of all sexes, ages, countries, and characters: and I must confess, that the incessant change of faces, the far greater number of which were strikingly beautiful, together with the illumination, the extent and majestic splendour of the place, with the continued sound of the music, makes an inconceivably delightful impression on the imagination; and I take the liberty to add, that, on seeing it now for the first time, I felt pretty nearly the same sensations, that I remember to have felt, when, in early youth, I first read the Fairy Tales.

Being however at length tired of the crowd, and being tired also, with always moving round and round in a circle, I sat myself down in one of the boxes, in order to take some refreshment, and was now contemplating at my ease, this prodigious collection and crowd of an happy, chearful world, who were here enjoying themselves devoid of care, when a waiter very civilly asked me what refreshment I wished to have, and in a few moments returned with what I asked for. To my astonishment, he would accept no money for these refreshments; which I could not comprehend, till he told me that everything was included in the half-crown I had paid at the door; and that I had only to command, if I wished for anything more; but that, if I pleased, I might give him as a present a trifling *douceur*. This I gave him with pleasure, as I could not help fancying, I was hardly entitled to so much civility and good attendance for one single half-crown.

I now went up into the gallery, and seated myself in one of the boxes there: and from thence becoming, all at once, a grave and moralizing spectator, I looked down on the concourse of people, who were still moving round and round in the fairy circle; and then I could easily distinguish several stars, and other orders, of knighthood; French queues and bags contrasted with plain English heads of hair, or professional wigs; old age and youth, nobility and commonalty, all passing each other in the motley swarm. An Englishman who joined me, during this my reverie, pointed out to me on my inquiring, princes, and lords with their dazzling stars; with which they eclipsed the less brilliant part of the company.

Here some moved round in an eternal circle to see and be seen; there a groupe of eager connoisseurs had placed themselves before the orchestra and were feasting their ears, while others, at the well-supplied tables, were regaling the parched roofs of their mouths, in a more substantial manner, and again others like myself were sitting alone, in the corner of a box in the gallery, making their remarks and reflexions on so interesting a scene.

I now and then indulged myself in the pleasure of exchanging, for some minutes, all this magnificence and splendour, for the gloom of the garden, in order to renew the pleasing surprize I experienced on my first entering the building. Thus I spent here some hours in the night, in a continual variation of entertainment; when the crowd now all at once began to lessen, and I also took a coach and drove home.

Midshipman Gardner (aged 12) in Action against the French, 20 October 1782

James Anthony Gardner

Owing to the light winds and the enemy repeatedly hauling up and then bearing away, it was near 6 p.m. before he formed his line. A three-decker (supposed to be the *Royal Louis*) leading his van began the action by firing into the *Goliath*, who led ours. The action continued from 6 p.m. until ¾ past 10; the van and rear chiefly engaged; the centre had little to do. The enemy's centre extended to our rear-most ship, so that eleven or twelve of them (the whole of their rear) never fired a shot. We had four killed and sixteen wounded; among the former Mr Robert Sturges, midshipman doing duty as mate, a gentleman highly respected and lamented by every officer and man on board. I was placed with another youngster under his care, and he took the greatest pains to teach us our duty. He was as brave a fellow as ever lived, and when his thigh was nearly shot off by the hip, he cheered the men when dying. It was a spent shot that killed him, and weighed 28 pounds; and what was remarkable, it took off at the same time the leg of a pig in the sty under the forecastle.

I had a very narrow escape while standing on the quarter deck with Captain Forrester of the marines. The first lieutenant (the late Admiral Alexander Fraser) came up to us, and while speaking a shot passed between us and stuck on the larboard side of the quarter deck. We were very close at the time, so that it could only have been a few inches from us. It knocked the speaking-trumpet out of Fraser's hand, and seemed to have electrified Captain Forrester and myself. The shot was cut out and weighed either 12 or 18 pounds – I forget which. Our rigging fore and aft was cut to pieces; the booms and boats also, and every timber-head on the forecastle, with the sheet and spare anchor stocks, were shot away, and the fluke of the latter. Our side, from the foremost gun to the after, was like a riddle, and it was astonishing that we had not more killed and wounded. Several shot-holes were under water, and our worthy old carpenter (Mr Cock) had very near been killed in the wing, and was knocked down by a splinter, but not materially hurt. The enemy set off in the night and could only be seen from the masthead in the morning. It was supposed they went for Cadiz.

A curious circumstance took place during the action. Two of the boys who had gone down for powder fell out in consequence of one attempting to take the box from the other, when a regular fight took place. It was laughable to see them boxing on the larboard side, and the ship in hot action on the starboard. One of our poor fellows was cut in two by a double-headed shot on the main deck, and the lining of his stomach (about the size of a pancake) stuck on the side of the launch, which was stowed amidships on the main deck with the sheep inside. The butcher who had the care of them, observing what was on the side of the boat, began to scrape it off with his nails, saying, 'Who the devil would have thought the fellow's paunch would have stuck so? I'm damned if I don't think it's glued on!'

The First Manned Flight in England, 15 September 1784

Vincent Lunardi

Lunardi, secretary to the Neapolitan ambassador, feared that the crowd would destroy his balloon if kept waiting too long, as they had that of the Frenchman de Moret the previous month. He made his ascent from the Artillery Ground and landed at South Mimms, Hertfordshire, to disembark his cat, which had suffered from the cold.

A little before two o'clock on Wednesday, Mr Biggin and myself were prepared for our expedition. His attention was allotted to the philosophical experiments and observations, mine to the conduct of the Machine, and the use of the vertical cars, in depressing the Balloon at pleasure.

The impatience of the multitude, made it unadvisable to proceed in filling the Balloon so as to give it the force it was intended to have: the process being therefore stopped, I retired for a few minutes to recollect and refresh myself previous to my departure, when a servant brought me a sudden account that by the falling of one of the masts which had been erected for the purpose of suspending the Balloon while filling, it had received a material injury which might possibly retard, if not prevent my voyage. I hastened instantaneously from the Armoury House, where I then was, and though I was happy to find that the accident was prevented by giving the falling fixture an opposite direction, yet I was so extremely shocked at the danger that menaced me, and the word I had received, that I did not possess myself or recover the effect of my apprehension during the remainder of my stay on the earth. The consequence was, that in the convulsion of my ideas, I forgot to supply myself with those instruments of observation which had been appointed for the voyage. On balancing the rising force of the Balloon, it was supposed incapable of taking up Mr Biggin with me, (whether he felt the most regret in relinquishing his design, or I in being deprived of his company it may be difficult to determine) but we were before a Tribunal, where an immediate decision was necessary, for hesitation and delay would have been construed into guilt, and the displeasure impending over us would have been fatal, if in one moment he had not the heroism to leave the gallery, and I the resolution to go alone. I now determined on my immediate ascension, being assured by the dread of any accident which might consign me and my Balloon to the fury of the populace, whose impatience had wrought them up to a degree of ferment. An affecting, because unpremeditated testimony of approbation and interest in my fate, was here given. The Prince of Wales, and the whole surrounding assembly, almost at one instant, took off their hats, hailed my resolution, and expressed the kindest and most cordial wishes for my safety and success. At five minutes after two, the last gun was fired, the cords divided, and the Balloon rose, the company returning my signals of adieu with the most unfeigned acclamations and applauses. The effect was that of a miracle on the multitudes which surrounded the place; and they passed from incredulity and menace into the most extravagant expressions of approbation and joy.

At the height of twenty yards, the Balloon was a little depressed by the wind, which had a fine effect; it held me over the ground for a few seconds, and seemed to pause majestically before its departure.

On discharging a part of the ballast, it ascended to the height of two hundred yards. As a multitude lay before me of a hundred and fifty thousand people, who had not seen my ascent from the ground, I had recourse to every stratagem to let them know I was in the gallery, and they literally rent the air with their acclamations and applause. In these stratagems I devoted my flag, and worked my oars, one of which was immediately broken, and fell from me, a pigeon too escaped, which, with a dog, and cat, were the only companions of my excursion.

When the thermometer had fallen from 68° to 61° I perceived a great difference in the temperature of the air. I became very cold and found it necessary to take a few glasses of wine. I likewise ate the leg of a chicken, but my bread and other provisions had been rendered useless by being mixed with the sand, which I carried as ballast.

When the thermometer was at fifty, the effect of the atmosphere and the combination of circumstances around produced a calm delight, which is inexpressible, and which no situation on earth could give. The stillness, extent, and magnificence of the scene rendered it highly awful. My horizon seemed a perfect circle; the terminating line several hundred miles in circumference. This I conjectured from the view of London; the extreme points of which formed an angle of only a few degrees. It was so reduced on the great scale before me, that I can find no simile to convey an idea of it. I could distinguish St Paul's and other churches from the houses. I saw the streets as lines, all animated with beings, whom I knew to be men and women, but which I should otherwise have had a difficulty in describing. It was an enormous bee-hive, but the industry of it was suspended. All the moving mass seemed to have no object but myself, and the transition from the suspicion, and perhaps contempt of the preceding hour, to the affectionate transport, admiration and glory of the present moment, was not without its effect on my mind.

Louis XVI and the French Royal Family, Prisoners at the Tuileries, 4 January 1790

Arthur Young

Louis attempted unsuccessfully to escape from Paris with his family in June 1791, and was guillotined on 21 January 1793, and the Dauphin, Louis-Charles, died in prison aged ten in 1795.

After breakfast walk in the gardens of the Tuileries, where there is the most extraordinary sight that either French or English eyes could ever behold at Paris. The King walking with six grenadiers of the *milice bourgeoise*, with an officer or two of his household and a page. The doors of the gardens are kept shut in respect to him, in order to exclude everybody but deputies or those who have admission tickets. When he entered the palace the doors of the gardens were thrown open for all without distinction, though the Queen was still walking with a lady of her court. She also was attended so closely by the *gardes bourgeoises*, that she could not speak, but in a low voice, without being heard by them. A mob followed her talking very loud, and paying no other apparent respect than that of taking off their hats wherever she passed, which was indeed more than I expected. Her Majesty does not appear to be in health; she seems to be much affected and shows it in her face; but the King is as plump as ease can render him. By his orders, there is a little garden railed off for the Dauphin to amuse himself in, and a small room is built in it to retire to in case of rain; here he was at work with his little hoe and rake, but not without a guard of two grenadiers. He is a very pretty good-natured-looking boy of five or six years old, with an agreeable countenance; wherever he goes, all hats are taken off to him, which I was glad to observe. All the family being kept thus close prisoners (for such they are in effect) afford, at first view, a shocking spectacle; and is really so if the act were not absolutely necessary to effect the revolution.

247

Chateaubriand Lands in the New World; Chesapeake Bay, 1791

François-René de Chateaubriand

Chateaubriand left France because of the Revolution, and sailed for America in the spring of 1791.

We walked towards the nearest house. Woods of balsam trees and Virginian cedars, mocking-birds, and cardinal tanagers proclaimed by their appearance and shade, their song and colour, that we were in a new clime. The house, which we reached after half an hour, was a cross between an English farmhouse and a West Indian hut. Herds of European cows were grazing in pastures surrounded by fences, on which striped squirrels were playing. Blacks were sawing up logs of wood, whites tending tobacco plants. A Negress of thirteen or fourteen, practically naked and singularly beautiful, opened the gate to us like a young Night. We bought some cakes of Indian corn, chickens, eggs, and milk, and returned to the ship with our demijohns and baskets. I gave my silk handkerchief to the little African girl: it was a slave who welcomed me to the soil of liberty.

Marie-Antoinette at the Opera, July 1792

Grace Elliott

After the 20th of June, the people who wished well to the King and Queen were desirous that her Majesty should sometimes appear in public, accompanied by the Dauphin, a most interesting, beautiful child, and her charming daughter, Madame Royale. In consequence of this she went to the Comédie Italienne with her children, Madame Elizabeth, the King's sister, and Madame Tourzelle, governess to the royal children. This was the very last time on which her Majesty appeared in public. I was there in my own box, nearly opposite the Queen's; and as she was so much more interesting than the play, I never took my eyes off her and her family. The opera which was given was *Les Evénemens Imprévus*, and Madame Dugazon played the *soubrette*. Her Majesty, from her first entering the house, seemed distressed. She was overcome even by the applause, and I saw her several times wipe the tears from her eyes.

The little Dauphin, who sat on her knee the whole night, seemed anxious to know the cause of his unfortunate mother's tears. She seemed to soothe him, and the audience appeared well disposed, and to feel for the cruel situation of their beautiful Queen. In one of the acts a duet is sung by the *soubrette* and the *valet*, where Madame Dugazon says: 'Ah! comme j'aime ma maîtresse'. As she looked particularly at the Queen at the moment she said this, some Jacobins, who had come into the playhouse, leapt upon the stage, and if the actors had not hid Madame Dugazon, they would have murdered her. They hurried the poor Queen and family out of the house, and it was all the Guards could do to get them safe into their carriages.

A Trip to Paris, July–August 1792

Richard Twiss

In every one of the towns between Calais and Paris a full-grown tree (generally a poplar) has been planted in the market place, with many of its boughs and leaves; these last being withered, it makes but a dismal appearance; on the top of this tree or pole is a red woollen or cotton night-cap, which is called the *Cap of Liberty*, with streamers about the pole, or red, blue and white ribbands. I saw several statues of saints, both within and without the churches (and in Paris likewise) with similar caps, and several crucifixes with the national cockade of ribbands tied to the left arm of the image on the cross, but not one with the cockade in its proper place; the reason of which I know not.

The churches in Paris are not much frequented on the weekdays, at present; I found a few old women on their knees in some of them, hearing mass; and, at the same time, at the other end of one of these churches commissaries were sitting and entering the names of volunteers for the army. The iron rails in the churches which part the choir from the nave, and also those which encompass chapels and tombs, are all ordered to be converted into heads for pikes.

Hitherto cockades of silk had been worn, the *aristocrats* wore such as were of a paler blue and red than those worn by the *democrats*, and the former were even distinguished by their carriages, on which a cloud was painted upon the arms, which entirely obliterated them (of these I saw above thirty in the evening *promenade* in the *Bois de Boulogne*), but on the 30th of July, every person was compelled by the people to wear a linen cockade, without any distinction in the red and blue colours.

I went once to Versailles; there is hardly anything in the palace but the bare walls, a very few of the looking-glasses, tapestry, and large pictures remaining, as it has now been near two years uninhabited. I crossed the great canal on foot; there was not a drop of water in it.

I went several times to the National Assembly; the *Tribunes*, or *Galleries* (of which there are three) entered warmly, by applauses and by murmurs and hisses, into the affairs which were treated of.

All the coats of arms which formerly decorated the gates of *Hôtels* are taken away, and even seals are at present engraven with cyphers only. The *Chevaliers de St Louis* still continue to wear the cross, or the ribband, at the button-hole; all other orders of knighthood are abolished. No liveries are worn by servants, that badge of slavery is likewise abolished; and also all corporation companies, as well as every other monopolizing society, and there are no longer any *Royal* tobacco or salt shops.

Books of all sorts are printed without any *approbation* or *privilege*. Many are exposed on stalls, which are very improper for the public eye. One of them was called the *Private Life of the Queen*, in two volumes, with obscene prints. The book itself is contemptible and disgusting, and might as well have been called *The Woman of Pleasure*. Of books of this sort I saw above thirty, with plates.

The common people are in general much better clothed than they were before the Revolution, which may be ascribed to their not being so grievously taxed as they were ... All those ornaments, which three years ago were worn of silver, are now of gold. All the women of lower class, even those who sit behind green-stalls, etc., wear gold ear-rings, with large drops, some of which cost two or three *louis*, and necklaces of the same. Many of the men wear plain gold earrings: those worn by officers and other gentlemen are usually as large as a half-crown piece. Even children of two years old have small gold drops in their ears.

The Execution of Louis XVI, 21 January 1793

Report by a Priest of His Majesty's Household

Henry Essex Edgeworth de Firmont

The unfortunate Louis XVI, foreseeing to what lengths the malice of his enemies was likely to go, and resolved to be prepared at all events, cast his eyes upon me, to assist him in his last moments, if condemned to die. He would not make any application to the ruling party, nor even mention my name without my consent. The message he sent me was touching beyond expression, and worded in a manner which I shall never forget. A King, though in chains, had a right to command, but he commanded not. My attendance was requested merely *as a pledge of my attachment for him, and as a favour, which he hoped I would not refuse. But as the service was likely to be attended with some danger for me, he dared not to insist, and only prayed (in case I deemed the danger to be too great) to point out to him a clergyman worthy of his confidence, but less known than I was myself, leaving the person absolutely to my choice* . . . Being obliged to take my party upon the spot, I resolved to comply with what appeared to be at that moment the call of Almighty God; and committing to His providence all the rest, I made answer to the most unfortunate of Kings, that whether he lived or died, I would be his friend to the last . . .

The King finding himself seated in the carriage, where he could neither speak to me nor be spoken to without witness, kept a profound silence. I presented him with my breviary, the only book I had with me, and he seemed to accept it with pleasure: he appeared anxious that I should point out to him the psalms that were most suited to his situation, and he recited them attentively with me. The *gendarmes*, without speaking, seemed astonished and confounded at the tranquil piety of their monarch, to whom they doubtless never had before approached so near.

The procession lasted almost two hours; the streets were lined with citizens, all armed, some with pikes and some with guns, and the carriage was surrounded by a body of troops, formed of the most desperate people of Paris. As another precaution, they had placed before the horses a number of drums, intended to drown any noise or murmur in favour of the King; but how could they be heard? Nobody appeared either at the doors or windows, and in the street nothing was to be seen, but armed citizens – citizens, all rushing towards the commission of a crime, which perhaps they detested in their hearts.

The carriage proceeded thus in silence to the Place de Louis XV, and stopped in the middle of a large space that had been left round the scaffold: this space was surrounded with cannon, and beyond, an armed multitude extended as far as the eye could reach. As soon as the King perceived that the carriage stopped, he turned and whispered to me, 'We are arrived, if I mistake not.' My silence answered that we were. One of the guards came to open the carriage door, and the *gendarmes* would have jumped out, but the King stopped them, and leaning his arm on my knee, 'Gentlemen,' said he, with the tone of majesty, 'I recommend to you this good man; take care that after my death no insult be offered to him – I charge you to prevent it.' . . . As soon as the King had left the carriage, three guards surrounded him, and would have taken off his clothes, but he repulsed them with haughtiness: he undressed himself, untied his neckcloth, opened his shirt, and arranged it himself. The guards, whom the determined countenance of the King had for a moment disconcerted, seemed to recover their audacity. They surrounded him again, and would have seized his hands. 'What are you attempting?' said the King, drawing back his hands. 'To bind you,' answered the wretches. 'To bind *me*,' said the King, with an indignant air. 'No! I shall never consent to that: do what you have been ordered, but you shall never bind me . . .'

The path leading to the scaffold was extremely rough and difficult to pass; the King was obliged to lean on my arm, and from the slowness with which he proceeded, I feared for a moment that his courage might fail; but what was my astonishment, when arrived at the last step, I felt that he suddenly let go my arm, and I saw him cross with a firm foot the breadth of the whole scaffold; silence, by his look alone, fifteen or twenty drums that were placed opposite to me; and in a voice so loud, that it must have been heard at the Pont Tournant, I heard him pronounce distinctly these memorable words: '*I die innocent of all the crimes laid to my charge; I pardon those who have occasioned my death; and I pray to God that the blood you are going to shed may never be visited on France.*'

He was proceeding, when a man on horseback, in the national

uniform, and with a ferocious cry, ordered the drums to beat. Many voices were at the same time heard encouraging the executioners. They seemed reanimated themselves, in seizing with violence the most virtuous of Kings, they dragged him under the axe of the guillotine, which with one stroke severed his head from his body. All this passed in a moment. The youngest of the guards, who seemed about eighteen, immediately seized the head, and showed it to the people as he walked round the scaffold; he accompanied this monstrous ceremony with the most atrocious and indecent gestures. At first an awful silence prevailed; at length some cries of 'Vive la République!' were heard. By degrees the voices multiplied, and in less than ten minutes this cry, a thousand times repeated, became the universal shout of the multitude, and every hat was in the air.

The Revolutionary Tribunal, Paris, October 1793

J. G. Millingen

In the centre of the hall, under a statue of justice, holding scales in one hand, and a sword in the other, with the book of laws by her side, sat Dumas, the President, with the other judges. Under them were seated the public accuser, Fouquier-Tinville, and his scribes. Three coloured ostrich plumes waved over their turned up hats, *à la Henri IV*, and they wore a tri-coloured scarf. To the right were benches on which the accused were placed in several rows, and *gendarmes*, with carbines and fixed bayonets by their sides. To the left was the jury.

Never can I forget the mournful appearance of these funereal processions to the place of execution. The march was opened by a detachment of mounted *gendarmes* – the carts followed; they were the same carts as those that are used in Paris for carrying wood; four boards were placed across them for seats, and on each board sat two, and sometimes three victims; their hands were tied behind their backs, and the constant jolting of the cart made them nod their heads up and down, to the great amusement of the spectators. On the front of the cart stood Samson, the executioner, or one of his sons or assistants; *gendarmes* on foot marched by the side; then followed a hackney-coach, in which was the *Rapporteur* and his clerk, whose duty it was to witness the execution, and then return to Fouquier-Tinville, the *Accusateur Publique*, to report the execution of what they called the law.

The process of execution was also a sad and heart-rending spectacle. In the middle of the Place de la Révolution was erected a guillotine, in front of a colossal statue of Liberty, represented seated on a rock, a Phrygian cap on her head, a spear in her hand, the other reposing on a shield. On one side of the scaffold were drawn out a sufficient number of carts, with large baskets painted red, to receive the heads and bodies of the victims. Those bearing the condemned moved on slowly to the foot of the guillotine; the culprits were led out in turn, and, if necessary, supported by two of the executioner's valets, as they were formerly called, but now denominated *élèves de l'Executeur des hautes oeuvres de la justice*; but their assistance was rarely required. Most of these unfortunates ascended the scaffold with a determined step – many of them looked up firmly on the menacing instrument of death, beholding for the last time the rays of the glorious sun, beaming on the polished axe; and I have seen some young men actually dance a few steps before they went up to be strapped to the perpendicular plane, which was then tilted to a horizontal plane in a moment, and ran on the grooves until the neck was secured and closed in by a moving board, when the head passed through what was called, in derision, *la lunette républicaine*; the weighty knife was then dropped with a heavy fall; and, with incredible dexterity and rapidity, two executioners tossed the body into the basket, while another threw the head after it.

Nelson Loses an Arm, Santa Cruz, Tenerife, 25 June 1797

William Hoste

At 1.00 a.m. commenced one of the heaviest cannonading I ever was witness to from the town upon our boats, likewise a very heavy fire of musketry, which continued without intermission for the space of four hours. At 2.00, Admiral Lord Nelson returned on board, being dreadfully wounded in the right arm with a grape-shot. I leave you to judge of my situation when I beheld our boat approach with him, who I may say has been a second father to me, his right arm dangling by his side, while with the other he helped himself to jump up the ship's side, and with a spirit that astonished everyone, told the surgeon to get his instruments ready, for he knew he must lose his arm, and that the sooner it was off the better. He underwent the amputation with the same firmness and courage that have always marked his character, and I am happy to say is now in a fair way of recovery.

The Battle of the Nile, 1 August 1798
By one of the Gun Crew of the Goliath

John Nichol

The Nile was one of Nelson's greatest victories. He attacked and destroyed a French squadron in Abu Qir Bay, near Alexandria, isolating Napoleon in Egypt and securing control of the Mediterranean.

The sun was just setting as we went into the bay, and a red and fiery sun it was. I would, if I had had my choice, been on the deck; there I would have seen what was passing, and the time would not have hung so heavy; but every man does his duty with spirit, whether his station be in the slaughter-house or in the magazine. (The seamen call the lower deck, near the main-mast, 'the slaughter-house', as it is amidships, and the enemy aim their fire principally at the body of the ship.) My station was in the powder-magazine with the gunner. As we entered the bay we stripped to our trousers, opened our ports, cleared, and every ship we passed gave them a broadside and three cheers. Any information we got was from the boys and women who carried the powder. They behaved as well as the men, and got a present for their bravery from the Grand Signior. When the French Admiral's ship blew up, the *Goliath* got such a shake we thought the after-part of her had blown up until the boys told us what it was. They brought us every now and then the cheering news of another French ship having struck [surrendered], and we answered the cheers on deck with heartfelt joy. In the heat of the action, a shot came right into the magazine, but did no harm, as the carpenters plugged it up, and stopped the water that was rushing in. I was much indebted to the gunner's wife, who gave her husband and me a drink of wine every now and then, which lessened our fatigue much. There were some of the women wounded, and one woman belonging to Leith died of her wounds, and was buried on a small island in the bay. One woman bore a son in the heat of the action; she belonged to Edinburgh.

When we ceased firing, I went on deck to view the state of the fleets, and an awful sight it was. The whole bay was covered with dead bodies, mangled, wounded, and scorched, not a bit of clothes on them except their trousers. There were a number of French, belonging to the French Admiral's ship, the *L'Orient*, who had swam to the *Goliath*, and were cowering under her forecastle. Poor fellows! they were brought on board, and Captain Foley ordered them down to the steward's room, to get provisions and clothing. One thing I observed in these Frenchmen quite different from anything I had before observed. In the American War, when we took a French ship, the *Duke de Chartres*, the prisoners were as merry as if they had taken us, only saying, '*Fortune de guerre* – you take me today, I take you tomorrow.' Those we now had on board were thankful for our kindness, but were sullen and as downcast as if each had lost a ship of his own.

The only incidents I heard of are two. One lad who was stationed by a salt-box, on which he sat to give out cartridges, and keep the lid close – it is a trying berth – when asked for a cartridge, he gave none, yet he sat upright; his eyes were open. One of the men gave him a push; he fell all his length on the deck. There was not a blemish on his body, yet he was quite dead, and was thrown overboard. The other, a lad who had the match in his hand to fire his gun. In the act of applying it, a shot took off his arm; it hung by a small piece of skin. The match fell to the deck. He looked to his arm, and seeing what had happened, seized the match in his left hand, and fired off the gun before he went to the cockpit to have it dressed. They were in our mess, or I might never have heard of it. Two of the mess were killed, and I knew not of it until the day after. Thus terminated the glorious first of August, the busiest night in my life.

Beggars, a Leech Gatherer, and Daffodils:
The Wordsworths at Grasmere, 1800–1802

Dorothy Wordsworth

On Tuesday, May 27th [1800], a very tall woman, tall much beyond the measure of tall women, called at the door. She had on a very long brown cloak, and a very white cap without Bonnet – her face was excessively brown, but it had plainly once been fair. She led a little bare-footed child about 2 years old by the hand and said her husband who was a tinker was gone before with the other children. I gave her a piece of Bread. Afterwards on my road to Ambleside, beside the Bridge at Rydale, I saw her husband sitting by the roadside, his two asses feeding beside him and the two young children at play upon the grass. The man did not beg. I passed on and about ¼ of a mile further I saw two boys before me, one about 10 the other about 8 years old at play chasing a butterfly. They were wild figures, not very ragged, but without shoes and stockings; the hat of the elder was wreathed round with yellow flowers, the younger whose hat was only a rimless crown, had stuck it round with laurel leaves. They continued at play till I drew very near and then they addressed me with the Beggars' cant and the whining voice of sorrow. I said I served your mother this morning. (The Boys were so like the woman who had called at the door that I could not be mistaken.) O! says the elder you could not serve my mother for she's dead and my father's on at the next town – he's a potter. I persisted in my assertion and that I would give them nothing. Says the elder Come, let's away, and away they flew like lightning. They had however sauntered so long in their road that they did not reach Ambleside before me, and I saw them go up to Matthew Harrison's house with their wallet upon the elder's shoulder, and creeping with a Beggar's complaining foot. On my return through Ambleside I met in the street the mother driving her asses; in the two Panniers of one of which were the two little children whom she was chiding and threatening with a wand which she used to drive on her asses, while the little things hung in wantonness over the Pannier's edge. The woman had told me in the morning that she was of Scotland, which her accent fully proved, but that she had lived (I think at Wigton), that they could not keep a house and so they travelled . . .

Friday, 3rd October. When Wm and I returned from accompanying Jones we met an old man almost double, he had on a coat thrown over his shoulders above his waistcoat and coat. Under this he carried a bundle and had an apron on and a night cap. His face was interesting. He had dark eyes and a long nose. John who afterwards met him at Wythburn took him for a Jew. He was of Scotch parents but had been born in the army. He had had a wife 'and a good woman and it pleased God to bless us with ten children'. All these were dead but one of whom he had not heard for many years, a sailor. His trade was to gather leeches, but now leeches are scarce and he had not strength for it. He lived by begging and was making his way to Carlisle where he should buy a few godly books to sell. He said leeches were very scarce partly owing to this dry season, but many years they have been scarce – he supposed it owing to their being much sought after, that they did not breed fast, and were of slow growth. Leeches were formerly 2/6 [per] 100; they are now 30/-. He had been hurt in driving a cart, his leg broke his body driven over his skull fractured. He felt no pain till he recovered from his first insensibility. 'It was then late in the evening, when the light was just going away.' . . .

Tuesday, 24th November, 1801. A rainy morning. We all were well except that my head ached a little and I took my Breakfast in bed. I read a little of Chaucer, prepared the goose for dinner, and then we all walked out. I was obliged to return for my fur tippet and Spenser it was so cold. We had intended going to Easedale but we shaped our course to Mr Gell's cottage. It was very windy and we heard the wind everywhere about us as we went along the Lane but the walls sheltered us. John Green's house looked pretty under Silver How. As we were going along we were stopped at once, at the distance perhaps of 50 yards from our favorite Birch tree. It was yielding to the gusty wind with all its tender twigs, the sun shone upon it and it glanced in the wind like a flying sunshiny shower. It was a tree in shape with stem and branches but it was like a Spirit of water. The sun went in and it resumed its purplish appearance the twigs still yielding to the wind but not so visibly to us. The other Birch trees that were near it looked bright and chearful, but it was a creature by its own self among them . . .

Thursday, 15th April, 1802. It was a threatening misty morning –

but mild. We set off after dinner from Eusemere. Mrs Clarkson went a short way with us but turned back. The wind was furious and we thought we must have returned. We first rested in the large Boat-house, then under a furze Bush opposite Mr Clarkson's. Saw the plough going in the field. The wind seized our breath, the Lake was rough. There was a Boat by itself floating in the middle of the Bay below Water Millock. We rested again in the Water Millock Lane. The hawthorns are black and green, the birches here and there greenish but there is yet more of purple to be seen on the Twigs. We got over into a field to avoid some cows – people working, a few primroses by the roadside, wood-sorrel flower, the anemone, scentless violets, strawberries, and that starry yellow flower which Mrs C. calls pile wort. When we were in the woods beyond Gowbarrow park we saw a few daffodils close to the water side. We fancied that the lake had floated the seeds ashore and that the little colony had so sprung up. But as we went along there were more and yet more and at last under the boughs of the trees, we saw that there was a long belt of them along the shore, about the breadth of a country turnpike road. I never saw daffodils so beautiful they grew among the mossy stones about and about them, some rested their heads upon these stones as on a pillow for weariness and the rest tossed and reeled and danced and seemed as if they verily laughed with the wind that blew upon them over the lake, they looked so gay ever glancing ever changing. This wind blew directly over the lake to them. There was here and there a little knot and a few stragglers a few yards higher up but they were so few as not to disturb the simplicity and unity and life of that one busy highway. We rested again and again. The Bays were stormy, and we heard the waves at different distances and in the middle of the water like the sea.

Nelson Turns a Blind Eye, Copenhagen, 2 April 1801

Colonel William Stewart

At Copenhagen Nelson was second-in-command to the elderly Admiral Sir Hyde Parker. An hour after disregarding Parker's signal, Nelson had overcome the Danish resistance and completed his victory.

Lord Nelson was at this time, as he had been during the whole Action, walking the starboard side of the quarter-deck; sometimes much animated, and at others heroically fine in his observations. A shot through the mainmast knocked a few splinters about us. He observed to me, with a smile, 'It is warm work, and this day may be the last to any of us at a moment'; and then stopping short at the gangway, he used an expression never to be erased from my memory, and said with emotion, 'but mark you, I would not be elsewhere for thousands.' When the signal, No. 39, was made, the Signal Lieutenant reported it to him. He continued his walk, and did not appear to take notice of it. The Lieutenant meeting his Lordship at the next turn asked, 'whether he should repeat it?' Lord Nelson answered, 'No, acknowledge it.' On the Officer returning to the poop, his Lordship called after him, 'Is No. 16 [the signal for close action] still hoisted?' The Lieutenant answering in the affirmative, Lord Nelson said, 'Mind you keep it so.' He now walked the deck considerably agitated, which was always known by his moving the stump of his right arm. After a turn or two, he said to me, in a quick manner, 'Do you know what's shown on board of the Commander-in-Chief, No. 39?' On asking him what that meant, he answered, 'Why, to leave off Action.' 'Leave off Action!' he repeated, and then added, with a shrug, 'Now, damn me if I do.' He also observed, I believe, to Captain Foley, 'You know, Foley, I have only one eye — I have a right to be blind sometimes', and then with an archness peculiar to his character, putting the glass to his blind eye, he exclaimed, 'I really do not see the signal.'

Childsplay in the Lake District, 27 September 1802

Samuel Taylor Coleridge

Hartley Coleridge was six in 1802, and Derwent two.

The river is full, and Lodore [a waterfall] is full, and silver-fillets come out of clouds and glitter in every ravine of all the mountains; and the hail lies like snow, upon their tops, and the impetuous gusts from Borrowdale snatch the water up high, and continually at the bottom of the lake it is not distinguishable from snow slanting before the wind – and under this seeming snow-drift the sunshine *gleams*, and over all the nether half of the Lake it is *bright* and *dazzles*, a cauldron of melted silver boiling! It is in very truth a sunny, misty, cloudy, dazzling, howling, omniform day, and I have been looking at as pretty a sight as a father's eyes could well see – Hartley and little Derwent running in the green where the gusts blow most madly, both with their hair floating and tossing, a miniature of the agitated trees, below which they were playing, inebriate both with the pleasure – Hartley whirling round for joy, Derwent eddying, half-willingly, half by the force of the gust, – driven backward, struggling forward, and shouting his little hymn of joy.

The Morning of Trafalgar: 10 a.m., 21 October 1805

Report of a Midshipman of the Neptune

Midshipman Badcock

Trafalgar, the decisive naval engagement of the Napoleonic wars, was fought to the west of Cadiz. Twenty of the thirty-three French and Spanish were destroyed or captured; none of the twenty-seven British ships was lost.

At this period the enemy were forming their double line in the shape of a crescent. It was a beautiful sight when the line was completed: their broadsides turned towards us showing their iron teeth, and now and then trying the range of a shot to ascertain the distance, that they might, the moment we came within point-blank (about six hundred yards) open their fire upon our van ships – no doubt with the hope of dismasting some of our leading vessels before they could close and break their line.

Some of the enemy's ships were painted like ourselves – with double yellow sides, some with a broad single red or yellow streak, others all black, and the noble *Santissima Trinidada* (138) [guns] with four distinct lines of red, with a white ribbon between them, made her seem to be a superb man-of-war, which, indeed, she was. Her appearance was imposing, her head splendidly ornamented with a colossal group of figures, painted white, representing the

Holy Trinity, from which she took her name. This magnificent ship was destined to be our opponent. She was lying to under topsails, top-gallant sails, royals, jib, and spanker; her courses were hauled up, and her lofty, towering sails looked beautiful, peering through the smoke as she awaited the onset. The flags of France and Spain, both handsome, chequered the line, waving defiance to that of Britain.

In our fleet Union Jacks and ensigns were made fast to the fore and fore-topmast-stays, as well as to the mizen rigging, besides one at the peak, in order that we might not mistake each other in the smoke, and to show the enemy our determination to conquer. Towards eleven our two lines were better formed, but still there existed long gaps in Vice-Admiral Collingwood's division. Lord Nelson's van was strong: three three-deckers – *Victory*, *Téméraire*, and *Neptune* – and four seventy-fours, their jib-booms nearly over the others' taffrails. The bands playing 'God Save the King', 'Rule Britannia', and 'Britons, Strike Home', the crews stationed on the forecastles of the different ships, cheering the ship ahead of them when the enemy began to fire, sent those feelings to our hearts that insured victory. About ten minutes before twelve, our antagonists opened their fire upon the *Royal Sovereign* (110), Vice-Admiral Collingwood, who most nobly, and unsupported for at least ten minutes, led his division into action, steering for the *Santa Anna* (112), which was painted all black, bearing the flag of Admiral Gravina, during which time all the enemy's line that could possibly bring a gun to bear were firing at her. She was the admiration of the whole fleet.

To show the great and master-mind of Nelson, who was thinking of everything, even in the momentous hour of battle, when most minds would have been totally absorbed in other matters, it was remarked by him that the enemy had the iron hoops round their masts painted black. Orders were issued by signal to whitewash those of his fleet, that in the event of all the ensigns being shot away, his ships might be distinguished by their white masts and hoops.

Trafalgar: Nelson Sends the Signal 'England Expects that Every Man This Day Will Do His Duty', Noon, 21 October 1805

Lieutenant George Brown

I was on the poop and quarter-deck whilst preparations for the fight were going on, and saw Lord Nelson, Captain Blackwood, and some other Captains of the frigates, in earnest conversation together, and a slip of paper in the hand of the former (which Captain Blackwood had looked at), yet I have no recollection that I ever saw it pass through other hands till it was given to Pasco, who, after referring to the telegraph signal book, took it back to his Lordship, and it was then that, I believe, the substitution of the words took place. I think (though not sure), the substitution was 'expects' for the word 'confides', the latter word not being in the telegraph book, and I think the word 'England' had been previously substituted for 'Nelson' for the same reason, at the suggestion of Captain Blackwood.

Trafalgar: Reception of the Signal, 21 October 1805

Report by a Marine Officer on HMS Ajax

Lieutenant Ellis

I was desired to inform those on the main-deck of the Admiral's signal. Upon acquainting one of the quartermasters of the order, he assembled the men with 'Avast there, lads, come and hear the Admiral's words.' When the men were mustered, I delivered with becoming dignity the sentence, rather anticipating that the effect on the men would be to awe them by its grandeur. Jack, however, did not appreciate it, for there were murmurs from some, whilst others in an audible whisper, murmured, 'Do our duty! Of course we'll do our duty! I've always done mine, haven't you? Let us come alongside of 'em, and we'll soon show whether we'll do our duty.' Still, the men cheered vociferously – more, I believe, from love and admiration of their Admiral and leader than from a full appreciation of this well-know

The Death of Lord Nelson, 21 October 1805

Dr William Beatty

Lady Hamilton, mentioned by the dying Nelson, was his mistress Emma Hamilton, who had borne him a daughter in 1800. Her husband, Sir William Hamilton, had died early in 1803.

It was from this Ship (the *Redoutable*) that Lord Nelson received his mortal wound. About fifteen minutes past one o'clock, which was in the heat of the engagement, he was walking the middle of the quarterdeck with Captain Hardy, and in the act of turning near the hatchway with his face towards the stern of the *Victory*, when the fatal ball was fired from the Enemy's mizen-top; which, from the situation of the two ships (lying on board of each other), was brought just abaft, and rather below, the *Victory*'s main-yard, and of course not more than fifteen yards distant from that part of the deck where his Lordship stood. The ball struck the epaulette on his left shoulder, and penetrated his chest. He fell with his face on the deck. Captain Hardy, who was on his right (the side furthest from the Enemy) and advanced some steps before his Lordship, on turning round, saw the Sergeant-Major (Secker) of Marines with two Seamen raising him from the deck; where he had fallen on the same spot on which, a little before, his Secretary had breathed his last, with whose blood his Lordship's clothes were much soiled. Captain Hardy expressed a hope that he was not severely wounded; to which the gallant Chief replied: 'They have done for me at last, Hardy.' 'I hope not,' answered Captain Hardy. 'Yes,' replied his Lordship, 'my backbone is shot through.'

Captain Hardy ordered the Seamen to carry the Admiral to the cockpit; and now two incidents occurred strikingly characteristic of this great man, and strongly marking that energy and reflection which in his heroic mind rose superior even to the immediate consideration of his present awful condition. While the men were carrying him down the ladder from the middle deck, his Lordship observed that the tiller ropes were not yet replaced; and desired one of the Midshipmen stationed there to go upon the quarterdeck and remind Captain Hardy of that circumstance, and request that new ones should be immediately rove. Having delivered this order, he took his handkerchief from his pocket and covered his face with it, that he might be conveyed to the cockpit at this crisis unnoticed by the crew . . .

The *Victory*'s crew cheered whenever they observed an Enemy's Ship surrender. On one of these occasions, Lord Nelson anxiously inquired what was the cause of it; when Lieutenant Pasco, who lay wounded at some distance from his Lordship, raised himself up, and told him that another Ship had struck: which appeared to give him much satisfaction. He now felt an ardent thirst; and frequently called for drink, and to be fanned with paper, making use of these words: 'Fan, fan,' and 'Drink, drink.' This he continued to repeat, when he wished for drink or the refreshment of cool air, till a very few minutes before he expired . . .

His Lordship now requested the Surgeon, who had been previously absent a short time attending Mr Rivers to return to the wounded, and give his assistance to such of them as he could be useful to; 'for,' said he, 'you can do nothing for me.' The Surgeon assured him that the Assistant Surgeons were doing everything that could be effected for those unfortunate men; but on his Lordship's several times repeating his injunctions to that purpose, he left him, surrounded by Doctor Scott, Mr Burke, and two of his Lordship's domestics. After the Surgeon had been absent a few minutes attending Lieutenants Peake and Reeves of the Marines, who were wounded, he was called by Doctor Scott to his Lordship, who said: 'Ah, Mr Beatty! I have sent for you to say, what I forgot to tell you before, that all power of motion and feeling below my breast are gone; and *you*', continued he, 'very well *know* I can live but a short time.' The emphatic manner in which he pronounced these last words left no doubt in the Surgeon's mind, that he adverted to the case of a man who had some months before received a mortal injury of the spine on board the *Victory*, and had laboured under similar privations of sense and muscular motion. The case had made a great impression on Lord Nelson: he was anxious to know the cause of such symptoms, which was accordingly explained to him; and he now appeared to apply the situation and fate of this man to himself. The Surgeon answered, 'My Lord, you told me so before': but he now examined the extremities, to ascertain the fact; when his Lordship said, 'Ah, Beatty! I am too certain of it: Scott and Burke have tried it already. *You know* I am gone.' The Surgeon replied: 'My Lord, unhappily for our Country, nothing can be done for you', and having made this declaration he was so much affected, that he turned round and withdrew a few steps to conceal his emotions. His Lordship said: 'I know it. I feel something rising in my breast,' putting his hand on his left side, 'which tells me I am gone.' Drink was recommended liberally, and Doctor Scott and Mr Burke fanned him with paper. He often exclaimed, 'God be praised, I have done my duty'; and upon the Surgeon's inquiring whether his pain was still very great, he declared, it continued so very severe, that he wished he was dead. 'Yet,' said he in a lower voice, 'one would like to live a little longer, too': and after a pause of a few minutes, he added in the same tone, 'What would become of poor Lady Hamilton, if she knew my situation!' . . .

Captain Hardy now came to the cockpit to see his Lordship a second time, which was after an interval of about fifty minutes from the conclusion of his first visit. Before he quitted the deck, he sent Lieutenant Hills to acquaint Admiral Collingwood with the lamentable circumstance of Lord Nelson's being wounded. Lord Nelson and Captain Hardy shook hands again: and while the Captain retained his Lordship's hand, he congratulated him, even in the arms of death, on his brilliant victory; 'which', said he, 'was complete'; though he did not know how many of the Enemy were captured, as it was impossible to perceive every Ship distinctly. He was certain however of fourteen or fifteen having surrendered. His Lordship answered, 'That is well, but I bargained for twenty': and then emphatically exclaimed, '*Anchor*, Hardy, *anchor!*' To this the Captain replied: 'I suppose, my Lord, Admiral Collingwood will now take upon himself the direction of affairs.' 'Not while I live, I hope, Hardy!' cried the dying Chief; and at that moment endeavoured ineffectually to raise himself from the bed. 'No,' added he; 'do *you* anchor, Hardy.' Captain Hardy then said: 'Shall *we* make the signal, Sir?' 'Yes,' answered his Lordship, 'for if I live, I'll anchor.' The energetic manner in which he uttered these his last orders to Captain Hardy, accompanied with his efforts to raise himself, evinced his determination never to resign the Command while he retained the exercise of his transcendent faculties, and that he expected Captain Hardy still to carry into effect the suggestions of his exalted mind; a sense of his duty overcoming the pains of death. He then told Captain Hardy, he felt that in a few minutes he should be no more; adding in a low tone, 'Don't throw me overboard, Hardy.' The Captain answered: 'Oh! no, certainly not.' 'Then,' replied his Lordship, 'you know what to do: and', continued he, 'take care of my dear Lady Hamilton, Hardy: take care of poor Lady Hamilton. Kiss me, Hardy.' The Captain now knelt down, and kissed his cheek; when his Lordship said, 'Now I am satisfied. Thank God, I have done my duty.' Captain Hardy stood for a minute or two in silent contemplation: he knelt down again, and kissed his Lordship's forehead. His Lordship said: 'Who is that?' The Captain answered: 'It is Hardy'; to which his Lordship replied, 'God bless you, Hardy!' . . . His thirst now increased; and he called for 'drink, drink,' 'fan, fan,' and 'rub, rub,' addressing himself in the last case to Doctor Scott, who had been rubbing his Lordship's breast with his hand, from which he found some relief. These words he spoke in a very rapid manner, which rendered his articulation difficult: but he every now and then, with evident increase of pain, made a greater effort with his vocal powers, and pronounced distinctly these last words: 'Thank God, I have done my duty'; and this great sentiment he continued to repeat as long as he was able to give it utterance.

Seeing the Elgin Marbles for the First Time, Summer 1808

A Revelation for an English Artist

B. R. Haydon

The Elgin Marbles, ancient Greek sculptures mainly from the Acropolis at Athens, were shipped to England between 1802 and 1812, amid furious public controversy, by Thomas Bruce, 7th Lord Elgin. The collection was not opened to the public until 1816.

To Park Lane then we went, and after passing through the hall and thence into an open yard, entered a damp, dirty penthouse where lay the marbles ranged within sight and reach. The first thing I fixed my eyes on was the wrist of a figure in one of the female groups, in which were visible, though in a feminine form, the radius and ulna. I was astonished, for I had never seen them hinted at in any female wrist in the antique. I darted my eye to the elbow, and saw the outer condyle visibly affecting the shape as in nature. I saw that the arm was in repose and the soft parts in relaxation. That combination of nature and idea which I had felt was so much wanting for high art was here displayed to midday conviction. My heart beat! If I had seen nothing else I had beheld sufficient to keep me to nature for the rest of my life. But when I turned to the Theseus and saw that every form was altered by action or repose, – when I saw that the two sides of his back varied, one side stretched from the shoulder-blade being pulled forward, and the other side compressed from the shoulder-blade being pushed close to the spine as he rested on his elbow, with the belly flat because the bowels fell into the pelvis as he sat, – and when, turning to the Ilyssus, I saw the belly protruded, from the figure lying on its side, – and again, when in the figure of the fighting metope I saw the muscle shown under the one armpit in that instantaneous action of darting out, and left out in the other armpits because not wanted – when I saw, in fact, the most heroic style of art combined with all the essential detail of actual life, the thing was done at once and for ever.

After the Battle of Roliça, 17 August 1808

Rifleman Harris

At Roliça, Portugal, the French general Delaborde fought a rearguard action against Sir Arthur Wellesley's English army.

The Rifles, indeed, fought well this day, and we lost many men. They seemed in high spirits, and delighted at having driven the enemy before them. Joseph Cochan was by my side, loading and firing very industriously, about this period of the day. Thirsting with heat and action, he lifted his canteen to his mouth.

'Here's to you, old boy,' he said as he took a pull at its contents. As he did so a bullet went through the canteen, and perforating his brain killed him in a moment. Another man fell close to him almost immediately, struck by a ball in the thigh.

Indeed, we caught it severely just here, and the old iron was also playing its part amongst our poor fellows very merrily. I saw a man named Symmonds struck full in the face by a round shot, and he came to the ground a headless trunk. Meanwhile, many large balls bounded along the ground amongst us so deliberately that we could occasionally evade them without difficulty. I could relate many more of the casualties I witnessed on this day, but the above will suffice.

When the roll was called after the battle, the females who missed their husbands came along the front of the line to inquire of the survivors whether they knew anything about them. Amongst other names I heard that of Cochan called, in a female voice, without being replied to. The name struck me, and I observed the poor woman who had called it, as she stood sobbing before us and apparently afraid to make further inquiries about her husband. No man had answered to his name, or had any account to give of his fate. I myself had observed him fall (as related before) whilst drinking from his canteen, but as I looked at the poor sobbing creature before me I felt unable to tell her of his death. At length Captain Leech observed her, and called out to the company, 'Does any man here know what has happened to Cochan? If so, let him speak out at once.'

Upon this order I immediately related what I had seen, and told the manner of his death. After a while Mrs Cochan appeared anxious to see the spot where her husband fell, and in the hope of still finding him alive asked me to accompany her over the field. She trusted, notwithstanding what I had told her, to find him yet alive.

'Do you think you could find it?' said Captain Leech, upon being referred to.

I told him I was sure I could, as I had remarked many objects whilst looking for cover during the skirmishing.

'Go, then,' said the captain, 'and show the poor woman the spot, as she seems so desirous of finding the body.'

I accordingly took my way over the ground we had fought upon, she following and sobbing after me; and quickly reaching the spot where her husband's body lay, I pointed it out to her.

She now soon discovered all her hopes were in vain. She embraced the stiffened corpse, and after rising and contemplating his disfigured face for some minutes, with hands clasped and tears streaming down her cheeks, she took a prayer book from her pocket, and kneeling down repeated the service for the dead over the body. When she had finished she appeared a good deal comforted; and I took the opportunity of beckoning to a pioneer I saw near with some other men, and together we dug a hole and quickly buried the body. Mrs Cochan then returned with me to the company to which her husband had been attached, and laid herself down upon the heath near us. The company to which Cochan had belonged (bereaved as she was) was now her home; and she marched and took equal fortune with us to Vimiera. She hovered about us during that battle, and then went with us to Lisbon, where she succeeded in procuring a passage to England.

The British Retreat to Corunna, 1–4 January 1809

Robert Blakeney

Advancing against Napoleon's army in Spain, Sir John Moore was forced to fall back on Corunna with fatigued and demoralized troops, pursued by the French under Soult. At Benevente, mentioned in this account, Moore had successfully withdrawn across the Esla, destroying the bridge.

Bembibre exhibited all the appearance of a place lately stormed and pillaged. Every door and window was broken, every lock and fastening forced. Rivers of wine ran through the houses and into the streets, where lay fantastic groups of soldiers (many of them with their firelocks broken), women, children, runaway Spaniards and muleteers, all apparently inanimate, except when here and there a leg or arm was seen to move, while the wine oozing from their lips and nostrils seemed the effect of gunshot wounds. Every floor contained the worshippers of Bacchus in all their different stages of devotion; some lay senseless, others staggered; there were those who prepared the libation by boring holes with their bayonets into the large wine vats, regardless of the quantity which flowed through the cellars and was consequently destroyed. The music was perfectly in character: savage roars announcing present hilarity were mingled with groans issuing from fevered lips disgorging the wine of yesterday; obscenity was public sport. But these scenes are too disgusting to be dwelt upon. We were employed the greatest part of the day [1 January 1809] in turning or dragging the drunken stragglers out of the houses into the streets and sending as many forward as could be moved. Our occupation next morning was the same; yet little could be effected with men incapable of standing, much less of marching forward. At length the cavalry reporting the near approach of the enemy, and Sir John Moore dreading lest

Napoleon's columns should intersect our line of march by pushing along the Foncevadon road, which joined our road not many miles in front of us, the reserve were ordered forward, preceded by the cavalry, and the stragglers were left to their fate. Here I must say that our division, imbibing a good deal of the bad example and of the wine left behind by the preceding columns, did not march out of Bembibre so strong as when they entered it.

We had proceeded but a short distance when the enemy's horsemen nearly approached the place; and then it was that the apparently lifeless stragglers, whom no exertion of ours was sufficient to rouse from their torpor, startled at the immediate approach of danger, found the partial use of their limbs. The road instantly became thronged by them; they reeled, staggered, and screaming threw down their arms. Frantic women held forth their babies, suing for mercy by the cries of defenceless innocence; but all to no purpose. The dragoons of the polite and civilized nation advanced, and cut right and left, regardless of intoxication, age or sex. Drunkards, women and children were indiscriminately hewn down – a dastardly revenge for their defeat at Benevente . . .

During this day's march [4 January] the misery and suffering attendant on wanton disorders and reckless debauchery among the men were awfully manifested; some were lying dead along the road, and many apparently fast approaching a similar fate. Cavalry horses too were continually being shot. One circumstance I shall mention which roused every feeling both of humanity and indignation. About seven or eight miles from Herrerias, seeing a group of soldiers lying in the snow, I immediately went forward to rouse them up and send them on to join their regiments. The group lay close to the roadside. On my coming up, a sad spectacle presented itself. Through exhaustion, depravity, or a mixture of both, three men, a woman and a child all lay dead, forming a kind of circle, their heads inwards. In the centre were still the remains of a pool of rum, made by the breaking of a cask of that spirit. The unfortunate people must have sucked more of the liquor than their constitutions could support. Intoxication was followed by sleep, from which they awoke no more; they were frozen to death.

Taken Prisoner at Corunna, 16 January 1809

Sir Charles Napier

The British victory at Corunna enabled Sir John Moore's army to embark and leave Spain, but Moore himself was mortally wounded. Sir Charles Napier, author of this account, survived to become conqueror of Sind.

I said to the four soldiers [Irish privates of the Fiftieth and Forty-Second], 'Follow me and we will cut through them.' Then with a shout I rushed forward. The Frenchmen had halted, but now ran on to us, and just as my spring was made the wounded leg failed, and I felt a stab in the back; it gave me no pain, but felt cold, and threw me on my face. Turning to rise, I saw the man who had stabbed me making a second thrust. Whereupon, letting go my sabre, I caught his bayonet by the socket, turned the thrust, and raising myself by the exertion, grasped his firelock with both hands, thus in mortal struggle regaining my feet. His companions had now come up, and I heard the dying cries of the four men with me, who were all instantly bayoneted. We had been attacked from behind by men not before seen, as we stood with our backs to a doorway, out of which must have rushed several men, for we were all stabbed in an instant, before the two parties coming up the road reached us. They did so, however, just as my struggle with the man who had wounded me was begun. That was a contest for life, and being the strongest I forced him between myself and his comrades, who appeared to be the men whose lives I had saved when they pretended to be dead on our advance through the village. They struck me with their muskets, clubbed and bruised me much, whereupon, seeing no help near, and being overpowered by numbers and in great pain from my wounded leg, I called out *Je me rend*, remembering the expression correctly from an old story of a fat officer whose name being James called out *Jemmy round*. Finding they had no disposition to spare me, I kept hold of the musket, vigorously defending myself with the body of the little Italian who had first wounded me; but I soon grew faint, or rather tired. At that moment a tall dark man came up, seized the end of the musket with his left hand, whirled his brass-hilted sabre round, and struck me a powerful blow on the head, which was bare, for my cocked hat had fallen off. Expecting the blow would finish me, I had stooped my head in hopes it might fall on my back, or at least on the thickest part of the head, and not on the left temple. So far I succeeded, for it fell exactly on the top, cutting me to the bone but not through it. Fire sparkled from my eyes. I fell on my knees, blinded but not quite losing my senses, and holding still on to the musket. Recovering in a moment I saw a florid, handsome young French drummer holding the arm of the dark Italian, who was in the act of repeating the blow. Quarter was then given; but they tore my pantaloons in tearing my watch and purse from my pocket and a little locket of hair which hung round my neck. But while this went on two of them were wounded, and the drummer, Guibert, ordered the dark man who had sabred me to take me to the rear. When we began to move, I resting on him because hardly able to walk, I saw him look back over his shoulder to see if Guibert was gone; and so did I, for his rascally face made me suspect him. Guibert's back was towards us; he was walking off, and the Italian again drew his sword, which he had before sheathed. I called out to the drummer, 'This rascal is going to kill me; brave Frenchmen don't kill prisoners.' Guibert ran back, swore furiously at the Italian, shoved him away, almost down, and putting his arms round my waist supported me himself. Thus this generous Frenchman saved me twice, for the Italian was bent upon slaying.

A Mastectomy, 30 September 1811

Fanny Burney

Fanny Burney [Madame d'Arblay] first felt pain in her breast in August 1810. Cancer was diagnosed, and Baron Larrey, Napoleon's surgeon, agreed to perform the operation. To spare her suspense, she was given very little notice. The 'M. d'A.' of the account is her husband, and Alexander her son.

One morning – the last of September, 1811, while I was in Bed, & M. d'A. was arranging some papers for his office, I received a Letter written by M. de Lally to a Journalist, in vindication of the honoured memory of his Father against the assertions of Mme du Deffand. I read it aloud to My Alexanders, with tears of admiration

& sympathy, & then sent it by Alex: to its excellent Author, as I had promised the preceding evening. I then dressed, aided, as usual for many months, by my maid, my right arm being condemned to total inaction; but not yet was the grand business over, when another Letter was delivered to me – another, indeed! – 'twas from M. Larrey, to acquaint me that at 10 o'clock he should be with me, properly accompanied, & to exhort me to rely as much upon his sensibility & his prudence, as upon his dexterity & his experience; he charged to secure the absence of M. d'A: & told me that the young Physician who would deliver me his *announce* would prepare for the operation, in which he must lend his aid: & also that it had been the decision of the consultation to allow me but two hours' notice. – Judge, my Esther, if I read this unmoved! – yet I had to disguise my sensations & intentions from M. d'A! – Dr Aumont, the Messenger & terrible Herald, was in waiting; M. d'A stood by my bedside; I affected to be long reading the Note, to gain time for forming some plan, & such was my terror of involving M. d'A. in the unavailing wretchedness of witnessing what I must go through, that it conquered every other, & gave me the force to act as if I were directing some third person. The detail would be too *Wordy*, as James says, but the *wholesale* is – I called Alex to my Bedside, & sent him to inform M. Barbier Neuville, chef du division du Bureau de M. d'A. that *the moment was come*, & I entreated him to write a summons upon urgent business for M. d'A. & to detain him till all should be over. Speechless & appalled, off went Alex, &, as I have since heard, was forced to sit down & sob in executing his commission. I then, by the maid, sent word to the young Dr Aumont that I could not be ready till one o'clock: & I finished my breakfast, & – not with much appetite, you will believe! forced down a crust of bread, & hurried off, under various pretences, M. d'A. He was scarcely gone, when M Du Bois arrived: I renewed my request for one o'clock: the rest came; all were fain to consent to the delay, for I had an apartment to prepare for my banished Mate. This arrangement, & those for myself, occupied me completely. Two engaged nurses were out of the way – I had a bed, Curtains, & heaven knows what to prepare – but business was good for my nerves. I was obliged to quit my room to have it put in order: – Dr Aumont would not leave the house; he remained in the Sallon, folding linen! – He had demanded 4 or 5 old & fine left off under Garments – I glided to our Book Cabinet: sundry necessary works

& orders filled up my time entirely till One O'clock, When all was ready — but Dr Moreau then arrived, with news that M. Dubois could not attend till three. Dr Aumont went away — & the Coast was clear. This, indeed, was a dreadful interval. I had no longer anything to do — I had only to think — TWO HOURS thus spent seemed never-ending. I would fain have written to my dearest Father — to You, my Esther — to Charlotte James — Charles — Amelia Lock — but my arm prohibited me: I strolled to the Sallon — I saw it fitted with preparations, & I recoiled — But I soon returned; to what effect disguise from myself what I must so soon know? — yet the sight of the immense quantity of bandages, compresses, spunges, Lint — made me a little sick: — I walked backwards & forwards till I quieted all emotion, & became, by degrees, nearly stupid — torpid, without sentiment or consciousness; — & thus I remained till the Clock struck three. A sudden spirit of exertion then returned, — I defied my poor arm, no longer worth sparing, & took my long banished pen to write a few words to M. d'A — & a few more for Alex, in case of a fatal result. These short billets I could only deposit safely, when the Cabriolets — one — two — three — four — succeeded rapidly to each other in stopping at the door. Dr Moreau instantly entered my room, to see if I were alive. He gave me a wine cordial, & went to the Sallon. I rang for my Maid & Nurses, — but before I could speak to them, my room, without previous message, was entered by 7 Men in black, Dr Larry, M. Dubois, Dr Moreau, Dr Aumont, Dr Ribe, & a pupil of Dr Larry, & another of M. Dubois. I was now awakened from my stupor — & by a sort of indignation — Why so many? & without leave? — But I could not utter a syllable. M. Dubois acted as Commander in Chief. Dr Larry kept out of sight; M. Dubois ordered a Bed stead into the middle of the room. Astonished, I turned to Dr Larry, who had promised that an Arm Chair would suffice; but he hung his head, & would not look at me. Two *old mattrasses* M. Dubois then demanded, & an old Sheet. I now began to tremble violently, more with distaste & horror of the preparations even than of the pain. These arranged to his liking, he desired me to mount the Bed stead. I stood suspended, for a moment, whether I should not abruptly escape — I looked at the door, the windows — I felt desperate — but it was only for a moment, my reason then took the command, & my fears & feelings struggled vainly against it. I called to my maid — she was crying, & the two Nurses stood, transfixed, at the door. Let those women all go! cried M. Dubois. This order recovered me my Voice – No, I cried, let them stay! *qu'elles restent*! This occasioned a little dispute, that re-animated me – The maid, however, & one of the nurses ran off – I charged the other to approach, & she obeyed. M. Dubois now tried to issue his commands *en militaire*, but I resisted all that were resistable – I was compelled, however, to submit to taking off my long robe de Chambre, which I had meant to retain – Ah, then, how did I think of my Sisters! – not one, at so dreadful an instant, at hand, to protect – adjust – guard me – I regretted that I had refused Mlle de Maisonneuve – Mlle Chastel – no one upon whom I could rely – my departed Angel! – how did I think of her! – how did I long – long for my Esther – my Charlotte! – My distress was, I suppose, apparent, though not my Wishes, for M. Dubois himself now softened, & spoke soothingly. Can *You*, I cried, feel for an operation that, to *You*, must seem so trivial? – Trivial? he repeated – taking up a bit of paper, which he tore, unconsciously, into a million of pieces, *oui – c'est peu de chose – mais – '* he stammered, & could not go on. No one else attempted to speak, but I was softened myself, when I saw even M. Dubois grow agitated, while Dr Larry kept always aloof, yet a glance showed me he was pale as ashes. I knew not, positively, then, the immediate danger, but every thing convinced me danger was hovering about me, & that this experiment could alone save me from its jaws. I mounted, therefore, unbidden, the Bed stead – & M. Dubois placed me upon the mattress, & spread a cambric handkerchief upon my face. It was transparent, however, & I saw, through it, that the Bed stead was instantly surrounded by the 7 men & my nurse. I refused to be held; but when, Bright through the cambric, I saw the glitter of polished Steel – I closed my Eyes. I would not trust to convulsive fear the sight of the terrible incision. A silence the most profound ensued, which lasted for some minutes, during which, I imagine, they took their orders by signs, & made their examination – Oh what a horrible suspension! – I did not breathe – & M. Dubois tried vainly to find any pulse. This pause, at length, was broken by Dr Larry, who, in a voice of solemn melancholy, said '*Qui me tiendra ce sein? –* '

No one answered; at least not verbally; but this aroused me from my passively submissive state, for I feared they imagined the whole breast infected – feared it too justly, – for, again through the Cambric, I saw the hand of M. Dubois held up, while his forefinger first described a straight line from top to bottom of the breast, secondly a Cross, & thirdly a Circle; intimating that the WHOLE was to be taken off. Excited by this idea, I started up, threw off my veil, &, in answer to the demand '*Qui me tiendra ce sein?*' cried '*C'est moi, Monsieur!*' & I held my hand under it, & explained the nature of my sufferings, which all sprang from one point, though they darted into every part. I was heard attentively, but in utter silence, & M. Dubois then replaced me as before, &, as before, spread my veil over my face. How vain, alas, my representation! immediately again I saw the fatal finger describe the Cross – & the circle – Hopeless, then, desperate, & self-given up, I closed once more my Eyes, relinquishing all watching, all resistance, all interference, & sadly resolute to be wholly resigned.

My dearest Esther, – & all my dears to whom she communicates this doleful ditty, will rejoice to hear that this resolution once taken, was firmly adhered to, in defiance of a terror that surpasses all description, & the most torturing pain. Yet – when the dreadful steel was plunged into the breast – cutting through veins – arteries – flesh – nerves – I needed no injunctions not to restrain my cries. I began a scream that lasted unintermittingly during the whole time of the incision – & I almost marvel that it rings not in my Ears still! so excruciating was the agony. When the wound was made, & the instrument was withdrawn, the pain seemed undiminished, for the air that suddenly rushed into those delicate parts felt like a mass of minute but sharp & forked poniards, that were tearing the edges of the wound – but when again I felt the instrument – describing a curve – cutting against the grain, if I may so say, while the flesh resisted in a manner so forcible as to oppose & tire the hand of the operator, who was forced to change from the right to the left – then, indeed, I thought I must have expired. I attempted no more to open my Eyes, – they felt as if hermettically shut, & so firmly closed, that the Eyelids seemed indented into the Cheeks. The instrument this second time withdrawn, I concluded the operation over – Oh no! presently the terrible cutting was renewed – & worse than ever, to separate the bottom, the foundation of this dreadful gland from the parts to which it adhered – Again all description would be baffled – yet again all was not over, – Dr Larry rested but his own hand, & – Oh Heaven! – I then felt the Knife rackling against the breast bone – scraping it! – This performed, while I yet remained in utterly speechless torture, I heard the Voice of Mr Larry, – (all others guarded a dead silence) in a tone nearly tragic, desire everyone present to pronounce if anything more remained to be done; The general voice was Yes, – but the finger of Mr Dubois – which I literally *felt* elevated over the wound, though I saw nothing, & though he touched nothing, so indescribably sensitive was the spot – pointed to some further requisition – & again began the scraping! – and, after this, Dr Moreau thought he discerned a peccant attom – and still, & still, M. Dubois demanded attom after attom – My dearest Esther, not for days, not for Weeks, but for Months I could not speak of this terrible business without nearly again going through it! I could not *think* of it with impunity! I was sick, I was disordered by a single question – even now, 9 months after it is over, I have a headache from going on with the account! & this miserable account, which I began 3 Months ago, at least, I dare not revise, nor read, the recollection is still so painful.

To conclude, the evil was so profound, the case so delicate, & the precautions necessary for preventing a return so numerous, that the operation, including the treatment & the dressing, lasted 20 minutes! a time, for sufferings so acute, that was hardly supportable – However, I bore it with all the courage I could exert, & never moved, nor stopt them, nor resisted, nor remonstrated, nor spoke – except once or twice, during the dressings, to say '*Ah Messieurs! que je vous plains!* – ' for indeed I was sensible to the feeling concern with which they all saw what I endured, though my speech was principally – *very* principally meant for Dr Larry. Except this, I uttered not a syllable, save, when so often they recommended, calling out '*Avertissez moi, Messieurs! avertissez moi!* – ' Twice, I believe, I fainted; at least, I have two total chasms in my memory of this transaction, that impede my tying together what passed. When all was done, & they lifted me up that I might be put to bed, my strength was so totally annihilated, that I was obliged to be carried, & could not even sustain my hands & arms, which hung as if I had been lifeless; while my face, as the Nurse has told me, was utterly colourless. This removal made me open my Eyes – & I then saw my good Dr Larry, pale nearly as myself, his face streaked with blood, & its expression depicting grief, apprehension, & almost horror.

When I was in bed, – my poor M. d'Arblay – who ought to write you himself his own history of this Morning – was called to me – & afterwards our Alex.

Napoleon Enters Moscow, 14 September 1812

Baron Claude François de Méneval

Retreating before Napoleon the Russians under Kutuzov adopted a scorched-earth policy, abandoning Moscow, which Napoleon entered unopposed. The premature onset of winter made his subsequent withdrawal from Moscow disastrous.

A curious and impressive sight was this sudden appearance of this great city, Asiatic rather than European, spreading out at the end of a desert and naked plain, topped with its twelve hundred spires and sky-blue cupolas, strewn with golden stars, and linked one to the other with gilded chains. This conquest had been dearly paid for, but Napoleon at that time lulled himself in the hope that he would be able to dictate peace there. The King of Naples, who entered it first, sent word to the Emperor that the city appeared to be deserted and that no civil or military functionary, nor nobleman, nor priest had presented himself. The Russian army had taken away the majority of the inhabitants of Moscow in its train. Some Russian and foreign dealers, who had managed to escape this order, came to see the Emperor and implored him to protect them against the pillaging with which they thought themselves menaced. There had remained in the city only a few thousand people belonging to the lowest classes of society, who had nothing to lose by awaiting the course of events.

Napoleon passed this night of September 14th in the Dorogomilow *faubourg*, and only entered Moscow on the morrow. This entry was not accompanied by that tumult which marks the taking possession of a great city. No noise disturbed the solitude of the city streets, save only the rumbling of the cannon and of the artillery *caissons*. Moscow seemed asleep in deep sleep, like one of those enchanted cities of which we read in Arabian tales. The streets through which we passed were lined with houses of fine appearance for the most part, with closed windows and doors. Palaces with colonnades, churches and beautiful buildings glittering with the luxury of Europe and of Asia raised themselves side by side with very modest habitations. All bespoke the ease and wealth of a great city enriched by trade and inhabited by a wealthy and numerous aristocracy. Some of the principal houses which we were able to enter were well appointed and well furnished, many even magnificently so, and their inhabitants did not appear to have abandoned them for ever.

The Emperor proceeded directly to the Kremlin, a large citadel placed in the centre of the town, on the top of a hill, surrounded with an embattled wall and flanked at intervals with towers armed with cannon. The Kremlin is a second city. It contains the imperial palace, the arsenal, the Senate palace, the archives, the principal public establishments, a large number of churches, temples filled with historical curiosities, objects serving for the coronation of the sovereigns, and lastly trophies and flags taken from the Turks. It is in one of the principal temples that are the tombs of the Tsars. In this imposing *fane* reigns a magnificence which is half barbaric and of a primitive character. The walls are covered with thick plates of gold and silver on which are figured in relief the principal incidents of the Sacred History. Enormous silver lamps of Byzantine shape hang from the arches of the building, large many-branched chandeliers of the same metal stand on pedestals on the floor. There is also to be seen in this sanctuary a portrait of the Holy Virgin attributed to St Luke, the frame of this picture is enriched with pearls and precious stones. A great bell-tower, known as the Ivan tower, was surmounted by a gigantic cross in the centre of which was enchased a cross of pure gold containing a fragment of the true cross. This cross and a number of curious objects which could be removed were to be sent to Paris from the Kremlin.

Hardly had the Emperor entered the Kremlin than fire broke out in the Kitaigorod, or Chinese city, an immense bazaar, surrounded by porticoes, in which were heaped up, in large shops or in cellars, the entrances to which were placed in the middle of the streets, precious goods of every kind, such as shawls, furs, Indian and Chinese tissues. Fruitless efforts were made to extinguish the flames, and the burning of the bazaar became the signal for a general conflagration in the city. This conflagration, spreading rapidly, devoured three-quarters of Moscow in three days. Each moment one saw smoke followed by flames breaking out of houses which had remained intact and in the end the fire broke out in every house in the city. The town was one mighty furnace from which sheaves of fire burst heavenwards lighting up the horizon with the glaring flames and spreading a burning heat. These masses of flame, mingling together, were rapidly caught up by a strong wind which spread them in every direction. They were accompanied by a succession of whistling noises and explosions caused by the falling walls and the explosion of inflammable materials which were stored in the shops and houses. To these roaring noises, to these sinister outbreaks added themselves the cries and yells of the wretched people who were caught by the flames in the houses which they had entered to pillage and which many escaped only to perish in the streets which formed a blazing labyrinth from which all escape was impossible. Motionless and in the silence of stupor we looked on at this horrible and magnificent spectacle, with the feeling of our absolute helplessness to render any assistance.

Death of a Climbing Boy, 29 March 1813

Evidence taken before the Parliamentary Committee on Climbing Boys, 1817

In 1817 a Committee of the House of Commons recommended that the use of climbing boys be prohibited, but the recommendation was not carried into effect.

On Monday morning, 29 March 1813, a chimney sweeper of the name of Griggs attended to sweep a small chimney in the brewhouse of Messrs Calvert and Co. in Upper Thames Street; he was accompanied by one of his boys, a lad of about eight years of age, of the name of Thomas Pitt. The fire had been lighted as early as 2 o'clock the same morning, and was burning on the arrival of Griggs and his little boy at eight. The fireplace was small, and an iron pipe projected from the grate some little way into the flue. This the master was acquainted with (having swept the chimneys in the brewhouse for some years), and therefore had a tile or two broken from the roof, in order that the boy might descend the chimney. He had no sooner extinguished the fire than he suffered the lad to go down; and the consequence, as might be expected, was his almost immediate death, in a state, no doubt, of inexpressible agony. The flue was of the narrowest description, and must have retained heat sufficient to have prevented the child's return to the top, even supposing he had not approached the pipe belonging to the grate, which must have been nearly red hot; this however was not clearly ascertained on the inquest, though the appearance of the body would induce an opinion that he had been unavoidably pressed against the pipe. Soon after his descent, the master, who remained on the top, was apprehensive that something had happened, and therefore desired him to come up; the answer of the boy was, 'I cannot come up, master, I must die here.' An alarm was given in the brewhouse immediately that he had stuck in the chimney, and a bricklayer who was at work near the spot attended, and after knocking down part of the brickwork of the chimney, just above the fireplace, made a hole sufficiently large to draw him through. A surgeon attended, but all attempts to restore life were ineffectual. On inspecting the body, various burns appeared; the fleshy part of the legs and a great part of the feet more particularly were injured; those parts too by which climbing boys most effectually ascend or descend chimneys, viz. the elbows and knees, seemed burnt to the bone; from which it must be evident that the unhappy sufferer made some attempts to return as soon as the horrors of his situation became apparent.

Wounded at Nivelle, 16 November 1813

Robert Blakeney

In the process of driving the French out of Spain, Wellington stormed Soult's positions on the river Nivelle. The allied loss was about 2,700; that of the French 4000.

Arriving immediately under the fort I perceived the enemy regularly drawn up behind trees cut down to the height of about five feet, the branches pointing forward, forming an abattis. I immediately turned about, and after receiving an appropriate salute retraced my steps with redoubled speed. I seized the king's colour carried by Ensign Montgomery, which I immediately halted; and called for the regimental Colour Ensign, McPherson, who answered, 'Here am I.' Having halted both colours in front of the foremost men, I prevented any from going forward. By these means we shortly presented a tolerably good front, and gave the men a few moments' breathing time. The whole operation did not take above ten minutes; but the men coming up every instant, each minute strengthened the front. At this exciting moment my gallant comrades, Lieutenants Vincent and L'Estrange, who stood by my side, remarked that if I did not allow the regiment to advance, the 61st Regiment would arrive at the redoubt as soon as we should. I immediately placed my cap on the point of my sword and passing to the front of the colours gave the word, 'Quick march. Charge!' We all rushed forward, excited by the old British cheer. But my personal advance was momentary; being struck by a shot which shattered both bones of my left leg, I came down. Vincent instantly asked what was the matter. I told him that my leg was broken, and that was all. I asked him to put the limb into a straight position, and to place me against a tree which stood close by; in this position I asked for my cap and sword, which had been struck from my hand in the fall; and then I cheered on the regiment as they gallantly charged into the redoubt.

The fort being carried, the regiment pursued the enemy down the opposite side of the hill, whilst I remained behind idly to look around me. The scene was beautifully romantic and heroically sublime. Groups of cavalry were seen judiciously, although apparently without regularity, dotted along the sides of every hill, watching an opportunity of falling on the discomfited foe. Our troops gallantly bore on over an unbroken series of intrenchments, thickly crowded with bayonets and kept lively by incessant fire. The awful passing events lay beneath my view; nor was there aught to interrupt my observation save a few bodily twitches, the pangs of prostrated ambition, and the shot and shells which burst close, or nearly cut the ground from under me.

Immediately after the redoubt was taken, under which I fell, another fort on our right, not yet attacked, turned some of its guns against the one just captured; and their shot and shell ploughing the ground all around me nearly suffocated me with dust and rubbish. Those who were not very severely wounded scrambled their way down the hill; but I might as well have attempted to carry a millstone as to drag my shattered leg after me. I therefore remained among the dead and dying, who were not few. My situation was not enviable. After some hours Assistant-Surgeon Simpson of the regiment appeared. I then got what is termed a field dressing; but unfortunately there were no leg splints; and so arm splints were substituted. Through this makeshift I suffered most severely during my descent. Some of the band coming up, I was put into a blanket and carried down the hill; but as we proceeded down this almost perpendicular descent, the blanket contracted from my weight in the middle, and then owing to the want of the proper long splints the foot drooped beyond the blanket's edge; it is almost impossible to imagine the torture which I suffered. Having gained the base of the hill towards dark, a cottage was fortunately discovered and into this I was carried.

Up to the noon of this day I congratulated myself on my good fortune in having served in the first and last battle fought in Spain, and proudly contemplated marching victoriously through France. I recalled too with pleasure and as if it were a propitious omen, that on this day five years ago I first trod Spanish ground. On November 16th, 1808, we marched into Fuentes de Oñoro, under the command of Sir John Moore. Then I was strong hale and joyous, with the glorious prospects of war favourably presented to view; but the afternoon of this, the fifth anniversary, proved a sad reverse. On this day I was carried out of Spain, borne in a blanket, broken in body and depressed in mind, with all my brilliant prospects like myself fallen to the ground. Such is glorious war.

After the field dressing Simpson departed in search of other wounded persons; and on his report of my wound two or three other medical officers sought me, fortunately in vain, that they might remove the limb. On the fourth day I was conveyed to a place where a hospital was established; but the inflammation of the leg was then so great (it was as big as my body) that no amputation could be attempted. A dressing took place which was long and painful, for I had bled so profusely while in the cottage that a cement hard as iron was formed round the limb, and before my removal it was absolutely necessary to cut me out of the bed on which I lay. After a considerable time passed in steeping with tepid water, the piece of mattress and sheet which I carried away from the cottage were removed; and now began the more painful operation of setting the leg. Staff-Surgeon Mathews and Assistant-Surgeon Graham, 31st Regiment, were the operators. Graham seized me by the knee and Mathews by the foot. They proposed that four soldiers should hold me during the operation; to this I objected, saying with a kind of boast that I was always master of my nerves. They now twisted and turned and extended my leg, aiming along it like a spirit level. The torture was dreadful; but though I ground my teeth and the big drops of burning perspiration rapidly chased each other, still I remained firm, and stifled every rising groan. After all was concluded I politely thanked Mathews, carelessly remarking that it was quite a pleasure to get wounded to be so comfortably dressed. This was mock heroism, for at the moment I trembled as if just taken from the rack.

Execution by Impalement: Latakia, 1813

Charles Lewis Meryon

The author of this account was a surgeon, travelling with Lady Hester Stanhope.

On the 19th of July, I was walking out of one of the gates of the town, about eight in the morning, when I came suddenly on a man who had been impaled an hour or two before, and was now dead, but still transfixed by the stake, which, as I saw on approaching him, came out about the sixth rib on the right side; but I was so shocked at this unexpected sight, that it was some minutes before I could recover myself sufficiently to go up to him. The stake was planted upright, seemed to be scarcely sharp, and was somewhat thicker than a hop-pole. I was told that it was forced up the body by repeated blows of a mallet, the malefactor having been bound on his face to a heavy pack-saddle, and an incision being made with a razor to facilitate the entrance of the stake. The body, yet alive, was set upright in a rude manner; for the Turks preserve no decorum in executions: from pity for his sufferings, after being a short time in this position, he was shot. His shirt, which was afterwards set on fire, in burning singed the whole of his body black; and thus he was left for two days. His crime was said to be the stealing of a bullock and the murder of one of his pursuers. Jewish, Christian, Drûze, and Ansáry criminals are alone subjected to this horrible punishment: Turks are beheaded.

The Retreat before Waterloo, 17 June 1815

Lieutenant W. B. Ingilby, Royal Horse Artillery

Napoleon's marshals Ney and de Grouchy had held Wellington at Quatre-Bras and defeated the Prussians at Ligny in secondary battles south of Waterloo on 16 June.

We marched before daylight, passed through Nivelles, meeting many wounded on the road, and arrived at Quatre Bras, where the affair of yesterday had been. The whole Army was gradually and successively arriving, and the French appeared in considerable force in our front. About noon Lord Arthur Hill, Aide-de-Camp to the Duke, mentioned that the Prussians had been defeated, and that their Army was in retreat. In the afternoon there appeared a considerable bustle among the Enemy's troops in our front, as if preparing for a move. The whole of our Infantry at this time were moving off to a position we understood to be a few miles to our rear.

The Cavalry formed in three lines: the Hussars in the first line, the Light Cavalry in the second, and in the third line the Heavy Cavalry. It suddenly became insufferably hot and close, and the sun became absolutely darkened by a very black cloud, while at the same time a heavy cloud of dust rising showed the advance of a very large body of Cavalry coming to reinforce the Enemy; they came from a direction on the right of the Enemy.

I had heard the same Aide-de-Camp say that Lord Uxbridge had positive orders not to have an affair of Cavalry.

The French Cavalry I have before adverted to now advanced boldly in great force, and for some time partially under cover of a wood, until their vedettes fired on our front line. We commenced a cannonade, which was promptly returned, and as the Enemy continued to advance and, I think, had commenced a deployment, an affair seemed inevitable.

The interest and even silence, until the Guns and skirmishers opened, up to this moment was intense, for it was not generally known that the Cavalry General was to avoid an affair.

At the last moment the order was given, and the whole commenced a rapid retreat in three Columns and by different roads. At this instant the heavy black cloud broke with a tremendous clap of thunder and torrent of rain. We formed the left Column in retreat. The road and ground became so quickly deluged with the heavy rain that was falling, that it became impracticable for the French Cavalry to press our Column in any force. In fact, out of the road in the track of our own Cavalry, the ground was poached into a complete puddle. Seeing this, and having lost the shoe from off a Gun horse, I halted and had it put on in spite of some skirmishers who began to press on us, but were kept at bay by our own skirmishers forming as if to charge them. This will show how impracticable it was for them to press us on this cross road. But at this moment I could see the centre Column on the main road on my right, and they apparently charging, accompanied, with much cheering. (This was the affair of the 7th Hussars, who were not successful, but the matter was retrieved by the Life Guards.) In our Column not a man was lost. The retreat for the Guns the whole way, with the exception of the Gun mentioned, was at a hard gallop for six or seven miles until we came upon the Infantry, in and getting into position. The rain continued very heavy throughout the night.

The same night I received instructions to set out by times in the morning to find a practicable road which should lead parallel to the main road, and through the wood of Soignies and by the left of Brussels, so that in case of further retreat Sir Hussey's Brigade might retire covering the left flank of the Army.

I left the bivouac just at dawn, and succeeded in making myself acquainted with a road practicable for our light Guns (six-pounders) and Cavalry. At a village I fell in with a body of four or five hundred Prussians, evidently of different Corps, and seemingly fugitives; however, they appeared as if collecting to march in the direction of the cannonade, which was commencing to be rather heavy. Numberless of the peasants had taken and were taking refuge in the wood of Soignies, with their women and children, cattle, pigs, sheep, and whatever valuables they could carry off. I went into Brussels; the streets were wholly deserted, except by the wounded that were straggling in from the Cavalry affair of yesterday and at Quatre Bras the day before; many were lying and seated about the steps of the houses as if unable to proceed further in search of a hospital. I managed to get a hasty breakfast in the Hotel d'Angleterre with a gentleman anxious for news, and who proved to be Admiral Malcolm. I carried off a cold fowl for the

Troop, who I knew had nothing, and which I reached about half-past ten o'clock, and immediately proceeded to make my report to Sir Hussey Vivian.

Waterloo, 18 June 1815: Dawn with the 7th Hussars

Sergeant-Major Edward Cotton

The field of Waterloo is an open, undulating plain; and on the day of the battle it was covered with splendid crops of rye, wheat, barley, oats, beans, peas, potatoes, turnips, tares and clover; some of which were of great height. There were a few patches of ploughed ground, intersected by two high roads, which branched off at Mont St Jean . . .

At break of day, all who were able began to be on the move. There were many who from cold and fatigue were unable to stir for some time. Some were cleaning arms, others fetching wood, water, straw, etc., from Mont St Jean – my present place of abode – some trying from the embers of our bivouac to light up fires, many of which had been entirely put out by the heavy rain. At this time there was a continual but irregular popping along the line, not unlike a skirmish. Our bivouac had a most unsightly appearance: both officers and men looked blue with cold; and our long beards with our wet and dirty clothing drying upon us was anything but comfortable. As morning advanced and all were in motion, one might imagine the whole plain itself to be undergoing a movement. Imagine 70,000 men huddled together. The buzzing resembled the distant roar of the sea against a rocky coast.

Waterloo, 18 June 1815: Charge of the Scots Greys and 92nd Highlanders, 2–3 p.m.

Lieutenant R. Winchester, 92nd Highlanders

At the commencement of the Action a Corps of Belgians of from 8000 to 10,000 men were formed in line in front of the 5th Division, but soon after they were attacked and their skirmishers driven in on their line, the whole of them retired through the 5th Division, and were seen no more during the Action. After this the Enemy made several severe attacks on the 5th Division. About two or three o'clock in the afternoon a Column between 3000 to 4000 men advanced to the hedge at the roadside which leads from the main road near La Haye Sainte beyond the left of our position. Previous to this the 92nd had been lying down under cover of the position when they were immediately ordered to stand to their arms, Major-General Sir Denis Pack calling out at the same time, '92nd, everything has given way on your right and left and you must charge this Column,' upon which he ordered four deep to be formed and closed in to the centre. The Regiment, which was then within about 20 yards of the Column, fired a volley into them. The Enemy on reaching the hedge at the side of the road had ordered arms, and were in the act of shouldering them when they received the volley from the 92nd.

The Scots Greys came up at this moment, and doubling round our flanks and through our centre where openings were made for them, both Regiments charged together, calling out 'Scotland for ever,' and the Scots Greys actually walked over this Column, and in less than three minutes it was totally destroyed, 2000, besides killed and wounded, of them having been made prisoners, and two of their Eagles captured. The grass field in which the Enemy was formed, which was only an instant before as green and smooth as the 15 acres in Phoenix Park, was in a few minutes covered with killed and wounded, knapsacks and their contents, arms, accoutrements, etc., literally strewed all over, that to avoid stepping on either one or the other was quite impossible; in fact one could hardly believe, had he not witnessed it, that such complete destruction could have been effected in so short a time.

Some of the French soldiers who were lying wounded were calling out '*Vive l'Empereur*,' and others firing their muskets at our men who had advanced past them in pursuit of the flying Enemy.

Waterloo, 18 June 1815: The Royal Horse Artillery Repulse Enemy Cavalry, late afternoon

Field Captain A. C. Mercer, Royal Horse Artillery

A heavy Column of Cavalry, composed of Grenadiers à Cheval and Cuirassiers, had just ascended the Plateau and was advancing upon us at a rapid pace, so that there scarcely appeared time even to get into action, and, if caught in column, of course we were lost.

However, the order was given to deploy, and each Gun as it came up immediately opened its fire; the two Infantry Squares at the same time commencing a feeble and desultory fire; for they were in such a state that I momentarily expected to see them disband.

Their ranks, loose and disjointed, presented gaps of several file in breadth, which the Officers and Sergeants were busily employed filling up by pushing and even thumping their men together; whilst these, standing like so many logs, with their arms at the recover, were apparently completely stupefied and bewildered. I should add that they were all perfect children. None of the privates, perhaps, were above 18 years of age. In spite of our fire the Column of Cavalry continued advancing at a *trot* until separated from us by scarcely more than the breadth of the little road, but at the very moment when we expected to be overwhelmed, those of the leading Squadrons suddenly turning, and endeavouring to make way to the rear, confusion took place, and the whole broke into a disorderly crowd. The scene that ensued is scarcely to be described. Several minutes elapsed ere they succeeded in quitting the Plateau, during which our fire was incessant, and the consequent carnage frightful, for each Gun (9 Prs) was loaded with a round and case shot; all of which, from the shortness of the distance, size of the object, and elevation of the ground on which they stood, *must* have taken effect.

Many, instead of seeking safety in retreat, wisely dashed through the intervals between our Guns, and made their way as we had seen others do; but the greater part, rendered desperate at finding themselves held, as it were, in front of the Battery, actually fought their way through their own ranks, and in the struggle we saw *blows* exchanged on all sides. At last the wreck of this formidable Column gained protection under the slope of the hill, leaving the

Plateau encumbered with their killed and wounded, and we then ceased firing, that our men, who were much fatigued with their exertions, might rest themselves and be fresh against the next attack, which we saw preparing; for they had not retired so far down the hill but that the tall caps of the Grenadiers of the leading Squadrons were visible above the brow.

The second attempt was preluded by a cloud of skirmishers, who, advancing to within a very short distance of our front, did us considerable mischief with their carbines and pistols, but their intention being evidently to draw out our fire, no notice was taken of them.

At length the Column, being re-formed, again ascended the Plateau, and advanced to attack us, but this time their pace scarcely exceeded a walk, or at most a gentle trot, too many obstacles lying in their way to admit of more rapid movement without confusion. This was in our favour. Experience having shown us the unerring and destructive effects of a close fire, we allowed the leading Squadrons to attain about half the distance between the brow of the slope and the road in our front before we commenced. It is scarcely necessary to say that the result was precisely similar to what has been already detailed. Again they fell into confusion, and again for several minutes were exposed to a deliberate fire of case shot within 20 yards, so that the heap of killed and wounded left on the ground, before great, was now enormous . . .

With respect to the appearance of the Field after the Action, not much can be said, for night closed in upon us very shortly, and we were too glad to lie down to think of looking about. That the ground was everywhere thickly strewed with the dead and dying (Men and Horses), wrecks of Gun and Ammunition Carriages, Arms, Caps, etc., will occur as a matter of course. I should, however, add that the heap of slaughter was far greater in front of our Battery than on any other part of the Field, so much so that Colonel Sir Augustus Fraser told me two days afterwards at Nivelles that in riding over the French Position he could distinctly see where G (our Letter) Troop had stood from the dark pile of bodies in front of it, which was such as even to form a remarkable feature in the Field.

Waterloo, 18 June 1815: Napoleon's Last Throw – Charge of the Imperial Guard, 7 p.m.

Captain H. W. Powell, First Foot Guards

There ran along this part of the position a cart road, on one side of which was a ditch and bank, in and under which the Brigade sheltered themselves during the cannonade, which might have lasted three-quarters of an hour. Without the protection of this bank every creature must have perished.

The Emperor [Napoleon] probably calculated on this effect, for suddenly the firing ceased, and as the smoke cleared away a most superb sight opened on us. A close Column of Grenadiers (about seventies in front) of *la Moyenne Garde*, about 6000 strong, led, as we have since heard, by Marshal Ney, were seen ascending the rise *au pas de charge* shouting '*Vive l'Empereur.*' They continued to advance till within fifty or sixty paces of our front, when the Brigade were ordered to stand up. Whether it was from the sudden and unexpected appearance of a Corps so near them, which must have seemed as starting out of the ground, or the tremendously heavy fire we threw into them, *La Garde*, who had never before failed in an attack *suddenly* stopped. Those who from a distance and more on the flank could see the affair, tell us that the effect of our fire seemed to force the head of the Column bodily back.

In less than a minute above 300 were down. They now wavered, and several of the rear divisions began to draw out as if to deploy, whilst some of the men in their rear beginning to fire over the heads of those in front was so evident a proof of their confusion, that Lord Saltoun (who had joined the Brigade, having had the whole of his Light Infantry Battalion dispersed at Hougoumont) holloaed out, 'Now's the time, my boys.' Immediately the Brigade sprang forward. *La Garde* turned and gave us little opportunity of trying the steel. We charged down the hill till we had passed the end of the orchard of Hougoumont, when our right flank became exposed to another heavy Column (as we afterwards understood of the *Chasseurs* of the *Garde*) who were advancing in support of the former Column. This circumstance, besides that our charge was isolated, obliged the Brigade to retire towards their original position.

Waterloo, 18 June 1815: The Finale

Captain J. Kincaid, Rifle Brigade

I shall never forget the scene which the field of battle presented about seven in the evening. I felt weary and worn out, less from fatigue than anxiety.

Our division, which had stood upwards of 5000 men at the commencement of the battle, had gradually dwindled down into a solitary line of skirmishers. The 27th regiment were lying literally dead, in square, a few yards behind us. My horse had received another shot through the leg, and one through the flap of the saddle, which lodged in his body, sending him a step beyond the pension list. The smoke still hung so thick about us that we could see nothing. I walked a little way to each flank to endeavour to get a glimpse of what was going on; but nothing met my eye except the mangled remains of men and horses, and I was obliged to return to my post as wise as I went.

I had never yet heard of a battle in which everybody was killed; but this seemed likely to be an exception, as all were going by turns . . .

Presently a cheer which we knew to be British commenced far to the right, and made everyone prick up his ears; it was Lord Wellington's long-wished-for orders to advance. It gradually approached, growing louder as it grew near. We took it up by instinct, charged through the hedge down upon the old knoll, sending our adversaries flying at the point of the bayonet. Lord Wellington galloped up to us at the instant, and our men began to cheer him; but he called out, 'No cheering, my lads, but forward, and complete our victory!'

This movement had carried us clear of the smoke; and to people who had been so many hours enveloped in darkness, in the midst of destruction, and naturally anxious about the result of the day, the scene which now met the eye conveyed a feeling of more exquisite gratification than can be conceived. It was a fine summer evening just before sunset. The French were flying in one confused mass. British lines were seen in close pursuit, and in admirable order, as far as the eye could reach to the right, while the plain to the left was filled with Prussians. The enemy made one last attempt at a stand on the rising ground to our right of La Belle Alliance; but a charge from General Adam's Brigade again threw them into a state of confusion, which was now inextricable, and their ruin was complete. Artillery, baggage, and everything belonging to them, fell into our hands. After pursuing them until dark, we halted about two miles beyond the field of battle, leaving the Prussians to follow up the victory.

Embalming a Patriarch, November 1815
An Unusual Task for a British Physician in the Lebanon

Charles Lewis Meryon

On Saturday, what was my surprise, on approaching the monastery, to find a crowd of people assembled at the church doors; and, on entering it, to see the dead patriarch sitting in a chair, with a crosier in his left hand and the New Testament in his right, whilst an incense pan smoked by his side. Prostrate, before and around him, were men and women, some of whom religiously approached the corpse, plucked a hair from the beard, or kissed the hand.

Messengers had been sent to the bishops of Sayda, Acre, Beyrout, and the other sees in the district. Theodosius, Bishop of Acre, happening to be at Beyrout, arrived about eleven in the morning just before me, and was giving the necessary orders for the funeral. I went into the room where he was. It is customary for the Greek Catholic Church to embalm its patriarchs: and this is generally done by the priests: but, as the offensive smell, which continued to arise from the last patriarch, whose body was deposited under the staircase in the chapel of Mar Elias, had convinced me that little or no care was used by the priests in doing it, I volunteered my services, which were accepted. I expected that some objection would have been made on the score of my being a heretic; but perhaps the priests were glad to get rid of a process so disagreeable to eyes unused to the dissection of dead bodies.

There was a receipt for preparing the drugs used in embalming kept at the see, which was forthwith sent to Sayda to be made up. The corpse was immediately carried into a vault or cellar near the door of the church. I was assisted by two peasants, who, together with the monks, showed as much indecency in the treatment of the body now lifeless as they had manifested obsequiousness and servility to it when breathing. I proposed that a flat table should be put upon trestles (such being the bedsteads of the monks themselves) to lay the corpse on: but their reply was, 'Why not on the ground?' I asked for silk thread to sew up the body: but they produced cotton, and said that would do well enough. I required a sponge and hot water: the latter they would not give themselves the trouble to bring, and the sponge they produced was as black as a coal. Who would be the future patriarch, not what would become of the dead one, was now all their consideration.

I opened the body. I removed each viscus, one by one, observing the external phenomena only, fearing to cut into them, lest the bystanders should speak of it among the populace, and I get stoned. Not one monk would attend, each declaring that he could not bear the sight: a lay brother came in once, to ask when the process would be over, and, having stolen a handkerchief, disappeared. The contents of the abdomen and chest being removed, I rubbed in the powdered ingredients over the interior surface of these cavities just as one salts down meat. Then, stuffing the whole with bran, I sewed up the body with the usual stitch; and, the thread being blue, the suture looked neat, which was the principal thing that excited admiration in the peasants. I took out the brains and filled the skull with powdered drugs. The integuments were then carefully drawn over and sewed up. The body was afterwards washed as clean as I could do it; for the bystanders were extremely indifferent to my reproaches for their irreverent conduct, and would afford me no assistance.

They now dressed the corpse in a pair of drawers, a *kombáz* (or gown) of white silk, with gold tinsel running through it; a silk band or cope, in the shape of a horse-shoe, which came over the shoulders from behind and reached to the ground, and a smaller one of the same kind over it, which two latter are episcopal emblems. To the right side in front was suspended a square board, covered with silk, resembling a dragoon's despatch bag. The mitre was then placed on his head; and the body, being tied in an armchair to keep it erect, was carried into the church, which was lighted up for the mass of the dead. It was eight o'clock in the evening, and I had been employed just five hours. A great concourse of people was assembled from the neighbouring villages. Not sure how some of them might be disposed to consider my interference in the religious rites of their church, I declined to attend the service. On the following morning, I mounted my horse, and rode back to Mar Elias.

Factory Conditions, c. 1815

Evidence of a Female Millhand to the Parliamentary Commissioners

Elizabeth Bentley

What age are you?
  Twenty-three.

Where do you live?
  At Leeds.

What time did you begin work at the factory?
  When I was six years old.

At whose factory did you work?
  Mr Burk's.

What kind of mill is it?
  Flax mill.

What was your business in that mill?
  I was a little doffer.

What were your hours of labour in that mill?
  From 5 in the morning till 9 at night, when they were thronged.

For how long a time together have you worked that excessive length of time?
  For about a year.

What were the usual hours of labour when you were not so thronged?
  From six in the morning till 7 at night.

What time was allowed for meals?
  Forty minutes at noon.

Had you any time to get your breakfast or drinking?

No, we had to get it as we could.

Do you consider doffing a laborious employment?
Yes.

Explain what you had to do?
When the frames are full, they have to stop the frames, and take the flyers off, and take the full bobbins off, and carry them to the roller, and then put empty ones on, and set the frame going again.

Does that keep you constantly on your feet?
Yes, there are so many frames and they run so quick.

Your labour is very excessive?
Yes, you have not time for anything.

Suppose you flagged a little, or were late, what would they do?
Strap us.

And they are in the habit of strapping those who are last in doffing?
Yes.

Constantly?
Yes.

Girls as well as boys?
Yes.

Have you ever been strapped?
Yes.

Severely?
Yes.

Is the strap used so as to hurt you excessively?
Yes it is . . . I have seen the overlooker go to the top end of the room, where the little girls hug the can to the backminders; he has taken a strap, and a whistle in his mouth, and sometimes he has got a chain and chained them, and strapped them all down the room.

What was his reason for that?
He was very angry.

Did you live far from the mill?
Yes, two miles.

Had you a clock?

No, we had not.

Were you generally there in time?

Yes, my mother has been up at 4 o'clock in the morning, and at 2 o'clock in the morning; the colliers used to go to their work at 3 or 4 o'clock, and when she heard them stirring she has got up out of her warm bed, and gone out and asked them the time; and I have sometimes been at Hunslet Car at 2 o'clock in the morning, when it was streaming down with rain, and we have had to stay till the mill was opened.

You are considerably deformed in person as a consequence of this labour?

Yes I am.

And what time did it come on?

I was about 13 years old when it began coming, and it has got worse since; it is five years since my mother died, and my mother was never able to get me a good pair of stays to hold me up, and when my mother died I had to do for myself, and got me a pair.

Were you perfectly straight and healthy before you worked at a mill?

Yes, I was as straight a little girl as ever went up and down town.

Were you straight till you were 13?

Yes, I was.

Did your deformity come upon you with much pain and weariness?

Yes, I cannot express the pain all the time it was coming.

Do you know of anybody that has been similarly injured in their health?

Yes, in their health, but not many deformed as I am.

It is very common to have weak ankles and crooked knees?

Yes, very common indeed.

This is brought on by stopping the spindle?

Yes.

Where are you now?

In the poorhouse.

State what you think as to the circumstances in which you have been placed during all this time of labour, and what you have considered about it as to the hardship and cruelty of it.

The witness was too much affected to answer the question.

Prison Visiting, 4 March 1817

Elizabeth Fry

Elizabeth Fry was a Quaker philanthropist and promoter of prison reform.

I have just returned from a most melancholy visit to Newgate, where I have been at the request of Elizabeth Fricker, previous to her execution [for robbery] tomorrow morning, at eight o'clock. I found her much hurried, distressed, and tormented in mind. Her hands cold, and covered with something like the perspiration preceding death, and in an universal tremor. The women who were with her said she had been so outrageous before our going that they thought a man must be sent for to manage her. However, after a serious time with her, her troubled soul became calmed. But is it for man thus to take the prerogative of the Almighty into his own hands? Is it not his place rather to endeavour to reform such; or restrain them from the commission of further evil? At least to afford poor erring fellow mortals, whatever may be their offences, an opportunity of proving their repentance by amendment of life. Besides this poor young woman, there are also six men to be hanged, one of whom has a wife near her confinement, also condemned, and seven young children. Since the awful report came down, he has become quite mad, from horror of mind. A strait waistcoat could not keep him within bounds: he had just bitten the turnkey; I saw the man come out with his hand bleeding, as I passed the cell.

Peterloo, 16 August 1819

Samuel Bamford

The mass meeting in St Peter's Field, Manchester, presided over by Henry Hunt, and seeking parliamentary reform, was dispersed, on the order of the magistrates, by the Manchester Yeomanry, the 15th Hussars and the Cheshire Volunteers. About 500 people were wounded and 11 killed.

In about half an hour after our arrival the sounds of music and reiterated shouts proclaimed the near approach of Mr Hunt and his party; and in a minute or two they were seen coming from Deansgate, preceded by a band of music and several flags. On the driving seat of a barouche sat a neatly dressed female, supporting a small flag, on which were some emblematical drawings and an inscription. Within the carriage were Mr Hunt, who stood up, Mr Johnson, of Smedley Cottage; Mr Moorhouse, of Stockport; Mr Carlile, of London; Mr John Knight, of Manchester; and Mr Saxton, a sub-editor of the *Manchester Observer*. Their approach was hailed by one universal shout from probably 80,000 persons. They threaded their way slowly past us and through the crowd, which Hunt eyed, I thought, with almost as much of astonishment as satisfaction. This spectacle could not be otherwise in his view than solemnly impressive. Such a mass of human beings he had not beheld till then. His responsibility must weigh on his mind. Their power for good or evil was irresistible, and who should direct that power? Himself alone who had called it forth. The task was great, and not without its peril. The meeting was indeed a tremendous one. He mounted the hustings; the music ceased; Mr Johnson proposed that Mr Hunt should take the chair; it was seconded, and carried by acclamation; and Mr Hunt, stepping towards the front of the stage, took off his white hat, and addressed the people.

Whilst he was doing so, I proposed to an acquaintance that, as the speeches and resolutions were not likely to contain anything new to us, and as we could see them in the papers, we should retire awhile and get some refreshment, of which I stood much in need, being not in very robust health. He assented, and we had got to nearly the outside of the crowd, when a noise and strange murmur arose towards the church. Some persons said it was the Blackburn people coming, and I stood on tiptoe and looked in the direction whence the noise proceeded, and saw a party of cavalry in blue and white uniform come trotting, sword in hand, round the corner of a garden wall, and to the front of a row of new houses, where they reined up in a line.

'The soldiers are here,' I said; 'we must go back and see what this means.' 'Oh,' someone made reply, 'they are only come to be ready if there should be any disturbance in the meeting.' 'Well, let us go back,' I said, and we forced our way towards the colours.

On the cavalry drawing up they were received with a shout of goodwill, as I understood it. They shouted again, waving their sabres over their heads; and then, slackening rein, and striking spur into their steeds, they dashed forward and began cutting the people.

'Stand fast,' I said, 'they are riding upon us; stand fast.' And there was a general cry in our quarter of 'Stand fast.' The cavalry were in confusion: they evidently could not, with all the weight of man and horse, penetrate that compact mass of human beings; and their sabres were plied to hew a way through naked held-up hands and defenceless heads; and then chopped limbs and wound-gaping skulls were seen; and groans and cries were mingled with the din of that horrid confusion. 'Ah! ah!' 'For shame! for shame!' was shouted. Then, 'Break! break! they are killing them in front, and they cannot get away'; and there was a general cry of 'Break! break.' For a moment the crowd held back as in a pause; then was a rush, heavy and resistless as a headlong sea, and a sound like low thunder, with screams, prayers, and imprecations from the crowd-moiled and sabre-doomed who could not escape.

By this time Hunt and his companions had disappeared from the hustings, and some of the yeomanry, perhaps less sanguinarily disposed than others, were busied in cutting down the flag-staves and demolishing the flags at the hustings.

On the breaking of the crowd the yeomanry wheeled, and, dashing whenever there was an opening, they followed, pressing and wounding. Many females appeared as the crowd opened; and striplings or mere youths also were found. Their cries were piteous and heart-rending, and would, one might have supposed, have disarmed any human resentment: but here their appeals were in vain. Women, white-vested maids, and tender youths, were indiscriminately sabred or trampled; and we have reason for believing that few were the instances in which that forbearance was vouchsafed which they so earnestly implored.

In ten minutes from the commencement of the havoc the field was an open and almost deserted space. The sun looked down through a sultry and motionless air. The curtains and blinds of the windows within view were all closed. A gentleman or two might occasionally be seen looking out from one of the new houses before mentioned, near the door of which a group of persons (special constables) were collected, and apparently in conversation; others were assisting the wounded or carrying off the dead. The hustings remained, with a few broken and hewed flag-staves erect, and a torn and gashed banner or two dropping; whilst over the whole field were strewed caps, bonnets, hats, shawls, and shoes, and other parts of male and female dress, trampled, torn, and bloody. The yeomanry had dismounted – some were easing their horses' girths, others adjusting their accoutrements, and some were wiping their sabres. Several mounds of human beings still remained where they had fallen, crushed down and smothered. Some of these still groaning, others with staring eyes, were gasping for breath, and others would never breathe more. All was silent save those low sounds, and the occasional snorting and pawing of steeds. Persons might sometimes be noticed peeping from attics and over the tall ridgings of houses, but they quickly withdrew, as if fearful of being observed, or unable to sustain the full gaze of a scene so hideous and abhorrent.

Cremation of the Poet Shelley, near Leghorn, 15 August 1822

Edward John Trelawny

Shelley had been drowned on 8 July 1822 when his yacht sank in a squall off Livorno.

Three white wands had been stuck in the sand to mark the Poet's grave, but as they were at some distance from each other, we had to cut a trench thirty yards in length, in the line of the sticks, to ascertain the exact spot, and it was nearly an hour before we came upon the grave.

In the mean time Byron and Leigh Hunt arrived in the carriage, attended by soldiers, and the Health Officer, as before [i.e. as on the previous day, when the body of Lieutenant Edward Williams, drowned with Shelley, was cremated]. The lonely and grand scenery that surrounded us so exactly harmonized with Shelley's genius, that I could imagine his spirit soaring over us. The sea, with the islands of Gorgona, Capraji, and Elba, was before us; old battlemented watchtowers stretched along the coast, backed by the marble-crested Apennines glistening in the sun, picturesque from their diversified outlines, and not a human dwelling was in sight. As I thought of the delight Shelley felt in such scenes of loneliness and grandeur whilst living, I felt we were no better than a herd of wolves or a pack of wild dogs, in tearing out his battered and naked body from the pure yellow sand that lay so lightly over it, to drag him back to the light of day; but the dead have no voice, nor had I power to check the sacrilege – the work went on silently in the deep and unresisting sand, not a word was spoken, for the Italians have a touch of sentiment, and their feelings are easily excited into sympathy. Even Byron was silent and thoughtful. We were startled and drawn together by a dull hollow sound that followed the blow of a mattock; the iron had struck a skull, and the body was soon uncovered. Lime had been strewn on it; this, or decomposition, had the effect of staining it of a dark and ghastly indigo colour. Byron asked me to preserve the skull for him; but remembering that he had formerly used one as a drinking-cup, I was determined Shelley's should not be so profaned. The limbs did not separate from the trunk, as in the case of Williams's body, so that the corpse was removed entire into the furnace. I had taken the precaution of having more and larger pieces of timber, in consequence of my experience of the day before of the difficulty of consuming a corpse in the open air with our apparatus. After the fire was well kindled we repeated the ceremony of the previous day; and more wine was poured over Shelley's dead body than he had consumed during his life. This with the oil and salt made the yellow flames glisten and quiver. The heat from the sun and fire was so intense that the atmosphere was tremulous and wavy. The corpse fell open and the heart was laid bare. The frontal bone of the skull, where it had been struck with the mattock, fell off; and, as the back of the head rested on the red-hot bottom bars of the furnace, the brains literally seethed, bubbled, and boiled as in a cauldron, for a very long time.

Byron could not face this scene, he withdrew to the beach and swam off to the *Bolivar*. Leigh Hunt remained in the carriage. The fire was so fierce as to produce a white heat on the iron, and to reduce its contents to grey ashes. The only portions that were not consumed were some fragments of bones, the jaw, and the skull, but what surprised us all, was that the heart remained entire. In snatching this relic from the fiery furnace, my hand was severely burnt; and had anyone seen me do the act I should have been put into quarantine.

Exit George IV, 1830

Mrs Arbuthnot

[23 April] – The King goes on much the same. The Doctors say he is a little better, but I think Halford is persuaded he will die. He gets black in the face & his pulse alters when he has these attacks on his breath, which they think shows something wrong about the heart. They took him out airing ten days ago &, when he got to the Lodge, he was so bad they were frightful to death & thought he would die. They gave him quantities of brandy, & he rallied so completely that he got into his carriage & drove 20 miles. His mode of living is really beyond belief. One day last week, at the hour of the servants' dinner, he called the Page in & said, 'Now you are going to dinner. Go down stairs & cut me off just such a piece of beef as you would like to have yourself, cut from the part you like the best yourself, & bring it me up.' The page accordingly went and fetched him an enormous quantity of roast beef, all of which he eat, & then slept for 5 hours.

One night he drank two glasses of hot ale & toast, three glasses of claret, some strawberries!! and a glass of brandy. Last night they gave him some physic and, after it, he drank three glasses of port wine & a glass of brandy. No wonder he is likely to die! But they say he will have all these things & nobody can prevent him. I dare say the wine would not hurt him, for with the Evil (which all the Royal Family have) it is necessary, I believe, to have a great deal of high food, but the mixture of *ale* & strawberries is enough to kill a horse . . .

[16 July] – I went yesterday to Windsor to the funeral of the late King. I went in the morning with Lady Georgiana Fane to Sir Andrew

Barnard's room in the Castle. He and Lord Fife went with us to see the Lying in State. It was in one of the old State Rooms in the Castle. The coffin was very fine and a most enormous size. They were very near having a frightful accident for, when the body was in the leaden coffin, the lead was observed to have bulged very considerably & in fact was in great danger of bursting. They were obliged to puncture the lead to let out the air & then to fresh cover it with lead. Rather an *unpleasant operation*, I should think, but the embalming must have been very ill done.

The Opening of the Liverpool to Manchester Railway, 15 September 1830

Frances Ann Kemble

The Liverpool to Manchester Railway was the first for which high-speed locomotives were designed. William Huskisson (1770–1830) whose death is described here, was a prominent politician.

We started on Wednesday last, to the number of about eight hundred people, in carriages. The most intense curiosity and excitement prevailed, and, though the weather was uncertain, enormous masses of densely packed people lined the road, shouting and waving hats and handkerchiefs as we flew by them. What with the sight and sound of these cheering multitudes and the tremendous velocity with which we were borne past them, my spirits rose to the true champagne height, and I never enjoyed anything so much as the first hour of our progress. I had been unluckily separated from my mother in the first distribution of places, but by an exchange of seats which she was enabled to make she rejoined me when I was at the height of my ecstasy, which was considerably damped by finding that she was frightened to death, and intent upon nothing but devising means of escaping from a situation which appeared to her to threaten with instant annihilation herself and all her travelling companions. While I was chewing the cud of this disappointment, which was rather bitter, as I had expected her to be as delighted as myself with our excursion, a man flew by us, calling out through a speaking-trumpet to stop the engine, for that somebody in the directors' carriage had sustained an injury. We were all stopped accordingly, and presently a hundred voices were heard exclaiming that Mr Huskisson was killed; the confusion that ensued is indescribable; the calling out from carriage to carriage to ascertain the truth, the contrary reports which were sent back to us, the hundred questions eagerly uttered at once, and the repeated and urgent demands for surgical assistance, created a sudden turmoil that was quite sickening. At last we distinctly ascertained that the unfortunate man's thigh was broken. From Lady Wilton, who was in the Duke's carriage, and within three yards of the spot where the accident happened, I had the following details, the horror of witnessing which we were spared through our situation behind the great carriage. The engine had stopped to take in a supply of water, and several of the gentlemen in the directors' carriage had jumped out to look about them. Lord Wilton, Count Batthyany, Count Matuscenitz, and Mr Huskisson among the rest were standing talking in the middle of the road, when an engine on the other line, which was parading up and down merely to show its speed, was seen coming down upon them like lightning. The most active of those in peril sprang back into their seats; Lord Wilton saved his life only by rushing behind the Duke's carriage, and Count Matuscenitz had but just leaped into it, with the engine all but touching his heels as he did so; while poor Mr Huskisson, less active from the effects of age and ill-health, bewildered, too, by the frantic cries of 'Stop the engine! Clear the track!' that resounded on all sides, completely lost his head, looked helplessly to the right and left, and was instantaneously prostrated by the fatal machine, which dashed down like a thunderbolt upon him, and passed over his leg, smashing and mangling it in the most horrible way. (Lady Wilton said she distinctly heard the crushing of the bone.) So terrible was the effect of the appalling accident that, except that ghastly 'crushing' and poor Mrs Huskisson's piercing shriek, not a sound was heard or a word uttered among the immediate spectators of the catastrophe. Lord Wilton was the first to raise the poor sufferer, and calling to aid his surgical skill, which is considerable, he tied up the severed artery, and, for a time at least, prevented death by loss of blood. Mr Huskisson was then placed in a carriage with his wife and Lord Wilton, and the engine, having been detached from the directors' carriage, conveyed them to Manchester. So great was the shock produced upon the whole party by this event, that the Duke of

Wellington declared his intention not to proceed, but to return immediately to Liverpool. However, upon its being represented to him that the whole population of Manchester had turned out to witness the procession, and that a disappointment might give rise to riots and disturbances, he consented to go on, and gloomily enough the rest of the journey was accomplished . . .

After this disastrous event the day became overcast, and as we neared Manchester the sky grew cloudy and dark, and it began to rain. The vast concourse of people who had assembled to witness the triumphant arrival of the successful travellers was of the lowest order of mechanics and artisans, among whom great distress and a dangerous spirit of discontent with the government at that time prevailed. Groans and hisses greeted the carriage, full of influential personages, in which the Duke of Wellington sat. High above the grim and grimy crowd of scowling faces a loom had been erected, at which sat a tattered, starved-looking weaver, evidently set there as a representative man, to protest against the triumph of machinery and the gain and glory which the wealthy Liverpool and Manchester men were likely to derive from it. The contrast between our departure from Liverpool and our arrival at Manchester was one of the most striking things I ever witnessed. The news of Mr Huskisson's fatal accident spread immediately, and his death, which did not occur till the evening, was anticipated by rumour.

Cholera in Manchester, 1832

Sir James Kay-Shuttleworth

I had requested the younger members of the staff, charged with the visitation of the outpatients of the infirmary, to give me the earliest information of the occurrence of any cases indicating the approach of cholera. I had a scientific wish to trace the mode of its propagation, and to ascertain if possible by what means it would be introduced into the town. My purpose also was to discover whether there was any, and if so what, link or connection between the physical and social evils, to which my attention had been so long directed.

A loop of the river Medlock swept round by a group of houses lying immediately below Oxford Road, and almost on the level of the black, polluted stream. This was a colony of Irish labourers and consequently known as Irishtown. I was requested by one of the staff of the outpatients of the infirmary to visit a peculiar case in one of these cottages. He gave me no description of it as we walked thither. On my arrival in a two-roomed house, I found an Irishman lying on a bed close to the window. The temperature of his skin was somewhat lower than usual, the pulse was weak and quick. He complained of no pain. The face was rather pale, and the man much dejected. None of the characteristic symptoms of cholera had occurred, but his attendant told me that the strength had gradually declined during the day, and that, seeing no cause for it, he had formed a suspicion of contagion. I sat by the man's bed for an hour, during which the pulse became gradually weaker. In a second hour it was almost extinct, and it became apparent that the patient would die. His wife and three children were in the room, and she was prepared by us for the too probable event. Thus the afternoon slowly passed away, and as evening approached I sent the young surgeon to have in readiness the cholera van not far away. We were surrounded by an excitable Irish population, and it was obviously desirable to remove the body as soon as possible, and then the family, and to lock up the house before any alarm was given. As twilight came on the sufferer expired without cramp or any other characteristic symptom. The wife had been soothed and she readily consented to be removed with her children to the hospital. Then suddenly the van drew up at the door, and in one minute, before the Irish were aware, drove away with its sad burden.

No case of Asiatic cholera had occurred in Manchester, yet notwithstanding the total absence of characteristic symptoms in this case, I was convinced that the contagion had arrived, and the patient had been its victim. The Knott Hill Hospital was a cotton factory stripped of its machinery, and furnished with iron bedsteads and bedding on every floor. On my arrival here I found the widow and her three children with a nurse grouped round a fire at one end of a gloomy ward. I ascertained that all necessary arrangements had been made for their comfort. They had an evening meal; the children were put to bed near the fire, except the infant which I left lying upon its mother's lap. None of them showed any sign of disease, and I left the ward to take some refreshment. On my return, or at a later visit before midnight, the infant had been sick in its mother's lap, had made a faint cry and had died. The mother was naturally full of terror and distress, for the child had had no medicine, had been fed only from its mother's breast, and, consequently, she could have no doubt that it perished from the same causes as its father. I sat with her and the nurse by the fire very late into the night. While I was there the children did not wake, nor seem in any way disturbed, and at length I thought I might myself seek some repose. When I returned about six o'clock in the morning, another child had severe cramps with some sickness, and while I stood by the bedside, it died. Then, later, the third and eldest child had all the characteristic symptoms of cholera and perished in one or two hours. In the course of the day the mother likewise suffered from a severe and rapid succession of the characteristic symptoms and died, so that within twenty-four hours the whole family was extinct, and it was not known that any other case of cholera had occurred in Manchester or its vicinity.

Birds in the Galapagos Archipelago, September 1835

Charles Darwin

I will conclude my description of the natural history of these islands, by giving an account of the extreme tameness of the birds.

This disposition is common to all the terrestrial species; namely, to the mocking-thrushes, the finches, wrens, tyrant-flycatchers, the dove, and carrion-buzzard. All of them often approached sufficiently near to be killed with a switch, and sometimes, as I myself tried, with a cap or hat. A gun is here almost superfluous; for with the muzzle I pushed a hawk off the branch of a tree. One day, whilst lying down, a mocking-thrush alighted on the edge of a pitcher, made of the shell of a tortoise, which I held in my hand, and began very quietly to sip the water; it allowed me to lift it from the ground whilst seated on the vessel: I often tried, and very nearly succeeded, in catching these birds by their legs. Formerly the birds appear to have been even tamer than at present. Cowley (in the year 1684) says that the 'Turtle-doves were so tame, that they would often alight upon our hats and arms, so as that we could take them alive: they not fearing man, until such time as some of our company did fire at them, whereby they were rendered more shy.' Dampier also, in the same year, says that a man in a morning's walk might kill six or seven dozen of these doves. At present, although certainly very tame, they do not alight on people's arms, nor do they suffer themselves to be killed in such large numbers. It is surprising that they have not become wilder; for these islands during the last hundred and fifty years have been frequently visited by buccaneers and whalers; and the sailors, wandering through the woods in search of tortoises, always take cruel delight in knocking down the little birds.

These birds, although now still more persecuted, do not readily become wild: in Charles Island, which had then been colonized about six years, I saw a boy sitting by a well with a switch in his hand, with which he killed the doves and finches as they came to drink. He had already procured a little heap of them for his dinner; and he said that he had constantly been in the habit of waiting by this well for the same purpose. It would appear that the birds in this archipelago, not having as yet learnt that man is a more dangerous animal than the tortoise or the Amblyrhynchus, disregard him, in the same manner as in England shy birds, such as magpies, disregard the cows and horses grazing in our fields.

The Coronation of Queen Victoria, 29 June 1838

Charles Greville

The Coronation (which, thank God, is over) went off very well. The day was fine, without heat or rain – the innumerable multitude which thronged the streets orderly and satisfied. The appearance of the Abbey was beautiful, particularly the benches of the Peeresses, who were blazing with diamonds. The entry of Soult [who had been one of Napoleon's marshals] was striking. He was saluted with a murmur of curiosity and applause as he passed through the nave, and nearly the same as he advanced along the choir. His appearance is that of a veteran warrior, and he walked alone, with his numerous suite following at a respectful distance, preceded by heralds and ushers, who received him with marked attention, more certainly than any of the other Ambassadors. The Queen looked very diminutive, and the effect of the procession itself was spoilt by being too crowded; there was not interval enough between the Queen and the Lords and others going before her. The Bishop of London (Blomfield) preached a very good sermon. The different actors in the ceremonial were very imperfect in their parts, and had neglected to rehearse them. Lord John Thynne, who officiated for the Dean of Westminster, told me that nobody knew what was to be done except the Archbishop and himself (who had rehearsed), Lord Willoughby (who is experienced in these matters), and the Duke of Wellington, and consequently there was a continual difficulty and embarrassment, and the Queen never knew what she was to do next. They made her leave her chair and enter into St Edward's Chapel before the prayers were concluded, much to the discomfiture of the Archbishop. She said to John Thynne, 'Pray tell me what I am to do, for they don't know'; and at the end, when the orb was put into her hand, she said to him, 'What am I to do with it?' 'Your Majesty is to carry it, if you please, in your hand.' 'Am I?' she said; 'it is very heavy.' The ruby ring was made for her little finger instead of the fourth, on which the rubric prescribes that it should be put. When the Archbishop was to put it on, she extended the former, but he said it must be on the latter. She said it was too small, and she could not get it on. He said it was right to put it there, and, as he insisted, she yielded, but had first to take off her other rings, and then this was forced on, but it hurt her very much, and as soon as the ceremony was over she was obliged to bathe her finger in iced water in order to get it off.

London Prostitutes, 1839

Flora Tristan

Flora Tristan, a Frenchwoman, and one of the first socialists and feminists, was on a fact-finding visit to England.

Between seven and eight o'clock one evening, accompanied by two friends armed with canes, I went to take a look at the new suburb which lies on either side of the long broad thoroughfare called Waterloo Road at the end of Waterloo Bridge. This neighbourhood is almost entirely inhabited by prostitutes and people who live off prostitution; it is courting danger to go there alone at night. It was a hot summer evening; in every window and doorway women were laughing and joking with their protectors. Half-dressed, some of them *naked to the waist*, they were a revolting sight, and the criminal, cynical expressions of their companions filled me with apprehension. These men are for the most part very good-looking – young, vigorous and well made – but their coarse and common air marks them as animals whose sole instinct is to satisfy their appetites.

Several of them accosted us and asked if we wanted a room. When we answered in the negative, one bolder than the rest demanded in a threatening tone, 'What are you doing here then, if you don't want a room for you and your lady friend?' I must confess I would not have liked to find myself alone with that man.

We went on our way and explored all the streets in the vicinity of Waterloo Road, then we sat upon the bridge to watch the women of the neighbourhood flock past, as they do every evening between the hours of eight and nine, on their way to the West End, where they ply their trade all through the night and return home between eight and nine in the morning. They infest the promenades and any other place where people gather, such as the approaches to the Stock Exchange, the various public buildings and the theatres, which they invade as soon as entry is reduced to half-price, turning all the corridors and foyers into their receiving-rooms. After the play they move on to the 'finishes'; these are squalid taverns or vast resplendent gin-palaces where people go to spend what remains of the night.

The 'finish' is as much a part of life in England as the beer-cellar in Germany or the elegant café in France. In the tavern the clerk and the shop assistant drink ale, smoke cheap tobacco and get drunk with tawdrily dressed women; in the gin-palace, fashionable gentlemen drink Cognac, punch, sherry, port, and French and Rhenish wines, smoke excellent Havana cigars, and flirt with beautiful young girls in splendid gowns. But in both places scenes of orgy are acted out in all their brutality and horror.

I had heard descriptions of the debauchery to be seen at finishes, but could never bring myself to believe them. Now I was in London for the fourth time with the firm resolve to discover everything for myself. I determined to overcome my repugnance and go in person to one of these finishes, so that I might judge for myself how far I could trust the various accounts I had been given. The same friends who had accompanied me to the Waterloo Road again offered to be my guides.

What goes on in these places ought to be seen, for it reveals the moral state of England better than any words could express. These splendid pleasure-houses have an appearance all their own. Those who frequent them seem to be dedicated to the night; they go to bed when the sun begins to light the horizon and awaken after it has set. From the outside, these 'gin-palaces' with their carefully fastened shutters seem to be quietly slumbering; but no sooner has the doorkeeper admitted you by the little door reserved for initiates than you are dazzled by the light of a thousand gas lamps. Upstairs there is a spacious salon divided down the middle; in one half there is a row of tables separated one from the other by wooden screens, as in all English restaurants, with upholstered seats like sofas on each side of the tables. In the other half there is a dais where the prostitutes parade in all their finery, seeking to arouse the men with their glances and remarks; when a gallant gentleman responds, they lead him off to one of the tables loaded with cold meats, hams, poultry, pastries and every manner of wines and spirits.

The finishes are the temples which English materialism raises to its gods; the servants who minister in them are dressed in rich liveries, and the capitalist owners reverently greet the male guests who come to exchange their gold for debauchery.

Towards midnight the regular clients begin to arrive; several finishes are frequented by men in high society, and this is where the cream of the aristocracy gather. At first the young noblemen recline on the sofas, smoking and exchanging pleasantries with the women; then, when they have drunk enough for the fumes of champagne and Madeira to go to their heads, the illustrious scions of the English nobility, the very honourable members of Parliament, remove their coats, untie their cravats, take off their waistcoats and braces, and proceed to set up their private boudoir in a public place. Why not make themselves at home, since they are paying out so much money for the right to display their contempt? As for any contempt *they* might inspire, they do not care in the least. The orgy rises to a crescendo; between four and five o'clock in the morning it reaches its height.

At this point it takes a good deal of courage to remain in one's seat, a mute spectator of all that takes place. What a worthy use these English lords make of their immense fortunes! How fine and generous they are when they have lost the use of their reason and offer fifty, even a hundred, guineas to a prostitute if she will lend herself to all the obscenities that drunkenness engenders.

For in a finish there is no lack of entertainment. One of the favourite sports is to *ply a woman with drink* until she falls dead drunk upon the floor, then to make her swallow a draught compounded of *vinegar, mustard,* and *pepper,* this invariably throws the poor creature into horrible convulsions, and her spasms and contortions provoke the *honourable company* to gales of laughter and infinite amusement. Another diversion much appreciated at these fashionable gatherings is to empty the contents of the nearest glass upon the women as they lie insensible on the ground. I have seen satin dresses of no recognizable colour, only a confused mass of stains: wine, brandy, beer, tea, coffee, cream, etc., daubed all over them in a thousand fantastic shapes – the handiwork of debauchery!

Death by Guillotine: Rome, 8 March 1845

Charles Dickens

The criminal, whose name Dickens does not give, had been condemned for robbing and murdering a Bavarian countess who was travelling as a pilgrim to Rome.

The beheading was appointed for fourteen and a half o'clock, Roman time: or a quarter before nine in the forenoon. I had two friends with me; and as we did not know but that the crowd might be very great, we were on the spot by half-past seven. The place of execution was near the church of San Giovanni decolláto (a doubtful compliment to Saint John the Baptist) in one of the impassable back streets without any footway, of which a great part of Rome is composed – a street of rotten houses, which do not seem to belong to anybody, and do not seem to have ever been inhabited, and certainly were never built on any plan, or for any particular purpose, and have no window-sashes, and are a little like deserted breweries, and might be warehouses but for having nothing in them. Opposite to one of these, a white house, the scaffold was built. An untidy, unpainted, uncouth, crazy-looking thing of course: some seven feet high, perhaps: with a tall, gallows-shaped frame rising above it, in which was the knife, charged with a ponderous mass of iron, all ready to descend, and glittering brightly in the morning sun, whenever it looked out, now and then, from behind a cloud.

There were not many people lingering about; and these were kept at a considerable distance from the scaffold, by parties of the Pope's dragoons. Two or three hundred foot-soldiers were under arms, standing at ease in clusters here and there; and the officers were walking up and down in twos and threes, chatting together, and smoking cigars.

At the end of the street, was an open space, where there would be a dust-heap, and piles of broken crockery, and mounds of vegetable refuse, but for such things being thrown anywhere and everywhere in Rome, and favouring no particular sort of locality. We got into a kind of wash-house, belonging to a dwelling-house on this spot; and standing there in an old cart, and on a heap of cart-wheels piled against the wall, looking, through a large grated window, at the scaffold, and straight down the street beyond it, until, in consequence of its turning off abruptly to the left, our perspective was brought to a sudden termination, and had a corpulent officer, in a cocked hat, for its crowning feature.

Nine o'clock struck, and ten o'clock struck, and nothing happened. All the bells of all the churches rang as usual. A little parliament of dogs assembled in the open space, and chased each other, in and out among the soldiers. Fierce-looking Romans of the lowest class, in blue cloaks, russet cloaks, and rags uncloaked, came and went, and talked together. Women and children fluttered, on the skirts of the scanty crowd. One large muddy spot was left quite bare, like a bald place on a man's head. A cigar-merchant, with an earthern pot of charcoal ashes in one hand, went up and down, crying his wares. A pastry-merchant divided his attention between the scaffold and his customers. Boys tried to climb up walls, and tumbled down again. Priests and monks elbowed a passage for themselves among the people, and stood on tiptoe for a sight of the knife: then went away. Artists, in inconceivable hats of the middle-ages, and beards (thank Heaven!) of no age at all, flashed picturesque scowls about them from their stations in the throng. One gentleman (connected with the fine arts, I presume) went up and down in a pair of Hessian-boots, with a red beard hanging down on his breast, and his long and bright red hair, plaited into two tails, one on either side of his head, which fell over his shoulders in front of him, very nearly to his waist, and were carefully entwined and braided!

Eleven o'clock struck; and still nothing happened. A rumour got about, among the crowd that the criminal would not confess; in which case, the priests would keep him until the Ave Maria (sunset); for it is their merciful custom never finally to turn the crucifix away from a man at that pass, as one refusing to be shriven, and consequently a sinner abandoned of the Saviour, until then. People began to drop off. The officers shrugged their shoulders and looked doubtful. The dragoons, who came riding up below our window, every now and then, to order an unlucky hackney-coach or cart away, as soon as it had comfortably established itself, and was covered with exulting people (but never before), became imperious, and quick-tempered. The bald place hadn't a straggling hair upon it; and the corpulent officer, crowning the perspective, took a world of snuff.

Suddenly, there was a noise of trumpets. 'Attention!' was among the foot-soldiers instantly. They were marched up to the scaffold and formed round it. The dragoons galloped to their near stations too. The guillotine became the centre of the wood of bristling bayonets and shining sabres. The people closed round nearer, on the flank of the soldiery. A long straggling stream of men and boys, who had accompanied the procession from the prison, came pouring into the open space. The bald spot was scarcely distinguishable from the rest. The cigar and pastry-merchants resigned all thoughts of business, for the moment, and abandoning themselves wholly to pleasure, got good situations in the crowd. The perspective ended, now, in a troop of dragoons. And the corpulent officer, sword in hand, looked hard at a church close to him, which he could see, but we, the crowd, could not.

After a short delay, some monks were seen approaching to the scaffold from this church; and above their heads, coming on slowly and gloomily, the effigy of Christ upon the cross, canopied with black. This was carried round the foot of the scaffold, to the front, and turned towards the criminal, that he might see it to the last. It was hardly in its place, when he appeared on the platform, barefooted; his hands bound; and with the collar and neck of his shirt cut away, almost to the shoulder. A young man – six-and-twenty – vigorously made, and well shaped. Face pale; small dark moustache; and dark brown hair.

He had refused to confess, it seemed, without first having his wife brought to see him; and they had sent an escort for her, which had occasioned the delay.

He immediately kneeled down, before the knife. His neck fitting into a hole, made for the purpose, in a cross plank, was shut down, by another plank above; exactly like the pillory. Immediately below him was a leathern bag. And into it his head rolled instantly.

The executioner was holding it by the hair, and walking with it round the scaffold, showing it to the people, before one quite knew that the knife had fallen heavily, and with a rattling sound.

When it had travelled round the four sides of the scaffold, it was set upon a pole in front – a little patch of black and white, for the long street to stare at, and the flies to settle on. The eyes were turned upward, as if he had avoided the sight of the leathern bag, and looked to the crucifix. Every tinge and hue of life had left it in that instant. It was dull, cold, livid, wax. The body also.

There was a great deal of blood. When we left the window, and went close up to the scaffold, it was very dirty; one of the two men who were throwing water over it, turning to help the other lift the body into a shell, picked his way as through mire. A strange appearance was the apparent annihilation of the neck. The head was taken off so close, that it seemed as if the knife had narrowly escaped crushing the jaw, or shaving off the ear; and the body looked as if there were nothing left above the shoulder.

Nobody cared, or was at all affected. There was no manifestation of disgust, or pity, or indignation, or sorrow.

American Slavery: Sale of Slaves, Virginia, December 1846

Dr Elwood Harvey

We attended a sale of land and other property, near Petersburg, Virginia, and unexpectedly saw slaves sold at public auction. The slaves were told they would not be sold, and were collected in front of the quarters, gazing on the assembled multitude. The land being sold, the auctioneer's loud voice was heard, 'Bring up the *niggers*!' A shade of astonishment and affright passed over their faces, as they stared first at each other, and then at the crowd of purchasers, whose attention was now directed to them. When the horrible truth was revealed to their minds that they were to be sold, and nearest relations and friends parted for ever, the effect was indescribably agonizing. Women snatched up their babes, and ran screaming into the huts. Children hid behind the huts and trees, and the men stood in mute despair. The auctioneer stood on the portico of the house, and the 'men and boys' were ranging in the yard for inspection. It was announced that no warranty of *soundness* was given, and purchasers must examine for themselves. A few old men were sold at prices from thirteen to twenty-five dollars, and it was painful to see old men, bowed with years of toil and suffering, stand up to be the jest of brutal tyrants, and to hear them tell their disease and worthlessness, fearing that they would be bought by traders for the Southern market.

A white boy, about fifteen years old, was placed on the stand. His hair was brown and straight, his skin exactly the same hue as other white persons, and no discernible trace of negro features in his countenance.

Some vulgar jests were passed on his colour, and two hundred dollars were bid for him; but the audience said 'that it was not enough to begin on for such a likely young nigger'. Several remarked that they 'would not have him as a gift'. Some said a white nigger was more trouble than he was worth. One man said it was wrong to sell *white* people. I asked him if it was more wrong than to sell black people. He made no reply. Before he was sold, his mother rushed from the house upon the portico, crying, in frantic grief, 'My son, O! my boy, they will take away my dear – .' Here her voice was lost, as she was rudely pushed back and the door closed. The sale was not for a moment interrupted, and none of the crowd appeared to be in the least affected by the scene. The poor boy, afraid to cry before so many strangers, who showed no signs of sympathy or pity, trembled, and wiped the tears from his cheeks with his sleeves. He was sold for about two hundred and fifty dollars. During the sale, the quarters resounded with cries and lamentations that made my heart ache. A woman was next called by name. She gave her infant one wild embrace before leaving it with an old woman, and hastened mechanically to obey the call; but stopped, threw her arms aloft, screamed, and was unable to move.

One of my companions touched my shoulder and said, 'Come, let us leave here; I can bear no more.' We left the ground. The man who drove our carriage from Petersburg had two sons who belonged to the estate – small boys. He obtained a promise that they should not be sold. He was asked if they were his only children; he answered; 'All that's left of eight.' Three others had been sold to the South, and he would never see or hear from them again.

American Slavery: Punishment of a Female Slave, New Orleans, c. 1846

Samuel Gridley Howe

The author, Samuel Gridley Howe, was a leading American educator, and a pioneer in the education of blind and handicapped children.

I have passed ten days in New Orleans, not unprofitably, I trust, in examining the public institutions – the schools, asylums, hospitals, prisons, etc. With the exception of the first, there is little hope of amelioration. I know not how much merit there may be in their system; but I do know that, in the administration of the penal code, there are abominations which should bring down the fate of Sodom upon the city. If Howard or Mrs Fry ever discovered so ill-administered a den of thieves as the New Orleans prison, they never described it. In the negroes' apartment I saw much which made me blush that I was a white man, and which, for a moment, stirred up an evil spirit in my animal nature. Entering a large paved courtyard, around which ran galleries filled with slaves of all ages, sexes, and colours, I heard the snap of a whip, every stroke of which sounded like the sharp crack of a pistol. I turned my head, and beheld a sight which absolutely chilled me to the marrow of my bones, and gave me, for the first time in my life, the sensation of my hair stiffening at the roots. There lay a black girl flat upon her face, on a board, her two thumbs tied, and fastened to one end, her feet tied and drawn tightly to the other end, while a strap passed over the small of her back, and, fastened around the board, compressed her closely to it. Below the strap she was entirely naked. By her side, and six feet off, stood a huge negro, with a long whip, which he applied with dreadful power and wonderful precision. Every stroke brought away a strip of skin, which clung to the lash, or fell quivering on the pavement, while the blood followed after it. The poor creature writhed and shrieked, and, in a voice which showed alike her fear of death and her dreadful agony, screamed to her master, who stood at her head, 'O, spare my life! don't cut my soul out!' But still fell the horrid lash; still strip after strip peeled off from the skin; gash after gash was cut in her living flesh, until it became a livid and bloody mass of raw and quivering muscle. It was with the greatest difficulty I refrained from springing upon the torturer, and arresting his lash; but, alas! what could I do, but turn aside to hide my tears for the sufferer, and my blushes for humanity? This was in a public and regularly organized prison; the punishment was one recognized and authorized by the law. But think you the poor wretch had committed a heinous offence, and had been convicted thereof, and sentenced to the lash? Not at all. She was brought by her master to be whipped by the common executioner, without trial, judge or jury, just at his beck or nod, for some real or supposed offence, or to gratify his own whim or malice. And he may bring her day after day, without cause assigned, and inflict any number of lashes he pleases, short of twenty-five, provided only he pays the fee. Or, if he choose, he may have a private whipping-board on his own premises, and brutalize himself there. A shocking part of this horrid punishment was its publicity, as I have said; it was in a courtyard surrounded by galleries, which were filled with coloured persons of all sexes – runaway slaves, committed for some crime, or slaves up for sale. You would naturally suppose they crowded forward, and gazed, horror-stricken, at the brutal spectacle below; but they did not; many of them hardly noticed it, and many were entirely indifferent to it. They went on in their childish pursuits, and some were laughing outright in the distant parts of the galleries; so low can man, created in God's image, be sunk in brutality.

The Irish Potato Famine: Victims of the Great Hunger, Castlehaven, 22 February 1847

Elihu Burritt

The Irish famine was the result of a devastating outbreak of potato blight which began in Europe in 1845. Of Ireland's population of 8 million about 1 million died of starvation and 1.5 million emigrated, mostly to the USA.

We entered a stinted den by an aperture about three feet high, and found one or two children lying asleep with their eyes open in the straw. Such, at least, was their appearance, for they scarcely winked while we were before them. The father came in and told his pitiful story of want, saying that not a morsel of food had they tasted for 24 hours. He lighted a wisp of straw and showed us one or two more children lying in another nook of the cave. Their mother had died, and he was obliged to leave them alone during most of the day, in order to glean something for their subsistence. We were soon among the most wretched habitations that I had yet seen, far worse than Skibbereen. Many of them were flat-roofed hovels, half buried in the earth, or built up against the rocks, and covered with rotten straw, seaweed or turf. In one which was scarcely seven feet square, we found five persons prostrate with the fever, and apparently near their end. A girl about sixteen, the very picture of despair, was the only one left who could administer any relief; and all she could do was to bring water in a broken pitcher to slake their parched lips. As we proceeded up a rocky hill overlooking the sea, we encountered new sights of wretchedness. Seeing a cabin standing somewhat by itself in a hollow, and surrounded by a moat of green filth, we entered it with some difficulty, and found a single child about three years old lying on a kind of shelf, with its little face resting upon the edge of the board and looking steadfastly out at the door as if for its mother. It never moved its eyes as we entered, but kept them fixed toward the entrance. It is doubtful whether the poor thing had a mother or father left to her; but it is more doubtful still whether those eyes would have relaxed their vacant gaze if both of them had entered at once with anything that could tempt the palate in their hands. No words can describe this peculiar appearance of the famished children. Never have I seen such bright, blue, clear eyes looking so steadfastly at nothing.

Flaubert and the Dancing Girls: Esna, Egypt, 6 March 1850

Gustave Flaubert

'Max' was Flaubert's travelling companion in Egypt, Maxime Du Camp; Joseph, Flaubert's Genoese dragoman. Almeh, meaning 'learned woman', was the name used for dancing girls and prostitutes.

While we were breakfasting, an *almeh* came to speak with Joseph. She was thin, with a narrow forehead, her eyes painted with antimony, a veil passed over her head and held by her elbows. She was followed by a pet sheep, whose wool was painted in spots with yellow henna. Around its nose was a black velvet muzzle. It was very woolly, its feet like those of a toy sheep, and it never left its mistress.

We go ashore. The town is like all the others, built of dried mud, smaller than Kena; the bazaars less rich. On the square, Albanian soldiers at a café. The postal authorities 'reside' on the square: that is, the *effendi* comes there to perform his functions. School above a mosque, where we go to buy some ink. First visit to the temple, where we stay but a moment. The houses have a kind of square tower, with poles thick with pigeons. In the doorways, a few *almehs*, fewer than at Kena, their dress less brilliant and their aspect less bold.

House of Kuchuk Hanem
Bambeh precedes us, accompanied by her sheep; she pushes open a door and we enter a house with a small courtyard and a stairway opposite the door. On the stairs, opposite us, surrounded by light and standing against the background of blue sky, a woman in pink trousers. Above, she wore only dark violet gauze.

She had just come from the bath, her firm breasts had a fresh smell, something like that of sweetened turpentine; she began by perfuming her hands with rose water.

We went up to the first floor. Turning to the left at the top of the stairs, we entered a square whitewashed room: two divans, two windows, one looking on the mountains, the other on the town.

... Kuchuk Hanem is a tall, splendid creature, lighter in colouring than an Arab; she comes from Damascus; her skin, particularly on her body, is slightly coffee-coloured. When she bends, her flesh ripples into bronze ridges. Her eyes are dark and enormous. Her eyebrows black, her nostrils open and wide; heavy shoulders, full, apple-shaped breasts. She wore a large tarboosh, ornamented on the top with a convex gold disk, in the middle of which was a small green stone imitating emerald; the blue tassel of her tarboosh was spread out fanwise and fell down over her shoulders; just in front of the lower edge of the tarboosh, fastened to her hair and going from one ear to the other, she had a small spray of white artificial flowers. Her black hair, wavy, unruly, pulled straight back on each side from a centre parting beginning at the forehead; small braids joined together at the nape of her neck. She has one upper incisor, right, which is beginning to go bad. For a bracelet she has two bands of gold, twisted together and interlaced, around one wrist. Triple necklace of large hollow gold beads. Earrings: gold disks, slightly convex, circumference decorated with gold granules. On her right arm is tattooed a line of blue writing.

She asks us if we would like a little entertainment, but Max says that first he would like to entertain himself alone with her, and they go downstairs. After he finishes, I go down and follow his example. Ground-floor room, with a divan and a *cafas* [an upturned palm-fibre basket] with a mattress.

Dance

The musicians arrive: a child and an old man, whose left eye is covered with a rag; they both scrape on the *rebabah*, a kind of small round violin with a metal leg that rests on the ground and two horse-hair strings. The neck of the instrument is very long in proportion to the rest. Nothing could be more discordant or disagreeable. The musicians never stop playing for an instant unless you shout at them to do so.

Kuchuk Hanem and Bambeh begin to dance. Kuchuk's dance is brutal. She squeezes her bare breasts together with her jacket. She puts on a girdle fashioned from a brown shawl with gold stripes, with three tassels hanging on ribbons. She rises first on one foot, then on the other – marvellous movement: when one foot is on the ground, the other moves up and across in front of the shin-bone – the whole thing with a light bound. I have seen this dance on old Greek vases.

Bambeh prefers a dance on a straight line; she moves with a lowering and raising of one hip only, a kind of rhythmic limping of great character. Bambeh has henna on her hands. She seems to be a devoted servant to Kuchuk. (She was a chambermaid in Cairo in an Italian household and understands a few words of Italian; her eyes are slightly diseased.) All in all, their dancing – except Kuchuk's step mentioned above – is far less good than that of Hasan el-Belbeissi, the male dancer in Cairo. Joseph's opinion is that all beautiful women dance badly.

At the café of *ces dames*. We take a cup of coffee. The place is like all such places – flat roof of sugar-cane stalks put together any which way. Kuchuk's amusement at seeing our shaven heads and hearing Max say: *Allah il allah*, etc.

We return to Kuchuk's house. The room was lighted by three wicks in glasses full of oil, inserted in tin sconces hanging on the wall. The musicians are in their places. Several glasses of *raki* are quickly drunk; our gift of liquor and the fact that we are wearing swords have their effect.

Arrival of Safiah Zugairah, a small woman with a large nose and eyes that are dark, deep-set, savage, sensual; her necklace of coins clanks like a country cart; she kisses our hands.

The four women seated in a line on the divan singing. The lamps cast quivering, lozenge-shaped shadows on the walls, the light is yellow. Bambeh wore a pink robe with large sleeves (all the costumes are light-coloured) and her hair was covered with a black kerchief such as the *fellahin* wear. They all sang, the *darabukehs* throbbed, and the monotonous rebecs furnished a soft but shrill bass; it was like a rather gay song of mourning.

Coup with Safia Zugairah ('Little Sophie') – I stain the divan. She is very corrupt and writhing, extremely voluptuous. But the best was the second copulation with Kuchuk. Effect of her necklace between my teeth. Her cunt felt like rolls of velvet as she made me come. I felt like a tiger.

Kuchuk dances the Bee. First, so that the door can be closed, the women send away Farghali and another sailor, who up to now have been watching the dances and who, in the background, constituted

324

the grotesque element of the scene. A black veil is tied around the eyes of the child, and a fold of his blue turban is lowered over those of the old man. Kuchuk shed her clothing as she danced. Finally she was naked except for a *fichu* which she held in her hands and behind which she pretended to hide, and at the end she threw down the *fichu*. That was the Bee. She danced it very briefly and said she does not like to dance that dance. Joseph, very excited, kept clapping his hands: *La, eu, nia, oh! eu, nia, oh!* Finally, after repeating for us the wonderful step she had danced in the afternoon, she sank down breathless on her divan, her body continuing to move slightly in rhythm. One of the women threw her her enormous white trousers striped with pink, and she pulled them on up to her neck. The two musicians were unblindfolded.

Inside the Crystal Palace: The Great Exhibition, 1851

Charlotte Brontë

Sir Joseph Paxton's Crystal Palace contained a floor area of more than 800,000 square feet and over 8 miles of display tables.

Yesterday I went for the second time to the Crystal Palace. We remained in it about three hours, and I must say I was more struck with it on this occasion than at my first visit. It is a wonderful place – vast, strange, new, and impossible to describe. Its grandeur does not consist in *one* thing, but in the unique assemblage of *all* things. Whatever human industry has created you find there, from the great compartments filled with railway engines and boilers, with mill machinery in full work, with splendid carriages of all kinds, with harness of every description, to the glass-covered and velvet-spread stands loaded with the most gorgeous work of the goldsmith and silversmith, and the carefully guarded caskets full of real diamonds and pearls worth hundreds of thousands of pounds. It may be called a bazaar or a fair, but it is such a bazaar or fair as Eastern genii might have created. It seems as if only magic could have gathered this mass of wealth from all the ends of the earth – as if none but supernatural hands could have arranged it thus, with such a blaze and contrast of colours and marvellous power of effect. The multitude filling the great aisles seems ruled and subdued by some invisible influence. Amongst the thirty thousand souls that peopled it the day I was there not one loud noise was to be heard, not one irregular movement seen; the living tide rolls on quietly, with a deep hum like the sea heard from the distance.

The Farringdon Watercress Market, 1851

Henry Mayhew

The shops in the market are shut, the gas-lights over the iron gates burn brightly, and every now and then you hear the half-smothered crowing of a cock, shut up in some shed or bird-fancier's shop. Presently a man comes hurrying along, with a can of hot coffee in each hand, and his stall on his head, and when he has arranged his stand by the gates, and placed his white mugs between the railings on the stone wall, he blows at his charcoal fire, making the bright sparks fly about at every puff he gives. By degrees the customers are creeping up, dressed in every style of rags; they shuffle up and down before the gates, stamping to warm their feet, and rubbing their hands together till they grate like sandpaper. Some of the boys have brought large hand-baskets, and carry them with the handles round their necks, covering the head entirely with the wicker-work as with a hood; others have their shallows fastened to their backs with a strap, and one little girl, with the bottom of her gown tattered into a fringe like a blacksmith's apron, stands shivering in a large pair of worn-out Vestris boots, holding in her blue hands a bent and rusty tea-tray. A few poor creatures have made friends with the coffee-man, and are allowed to warm their fingers at the fire under the cans, and as the heat strikes into them, they grow sleepy and yawn.

The market – by the time we reach it – has just begun; one dealer has taken his seat, and sits motionless with cold – for it wants but a month to Christmas – with his hands thrust deep into the pockets of his grey driving coat. Before him is an opened hamper, with a candle fixed in the centre of the bright green cresses, and as it shines through the wicker sides of the basket, it casts curious patterns on the ground – as a night shade does. Two or three customers, with their 'shallows' slung over their backs, and their hands poked into the bosoms of their gowns, are bending over the hamper, the light from which tinges their swarthy features, and they rattle their halfpence and speak coaxingly to the dealer, to hurry him in their bargains.

Just as the clocks are striking five, a stout saleswoman enters the gates, and instantly a country-looking fellow, in a waggoner's cap and smock-frock, arranges the baskets he has brought up to London. The other ladies are soon at their posts, well wrapped up in warm cloaks, over their thick shawls, and sit with their hands under their aprons, talking to the loungers, whom they call by their names. Now the business commences; the customers come in by twos and threes, and walk about, looking at the cresses, and listening to the prices asked. Every hamper is surrounded by a black crowd, bending over till their heads nearly meet, their foreheads and cheeks lighted up by the candle in the centre. The saleswomen's voices are heard above the noise of the mob, sharply answering all objections that may be made to the quality of their goods. 'They're rather spotty, mum,' says an Irishman, as he examines one of the leaves. 'No more spots than a new-born babe, Dennis,' answers the lady tartly, and then turns to a newcomer. At one basket, a street-seller in an old green cloak has spread out a rusty shawl to receive her bunches, and by her stands her daughter, in a thin cotton dress, patched like a quilt. 'Ah! Mrs Dolland,' cried the saleswoman in a gracious tone, 'can you keep yourself warm? it bites the fingers like biling water, it do.' At another basket, an old man, with long grey hair streaming over a kind of policeman's cape, is bitterly complaining of the way he has been treated by another sales-woman. 'He bought a lot of her, the other morning, and by daylight they were quite white; for he only made threepence on his best day.' 'Well, Joe,' returns the lady, 'you should come to them as knows you, and allers treats you well.'

As the morning twilight came on, the paved court was crowded with purchasers. The sheds and shops at the end of the market grew every moment more distinct, and a railway-van, laden with carrots, came rumbling into the yard. The pigeons, too, began to fly on to the sheds, or walk about the paving-stones, and the gas-man came round with his ladder to turn out the lamps. Then every one was pushing about; the children crying, as their naked feet were trodden upon, and the women hurrying off, with their baskets or shawls filled with cresses, and the bunch of rushes in their hands. In one corner of the market, busily tying up their bunches, were three or four girls seated on the stones, with their legs curled up under them, and the ground near them was green with the leaves they had thrown away. A saleswoman, seeing me looking at the group, said to me, 'Ah! you should come here of a summer's morning, and then you'd see 'em, sitting tying up, young and old, upwards of a hundred poor things as thick as crows in a ploughed field.'

As it grew late, and the crowd had thinned, none but the very poorest of the cress-sellers were left. Many of these had come without money, others had their halfpence tied up carefully in their shawl-ends, as though they dreaded the loss. A sickly-looking boy, of about five, whose head just reached above the hampers, now crept forward, treading with his blue naked feet over the cold stones as a cat does over wet ground. At his elbows and knees, his skin showed in gashes through the rents in his clothes, and he looked so frozen, that the buxom saleswoman called to him, asking if his mother had gone home. The boy knew her well, for without answering her question, he went up to her, and, as he stood shivering on one foot, said, 'Give us a few old cresses, Jinney,' and in a few minutes was running off with a green bundle under his arm.

As you walk home – although the apprentice is knocking at the master's door – the little watercress girls are crying their goods in every street. Some of them are gathered round the pumps, washing the leaves and piling up the bunches in their baskets, that are tattered and worn as their own clothing; in some of the shallows the holes at the bottom have been laced up or darned together with rope and string, or twigs and split laths have been fastened across; whilst others are lined with oilcloth, or old pieces of sheet-tin. Even by the time the cress-market is over, it is yet so early that the maids are beating the mats in the road, and mechanics, with their tool-baskets slung over their shoulders, are still hurrying to their work.

Louis Napoleon's Troops Subdue Paris,
4 December 1851

Victor Hugo

*President of the Second Republic, Louis Napoleon made himself
Emperor Napoleon III by a* coup d'état *on 2 December 1851,
defeating the Republicans in subsequent street fighting in Paris.*

From twelve to two o'clock there was in this enormous city given
over to the unknown an indescribable and fierce expectation. All
was calm and awe-striking. The regiments and the limbered
batteries quitted the faubourg and stationed themselves noiselessly
around the boulevards. Not a cry in the ranks of the soldiery. An
eye-witness said, 'The soldiers march with quite a jaunty air.' On
the Quai de la Ferronnerie, heaped up with regiments ever since the
morning of the 2nd of December, there now only remained a post
of Municipal Guards. Everything ebbed back to the centre, the
people as well as the army; the silence of the army had ultimately
spread to the people. They watched each other.

Each soldier had three days' provisions and six packets of
cartridges.

It has since transpired that at this moment 10,000 francs were
daily spent in brandy for each brigade.

Towards one o'clock, Magnan went to the Hôtel de Ville, had
the reserve limbered under his own eyes, and did not leave until all
the batteries were ready to march.

Certain suspicious preparations grew more numerous. Towards
noon the State workmen and the hospital corps had established a
species of huge ambulance at No. 2, Faubourg Montmartre. A great
heap of litters was piled up there. 'What is all this for?' asked the
crowd . . .

At two o'clock five brigades, those of Cotte, Bourgon, Canrobert,
Dulac, and Reybell, five batteries of artillery, 16,400 men, infantry
and cavalry, lancers, cuirassiers, grenadiers, gunners, were
echelloned without any ostensible reason between the Rue de la
Paix and the Faubourg Poissonnière. Pieces of cannon were pointed
at the entrance of every street; there were eleven in position on the
Boulevard Poissonnière alone. The foot soldiers had their guns to
their shoulders, the officers their swords drawn. What did all this

mean? It was a curious sight, well worth the trouble of seeing, and on both sides of the pavements, on all the thresholds of the shops, from all the storeys of the houses, an astonished, ironical, and confiding crowd looked on.

Little by little, nevertheless, this confidence diminished, and irony gave place to astonishment; astonishment changed to stupor. Those who have passed through that extraordinary minute will not forget it. It was evident that there was something underlying all this. But what? Profound obscurity. Can one imagine Paris in a cellar? People felt as though they were beneath a low ceiling. They seemed to be walled up in the unexpected and the unknown. They seemed to perceive some mysterious will in the background. But after all they were strong; they were the Republic, they were Paris; what was there to fear? Nothing. And they cried, 'Down with Bonaparte!' The troops continued to keep silence, but the swords remained outside their scabbards, and the lighted matches of the cannon smouldered at the corners of the streets. The cloud grew blacker every minute, heavier and more silent. This thickening of the darkness was tragical. One felt the coming crash of a catastrophe, and the presence of a villain; snake-like treason writhed during this night, and none can foresee where the downward slide of a terrible design will stop when events are on a steep incline.

What was coming out of this thick darkness?

Suddenly, at a given signal, a musket shot being fired, no matter where, no matter by whom, the shower of bullets poured upon the crowd. A shower of bullets is also a crowd; it is death scattered broadcast. It does not know whither it goes, nor what it does; it kills and passes on.

In the twinkling of an eye there was a butchery on the boulevard a quarter of a league long. Eleven pieces of cannon wrecked the Sallandrouze carpet warehouse. The shot tore completely through twenty-eight houses. The baths of Jouvence were riddled. There was a massacre at Tortoni's. A whole quarter of Paris was filled with an immense flying mass, and with a terrible cry.

New Year's Day was not far off, some shops were full of New Year's gifts. In the Passage du Saumon, a child of thirteen, flying before the platoon-firing, hid himself in one of these shops, beneath a heap of toys. He was captured and killed. Those who killed him laughingly widened his wounds with their swords. A woman told me, 'The cries of the poor little fellow could be heard all through the passage.' Four men were shot before the same shop. The officer said to them, 'This will teach you to loaf about.' A fifth, named Mailleret, who was left for dead, was carried the next day with eleven wounds to the Charité. There he died.

They fired into the cellars by the air-holes.

A workman, a currier, named Moulins, who had taken refuge in one of these shot-riddled cellars, saw through the cellar air-hole a passer-by, who had been wounded in the thigh by a bullet, sit down on the pavement with the death rattle in his throat, and lean against a shop. Some soldiers who heard this rattle ran up and finished off the wounded man with bayonet thrusts.

One brigade killed the passers-by from the Madeleine to the Opéra, another from the Opéra to the Gymnase; another from the Boulevard Bonne Nouvelle to the Porte Saint-Denis; the 75th of the Line having carried the barricade of the Porte Saint-Denis, it was no longer a fight, it was a slaughter. The massacre radiated – a word horribly true – from the boulevard into all the streets. It was a devil-fish stretching out its feelers. Flight? Why? Concealment? To what purpose? Death ran after you quicker than you could fly. In the Rue Pagevin a soldier said to a passer-by, 'What are you doing here?' 'I am going home.' The soldier kills the passer-by. In the Rue des Marais they kill four young men in their own courtyard. Colonel Espinasse exclaimed, 'After the bayonet, cannon!' Colonel Rochefort exclaimed, 'Thrust, bleed, slash!' and he added, 'It is an economy of powder and noise.' Before Barbedienne's establishment an officer was showing his gun, an arm of considerable precision, admiringly to his comrades, and he said, 'With this gun I can score magnificent shots between the eyes.' Having said this, he aimed at random at someone, and succeeded. The carnage was frenzied.

At the corner of the Rue du Sentier an officer of Spahis, with his sword raised, cried out, 'This is not the sort of thing! You do not understand at all. Fire on the women.' A woman was flying, she was with child, she falls, they deliver her by the means of the butt-ends of their muskets. Another, perfectly distracted, was turning the corner of a street. She was carrying a child. Two soldiers aimed at her. One said, 'At the woman!' And he brought down the woman. The child rolled on the pavement. The other soldier said, 'At the child!' And he killed the child.

In the Rue Mandar, there was, stated an eye-witness, 'a rosary of corpses', reaching as far as the Rue Neuve Saint-Eustache. Before the house of Odier twenty-six corpses, thirty before the Hotel Montmorency. Fifty-two before the Variétés, of whom eleven were women. In the Rue Grange-Batelière there were three naked corpses. No. 19, Faubourg Montmartre, was full of dead and wounded.

A woman, flying and maddened, with dishevelled hair and her arms raised aloft, ran along the Rue Poissonnière, crying, 'They kill! they kill! they kill! they kill! they kill!'

I was anxious to know what I ought to do. Certain treasons, in order to be proved, need to be investigated. I went to the field of murder.

I reached the boulevard; the scene was indescribable. I witnessed this crime, this butchery, this tragedy. I saw that rain of blind death, I saw the distracted victims fall around me in crowds. It is for this that I have signed myself in this book AN EYE-WITNESS.

Victoria and Albert in the Highlands, 11 October 1852

Queen Victoria

After luncheon, Albert decided to walk through the wood for the last time, to have a last chance, and allowed Vicky [the Princess Royal] and me to go with him. At half-past three o'clock we started, got out at Grant's, and walked up part of Carrop, intending to go along the upper path, when a stag was heard to roar, and we all turned into the wood. We crept along, and got into the middle path. Albert soon left us to go lower, and we sat down to wait for him; presently we heard a shot – then complete silence – and, after another pause of some little time, three more shots. This was again succeeded by complete silence. We sent someone to look, who shortly after returned, saying the stag had been twice hit and they were after him. Macdonald next went, and in about five minutes we heard 'Solomon' give tongue, and knew he had the stag at bay. We listened a little while, and then began moving down hoping to arrive in time; but the barking had ceased, and Albert had already killed the stag; and on the road he lay, a little way beyond Invergelder – the beauty that we had admired yesterday evening.

He was a magnificent animal, and I sat down and scratched a little
sketch of him on a bit of paper that Macdonald had in his pocket,
which I put on a stone – while Albert and Vicky, with the others,
built a little cairn to mark the spot. We heard, after I had finished
my little scrawl, and the carriage had joined us, that another stag
had been seen near the road; and we had not gone as far as the
'Irons', before we saw one below the road, looking so handsome.
Albert jumped out and fired – the animal fell, but rose again, and
went on a little way, and Albert followed. Very shortly after,
however, we heard a cry, and ran down and found Grant and
Donald Stewart pulling up a stag with a very pretty head. Albert
had gone on, Grant went after him, and I and Vicky remained with
Donald Stewart, the stag, and the dogs. I sat down to sketch, and
poor Vicky, unfortunately, seated herself on a wasp's nest, and was
much stung. Donald Stewart rescued her, for I could not, being
myself too much alarmed. Albert joined us in twenty minutes,
unaware of having killed the stag. What a delightful day!

The Japanese are Introduced to Western Technology, March 1854

Commodore Matthew C. Perry

*The author, Commodore Perry, commanded the US naval force
that opened Japan to Western influence.*

During our stay in Edo Bay, all the officers and members of the
crews had frequent opportunities of mingling freely with the
people, both ashore and on board, as many of the natives visited the
ships in the business of bringing water and provisions, and on
official matters.

For the first few days after our arrival at Yokohama, Mr Gay, the
chief engineer of *Mississippi*, assisted by First Assistant Engineer
Danby, with the requisite number of mechanics, was employed in
unpacking and putting in working order the locomotive engine,
whilst Messrs Draper and Williams were equally busy in preparing
to erect the telegraphic posts for the extension of the magnetic lines.
Dr Morrow was also engaged in unpacking and arranging the
agricultural implements, all intended for presentation to the

Emperor, after being first exhibited and explained.

The Japanese authorities offered every facility. Sheds were prepared for sheltering the various articles from the weather; a flat piece of ground was assigned to the engineers for laying down the track of the locomotive. Posts were brought and erected as directed by Messrs Draper and Williams, and telegraphic wires of nearly a mile in a direct line were soon extended in as perfect a manner as could have been done in the United States. One end of the wire was at the treaty house, the other at a building allotted for the purpose, and communication was soon opened between the two operators in the English, Dutch, and Japanese languages, very much to the amazement of the spectators.

Meanwhile the implements of husbandry had been put together and exhibited, the track laid down, and the beautiful little engine with its tiny car set in motion. It could be seen from the ship, flying round its circular path exciting the utmost wonder in the minds of the Japanese. Although this perfect piece of machinery was with its car finished in the most tasteful manner, it was much smaller than I had expected it would have been, the car being incapable of admitting with any comfort even a child of six years. The Japanese therefore who rode upon it were seated upon the roof, whilst the engineer placed himself upon the tender.

The Battle of Balaclava and the Charge of the Light Brigade, 25 October 1854

William Howard Russell

If the exhibition of the most brilliant valour, of the excess of courage, and of a daring which would have reflected lustre on the best days of chivalry can afford full consolation for the disaster of today, we can have no reason to regret the melancholy loss which we sustained in a contest with a savage and barbarian enemy.

I shall proceed to describe, to the best of my power, what occurred under my own eyes, and to state the facts which I have heard from men whose veracity is unimpeachable, reserving to myself the exercise of the right of private judgement in making public and in suppressing the details of what occurred on this memorable day . . .

It will be remembered that in a letter sent by last mail from this it was mentioned that eleven battalions of Russian infantry had crossed the Tchernaya, and that they threatened the rear of our position and our communication with Balaclava. Their bands could be heard playing at night by travellers along the Balaclava road to the camp, but they 'showed' but little during the day and kept up among the gorges and mountain passes through which the roads to Inkermann, Simpheropol, and the south-east of the Crimea wind towards the interior. It will be recollected also that the position we occupied in reference to Balaclava was supposed by most people to be very strong — even impregnable. Our lines were formed by natural mountain slopes in the rear, along which the French had made very formidable intrenchments. Below those intrenchments, and very nearly in a right line across the valley beneath, are four conical hillocks, one rising above the other as they recede from our lines . . . On the top of each of these hills the Turks had thrown up earthen redoubts, defended by 250 men each, and armed with two or three guns — some heavy ship guns — lent by us to them, with one artilleryman in each redoubt to look after them. These hills cross the valley of Balaclava at the distance of about two and a half miles from the town. Supposing the spectator then to take his stand on one of the heights forming the rear of our camp before Sebastopol, he would see the town of Balaclava, with its scanty shipping, its narrow strip of water, and its old forts on his right hand; immediately below he would behold the valley and plain of coarse meadowland, occupied by our cavalry tents, and stretching from the base of the ridge on which he stood to the foot of the formidable heights on the other side; he would see the French trenches lined with Zouaves a few feet beneath, and distant from him, on the slope of the hill; a Turkish redoubt lower down, then another in the valley, then in a line with it some angular earthworks, then, in succession, the other two redoubts up Canrobert's Hill.

At the distance of two or two and a half miles across the valley there is an abrupt rocky mountain range of most irregular and picturesque formation, covered with scanty brushwood here and there, or rising into barren pinnacles and plateaux of rock. In outline and appearance, this position of the landscape is wonderfully like the Trossachs. A patch of blue sea is caught in between the overhanging cliffs of Balaclava as they close in the entrance to the harbour on the right. The camp of the Marines pitched on the hillsides more than one thousand feet above the level of the sea is opposite to you as your back is turned to Sebastopol and your right side towards Balaclava. On the road leading up the valley, close to the entrance of the town and beneath these hills, is the encampment of the 93rd Highlanders.

The cavalry lines are nearer to you below, and are some way in advance of the Highlanders, and nearer to the town than the Turkish redoubts. The valley is crossed here and there by small waves of land. On your left the hills and rocky mountain ranges gradually close in toward the course of the Tchernaya, till at three or four miles' distance from Balaclava the valley is swallowed up in a mountain gorge and deep ravines, above which rise tier after tier of desolate whitish rock garnished now and then by bits of scanty herbage, and spreading away towards the east and south, where they attain the alpine dimensions of Tschatir Dagh. It is very easy for an enemy at the Belbek, or in command of the road of Mackenzie's Farm, Inkermann, Simpheropol, or Bakhchisarai, to debouch through these gorges at any time upon this plain from the neck of the valley, or to march from Sebastopol by the Tchernaya and to advance along it towards Balaclava, till checked by the Turkish redoubts on the southern side or by the fire from the French works on the northern side, i.e., the side which in relation to the valley of Balaclava forms the rear of our position.

At half past seven o'clock this morning an orderly came galloping in to the headquarters camp from Balaclava, with the news that at dawn a strong corps of Russian horse supported by guns and battalions of infantry had marched into the valley, and had already nearly dispossessed the Turks of the redoubt No. 1 (that on Canrobert's Hill, which is farthest from our lines) and that they were opening fire on the redoubts Nos. 2, 3 and 4, which would speedily be in their hands unless the Turks offered a stouter resistance than they had done already.

Orders were dispatched to Sir George Cathcart and to HRH the Duke of Cambridge to put their respective divisions, the 4th and 1st, in motion for the scene of action, and intelligence of the advance of the Russians was also furnished to General Canrobert. Immediately on receipt of the news the General commanded General Bosquet to get the Third Division under arms, and sent a strong body of artillery and some 200 Chasseurs d'Afrique to assist us in holding the valley. Sir Colin Campbell, who was in command of Balaclava, had drawn up the 93rd Highlanders a little in front of the road to the town at the first news of the advance of the enemy. The marines on the heights got under arms; the seamen's batteries and marines' batteries on the heights close to the town were manned, and the French artillerymen and the Zouaves prepared for action along their lines. Lord Lucan's little camp was the scene of great excitement. The men had not had time to water their horses; they had not broken their fast from the evening of the day before, and had barely saddled at the first blast of the trumpet, when they were drawn up on the slope behind the redoubts in front of the camp to operate on the enemy's squadrons. It was soon evident that no reliance was to be placed on the Turkish infantrymen or artillerymen. All the stories we had heard about their bravery behind stone walls and earthworks proved how differently the same or similar people fight under different circumstances. When the Russians advanced the Turks fired a few rounds at them, got frightened at the distance of their supports in the rear, looked round, received a few shots and shell, and then 'bolted', and fled with an agility quite at variance with the commonplace notions of oriental deportment on the battlefield. But Turks on the Danube are very different beings from Turks in the Crimea, as it appears that the Russians of Sebastopol are not at all like the Russians of Silistria.

Soon after eight Lord Raglan and his staff turned out and cantered towards the rear of our position. The booming of artillery, the spattering roll of musketry, were heard rising from the valley, drowning the roar of the siege guns in front before Sebastopol. As I rode in the direction of the firing over the thistles and large stones which cover the undulating plain which stretches away towards Balaclava, on a level with the summit of the ridges above it, I observed a French light infantry regiment (the 27th, I think) advancing with admirable care and celerity from our right towards the ridge near the telegraph house, which was already lined with companies of French infantry, while mounted officers scampered along its broken outline in every direction.

General Bosquet, a stout soldierlike-looking man, who reminds one of the old *genre* of French generals as depicted at Versailles, followed, with his staff and small escort of Hussars, at a gallop. Faint white clouds rose here and there above the hill from the cannonade below. Never did the painter's eye rest upon a more beautiful scene than I beheld from the ridge. The fleecy vapours still hung around the mountain tops and mingled with the ascending volumes of smoke; the patch of sea sparkled freshly in the rays of the morning sun, but its light was eclipsed by the flashes which gleamed from the masses of armed men below.

Looking to the left towards the gorge we beheld six compact masses of Russian infantry which had just debouched from the mountain passes near the Tchernaya, and were slowly advancing with solemn stateliness up the valley. Immediately in their front was a regular line of artillery, of at least twenty pieces strong. Two batteries of light guns were already a mile in advance of them, and were playing with energy on the redoubts, from which feeble puffs of smoke came at long intervals. Behind the guns, in front of the infantry, were enormous bodies of cavalry. They were in six compact squares, three on each flank, moving down *en échelon* towards us, and the valley was lit up with the blaze of their sabres and lance points and gay accoutrements. In their front, and extending along the intervals between each battery of guns, were clouds of mounted skirmishers, wheeling and whirling in the front of their march like autumn leaves tossed by the wind. The Zouaves close to us were lying like tigers at the spring, with ready rifles in hand, hidden chin deep by the earthworks which run along the line of these ridges on our rear, but the quick-eyed Russians were manoeuvring on the other side of the valley, and did not expose their columns to attack. Below the Zouaves we could see the Turkish gunners in the redoubts, all in confusion as the shells burst over them. Just as I came up the Russians had carried No. 1 redoubt, the farthest and most elevated of all, and their horsemen were chasing the Turks across the interval which lay between it and redoubt No. 2. At that moment the cavalry, under Lord Lucan, were formed in glittering masses – the Light Brigade, under Lord Cardigan, in advance of the Heavy Brigade, under Brigadier-General Scarlett, in reserve. They were drawn up just in front of their encampment, and were concealed from the view of the enemy by a slight 'wave' in the plain. Considerably to the rear of their right, the 93rd Highlanders were drawn up in line, in front of the approach to Balaclava. Above and behind them on the heights, the marines were visible through the glass, drawn up under arms, and the gunners could be seen ready in the earthworks, in which were placed the heavy ships' guns. The 93rd had originally been advanced somewhat more into the plain, but the instant the Russians got possession of the first redoubt they opened fire on them from our own guns, which inflicted some injury, and Sir Colin Campbell 'retired' his men to a better position. Meantime the enemy advanced his cavalry rapidly. To our inexpressible disgust we saw the Turks in redoubt No. 2 fly at their approach. They ran in scattered groups across towards redoubt No. 3, and towards Balaclava, but the horse-hoof of the Cossacks was too quick for them, and sword and lance were busily plied among the retreating band. The yells of the pursuers and pursued were plainly audible. As the Lancers and Light Cavalry of the Russians advanced they gathered up their skirmishers with great speed and in excellent order – the shifting trails of men, which played all over the valley like moonlight on water, contracted, gathered up, and the little *peloton* in a few moments became a solid column. Then up came their guns, in rushed their gunners to the abandoned redoubt, and the guns of No. 2 redoubt soon played with deadly effect upon the dispirited defenders of No. 3 redoubt. Two or three shots in return from the earthworks, and all is silent. The Turks swarm over the earthworks and run in confusion towards the town, firing their muskets at the enemy as they run. Again the solid column of cavalry opens like a fan, and resolves itself into the 'long spray' of skirmishers. It laps the flying Turks, steel flashes in the air, and down go the poor Muslim quivering on the plain, split through fez and musket-guard to the chin and breast-belt. There is no support for them. It is evident the Russians have been too quick for us. The Turks have been too quick also, for they have not held their redoubts long enough to enable us to bring them help. In vain the naval guns on the heights fire on the Russian cavalry; the distance is too great for shot or shell to reach. In vain the Turkish gunners in the earthern batteries which are placed along the French intrenchments strive to protect their flying countrymen; their shot fly wide and short of the swarming masses. The Turks betake themselves towards the Highlanders, where they check their flight and form into companies on the flanks of the Highlanders.

As the Russian cavalry on the left of their line crown the hill, across the valley they perceive the Highlanders drawn up at the distance of some half-mile, calmly awaiting their approach. They halt, and squadron after squadron flies up from the rear, till they have a body of some 1500 men along the ridge – Lancers and Dragoons and Hussars. Then they move *en échelon* in two bodies, with another in reserve. The cavalry who have been pursuing the Turks on the right are coming up the ridge beneath us, which conceals our cavalry from view. The heavy brigade in advance is drawn up in two columns. The first column consists of the Scots Greys and of their old companions in glory, the Enniskillens; the second of the 4th Royal Irish, of the 5th Dragoon Guards, and of the 1st Royal Dragoons. The Light Cavalry Brigade is on their left in two lines also. The silence is oppressive; between the cannon bursts, one can hear the champing of bits and the clink of sabres in the valley below. The Russians on their left drew breath for a moment, and then in one grand line dashed at the Highlanders. The ground flies beneath their horses' feet – gathering speed at every stride they dash on towards that thin red streak topped with a line of steel. The Turks fire a volley at 800 yards, and run. As the Russians come within 600 yards, down goes that line of steel in front, and out rings a rolling volley of Minié musketry. The distance is too great. The Russians are not checked, but still sweep onwards with the whole force of horse and man, through the smoke, here and there knocked over by the shot of our batteries above. With breathless suspense everyone awaits the bursting of the wave upon the line of Gaelic rock; but ere they came within 150 yards, another deadly volley flashes from the levelled rifles, and carries death and terror into the Russians. They wheel about, open files right and left, and fly back faster than they came.

'Bravo Highlanders! well done!' shout the excited spectators; but events thicken. The Highlanders and their splendid front are soon forgotten. Men scarcely have a moment to think of this fact that the 93rd never altered their formation to receive that tide of horsemen.

'No,' said Sir Colin Campbell, 'I did not think it worth while to form them even four deep!'

The ordinary British line, two deep, was quite sufficient to repel the attack of these Muscovite chevaliers. Our eyes were, however, turned in a moment on our own cavalry. We saw Brigadier General Scarlett ride along in front of his massive squadrons. The Russians – evidently *corps d'élite* – their light-blue jackets embroidered with silver lace, were advancing on their left at an easy gallop, towards the brow of the hill. A forest of lances glistened in their rear, and several squadrons of grey-coated dragoons moved up quickly to support them as they reached the summit. The instant they came in sight the trumpets of our cavalry gave out the warning blast which told us all that in another moment we would see the shock of battle beneath our very eyes. Lord Raglan, all his staff and escort, and groups of officers, the Zouaves, the French generals and officers, and bodies of French infantry on the height, were spectators of the scene as though they were looking on the stage from the boxes of a theatre. Nearly everyone dismounted and sat down, and not a word was said.

The Russians advanced down the hill at a slow canter, which they changed to a trot and at last nearly halted. The first line was at least double the length of ours – it was three times as deep. Behind them was a similar line, equally strong and compact. They evidently despised their insignificant-looking enemy, but their time was come.

The trumpets rang out through the valley, and the Greys and Enniskillens went right at the centre of the Russian cavalry. The space between them was only a few hundred yards; it was scarce enough to let the horses 'gather way', nor had the men quite space sufficient for the full play of their sword arms. The Russian line brings forward each wing as our cavalry advance and threaten to annihilate them as they pass on. Turning a little to their left, so as to meet the Russians' right, the Greys rush on with a cheer that thrills to every heart – the wild shout of the Enniskillens rises through the air at the same moment. As lightning flashes through a cloud the Greys and Enniskillens pierced through the dark masses of the Russians. The shock was but for a moment. There was a clash of steel and a light play of sword blades in the air, and then the Greys and the redcoats disappear in the midst of the shaken and quivering columns. In another moment we see them merging and dashing on with diminished numbers, and in broken order, against the second line, which is advancing against them to retrieve the fortune of the charge.

It was a terrible moment. 'God help them! They are lost!' was the exclamation of more than one man, and the thought of many. With unabated fire the noble hearts dashed at their enemy – it was a fight of heroes. The first line of Russians which had been smashed utterly by our charge, and had fled off at one flank and towards the centre, were coming back to swallow up our handful of men. By sheer steel and sheer courage Enniskillen and Scot were winning their desperate way right through the enemy's squadrons, and already grey horses and redcoats had appeared right at the rear of the second mass, when, with irresistible force, like one bolt from a bow, the 1st Royals, the 4th Dragoon Guards, and the 5th Dragoon Guards rushed at the remnants of the first line of the enemy, went through it as though it were made of pasteboard, and dashing on the second body of Russians, as they were still disordered by the terrible assault of the Greys and their companions, put them to utter rout. This Russian horse in less than five minutes after it met our dragoons was flying with all its speed before a force certainly not half its strength.

A cheer burst from every lip – in the enthusiasm officers and men took off their caps and shouted with delight, and thus keeping up the scenic character of their position, they clapped their hands again and again . . .

And now occurred the melancholy catastrophe which fills us all with sorrow. It appears that the Quartermaster General, Brigadier Airey, thinking that the Light Cavalry had not gone far enough in front when the enemy's horse had fled, gave an order in writing to Captain Nolan, 15th Hussars, to take to Lord Lucan, directing His Lordship 'to advance' his cavalry nearer to the enemy. A braver soldier than Captain Nolan the army did not possess. He was known to all his arm of the service for his entire devotion to his profession, and his name must be familiar to all who take interest in our cavalry for his excellent work published a year ago on our drill and system of remount and breaking horses. I had the pleasure of his acquaintance, and I know he entertained the most exalted opinions respecting the capabilities of the English horse soldier. Properly led, the British Hussar and Dragoon could in his mind break square, take batteries, ride over columns of infantry, and pierce any other cavalry in the world, as if they were made of straw. He thought they had not had the opportunity of doing all that was in their power, and that they had missed even such chances as they had offered to them – that, in fact, they were in some measure disgraced. A matchless rider and a first-rate swordsman, he held in contempt, I am afraid, even grape and canister. He rode off with his orders to Lord Lucan. He is now dead and gone.

God forbid I should cast a shade on the brightness of his honour, but I am bound to state what I am told occurred when he reached His Lordship. I should premise that, as the Russian cavalry retired, their infantry fell back towards the head of the valley, leaving men in three of the redoubts they had taken and abandoning the fourth. They had also placed some guns on the heights over their position, on the left of the gorge. Their cavalry joined the reserves, and drew up in six solid divisions, in an oblique line, across the entrance to the gorge. Six battalions of infantry were placed behind them, and about thirty guns were drawn up along their line, while masses of infantry were also collected on the hills behind the redoubts on our right. Our cavalry had moved up to the ridge across the valley, on our left, as the ground was broken in front, and had halted in the order I have already mentioned.

When Lord Lucan received the order from Captain Nolan and had read it, he asked, we are told, 'Where are we to advance to?'

Captain Nolan pointed with his finger to the line of the Russians, and said, 'There are the enemy, and there are the guns, sir, before them. It is your duty to take them,' or words to that effect, according to the statements made since his death.

Lord Lucan with reluctance gave the order to Lord Cardigan to advance upon the guns, conceiving that his orders compelled him to do so. The noble Earl, though he did not shrink, also saw the fearful odds against him. Don Quixote in his tilt against the windmill was not near so rash and reckless as the gallant fellows who prepared without a thought to rush on almost certain death.

It is a maxim of war that 'cavalry never act without support', that 'infantry should be close at hand when cavalry carry guns, as the effect is only instantaneous', and that it is necessary to have on the flank of a line of cavalry some squadrons in column, the attack on the flank being most dangerous. The only support our Light Cavalry had was the reserve of Heavy Cavalry at a great distance behind them – the infantry and guns being far in the rear. There were no squadrons in column at all, and there was a plain to charge over before the enemy's guns were reached of a mile and a half in length.

At ten past eleven our Light Cavalry Brigade rushed to the front. They numbered as follows, as well as I could ascertain:

	MEN
4th Light Dragoons	118
8th Irish Hussars	104
11th Prince Albert's Hussars	110
13th Light Dragoons	130
17th Lancers	145

Total 607 sabres

The whole brigade scarcely made one effective regiment, according to the numbers of continental armies; and yet it was more than we could spare. As they passed towards the front, the Russians opened on them from the guns in the redoubts on the right, with volleys of musketry and rifles.

They swept proudly past, glittering in the morning sun in all the pride and splendour of war. We could hardly believe the evidence of our senses! Surely that handful of men were not going to charge an army in position? Alas! it was but too true – their desperate valour knew no bounds, and far indeed was it removed from its so-called better part – discretion. They advanced in two lines, quickening their pace as they closed towards the enemy. A more fearful spectacle was never witnessed than by those who, without the power to aid, beheld their heroic countrymen rushing to the arms of death. At the distance of 1200 yards the whole line of the enemy belched forth, from thirty iron mouths, a flood of smoke and flame, through which hissed the deadly balls. Their flight was marked by instant gaps in our ranks, by dead men and horses, by steeds flying wounded or riderless across the plain. The first line was broken – it was joined by the second, they never halted or checked their speed an instant. With diminished ranks, thinned by those thirty guns, which the Russians had laid with the most deadly accuracy, with a halo of flashing steel above their heads, and with a cheer which was many a noble fellow's death cry, they flew into the smoke of the batteries; but ere they were lost from view, the plain was strewed with their bodies and with the carcasses of horses. They were exposed to an oblique fire from the batteries on the hills on both sides, as well as to a direct fire of musketry.

Through the clouds of smoke we could see their sabres flashing as they rode up to the guns and dashed between them, cutting down the gunners as they stood. The blaze of their steel, as an officer standing near me said, was 'like the turn of a shoal of mackerel'. We saw them riding through the guns, as I have said; to our delight we saw them returning, after breaking through a column of Russian infantry, and scattering them like chaff, when the flank fire of the battery on the hill swept them down, scattered and broken as they were. Wounded men and dismounted troopers flying towards us told the sad tale – demigods could not have done what they had failed to do. At the very moment when they were about to retreat, an enormous mass of lancers was hurled upon their flank. Colonel Shewell, of the 8th Hussars, saw the danger, and rode his few men straight at them, cutting his way through with fearful loss. The other regiments turned and engaged in a desperate encounter. With courage too great almost for credence, they were breaking their way through the columns which enveloped them, when there took place an act of atrocity without parallel in the modern warfare of civilized nations. The Russian gunners, when the storm of cavalry passed, returned to their guns. They saw their own cavalry mingled with the troopers who had just ridden over them, and to the eternal disgrace of the Russian name the miscreants poured a murderous volley of grape and canister on the mass of struggling men and horses, mingling friend and foe in one common ruin. It was as much as our Heavy Cavalry Brigade could do to cover the retreat of the miserable remnants of that band of heroes as they returned to the place they had so lately quitted in all the pride of life.

At twenty-five to twelve not a British soldier, except the dead and dying, was left in front of these bloody Muscovite guns. Our loss, as far as it could be ascertained in killed, wounded, and missing at two o'clock today, was as follows:

	Went into Action Strong	Returned from Action	Loss
4th Light Dragoons	118	39	79
8th Hussars	104	38	66
11th Hussars	110	25	85
13th Light Dragoons	130	61	69
17th Lancers	145	35	110
	607	198	409

The Indian Mutiny: Scene of the Massacre of British Women and Children at Cawnpore, 21 July 1857

Report of an Officer in General Havelock's Relieving Force

The Mutiny began at Meerut but spread to other cities including Cawnpore where the Nana Sahib, the native ruler, massacred the entire garrison including 200 women and children who were hacked to death in a house known as the Bibigarh.

I was directed to the house where all the poor miserable ladies had been murdered. It was alongside the Cawnpore hotel, where the Nana [i.e. Nana Sahib] lived. I never was more horrified! The place was one mass of blood. I am not exaggerating when I tell you that the soles of my boots were more than covered with the blood of these poor wretched creatures. Portions of their dresses, collars, children's socks, and ladies' round hats lay about, saturated with their blood; and in the sword-cuts on the wooden pillars of the room long dark hair was carried by the edge of the weapon, and there hung their tresses – a most painful sight! I have often wished since that I had never been there, but sometimes wish that every soldier was taken there that he might witness the barbarities our poor countrywomen had suffered. Their bodies were afterwards dragged out and thrown down a well outside the building where their limbs were to be seen sticking out in a mass of gory confusion . . .

Those poor ladies were massacred on the 15th, after we had thrashed the blackguards at the bridge. The collector, who gave the order for their death, was taken prisoner the day before yesterday, and now hangs from a branch about 200 yards off the roadside. His death was, accidentally, a most painful one, for the rope was badly adjusted, and when he dropped, the noose closed over his jaw. His hands then got loose, and he caught hold of the rope and struggled to get free; but two men took hold of his legs, and jerked his body until his neck broke. This seems to me the just reward he should have got on earth for his barbarity.

The Indian Mutiny: Retribution for the Massacre, July 1857

General Havelock

Whenever a rebel is caught he is immediately tried, and unless he can prove a defence he is sentenced to be hanged at once; but the chief rebels or ringleaders I make first clean up a certain portion of the pool of blood, still two inches deep, in the shed where the fearful murder and mutilation of women and children took place. To touch blood is most abhorrent to the high-caste natives, they think by doing so they doom their souls to perdition. Let them think so. My object is to inflict a fearful punishment for a revolting, cowardly, barbarous deed, and to strike terror into these rebels. The first I caught was a subahdar, or native officer, a high-caste Brahmin, who tried to resist my order to clean up the very blood he had helped to shed; but I made the Provost-Marshal do his duty, and a few lashes soon made the miscreant accomplish his task. When done, he was taken out and immediately hanged, and after death buried in a ditch at the roadside. No one who has witnessed the scenes of murder, mutilation, and massacre can ever listen to the word 'mercy' as applied to these fiends. The well of mutilated bodies – alas! containing upwards of 200 women and children – I have had decently covered in and built up as one large grave.

The Indian Mutiny: Household Arrangements in Besieged Lucknow, 1857

Adelaide Case

The siege of Lucknow lasted from 1 July to 17 November, when Sir Colin Campbell's relieving force entered the city.

Thursday, 20 August. A good deal of shelling has been going on this morning, but it is mostly our own . . . It rained in the evening a good deal. A poor little child next door to us died of cholera; it was only taken ill about one o'clock and it was dead before seven. The poor mother was in a dreadful state just before it died, and afterwards perfectly calm. While we were undressing she came and asked if we had an empty box we could give her to bury the poor little thing in. We had not one long enough . . .

Thursday, 27 August. Colonel Inglis had a most merciful escape last night. He was standing on the bastion at Mr Gubbins's house, close to Mr Webb when he was killed. They saw the round shot coming, and went down to avoid it, but it hit Mr Webb, and a native who was with him, killing them both instantaneously. It makes one shudder to think how death is hovering about and around us all; busy indeed has he been amongst this little garrison. Mrs Thornhill had a little girl last night. Sir Henry Lawrence's things are being sold today [he had recently been killed]; heard of a ham being sold for £7 and a tin of soup sufficient only for one day's dinner for £1.5s.!!! Money has ceased to be of any value, and people are giving unheard-of prices for stores of any kind – one dozen brandy £20; one small box of vermicelli, £5; four small cakes of chocolate, £2.10s.!!! . . .

Monday, 5 October. Today we have begun to restrict ourselves to two chuppatties each a day; and soon, I fear, we shall have to eat horseflesh; but as yet we have beef and rice. I have been hungry today, and could have eaten more, had I had it. Seven men and three officers came in today from the Fureed Bux, badly wounded. Mrs Roberts came to see us this morning, and told us the chloroform at the hospital is all gone. Mrs Omiley's children both died in one hour a day or two ago . . .

Sunday, 18 October. We have been out of soap for some days and are now obliged to wash with what is called 'bason' (ground grain made into a paste with water). It is a nice clean thing, and the best substitute for soap.

Single Combat in the Caucasus, 1858

Alexandre Dumas

After an hour and a half we reached the fortress of Shedrinskaia, where we halted to rest our horses and change our guard. This time we were given twelve, and as we rode on again, following the bank of the Terek which adjoins the road at this spot, two of our Cossacks went ahead of us, two brought up the rear, and the others galloped beside us, four on each side. To my right, as far as I could see, stretched dense thickets some three feet high, with an occasional tall tree of a different kind towering above them. To my left, the same thick bushes ran from the edge of the road to the river bank.

Suddenly a flight of partridge rose from the bushes by the river and I could not resist the chance of a shot or two, so I quickly took the bullets from my gun and slipped in a couple of light cartridges. Though the chief Cossack strongly protested that it would be risky to leave the road, I dismounted, went a dozen yards into the bushes and fired. One bird fell. 'Did you see where it came down, Moynet?' I cried. 'The sun's in my eyes. I know I hit one, but that's all.'

'Wait a minute. I'll come and help you look,' he replied, but before he could reach me I heard another shot fired a hundred yards away. I saw a puff of smoke and at the same moment heard a bullet whistle through the upper branches of the bushes that engulfed us to the waist, and only a couple of feet away. We ran back, and saw that the bullet had hit one of the horses, breaking its foreleg high up near the body. I had already loaded my gun with fresh bullets as I ran; a Cossack was holding my mount by the bridle; I swung into the saddle and stood in my stirrups to get a wider view. What surprised me, from what I had heard of the habits of Chechen bandits, was their delay in attacking us. Usually they charge down on an enemy as soon as their first shot is fired.

At this moment we saw seven or eight men filing up from the bank of the Terek. Our Cossacks gave a cheer and raced off towards them, but then another man emerged from the thicket where he had shot at us. He made no attempt to escape, but stood his ground, brandishing his gun above his head and shouting: '*Abreck!*'

'*Abreck!*' our Cossacks shouted in reply, and reined in their horses to a standstill.

'What does that mean?' I asked Kalino.

'It means that he is sworn to seek out danger and never to turn his back to an enemy. He is challenging one of our Cossacks to single combat.'

'Tell them I'll give twenty roubles to the man who accepts that challenge,' I cried.

Kalino took my message to our men and there was a short silence while they looked at each other as if to choose the bravest one among them. Meanwhile, a couple of hundred yards away, the challenger was putting his horse through a complicated series of evolutions and still shouting '*Abreck!*'

'*Sacrebleu!* Pass me my carbine, Kalino,' I exclaimed. 'I'd love to bring him down, the arrogant rascal!'

'Don't do anything like that,' he advised. 'You're going to see something well worth watching. Our Cossacks are just discussing which of them is to tackle him. They've recognized him as a champion well known in these mountains. Wait! Here's one of our men coming now.'

The Cossack whose horse had been shot had tried to get the animal on its feet again, but with no success. Now he was walking over to put his case before me, as leader of the expedition. According to custom he had a personal right to do so, in view of his loss. These Cossacks provide their own horses and weapons, out of their soldier's pay. When a horse is killed in action, the man's commanding officer gives him a government grant of twenty-two roubles, but since a reasonably good horse costs at least thirty the soldier will be eight roubles or more out of pocket. Our Cossack therefore claimed that he had the best right to try and win the twenty roubles I had offered. With luck, it would leave him ten roubles in hand. Had he my permission to fight the man who had wounded his horse? The suggestion seemed to me fair and just, so I expressed my approval.

Meanwhile, the mountain tribesman had been riding round us in ever-narrowing circles and was now quite close. The eyes of our Cossacks flashed, but not one of them dishonoured the code that forbade him to shoot, once the challenge had been accepted. Their captain spoke a word or two to the man who had just left us, then said: 'All right, then. Off you go, my lad!'

'But I haven't got a horse!' the Cossack replied. 'Who will lend me one?' His comrades stood silent, for if a borrowed horse were killed it was doubtful whether the government would make any grant to the owner. Appreciating their difficulty, which Kalino explained to me, I jumped down from my own mount, one of the best in the cavalry stables. 'Here you are,' I cried. 'Take mine!' Instantly the Cossack leapt into the saddle and was off.

Another Cossack came up to me. 'What does he say?' I asked

Kalino, who replied: 'He wants to know whether, if any harm comes to his comrade, he can take his place?'

'He's in rather a hurry, it seems to me; but still, I agree.'

The Cossack returned to his place and began checking his weapons as if he expected his turn to arrive at any moment. By this time, the first man was already close enough to fire, but his opponent made his horse rear so that the bullet struck it in the shoulder. His return shot carried away the Cossack's fur hat. Now they both slung their guns over their shoulders and seized their swords. The mountaineer managed his wounded horse so cleverly that, though blood was streaming down its chest, it showed no sign of weakness and responded instantly to the bridle, the pressure of its master's knees and the sound of his voice. Now the men were fighting hand to hand, and for a moment I thought our Cossack had run his enemy through, for I saw the point of the blade shine behind his back. But he had only thrust it through his jerkin. In the next few minutes it was impossible to see what was happening, but then came a pause, and slowly our Cossack slipped from his saddle. That is, his body slumped to the ground. His head, dripping with blood, was waved at us with a fierce cry of triumph, then tied to the saddle-bow of his conqueror. His horse, now riderless, circled back to join us and its stable companions.

I turned to the Cossack who had asked to be the next. He was quietly smoking his pipe, but he nodded and said: 'All right! I'm going.'

Then he, in turn, gave a yell of defiance to show that he now challenged the victor, and the *abreck* paused in his dance of triumph to face his new opponent. 'All right,' I cried to the Cossack. 'Now I'll make it thirty roubles.' He simply winked at me and rode away, still puffing at his pipe, but I noticed that no smoke escaped his lips and thought he must be swallowing it. Then he galloped off.

The *abreck* had had no chance to reload, and our Cossack, at a range of forty yards, shouldered his gun. We saw a puff of smoke but heard no bullet, and so concluded that his gun had misfired. By now, the mountaineer had reloaded and we saw him fire, but the Cossack made his horse swerve and so avoided the bullet, though the range was now only a few yards. Then we saw the Cossack fire again, and by the sudden jerk of the mountaineer's body we knew he had been hit. He dropped the bridle and saved himself from falling by clasping both arms round the neck of his horse. The poor animal, with no help from its rider and maddened by its own wound, bolted towards the river. We were on the point of riding off in pursuit when we saw the body of the mountaineer slipping slowly to the ground.

Our Cossack, fearing that this might be a trick and that his opponent was not really dead, circled round the fallen man, trying to see his face. But he had fallen with his face to the ground. Accordingly, ten paces away, he fired one more shot at the enemy, but the bullet was wasted. The mountain champion was dead indeed. The Cossack dismounted, drew his sword, bent over the body and a moment later stood waving the severed head, while the other Cossacks cheered wildly. He had not only won thirty roubles, he had saved the honour of his regiment and avenged his comrade.

A moment later, the mountaineer was stripped naked. The Cossack wrapped his clothes in a bundle, slung it over the back of the wounded horse, which made no attempt to escape, remounted his own horse and rode back to us. There was one question I was longing to ask him. 'We all saw your gun misfire, yet you did not reload. How, then, could you manage to fire another shot?'

The Cossack laughed. 'But my gun did not misfire!'

'Yes, it did!' his comrades insisted. 'We all saw the smoke!'

'That's what I wanted you to think, you and that *abreck*, but really it was the smoke from my pipe. I kept it in my mouth on purpose.'

'Here are your thirty roubles,' I replied, counting them into his hand, 'but it seems to me you're a pretty tricky customer!'

Explosion on Board Brunel's *Great Eastern* Steamship, 12 September 1859

George Augustus Sala

The prototype of the modern ocean liner, Brunel's Great Eastern *(18,914 tons) was the largest ship in the world at the time of its launching in 1858.*

We had dined. It was six o'clock, and we were off Hastings, at about seven miles' distance from the shore. The majority of the passengers, having finished their repast, had gone on deck. The ladies had retired, and, as we conjectured, according to their usual custom, to their boudoir. The dining saloon was deserted, save by a small knot of joyous guests, all known to each other, who had gathered round the most popular of the directors, Mr Ingram. That gentleman, his hand on the shoulder of his young son, was listening, not apparently unpleased, to the eloquence of a friend, who was decanting on his merits while proposing his health. The glasses were charged; the orator's peroration had culminated; the revellers were upstanding; when – as if the fingers of a man's hand had come out against the cabin wall, and written, as in sand, that the Medes and Persians were at the gate, the verberation of a tremendous explosion was heard. The reverberation followed. Then came – to our ears, who were in the dining room – a tremendous crash, not hollow, as of thunder, but solid, as of objects that offered resistance. Then a sweeping, rolling, swooping, rumbling sound, as of cannon balls scudding along the deck above. Remember, I am only describing *now* my personal experience and sensations. The rumbling noise was followed by the smash of the dining saloon skylights, and the irruption of a mass of fragments of wood and iron, followed by a thick cloud of powdered glass, and then by coaldust. My garments are full of the first, my hair and eyebrows of the last, now. There was but one impulse, one question – to go on deck; to ask, 'What can it be?' To me, the crash was greater than the explosion; and I thought more of a collision, or of the fall of one of the huge yards, than of an explosion; but my next neighbour cried out, 'The boiler has burst!' On gaining the deck I could at first see nothing but billows of steam rolling towards us. Then along the deck I saw the engine hose rapidly drawn along, and in another moment dozens of men were seizing it and carrying it forward. The wind was blowing tolerably strong, and when the steam cleared away a little in my immediate vicinity, there came an eddying shower of splinters, fragments of gilt moulding, shreds of ornamental paper, and tatters of crimson curtains. Several gentlemen now exerted themselves in the most praiseworthy manner to get the passengers aft; the danger was evidently forward; a thick cloud of steam there concealed all objects; but there was smoke as well as vapour, and I thought the ship was on fire. As men and passengers came rushing by I heard ejaculations of 'Fire', 'The boilers', 'The donkey engine has burst'; but these were more matters of question and answer than evidences of terror. There seemed to be amazement and curiosity, but – among the passengers at least – not the slightest panic . . .

The effects of the catastrophe soon became lamentably apparent. One by one, borne on the shoulders or in the arms of their comrades, or, in one or two cases, staggering past, came by the unfortunate men who had been scalded in the stokehole. The face of one was utterly without human semblance, and looked simply like a mass of raw beefsteak. Another was so horribly scalded about the groin, that the two hands might be laid in the raw cavity, and scraps of his woollen undergarment were mixed up with hanks of boiled flesh. Another I saw had his trousers scalded away from the mid-thigh; his two legs, bare from thigh to heel, were continuous scalds, the skin and flesh hanging here and there. As they raised another man, the flesh of his hands came away in the grasp of those who held him, and he looked as though he had two bloody gloves on. There were some cases of severe contusions, and cuts from fractured glass; but curiously enough, not one instance of broken limb. Some of the sufferers were hysterical, laughing and crying in a pitiable manner. When in the hospital, or sick bay, the agony of some was so intolerable that – all gently and soothingly as it was done – they had to be held down. The remedies applied were linseed oil and cotton-wool, continuously renewed.

Descending to the lower deck, the scene irresistibly reminded one of the interior of the area of Covent Garden Theatre after the fire of 1856. The vast expanse between decks was one heap of fragments. You trod upon one vast sultry mass of ruin and desolation. The nests of sleeping berths, the corridors and staircases were all (save the main one) gone. The cabin which with two friends I had occupied no longer existed. With all in the same block it had been blown entirely away. A portmanteau belonging to your correspondent was subsequently recovered from the *débâcle*; but my two companions lost everything they possessed on board. Forward, in this lower deck, you saw the great, gaping pit, which had vomited forth the fruits of the 'collapse'. It was an infernal region, that horrible hole. The bed of the accursed 'jacket', with torn and jagged ends, was still visible. In the hole, were beams and girders, planks and rails, and gigantic steampipes twisted double like disused speaking trumpets. The huge iron plates at the root of the funnel were torn or crumpled up like writing paper. The great wrought-iron girders supporting the lower deck were curved and bent; the flooring of the deck itself was, in part, upheaved, and disclosed ominous gaps. The boilers had sustained no injury. Weeks' time and thousands of pounds in expenditure must be consumed ere the *Great Eastern*'s proprietors will be able to repair the damage done to her 'main cabin fittings'.

Neither ship – as a ship – nor paddles, nor screw, were injured. At first there was an expressed intention to put into the nearest haven; but this idea was abandoned, and the *Great Eastern* proceeded on her voyage to Portland.

The *Times* Correspondent Helps Garibaldi Liberate Palermo, 27–31 May 1860

Nandor Eber

The conquest of Sicily by Garibaldi and his thousand guerrilla 'Redshirts' led to the liberation of Italy and the abdication of Francis II, last of the Bourbon kings of Naples. The bombardment of Palermo by the Neapolitans, described at the end of this account, ceased on 6 June when 20,000 Neapolitan troops, supported by nine frigates, surrendered.

Palermo, 27 May 1860. It is 2 p.m., and I am writing to you with the bombshells flying above my head through the air. In my last letter from this place of the 25th ult. I tried to give you a sketch of the position here, but could tell you little enough beyond conjectures about what was going on outside. I can now supply this deficiency, and tell you all that happened since Garibaldi's landing, till yesterday, from the very best authority; of the events since yesterday I can speak as an eye-witness. They will prove to you that Garibaldi's star, so far from being in the decline, seems rising brighter every day, and that if Sicily becomes free it will be owing to him . . .

He arrived yesterday morning at Misilmeri, on the high road to Catania, where he had given rendezvous to all the chieftains or captains on that side of the mountain chain. I was sick of uncertain rumours, which alone were to be got at in town, and which would leave your readers in darkness about the true state of things.

Besides, knowing a little of the gallant General's tactics, I had a strong suspicion that something was impending which could be better seen from without than from inside the town, so I determined to see whether I could not get there.

A drive of half an hour or more, in a gentle descent, with a lovely valley beneath, and beautiful mountain scenery in front, brought me to the town of Misilmeri, a wretched little place, altogether wanting in character. In the little square held out on one side the committee, which forms a kind of provisional government, and on the other, up some wooden steps fixed outside, was enthroned the chief of the staff of Garibaldi's expedition in primitive simplicity. Colonel Sirtori was just giving a pass to two young American officers from the United States steamship *Iroquois*, without which no one was allowed to enter the camp. As he had likewise given them an officer as guide, I joined them, and up we sauntered towards the heights leading to the Gebel Rosso and the pass of the Mezzagna. We had soon left behind us the few remaining houses and the ruins of the feudal castle to the left, the white limestone walls of which had something in them that reminded you of a skeleton. The ground all about is planted with olive trees, vines, and different sorts of grain, which all grow luxuriantly in spite of the stony nature of the place. The General had pitched his camp on a tolerably extensive plateau, just above the ruins, looking down on one side towards the plain and the range which ends at Cape Zaffarana, while on the other side the peaks of the Gebel Rosso and the pass of Mezzagna were visible across a depression in the ground, looking very much like an extinct crater, and now partially filled with water, owing to the copious rains which had fallen during the last few days. It was one of those panoramas which suggests naturally your pitching your tent there – that is, if you have one. The word tent is erased from the military dictionary of Garibaldi. However, a popular general has to yield at times to his soldiers, and so he could not prevent them from sticking into the ground four of the lances with which the squadron who have no muskets are armed, and from throwing over it a blanket. Under the tent you could see the gaucho saddle arranged as a pillow, and the black sheepskin covering as a bed. As for everyone else there were the olive trees affording shade, plenty of stones for pillows, and perhaps for every tenth man a cloak or blanket. All around were picketed the horses, most of them entire, and behaving accordingly.

The General himself was not there when we arrived but had taken one of his morning strolls, but in front of his tent there were all his trusty followers . . .

Well, all this motley crew increased now by the two young American naval men, and soon after joined by three British naval officers, was collected round a common nucleus – a smoking kettle with the larger part of a calf in it, and a liberal allowance of onions, a basket with heaps of fresh bread, and a barrel containing Marsala. Everyone helped himself in the most communistic manner, using fingers and knife, and drinking out of the solitary tin pot. It is only in this irregular warfare that you see these scenes in their greatest perfection. The long marches and counter-marches, rains, fights, and sleeping on the ground had made almost everyone worthy to figure in a picture by Murillo, with all those grand Sicilian mountains, not unlike those of Greece, forming a background such as no picture can reproduce.

Soon after my arrival Garibaldi made his appearance, and received his foreign visitors with that charming, quiet simplicity which characterizes him, lending himself with great complaisance to the invariably recurring demands of autographs, and answering the numerous questions which were naturally put to him. It was only after the departure of his guests that the General resumed business. The question debated was nothing more or less than to venture on a *coup de main* on Palermo the same night . . .

The first idea was to make the attack in the middle of the night – the Neapolitans don't like a stir at night, and there was every chance of a panic among them; but there was some danger that way likewise for the Sicilian insurgents and it was thought best to make such arrangements as would bring the force at dawn to the gates of the town. According to the original and better plan of the General himself and his Adjutant-General, Colonel Turr, the movement was to have been made along the main road from Misilmeri, broad enough to admit of considerable development of the columns and commodious in every respect. The native captains, however, suggested the Pass of Mezzagna, which descends from the heights behind Gebel Rosso into the plain of Palermo. According to their statements it was much shorter, and by no means difficult. Their statements were believed, and the whole force received orders to be concentrated by nightfall on the summit of the pass, crowned with a church.

According to the first disposition the troops brought by the General himself were to lead the way, and the *squadre* to follow; but some of the chiefs begged it as a favour for their corps to have the honour of being first in the town – a claim which could not be very well refused. The plan was therefore modified. The guides, and three men from each company of the Cacciatori delle Alpi, were formed into an *avant-garde*, confided to Major Tüköri, a Hungarian officer, who distinguished himself under General Kméty on the 29th of September at Kars. Behind this *avant-garde* followed the Sicilians, commanded by La Maga, an emigrant, who had come over with Garibaldi. The second line was led by the riflemen of Genoa – excellent shots all, armed with the Swiss carbine. Behind them came the two battalions of Cacciatori delle Alpi, and in the rear the rest of the Sicilians.

The order having been distributed, the different bands gradually worked their way towards the summit of the pass. The packing up at headquarters did not take much time; it soon after broke up its camp and followed the troops. I was mounted on a regular Rosinante, with a halter passed round the jaw, and provided with a saddle which seemed to have been formed to fit on the vertebrae of my lean black charger. A blanket was, however, found in due time, and on the whole I cannot complain. The road up to the pass winds along rows of gigantic cactus hedges, which give a thoroughly Eastern character to the country. It was just sunset when we arrived at the top when, through a gap, we could see the bay and town of Palermo and the sea beyond, looking more like a fairy picture than reality. All the mountains, with their rugged points naturally of a reddish tint, seemed to have drunk in the rays of the setting sun, and exhibited that rosy colour which I had thought hitherto a special gift of the plain of Attica. While you had this charming scene before you, you looked behind, as it were, into the hearts of the mountains. It was one of the finest spots I ever saw, and all the country was fragrant with spring flowers, the perfume of which came out with redoubled vigour as soon as the sun had set. It proved a bad road for the expedition, that mountain pass, but it was lovely to look upon.

In order to entertain the Neapolitans with the idea that all was safe on that side, the usual large fires were kindled on the tops of the mountains, and kept up long after our departure by men left behind for that purpose. Garibaldi went up to look at the position underneath, or perhaps to indulge in that kind of reverie to which he is subject in such solemn moments, and which ends in a concentration of all his faculties on the sole aim he has before him.

The evening gun in the fort had long been re-echoed by the mountains, and the moon had risen clear and bright above our heads, giving a new charm to this lovely scenery, before we stirred.

During this interval the *Picciotti* (youngsters), as the patriots are called, were put into some kind of order which, you will believe me, was no easy matter in the comparative darkness which prevailed; no chief knowing his men, and the men not recognizing their chief – everyone acting for someone else, and no one able to give an answer. With the exception of the troops brought over by Garibaldi, all the rest seemed an entangled mass almost impossible to unravel. However, by degrees those belonging to the same chief found themselves together, and the march began at 10 p.m. Either the Sicilian chieftains had never looked at the pass of Mezzagna, or else they have curious ideas of a road; the whole is nothing but a track among big stones crossing and recrossing the bed of a mountain torrent, following not unfrequently the bed of the torrent, leading over smooth masses of stones and across most awkward gaps – all this, at an angle of 25 degrees, to be passed on horseback at night! Even the men could only go singly, which made our line of a frightful length, and caused continual delays and stoppages. The General vowed never to believe another Sicilian report on the state of a mountain road. However, in the end we reached the plain, and came in among the olive trees below, with few falls among the sure-footed horses. A halt was made until all the columns had descended, and during this halt an incident occurred which did not promise much for the future behaviour of our *Picciotti*. The horses in Sicily are left for the most part entire, hence continual fighting and considerable neighing, which was so inconvenient in a night expedition of this kind that several of the most vicious steeds had to be sent back. One of them still remained and began its antics; the rider lost patience, which made matters worse. Those nearest threw themselves back in haste, and communicated the movement to those behind. These, many of whom had sat down and begun to doze, mistook in their dreams, probably, the trees for Neapolitans, the stars for so many shells, and the moon for a colossal fireball; at any rate, the majority of them were with one bound in the thickets on both sides of the road, several fired off their muskets in their fright, and very little was wanting to cause a general panic. Everyone did what he could to restore confidence, but the effect was produced and reacted, as you will see by and by. Another incident occurred, which might have led to the failure of the whole expedition. The Sicilian guides who were with the *avant-garde* missed the road, and instead of taking a by-road which led into the main road we had to pursue, they continued on the road near the hillside, which would have brought us just where the Neapolitans were in the greatest strength. The mistake was perceived in time and repaired, but not without considerable loss of time. At last the column emerged on to the main road, which is broad, and skirted by high garden walls. As we had lost considerable time with all these *contretemps* and as dawn was approaching, we had to make haste, but, whether from fatigue or the impression of the night panic, the *Picciotti* could not be brought to move very fast. It was just the first glimmer of dawn when we passed the first houses, which extend in this direction a long way out of the town of Palermo. The *squadri*, who ought to have known the locality better, began shouting and '*evviva*ing', just as if we had been close to the gates. Had it not been for this blunder the *avant-garde* might have surprised the post on the bridge of the Ammiragliato, and probably penetrated into the town without the loss of a man. As it was, the shouting not only roused those on guard on the bridge, but likewise gave an opportunity to the Neapolitans to strengthen the force at the gate of Termini, and to make all their dispositions for a defence from the flank.

Instead, therefore, of surprising the post on the bridge, the *avant-garde* was received by a well-sustained fire, not only in front, but from the houses in their flanks. At the first sound of the musketry most of the *Picciotti* were across the garden walls, but not with the view of firing from behind them, leaving thus the thirty or forty men of the *avant-garde* all isolated in the large exposed street which leads to the bridge. The first battalion of the Cacciatori was sent up, and as it did not carry the position fast enough, the second was sent after it soon after. While these were driving back the Neapolitans, everyone did his best to drive the *Picciotti* forward. It was not so easy, in the beginning especially, when the sound of cannon was heard in front, although its effects were scarcely visible. However the *Picciotti*, who remind me very much of Arnout Bashi-bazouks, can be led on after the first unpleasant sensation has passed away, especially when they see that it is not all shots that kill or wound, not even the cannon shots, which make so formidable a noise. They could see this to perfection this morning, for although the Neapolitan rifles are scarcely inferior to the best firearms, I never saw so little damage done by so much shooting. Everyone put himself to work, therefore, to lead and urge on the *Picciotti*, driving them out of the sheltered places by all kinds of contrivances, and often by blows and main force. After some trouble most of them were safely brought through the open space before the bridge, but the general tendency was to go under rather than above the bridge, which is, like all bridges over torrents, high, and was in this instance exposed to a heavy crossfire from the Piana di Borazzo, where the Neapolitans had a loop-holed wall and some guns mounted, which threw a few ill-aimed shells. While the General himself and many of his staff did their best to make them leave this shelter again and proceed, the *avant-garde* had chased back the Neapolitans to the *stradone* which runs down to the sea just in front of the Porta di Termini. The Neapolitan fort at the gate, considerably reinforced, opened a hot fire, which swept down the long avenue of houses leading to the bridge, while at the same time the two guns and the troops posted at the Porta Sant'Antonio brought a crossfire to bear on the attackers. But this was no obstacle to the brave fellows who led the way. They did not lose time with firing, but rushed on with the bayonet. The commander of the *avant-garde*, Major Tüköri, and three of the guides, were the first across the sandbag barricade in the town, but the leader was wounded by a shot, which shattered his left knee. Otherwise the loss had been trifling. While the *avant-garde* and the Cacciatori chased the Neapolitans from spot to spot, the Palermitans began likewise to stir but, justice compels me to say, only in the parts which the troops had left.

The same scene as at the bridge was repeated at the crossing of the *stradone* by the *Picciotti* who followed in a straggling movement. And yet it was important to get into the town, in order not to be outflanked or taken in the rear by the Neapolitans holding the Piana di Borazzo. In order to avert this danger the order was given to some of the bands to get behind the garden walls which line the road by which the Neapolitans might have come down on our left. These diversions, and probably the dislike to fight in the open, were sufficient to parry this danger until the greatest part of the stragglers had passed. At the same time a barricade was thrown up in the rear with anything which could be laid hold of. This work pleased the *Picciotti* so well that they began throwing up a barricade in the front likewise. At any rate they blocked up a part of the road before they could be prevented.

But the most critical thing was decidedly the crossing of the *stradone*, where the crossfire was kept up, and all kinds of dodges were resorted to to make them risk this *salto*, which they thought mortal. I and one of the followers of Garibaldi held out one of the men by main force exposed to the fire, which soon made him run across. It was here, above all, that the bad firing of the Neapolitans told. I was looking on for some time, and did not see a single man even wounded. In order to encourage the *Picciotti*, one of the Genoese riflemen took four or five chairs, planted the tricolour on one of them, and sat down upon it for some time. The thing took at last decidedly, and you saw the *Picciotti* stopping in the road to fire off their muskets.

Close to the Porta di Termini is the Vecchia Fiera – the old marketplace. This was the first point where Garibaldi stopped. One must know these Sicilians to have an idea of the frenzy, screaming, shouting, crying, and hugging; all would kiss his hand and embrace his knees. Every moment brought new masses, which debouched in troops from one of the streets, anxious to have their turn. As the Cacciatori gradually cleared the lower part of the town most of the inhabitants came to have a look, and give a greeting to the liberator of Palermo and Sicily. The entrance was effected about half-past 5 a.m., and by noon more than one half of the town was clear of the troops. But two hours before this was effected the citadel had opened its fire on the town, at first moderately enough, but soon after with great vigour, firing large 13-inch shells, red-hot shot, and every other projectile calculated to do the greatest possible damage. About noon or so the ships in the harbour opened their fire, and between the two they contrived to destroy a great number of houses in the lower part of the town, killing and wounding a large number of people of all ages and both sexes. Two of the large shells were sent right into the hospital, and exploded in one of the wards. Everywhere you perceived ruins and conflagrations, dead and wounded, not a few of whom must have perished among the ruins of their houses. It was especially the part of the town near the Piazza Bologni, and some of the adjoining streets, which was ill treated. If the object of the Neapolitans was to inspire terror, they certainly succeeded. Whoever could took refuge in whatever he thought the most bomb-proof place, and those who could not you saw crying, praying and wringing their hands in the streets. It was a pitiable sight, indeed, and it did more harm to inoffensive people than to those who might have retaliated.

Evening. The bombardment is still kept up, with only short intervals, especially from the Castle. All those who came in this morning with Garibaldi are dead beat, having had no sleep last night, and plenty of work since. The general himself is reposing on the platform which surrounds the large fountain in the Piazza del Pretorio, where the committee is sitting *en permanence.* This committee, the same which carried on the whole movement from the beginning, has constituted itself as a Provisional Government, under the dictatorship of Garibaldi.

The town is illuminated, and presents during the intervals of the bombardment an animated appearance; but all the shops are still closed. The illumination, with the antique-shaped glass lamps suspended from the balconies, presents a very pretty effect, rather heightened by the shells flying through the clear sky.

Derby Day, 28 May 1861
A French Visitor's View

Hippolyte Taine

The 1861 Derby was won by Kettledrum at 16 to 1, from the favourite, Dundee.

Races at Epsom: it is the Derby Day, a day of jollification; Parliament does not sit; for three days all the talk has been about horses and their trainers.

We start from Waterloo station. The sky is cloudless, free from mist; my English neighbours remark that they have never seen such a day in London. All around may be witnessed green husbandry, meadows encompassed with hedges, and the hedgerow is often interspersed with trees. The splendour of this green, the mass and the vigour of lustrous golden, bursting flowers, are extraordinary. Velvets constellated with diamonds, watered silks, the most magnificent embroideries do not match this deep hue; the colour is excessive, beyond the reach of painting; but never have the blooming and blossoming of plants, the luxury and the joy of the adorned earth, dazzled me with such bright pomp.

Epsom course is a large, green plain, slightly undulating; on one side are reared three public stands and several other smaller ones. In front, tents, hundreds of shops, temporary stables under canvas, and an incredible confusion of carriages, of horses, of horsemen, of private omnibuses; there are perhaps 200,000 human heads here. Nothing beautiful or even elegant; the carriages are ordinary vehicles, and toilettes are rare; one does not come here to exhibit them but to witness a spectacle: the spectacle is interesting only on account of its size. From the top of the Stand the enormous ant-heap swarms, and its din ascends. But beyond, on the right, a row of large trees, behind them the faint bluish undulations of the verdant country, make a magnificent frame to a mediocre picture. Some clouds as white as swans float in the sky, and their shadow sweeps over the grass; a light mist, charged with sunshine, flits in the distance, and the illuminated air, like a glory, envelops the plain, the heights, the vast area, and all the disorder of the human carnival.

It is a carnival, in fact; they have come to amuse themselves in a noisy fashion. Everywhere are gypsies, comic singers and dancers disguised as negroes, shooting galleries where bows and arrows or guns are used, charlatans who by dint of eloquence palm off watch chains, games of skittles and sticks, musicians of all sorts, and the most astonishing row of cabs, barouches, droskies, four-in-hands, with pies, cold meats, melons, fruits, wines, especially champagne. They unpack; they proceed to drink and eat; that restores the creature and excites him; coarse joy and open laughter are the result of a full stomach. In presence of this ready-made feast the aspect of the poor is pitiable to behold; they endeavour to sell you penny dolls, remembrances of the Derby; to induce you to play at Aunt Sally, to black your boots. Nearly all of them resemble wretched, hungry, beaten, mangy dogs, waiting for a bone, without hope of finding much on it. They arrived on foot during the night, and count upon dining off crumbs from the great feast. Many are lying on the ground, among the feet of the passers-by, and sleep open-mouthed, face upwards. Their countenances have an expression of stupidity and of painful hardness. The majority of them have bare feet, all are terribly dirty, and most absurd-looking; the reason is that they wear gentlemen's old clothes, worn-out fashionable dresses, small bonnets, formerly worn by young ladies. The sight of these cast-off things, which have covered several bodies, becoming more shabby in passing from one to the other, always makes me uncomfortable. To wear these old clothes is degrading; in doing so the human being shows or avows that he is the off-scouring of society. Among us [the French] a peasant, a workman, a labourer, is a different man, not an inferior person; his blouse belongs to him, as my coat belongs to me – it has clothed no one but him. The employment of ragged clothes is more than a peculiarity; the poor resign themselves here to be the footstool of others.

One of these women, with an old shawl that appeared to have been dragged in the gutter, with battered head-gear, which had been a bonnet, made limp by the rain, with a poor, dirty, pale baby in her arms, came and prowled round our omnibus, picked up a castaway bottle, and drained the dregs. Her second girl, who could walk, also picked up and munched a rind of melon. We gave them a shilling and cakes. The humble smile of thankfulness they returned, it is impossible to describe. They had the look of saying, like Sterne's poor donkey, 'Do not beat me, I beseech you – yet you may beat me if you wish.' Their countenances were burned, tanned by the sun; the mother had a scar on her right cheek, as if she had been struck by a boot; both of them, the child in particular, were grown wild and stunted. The great social mill crushes and grinds here, beneath its steel gearing, the lowest human stratum.

However, a bell rings, and the race is about to begin. The three or four hundred policemen clear the course; the stands are filled, and the meadow in front of them is but a large black patch. We ascend to our places; nothing seems at all imposing. At this distance the crowd is an ant-heap; the horsemen and carriages which move forward and cross each other resemble beetles, May-bugs, large sombre drones on a green cloth. The jockeys in red, in blue, in yellow, in mauve, form a small group apart, like a swarm of butterflies which has alighted. Probably I am wanting in enthusiasm, but I seem to be looking at a game of insects. Thirty-four run; after three false starts they are off; fifteen or twenty keep together, the others are in small groups, and one sees them moving down the far side of the circuit. To the eye the speed is not very great; it is that of a railway train seen at a distance of half a league – when the carriages look like toy coaches which a child pulls along on a string. For several minutes the brown patch, dotted with red and bright spots, moves steadily over the distant green. It turns; one perceives the first group approach. 'Hats off!' and all heads are uncovered, and everyone rises; a repressed 'hurrah' runs through the stands. The frigid faces are on fire; brief, nervous gestures suddenly stir the phlegmatic bodies; below, in the betting ring, the agitation is extraordinary – like a general St Vitus's dance; picture a mass of puppets receiving an electric shock, and gesticulating with all their members like mad semaphores. But the most curious spectacle is the human tide which instantly pours forth and rolls over the course behind the runners, like a wave of ink; the black, motionless crowd has suddenly become molten; in a moment it spreads itself over a vast area. The policemen make a barrier in two or three ranks, using force when necessary to guard the square to which the jockeys and horses are led. Measures are taken to weigh and see that all is right . . .

We descend; there is a hustling and crushing in the staircases, at the refreshment counters; but most of the carriages are provisioned for the day, and the people feast in the open air in small knots . . . Over the whole downs jaws are at work, bottles are emptied, and towards evening the carnival is in full swing. Twenty-four gentlemen triumphantly range on their omnibus seventy-five bottles which they have emptied. Groups pelt each other with chicken bones, lobster shells, pieces of turf. Two parties of gentlemen have descended from their omnibuses and engaged in a fight, ten against ten; one of them gets two teeth broken . . .

On our return, the road is hidden by dust; the fields, near the roadside, are reddened by feet; everybody returns frightfully dirty, and powdered with white; there are drunken people along the whole road; up to eight o'clock in the evening they might be seen staggering and sick on Hyde Park Corner; their comrades support them, laughing, and the spectators' faces do not betoken disgust. Today everything is allowable, it is an outlet for a year of repression.

The American Civil War: General Grant Besieges the Confederate Forces in Vicksburg, May 1863

Special Correspondent, *Cleveland Herald*, Ohio

The capture of Vicksburg, Mississippi, on 4 July by General Ulysses S. Grant was a fatal blow for the Confederate Southern states, and brought the Mississippi under Union control.

Let us climb the parapet and see the siege by moonlight. In front of us, beyond the enemy's works, but hidden from us, lies the city of Vicksburg. Look carefully, and you can distinguish the spires of the courthouse and two or three churches. The rebels had a signal station on the former when we came, but our shells made it too warm for them, and they withdrew. The mortars are playing tonight, and they are well worth seeing. We watch a moment, and in the direction of Young's Point, beyond the city, suddenly up shoots a flash of light, and in a moment the ponderous shell, with its fuse glowing and sparkling, rises slowly from behind the bluffs; up, up, it goes, as though mounting to the zenith, over it comes towards us, down through its flight trajectory into the city, and explodes with a shock that jars the ground for miles. There are women and tender children where those shells fall, but war is war.

Sherman's eight-inch monsters are grumbling far way on the right. Nearer, McPherson's, too, are playing – we can even see the cannoneers beside them at each flash. Ours will open at midnight; then there will be music to your heart's content. Meanwhile, let us go to the front. A hundred yards to the right of where we now are we enter a deep trench. Following this, as it winds down around the hill, we reach the opening of a cave or mine. The air within is damp and close, like that of a vault. Candles are burning dimly at intervals, and we hear a hum of voices far within and out of sight. We proceed, and presently meet two men carrying a barrow of earth, for our boys are at work night and day. Finally, we reach the moonlight again, and emerge into a wide, deep trench, cut across the line of the covered way. This is open, and filled with troops, who protect the working party. A heavy parapet of cotton bales and earth is built on the side towards the enemy, and we must mount them to look over.

We are now within sociable distance of the chivalry. Those men lying on the ground, ten to thirty yards from us, are our boys, our advance pickets; but that grey fellow, with the bright musket, which glistens so, a few steps beyond, is a 'reb.', long-haired and hot-blooded, one of Wall's famous Texas legion – a bulldog to fight, you may be sure.

Now jump down and enter the mouth of the other mine, which leads toward the salient of the enemy's work. Stumbling along, we reach the end where the men are digging. The candle burns very dimly – the air is almost stifling. Never mind, let us watch them. See that slender, bright-looking fellow swinging that pick. Great beaded drops of perspiration trickle down his face; there is not a dry thread in his coarse, grey shirt; but no matter, the pick swings, and each stroke slices down six inches of the tough subsoil of Mississippi. That fellow was 'Jim', once a tender-handed, smooth-faced, nice young man, whose livery-stable, billiard and cigar bills were a sore trial to his worthy governor. Jim says that he used to wear gloves and 'store-clothes', and that girls called him good-looking, but that's played out now; he is going for Uncle Sam.

But we return to the fresh air. Look over the parapet again towards the turret, where we saw the rebel picket. Do you see the little grey mounds which cover the hillside so thickly? – ten, twenty, thirty, you can count on a few square rods. Ah, my friend, this is sacred ground you are looking upon. There our boys charged; there they were slain in heaps; but they pressed on, and leaped into the ditch. They climbed the parapet, and rolled back into eternity. Others followed them; their flag was planted, and they sprang over, to meet their certain death. An hour passed, and *one* returned; the rest were dead.

Gettysburg: The Confederate Bombardment, 3 July 1863

Samuel Wilkeson writes his despatch beside the body of his son, Lieutenant Bayard Wilkeson, killed in the first day's fighting

Samuel Wilkeson

Gettysburg, fought 35 miles south-west of Harrisburg, Pennsylvania, was the turning point of the Civil War. After three days' battle the Confederate army, which had invaded the North under General Robert E. Lee, was forced to withdraw. About 23,000 Northern troops fell and 20,000 Southerners.

Who can write the history of a battle whose eyes are immovably fastened upon a central figure of transcendingly absorbing interest – the dead body of an oldest born, crushed by a shell in a position where a battery should never have been sent, and abandoned to death in a building where surgeons dared not to stay? . . .

For such details as I have the heart for. The battle commenced at daylight, on the side of the horseshoe position, exactly opposite to that which Ewell had sworn to crush through. Musketry preceded the rising of the sun. A thick wood veiled this fight, but out of the leafy darkness arose the smoke and the surging and swelling of the fire . . .

Suddenly, and about ten in the forenoon, the firing on the east side and everywhere about our lines ceased. A silence of deep sleep fell upon the field of battle. Our army cooked, ate and slumbered. The rebel army moved 120 guns to the west, and massed there Longstreet's corps and Hill's corps to hurl them upon the really weakest point of our entire position.

Eleven o'clock – twelve o'clock – one o'clock. In the shadow cast by the tiny farmhouse, sixteen by twenty, where General Meade had made his headquarters, lay wearied staff officers and tired reporters. There was not wanting to the peacefulness of the scene the singing of a bird, which had a nest in a peach tree within the tiny yard of the whitewashed cottage. In the midst of its warbling a shell screamed over the house, instantly followed by another and another, and in a moment the air was full of the most complete artillery prelude to an infantry battle that was ever exhibited. Every size and form of shell known to British and to American gunnery shrieked, moaned, whirled, whistled, and wrathfully fluttered over our ground . . . Through the midst of the storm of screaming and exploding shells an ambulance, driven by its frenzied conductor at full speed, presented to all of us the marvellous spectacle of a horse going rapidly on three legs. A hinder one had been shot off at the hock . . . During this fire the houses at twenty and thirty feet distant were receiving their death, and soldiers in Federal blue were torn to pieces in the road and died with the peculiar yells that blend the extorted cry of pain with horror and despair. Not an orderly, not an ambulance, not a straggler was to be seen upon the plain swept by this tempest of orchestral death thirty minutes after it commenced.

The Great March: General Sherman Lays Waste the South, October 1864 – February 1865

George Nichols

General Sherman, author of the phrase 'War is hell', led the Union forces on their crushing campaign through the South in 1864–5.

When General Sherman was in pursuit of Hood, he stood one evening [5 October 1864] upon the top of Pine Knob, eagerly watching the Western horizon for indications of the presence of an army. Cox had just arrived upon the ground with the head of his column, by a detour round the eastern base of Kenesaw. Welcoming him, General Sherman pointed in the direction of the Allatoona and Dallas Road, and said, 'General Cox, I wish you to push out upon that road until you strike the Dallas Road. Let me know the position of your head of column by a flame and smoke. Burn barns, houses, anything; but let me see from this point where you are.'

General Cox instantly departed. In a few minutes a blue column of smoke rose up into the still air, and then another, and yet again another – stretching out and winding among the hills and valleys, creeping up out of the forest, and gradually lost in the grey and purple twilight. No sound of cannon disturbed the exquisite beauty of the scene, and these silent witnesses of the forward steps of our soldiers told us that no enemy was near . . .

12 February 1865. Tonight we are encamped upon the place of one of South Carolina's most high-blooded chivalry – one of those persons who believed himself to have been brought into the world to rule over his fellow creatures, a sort of Grand Pasha, and all that sort of thing. How the negro pioneers are making away with the evergreens and rosebushes of his artistically arranged walks, flower beds and drives! These black men in blue are making brooms of his pet shrubs, with which they clear the ground in front of the tents . . .

19 February, Columbia. General Sherman has given orders for the farther destruction of all public property in the city, excepting the new capitol, which will not be injured. I think the General saves this building more because it is a beautiful work of art than for any other reason. The arsenal, railroad, depots, storehouses, magazines, public property, and cotton to the amount of 20,000 bales, are today destroyed. There is not a rail upon any of the roads within twenty miles of Columbia but will be twisted into corkscrews before the sun sets.

The Great March: General Sherman's 'Bummers', March 1865

Elias Smith

In rear of each Division followed the foragers, or 'bummers', as they are called by the soldiers, constituting a motley group which strongly recalls the memory of Falstaff's ragged army, though they are by no means men in buckram. The men having worn out all their clothing and shoes during the march, were obliged to provide themselves the best way they could as they went along.

Here came men strutting in mimic dignity in an old swallow-tailed coat, with plug hats, the tops knocked in; there a group in seedy coats and pants of Rebel grey, with arms and legs protruding beyond all semblance of fit or of fashion; short jackets, long-tailed surtouts, and coats of every cast with broad tails, narrow tails, and no tails at all – all of the most antiquated styles. Some wore women's bonnets, or young ladies' hats, with streamers of faded ribbons floating fantastically in the wind.

The procession of vehicles and animals was of the most grotesque description. There were donkeys large and small, almost smothered, under burdens of turkeys, geese and other kinds of poultry, ox carts, skinny horses pulling in the fills of some parish doctors, old sulkies, farm wagons and buggies, hacks, chaises, rockaways, aristocratic and family carriages, all filled with plunder and provisions.

There was bacon, hams, potatoes, flour, pork, sorghum, and freshly slaughtered pigs, sheep, and poultry dangling from saddle tree and wagon, enough, one would suppose, to feed the army for a fortnight.

The Murder of President Lincoln, 14 April 1865

Walt Whitman

The assassin, John Wilkes Booth, was a professional actor, a vigorous supporter of the South and advocate of slavery. He escaped after the murder but was hunted down and killed in a Virginia tobacco barn twelve days later.

The day, April 14, 1865, seems to have been a pleasant one throughout the whole land – the moral atmosphere pleasant too – the long storm, so dark, so fratricidal, full of blood and doubt and gloom, over and ended at last by the sunrise of such an absolute National victory, and utter breaking down of Secessionism – we almost doubted our own senses! Lee had capitulated beneath the apple-tree of Appomattox. The other armies, the flanges of the revolt, swiftly followed . . . And could it really be, then? Out of all the affairs of this world of woe and passion, of failure and disorder and dismay, was there really come the confirmed, unerring sign of plan, like a shaft of pure light – of rightful rule – of God? . . . So the day, as I say, was propitious. Early herbage, early flowers, were out. (I remember where I was stopping at the time, the season being advanced, there were many lilacs in full bloom. By one of those caprices that enter and give tinge to events without being at all a part of them, I find myself always reminded of the great tragedy of that day by the sight and odour of these blossoms. It never fails.)

But I must not dwell on accessories. The deed hastens. The

popular afternoon paper of Washington, the little *Evening Star*, had spattered all over its third page, divided among the advertisements in a sensational manner in a hundred different places, *The President and his Lady will be at the Theatre this evening* . . . (Lincoln was fond of the theatre. I have myself seen him there several times. I remember thinking how funny it was that He, in some respects, the leading actor in the greatest and stormiest drama known to real history's stage, through centuries, should sit there and be so completely interested and absorbed in those human jackstraws, moving about with their silly little gestures, foreign spirit, and flatulent text.)

On this occasion the theatre was crowded, many ladies in rich and gay costumes, officers in their uniforms, many well-known citizens, young folks, the usual clusters of gas-lights, the usual magnetism of so many people, cheerful, with perfumes, music of violins and flutes – (and over all, and saturating all, that vast vague wonder, *Victory*, the Nation's Victory, the triumph of the Union, filling the air, the thought, the sense, with exhilaration more than all perfumes.)

The President came betimes, and, with his wife, witnessed the play, from the large stage-boxes of the second tier, two thrown into one, and profusely draped with the National flag. The acts and scenes of the piece – one of those singularly written compositions which have at least the merit of giving entire relief to an audience engaged in mental action or business excitements and cares during the day, as it makes not the slightest call on either the moral, emotional, aesthetic, or spiritual nature – a piece, (*Our American Cousin*) in which, among other characters, so called, a Yankee, certainly such a one as was never seen, or the least like it ever seen, in North America, is introduced in England, with a varied fol-de-rol of talk, plot, scenery, and such phantasmagoria as goes to make up a modern popular drama – had progressed through perhaps a couple of its acts, when in the midst of this comedy, or tragedy, or non-such, or whatever it is to be called, and to off-set it or finish it out, as if in Nature's and the Great Muse's mockery of those poor mimes, comes interpolated that Scene, not really or exactly to be described at all (for on the many hundreds who were there it seems to this hour to have left little but a passing blur, a dream, a blotch) – and yet partially to be described as I now proceed to give it . . . There is a scene in the play representing a modern parlour, in which

two unprecedented English ladies are informed by the unprecedented and impossible Yankee that he is not a man of fortune,
and therefore undesirable for marriage-catching purposes; after
which, the comments being finished, the dramatic trio make exit,
leaving the stage clear for a moment. There was a pause, a hush as it
were. At this period came the murder of Abraham Lincoln. Great as
that was, with all its manifold train, circling round it, and
stretching into the future for many a century, in the politics,
history, art, of the New World, in point of fact the main thing, the
actual murder, transpired with the quiet and simplicity of any
commonest occurrence – the bursting of a bud or pod in the growth
of vegetation, for instance. Through the general hum following the
stage pause, with the change of positions, came the muffled sound
of a pistol shot, which not one hundredth part of the audience
heard at the time – and yet a moment's hush – somehow, surely a
vague startled thrill – and then, through the ornamented,
draperied, starred and striped space-way of the President's box, a
sudden figure, a man raises himself with hands and feet, stands a
moment on the railing, leaps below to the stage (a distance of
perhaps fourteen or fifteen feet) falls out of position, catching his
boot-heel in the copious drapery (the American flag), falls on one
knee, quickly recovers himself, rises as if nothing had happened (he
really sprains his ankle, but unfelt then) – and so the figure, Booth,
the murderer, dressed in plain black broadcloth, bare-headed, with
a full head of glossy, raven hair, and his eyes like some mad
animal's flashing with light and resolution, yet with a certain
strange calmness, holds aloft in one hand a large knife – walks
along not much back from the footlights – turns fully toward the
audience his face of statuesque beauty, lit by those basilisk eyes,
flashing with desperation, perhaps insanity – launches out in a firm
and steady voice the words, *Sic semper tyrannis* – and then walks
with neither slow nor very rapid pace diagonally across to the back
of the stage, and disappears . . . (Had not all this terrible scene –
making the mimic ones preposterous – had it not all been
rehearsed, in blank, by Booth, beforehand?)

A moment's hush, incredulous – a scream – the cry of *Murder* –
Mrs Lincoln leaning out of the box, with ashy cheeks and lips, with
involuntary cry, pointing to the retreating figure, *He has killed the
President* . . . And still a moment's strange, incredulous suspense –
and then the deluge! – then that mixture of horror, noises,

uncertainty – (the sound, somewhere back, of a horse's hoofs clattering with speed) – the people burst through chairs and railings, and break them up – that noise adds to the queerness of the scene – there is inextricable confusion and terror – women faint – quite feeble persons fall, and are trampled on – many cries of agony are heard – the broad stage suddenly fills to suffocation with a dense and motley crowd, like some horrible carnival – the audience rush generally upon it – at least the strong men do – the actors and actresses are all there in their play costumes and painted faces, with mortal fright showing through the rouge, some trembling – some in tears – the screams and calls, confused talk – redoubled, trebled – two or three manage to pass up water from the stage to the President's box – others try to clamber up – etc., etc., etc.

In the midst of all this, the soldiers of the President's Guard, with others, suddenly drawn to the scene, burst in – (some two hundred altogether) – they storm the house, through all the tiers, especially the upper ones, inflamed with fury, literally charging the audience with fixed bayonets, muskets and pistols, shouting *Clear out! clear out! you sons of –* . . . Such the wild scene, or a suggestion of it rather, inside the playhouse that night.

Outside, too, in the atmosphere of shock and craze, crowds of people, filled with frenzy, ready to seize any outlet for it, come near committing murder several times on innocent individuals. One such case was especially exciting. The infuriated crowd, through some chance, got started against one man, either for words he uttered, or perhaps without any cause at all, and were proceeding at once to actually hang him on a neighbouring lamp-post, when he was rescued by a few heroic policemen, who placed him in their midst and fought their way slowly and amid great peril toward the Station House . . . It was a fitting episode of the whole affair. The crowd rushing and eddying to and fro – the night, the yells, the pale faces, many frightened people trying in vain to extricate themselves – the attacked man, not yet freed from the jaws of death, looking like a corpse – the silent resolute half-dozen policemen, with no weapons but their little clubs, yet stern and steady through all those eddying swarms – made indeed a fitting side-scene to the grand tragedy of the murder . . . They gained the Station House with the protected man, whom they placed in security for the night, and discharged him in the morning.

And in the midst of that night-pandemonium of senseless hate, infuriated soldiers, the audience and the crowd – the stage, and all its actors and actresses, its paint-pots, spangles, and gas-lights – the life-blood from those veins, the best and sweetest of the land, drips slowly down, and death's ooze already begins its little bubbles on the lips . . . Such, hurriedly sketched, were the accompaniments of the death of President Lincoln. So suddenly and in murder and horror unsurpassed he was taken from us. But his death was painless.

Americans Abroad, 1867

Mark Twain

The author was sailing on the excursion steamship Quaker City, *as travel correspondent for* Alta California, *California's largest paper.*

Bad news came. The commandant of the Piraeus came in his boat and said we must either depart or else get outside the harbour and remain imprisoned in our ship, under rigid quarantine, for eleven days! So we took up the anchor and moved outside, to lie a dozen hours or so taking in supplies and then sail for Constantinople. It was the bitterest disappointment we had yet experienced. To lie a whole day in sight of the Acropolis and yet be obliged to go away without visiting Athens! Disappointment was hardly a strong enough word to describe the circumstances.

All hands were on deck all the afternoon, with books and maps and glasses, trying to determine which 'narrow rocky ridge' was the Areopagus, which sloping hill the Pnyx, which elevation the Museum Hill, and so on. And we got things confused. Discussion became heated, and party spirit ran high. Church members were gazing with emotion upon a hill which they said was the one St Paul preached from, and another faction claimed that that hill was Hymettus, and another that is was Pentelikon! After all the trouble, we could be certain of only one thing – the square-topped hill was the Acropolis and the grand ruin that crowned it was the Parthenon, whose picture we knew in infancy in the school books.

We inquired of everybody who came near the ship whether there were guards in the Piraeus, whether they were strict, what the chances were of capture should any of us slip ashore, and in case any of us made the venture and were caught, what would be probably done to us? The answers were discouraging: There was a strong guard or police force; the Piraeus was a small town, and any stranger seen in it would surely attract attention – capture would be certain. The commandant said the punishment would be 'heavy'; when asked, 'How heavy?' he said it would be 'very severe' – that was all we could get out of him.

At eleven o'clock at night, when most of the ship's company were abed, four of us stole softly ashore in a small boat, a clouded moon favouring the enterprise, and started two and two, and far apart, over a low hill, intending to go clear around the Piraeus, out of the range of its police. Picking our way so stealthily over that rocky, nettle-grown eminence made us feel a good deal as if I were on my way somewhere to steal something. My immediate comrade and I talked in an undertone about quarantine laws and their penalties, but we found nothing cheering in the subject . . .

Seeing no road, we took a tall hill to the left of the distant Acropolis for a mark and steered straight for it over all obstructions, and over a little rougher piece of country than exists anywhere else outside the state of Nevada, perhaps. Part of the way it was covered with small, loose stones – we trod on six at a time and they all rolled. Another part of it was dry, loose, newly ploughed ground. Still another part of it was a long stretch of low grapevines, which were tanglesome and troublesome, and which we took to be brambles. The Attic Plain, barring the grapevines, was a barren, desolate, unpoetical waste – I wonder what it was in Greece's Age of Glory, five hundred years before Christ.

In the neighbourhood of one o'clock in the morning, when we were heated with fast walking and parched with thirst, Denny exclaimed, 'Why, these weeds are grapevines!' And in five minutes we had a score of bunches of large, white, delicious grapes, and were reaching down for more when a dark shape rose mysteriously up out of the shadows beside us and said, 'Ho!' And so we left.

In ten minutes more we struck into a beautiful road, and unlike some others we had stumbled upon at intervals, it led in the right direction. We followed it. It was broad and smooth and white, handsome and in perfect repair, and shaded on both sides for a mile or so with single ranks of trees and also with luxuriant vineyards.

Twice we entered and stole grapes, and the second time somebody shouted at us from some invisible place. Whereupon we left again. We speculated in grapes no more on that side of Athens.

Shortly we came upon an ancient stone aqueduct built upon arches, and from that time forth we had ruins all about us – we were approaching our journey's end. We could not see the Acropolis now or the high hill, either, and I wanted to follow the road till we were abreast of them, but the others overruled me, and we toiled laboriously up the stony hill immediately in our front – and from its summit saw another – climbed it and saw another! It was an hour of exhausting work. Soon we came upon a row of open graves cut in the solid rock (for a while one of them served Socrates for a prison); we passed around the shoulder of the hill, and the citadel, in all its ruined magnificence, burst upon us! We hurried across the ravine and up a winding road and stood on the old Acropolis, with the prodigious walls of the citadel towering above our heads. We did not stop to inspect their massive blocks of marble or measure their height or guess at their extraordinary thickness, but passed at once through a great arched passage like a railway tunnel and went straight to the gate that leads to the ancient temples. It was locked! So, after all, it seemed that we were not to see the great Parthenon face to face. We sat down and held a council of war. Result: the gate was only a flimsy structure of wood – we would break it down. It seemed like desecration, but then we had travelled far, and our necessities were urgent. We could not hunt up guides and keepers – we must be on the ship before daylight. So we argued. This was all very fine, but when we came to break the gate, we could not do it. We moved around an angle of the wall and found a low bastion: eight feet high without, ten or twelve within. Denny prepared to scale it, and we got ready to follow. By dint of hard scrambling he finally straddled the top, but some loose stones crumbled away and fell with a crash into the court within. There was instantly a banging of doors and a shout. Denny dropped from the wall in a twinkling, and we retreated in disorder to the gate. Xerxes took that mighty citadel four hundred and eighty years before Christ, when his five millions of soldiers and camp followers followed him to Greece, and if we four Americans could have remained unmolested five minutes longer, we would have taken it too.

The garrison had turned out – four Greeks. We clamoured at the gate, and they admitted us. (Bribery and corruption.)

We crossed a large court, entered a great door, and stood upon a pavement of purest white marble, deeply worn by footprints. Before us in the flooding moonlight rose the noblest ruins we had ever looked upon – the Propylaea; a small Temple of Minerva; the Temple of Hercules; and the grand Parthenon. (We got these names from the Greek guide, who didn't seem to know more than seven men ought to know.) These edifices were all built of the whitest Pentelik marble, but have a pinkish stain upon them now. Where any part is broken, however, the fracture looks like fine loaf sugar. Six caryatids, or marble women, clad in flowing robes, support the portico of the Temple of Hercules, but the porticoes and colonnades of the other structures are formed of massive Doric and Ionic pillars, whose flutings and capitals are still measurably perfect, notwithstanding the centuries that have gone over them and the sieges they have suffered. The Parthenon originally was two hundred and twenty-six feet long, one hundred wide, and seventy high, and had two rows of great columns, eight in each, at either end, and single rows of seventeen each down the sides, and was one of the most graceful and beautiful edifices ever erected.

Most of the Parthenon's imposing columns are still standing, but the roof is gone. It was a perfect building two hundred and fifty years ago, when a shell dropped into the Venetian magazine stored here, and the explosion which followed wrecked and unroofed it. I remember but little about the Parthenon, and I have put in one or two facts and figures for the use of other people with short memories. Got them from the guidebook.

As we wandered thoughtfully down the marble-paved length of this stately temple the scene about us was strangly impressive. Here and there in lavish profusion were gleaming white statues of men and women, propped against blocks of marble, some of them armless, some without legs, others headless – but all looking mournful in the moonlight and startlingly human! They rose up and confronted the midnight intruder on every side – they stared at him with stony eyes from unlooked-for nooks and recesses; they peered at him over fragmentary heaps far down the desolate corridors; they barred his way in the midst of the broad forum and solemnly pointed with handless arms the way from the sacred fane; and through the roofless temple the moon looked down and banded the floor and darkened the scattered fragments and broken statues with the slanting shadows of the columns . . .

The full moon was riding high in the cloudless heavens now. We sauntered carelessly and unthinkingly to the edge of the lofty battlements of the citadel and looked down – a vision! And such a vision! Athens by moonlight! The prophet that thought the spendours of the New Jerusalem were revealed to him surely saw this instead! It lay in the level plain right under our feet – all spread abroad like a picture – and we looked down upon it as we might have looked from a balloon. We saw no semblance of a street, but every house, every window, every clinging vine, every projection, was as distinct and sharply marked as if the time were noonday; and yet there was no glare, no glitter, nothing harsh or repulsive – the noiseless city was flooded with the mellowest light that ever streamed from the moon, and seemed like some living creature wrapped in peaceful slumber. On its further side was a little temple, whose delicate pillars and ornate front glowed with a rich lustre that chained the eye like a spell; and nearer by, the palace of the king reared its creamy walls out of the midst of a great garden of shrubbery that was flecked all over with a random shower of amber lights – a spray of golden sparks that lost their brightness in the glory of the moon and glinted softly upon the sea of dark foliage like the pallid stars of the Milky Way. Overhead the stately columns, majestic still in their ruin – under foot the dreaming city – in the distance the silver sea – not on the broad earth is there another picture half so beautiful!

The Suppression of the Paris Commune, 23–24 May 1871

Archibald Forbes

When the elections of February 1871 produced a National Assembly with a Royalist majority, the republican Parisians set up a commune to resist the Versailles government. Versaillist troops entered Paris on 21 May, and in the 'bloody week' that followed 20,000 communards (or 'federals', as they were also called) were killed, either in the street fighting or in summary executions.

Paris, Tuesday, 23 May, Five o'clock. The firing is furious and confusing all round. At the Opera House it is especially strong. I see troops and man after man skulking along the parapet of its roof. They have packs on, so I think they are Versaillists; but I cannot see their breeches and so cannot be certain. The *drapeau rouge* still waves from the statue on the summit of the New Opera House. The Federals are massed now at the top of the Rue Lafitte and firing down toward the boulevards. This must mean that the Versaillists are on the boulevards now. On account of the Versaillist fire the Federals cannot well come out into the Rue de Provence, and everywhere they seem between the devil and the deep sea. The people in the Porte Cochère are crying bravo and clapping their hands, because they think the Versaillists are winning.

Twenty minutes past five. They were Versaillists that I saw on the parapet of the New Opera. There is a cheer; the people rush out into the fire and clap their hands. The tricolor is waving on the hither end of the Opera House. I saw the man stick it up. The red flag still waves at the other end. A ladder is needed to remove it. Ha! you are a good plucky one, if all the rest were cowards. You deserve to give the army a good name. A little grig of a fellow in red breeches, he is one of the old French linesman breed. He scuttles forward to the corner of the Rue Halévy in the Boulevard Haussmann, takes up his post behind a tree, and fires along the Boulevard Haussmann towards the Rue Taitbout. When is a Frenchman not dramatic? He fires with an air; he loads with an air; he fires again with a flourish, and is greeted with cheering and clapping of hands. Then he beckons us back dramatically, for he meditates firing up the Rue de Lafayette, but changes his mind and blazes away again up Haussmann. Then he turns and waves on his fellows as if he were on the boards of a theatre, the Federal bullets cutting the bark and leaves all around him. He is down. The woman and I dart out from our corner and carry him in. He is dead, with a bullet through the forehead.

Twenty-five minutes to six. The scene is intensely dramatic. A Versaillist has got a ladder and is mounting the statue of Apollo on the front elevation of the New Opera House. He tears down the *drapeau rouge* just as the Versailles troops stream out of the Chaussée d'Antin across the Boulevard Haussmann, and down the Rue Meyerbeer and the continuation of the Chaussée d'Antin. The people rushed from their houses with bottles of wine; money was showered into the streets. The women fell on the necks of the sweaty, dusty men in red breeches, and hugged them amid shouts of *Vive la ligne*. The soldiers fraternized warmly; drank and pressed forward. Their discipline was admirable. They formed in companies behind the next barricade and obeyed the officer at once when he called them from conviviality. Now the wave of Versaillists is over us for good, and the red breeches are across the Great Boulevard and going at the Place Vendôme. Everybody seems wild with joy, and Communist cards of citizenship are being torn up wholesale. It is not *citoyen* now under pain of suspicion. You may say *monsieur* if you like.

Ten p.m. Much has been done since the hour at which I last dated. The Versaillist soldiers, pouring down in one continuous stream by the Chaussée d'Antin, horse, foot, and artillery, crossed the Great Boulevard, taking the insurgents in flank, not without considerable fighting and a good deal of loss, for the Federals fought like wildcats wherever they could get the ghost of a cover. Anxious to ascertain whether there was any prospect of an Embassy bag to Versailles, I started up the now quiet Boulevard Haussmann, and by tacks and dodges got down into the Rue de Miromesnil, which debouches in the faubourg opposite the Palace of the Elysée. Shells were bursting very freely in the neighbourhood, but the matter was urgent, and I pressed on up to the Rue du Faubourg Saint-Honoré, and looked round the corner for a second. Had I looked a second longer, I should not have been writing these lines. A shell splinter whizzed past me as I drew back, close enough to blow my beard aside. The street was a pneumatic tube for shellfire. Nothing could have lived in it. I fell back, thinking I might get over to the Embassy as the firing died away, and waited in the entry of an ambulance for an hour. There were not a few ambulances about this spot. I saw, for a quarter of an hour, one wounded man carried into the one I was near every minute, for I timed the stretchers by my watch. Looking into others, I could see the courtyards littered with mattresses and groaning men. A few but not many corpses, chiefly of National Guards, lay in the streets, behind the barricades, and in the gutters.

As I returned to the Hôtel de la Chaussée d'Antin, I had to cross the line of artillery pouring southward from the Church of the Trinity, and so down the Rue Halévy, toward the quarter where the sound indicated hot fighting was still going on. The artillerymen received a wild ovation from the inhabitants of the Chaussée d'Antin. The men gave them money, the women tendered them bottles of wine. All was *gaudeamus*. Where, I wonder, had the people secreted the tricolor all these days of the Commune? It now waved from every window, and flapped in the still night air, as the shouts of *Vive la ligne* gave it a lazy throb.

Wednesday. And so evening wore into night, and night became morning. Ah! this morning! Its pale flush of aurora bloom was darkest, most sombre night for the once proud, now stricken and humiliated, city. When the sun rose, what saw he? Not a fair fight – on that within the last year Sol has looked down more than once. But black clouds flouted his rays – clouds that rose from the Palladium of France. Great God! that men should be so mad as to strive to make universal ruin because their puny course of factiousness is run! The flames from the Palace of the Tuileries, kindled by damnable petroleum, insulted the soft light of the morning and cast lurid rays on the grimy recreant Frenchmen who skulked from their dastardly incendiarism to pot at countrymen from behind a barricade. How the place burned! The flames revelled in the historical palace, whipped up the rich furniture, burst out the plate-glass windows, brought down the fantastic roof. It was in the Prince Imperial's wing facing the Tuileries Gardens where the demon of fire first had his dismal sway. By eight o'clock the whole of the wing was nearly burned out. As I reached the end of the Rue Dauphine the red belches of flames were bursting out from the corner of the Tuileries facing the private gardens and the Rue de Rivoli: the rooms occupied by the King of Prussia and his suite on the visit to France the year of the Exhibition. There is a furious jet of flame pouring out of the window where Bismarck used to sit and smoke. Crash! Is it an explosion or a fall of flooring that causes this burst of black smoke and red sparks in our faces? God knows what fell devices may be within that burning pile; it were well surely to give it a wide berth.

And so eastward to the Place du Palais-Royal, which is still unsafe by reason of shot and shell from the neighbourhood of the Hôtel de Ville. And there is the great archway by which troops were wont to enter into the Place du Carrousel – is the fire there yet? Just there, and no more; could the archway be cut, the Louvre, with its artistic riches, might still be spared. But there are none to help. The troops are lounging supine in the rues; intent – and who shall blame weary, powder-grimed men? – on bread and wine. And so the devastator leaps from chimney to chimney, from window to window. He is over the archway now, and I would not give two hours' purchase for all the riches of the Louvre. In the name of modern vandalism, what means that burst of smoke and jet of fire? Alas for art; the Louvre is on fire independently. And so is the Palais-Royal and the Hôtel de Ville, where the rump of the Commune are cowering amidst their incendiarism; and the Ministry of Finance, and many another public and private building besides.

I turn from the spectacle sad and sick, to be sickened yet further by another spectacle. The Versaillist troops collected about the foot of the Rue Saint-Honoré were enjoying the fine game of Communist hunting. The Parisians of civil life are caitiffs to the last drop of their thin, sour, white blood. But yesterday they had cried *Vive la Commune!* and submitted to be governed by this said Commune. Today they rubbed their hands with livid currish joy to have it in their power to denounce a Communist and reveal his hiding place. Very eager at this work are the dear creatures of women. They know the rat-holes into which the poor devils have got, and they guide to them with a fiendish glee which is a phase of the many-sided sex. *Voila!* the braves of France returned to a triumph after a shameful captivity! They have found him, the miserable! Yes, they drag him out from one of the purlieus which Haussmann had not time to sweep away, and a guard of six of them hem him round as they march him into the Rue Saint-Honoré. A tall, pale, hatless man, with something not ignoble in his carriage. His lower lip is trembling, but his brow is firm, and the eye of him has some pride and defiance in it. They yell – the crowd – 'Shoot him; shoot him!' – the demon women most clamorous, of course. An arm goes into the air; there are on it the stripes of a non-commissioned officer, and there is a stick in the fist. The stick falls on the head of the pale man in black. Ha! the infection has caught; men club their rifles, and bring them down on that head, or clash them into splinters in their lust for murder. He is down; he is up again; he is down again; the thuds of the gunstocks on him sounding just as the sound when a man beats a cushion with a stick. A certain British impulse, stronger than consideration for self, prompts me to run forward.

But it is useless. They are firing into the flaccid carcass now, thronging about it like blowflies on a piece of meat. His brains spurt on my boot and plash into the gutter, whither the carrion is bodily chucked, presently to be trodden on and rolled on by the feet of multitudes and wheels of gun carriages.

Womanhood, then, is not quite dead in that band of bedlamites who had clamoured 'Shoot him.' Here is one in hysterics; another, with wan, scared face, draws out of the press an embryo bedlamite, her offspring, and, let us hope, goes home. But surely all manhood is dead in the soldiery of France to do a deed like this. An officer – one with a bull throat and the eyes of Algiers – stood by and looked on at the sport, sucking a cigar meanwhile.

The merry game goes on. Denouncing becomes fashionable, and denouncing is followed in the French natural sequence by braining. Faugh! let us get away from the truculent cowards and the bloody gutters, and the yelling women, and the Algerian-eyed officers. Here is the Place Vendôme, held, as I learn on credible authority, by twenty-five Communists and a woman, against all that Versailles found it in its heart to do, for hours. In the shattered Central Place Versaillist sentries are stalking about the ruins of the column. They have accumulated, too, some forces in the rat-trap. There is one corpse in the gutter buffeted and besmirched – the corpse, as I learn, of the Communist captain of a barricade who held it for half an hour single-handed against the braves of France, and then shot himself. The braves have, seemingly, made sure of him by shooting him and the clay, which was once a man, over and over again.

And how about the chained wildcats in the Hôtel de Ville? Their backs are to the wall, and they are fighting now, not for life, but that they may do as much evil as they can before their hour comes – as come it will before the minute hand of my watch makes many more revolutions. The Versaillists do not dare to rush at the barricades around the Hôtel de Ville; they are at once afraid of their skins and explosions. But they are mining, circumventing, burrowing, and they will be inside the cordon soon. Meanwhile the holders of the Hôtel de Ville are pouring out death and destruction over Paris in miscellaneous wildness. Now it is a shell in the Champs-Elysées; now one in the already shattered Boulevard Haussmann; now one somewhere about the Avenue Reine Hortense. It is between the devil and the deep sea with the people in the Hôtel de Ville. One enemy with weapons in his hand is outside; another, fire, and fire kindled by themselves, is inside. Will they roast, or seek death on a bayonet point?

It is hard to breathe in an atmosphere mainly of petroleum smoke. There is a sun, but his heat is dominated by the heat of the conflagrations. His rays are obscured by the lurid, blue-black smoke that is rising with a greasy fatness everywhere into the air. Let us out of it, for goodness' sake. I take horse, and ride off by the river bank toward the Point-du-Jour, leaving at my back the still loud rattle of the firing and the smoke belches. I ride on to the Point-du-Jour through Dombrowski's 'second line of defence' by the railway viaduct. Poor Dombrowski! a good servant to bad masters. I should like to know his fate for certain. Versaillists have told me that they saw him taken prisoner yesterday morning, dragged on to the Trocadéro, and there shot in cold blood in the face of day, looking dauntlessly into the muzzles of the chassepots. Others say he is wounded and a prisoner.

As I ride up the broad slope of the avenue between Viroflay and Versailles, I pass a very sorrowful and dejected company. In file after file of six each march the prisoners of the Commune – there are over two thousand of them together – patiently, and it seems to me with some consciousness of pride they march, linked closely arm in arm. Among them are many women, some of them the fierce barricade Hecates, others mere girls, soft and timid, who are here seemingly because a parent is here too. All are bareheaded and foul with dust, many powder-stained too, and the burning sun beats down on bald foreheads. Not the sun alone beats down, but the flats of sabres wielded by the dashing Chasseurs d'Afrique, who are the escort of these unfortunates. Their experiences might have taught them decency to the captives. No sabre blades had descended on their pates in that long, dreary march from Sedan to their German captivity; they were the prisoners of soldiers. But they are prisoners now no longer, as they caper on their wiry Arab stallions, and in their pride of cheap victory, they belabour unmercifully the miserables of the Commune. In front are three or four hundred prisoners, lashed together with ropes, and among these are not a few men in red breeches, deserters taken red-handed. I marvel that they are here at all, and not dead in the streets of Paris.

As I drive along the green margin of the placid Seine to Saint-Denis, the spectacle which the capital presents is one never to be forgotten. On its white houses the sun still smiles. But up through the sunbeams struggle and surge ghastly swart waves and folds and pillars of dense smoke; not one or two, but I reckon them on my fingers till I lose the count. Ha! there is a sharp crack, and then a dull thud on the air. No artillery that, surely some great explosion, which must have rocked Paris to its base. There rises a convolvulus-shaped volume of whiter smoke, with a jetlike spurt, such as men describe when Vesuvius bursts into eruption, and then it breaks into fleecy waves and eddies away to the horizon all round as the ripple of a stone thrown into a pool spreads to the margin of the water. The crowds of Germans who sit by the Seine, stolidly watching, are startled into a burst of excitement – the excitement might well be worldwide. 'Paris the beautiful' is Paris the ghastly, Paris the battered, Paris the burning, Paris the blood-spattered, now. And this is the nineteenth century, and Europe professes civilization, and France boasts of culture, and Frenchmen are braining one another with the butt ends of muskets, and Paris is burning. We want but a Nero to fiddle.

The Paris Commune: The Finale, 29 May 1871

Archibald Forbes

The Mur des Fédérés, against which the communards were shot, is still a place of pilgrimage for the French Left.

Travelling to England, and writing hard all the way in train and boat, I reached London on the early morning of Thursday, May 25th, and was back in Paris the following day. All was then virtually over. The hostages in La Roquette had been shot, and the Hôtel de Ville had fallen on the afternoon of the day I had left. When I returned the Communists were at their last gasp in the Château d'Eau, the Buttes de Chaumont, and Père-Lachaise. On the afternoon of the 28th, after just one week of fighting, Marshal MacMahon announced, 'I am absolute master of Paris.' On the following morning I visited Père-Lachaise, where the very last shots had been fired. Bivouac fires had been fed with the souvenirs of pious sorrow, and the trappings of woe had been torn down to be used as bedclothes. But there had been no great amount of fighting in the cemetery itself. An infallible token of close and heavy firing

are the dents of many bullets, and of those there were comparatively few in Père-Lachaise. Shells, however, had fallen freely, and
the results were occasionally very ghastly. But the ghastliest sight in
Père-Lachaise was in the south-eastern corner, where, close to the
boundary wall, there had been a natural hollow. The hollow was
now filled up by dead. One could measure the dead by the rood.
There they lay, tier above tier, each successive tier powdered over
with a coating of chloride of lime – two hundred of them patent to
the eye, besides those underneath hidden by the earth covering layer
after layer. Among the dead were many women. There, thrown up
in the sunlight, was a well-rounded arm with a ring on one of the
fingers; there, again, was a bust shapely in death. And yonder were
faces which to look upon made one shudder – faces distorted out of
humanity with ferocity and agony combined. The ghastly effect of
the dusty white powder on the dulled eyes, the gnashed teeth, and
the jagged beards cannot be described. How died these men and
women? Were they carted hither and laid out in this dead-hole of
Père-Lachaise? Not so: the hole had been replenished from close by.
Just yonder was where they were posted up against that section of
pock-pitted wall – there was no difficulty in reading the open book
– and were shot to death as they stood or crouched.

Stanley Finds Livingstone, 10 November 1871

H. M. Stanley

*David Livingstone, Scots missionary and explorer, headed an
expedition to central Africa in 1866, reaching Lake Tanganyika in
February 1869. Some of his followers deserted, and concocted the
story that he had been killed by the Ngoni. The New York Herald
sent a correspondent, Henry M. Stanley, to Africa to find him.*

A couple of hours brought us to the base of a hill, from the top of
which the Kirangozi said we could obtain a view of the great
Tanganyika Lake. Heedless of a rough path or of the toilsome
steep, spurred onward by the cheery promise, the ascent was
performed in a short time. I was pleased at the sight; and, as we
descended, it opened more and more into view until it was revealed
at last as a grand inland sea, bounded westward by an appalling

and black-blue range of mountains, and stretching north and south without bounds, a grey expanse of water.

From the western base of the hill was a three hours' march, though no march ever passed off so quickly. The hours seemed to have been quarters, we had seen so much that was novel and rare to us who had been travelling so long on the highlands. The mountains bounding the lake on the eastward receded and the lake advanced. We had crossed the Ruche, or Linche, and its thick belt of tall matted grass. We had plunged into a perfect forest of them and had entered into the cultivated fields which supply the port of Ujiji with vegetables, etc., and we stood at last on the summit of the last hill of the myriads we had crossed, and the port of Ujiji, embowered in palms, with the tiny waves of the silver waters of the Tanganyika rolling at its feet, was directly below us.

We are now about descending – in a few minutes we shall have reached the spot where we imagine the object of our search – our fate will soon be decided. No one in that town knows we are coming; least of all do they know we are so close to them. If any of them ever heard of the white man at Unyanyembe they must believe we are there yet . . .

Well, we are but a mile from Ujiji now, and it is high time we should let them know a caravan is coming; so 'Commence firing' is the word passed along the length of the column, and gladly do they begin. They have loaded their muskets half full, and they roar like the broadside of a line-of-battle ship. Down go the ramrods, sending huge charges home to the breech, and volley after volley is fired. The flags are fluttered; the banner of America is in front, waving joyfully; the guide is in the zenith of his glory. The former residents of Zanzita will know it directly and will wonder – as well they may – as to what it means. Never were the Stars and Stripes so beautiful to my mind – the breeze of the Tanganyika has such an effect on them. The guide blows his horn, and the shrill, wild clangour of it is far and near; and still the cannon muskets tell the noisy seconds. By this time the Arabs are fully alarmed; the natives of Ujiji, Waguha, Warundi, Wanguana, and I know not whom hurry up by the hundreds to ask what it all means – this fusillading, shouting, and blowing of horns and flag flying. There are Yambos shouted out to me by the dozen, and delighted Arabs have run up breathlessly to shake my hand and ask anxiously where I come from. But I have no patience with them. The expedition goes far too slow. I should like to settle the vexed question by one personal view. Where is he? Has he fled?

Suddenly a man – a black man – at my elbow shouts in English, 'How do you do, sir?'

'Hello, who the deuce are you?'

'I am the servant of Dr Livingstone,' he says; and before I can ask any more questions he is running like a madman towards the town.

We have at last entered the town. There are hundreds of people around me – I might say thousands without exaggeration, it seems to me. It is a grand triumphal procession. As we move, they move. All eyes are drawn towards us. The expedition at last comes to a halt; the journey is ended for a time; but I alone have a few more steps to make.

There is a group of the most respectable Arabs, and as I come nearer I see the white face of an old man among them. He has a cap with a gold band around it, his dress is a short jacket of red blanket cloth, and his pants – well, I didn't observe. I am shaking hands with him. We raise our hats, and I say:

'Dr Livingstone, I presume?'

And he says, 'Yes.'

The Turkish Atrocities in Bulgaria, 2 August 1876
The Daily News *Correspondent Reaches Batak*

J. A. MacGahan

The Bulgarian revolt of 1876 was savagely suppressed by Turkish troops, especially the ill-disciplined irregulars known as Bashi-Bazouks. The horror aroused by MacGahan's reports helped to bring about the autonomous state of Bulgaria in 1878 at the Congress of Berlin.

Down in the bottom of one of these hollows we could make out a village, which our guide informed us it would still take us an hour and a half to reach, although it really seemed to be very near. This was the village of Batak, which we were in search of. The hillsides were covered with little fields of wheat and rye, that were golden with ripeness. But although the harvest was ripe, and over ripe, although in many places the well-filled ears had broken down the fast-decaying straw that could no longer hold them aloft, and were now lying flat, there was no sign of reapers trying to save them. The fields were as deserted as the little valley, and the harvest was rotting in the soil. In an hour we had neared the village.

As we approached our attention was directed to some dogs on a slope overlooking the town. We turned aside from the road, and, passing over the debris of two or three walls, and through several gardens, urged our horses up the ascent towards the dogs. They barked at us in an angry manner, and then ran off into the adjoining fields. I observed nothing peculiar as we mounted, until my horse stumbled. When looking down I perceived he had stepped on a human skull partly hid among the grass. It was quite dry and hard, and might, to all appearances, have been there for two or three years, so well had the dogs done their work. A few steps further there was another, and beside it part of a skeleton, likewise white and dry. As we ascended, bones, skeletons, and skulls became more frequent, but here they had not been picked so clean, for there were fragments of half-dry, half-putrid flesh still clinging to them. At last we came to a kind of little plateau or shelf on the hillside, where the ground was nearly level, with the exception of a little indentation where the head of a hollow broke through. We rode towards this, with the intention of crossing it, but all suddenly drew rein with an exclamation of horror, for right before us, almost beneath our horses' feet, was a sight that made us shudder. It was a heap of skulls, intermingled with bones from all parts of the human body, skeletons, nearly entire, rotting clothing, human hair, and putrid flesh lying there in one foul heap, around which the grass was growing luxuriantly. It emitted a sickening odour, like that of a dead horse, and it was here the dogs had been seeking a hasty repast when our untimely approach interrupted them.

In the midst of this heap I could distinguish one slight skeleton form still enclosed in a chemise, the skull wrapped about with a coloured handkerchief, and the bony ankles encased in the embroidered footless stockings worn by the Bulgarian girls. We looked about us. The ground was strewed with bones in every direction, where the dogs had carried them off to gnaw them at their leisure. At the distance of a hundred yards beneath us lay the town. As seen from our standpoint, it reminded one somewhat of the ruins of Herculaneum or Pompeii.

There was not a roof left, not a whole wall standing; all was a mass of ruins, from which arose, as we listened, a low plaintive wail, like the 'keening' of the Irish over their dead, that filled the little valley and gave it voice . . .

On the other side of the way were the skeletons of two children lying side by side, partly covered with stones, and with frightful sabre cuts in their little skulls. The number of children killed in these massacres is something enormous. They were often spitted on bayonets, and we have several stories from eye witnesses who saw little babies carried about the streets, both here and at Otluk-kui, on the point of bayonets. The reason is simple. When a Mahometan has killed a certain number of infidels, he is sure of Paradise, no matter what his sins may be. Mahomet probably intended that only armed men should count, but the ordinary Mussulman takes the precept in broader acceptation, and counts women and children as well. Here in Batak the Bashi-Bazouks, in order to swell the count, ripped open pregnant women, and killed the unborn infants. As we approached the middle of the town, bones, skeletons, and skulls became more numerous. There was not a house beneath the ruins of which we did not perceive human remains, and the street besides was strewn with them. Before many of the doorways women were walking up and down wailing their funeral chant. One of them caught me by the arm and led me inside of the walls, and there in one corner, half covered with stones and mortar, were the remains of another young girl, with her long hair flowing wildly about among the stones and dust. And the mother fairly shrieked with agony, and beat her head madly against the wall. I could only turn round and walk out sick at heart, leaving her alone with her skeleton. A few steps further on sat a woman on a doorstep, rocking herself to and fro, and uttering moans heartrending beyond anything I could have imagined. Her head was buried in her hands, while her fingers were unconsciously twisting and tearing her hair as she gazed into her lap, where lay three little skulls with the hair still clinging to them. How did the mother come to be saved, while the children were slaughtered? Who knows? Perhaps she was away from the village when the massacre occurred. Perhaps she had escaped with a babe in her arms, leaving these to be saved by the father; or perhaps, most fearful, most pitiful of all, she had been so terror-stricken that she had abandoned the three poor little ones to their fate and saved her own life by flight. If this be so, no wonder she is tearing her hair in that terribly unconscious way as she gazes at the three little heads lying in her lap . . .

The church was not a very large one, and it was surrounded by a low stone wall, enclosing a small churchyard about fifty yards wide by seventy-five long. At first we perceive nothing in particular, and the stench is so great that we scarcely care to look about us, but we see that the place is heaped up with stones and rubbish to the height of five or six feet above the level of the street, and upon inspection we discover that what appeared to be a mass of stones and rubbish is in reality an immense heap of human bodies covered over with a thin layer of stones. The whole of the little churchyard is heaped up with them to the depth of three or four feet, and it is from here that the fearful odour comes. Some weeks after the massacre, orders were sent to bury the dead. But the stench at that time had become so deadly that it was impossible to execute the order, or even to remain in the neighbourhood of the village. The men sent to perform the work contented themselves with burying a few bodies, throwing a little earth over others as they lay, and here in the churchyard they had tried to cover this immense heap of festering humanity by throwing in stones and rubbish over the walls, without daring to enter. They had only partially succeeded. The dogs had been at work there since, and now could be seen projecting from this monster grave, heads, arms, legs, feet, and hands, in horrid confusion. We were told there were three thousand people lying here in this little churchyard alone, and we could well believe it. It was a fearful sight – a sight to haunt one through life. There were little curly heads there in that festering mass, crushed down by heavy stones; little feet not as long as your finger on which the flesh was dried hard, by the ardent heat before it had time to decompose; little baby hands stretched out as if for help; babes that had died wondering at the bright gleam of sabres and the red hands of the fierce-eyed men who wielded them; children who had died shrinking with fright and terror; young girls who had died weeping and sobbing and begging for mercy; mothers who died trying to shield their little ones with their own weak bodies, all lying there together, festering in one horrid mass. They were silent enough now. There are no tears nor cries, no weeping, no shrieks of terror, nor prayers for mercy. The harvests are rotting in the fields, and the reapers are rotting here in the churchyard.

An Immigrant Crosses America, 23 August 1879

Robert Louis Stevenson

Having travelled steerage to New York aboard the Devonia, *Stevenson crossed the continent to California on an immigrant train.*

It had thundered on the Friday night, but the sun rose on Saturday without a cloud. We were at sea – there is no other adequate expression – on the plains of Nebraska. I made my observatory on the top of a fruit wagon, and sat by the hour upon that perch to spy about me, and to spy in vain for something new. It was a world almost without a feature; an empty sky, an empty earth; front and back, the line of railway stretched from horizon to horizon, like a cue across a billiard-board; on either hand, a green plain ran till it touched the skirts of heaven. Along the track innumerable wild sunflowers, no bigger than a crownpiece, bloomed in a continuous flowerbed; grazing beasts were seen upon the prairie at all degrees of distance and diminution; and now and again we might perceive a few dots beside the railroad, which grew more and more distinct as we grew nearer, till they turned into wooden cabins, and then dwindled and dwindled in our wake until they melted into their surroundings, and we were once more alone upon the billiard-board. The train toiled over this infinity like a snail; and being the one thing moving, it was wonderful what huge proportions it began to assume in our regard. It seemed miles in length, and either end of it within but a step of the horizon. Even my own body or my own head seemed a great thing in that emptiness. I note the feeling the more readily as it is the contrary of what I have read of in the experience of others. Day and night, above the roar of the train, our ears were kept busy with the incessant chirp of grasshoppers; a noise like the winding up of countless clocks and watches, which began after a while to seem proper to that land.

Paul Gauguin Marries: Tahiti, 1892

Paul Gauguin

Journey round the island – Leaving the coast road I plunge into a thicket that leads far into the mountains. Arrive at a small valley. Several people live there and want to go on living in the old way –

I move on. Arrived in Taravao (far end of the island) the gendarme lends me his horse, I ride along the east coast, not much frequented by Europeans. Arrived at Faone, the small district that comes before that of Itia, a native hails me. 'Hey! man who makes men,' (he knows that I am a painter), 'come and eat with us (*Haere mai ta maba*)' – the phrase of welcome. I do not need to be asked twice, his face is so gentle. I dismount from the horse, he takes it and ties it to a branch, without any servility, simply and efficiently. I go into a house where several men, women and children are gathered, sitting on the ground chatting and smoking – 'Where are you going?' says a fine Maori woman of about forty. 'I'm going to Itia.' 'What for?' An idea passed through my brain. I answered, 'To look for a wife. Itia has plenty, and pretty ones.' 'Do you want one?' 'Yes.' 'If you like I'll give you one. She's my daughter.'

'Is she young?' 'Ae.' –

'Is she pretty?' 'Ae.' –

'Is she in good health?' 'Ae.' –

'Good, go and fetch her for me.'

She went away for a quarter of an hour; and as they brought the Maori meal of wild bananas and some crayfish, the old woman returned, followed by a tall young girl carrying a small parcel. Through her excessively transparent dress of pink muslin the golden skin of her shoulders and arms could be seen. Two nipples thrust out firmly from her chest. Her charming face appeared to me different from the others I had seen on the island up to the present, and her bushy hair was slightly crinkled. In the sunshine an orgy of chrome yellows. I found out that she was of Tonga origin.

When she had sat down beside me I asked her some questions: 'You aren't afraid of me?' '*Aita* (no).'

'Would you like to live always in my hut?' '*Eha*.'

'You've never been ill?' '*Aita*.'

That was all. And my heart throbbed as, impassively, she laid out on the ground before me, on a large banana-leaf, the food that was offered me. Though hungry, I ate timidly. That girl – a child of about thirteen – enchanted me and scared me: what was going on in her soul? and at this contract so hastily thought of and signed I felt a shy hesitation about the signing – I, nearly an old man. Perhaps the mother had ordered it, with her mind on money. And yet in that tall child the independent pride of all that race . . . the serenity of a thing deserving praise. The mocking, though tender, lip showed clearly that the danger was for me, not for her. I left the hut, I will not say without fear, took my horse and mounted. The girl followed behind; the mother, a man and two young women – her aunts, she said – followed also. We took the road back to Taravao, nine kilometres from Faone – After a kilometre I was told: '*Parahi teie* (Stop here).' I dismounted and entered a large hut, well kept and smelling almost of opulence. The opulence of the wealth of the earth. Pretty mats on the ground, on top of straw . . . A family, quite young and as gracious as could be, lived there, and the girl sat down next to her mother, whom she introduced to me. A silence. Cool water, which we drank in turn like a libation. And the young mother said to me, with tears in her eyes, 'Are you kind?' . . .

When I had examined my conscience I answered uneasily, 'Yes.'

'Will you make my daughter happy?' 'Yes.'

'In eight days let her come back. If she is not happy she will leave you.'

A long silence – We emerged and again I moved off on horseback. They followed behind. On the road we met several people. 'Well, well, you're the *vahine* of a Frenchman now, are you? Be happy. Good luck.'

That matter of two mothers worried me. I asked the old woman who had offered me her daughter, 'Why did you tell me a lie?' Tehaurana's mother (that was my wife's name) answered, 'The other is also her mother, her nursing mother.'

We reached Taravao. I gave the gendarme back his horse.

His wife (a Frenchwoman) said to me (not indeed maliciously, but tactlessly), 'What! have you brought back a trollop with you?' And her eyes undressed the impassive girl, now grown haughty: decrepitude was staring at the new flowering, the virtue of the law was breathing impurely upon the native but pure unashamedness of trust, faith. And against that so blue sky I saw with grief this dirty cloud of smoke. I felt ashamed of my race, and my eyes turned away from that mud – quickly I forgot it – to gaze upon this gold which already I loved – I remember that. The family farewells took place at Taravao, at the house of the Chinese who there deals in everything – men and beasts. My fiancée and I took the public carriage, which brought us to Mataiea, twenty-five kilometres from there – my home.

The Graeco-Turkish War: The Siege of Prevesa, 18 April 1897

Richard Harding Davis

The Graeco-Turkish war, which followed a Greek attempt to annexe Crete, ended with the defeat of the Greeks in May 1897. Prevesa, in western Greece, had been taken by the Turks in 1798, and was not recaptured by the Greeks until 1913.

The siege of Prevesa began on the 18th of April, and the Greek officers on the warships continued the siege until the armistice.

It was hard to believe that war existed in that part of Greece; it was difficult to see how, with such a background, men could act a part so tragic; for the scene was set for a pastoral play – perhaps for a comic opera. If Ireland is like an emerald, this part of Greece is like an opal; for its colours are as fierce and brilliant as are those of the opal, and are hidden, as they are, with misty white clouds that soften and beautify them. Against the glaring blue sky are the snow-topped mountains, and below the snow line green pasture-lands glowing with great blocks of purple furze and yellow buttercups and waving wheat, that changes when the wind blows, and is swayed about like waves of smoke. In the high grass are the light-blue flowers of the flax, on tall, bending stalks, and white flowers with hearts of yellow, and miles of scarlet poppies, and above them tall, dark poplars and the greyish-green olive trees. The wind from the Adriatic and the Gulf of Arta sweeps over this burning landscape in great, generous waves, cooling the hot air and stirring the green leaves and the high grass and the bending flowers with the strong, fresh breath of the sea.

White clouds throw shadows over the whole as they sweep past or rest on the hills of grey stones, where the yellow sheep look, from the path below, like fat grains of corn spilled on a green billiard cloth. You may ride for miles through this fair country and see no moving thing but the herds of silken-haired goats and yellow sheep, and the shepherds leaning on their long rifles, and looking, in their tights and sleeveless cloaks and embroidered jackets, like young princes of the soil.

It is hard to imagine men fighting fiercely and with bloodshot eyes in such a place; and, as a matter of fact, no men were fighting there, except in a measured, leisurely, and well-bred way. Over in Thessaly, for all we know here, there was war, and all that war entails; but by the Arta the world went on much as it had before – the sheep-bells tinkled from every hillside, the soldiers picnicked under the shade of the trees, and the bombardment of Prevesa continued, with interruptions of a day at a time, and the answering guns of the Turks returned the compliment in an apologetic and desultory fashion. Sometimes it almost seemed – so bad was the aim of the Turkish soldiers – that they were uncertain as to whether or not they had loaded their pieces, and were pulling the lanyards in order to find out, being too lazy to open the breech and look.

A Seaside Holiday, Norfolk Coast, August 1897

W. H. Hudson

The little town was overcrowded with late summer visitors, all eager for the sea yet compelled to waste so much precious time shut up in apartments, and at every appearance of a slight improvement in the weather they would pour out of the houses and the green slope would be covered with a crowd of many hundreds, all hurrying down to the beach. The crowd was composed mostly of women – about three to every man, I should say – and their children; and it was one of the most interesting crowds I had ever come across on account of the large number of persons in it of a peculiarly fine type, which chance had brought together at that spot. It was the large English blonde, and there were so many individuals of this type that they gave a character to the crowd, so that those of a different physique and colour appeared to be fewer than they were and were almost overlooked. They came from various places about the country, in the north and the Midlands, and appeared to be of the well-to-do classes; they, or many of them, were with their families but without their lords. They were mostly tall and large in every way, very white-skinned, with light or golden hair and large light-blue eyes. A common character of these women was their quiet reposeful manner; they walked and talked and rose up and sat down and did everything, in fact, with an air of deliberation; they gazed in a slow steady way at you, and were dignified, some even majestic, and were like a herd of large beautiful white cows. The children too, especially the girls, some almost as tall as their large mothers, though still in short frocks, were very fine. The one pastime of these was paddling, and it was a delight to see their bare feet and legs. The legs of those who had been longest on the spot – probably several weeks in some instances – were of a deep nutty-brown hue suffused with pink; after these a gradation of colour, light brown tinged with buff, pinkish buff and cream, like the Gloire de Dijon rose; and so on to the delicate tender pink of the clover blossom; and, finally, the purest ivory white of the latest arrivals whose skins had not yet been caressed and coloured by sun and wind.

The Attack on the Atbara, 10 April 1898

George W. Steevens

Kitchener had been appointed Sirdar (Commander-in-Chief) of the army in Egypt in 1892. His advance to the Atbara river was part of his campaign against the separatist Sudanese forces of al-Mahdi.

As the first rays of sunrise glinted on the desert pebbles, the army rose up and saw that it was in front of the enemy. All night it had moved blindly, in faith. At six in the evening the four brigades were black squares on the rising desert outside the bushes of Umdabea Camp, and they set out to march. Hard gravel underfoot, full moon overhead, about them a coy horizon that seemed immeasurable, yet revealed nothing. The squares tramped steadily for an hour. Then all lay down, so that the other brigades were swallowed up into the desert, and the faces of the British square were no more than shadows in the white moonbeams. The square was unlocked, and first the horses were taken down to water, then the men by half-battalions. We who had water ate some biscuits, put our heads on saddle-bags, rolled our bodies in blankets, and slept a little.

The next thing was a long rustle overhead; stealing in upon us, urgently whispering us to rise and mount and move. The moon had passed overhead. It was one o'clock. The square rustled into life and motion, bent forward, and started, half asleep. No man spoke, and no light showed, but the sand-muffled trampling and the moon-veiled figures forbade the fancy that it was all a dream. The shape of lines of men – now close, now broken, and closing up again as the ground broke or the direction changed – the mounted officers, and the hushed order, 'Left shoulder forward', the scrambling Maxim mules, the lines of swaying camels, their pungent smell, and the rare neigh of a horse, the other three squares like it, which we knew of but could not see – it was just the same war machine as we had seen all these days on parade. Only this time it was in deadly earnest, moving stealthily but massively forward towards an event that none of us could quite certainly foretell.

We marched till something after four, then halted, and the men lay down again and slept. The rest walked up and down, talking to one and another, wondering in half-voices *were they there*, would they give us a fight or should we find their lines empty, how would the fight be fought, and, above all, how were we to get over their zariba. For Mahmud's zariba was pictured very high, and very thick and very prickly, which sounded awkward for the Cameron Highlanders, who were to assault it. Somebody had proposed burning it, either with war-rockets or paraffin and safety matches; somebody else suggested throwing blankets over it, though how you throw blankets over a ten by twenty feet hedge of camel-thorn, and what you do next when you have thrown them the inventor of the plan never explained; others favoured scaling ladders, apparently to take headers off on to the thorns and the enemy's spears, and even went so far as to make a few; most were for the simpler plan of just taking hold of it and pulling it apart. But how many of the men who pulled would ever get through the gap?

We could see their position quite well by now – the usual river fringe of grey-green palms meeting the usual desert fringe of yellow-grey mimosa. And the smoke-grey line in front of it all must be their famous zariba. Before its right centre fluttered half-a-dozen flags, white and pale blue, yellow and pale chocolate. The line went on till it was not half a mile from the flags. Then it halted.

Thud! went the first gun, and phutt! came faintly back, as its shell burst on the zariba into a wreathed round cloud of just the zariba's smoky grey. I looked at my watch, and it marked 6.20. The battle that had now menaced, now evaded us for a month – the battle had begun.

The bugle sang out the advance. The pipes screamed war, and the line started forward, like a ruler drawn over the tussock-broken sand. Up a low ridge they moved forward: when would the dervishes fire? The Camerons were to open from the top of the ridge, only 300 yards short of the zariba; up and up, forward and forward: when would they fire? Now the line crested the ridge; the men knelt down. 'Volley-firing by sections' – and crash it came. It came from both sides, too, almost the same instant. Wht–t, wht–t, wht–t piped the bullets overhead: the line knelt very firm, and aimed very steady, and crash, crash, crash, they answered it.

Oh! A cry more of dismayed astonishment than of pain, and a man was upon his feet and over on his back and the bearers were dashing in from the rear. He was dead before they touched him, but already they found another for the stretcher. Then bugle again, and up and on: the bullets were swishing and lashing now like rain on the river. But the line of khaki and purple tartan never bent nor swayed; it just went slowly forward like a ruler. The officers at its head strode self-containedly; they might have been on the hill after grouse; only from their locked faces turned unswervingly towards the bullets could you see that they knew and had despised the danger. And the unkempt, unshaven Tammies, who in camp seemed little enough like covenanters or Ironsides, were now quite transformed. It was not so difficult to go on – the pipes picked you up and carried you on – but it was difficult not to hurry: yet whether they aimed or advanced they did it orderly, gravely, without speaking. The bullets had whispered to raw youngsters in one breath the secret of all the glories of the British Army.

Forward and forward, more swishing about them and more crashing from them. Now they were moving, always without hurry, down a gravelly incline. Three men went down without a cry at the very foot of the Union Jack, and only one got to his feet again; the flag shook itself and still blazed splendidly. Next, a supremely furious gust of bullets, and suddenly the line stood fast. Before it was a loose low hedge of dry camel-thorn – the zariba, the redoubt-able zariba. That it? A second they stood in wonder, and then, 'Pull it away,' suggested somebody. Just half-a-dozen tugs; and the impos-sible zariba was a gap and a scattered heap of brushwood. Beyond is a low stockade and trenches, but what of that? Over and in! Hurrah, hurrah, hurrah!

Now fall in, and back to the desert outside. And unless you are congenitally amorous of horrors don't look too much about you. Black spindle-legs curled up to meet red-gimbleted black faces, donkeys headless and legless or sieves of shrapnel, camels with necks writhed back on to their humps, rotting already in pools of blood and bile-yellow water, heads without faces and faces without any-thing below, cobwebbed arms and legs, and black skins grilled to crackling on smouldering palm-leaf – don't look at it. Here is the Sirdar's white star and crescent on red; here is the Sirdar, who created this battle, this clean-jointed, well-oiled, smooth-running clockwork-perfect masterpiece of a battle. Not a flaw, not a check, not a jolt; and not a fleck on its shining success. Once more, hurrah, hurrah, hurrah.

The Battle of Omdurman 2 September 1898

Winston Churchill

At Omdurman Kitchener crushed the Sudanese separatist move-ment, using machine-guns, artillery and naval guns against the simply armed Mahdist forces. About 20,000 were killed and wounded; British casualties were 500.

I took six men and a corporal. We trotted fast over the plain and soon began to breast the unknown slopes of the ridge. There is nothing like the dawn. The quarter of an hour before the curtain is lifted upon an unknowable situation is an intense experience of war. Was the ridge held by the enemy or not? Were we riding through the gloom into thousands of ferocious savages? Every step might be deadly; yet there was no time for over-much precaution. The regiment was coming on behind us, and dawn was breaking. It was already half light as we climbed the slope. What should we find at the summit? For cool, tense excitement I commend such moments.

Now we are near the top of the ridge. I make one man follow a hundred yards behind, so that whatever happens, he may tell the tale. There is no sound but our own clatter. We have reached the crest line. We rein in our horses. Every minute the horizon extends; we can already see 200 yards. Now we can see perhaps a quarter of a mile. All is quiet; no life but our own breathes among the rocks and sand hummocks of the ridge. No ambuscade, no occupation in force! The farther plain is bare below us: we can now see more than half a mile.

So they have all decamped! Just what we said! All bolted off to Kordofan; no battle! But wait! The dawn is growing fast. Veil after veil is lifted from the landscape. What is this shimmering in the distant plain? Nay — it is lighter now — what are these dark markings beneath the shimmer? *They are there!* These enormous black smears are thousands of men; the shimmering is the glinting of their weapons. It is now daylight. I slip off my horse; I write in my field service notebook, 'The Dervish army is still in position a mile and a half south-west of Jebel Surgham.' I send this message by the corporal direct as ordered to the Commander-in-Chief. I mark it XXX. In the words of the drill book 'with all despatch', or as one would say, 'Hell for leather.'

A glorious sunrise is taking place behind us; but we are admiring something else. It is already light enough to use field-glasses. The dark masses are changing their values. They are already becoming lighter than the plain; they are fawn-coloured. Now they are a kind of white, while the plain is dun. In front of us is a vast array four or five miles long. It fills the horizon till it is blocked out on our right by the serrated silhouette of Surgham Peak. This is an hour to live. We mount again, and suddenly new impressions strike the eye and mind. These masses are not stationary. They are advancing, and they are advancing fast. A tide is coming in. But what is this sound which we hear: a deadened roar coming up to us in waves? They are cheering for God, his Prophet and his holy Khalifa. They think they are going to win. We shall see about that presently. Still I must admit that we check our horses and hang upon the crest of the ridge for a few moments before advancing down its slopes.

But now it is broad morning and the slanting sun adds brilliant colour to the scene. The masses have defined themselves into swarms of men, in ordered ranks bright with glittering weapons, and above them dance a multitude of gorgeous flags. We see for ourselves what the Crusaders saw . . . From where we sat on our horses we could see both sides. There was our army ranked and massed by the river. There were the gunboats lying expectant in the stream. There were all the batteries ready to open. And meanwhile on the other side, this large oblong gay-coloured crowd in fairly good order climbed swiftly up to the crest of exposure. We were about 2,500 yards from our own batteries, but little more than 200 from their approaching target. I called these Dervishes 'The White Flags'. They reminded me of the armies in the Bayeux tapestries, because of their rows of white and yellow standards held upright. Meanwhile the Dervish centre far out in the plain had come within range, and one after another the British and Egyptian batteries opened upon it. My eyes were riveted by a nearer scene. At the top of the hill 'The White Flags' paused to rearrange their ranks and drew out a broad and solid parade along the crest. Then the cannonade turned upon them. Two or three batteries and all the gunboats, at least thirty guns, opened an intense fire. Their shells shrieked towards us and burst in scores over the heads and among the masses of the White Flagmen. We were so close, as we sat spellbound on our horses, that we almost shared their perils. I saw the full blast of Death strike this human wall. Down went their standards by dozens and their men by hundreds. Wide gaps and shapeless heaps appeared in their array. One saw them jumping and tumbling under the shrapnel bursts; but none turned back. Line after line they all streamed over the shoulder and advanced towards our zeriba, opening a heavy rifle fire which wreathed them in smoke.

Hitherto no one had taken any notice of us; but I now saw Baggara horsemen in twos and threes riding across the plain on our left towards the ridge. One of these patrols of three men came within pistol range. They were dark, cowled figures, like monks on horseback – ugly, sinister brutes with long spears. I fired a few shots at them from the saddle, and they sheered off. I did not see why we should not stop out on this ridge during the assault. I thought we could edge back towards the Nile and so watch both sides while keeping out of harm's way. But now arrived a positive order from Major Finn saying 'Come back at once into the zeriba as the infantry are about to open fire.' We should in fact have been safer on the ridge, for we only just got into the infantry lines before the rifle-storm began . . .

As soon as the fire began to slacken and it was said on all sides that the attack had been repulsed, a General arrived with his staff at a gallop with instant orders to mount and advance. In two minutes the four squadrons were mounted and trotting out of the zeriba in a southerly direction. We ascended again the slopes of Jebel Surgham which had played its part in the first stages of the action, and from its ridges soon saw before us the whole plain of Omdurman with the vast mud city, its minarets and domes, spread before us six or seven miles away. After various halts and reconnoitrings we found ourselves walking forward in what is called 'column of troops'. There are four troops in a squadron and four squadrons in a regiment. Each of these troops now followed the other. I commanded the second troop from the rear, comprising between twenty and twenty-five Lancers.

Everyone expected that we were going to make a charge. That was the one idea that had been in all minds since we had started from Cairo. Of course there would be a charge. In those days, before the Boer War, British cavalry had been taught little else. Here was clearly the occasion for a charge. But against what body of enemy, over what ground, in which direction or with what purpose, were matters hidden from the rank and file. We continued to pace forward over the hard sand, peering into the mirage-twisted plain in a high state of suppressed excitement. Presently I noticed, 300 yards away on our flank and parallel to the line on which we were advancing, a long row of blue-black objects, two or three yards apart. I thought there were about a hundred and fifty. Then I became sure that these were men – enemy men – squatting on the ground. Almost at the same moment the trumpet sounded 'Trot', and the whole long column of cavalry began to jingle and clatter across the front of these crouching figures. We were in the lull of the battle and there was perfect silence. Forthwith from every blue-black blob came a white puff of smoke, and a loud volley of musketry broke the odd stillness. Such a target at such a distance could scarcely be missed, and all along the column here and there horses bounded and a few men fell.

The intentions of our Colonel had no doubt been to move round the flank of the body of Dervishes he had now located, and who, concealed in a fold of the ground behind their riflemen, were invisible to us, and then to attack them from a more advantageous quarter; but once the fire was opened and losses began to grow, he must have judged it inexpedient to prolong his procession across the open plain. The trumpet sounded 'Right wheel into line', and all the sixteen troops swung round towards the blue-black riflemen. Almost immediately the regiment broke into a gallop, and the 21st Lancers were committed to their first charge in war!

I propose to describe exactly what happened to me: what I saw and what I felt. The troop I commanded was, when we wheeled into line, the second from the right of the regiment. I was riding a handy, sure-footed, grey Arab polo pony. Before we wheeled and began to gallop, the officers had been marching with drawn swords. On account of my shoulder I had always decided that if I were involved in hand-to-hand fighting, I must use a pistol and not a sword. I had purchased in London a Mauser automatic pistol, then the newest and latest design. I had practised carefully with this during our march and journey up the river. This then was the weapon with which I determined to fight. I had first of all to return my sword into its scabbard, which is not the easiest thing to do at a gallop. I had then to draw my pistol from its wooden holster and bring it to full cock. This dual operation took an appreciable time, and until it was finished, apart from a few glances to my left to see what effect the fire was producing, I did not look up at the general scene.

Then I saw immediately before me, and now only half the length of a polo ground away, the row of crouching blue figures firing frantically, wreathed in white smoke. On my right and left my neighbouring troop leaders made a good line. Immediately behind was a long dancing row of lances couched for the charge. We were going at a fast but steady gallop. There was too much trampling and rifle fire to hear any bullets. After this glance to the right and left and at my troop, I looked again towards the enemy. The scene appeared to be suddenly transformed. The blue-black men were still firing, but behind them there now came into view a depression like a shallow sunken road. This was crowded and crammed with men rising up from the ground where they had hidden. Bright flags appeared as if by magic, and I saw arriving from nowhere Emirs on horseback among and around the mass of the enemy. The Dervishes appeared to be ten or twelve deep at the thickest, a great grey mass gleaming with steel, filling the dry watercourse. In the same twinkling of an eye I saw also that our right overlapped their left, that my troop would just strike the edge of their array, and that the troop on my right would charge into air. My subaltern comrade on the right, Wormald of the 7th Hussars, could see the situation too; and we both increased our speed to the very fastest gallop and curved inwards like the horns of the moon. One really had not time to be frightened or to think of anything else but these particular necessary actions which I have described. They completely occupied mind and senses.

The collision was now very near. I saw immediately before me, not ten yards away, the two blue men who lay in my path. They were perhaps a couple of yards apart. I rode at the interval between them. They both fired. I passed through the smoke conscious that I was unhurt. The trooper immediately behind me was killed at this place and at this moment, whether by these shots or not I do not know. I checked my pony as the ground began to fall away beneath his feet. The clever animal dropped like a cat four or five feet down on the sandy bed of the watercourse, and in this sandy bed I found myself surrounded by what seemed to be dozens of men. They were not thickly packed enough at this point for me to experience any actual collision with them. Whereas Grenfell's troop next but one on my left was brought to a complete standstill and suffered very heavy losses, we seemed to push our way through as one has sometimes seen mounted policemen break up a crowd. In less time than it takes to relate, my pony had scrambled up the other side of the ditch. I looked round.

Once again I was on the hard, crisp desert, my horse at a trot. I had the impression of scattered Dervishes running to and fro in all directions. Straight before me a man threw himself on the ground. The reader must remember that I had been trained as a cavalry soldier to believe that if ever cavalry broke into a mass of infantry, the latter would be at their mercy. My first idea therefore was that the man was terrified. But simultaneously I saw the gleam of his curved sword as he drew it back for a ham-stringing cut. I had room and time enough to turn my pony out of his reach, and leaning over on the off side I fired two shots into him at about three yards. As I straightened myself in the saddle, I saw before me another figure with uplifted sword. I raised my pistol and fired. So close were we that the pistol itself actually struck him. Man and sword disappeared below and behind me. On my left, ten yards away, was an Arab horseman in a bright-coloured tunic and steel helmet, with chain-mail hangings. I fired at him. He turned aside. I pulled my horse into a walk and looked around again . . . There was a mass of Dervishes about forty or fifty yards away on my left. They were huddling and clumping themselves together, rallying for mutual protection. They seemed wild with excitement, dancing about on their feet, shaking their spears up and down. The whole scene seemed to flicker. I have an impression, but it is too fleeting to define, of brown-clad Lancers mixed up here and there with this surging mob. The scattered individuals in my immediate neighbour-hood made no attempt to molest me. Where was my troop? Where were the other troops of the squadron? Within a hundred yards of me I could not see a single officer or man. I looked back at the Dervish mass. I saw two or three riflemen crouching and aiming their rifles at me from the fringe of it. Then for the first time that morning I experienced a sudden sensation of fear. I felt myself absolutely alone. I thought these riflemen would hit me and the rest devour me like wolves. What a fool I was to loiter like this in the midst of the enemy! I crouched over the saddle, spurred my horse into a gallop and drew clear of the *mêlée*. Two or three hundred yards away I found my troop all ready faced about and partly formed up.

The Spanish-American War: The Battle of El Caney, Cuba, 1 July 1898

James Creelman

The Spanish-American War ended Spanish colonial rule in the Americas. While US troops, including Theodore Roosevelt and his 'Rough Riders', took the fortified village of El Caney, the Spanish Caribbean fleet was completely destroyed by the US Navy outside Santiago harbour.

From the torn hammock on which I lay among my comrades, under a strip of rain-soaked canvas, the tall figure of General Lawton could be seen moving in the grey dawning light, toward the mud-clogged road along which the American forces had been marching all night, in the direction of Santiago de Cuba, where the Spaniards stood in the trenches and fortifications awaiting the attack. The battle which ended the rule of Spain in the western world, after four centuries of glory and shame, was about to begin.

A sturdy little New York war artist, clad in a red blanket – the only dry thing in our camp – made his way through the bushes to a neighbouring stream and returned with our canteens filled.

'No time to lose,' he said. 'Lawton will open on El Caney at sunrise. His battery is in position now. Better not wait for breakfast. We have no fire, anyhow. Turn out, fellows – you've been asleep three hours.' And the damp and sleepy correspondents arose to face another day's work.

Presently we were trudging along in the mire, tortured by the sour smells of the trampled vegetation, which yesterday's fierce sun had fermented, and the tropical fever, from which few escaped.

Monstrous land-crabs, green and scarlet, with leprous blotches of white, writhed across our path. Birds sang softly in the tangled chaparral and tall grass. Crimson and yellow blossoms glowed in the dense green growths. Troops of vultures wheeled lazily against the dawn-tinged clouds, or sat in the tall coconut palms. As the sun rose, it struck sparkles from the dripping foliage. But hunger and fever and news-eager journalism had no eye for these things. Before us were thousands of men preparing to die; nine miles behind us were steam vessels ready to carry our despatches to the cable station in Jamaica; and in New York were great multitudes, waiting to know the result of the battle.

The Battle of El Caney: The Aftermath, 2 July 1898

Stephen Crane

Pushing through the throng in the plaza, we came in sight of the door of the church, and here was a strange scene. The church had been turned into a hospital for Spanish wounded who had fallen into American hands. The interior of the church was too cave-like in its gloom for the eyes of the operating surgeons, so they had had the altar-table carried to the doorway, where there was a bright light. Framed then in the black archway was the altar-table with the figure of a man upon it. He was naked save for a breech-clout, and so close, so clear was the ecclesiastic suggestion that one's mind leaped to a fantasy that this thin, pale figure had just been torn down from a cross. The flash of the impression was like light, and for this instant it illumined all the dark recesses of one's remotest idea of sacrilege, ghastly and wanton. I bring this to you merely as an effect, an effect of mental light and shade, if you like; something done in thought similar to that which the French impressionists do in colour; something meaningless and at the same time overwhelming, crushing, monstrous. 'Poor devil; I wonder if he'll pull through,' said Leighton. An American surgeon and his assistants were intent over the prone figure. They wore white aprons. Something small and silvery flashed in the surgeon's hand. An assistant held the merciful sponge close to the man's nostril, but he was writhing and moaning in some horrible dream of his artificial sleep. As the surgeon's instrument played, I fancied that the man dreamed that he was being gored by a bull. In his pleading, delirious babble occurred constantly the name of the Virgin, the Holy Mother. 'Good morning,' said the surgeon. He changed his knife to his left hand and gave me a wet palm. The tips of his fingers were wrinkled, shrunken, like those of a boy who has been in swimming too long.

Jumping a Train, 20 March 1899

W. H. Davies

The snow was still deep and the mornings and evenings cold when, a week after this, we reached Ottawa. This slow travelling was not at all to my liking, and I often persuaded my companion to make more haste towards Winnipeg. This he agreed to do; so the next morning we jumped a freight train, determined to hold it for the whole day. Unfortunately it was simply a local train, and being very slow, having to stop on the way at every insignificant little station, we left it, at a town called Renfrew, intending that night to beat a fast overland passenger train, which would convey us four or five hundred miles before daybreak. With this object we sat in the station's waiting room until evening, and then, some twenty minutes before the train became due, we slipped out unobserved and took possession of an empty car, stationary some distance away, from which place we would see the train coming, and yet be unseen from the station's platform. This train would soon arrive, for passengers were already pacing the platform, the luggage was placed in readiness, and a number of curious people, having nothing else to do, had assembled here to see the coming and going of the train. At last we heard its whistle, and, looking out, we saw the headlight in the distance, drawing nearer and nearer. It steamed into the station without making much noise, for the rails were slippery, there still being much ice and snow on the track. 'Come,' I said to Jack, 'there is no time to lose'; and we quickly jumped out of the empty car.

This fast passenger train carried a blind baggage car, which means that the end nearest to the engine was blind in having no door. Our object was to suddenly appear from a hiding place, darkness being favourable, and leap on the step of this car, and from that place to the platform; this being done when the train was in motion, knowing that the conductor, who was always on the watch for such doings, rarely stopped the train to put men off, even when sure of their presence. If he saw us before the train started, he would certainly take means to prevent us from riding. When we had once taken possession of this car, no man could approach us until we reached the next stopping place, which would probably be fifty miles, or much more. At that place we would dismount, conceal ourselves, and, when it was again in motion, make another leap for our former place. Of course, the engineer and firemen could reach us, but these men were always indifferent, and never interfered, their business being ahead instead of behind the engine.

The train whistled almost before we were ready, and pulled slowly out of the station. I allowed my companion the advantage of being the first to jump, owing to his maimed hand. The train was now going faster and faster, and we were forced to keep pace with it. Making a leap he caught the handle bar and sprang lightly on the step, after which my hand quickly took possession of this bar, and I ran with the train, prepared to follow his example. To my surprise, instead of at once taking his place on the platform, my companion stood thoughtlessly irresolute on the step, leaving me no room to make the attempt. But I still held to the bar, though the train was now going so fast that I found great difficulty in keeping step with it. I shouted to him to clear the step. This he proceeded to do, very deliberately, I thought. Taking a firmer grip on the bar, I jumped, but it was too late, for the train was now going at a rapid rate. My foot came short of the step, and I fell, and, still clinging to the handle bar, was dragged several yards before I relinquished my hold. And there I lay for several minutes, feeling a little shaken, whilst the train passed swiftly on into the darkness.

Even then I did not know what had happened, for I attempted to stand, but found that something had happened to prevent me from doing this. Sitting down in an upright position, I then began to examine myself, and now found that the right foot was severed from the ankle. This discovery did not shock me so much as the thoughts which quickly followed. For, as I could feel no pain, I did not know but what my body was in several parts, and I was not satisfied until I had examined every portion of it. Seeing a man crossing the track, I shouted to him for assistance. He looked in one direction and another, not seeing me in the darkness, and was going his way when I shouted again. This time he looked full my way, but instead of coming nearer, he made one bound in the air, nearly fell, scrambled to his feet, and was off like the shot from a gun. This man was sought after for several weeks, by people curious to know who he was, but was never found, and no man came forward to say – 'I am he.' Having failed to find this man, people at last began to think I was under a ghostly impression. Probably that was the other man's impression, for who ever saw Pity make the same speed as Fear?

Another man, after this, approached, who was a workman on the line, and at the sound of my voice he seemed to understand at once what had occurred. Coming forward quickly, he looked me over, went away, and in a minute or two returned with the assistance of several others to convey me to the station. A number of people were still there; so that when I was placed in the waiting room to bide the arrival of a doctor, I could see no other way of keeping a calm face before such a number of eyes than by taking out my pipe and smoking, an action which, I am told, caused much sensation in the local press.

The Boer War: The Suffering of the Civilian Population, Mafeking, April–May 1900

J. E. Neilly

The garrison at Mafeking, besieged by Boers from 12 October 1899 to 17 May 1900, was commanded by Colonel Robert (later Lord) Baden-Powell.

It was not pleasant to mix among the people of the kraals. Hunger had them in its grip, and many of them were black spectres and living skeletons. I saw them crawling along on legs like the stems of well-blackened 'cutties', with their ribs literally breaking through their shrivelled skin – men, women, and children. I saw them, too, fall down on the veldt and lie where they had fallen, too weak to go on their way. The sufferers were mostly little boys – mere infants ranging in age from four or five upwards. When the famine struck the place they were thrown out of the huts by their parents to live or die, sink or swim . . .

When the Colonel got to know of the state of affairs he instituted soup kitchens, where horses were boiled in huge cauldrons, and the savoury mess doled out in pints and quarts to all comers. Some of the people – those employed on works – paid for the food; the remainder, who were in the majority, obtained it free. One of those kitchens was established in the Stadt, and I several times went down there to see the unfortunates fed.

Words could not portray the scene of misery. The best thing I can do is to ask you to fancy five or six hundred human frameworks of both sexes and all ages, from the tender infant upwards, dressed in the remains of tattered rags, standing in lines, each holding an old blackened can or beef tin, awaiting turn to crawl painfully up to the kitchen where the food was distributed. Having obtained the horse soup, fancy them tottering off a few yards and sitting down to wolf up the life-fastening mess, and lick the tins when they had finished. It was one of the most heart-rending sights I ever witnessed, and I have seen many . . .

When a flight of locusts came it was regarded as a godsend – this visitation that is looked upon by the farmer as hardly less of a curse than the rinderpest or drought. The starving ones gathered the insects up in thousands, stripped them of their heads, legs, and wings, and ate the bodies. They picked up meat-tins and licked them; they fed like outcast curs. They went farther than the mongrel. When a dog gets a bone he polishes it white and leaves it there. Day after day I heard outside my door continuous thumping sounds. They were caused by the living skeletons who, having eaten all that was outside the bones, smashed them up with stones and devoured what marrow they could find. They looked for bones on the dust-heaps, on the roads everywhere, and I pledge my word that I saw one poor fellow weakly follow a dog with a stone and with unerring aim strike him on the ribs, which caused the lean and hungry brute to drop a bone, which the Kafir carried off in triumph to the kerb, where he smashed it and got what comfort he could from it.

Queen Victoria's Last Journey, 1 February 1901

Cissy, Countess of Denbigh

Victoria died at Osborne, Isle of Wight, on 22 January 1901

I think you will like to hear of my going down to Southampton to see the passing of our dear Queen from Osborne to Portsmouth.

I went on the *Scot*, where both Houses were embarked. We steamed out, and took up our position between the last British ship and the first foreign ships of war, on the south side of the double line down which the procession was to pass. The day was one of glorious sunshine, with the smoothest and bluest of seas. After a while a black torpedo destroyer came dashing down the line signalling that the *Alberta* was leaving Osborne and from every ship, both British and foreign, boomed out the minute guns for close on an hour before the procession reached us. The sun was now (3 p.m.) beginning to sink, and a wonderful golden pink appeared in the sky and as the smoke slowly rose from the guns it settled in one long festoon behind them, over Haslar, a purple festoon like the purple hangings ordered by the King.

Then slowly down the long line of battleships came eight torpedo destroyers, dark gliding forms, and after them the white *Alberta* looking very small and frail next the towering battleships. We could see the motionless figures standing round the white pall which, with the crown and orb and sceptre, lay upon the coffin. Solemnly and slowly, it glided over the calm blue water, followed by the other three vessels, giving one a strange choke, and a catch in one's heart as memory flew back to her triumphal passage down her fleet in the last Jubilee review. As slowly and as silently as it came the cortège passed away into the haze: with the solemn booming of the guns continuing every minute till Portsmouth was reached. A wonderful scene and marvellously impressive, leaving behind it a memory of peace and beauty and sadness which it is impossible to forget.

The First Radio Signal across the Atlantic, 12 December 1901

Guglielmo Marconi

Marconi awaited the signal from Poldhu, Cornwall, in a hut on the cliffs at St John's, Newfoundland.

Shortly before mid-day I placed the single earphone to my ear and started listening. The receiver on the table before me was very crude – a few coils and condensers and a coherer – no valves, no amplifiers, not even a crystal. But I was at last on the point of putting the correctness of all my beliefs to test. The answer came at 12.30 when I heard, faintly but distinctly, *pip-pip-pip*. I handed the phone to Kemp: 'Can you hear anything?' I asked. 'Yes,' he said, 'the letter S' – he could hear it. I knew then that all my anticipations had been justified. The electric waves sent out into space from Poldhu had traversed the Altantic – the distance, enormous as it seemed then, of 1,700 miles – unimpeded by the curvature of the earth. The result meant much more to me than the mere successful realization of an experiment. As Sir Oliver Lodge has stated, it was an epoch in history. I now felt for the first time absolutely certain that the day would come when mankind would be able to send messages without wires not only across the Atlantic but between the farthermost ends of the earth.

A Roundabout in Montmartre, 4 November 1903

Arnold Bennett

At the Montmartre Fair, now in progress, I was much struck by the charming effect of the roundabout opposite the Moulin Rouge: The machine in full swing, the pigs galloping one way and the ceiling of the machine going the other brilliantly lit by electric light in clusters and in single arc lamps. Two young, fair, and pretty *cocottes* with red lips and white teeth, brilliantly dressed, sitting *sans gêne* in one of the cars, in the full glare, showing well against red velvet cushions of the car, and throwing those peculiarly French coloured paper-streamers into the crowd; these streamers have the effect of fireworks, rockets, in the sky – a line of fire. The whole machine is gradually covered with them, and becomes a sort of cocoon, and they stream round after it in thousands and lie thick in the road.

Bloody Sunday: St Petersburg, 22 January 1905

A Young Priest, Father Gapon, Leads a Peaceful March to the Winter Palace

Father Gapon

This massacre of peaceful demonstrators sparked off strikes and protests throughout Russia, and the Tsar was forced to issue a manifesto promising to convene a national parliament.

'Shall we go straight toward the gate, or by a roundabout route to avoid the soldiers?' I was asked. I shouted huskily, 'No; straight through them. Courage! Death or Freedom!' and the crowd shouted in return, 'Hurrah!' We then started forward, singing in one mighty, solemn voice the Tsar's hymn, 'God Save thy People'. But when we came to the line, 'Save Nicholas Alexandrovitch', some of the men who belonged to the Socialist Party were wicked enough to substitute the words 'Save George Appolonovich' [Gapon], while others simply repeated the words, 'Death or Freedom!' The procession moved in a compact mass. In front of me were my two bodyguards and a young fellow with dark eyes from whose face his hard labouring life had not yet wiped away the light of youthful gaiety. On the flanks of the crowd ran the children. Some of the women insisted on walking in the first rows, in order, as they said, to protect me with their bodies, and force had to be used to remove them. I may mention also as a significant fact that at the start the police not only did not interfere with the procession, but moved with us with bared heads in recognition of the religious emblems. Two local police officers marched bareheaded in front of us, preventing any hindrance to our advance and forcing a few carriages that we met to turn aside in our favour. In this way we approached the Narva Gate, the crowd becoming denser as we progressed, the singing more impressive, and the whole scene more dramatic.

At last we reached within two hundred paces of where the troops stood. Files of infantry barred the road, and in front of them a company of cavalry was drawn up, with their swords shining in the sun. Would they dare to touch us? For a moment we trembled, and then started forward again.

Suddenly the company of Cossacks galloped rapidly towards us with drawn swords. So, then, it was to be a massacre after all! There was no time for consideration, for making plans, or giving orders. A cry of alarm arose as the Cossacks came down upon us. Our front ranks broke before them, opening to right and left, and down this lane the soldiers drove their horses, striking on both sides. I saw the swords lifted and falling, the men, women and children dropping to the earth like logs of wood, while moans, curses and shouts filled the air. It was impossible to reason in the fever of this crisis. At my order the front rows formed again in the wake of the Cossacks, who penetrated farther and farther, and at last emerged from the end of the procession.

Again we started forward, with solemn resolution and rising rage in our hearts. The Cossacks turned their horses and began to cut their way through the crowd from the rear. They passed through the whole column and galloped back towards the Narva Gate, where – the infantry having opened their ranks and let them through – they again formed line. We were still advancing, though the bayonets raised in threatening rows seemed to point symbolically to our fate. A spasm of pity filled my heart, but I felt no fear. Before we started, my dear friend, the workman K——, had said to me, 'We are going to give your life as a sacrifice.' So be it!

We were not more than thirty yards from the soldiers, being separated from them only by the bridge over the Tarakanovskii Canal, which here marks the border of the city, when suddenly, without any warning and without a moment's delay, was heard the dry crack of many rifle-shots. I was informed later on that a bugle was blown, but we could not hear it above the singing, and even if we had heard it we should not have known what it meant.

Vasiliev, with whom I was walking hand in hand, suddenly left hold of my arm and sank upon the snow. One of the workmen who carried the banners fell also. Immediately one of the two police officers to whom I had referred shouted out, 'What are you doing? How dare you fire upon the portrait of the Tsar?' This, of course, had no effect, and both he and the other officer were shot down – as I learned afterwards, one was killed and the other dangerously wounded.

I turned rapidly to the crowd and shouted to them to lie down, and I also stretched myself out upon the ground. As we lay thus another volley was fired, and another, and yet another, till it seemed as though the shooting was continuous. The crowd first kneeled and then lay flat down, hiding their heads from the rain of bullets, while the rear rows of the procession began to run away. The smoke of the fire lay before us like a thin cloud, and I felt it stiflingly in my throat. An old man named Lavrentiev, who was carrying the Tsar's portrait, had been one of the first victims. Another old man caught the portrait as it fell from his hands and carried it till he too was killed by the next volley. With his last gasp the old man said, 'I may die, but I will see the Tsar.' One of the banner-carriers had his arm broken by a bullet. A little boy of ten years, who was carrying a church lantern, fell pierced by a bullet, but still held the lantern tightly and tried to rise again, when another shot struck him down. Both the smiths who had guarded me were killed, as well as all those who were carrying the icons and banners; and all these emblems now lay scattered on the snow. The soldiers were actually shooting into the courtyards of the adjoining houses, where the crowd tried to find refuge and, as I learned afterwards, bullets even struck persons inside, through the windows.

At last the firing ceased. I stood up with a few others who remained uninjured and looked down at the bodies that lay prostrate around me. I cried to them, 'Stand up!' But they lay still. I could not at first understand. Why did they lie there? I looked again, and saw that their arms were stretched out lifelessly, and I saw the scarlet stain of blood upon the snow. Then I understood. It was horrible. And my Vasiliev lay dead at my feet.

Horror crept into my heart. The thought flashed through my mind, 'And this is the work of our Little Father, the Tsar.' Perhaps this anger saved me, for now I knew in very truth that a new chapter was opened in the book of the history of our people. I stood up, and a little group of workmen gathered round me again. Looking backward, I saw that our line, though still stretching away into the distance, was broken and that many of the people were fleeing. It was in vain that I called to them, and in a moment I stood there, the centre of a few scores of men, trembling with indignation amid the broken ruins of our movement.

The San Francisco Earthquake, 17 April 1906

Jack London

The earthquake and subsequent fire made 225,000 homeless.

San Francisco is gone! Nothing remains of it but memories and a fringe of dwelling houses on the outskirts. Its industrial section is wiped out. Its social and residential section is wiped out. The factories and warehouses, the great stores and newspaper buildings, the hotels and the palaces of the nabobs, are all gone. Remains only the fringe of dwelling houses on the outskirts of what was once San Francisco.

Within an hour after the earthquake shock the smoke of San Francisco's burning was a lurid tower visible a hundred miles away. And for three days and nights this lurid tower swayed in the sky, reddening the sun, darkening the sky, and filling the land with smoke.

On Wednesday morning at a quarter past five came the earthquake. A minute later the flames were leaping upward. In a dozen different quarters south of Market Street, in the working-class ghetto, and in the factories, fires started. There was no opposing the flames. There was no organization, no communication. All the cunning adjustments of a twentieth-century city had been smashed by the earthquake. The streets were humped into ridges and depressions and piled with debris of fallen walls. The steel rails were twisted into perpendicular and horizontal angles. The telephone and telegraph systems were disrupted. And the great water mains had burst. All the shrewd contrivances and safeguards of man had been thrown out of gear by thirty seconds' twitching of the earth crust.

By Wednesday afternoon, inside of twelve hours, half the heart of the city was gone. At that time I watched the vast conflagration from out on the bay. It was dead calm. Not a flicker of wind stirred. Yet from every side wind was pouring in upon the city. East, west, north, and south, strong winds were blowing upon the doomed city. The heated air rising made an enormous suck. Thus did the fire of itself build its own colossal chimney through the atmosphere. Day and night this dead calm continued, and yet, near to the flames, the wind was often half a gale, so mighty was the suck.

The edict which prevented chaos was the following proclamation by Mayor E. E. Schmitz:

'The Federal Troops, the members of the Regular Police Force, and all Special Police Officers have been authorized to KILL any and all persons found engaged in looting or in the commission of any other crime.

'I have directed all the Gas and Electric Lighting Companies not to turn on gas or electricity until I order them to do so; you may therefore expect the city to remain in darkness for an indefinite time.

'I request all citizens to remain at home from darkness until daylight of every night until order is restored.

'I warn all citizens of the danger of fire from damaged or destroyed chimneys, broken or leaking gas pipes or fixtures, or any like cause.'

Wednesday night saw the destruction of the very heart of the city. Dynamite was lavishly used, and many of San Francisco's proudest structures were crumbled by man himself into ruins, but there was no withstanding the onrush of the flames. Time and again successful stands were made by the fire fighters, and every time the flames flanked around on either side, or came up from the rear, and turned to defeat the hard-won victory . . .

At nine o'clock Wednesday evening I walked down through miles and miles of magnificent buildings and towering skyscrapers. Here was no fire. All was in perfect order. The police patrolled the streets. Every building had its watchman at the door. And yet it was doomed, all of it. There was no water. The dynamite was giving out. And at right-angles two different conflagrations were sweeping down upon it.

At one o'clock in the morning I walked down through the same section. Everything still stood intact. There was no fire. And yet there was a change. A rain of ashes was falling. The watchmen at the doors were gone. The police had been withdrawn. There were no firemen, no fire engines, no men fighting with dynamite. The district had been absolutely abandoned. I stood at the corner of Kearney and Market, in the very innermost heart of San Francisco. Kearney Street was deserted. Half-a-dozen blocks away it was burning on both sides. The street was a wall of flame. And against this wall of flame, silhouetted sharply, were two United States cavalrymen sitting their horses, calmly watching. That was all. Not another person was in sight. In the intact heart of the city two troopers sat their horses and watched.

Surrender was complete. There was no water. The sewers had long since been pumped dry. There was no dynamite. Another fire had broken out further uptown, and now from three sides conflagrations were sweeping down. The fourth side had been burned earlier in the day. In that direction stood the tottering walls of the Examiner Building, the burned-out Call Building, the smouldering ruins of the Grand Hotel, and the gutted, devastated, dynamited Palace Hotel.

The following will illustrate the sweep of the flames and the inability of men to calculate their spread. At eight o'clock Wednesday evening I passed through Union Square. It was packed with refugees. Thousands of them had gone to bed on the grass. Government tents had been set up, supper was being cooked, and the refugees were lining up for free meals.

At half-past one in the morning three sides of Union Square were in flames. The fourth side, where stood the great St Francis Hotel, was still holding out. An hour later, ignited from top and sides, the St Francis was flaming heavenward. Union Square, heaped high with mountains of trunks, was deserted. Troops, refugees, and all had retreated.

It was at Union Square that I saw a man offering a thousand dollars for a team of horses. He was in charge of a truck piled high with trunks from some hotel. It had been hauled here into what was considered safety, and the horses had been taken out. The flames were on three sides of the square, and there were no horses.

Also, at this time, standing beside the truck, I urged a man to seek safety in flight. He was all but hemmed in by several conflagrations. He was an old man and he was on crutches. Said he: 'Today is my birthday. Last night I was worth thirty thousand dollars. I bought five bottles of wine, some delicate fish, and other things for my birthday dinner. I have had no dinner, and all I own are these crutches.'

I convinced him of his danger and started him limping on his way. An hour later, from a distance, I saw the truckload of trunks burning merrily in the middle of the street.

On Thursday morning, at a quarter past five, just twenty-four hours after the earthquake, I sat on the steps of a small residence of Nob Hill. With me sat Japanese, Italians, Chinese, and Negroes – a bit of the cosmopolitan flotsam of the wreck of the city. All about were the palaces of the nabob pioneers of Forty-nine. To the east and south, at right-angles, were advancing two mighty walls of flame.

I went inside with the owner of the house on the steps of which I sat. He was cool and cheerful and hospitable. 'Yesterday morning,' he said, 'I was worth six hundred thousand dollars. This morning this house is all I have left. It will go in fifteen minutes.' He pointed to a large cabinet. 'That is my wife's collection of china. This rug upon which we stand is a present. It cost fifteen hundred dollars. Try that piano. Listen to its tone. There are few like it. There are no horses. The flames will be here in fifteen minutes.'

Outside, the old Mark Hopkins residence, a palace, was just catching fire. The troops were falling back and driving refugees before them. From every side came the roaring of flames, the crashing of walls, and the detonations of dynamite.

I passed out of the house. Day was trying to dawn through the smoke pall. A sickly light was creeping over the face of things. Once only the sun broke through the smoke pall, blood-red, and showing quarter its usual size. The smoke pall itself, viewed from beneath, was a rose colour that pulsed and fluttered with lavender shades. Then it turned to mauve and yellow and dun. There was no sun. And so dawned the second day on stricken San Francisco.

The First Channel Flight, 25 July 1909

Louis Blériot

Blériot's 28-h.p. monoplane averaged 46 mph, making the crossing in 40 minutes. It was later exhibited at Selfridge's and 120,000 people filed past it in four days.

In the early morning of Sunday, 25 July 1909, I left my hotel at Calais and drove out to the field where my aeroplane was garaged. On the way I noted that the weather was favourable to my endeavour. I therefore ordered the destroyer *Escopette*, placed at my disposal by the French Government, to go to sea. I examined my aeroplane. I started the engine, and found it worked well. At half-past four we could see all round. Daylight had come. My thoughts were only upon the flight, and my determination to accomplish it this morning.

Four thirty-five. *Tout est prêt!* In an instant I am in the air, my engine making 1,200 revolutions – almost its highest speed – in order that I may get quickly over the telegraph wires along the edge of the cliff. As soon as I am over the cliff I reduce my speed. There is now no need to force my engine. I begin my flight, steady and sure, towards the coast of England. I have no apprehensions, no sensations, *pas du tout*. The *Escopette* has seen me. She is driving ahead across the Channel at full speed. She makes perhaps 26 miles per hour. What matters? I am making over 40 mph. Rapidly I overtake her, travelling at a height of 250 feet. The moment is supreme, yet I surprised myself by feeling no exultation. Below me is the sea; the motion of the waves is not pleasant. I drive on. Ten minutes go. I turn my head to see whether I am proceeding in the right direction. I am amazed. There is nothing to be seen – neither the destroyer, nor France, nor England. I am alone. I am lost.

Then I saw the cliffs of Dover! Away to the west was the spot where I had intended to land. The wind had taken me out of my course. I turned and now I was in difficulties, for the wind here by the cliffs was much stronger, and my speed was reduced as I fought against it. My beautiful aeroplane responded. I saw an opening and I found myself over dry land. I attempted a landing, but the wind caught me and whirled me round two or three times. At once I stopped my motor, and instantly my machine fell straight on the ground. I was safe on your shore. Soldiers in khaki ran up, and also a policeman. Two of my compatriots were on the spot. They kissed my cheeks. I was overwhelmed.

Suffragette Lady Constance Lytton, Disguised as a Lower-Class Woman, Jane Warton, is Forcibly Fed in Walton Gaol, Liverpool, 18 January 1910

Constance Lytton

I was visited again by the Senior Medical Officer, who asked me how long I had been without food. I said I had eaten a buttered scone and a banana sent in by friends to the police station on Friday at about midnight. He said, 'Oh, then, this is the fourth day; that is too long, I shall feed you, I must feed you at once,' but he went out and nothing happened till about six o'clock in the evening, when he returned with, I think, five wardresses and the feeding apparatus. He urged me to take food voluntarily. I told him that was absolutely out of the question, that when our legislators ceased to resist enfranchising women then I should cease to resist taking food in prison. He did not examine my heart nor feel my pulse; he did not ask to do so, nor did I say anything which could possibly induce him to think I would refuse to be examined. I offered no resistance to being placed in position, but lay down voluntarily on the plank bed. Two of the wardresses took hold of my arms, one held my head and one my feet. One wardress helped to pour the food. The doctor leant on my knees as he stooped over my chest to get at my mouth. I shut my mouth and clenched my teeth. I had looked forward to this moment with so much anxiety lest my identity should be discovered beforehand, that I felt positively glad when the time had come. The sense of being overpowered by more force than I could possibly resist was complete, but I resisted nothing except with my mouth. The doctor offered me the choice of a wooden or steel gag; he explained elaborately, as he did on most subsequent occasions, that the steel gag would hurt and the wooden one not, and he urged me not to force him to use the steel gag. But I did not speak nor open my mouth, so that after playing about for a moment or two with the wooden one he finally had recourse to the steel. He seemed annoyed at my resistance and he broke into a temper as he plied my teeth with the steel implement. He found that on either side at the back I had false teeth mounted on a bridge which did not take out. The superintending wardress asked if I had any false teeth, if so, that they must be taken out; I made no answer and the process went on. He dug his instrument down on to the sham tooth, it pressed fearfully on the gum. He said if I resisted so much with my teeth, he would have to feed me through the nose. The pain of it was intense and at last I must have given way for he got the gag between my teeth, when he proceeded to turn it much more than necessary until my jaws were fastened wide apart, far more than they could go naturally. Then he put down my throat a tube which seemed to me much too wide and was something like four feet in length. The irritation of the tube was excessive. I choked the moment it touched my throat until it had got down. Then the food was poured in quickly; it made me sick a few seconds after it was down and the action of the sickness made my body and legs double up, but the wardresses instantly pressed back my head and the doctor leant on my knees. The horror of it was more than I can describe. I was sick over the doctor and wardresses, and it seemed a long time before they took the tube out. As the doctor left he gave me a slap on the cheek, not violently, but, as it were, to express his contemptuous disapproval, and he seemed to take for granted that my distress was assumed. At first it seemed such an utterly contemptible thing to have done that I could only laugh in my mind. Then suddenly I saw Jane Warton lying before me, and it seemed as if I were outside of her. She was the most despised, ignorant and helpless prisoner that I had seen. When she had served her time and was out of the prison, no one would believe anything she said, and the doctor when he had fed her by force and tortured her body, struck her on the cheek to show how he despised her! That was Jane Warton, and I had come to help her.

When the doctor had gone out of the cell, I lay quite helpless. The wardresses were kind and knelt round to comfort me, but there was nothing to be done, I could not move, and remained there in what, under different conditions, would have been an intolerable mess. I had been sick over my hair, which, though short, hung on either side of my face, all over the wall near my bed, and my clothes seemed saturated with it, but the wardresses told me they could not get me a change that night as it was too late, the office was shut. I lay quite motionless, it seemed paradise to be without the suffocating tube, without the liquid food going in and out of my body and without the gag between my teeth. Presently the wardresses all left me, they had orders to go, which were carried out with the usual promptness. Before long I heard the sounds of the forced feeding in the next cell to mine. It was almost more than I could bear, it was Elsie Howey, I was sure. When the ghastly process was over and all quiet, I tapped on the wall and called out at the top of my voice, which wasn't much just then, 'No surrender,' and there came the answer past any doubt in Elsie's voice, 'No surrender.'

The Arrest of Dr Crippen, 31 July 1910

Captain H. G. Kendall

Wife-murderer Crippen was the first criminal to be hunted down by wireless. He was executed, but Ethel le Neve, charged as an accessory, was acquitted. The narrator is Captain Kendall, master of the Canadian Pacific liner Montrose.

The *Montrose* was in port at Antwerp when I read in the *Continental Daily Mail* that a warrant had been issued for Crippen and le Neve. They were reported to have been traced to a hotel in Brussels but had then vanished again.

Soon after we sailed for Quebec I happened to glance through the porthole of my cabin and behind a lifeboat I saw two men. One was squeezing the other's hand. I walked along the boat deck and got into conversation with the elder man. I noticed that there was a mark on the bridge of his nose through wearing spectacles, that he had recently shaved off a moustache, and that he was growing a beard. The young fellow was very reserved, and I remarked about his cough.

'Yes,' said the elder man, 'my boy has a weak chest, and I'm taking him to California for his health.'

I returned to my cabin and had another look at the *Daily Mail*. I studied the description and photographs issued by Scotland Yard. Crippen was 50 years of age, 5 ft 4 ins high, wearing spectacles and a moustache; Miss le Neve was 27, 5 ft 5 ins, slim, with pale complexion. I then examined the passenger list and ascertained that the two passengers were travelling as 'Mr Robinson and son'. I arranged for them to take meals at my table.

When the bell went for lunch I tarried until the coast was clear, then slipped into the Robinsons' cabin unobserved, where I noticed two things: that the boy's felt hat was packed round the rim to make it fit, and that he had been using a piece of a woman's bodice as a face flannel. That satisfied me. I went down to the dining saloon and kept my eyes open. The boy's manners at table were ladylike. Later, when they were promenading the saloon deck, I went out and walked behind them, and called out, 'Mr Robinson!' I had to shout the name several times before the man turned and said to me, 'I'm sorry, Captain, I didn't hear you – this cold wind is making me deaf.'

In the next two days we developed our acquaintance. Mr Robinson was the acme of politeness, quiet-mannered, a non-smoker; at night he went on deck and roamed about on his own. Once the wind blew up his coat tails and in his hip pocket I saw a revolver. After that I also carried a revolver, and we often had pleasant little tea parties together in my cabin, discussing the book he was reading, which was *The Four Just Men*, a murder mystery by Edgar Wallace – and when that little fact was wirelessed to London and published it made Edgar Wallace's name ring, so agog was everybody in England over the Crippen case.

That brings me to the wireless. On the third day out I gave my wireless operator a message for Liverpool: *One hundred and thirty miles west of Lizard ... have strong suspicions that Crippen London cellar murderer and accomplice are among saloon passengers ... Accomplice dressed as boy; voice, manner, and build undoubtedly a girl.*

I remember Mr Robinson sitting in a deckchair, looking at the wireless aerials and listening to the crackling of our crude spark-transmitter, and remarking to me what a wonderful invention it was.

I sent several more reports, but our weak transmitting apparatus was soon out of communication with land. We could hear other ships at a great distance, however, and you may imagine my excitement when my operator brought me a message he had intercepted from a London newspaper to its representative aboard the White Star liner *Laurentic* which was also heading westward across the Atlantic: *What is Inspector Dew doing? Is he sending and receiving wireless messages? Is he playing games with passengers? Are passengers excited over chase? Rush reply.*

This was the first I knew that my message to Liverpool had caused Inspector Dew to catch the first boat out – the *Laurentic*. With her superior speed I knew she would reach the Newfoundland coast before me. I hoped that if she had any news for me the *Laurentic* would leave it at the Belle Island station to be transmitted to me as soon as I passed that point on my approach to Canada.

She had news indeed: *Will board you at Father Point . . . strictly confidential . . . from Inspector Dew, Scotland Yard, on board* Laurentic.

I replied: *Shall arrive Father Point about 6 a.m. tomorrow . . . should advise you to come off in small boat with pilot, disguised as pilot . . .*

This was confirmed. The last night was dreary and anxious, the sound of our fog-horn every few minutes adding to the monotony. The hours dragged on as I paced the bridge; now and then I could see Mr Robinson strolling about the deck. I had invited him to get up early to see the 'pilots' come aboard at Father Point in the River St Lawrence. When they did so they came straight to my cabin. I sent for Mr Robinson. When he entered I stood with the detective facing the door, holding my revolver inside my coat pocket. As he came in, I said, 'Let me introduce you.'

Mr Robinson put out his hand, the detective grabbed it, at the same time removing his pilot's cap, and said, 'Good morning, Dr Crippen. Do you know me? I'm Inspector Dew, from Scotland Yard.'

Crippen quivered. Surprise struck him dumb. Then he said, 'Thank God it's over. The suspense has been too great. I couldn't stand it any longer.'

The Siege of Sidney Street, 3 January 1911

Philip Gibbs

Pursuing a gang of jewel robbers who had killed a policeman, the police cornered suspects, including, it was thought, a dangerous criminal called 'Peter the Painter', in 100 Sidney Street, Mile End Road. The affair caused an outcry against foreign immigrants, political refugees, and the East End anarchist underworld of Russian and German Jews, to which the Sidney Street gunmen were thought to belong.

For some reason, which I have forgotten, I went very early that morning to the *Chronicle* office, and was greeted by the news editor with the statement that a hell of a battle was raging in Sidney Street. He advised me to go and look at it.

I took a taxi, and drove to the corner of that street, where I found a dense crowd observing the affair as far as they dared peer round the angle of the walls from adjoining streets. Heedless at the moment of danger, which seemed to me ridiculous, I stood boldly opposite Sidney Street and looked down its length of houses. Immediately in front of me four soldiers of one of the Guards' regiments lay on their stomachs, protected from the dirt of the road by newspaper 'sandwich' boards, firing their rifles at a house halfway down the street. Another young Guardsman, leaning against a wall, took random shots at intervals while he smoked a Woodbine. As I stood near him, he winked and said, 'What a game!'

It was something more than a game. Bullets were flicking off the wall like peas, plugging holes into the dirty yellow brick, and ricocheting fantastically. One of them took a neat chip out of a policeman's helmet, and he said, 'Well, I'll be blowed!' and laughed in a foolish way. It was before the war, when we learned to know more about the meaning of bullets. Another struck a stick on which a journalistic friend of mine was leaning in an easy, graceful way. His support and his dignity suddenly departed from him.

'That's funny!' he said seriously, as he saw his stick neatly cut in half at his feet.

A cinematograph operator, standing well inside Sidney Street, was winding his handle vigorously, quite oblivious of the whiz of bullets, which were being fired at a slanting angle from the house, which seemed to be the target of the prostrate Guardsmen.

A large police inspector, of high authority, shouted a command to his men.

'What's all that nonsense? Clear the people back! Clear 'em right back! We don't want a lot of silly corpses lying round.'

A cordon of police pushed back the dense crowd, treading on the toes of those who would not move fast enough.

I found myself in a group of journalists.

'Get back there!' shouted the police.

But we were determined to see the drama out. It was more sensational than any 'movie' show. Immediately opposite was a tall gin palace – 'The Rising Sun'. Some strategist said, 'That's the place for us!' We raced across before the police could outflank us.

A Jew publican stood in the doorway, sullenly.

'Whatcher want?' he asked.

'Your roof,' said one of the journalists.

'A quid each, and worth it,' said the Jew.

At that time, before the era of paper money, some of us carried golden sovereigns in our pockets, one to a 'quid'. Most of the others did, but, as usual, I had not more than eighteenpence. A friend lent me the necessary coin, which the Jew slipped into his pocket as he let me pass. Twenty of us, at least, gained access to the roof of 'The Rising Sun'.

It was a good vantage point, or O.P., as we should have called it later in history. It looked right across to the house in Sidney Street in which Peter the Painter and his friends were defending themselves to the death – a tall, thin house of three storeys, with dirty window blinds. In the house immediately opposite were some more Guardsmen, with pillows and mattresses stuffed into the windows in the nature of sandbags as used in trench warfare. We could not see the soldiers, but we could see the effect of their intermittent fire, which had smashed every pane of glass and kept chipping off bits of brick in the anarchists' abode.

The street had been cleared of all onlookers, but a group of detectives slunk along the walls on the anarchists' side of the street at such an angle that they were safe from the slanting fire of the enemy. They had to keep very close to the wall, because Peter and his pals were dead shots and maintained something like a barrage fire with their automatics. Any detective or policeman who showed himself would have been sniped in a second, and these men were out to kill.

The thing became a bore as I watched it for an hour or more, during which time Mr Winston Churchill, who was then Home Secretary, came to take command of active operations, thereby causing an immense amount of ridicule in next day's papers. With a bowler hat pushed firmly down on his bulging brow, and one hand in his breast pocket, like Napoleon on the field of battle, he peered round the corner of the street, and afterwards, as we learned, ordered up some field guns to blow the house to bits.

That never happened for a reason which we on 'The Rising Sun' were quick to see.

In the top-floor room of the anarchists' house we observed a gas jet burning, and presently some of us noticed the white ash of burnt paper fluttering out of a chimney pot.

'They're burning documents,' said one of my friends.

They were burning more than that. They were setting fire to the house, upstairs and downstairs. The window curtains were first to catch alight, then volumes of black smoke, through which little tongues of flame licked up, poured through the empty window frames. They must have used paraffin to help the progress of the fire, for the whole house was burning with amazing rapidity.

'Did you ever see such a game in London!' exclaimed the man next to me on the roof of the public house.

For a moment I thought I saw one of the murderers standing on the window sill. But it was a blackened curtain which suddenly blew outside the window frame and dangled on the sill.

A moment later I had one quick glimpse of a man's arm with a pistol in his hand. He fired and there was a quick flash. At the same moment a volley of shots rang out from the Guardsmen opposite. It is certain that they killed the man who had shown himself, for afterwards they found his body (or a bit of it) with a bullet through the skull. It was not long afterwards that the roof fell in with an upward rush of flame and sparks. The inside of the house from top to bottom was a furnace.

The detectives, with revolvers ready, now advanced in Indian file. One of them ran forward and kicked at the front door. It fell in, and a sheet of flame leaped out. No other shot was fired from within. Peter the Painter and his fellow bandits were charred cinders in the bonfire they had made.

South Polar Expedition: Captain Scott's Diary, March 1912

Captain Scott

Scott and his four remaining companions had reached the pole on 18 January, only to find that Roald Amundsen had preceded them by about a month. On 12 November searchers found the tent with the frozen bodies.

Impressions

The seductive folds of the sleeping-bag.

The hiss of the primus and the fragrant steam of the cooker issuing from the tent ventilator.

The small green tent and the great white road.

The whine of a dog and the neigh of our steeds.

The driving cloud of powdered snow.

The crunch of footsteps which break the surface crust.

The wind-blown furrows.

The blue arch beneath the smoky cloud.

The crisp ring of the ponies' hoofs and the swish of the following sledge.

The droning conversation of the march as driver encourages or chides his horse.

The patter of dog pads.

The gentle flutter of our canvas shelter.

Its deep booming sound under the full force of a blizzard.

The drift snow like finest flour penetrating every hole and corner – flickering up beneath one's head covering, pricking sharply as a sand blast.

The sun with blurred image peeping shyly through the wreathing drift giving pale shadowless light.

The eternal silence of the great white desert. Cloudy columns of snow drift advancing from the south, pale yellow wraiths, heralding the coming storm, blotting out one by one the sharp-cut lines of the land . . .

Friday, 16 March or Saturday, 17. Lost track of dates, but think the last correct. Tragedy all along the line. At lunch, the day before yesterday, poor Titus Oates said he couldn't go on; he proposed we should leave him in his sleeping-bag. That we could not do, and induced him to come on, on the afternoon march. In spite of its awful nature for him he struggled on and we made a few miles. At night he was worse and we knew the end had come.

Should this be found I want these facts recorded. Oates's last thoughts were of his Mother, but immediately before he took pride in thinking that his regiment would be pleased with the bold way in which he met his death. We can testify to his bravery. He has borne intense suffering for weeks without complaint, and to the very last was able and willing to discuss outside subjects. He did not – would not – give up hope to the very end. He was a brave soul. This was the end. He slept through the night before last, hoping not to wake; but he woke in the morning – yesterday. It was blowing a blizzard. He said, 'I am just going outside and may be some time.' He went out into the blizzard and we have not seen him since.

I take this opportunity of saying that we have stuck to our sick companions to the last. In case of Edgar Evans, when absolutely out of food and he lay insensible, the safety of the remainder seemed to demand his abandonment, but Providence mercifully removed him at this critical moment. He died a natural death, and we did not leave him till two hours after his death. We knew that poor Oates was walking to his death, but though we tried to dissuade him, we knew it was the act of a brave man and an English gentleman. We all hope to meet the end with a similar spirit, and assuredly the end is not far.

I can only write at lunch and then only occasionally. The cold is intense, −40° at midday. My companions are unendingly cheerful, but we are all on the verge of serious frostbites, and though we constantly talk of fetching through I don't think any one of us believes it in his heart.

We are cold on the march now, and at all times except meals. Yesterday we had to lay up for a blizzard and today we move dreadfully slowly. We are at No. 14 pony camp, only two pony marches from One Ton Depot. We leave here our theodolite, a camera, and Oates's sleeping-bags. Diaries, etc., and geological specimens carried at Wilson's special request, will be found with us or on our sledge.

Sunday, 18 March. Today, lunch, we are 21 miles from the depot. Ill fortune presses, but better may come. We have had more wind and drift from ahead yesterday; had to stop marching; wind N.W., force 4, temp. −35°. No human being could face it, and we are worn out *nearly*.

My right foot has gone, nearly all the toes − two days ago I was proud possessor of best feet. These are the steps of my downfall. Like an ass I mixed a small spoonful of curry powder with my melted pemmican − it gave me violent indigestion. I lay awake and in pain all night; woke and felt done on the march; foot went and I didn't know it. A very small measure of neglect and have a foot which is not pleasant to contemplate. Bowers takes first place in condition, but there is not much to choose after all. The others are still confident of getting through − or pretend to be − I don't know! We have the last *half* fill of oil in our primus and a very small quantity of spirit − this alone between us and thirst. The wind is fair for the moment, and that is perhaps a fact to help. The mileage would have seemed ridiculously small on our outward journey.

Monday, 19 March. Lunch. We camped with difficulty last night and were dreadfully cold till after our supper of cold pemmican and biscuit and a half a pannikin of cocoa cooked over the spirit. Then, contrary to expectation, we got warm and all slept well. Today we started in the usual dragging manner. Sledge dreadfully heavy. We are 15½ miles from the depot and ought to get there in three days. What progress! We have two days' food but barely a day's fuel. All our feet are getting bad − Wilson's best, my right foot worse, left all right. There is no chance to nurse one's feet till we can get hot food into us. Amputation is the least I can hope for now, but will the trouble spread? That is the serious question. The weather doesn't give us a chance − the wind from N. to N.W. and −40° temp. today.

Wednesday, 21 March. Got within 11 miles of depot Monday night; had to lay up all yesterday in severe blizzard. Today forlorn hope, Wilson and Bowers going to depot for fuel.

Thursday, 22 and 23 March. Blizzard bad as ever − Wilson and Bowers unable to start − tomorrow last chance − no fuel and only one or two of food left − must be near the end. Have decided it shall be natural − we shall march for the depot with or without our effects and die in our tracks.

Thursday, 29 March. Since the 21st we have had a continuous gale from W.S.W. and S.W. We had fuel to make two cups of tea apiece and bare food for two days on the 20th. Every day we have been ready to start for our depot *11 miles* away, but outside the door of the tent it remains a scene of whirling drift. I do not think we can hope for any better things now. We shall stick it out to the end, but we are getting weaker, of course, and the end cannot be far.

It seems a pity, but I do not think I can write more.

R. SCOTT

For God's sake look after our people.

The *Titanic*: A Fireman's Story, 15 April 1912

Harry Senior

The 'unsinkable' Titanic had only 1,178 lifeboat spaces for the 2,224 people aboard. A total of 1,513 lives were lost – a high proportion of them steerage passengers.

I was in my bunk when I felt a bump. One man said, 'Hello. She has been struck.' I went on deck and saw a great pile of ice on the well deck before the forecastle, but we all thought the ship would last some time, and we went back to our bunks. Then one of the firemen came running down and yelled, 'All muster for the lifeboats.' I ran on deck, and the Captain said, 'All firemen keep down on the well deck. If a man comes up I'll shoot him.'

Then I saw the first lifeboat lowered. Thirteen people were on board, eleven men and two women. Three were millionaires, and one was Ismay [J. Bruce Ismay, Managing Director of the White Star Line; a survivor].

Then I ran up on to the hurricane deck and helped to throw one of the collapsible boats on to the lower deck. I saw an Italian woman holding two babies. I took one of them, and made the woman jump overboard with the baby, while I did the same with the other. When I came to the surface the baby in my arms was dead. I saw the woman strike out in good style, but a boiler burst on the *Titanic* and started a big wave. When the woman saw that wave, she gave up. Then, as the child was dead, I let it sink too.

I swam around for about half an hour, and was swimming on my back when the *Titanic* went down. I tried to get aboard a boat, but some chap hit me over the head with an oar. There were too many in her. I got around to the other side of the boat and climbed in.

The *Titanic*: The Wireless Operator's Story, 15 April 1912

Harold Bride

From aft came the tunes of the band. It was a ragtime tune. I don't know what. Then there was 'Autumn' . . . I went to the place I had seen the collapsible boat on the boat deck, and to my surprise I saw the boat, and the men still trying to push it off. I guess there wasn't a sailor in the crowd. They couldn't do it. I went up to them and was just lending a hand when a large wave came awash of the deck. The big wave carried the boat off. I had hold of an oarlock and I went with it. The next I knew I was in the boat. But that was not all. I was in the boat, and the boat was upside-down, and I was under it. And I remember realizing I was wet through and that whatever happened I must not breathe, for I was under water. I knew I had to fight for it, and I did. How I got out from under the boat I do not know but I felt a breath of air at last. There were men all around me – hundreds of them. The sea was dotted with them, all depending on their lifebelts. I felt I simply had to get away from the ship. She was a beautiful sight then. Smoke and sparks were rushing out of her funnel. There must have been an explosion, but we heard none. We only saw the big stream of sparks. The ship was turning gradually on her nose – just like a duck that goes for a dive. I had only one thing on my mind – to get away from the suction. The band was still playing. I guess all of them went down. They were playing 'Autumn' then. I swam with all my might. I suppose I was 150 feet away when the *Titanic*, on her nose, with her after-quarter sticking straight up in the air, began to settle – slowly.

When at last the waves washed over her rudder there wasn't the least bit of suction I could feel. She must have kept going just so slowly as she had been . . . I felt after a little while like sinking. I was very cold. I saw a boat of some kind near me, and put all my strength into an effort to swim to it. It was hard work. I was all done when a hand reached out from the boat and pulled me aboard. It was our same collapsible. The same crowd was on it. There was just room for me to roll on the edge. I lay there not caring what happened. Somebody sat on my legs. They were wedged in between slats and were being wrenched. I had not the heart left to ask the man to move. It was a terrible sight all around – men swimming and sinking.

I lay where I was, letting the man wrench my feet out of shape. Others came near. Nobody gave them a hand. The bottom-up boat already had more men than it would hold, and it was sinking. At first the larger waves splashed over my clothing. Then they began to splash over my head, and I had to breathe when I could. As we floated around on our capsized boat and I kept straining my eyes for a ship's lights, somebody said, 'Don't the rest of you think we ought to pray?' The man who made the suggestion asked what the religion of the others was. Each man called out his religion. One was a Catholic, one a Methodist, one a Presbyterian. It was decided the most appropriate prayer for all was the Lord's Prayer. We spoke it over in chorus with the man who first suggested that we pray as the leader. Some splendid people saved us. They had a right-side-up boat and it was full to capacity. Yet they came to us and loaded us all into it. I saw some lights off in the distance and knew a steamship was coming to our aid.

The *Titanic*: From a Lifeboat, 15 April 1912

Mrs D. H. Bishop

We did not begin to understand the situation till we were perhaps a mile or more away from the *Titanic*. Then we could see the rows of lights along the decks begin to slant gradually upward from the bow. Very slowly the lines of light began to point downward at a greater and greater angle. The sinking was so slow that you could not perceive the lights of the deck changing their position. The slant seemed to be greater about every quarter of an hour. That was the only difference.

In a couple of hours, though, she began to go down more rapidly.

Then the fearful sight began. The people in the ship were just beginning to realize how great their danger was. When the forward part of the ship dropped suddenly at a faster rate, so that the upward slope became marked, there was a sudden rush of passengers on all the decks towards the stern. It was like a wave. We could see the great black mass of people in the steerage sweeping to the rear part of the boat and breaking through into the upper decks. At the distance of about a mile we could distinguish everything through the night, which was perfectly clear. We could make out the increasing excitement on board the boat as the people, rushing to and fro, caused the deck lights to disappear and reappear as they passed in front of them.

This panic went on, it seemed, for an hour. Then suddenly the ship seemed to shoot up out of the water and stand there perpendicularly. It seemed to us that it stood upright in the water for four full minutes.

Then it began to slide gently downwards. Its speed increased as it went down head first, so that the stern shot down with a rush.

The lights continued to burn till it sank. We could see the people packed densely in the stern till it was gone . . .

As the ship sank we could hear the screaming a mile away. Gradually it became fainter and fainter and died away. Some of the lifeboats that had room for more might have gone to their rescue, but it would have meant that those who were in the water would have swarmed aboard and sunk her.

The Lemon Gardens under Cover for Winter: Gargnano, Lago di Garda, February 1913

D. H. Lawrence

In the morning I often lie in bed and watch the sunrise. The lake lies dim and milky, the mountains are dark blue at the back, while over them the sky gushes and glistens with light. At a certain place on the mountain ridge the light burns gold, seems to fuse a little groove on the hill's rim. It fuses and fuses at this point, till of a sudden it comes, the intense, molten, living light. The mountains melt suddenly, the light steps down, there is a glitter, a spangle, a clutch of spangles, a great unbearable sun-track flashing across the milky lake, and the light falls on my face. Then, looking aside, I hear the little slotting noise which tells me they are opening the lemon gardens, a long panel here and there, a long slot of darkness at irregular intervals between the brown wood and the glass stripes.

'*Voulez-vous*' – the Signore bows me in with outstretched hand – '*voulez-vous entrer, monsieur?*'

I went into the lemon-house, where the poor trees seem to mope in the darkness. It is an immense, dark, cold place. Tall lemon trees, heavy with half-visible fruit, crowd together, and rise in the gloom. They look like ghosts in the darkness of the underworld, stately, and as if in life, but only grand shadows of themselves. And lurking here and there, I see one of the pillars. But he, too, seems a shadow, not one of the dazzling white fellows I knew. Here we are trees, men, pillars, the dark earth, the sad black paths, shut in in this enormous box. It is true, there are long strips of window and slots of space, so that the front is striped, and an occasional beam of light fingers the leaves of an enclosed tree and the sickly round lemons. But it is nevertheless very gloomy.

'But it is much colder in here than outside,' I said.

'Yes,' replied the Signore, 'now. But at night – I *think* – '

I almost wished it were night to try. I wanted to imagine the trees cosy. They seemed now in the underworld. Between the lemon trees, beside the path, were little orange trees, and dozens of oranges hanging like hot coals in the twilight. When I warm my hands at them the Signore breaks me off one twig after another, till I have a bunch of burning oranges among dark leaves, a heavy bouquet. Looking down the Hades of the lemon-house, the many ruddy-clustered oranges beside the path remind me of the lights of a village along the lake at night, while the pale lemons above are the stars. There is a subtle, exquisite scent of lemon flowers. Then I notice a citron. He hangs heavy and bloated upon so small a tree, that he seems a dark green enormity. There is a great host of lemons overhead, half visible, a swarm of ruddy oranges by the path, and here and there a fat citron. It is almost like being under the sea.

Colombo Curry, 11 November 1913

Anna Buchan

The author, Anna Buchan, John Buchan's sister, was sailing to India aboard the SS Scotia.

In Colombo we got rickshaws and drove out to the Galle Face Hotel, a beautiful place with the surf thundering on the beach outside. If I were rich I would always ride in a rickshaw. It is a delightful way of getting about, and as we were trotted along a fine, broad road, small brown boys ran alongside and pelted us with big waxy, sweet-smelling blossoms. We did enjoy it so. At the Galle Face in a cool and lofty dining hall we had an excellent and varied breakfast, and ate real proper Eastern curry for the first time. Another new experience! I don't like curry at home, curry as English cooks know it – a greasy make-up of cold joint served with sodden rice, but this was different. First, rice was handed around, every particle firm and separate and white, and then a rich brown mixture with prawns and other interesting ingredients, which was the curry. You mix the curry with the rice when a whole trayful of condiments is offered to eat with it, things like very thin water biscuits, Bombay duck – all sorts of chutney, and when you have mixed everything up together the result is one of the nicest dishes it has been my lot to taste. Note also, you eat it with a fork and spoon, not with a fork alone as mere provincials do!

GBS at his Mother's Funeral, 22 February 1914

George Bernard Shaw

Why does a funeral always sharpen one's sense of humor and rouse one's spirits? This one was a complete success. No burial horrors. No mourners in black, snivelling and wallowing in induced grief. Nobody knew except myself, Barker & the undertaker. Since I could not have a splendid procession with lovely colors and flashing life and triumphant music, it was best with us three. I particularly mention the undertaker because the humor of the occasion began with him. I went down in the tube to Golders Green with Barker, and walked to the crematorium; and there came also the undertaker presently with his hearse, which had walked (the horse did) conscientiously at a funeral pace through the cold; though my mother would have preferred an invigorating trot. The undertaker approached me in the character of a man shattered with grief; and I, hard as nails and in loyally high spirits (rejoicing irrepressibly in my mother's memory), tried to convey to him that this professional chicanery, as I took it to be, was quite unnecessary. And lo! it wasnt professional chicanery at all. He had done all sorts of work for her for years, and was actually and really in a state about losing her, not merely as a customer, but as a person he liked and was accustomed to. And the coffin was covered with violet cloth – no black.

I must rewrite the burial service; for there are things in it that are deader than anyone it has ever been read over; but I had it read not only because the parson must live by his fees, but because with all its drawbacks it is the most beautiful thing that can be read as yet. And the parson did not gabble and hurry in the horrible manner common on such occasions. With Barker & myself for his congregation (and Mamma) he did it with his utmost feeling and sincerity. We could have made him perfect technically in two rehearsals; but he was excellent as it was; and I shook his hand with unaffected gratitude in my best manner.

At the passage 'earth to earth, ashes to ashes, dust to dust,' there was a little alteration of the words to suit the process. A door opened in the wall; and the violet coffin mysteriously passed out through it and vanished as it closed. People think that door the door of the furnace; but it isnt. I went behind the scenes at the end of the service and saw the real thing. People are afraid to see it; but it is wonderful. I found there the violet coffin opposite another door, a real unmistakable furnace door. When it lifted there was a plain little chamber of cement and firebrick. No heat. No noise. No roaring draught. No flame. No fuel. It looked cool, clean, sunny, though no sun could get there. You would have walked in or put your hand in without misgiving. Then the violet coffin moved again and went in, feet first. And behold! The feet burst miraculously into streaming ribbons of garnet-colored lovely flame, smokeless and eager, like pentecostal tongues, and as the whole coffin passed in it sprang into flame all over; and my mother became that beautiful fire.

The door fell; and they said that if we wanted to see it all through, we should come back in an hour and a half. I remembered the wasted little figure with the wonderful face, and said 'Too long' to myself; but we went off and looked at the Hampstead Garden Suburb (in which I have shares), and telephoned messages to the theatre, and bought books, and enjoyed ourselves generally . . .

The end was wildly funny: she would have enjoyed it enormously. When we returned we looked down through an opening in the floor to a lower floor close below. There we saw a roomy kitchen, with a big cement table and two cooks busy at it. They had little tongs in their hands, and they were deftly and busily picking nails and scraps of coffin handles out of Mamma's dainty little heap of ashes and samples of bone. Mamma herself being at that moment leaning over beside me, shaking with laughter. Then they swept her up into a sieve, and shook her out; so that there was a heap of dust and a heap of calcined bone scraps. And Mamma said in my ear, 'Which of the two heaps is me, I wonder!'

And that merry episode was the end, except for making dust of the bone scraps and scattering them on a flower bed.

O grave, where is thy victory?

The Murder of the Archduke Franz Ferdinand at Sarajevo, 28 June 1914

By One of the Conspirators

Borijove Jevtic

The assassination gave Austro-Hungary the excuse it wanted to attack Serbia, and so precipitated World War I. Princip, aged nineteen, was sentenced to twenty years' imprisonment − the maximum penalty for a minor. Suffering from tuberculosis of the bone, he died in hospital in 1918.

A tiny clipping from a newspaper mailed without comment from a secret band of terrorists in Zagreb, a capital of Croatia, to their comrades in Belgrade, was the torch which set the world afire with war in 1914. That bit of paper wrecked old proud empires. It gave birth to new, free nations.

I was one of the members of the terrorist band in Belgrade which received it and, in those days, I and my companions were regarded as desperate criminals. A price was on our heads. Today my little band is seen in a different light, as pioneer patriots. It is recognized that our secret plans hatched in an obscure café in the capital of old Serbia, have led to the independence of the new Yugoslavia, the united nation set free from Austrian domination.

The little clipping was from the *Srobobran*, a Croatian journal of limited circulation, and consisted of a short telegram from Vienna. This telegram declared that the Austrian Archduke Franz Ferdinand would visit Sarajevo, the capital of Bosnia, 28 June, to direct army manoeuvres in the neighbouring mountains.

It reached our meeting place, the café called Zeatna Moruana, one night the latter part of April, 1914 . . . At a small table in a very humble café, beneath a flickering gas jet we sat and read it. There was no advice nor admonition sent with it. Only four letters and two numerals were sufficient to make us unanimous, without discussion, as to what we should do about it. They were contained in the fateful date, 28 June.

How dared Franz Ferdinand, not only the representative of the oppressor but in his own person an arrogant tyrant, enter Sarajevo on that day? Such an entry was a studied insult.

28 June is a date engraved deeply in the heart of every Serb, so that the day has a name of its own. It is called the vidovnan. It is the day on which the old Serbian kingdom was conquered by the Turks at the battle of Amselfelde in 1389. It is also the day on which in the second Balkan War the Serbian arms took glorious revenge on the Turk for his old victory and for the years of enslavement.

That was no day for Franz Ferdinand, the new oppressor, to venture to the very doors of Serbia for a display of the force of arms which kept us beneath his heel.

Our decision was taken almost immediately. Death to the tyrant!

Then came the matter of arranging it. To make his death certain twenty-two members of the organization were selected to carry out the sentence. At first we thought we would choose the men by lot. But here Gavrilo Princip intervened. Princip is destined to go down in Serbian history as one of her greatest heroes. From the moment Ferdinand's death was decided upon he took an active leadership in its planning. Upon his advice we left the deed to members of our band who were in and around Sarajevo under his direction and that of Gabrinovic, a linotype operator on a Serbian newspaper. Both were regarded as capable of anything in the cause.

The fateful morning dawned. Two hours before Franz Ferdinand arrived in Sarajevo all the twenty-two conspirators were in their allotted positions, armed and ready. They were distributed 500 yards apart over the whole route along which the Archduke must travel from the railroad station to the town hall.

When Franz Ferdinand and his retinue drove from the station they were allowed to pass the first two conspirators. The motor cars were driving too fast to make an attempt feasible and in the crowd were Serbians: throwing a grenade would have killed many innocent people.

When the car passed Gabrinovic, the compositor, he threw his grenade. It hit the side of the car, but Franz Ferdinand with presence of mind threw himself back and was uninjured. Several officers riding in his attendance were injured.

The cars sped to the Town Hall and the rest of the conspirators did not interfere with them. After the reception in the Town Hall General Potiorek, the Austrian Commander, pleaded with Franz Ferdinand to leave the city, as it was seething with rebellion. The Archduke was persuaded to drive the shortest way out of the city and to go quickly.

The road to the manoeuvres was shaped like the letter V, making a sharp turn at the bridge over the River Nilgacka. Franz Ferdinand's car could go fast enough until it reached this spot but here it was forced to slow down for the turn. Here Princip had taken his stand.

As the car came abreast he stepped forward from the curb, drew his automatic pistol from his coat and fired two shots. The first struck the wife of the Archduke, the Archduchess Sofia, in the abdomen. She was an expectant mother. She died instantly.

The second bullet struck the Archduke close to the heart.

He uttered only one word; 'Sofia' – a call to his stricken wife. Then his head fell back and he collapsed. He died almost instantly.

The officers seized Princip. They beat him over the head with the flat of their swords. They knocked him down, they kicked him, scraped the skin from his neck with the edges of their swords, tortured him, all but killed him.

Then he was taken to the Sarajevo gaol. The next day he was transferred to the military prison and the round-up of his fellow conspirators proceeded, although he denied that he had worked with anyone.

He was confronted with Gabrinovic, who had thrown the bomb. Princip denied he knew him. Others were brought in, but Princip denied the most obvious things.

The next day they put chains on Princip's feet, which he wore till his death.

His only sign of regret was the statement that he was sorry he had killed the wife of the Archduke. He had aimed only at her husband and would have preferred that any other bullet should have struck General Potiorek.

The Austrians arrested every known revolutionary in Sarajevo and among them, naturally, I was one. But they had no proof of my connection with the crime. I was placed in the cell next to Princip's, and when Princip was taken out to walk in the prison yard I was taken along as his companion.

The Vulture, July 1914

Osbert Sitwell

Sir Basil Zaharoff, original name Basileios Zacharias, millionaire armaments dealer, was made a Knight Grand Cross of the Order of the Bath after the war.

I was having luncheon at a table alone, when an acquaintance asked me if he might sit at it, as the room was full. Our talk was dull, neutral, with no life in it, but towards the end of the meal he turned to me and said quietly, 'Do you see the man over there, by the window, with a beaky nose, and a white moustache and imperial? Wearing a pink carnation? Well, he's a very remarkable man. Look at him carefully, and I'll tell you about him.'

Glancing in the direction indicated, I saw a rather tall, broadly built man, with a strange yellow face, strongly marked features, and pale, sunken eyes. He was dressed in a well-cut English suit, and had taken trouble, it could be seen, about his clothes generally. It was difficult racially to place him. He did not seem to be a Jew, he was too tall and sturdily built; but apart from his frame, there was about him an oriental air. He might have been a Turk or a Cypriot

— I have since seen money-changers in Cyprus who a little resemble him.

'There must be something up,' my informant continued, 'or he wouldn't be here! His arrival is always a sign of trouble, and every European Chancellery makes a point of knowing where he is. His name is Basil Zaharoff.'

Certainly there was something both evil and imposing about his figure: and as he grew older, the shell hardened and became more typical. His personal appearance should have put all with whom he came into contact on their guard – it is, indeed, singular that western man, while refusing to place credence in anything that he cannot see, while rejecting absolutely omens, prophecies and visions, should at the same time, as he so often does, deny the evidence of his own eyes. This armament-monger most exactly resembled a vulture, and it is no good pretending, in order to avoid the obvious parallel, that he did not. To some it may cause surprise that a man who traded in weapons of death and the prospects of war, and grew fat-bodied on the result of them, should have resembled the scaly-necked bird; but whether or no it seems strange, depends on one's view of the world, and of the immense and startling range of analogy, simile and image that it offers. There, in any case, the likeness was, for all to behold: the beaky face, the hooded eye, the wrinkled neck, the full body, the impression of physical power and of the capacity to wait, the sombre alertness . . .

The German Army Marches through Brussels, 21 August 1914

Richard Harding Davis

Belgian neutrality had been guaranteed by the European powers, but was ignored by the Germans, intent on reaching the Channel ports and Paris.

The entrance of the German army into Brussels has lost the human quality. It was lost as soon as the three soldiers who led the army bicycled into the Boulevard du Régent and asked the way to the Gare du Nord. When they passed the human note passed with them.

What came after them, and twenty-four hours later is still coming, is not men marching, but a force of nature like a tidal wave, an avalanche or a river flooding its banks. At this minute it is rolling through Brussels as the swollen waters of the Conemaugh Valley swept through Johnstown.

At the sight of the first few regiments of the enemy we were thrilled with interest. After for three hours they had passed in one unbroken steel-grey column we were bored. But when hour after hour passed and there was no halt, no breathing time, no open spaces in the ranks, the thing became uncanny, inhuman. You returned to watch it, fascinated. It held the mystery and menace of fog rolling toward you across the sea.

The grey of the uniforms worn by both officers and men helped this air of mystery. Only the sharpest eye could detect among the thousands that passed the slightest difference. All moved under a cloak of invisibility. Only after the most numerous and severe tests at all distances, with all materials and combinations of colours that give forth no colour, could this grey have been discovered. That it was selected to clothe and disguise the German when he fights is typical of the German staff in striving for efficiency to leave nothing to chance, to neglect no detail.

After you have seen this service uniform under conditions entirely opposite you are convinced that for the German soldier it is his strongest weapon. Even the most expert marksman cannot hit a target he cannot see. It is a grey green, not the blue grey of our Confederates. It is the grey of the hour just before daybreak, the grey of unpolished steel, of mist among green trees.

I saw it first in the Grand Place in front of the Hôtel de Ville. It was impossible to tell if in that noble square there was a regiment or a brigade. You saw only a fog that melted into the stones, blended with the ancient house fronts, that shifted and drifted, but left you nothing at which you could point.

Later, as the army passed below my window, under the trees of the Botanical Park, it merged and was lost against the green leaves. It is no exaggeration to say that at a hundred yards you can see the horses on which the uhlans ride, but you cannot see the men who ride them.

If I appear to overemphasize this disguising uniform it is because of all the details of the German outfit it appealed to me as one of the most remarkable. The other day when I was with the rearguard of the French Dragoons and Cuirassiers and they threw out pickets, we could distinguish them against the yellow wheat or green gorse at half a mile, while these men passing in the street, when they have reached the next crossing, become merged into the grey of the paving stones and the earth swallows them. In comparison the yellow khaki of our own American army is about as invisible as the flag of Spain.

Yesterday Major General von Jarotsky, the German Military Governor of Brussels, assured Burgomaster Max that the German army would not occupy the city, but would pass through it. It is still passing. I have followed in campaigns six armies, but excepting not even our own, the Japanese, or the British, I have not seen one so thoroughly equipped. I am not speaking of the fighting qualities of any army, only of the equipment and organization. The German army moved into this city as smoothly and as compactly as an Empire State Express. There were no halts, no open places, no stragglers.

This army has been on active service three weeks, and so far there is not apparently a chin strap or a horseshoe missing. It came in with the smoke pouring from cookstoves on wheels, and in an hour had set up post-office wagons, from which mounted messengers galloped along the line of columns, distributing letters, and at which soldiers posted picture postcards.

The infantry came in in files of five, two hundred men to each company; the Lancers in columns of four, with not a pennant missing. The quick-firing guns and fieldpieces were one hour at a time in passing, each gun with its caisson and ammunition wagon taking twenty seconds in which to pass.

The men of the infantry sang 'Fatherland, My Fatherland'. Between each line of song they took three steps. At times two thousand men were singing together in absolute rhythm and beat. When the melody gave way the silence was broken only by the stamp of iron-shod boots, and then again the song rose. When the singing ceased, the bands played marches. They were followed by the rumble of siege guns, the creaking of wheels, and of chains clanking against the cobblestones and the sharp bell-like voices of the bugles.

For seven hours the army passed in such solid columns that not once might a taxicab or trolley car pass through the city. Like a river of steel it flowed, grey and ghostlike. Then, as dusk came and as thousands of horses' hoofs and thousands of iron boots continued to tramp forward, they struck tiny sparks from the stones, but the horses and the men who beat out the sparks were invisible.

At midnight pack wagons and siege guns were still passing. At seven this morning I was awakened by the tramp of men and bands playing jauntily. Whether they marched all night or not I do not know; but now for twenty-six hours the grey army has rumbled by with the mystery of fog and the pertinacity of a steam roller.

War Frenzy in St Petersburg, August, 1914

Sergyei N. Kurnakov

There was a crowd in front of a newspaper office. Every few minutes a momentous phrase scribbled in charcoal appeared in the window: 'ENGLAND GIVES UP PEACE NEGOTIATIONS. Germany invades Belgium. Mobilization progressing with Great Enthusiasm.' And at 7.50 p.m.:

'GERMANY DECLARES WAR ON RUSSIA.'

Spontaneously the crowd started singing the national anthem. The little pimply clerk who had pasted up the irrevocable announcement was still standing in the window, enjoying his vicarious importance. The people were staring at the sprawling words, as if trying to understand what they actually meant as far as each personal little life was concerned.

Then the edges of the crowd started breaking off and drifting in one direction, up the Nevsky Prospect. I heard the phrase 'German Embassy' repeated several times. I walked slowly that way.

The mob pulled an officer from his cab and carried him in triumph.

I went into a telephone box and called up Stana.

'Yes, it's been declared . . . I don't know what I am going to do yet . . . All right, I'll be over about midnight.'

I did not like the way her receiver clicked; there seemed to be contempt in it.

When I got to the St Isaac Square it was swarming with people. It must have been about nine o'clock, for it was pretty light yet – the enervating, exciting twilight of the northern nights.

The great greystone monstrosity of the German Embassy was facing the red granite of St Isaac's Cathedral. The crowds were pressing around waiting for something to happen. I was watching a young naval officer being pawed by an over-patriotic group when the steady hammering of axes on metal made me look up at the Embassy roof, which was decorated with colossal figures of overfed German warriors holding bloated carthorses. A flagstaff supported a bronze eagle with spread wings.

Several men were busily hammering at the feet of the Teutons. The very first strokes pitched the mob to a frenzy: the heroic figures were hollow!

'They are empty! . . . A good omen! . . . Another German bluff! . . . We'll show them! . . . Hack them all down! . . . No, leave the horses standing! . . . The national anthem! . . . Lord, Save Thy People!'

The axes were hammering faster and faster. At last one warrior swayed, pitched forward, and crashed to the pavement one hundred feet below. A tremendous howl went up, scaring a flock of crows off the gilded dome of St Isaac's. The turn of the eagle came; the bird came hurtling down, and the battered remains were immediately drowned in the nearby Moika river.

But obviously the destruction of the symbols was not enough. A quickly organized gang smashed a side door of the Embassy.

I could see flashlights and torches moving inside, flitting to the upper storeys. A big window opened and spat a great portrait of the Kaiser at the crowd below. When it reached the cobblestones, there was just about enough left to start a good bonfire. A rosewood grand piano followed, exploded like a bomb; the moan of the broken strings vibrated in the air for a second and was drowned: too many people were trying to outshout their own terror of the future.

'Deploy! . . . Trot! . . . Ma—a—arch!'

A troop of mounted *gendarmes* was approaching from the other end of the square. The crowd opened up like the Red Sea for the Israelites. A new crowd carrying the portrait of the Emperor and singing a hymn was advancing slowly towards the *gendarmes*. Their officer halted the men and stiffened at the salute; this was the only thing he did towards restoring order. The bonfire was being fed by the furniture, books, pictures, and papers which came hurtling through the windows of the Embassy.

The emblazoned crockery of state came crashing, and the shattering sound whipped the crowd into a new wave of hysteria.

A woman tore her dress at the collar, fell on her knees with a shriek, and pressed her naked breasts against the dusty boots of a young officer in campaign uniform.

'Take me! Right here, before these people! Poor boy . . . you will give your life . . . for God . . . for the Tsar . . . for Russia!'

Another shriek, and she fainted. Men and women were running aimlessly around the bonfire . . . Is it an effect of light and shadow, or do I really see high cheekbones, slanting eyes, and the conic fur caps of Aladin Mirza's horde?

Whew! . . . I let out the breath I had been holding unconsciously during the entire bacchanal.

Improving Morale, 12 September 1914

Brigadier General E. L. Spears

General de Maud'huy had just been roused from sleep on the straw of a shed and was standing in the street, when a little group of unmistakable purport came round the corner. Twelve soldiers and an NCO, a firing party, a couple of gendarmes, and between them an unarmed soldier. My heart sank and a feeling of horror overcame me. An execution was about to take place. General de Maud'huy gave a look, then held up his hand so that the party halted, and with his characteristic quick step went up to the doomed man. He asked what he had been condemned for. It was for abandoning his post. The General then began to talk to the man. Quite simply he explained discipline to him. Abandoning your post was letting down your pals, more, it was letting down your country that looked to you to defend her. He spoke of the necessity of example, how some could do their duty without prompting but others, less strong, had to know and understand the supreme cost of failure. He told the condemned man that his crime was not venial, not low, and that he must die as an example, so that others should not fail. Surprisingly the wretch agreed, nodded his head. The burden of infamy was lifted from his shoulders. He saw a glimmer of something, redemption in his own eyes, a real hope, though he knew he was to die.

Maud'huy went on, carrying the man with him to comprehension that any sacrifice was worth while if it helped France ever so little. What did anything matter if he knew this?

Finally de Maud'huy held out his hand: 'Yours also is a way of dying for France,' he said. The procession started again, but now the victim was a willing one.

The sound of a volley in the distance announced that all was over. General de Maud'huy wiped the beads of perspiration from his brow, and for the first time perhaps his hand trembled as he lit his pipe.

A Suffolk Farmhand at Gallipoli, June 1915

Leonard Thompson

The Allied attack on Gallipoli and the Dardanelles was meant, initially, to relieve pressure on the Russians by attracting the attention of the Turkish Army. Australian, New Zealand and Indian divisions took part, as well as British. British and Commonwealth casualties were 213,980.

We arrived at the Dardanelles and saw the guns flashing and heard the rifle fire. They heaved our ship, the *River Clyde*, right up to the shore. They had cut a hole in it and made a little pier, so we were able to walk straight off and on to the beach. We all sat there – on the Hellespont! – waiting for it to get light. The first things we saw were big wrecked Turkish guns, the second a big marquee. It didn't make me think of the military but of the village fêtes. Other people must have thought like this because I remember how we all rushed up to it, like boys getting into a circus, and then found it all laced up. We unlaced it and rushed in. It was full of corpses. Dead Englishmen, lines and lines of them, and with their eyes wide open. We all stopped talking. I'd never seen a dead man before and here I was looking at two or three hundred of them. It was our first fear. Nobody had mentioned this. I was very shocked. I thought of Suffolk and it seemed a happy place for the first time.

Later that day we marched through open country and came to within a mile and half of the front line. It was incredible. We were there – at the war! The place we had reached was called 'dead ground' because it was where the enemy couldn't see you. We lay in little square holes, myself next to James Sears from the village. He was about thirty and married. That evening we wandered about on the dead ground and asked about friends of ours who had arrived a month or so ago. 'How is Ernie Taylor?' – 'Ernie? – he's gone.' 'Have you seen Albert Paternoster?' – 'Albert? – he's gone.' We learned that if 300 had 'gone' but 700 were left, then this wasn't too bad. We then knew how unimportant our names were.

I was on sentry that night. A chap named Scott told me that I must only put my head up for a second but that in this time I must see as much as I could. Every third man along the trench was a sentry. The next night we had to move on to the third line of trenches and we heard that the Gurkhas were going over and that we had to support their rear. But when we got to the communication trench we found it so full of dead men that we could hardly move. Their faces were quite black and you couldn't tell Turk from English. There was the most terrible stink and for a while there was nothing but the living being sick on to the dead. I did sentry again that night. It was one–two–sentry, one–two–sentry all along the trench, as before. I knew the next sentry up quite well. I remembered him in Suffolk singing to his horses as he ploughed. Now he fell back with a great scream and a look of surprise – dead. It is quick, anyway, I thought. On June 4th we went over the top. We took the Turks' trench and held it. It was called Hill 13. The next day we were relieved and told to rest for three hours, but it wasn't more than half an hour before the relieving regiment came running back. The Turks had returned and recaptured their trench. On June 6th my favourite officer was killed and no end of us butchered, but we managed to get hold of Hill 13 again. We found a great muddle, carnage and men without rifles shouting '*Allah! Allah!*', which is God's name in the Turkish language. Of the sixty men I had started out to war from Harwich with, there were only three left.

We set to work to bury people. We pushed them into the sides of the trench but bits of them kept getting uncovered and sticking out, like people in a badly made bed. Hands were the worst; they would escape from the sand, pointing, begging – even waving! There was one which we all shook when we passed, saying, 'Good morning', in a posh voice. Everybody did it. The bottom of the trench was springy like a mattress because of all the bodies underneath. At night, when the stench was worse, we tied crêpe round our mouths and noses. This crêpe had been given to us because it was supposed to prevent us being gassed. The flies entered the trenches at night and lined them completely with a density which was like moving cloth. We killed millions by slapping our spades along the trench walls but the next night it would be just as bad. We were all lousy and we couldn't stop shitting because we had caught dysentery. We wept, not because we were frightened but because we were so dirty.

Mobile Hospital Unit with the Russian Army, Galicia, 2 June 1915

Hugh Walpole

The dawn was beautiful. Soon after we went off to look for the battle. The cannons were booming now in the forest. We went off in our haycarts to look for them. We got right into the forests which were lovely in the early morning, the sky red and gold, the birds singing. Although the cannon sounded so near we found nothing there and went off to another part. Here we found plenty, and soon we were settled just behind a trench with a battery banging in our ear. The soldiers had settled into the trench as though they had been born in it and they looked at us with a kind of amiable indifference. Then came a long wait. I got a bad headache from the noise of the battery and felt lonely and miserable – not frightened, though shrapnel was singing over our heads. After five we moved down to another trench where I sat until dark. Nice old colonel here – fine old farm with a beautiful old tree – all very merry here, beautiful hot suppers, soldiers sewing, laughing, waiting. Old Colonel tells stories about lovely women when the noise pauses. At dark set off to find dead. This really rather alarming, the hedges filled with silent soldiers, the moonlight making everything unreal and unsafe. We found our men then were met by an officer with a large silent company behind him who told us that we must hurry as they were going to begin an attack. We *did* hurry, and just as we got our carts out of the position and began to climb the hill, the whole landscape behind us, which had been dead still, cracked into sound. The cannon broke out on every side of us – fire and flashes and coloured lights and a noise as though the sky, made of china, had broken into a million pieces and fallen — a magnificent unforgettable spectacle.

With Austrian Cavalry on the Eastern Front, August 1915

Oskar Kokoschka

There was something stirring at the edge of the forest. Dismount! Lead horses! Our line was joined by volunteers, and we beat forward into the bushes as if we were going out to shoot pheasant. The enemy was withdrawing deeper into the forest, firing only sporadically. So we had to mount again, which was always the worst part, for since conscription had been introduced the requisitioned horses were as gun-shy as the reservists who had been called up were wretched horsemen. After all, most of them were used to sitting only on an office chair. In the forest suddenly we were met by a hail of bullets so near and so thick that one seemed to see each bullet flitting past; it was like a startled swarm of wasps. Charge! Now the great day had come, the day for which I too had been longing. I still had enough presence of mind to urge my mount forward and to one side, out of the throng of other horses that had now gone wild, as if chased by ghosts, the congestion being made worse by more coming up from the rear and galloping over the fallen men and beasts. I wanted to settle this thing on my own and to look the enemy straight in the face. A hero's death — fair enough! But I had no wish to be trampled to death like a worm. The Russians had lured us into a trap. I had actually set eyes on the Russian machine-gun before I felt a dull blow on my temple.

The sun and the moon were both shining at once and my head ached like mad. What on earth was I to do with this scent of flowers? Some flower — I couldn't remember its name however I racked my brains. And all that yelling round me and the moaning of the wounded, which seemed to fill the whole forest — that must have been what brought me round. Good lord, they must be in agony! Then I became absorbed by the fact that I couldn't control the cavalry boot with the leg in it, which was moving about too far away, although it belonged to me. I recognized the boot by the spur: contrary to regulations, my spurs had no sharp rowels. Over on the grass there were two captains in Russian uniform dancing a ballet, running up and kissing each other on the cheeks like two young girls. That would have been against regulations in our army. I had a tiny round hole in my head. My horse, lying on top of me, had lashed out one last time before dying, and that had brought me to my senses. I tried to say something, but my mouth was stiff with blood, which was beginning to congeal. The shadows all round me were growing huger and huger, and I wanted to ask how it was that the sun and moon were both shining at the same time. I wanted to point at the sky, but my arm wouldn't move. Perhaps I lay there unconscious for several days.

Lance-Corporal Baxter Wins the DCM, Western Front, September 1915

Robert Graves

From the morning of September 24th to the night of October 3rd, I had in all eight hours of sleep. I kept myself awake and alive by drinking about a bottle of whisky a day. I had never drunk it before, and have seldom drunk it since; it certainly helped me then. We had no blankets, greatcoats, or waterproof sheets, nor any time or material to build new shelters. The rain poured down. Every night we went out to fetch in the dead of the other battalions. The Germans continued indulgent and we had few casualties. After the first day or two the corpses swelled and stank. I vomited more than once while superintending the carrying. Those we could not get in from the German wire continued to swell until the wall of the stomach collapsed, either naturally or when punctured by a bullet; a disgusting smell would float across. The colour of the dead faces changed from white to yellow-grey, to red, to purple, to green, to black, to slimy.

On the morning of the 27th a cry arose from No Man's Land. A wounded soldier of the Middlesex had recovered consciousness after two days. He lay close to the German wire. Our men heard it and looked at each other. We had a tender-hearted lance-corporal named Baxter. He was the man to boil up a special dixie for the sentries of his section when they came off duty. As soon as he heard the wounded Middlesex man, he ran along the trench calling for a volunteer to help fetch him in. Of course, no one would go; it was death to put one's head over the parapet. When he came running to ask me I excused myself as being the only officer in the company. I would come out with him at dusk, I said – not now. So he went alone. He jumped quickly over the parapet, then strolled across No Man's Land, waving a handkerchief; the Germans fired to frighten him, but since he persisted they let him come up close. Baxter continued towards them and, when he got to the Middlesex man, stopped and pointed to show the Germans what he was at. Then he dressed the man's wounds, gave him a drink of rum and some biscuit that he had with him, and promised to be back again at nightfall. He did come back, with a stretcher party, and the man eventually recovered. I recommended Baxter for the Victoria Cross, being the only officer who had witnessed the action, but the authorities thought it worth no more than a Distinguished Conduct Medal.

Gallipoli: The Allied Evacuation, 19 December 1915

Norman King-Wilson

The abandonment of the Gallipoli Campaign brought about the resignation of Churchill, the chief supporter of the venture.

On the morning of the 19th I got my final orders. By 8 p.m. only eleven men and myself of the FA [Field Ambulance] remained. The men in the trenches spent the last day turning every dugout into a death trap and the most innocent-looking things into infernal machines. Some dugouts would blow up when the doors were opened. A drafting table had several memorandum books lying on it each with electrical connections to an explosive charge sufficient to destroy a platoon. A gramophone, wound up and with record on, ready to be started, was left in one dugout so contrived that the end of the tune meant the death of the listeners. Piles of bully beef tins, turned into diabolical engines of destruction, lay scattered about. In front of the trenches lay miles of trip mines. Hundreds of rifles lay on the top of the parapet, with string tied to trigger, supporting a tin can, into which water from another tin dripped. Flares were arranged in the same way. Really I never thought the British Tommy possessed such diabolical ingenuity.

That evening the 4th CCS [Casualty Clearing Station] officers and myself dined well on supplies left for us. We had a roaring fire in a big dugout, burning someone else's house. We laughed and yarned and jested, waiting, waiting for God knows what, but for something to break the silence that oppressed that vast empty graveyard, not only the graveyard of thousands of good men, but of England's hope in the Dardanelles. The hills seemed to tower in silent might in the pale, misty moonlight, and the few lights upon them flickered like the ghosts of the army that had gone.

U-Boat 202 Attacks, April 1916

Adolf K. G. E. von Spiegel

The steamer appeared to be close to us and looked colossal. I saw the captain walking on his bridge, a small whistle in his mouth. I saw the crew cleaning the deck forward, and I saw, with surprise and a slight shudder, long rows of wooden partitions right along all the decks, from which gleamed the shining black and brown backs of horses.

'Oh, heavens, horses! What a pity, those lovely beasts!

'But it cannot be helped,' I went on thinking. 'War is war, and every horse the fewer on the Western front is a reduction of England's fighting power.' I must acknowledge, however, that the thought of what must come was a most unpleasant one, and I will describe what happened as briefly as possible.

There were only a few more degrees to go before the steamer would be on the correct bearing. She would be there almost immediately; she was passing us at the proper distance, only a few hundred metres away.

'Stand by for firing a torpedo!' I called down to the control room.

That was a cautionary order to all hands on board. Everyone held his breath.

Now the bows of the steamer cut across the zero line of my periscope – now the forecastle – the bridge – the foremast – funnel –

'FIRE!'

A slight tremor went through the boat – the torpedo had gone.

'Beware, when it is released!'

The death-bringing shot was a true one, and the torpedo ran towards the doomed ship at high speed. I could follow its course exactly by the light streak of bubbles which was left in its wake.

'Twenty seconds,' counted the helmsman, who, watch in hand, had to measure the exact interval of time between the departure of the torpedo and its arrival at its destination.

'Twenty-three seconds.' Soon, soon this violent, terrifying thing would happen. I saw that the bubble-track of the torpedo had been discovered on the bridge of the steamer, as frightened arms pointed towards the water and the captain put his hands in front of his eyes and waited resignedly. Then a frightful explosion followed, and we were all thrown against one another by the concussion, and then, like Vulcan, huge and majestic, a column of water two hundred metres high and fifty metres broad, terrible in its beauty and power, shot up to the heavens.

'Hit abaft the second funnel,' I shouted down to the control room.

Then they fairly let themselves go down below. There was a real wave of enthusiasm, arising from hearts freed from suspense, a wave which rushed through the whole boat and whose joyous echoes reached me in the conning tower. And over there? War is a hard task master. A terrible drama was being enacted on board the ship, which was hard hit and in a sinking condition. She had a heavy and rapidly increasing list towards us.

All her decks lay visible to me. From all the hatchways a storming, despairing mass of men were fighting their way on deck, grimy stokers, officers, soldiers, grooms, cooks. They all rushed, ran, screamed for boats, tore and thrust one another from the ladders leading down to them, fought for the lifebelts and jostled one another on the sloping deck. All amongst them, rearing, slipping horses are wedged. The starboard boats could not be lowered on account of the list; everyone therefore ran across to the port boats, which, in the hurry and panic, had been lowered with great stupidity either half full or overcrowded. The men left behind were wringing their hands in despair and running to and fro along the decks; finally they threw themselves into the water so as to swim to the boats.

Then – a second explosion, followed by the escape of white hissing steam from all hatchways and scuttles. The white steam drove the horses mad. I saw a beautiful long-tailed dapple-grey horse take a mighty leap over the berthing rails and land into a fully laden boat. At that point I could not bear the sight any longer, and I lowered the periscope and dived deep.

The Battle of Jutland: 'X' Turret, Battlecruiser *Queen Mary*, 31 May 1916

Ernest Francis

Jutland, the only major encounter between the British and German fleets in World War I, was claimed as a victory by both sides – by the Germans because they destroyed many more ships and men; by the British because they retained control of the North Sea.

The gun crews were absolutely perfect, inclined to be a little slow in loading, but I gave them a yell and pointed out to them that I wanted a steady stride. After that everything went like clockwork ... My number 3 said, 'PO Francis, can you see what we are up against?' Well I had been anxious to have a look round, but could not spare the time, but as soon as my gun had fired and while the loading was being completed, I had a look through the periscopes, and it seemed to me that there were hundreds of masts and funnels. I dropped back into my seat and laid my gun by pointer, being in director firing, and while the loading was being completed again, I told them there were a few battle cruisers out, not wishing to put a damper on them in any way; not that I think it would have done so, as they were all splendid fellows and backed me up magnificently.

Up till now I had not noticed any noise, such as being struck by a shell, but afterwards there was a heavy blow, struck, I should imagine, in the after 4-inch battery, and a lot of dust and pieces flying around on the top of 'X' turret. My attention was called by the turret trainer, AB Long, who reported the front glass of his periscope blocked up. This was not very important because we were in director training, but some one in rear heard him report his glass foul and without orders dashed on top and cleared it. He must have been smashed up as he did, for he fell in front of the periscope and then apparently fell on to the turret. I wish I knew his name, poor chap, but it's no use guessing.

Another shock was felt shortly after this, but it did not affect the turret, so no notice was taken. Then the T.S. reported to Lieutenant Ewert that the third ship of the line was dropping out. First blood to *Queen Mary*. The shout they gave was good to hear. I could not resist giving a quick look at her, at their request, and I found that the third ship of the line was going down by the bows. I felt the turret travel a bit faster than she had been moving, and surmised we must have shifted on to the fourth ship of the line; being in director firing, no orders were required for training.

I looked again and found the third ship of the line was gone, so I turned to the spare gun layer, PO Killick, who was recording the number of rounds fired, and he said thirty some odd figures, I didn't catch the exact number. A few more rounds were fired when I took another look through my telescope and there was quite a fair distance between the second ship and what I believed was the fourth ship, due I think to the third ship going under. Flames were belching from what I took to be the fourth ship of the line, then came the big explosion which shook us a bit, and on looking at the pressure gauge I saw the pressure had failed. Immediately after that came, what I term, the big smash, and I was dangling in the air on a bowline, which saved me from being thrown down on the floor of the turret. These bowlines were an idea I brought into my turret and each man in the gunhouse was supplied with one, and as far as I noticed the men who had them on were not injured in the big smash. Nos. 2 and 3 of the left gun slipped down under the gun and the gun appeared to me to have fallen through its trunnions and smashed up these two numbers.

Everything in the ship went as quiet as a church, the floor of the turret was bulged up and the guns were absolutely useless. I must mention here that there was not a sign of excitement. One man turned to me and said, 'What do you think has happened?' I said, 'Steady, everyone, I will speak to Mr Ewert.' I went back to the Cabinet and said, 'What do you think has happened, Sir?' He said, 'God knows!' 'Well, Sir,' I said, 'it's no use keeping them all down here. Why not send them up on the 4-inch guns, and give them a chance to fight it out? As soon as the Germans find we are out of action they will concentrate on us and we shall all be going sky high.' He said, 'Yes, good idea, just see if the 4-inch guns aft are still standing.'

I put my head through the hole in the roof of the turret and nearly fell through again. The after 4-inch battery was smashed out of all recognition, and then I noticed that the ship had got an awful list to port. I dropped back again into the turret and told Lieutenant Ewert the state of affairs. He said, 'Francis, we can do no more than give them a chance, clear the turret.'

'Clear the turret,' I said, and out they went. PO Stares was the last I saw coming up from the Working Chamber, and I asked him whether he had passed the order to the Magazine and Shell Room, and he told me it was no use as the water was right up to the trunk leading to the shell room, so the bottom of the ship must have been torn out of her. Then I said, 'Why didn't you come up?' He simply said, 'There was no order to leave the turret.'

I went through the Cabinet and out on top and Lieutenant Ewert was following me; suddenly he stopped and went back into the turret. I believe he went back because he thought someone was inside . . .

I was halfway down the ladder at the back of the turret when Lieutenant Ewert went back. The ship had an awful list to port by this time, so much so that men getting off the ladder went sliding down to port. I got to the bottom rung of the ladder and could not, by my own efforts, reach the stanchions lying on the deck from the ship's side, starboard side. I knew if I let go I should go sliding down to port like some of the others must have done, and probably get smashed up sliding down. Two of my turret's crew, seeing my difficulty, came to my assistance. They were AB Long, Turret Trainer, and AB Lane, left gun No 4. Lane held Long at full length from the ship's side and I dropped from the ladder, caught Long's legs and so gained the starboard side. These two men had no thought for their own safety; they knew I wanted assistance and that was good enough for them. They were both worth a VC twice over.

When I got to the ship's side, there seemed to be quite a fair crowd, and they didn't appear to be very anxious to take to the water. I called out to them, 'Come on you chaps, who's coming for a swim?' Someone answered, 'She will float for a long time yet,' but something, I don't pretend to know what it was, seemed to be urging me to get away, so I clambered over the slimy bilge keel and fell off into the water, followed I should think by about five more men. I struck away from the ship as hard as I could and must have covered nearly fifty yards when there was a big smash, and stopping and looking round, the air seemed to be full of fragments and flying pieces.

A large piece seemed to be right above my head, and acting on impulse, I dipped under to avoid being struck, and stayed under as long as I could, and then came to the top again, and coming behind me I heard a rush of water, which looked very like surf breaking on a beach and I realized it was the suction or backwash from the ship which had just gone. I hardly had time to fill my lungs with air when it was on me. I felt it was no use struggling against it, so I let myself go for a moment or two, then I struck out, but I felt it was a losing game and remarked to myself, 'What's the use of you struggling, you're done,' and I actually ceased my efforts to reach the top, when a small voice seemed to say, 'Dig out.'

I started afresh, and something bumped against me. I grasped it and afterwards found it was a large hammock, but I felt I was getting very weak and roused myself sufficiently to look around for something more substantial to support me. Floating right in front of me was what I believe to be the centre bulk of our Pattern 4 target. I managed to push myself on the hammock close to the timber and grasped a piece of rope hanging over the side. My next difficulty was to get on top and with a small amount of exertion I kept on. I managed to reeve my arms through a strop and I must have become unconscious.

When I came to my senses again I was halfway off the spar but I managed to get back again. I was very sick and seemed to be full of oil fuel. My eyes were blocked up completely with it and I could not see. I suppose the oil had got a bit crusted and dry. I managed by turning back the sleeve of my jersey, which was thick with oil, to expose a part of the sleeve of my flannel, and thus managed to get the thick oil off my face and eyes, which were aching awfully. Then I looked and I believed I was the only one left of that fine Ship's Company. What had really happened was the *Laurel* had come and picked up the remainder and not seeing me got away out of the zone of fire, so how long I was in the water I do not know. I was miserably cold, but not without hope of being picked up, as it seemed to me that I had only to keep quiet and a ship would come for me.

After what seemed ages to me, some destroyers came racing along, and I got up on the spar, steadied myself for the moment, and waved my arms. The *Petard*, one of our big destroyers, saw me and came over, but when I got on the spar to wave to them, the swell rolled the spar over and I rolled off. I was nearly exhausted again getting back. The destroyer came up and a line was thrown to me, which, needless to say, I grabbed hold of for all I was worth, and was quickly hauled up on to the deck of the destroyer.

The Somme: 21st Casualty Clearing Station, 1–3 July 1916

A Padre's View

The Reverend John M. S. Walker

At the Somme (1 July – 13 November 1916) the British sustained 60,000 casualties on the first day. In October torrential rains turned the battlefield to a quagmire. By mid-November the Allies had advanced 5 miles at a cost of 450,000 German, 200,000 French and 420,000 British lives.

Saturday, 1 July. 7.30, the heavens and earth were rolling up, the crazy hour had begun, every gun we owned fired as hard as ever it could for more than an hour. From a hill near Veils over us to left and right great observation balloons hung, eighteen in view. Aeroplanes dashed about, morning mist and gun smoke obscured the view. We got back for a late breakfast and soon the wounded by German shells came in, then all day long cars of dying and wounded, but all cheerful for they told us of a day of glorious successes. They are literally piled up – beds gone, lucky to get space on floor of tent, hut or ward, and though the surgeons work like Trojans many must yet die for lack of operation. All the CCSs [Casualty Clearing Stations] are overflowing.

Later. We have 1,500 in and still they come, 300–400 officers, it is a sight – chaps with fearful wounds lying in agony, many so patient, some make a noise, one goes to a stretcher, lays one's hand on the forehead, it is cold, strike a match, he is dead – here a Communion, there an absolution, there a drink, there a madman, there a hot-water bottle and so on – one madman was swearing and kicking, I gave him a drink, he tried to bite my hand and squirted the water from his mouth into my face – well, it is an experience beside which all previous experience pales. Oh I am tired, excuse writing.

2 July. What a day, I had no corner in the hospital even for Holy Communion, the Colonel said that no services might be under cover, fortunately it was fine so rigged up my packing-case altar on a wood behind the sisters' camp. Then all day squatting or kneeling by stretchers administering Holy Communion, etc. Twice I went to bury, of course we used the trench we had prepared in a field adjoining. I first held a service of consecration, when I turned round the old man labouring in the field was on his knees in the soil. I buried thirty-seven but have some left over till tomorrow. Saddest place of all is the moribund ward, two large tents laced together packed with dying officers and men, here they lie given up as hopeless, of course they do not know it. But I can't write. I am too tired and I have some patients' letters.

3 July. Now I know something of the horrors of war, the staff is redoubled but what of that, imagine 1,000 badly wounded *per diem.* The surgeons are beginning to get sleep, because after working night and day they realize we may be at this for some months, as Verdun. We hear of great successes but there are of course setbacks and one hears of ramparts of dead English and Germans. Oh, if you could see our wards, tents, huts, crammed with terrible wounds — see the rows of abdominals and lung penetrations dying — you meet a compound fracture of femur walking about — in strict confidence, please, I got hold of some morphia and I go to that black hole of Calcutta (Moribund) and use it or I creep into the long tents where two or three hundred Germans lie, you can imagine what attention they get with our own neglected, the cries and groans are too much to withstand and I cannot feel less pity for them than for our own.

The First Tanks in Action, 15 September 1916

Bert Chaney

The British Mark I tanks were American Holt tractors, adapted for military use, weighing 30 tons and capable of about 4 mph. Thirty-six of them spearheaded the British attempt, on 15 September, to break through on the Somme.

We heard strange throbbing noises, and lumbering slowly towards us came three huge mechanical monsters such as we had never seen before. My first impression was that they looked ready to topple on their noses, but their tails and the two little wheels at the back held them down and kept them level. Big metal things they were, with two sets of caterpillar wheels that went right round the body. There was a bulge on each side with a door in the bulging part, and machine-guns on swivels poked out from either side. The engine, a petrol engine of massive proportions, occupied practically all the inside space. Mounted behind each door was a motor-cycle type of saddle seat and there was just about enough room left for the belts of ammunition and the drivers . . .

Instead of going on to the German lines the three tanks assigned to us straddled our front line, stopped and then opened up a murderous machine-gun fire, enfilading us left and right. There they sat, squat monstrous things, noses stuck up in the air, crushing the sides of our trench out of shape with their machine-guns swivelling around and firing like mad.

Everyone dived for cover, except the colonel. He jumped on top of the parapet, shouting at the top of his voice, 'Runner, runner, go tell those tanks to stop firing at once. At once, I say.' By now the enemy fire had risen to a crescendo but, giving no thought to his own personal safety as he saw the tanks firing on his own men, he ran forward and furiously rained blows with his cane on the side of one of the tanks in an endeavour to attract their attention.

Although, what with the sounds of the engines and the firing in such an enclosed space, no one in the tank could hear him, they finally realized they were on the wrong trench and moved on, frightening the Jerries out of their wits and making them scuttle like frightened rabbits.

The End of Zeppelin L31, 1 October 1916

Michael MacDonagh

I saw last night what is probably the most appalling spectacle associated with the war which London is likely to provide – the bringing down in flames of a raiding Zeppelin.

I was late at the office, and leaving it just before midnight was crossing to Blackfriars Bridge to get a tramcar home, when my attention was attracted by frenzied cries of 'Oh! Oh! She's hit!' from some wayfarers who were standing in the middle of the road gazing at the sky in a northern direction. Looking up the clear run of New Bridge Street and Farringdon Road I saw high in the sky a concentrated blaze of searchlights, and in its centre a ruddy glow which rapidly spread into the outline of a blazing airship. Then the searchlights were turned off and the Zeppelin drifted perpendicularly in the darkened sky, a gigantic pyramid of flames, red and orange, like a ruined star falling slowly to earth. Its glare lit up the streets and gave a ruddy tint even to the waters of the Thames.

The spectacle lasted two or three minutes. It was so horribly fascinating that I felt spellbound – almost suffocated with emotion, ready hysterically to laugh or cry. When at last the doomed airship vanished from sight there arose a shout the like of which I never heard in London before – a hoarse shout of mingled execration, triumph and joy; a swelling shout that appeared to be rising from all parts of the metropolis, ever increasing in force and intensity. It was London's *Te Deum* for another crowning deliverance. Four Zeppelins destroyed in a month! . . .

On getting to the office this morning I was ordered off to Potter's Bar, Middlesex, where the Zeppelin had been brought down, about thirteen miles from London. These days trains are infrequent and travel slowly as a war economy. The journey from King's Cross was particularly tedious. The train I caught was packed. My compartment had its twenty seats occupied and ten more passengers found standing room in it. The weather, too, was abominable. Rain fell persistently. We had to walk the two miles to the place where the Zeppelin fell, and over the miry roads and sodden fields hung a thick, clammy mist . . .

I got from a member of the Potter's Bar anti-aircraft battery an account of the bringing down of the Zeppelin. He said the airship was caught in the beams of three searchlights from stations miles apart, and was being fired at by three batteries also from distances widely separated. She turned and twisted, rose and fell, in vain attempts to escape to the shelter of the outer darkness. None of the shells reached her. Then an aeroplane appeared and dropped three flares – the signal to the ground batteries to cease firing as he was about to attack. The airman, flying about the Zeppelin, let go rounds of machine-gun fire at her without effect, until one round fired into her from beneath set her on fire, and down she came a blazing mass, roaring like a furnace, breaking as she fell into two parts which were held together by internal cables until they reached the ground.

The framework of the Zeppelin lay in the field in two enormous heaps, separated from each other by about a hundred yards. Most of the forepart hung suspended from a tree . . .

The crew numbered nineteen. One body was found in the field some distance from the wreckage. He must have jumped from the doomed airship from a considerable height. So great was the force with which he struck the ground that I saw the imprint of his body clearly defined in the stubbly grass. There was a round hole for the head, then deep impressions of the trunk, with outstretched arms, and finally the widely separated legs. Life was in him when he was picked up, but the spark soon went out. He was, in fact, the Commander, who had been in one of the gondolas hanging from the airship . . .

With another journalist I went to the barn where the bodies lay. As we approached we heard a woman say to the sergeant of the party of soldiers in charge, 'May I go in? I would like to see a dead German.' 'No, madam, we cannot admit ladies,' was the reply. Introducing myself as a newspaper reporter, I made the same request. The sergeant said to me, 'If you particularly wish to go in you may. I would, however, advise you not to do so. If you do you will regret your curiosity.' I persisted in my request . . .

Explaining to the sergeant that I particularly wanted to see the body of the Commander, I was allowed to go in. The sergeant removed the covering from one of the bodies which lay apart from the others. The only disfigurement was a slight distortion of the face. It was that of a young man, clean-shaven. He was heavily clad in a dark uniform and overcoat, with a thick muffler round his neck.

I knew who he was. At the office we had had official information of the identity of the Commander and the airship (though publication of both particulars was prohibited), and it was this knowledge that had determined me to see the body. The dead man was Heinrich Mathy, the most renowned of the German airship commanders, and the perished airship was his redoubtable L31. Yes, there he lay in death at my feet, the bugaboo of the Zeppelin

raids, the first and most ruthless of these Pirates of the Air bent on
our destruction.

Birds on the Western Front, 1916

H. H. Munro ('Saki')

Munro, the author, was killed at Beaumont-Hamel on 14 November 1916.

Considering the enormous economic dislocation which the war
operations have caused in the regions where the campaign is raging,
there seems to be very little corresponding disturbance in the bird
life of the same districts. Rats and mice have mobilized and
swarmed into the fighting line, and there has been a partial
mobilization of owls, particularly barn owls, following in the wake
of the mice, and making laudable efforts to thin out their numbers.
What success attends their hunting one cannot estimate; there are
always sufficient mice left over to populate one's dug-out and make
a parade-ground and race-course of one's face at night. In the
matter of nesting accommodation the barn owls are well provided
for; most of the still intact barns in the war zone are requisitioned
for billeting purposes, but there is a wealth of ruined houses, whole
streets and clusters of them, such as can hardly have been available
at any previous moment of the world's history since Nineveh and
Babylon became humanly desolate. Without human occupation
and cultivation there can have been no corn, no refuse, and
consequently very few mice, and the owls of Niveveh cannot have
enjoyed very good hunting; here in Northern France the owls have
desolation and mice at their disposal in unlimited quantities, and as
these birds breed in winter as well as in summer, there should be a
goodly output of war owlets to cope with the swarming generations
of war mice.

Apart from the owls one cannot notice that the campaign is
making any marked difference in the bird life of the countryside.
The vast flocks of crows and ravens that one expected to find in the
neighbourhood of the fighting line are non-existent, which is
perhaps rather a pity. The obvious explanation is that the roar and
crash and fumes of high explosives have driven the crow tribe in

panic from the fighting area; like many obvious explanations, it is not a correct one. The crows of the locality are not attracted to the battlefield, but they certainly are not scared away from it. The rook is normally so gun-shy and nervous where noise is concerned that the sharp banging of a barn door or the report of a toy pistol will sometimes set an entire rookery in commotion; out here I have seen him sedately busy among the refuse heaps of a battered village, with shells bursting at no great distance, and the impatient-sounding, snapping rattle of machine-guns going on all round him; for all the notice that he took he might have been in some peaceful English meadow on a sleepy Sunday afternoon. Whatever else German frightfulness may have done it has not frightened the rook of North-Eastern France; it has made his nerves steadier than they have ever been before, and future generations of small boys, employed in scaring rooks away from the sown crops in the region, will have to invent something in the way of super-frightfulness to achieve their purpose. Crows and magpies are nesting well within the shell-swept area, and over a small beech copse I once saw a pair of crows engaged in hot combat with a pair of sparrow-hawks, while considerably higher in the sky, but almost directly above them, two Allied battle planes were engaging an equal number of enemy aircraft.

Unlike the barn owls, the magpies have had their choice of building sites considerably restricted by the ravages of war; the whole avenues of poplars, where they were accustomed to construct their nests, have been blown to bits, leaving nothing but dreary-looking rows of shattered and splintered trunks to show where once they stood. Affection for a particular tree has in one case induced a pair of magpies to build their bulky, domed nest in the battered remnants of a poplar of which so little remained standing that the nest looked almost bigger than the tree; the effect rather suggested an archiepiscopal enthronement taking place in the ruined remains of Melrose Abbey. The magpie, wary and suspicious in his wild state, must be rather intrigued at the change that has come over the erstwhile fearsome not-to-be-avoided human, stalking everywhere over the earth as its possessor, who now creeps about in screened and sheltered ways, as chary of showing himself in the open as the shyest of wild creatures.

The buzzard, the earnest seeker after mice, does not seem to be taking any war risks, at least I have never seen one out here, but kestrels hover about all day in the hottest parts of the line, not in the least disconcerted, apparently, when a promising mouse-area suddenly rises in the air in a cascade of black or yellow earth. Sparrow-hawks are fairly numerous, and a mile or two back from the firing line I saw a pair of hawks that I took to be red-legged falcons, circling over the top of an oak copse. According to investigations made by Russian naturalists, the effect of the war on bird life on the Eastern front has been more marked than it has been over here. 'During the first year of the war rooks disappeared, larks no longer sang in the fields, the wild pigeon disappeared also.' The skylark in this region has stuck tenaciously to the meadows and crop-lands that have been seamed and bisected with trenches and honeycombed with shell-holes. In the chill, misty hour of gloom that precedes a rainy dawn, when nothing seemed alive except a few wary waterlogged sentries and many scuttling rats, the lark would suddenly dash skyward and pour forth a song of ecstatic jubilation that sounded horribly forced and insincere. It seemed scarcely possible that the bird could carry its insouciance to the length of attempting to rear a brood in that desolate wreckage of shattered clods and gaping shell-holes, but once, having occasion to throw myself down with some abruptness on my face, I found myself nearly on the top of a brood of young larks. Two of them had already been hit by something, and were in rather a battered condition, but the survivors seemed as tranquil and comfortable as the average nestling.

At the corner of a stricken wood (which has had a name made for it in history, but shall be nameless here), at a moment when lyddite and shrapnel and machine-gun fire swept and raked and bespattered that devoted spot as though the artillery of an entire division had suddenly concentrated on it, a wee hen chaffinch flitted wistfully to and fro, amid splintered and falling branches that had never a green bough left on them. The wounded lying there, if any of them noticed the small bird, may well have wondered why anything having wings and no pressing reason for remaining should have chosen to stay in such a place. There was a battered orchard alongside the stricken wood, and the probable explanation of the bird's presence was that it had a nest of young ones whom it was too scared to feed, too loyal to desert. Later on, a small flock of chaffinches blundered into the wood, which they were doubtless in the habit of using as a highway to their feeding grounds; unlike the solitary hen bird, they made no secret of their desire to get away as fast as their dazed wits would let them. The only other bird I ever saw there was a magpie, flying low over the wreckage of fallen tree limbs; 'one for sorrow,' says the old superstition. There was sorrow enough in that wood.

The English gamekeeper, whose knowledge of wild life usually runs on limited and perverted lines, has evolved a sort of religion as to the nervous debility of even the hardiest game birds; according to his beliefs a terrier trotting across a field in which a partridge is nesting, or a mouse-hawking kestrel hovering over the hedge, is sufficient cause to drive the distracted bird off its eggs and send it whirring into the next county.

The partridge of the war zone shows no signs of such sensitive nerves. The rattle and rumble of transport, the constant coming and going of bodies of troops, the incessant rattle of musketry and deafening explosions of artillery, the night-long flare and flicker of star-shells, have not sufficed to scare the local birds away from their chosen feeding grounds, and to all appearances they have not been deterred from raising their broods. Gamekeepers who are serving with the colours might seize the opportunity to indulge in a little useful nature study.

Gassed: Messines Ridge, 7 June 1917

William Pressey

From 1915 to 1918 the Germans used a succession of poison gases – chlorine, phosgene and mustard gas – each of which was promptly duplicated on the Allied side.

We had been shooting most of the night and the Germans had been hitting back with shrapnel, high explosive and gas shells. With the terrific noise and blinding flashes of gunfire, if a lull occurred for only a few minutes and you were leaning against something, you had just to close your eyes and you were asleep. Nearing daylight we were told to rest. We dived into the dugout, I pulled off my tunic and boots and was asleep in no time at all.

I was awakened by a terrific crash. The roof came down on my chest and legs and I couldn't move anything but my head. I thought,

'So this is it, then.' I found I could hardly breathe. Then I heard voices. Other fellows with gas helmets on, looking very frightening in the half-light, were lifting timber off me and one was forcing a gas helmet on me. Even when you were all right, to wear a gas helmet was uncomfortable, your nose pinched, sucking air through a canister of chemicals. As I was already choking I remember fighting against having this helmet on.

The next thing I knew was being carried on a stretcher past our officers and some distance from the guns. I heard someone ask, 'Who's that?' 'Bombardier Pressey, sir.' 'Bloody hell.' I was put into an ambulance and taken to the base, where we were placed on the stretchers side by side on the floor of a marquee, with about twelve inches in between. I suppose I resembled a kind of fish with my mouth open gasping for air. It seemed as if my lungs were gradually shutting up and my heart pounded away in my ears like the beat of a drum. On looking at the chap next to me I felt sick, for green stuff was oozing from the side of his mouth.

To get air into my lungs was real agony and the less I got the less the pain. I dozed off for short periods but seemed to wake in a sort of panic. To ease the pain in my chest I may subconsciously have stopped breathing, until the pounding of my heart woke me up. I was always surprised when I found myself awake, for I felt sure that I would die in my sleep. So little was known about treatment for various gases, that I never had treatment for phosgene, the type I was supposed to have had. And I'm sure that the gas some of the other poor fellows had swallowed was worse than phosgene. Now and then orderlies would carry out a stretcher.

The Battle of Langemarck, 27 August 1917

Edwin Campion Vaughan

Up the road we staggered, shells bursting around us. A man stopped dead in front of me, and exasperated I cursed him and butted him with my knee. Very gently he said, 'I'm blind, sir,' and turned to show me his eyes and nose torn away by a piece of shell. 'Oh God! I'm sorry, sonny,' I said. 'Keep going on the hard part,' and left him staggering back in his darkness. At the Triangle the shelling was lighter and the rifle fire far above our heads. Around us were numerous dead, and in shell-holes where they had crawled to safety were wounded men. Many others, too weak to move, were lying where they had fallen and they cheered us faintly as we passed: 'Go on boys! Give 'em hell!' Several wounded men of the 8th Worcesters and 7th Warwicks jumped out of their shell-holes and joined us.

A tank had churned its way slowly round behind Springfield and opened fire; a moment later I looked and nothing remained of it but a crumpled heap of iron; it had been hit by a large shell. It was now almost dark and there was no firing from the enemy; ploughing across the final stretch of mud, I saw grenades bursting around the pillbox and a party of British rushed in from the other side. As we all closed in, the Boche garrison ran out with their hands up; in the confused party I recognized Reynolds of the 7th Battalion, who had been working forward all the afternoon. We sent the sixteen prisoners back across the open but they had only gone a hundred yards when a German machine-gun mowed them down.

Reynolds and I held a rapid conference and decided that the cemetery and Spot Farm were far too strongly held for us to attack, especially as it was then quite dark; so we formed a line with my party on the left in touch with the Worcesters, who had advanced some 300 yards further than we, and Reynolds formed a flank guard back to the line where our attack had broken. I entered Springfield, which was to be my HQ.

It was a strongly built pillbox, almost undamaged; the three defence walls were about ten feet thick, each with a machine-gun position, while the fourth wall, which faced our new line, had one small doorway – about three feet square. Crawling through this I found the interior in a horrible condition; water in which floated indescribable filth reached our knees; two dead Boche sprawled face downwards and another lay across a wire bed. Everywhere was dirt and rubbish and the stench was nauseating.

On one of the machine-gun niches lay an unconscious German officer, wearing two black and white medal ribbons; his left leg was torn away, the bone shattered and only a few shreds of flesh and muscle held it on. A tourniquet had been applied, but had slipped and the blood was pouring out. I commenced at once to readjust this and had just stopped the bleeding when he came round and gazed in bewilderment at my British uniform. He tried to struggle up, but was unable to do so and, reassuring him, I made him comfortable, arranging a pillow out of a Boche pack. He asked me faintly what had happened, and in troops' German I told him 'Drei caput – others Kamerad,' at which he dropped back his head with a pitiful air of resignation. I offered him my waterbottle, but when he smelled the rum he would not touch it, nor would he take whisky from my flask, but when one of my troops gave him water he gulped it greedily.

Then he became restless, twisting and turning so that his leg kept rolling off the platform and dragging from his hip; I took it on to my knees and moved it gently with him until at last he lay quiet. On one of the beds was a German flash lamp and I sent a fellow out to signal to our lines '8th Warwick in Springfield'. Time after time he sent it, but there was no acknowledgement. All was quiet around us now, but the Germans were still shelling the St Julien road. Suddenly I heard a commotion at the doorway and two fellows crawled in dragging a stretcher which they hoisted on to the wire bed in front of me. It was an officer of the 8th Worcester who greeted me cheerily.

'Where are you hit?' I asked.

'In the back near the spine. Could you shift my gas helmet from under me?'

I cut away the satchel and dragged it out; then he asked for a cigarette. Dunham produced one and he put it between his lips; I struck a match and held it across, but the cigarette had fallen on his chest and he was dead.

I picked up a German automatic from the bed and in examining it, loosed off a shot which hit the concrete near the Boche's head; he gave a great start and turned towards me, smiling faintly when he saw that it was accidental. Then he commenced to struggle to reach his tunic pocket; I felt in it for him and produced three pieces of sugar. Taking them in his trembling hand, he let one fall into the water, gazing regretfully after it; another he handed to me. It was crumbling and saturated with blood so I slipped it into my pocket whilst pretending to eat it. I now produced some bread and meat; he would not have any, but I ate heartily sitting on the wire bed with my feet in the water and my hands covered in mud and blood . . .

Now with a shrieking and crashing, shells began to descend upon us from our own guns, while simultaneously German guns began to shell their own lines. In my haversack all this time I had been carrying a treasure which I now produced – a box of 100 Abdulla Egyptians. I had just opened the box when there was a rattle of rifles outside and a voice yelled, 'Germans coming over, sir!' Cigarettes went flying into the water as I hurled myself through the doorway and ran forward into the darkness where my men were firing. I almost ran into a group of Germans and at once shouted, 'Ceasefire!' for they were unarmed and were 'doing Kamerad'.

The poor devils were terrified; suspicious of a ruse I stared into the darkness while I motioned them back against the wall with my revolver. They thought I was going to shoot them and one little fellow fell on his knees babbling about his wife and 'zwei Kinder'. Going forward I found that several of the party were dead and another died as I dragged him in. The prisoners clustered round me, bedraggled and heart-broken, telling me of the terrible time they had been having, 'Nichts essen,' 'Nichts trinken,' always shells, shells, shells! They said that all of their company would willingly come over. I could not spare a man to take them back, so I put them into shell-holes with my men who made great fuss of them, sharing their scanty rations with them.

Re-entering the pillbox I found the Boche officer quite talkative. He told me how he had kept his garrison fighting on, and would never have allowed them to surrender. He had seen us advancing and was getting his guns on to us when a shell from the tank behind had come through the doorway, killed two men and blown his leg off. His voice trailed away and he relapsed into a stupor. So I went out again into the open and walked along our line; a few heavies were still pounding about us, but a more terrible sound now reached my ears.

From the darkness on all sides came the groans and wails of wounded men; faint, long, sobbing moans of agony, and despairing shrieks. It was too horribly obvious that dozens of men with serious wounds must have crawled for safety into new shell-holes, and now the water was rising about them and, powerless to move, they were slowly drowning. Horrible visions came to me with those cries – of Woods and Kent, Edge and Taylor, lying maimed out there trusting that their pals would find them, and now dying terribly, alone amongst the dead in the inky darkness. And we could do nothing to help them; Dunham was crying quietly beside me, and all the men were affected by the piteous cries.

The Execution of Mata Hari, 18 October 1917

Henry G. Wales

Mata Hari (b. 1876) was apparently a double agent, but the extent of her espionage activities remains uncertain.

Mata Hari, which is Javanese for Eye-of-the-Morning, is dead. She was shot as a spy by a firing squad of Zouaves at the Vincennes Barracks. She died facing death literally, for she refused to be blindfolded.

Gertrud Margarete Zelle, for that was the real name of the beautiful Dutch-Javanese dancer, did appeal to President Poincaré for a reprieve, but he refused to intervene.

The first intimation she received that her plea had been denied was when she was led at daybreak from her cell in the Saint-Lazare prison to a waiting automobile and then rushed to the barracks where the firing squad awaited her.

Never once had the iron will of the beautiful woman failed her. Father Arbaux, accompanied by two sisters of charity, Captain Bouchardon, and Maître Clunet, her lawyer, entered her cell, where she was still sleeping – a calm, untroubled sleep, it was remarked by the turnkeys and trusties.

The sisters gently shook her. She arose and was told that her hour had come.

'May I write two letters?' was all she asked.

Consent was given immediately by Captain Bouchardon, and pen, ink, paper, and envelopes were given to her.

She seated herself at the edge of the bed and wrote the letters with feverish haste. She handed them over to the custody of her lawyer.

Then she drew on her stockings, black, silken, filmy things, grotesque in the circumstances. She placed her high-heeled slippers on her feet and tied the silken ribbons over her insteps.

She arose and took the long black velvet cloak, edged around the bottom with fur and with a huge square fur collar hanging down the back, from a hook over the head of her bed. She placed this cloak over the heavy silk kimono which she had been wearing over her nightdress.

Her wealth of black hair was still coiled about her head in braids.

She put on a large, flapping black felt hat with a black silk ribbon and bow. Slowly and indifferently, it seemed, she pulled on a pair of black kid gloves. Then she said calmly:

'I am ready.'

The party slowly filed out of her cell to the waiting automobile.

The car sped through the heart of the sleeping city. It was scarcely half-past five in the morning and the sun was not yet fully up.

Clear across Paris the car whirled to the Caserne de Vincennes, the barracks of the old fort which the Germans stormed in 1870.

The troops were already drawn up for the execution. The twelve Zouaves, forming the firing squad, stood in line, their rifles at ease. A subofficer stood behind them, sword drawn.

The automobile stopped, and the party descended, Mata Hari last. The party walked straight to the spot, where a little hummock of earth reared itself seven or eight feet high and afforded a background for such bullets as might miss the human target.

As Father Arbaux spoke with the condemned women, a French officer approached, carrying a white cloth.

'The blindfold,' he whispered to the nuns who stood there and handed it to them.

'Must I wear that?' asked Mata Hari, turning to her lawyer, as her eyes glimpsed the blindfold.

Maître Clunet turned interrogatively to the French officer.

'If Madame prefers not, it makes no difference,' replied the officer, hurriedly turning away.

Mata Hari was not bound and she was not blindfolded. She stood gazing steadfastly at her executioners, when the priest, the nuns, and her lawyer stepped away from her.

The officer in command of the firing squad, who had been watching his men like a hawk that none might examine his rifle and try to find out whether he was destined to fire the blank cartridge which was in the breech of one rifle, seemed relieved that the business would soon be over.

A sharp, crackling command, and the file of twelve men assumed rigid positions at attention. Another command, and their rifles were at their shoulders; each man gazed down his barrel at the breast of the woman which was the target.

She did not move a muscle.

The underofficer in charge had moved to a position where from the corners of their eyes they could see him. His sword was extended in the air.

It dropped. The sun – by this time up – flashed on the burnished blade as it described an arc in falling. Simultaneously the sound of the volley rang out. Flame and a tiny puff of greyish smoke issued from the muzzle of each rifle. Automatically the men dropped their arms.

At the report Mata Hari fell. She did not die as actors and moving-picture stars would have us believe that people die when they are shot. She did not throw up her hands nor did she plunge straight forward or straight back.

Instead she seemed to collapse. Slowly, inertly, she settled to her knees, her head up always, and without the slightest change of expression on her face. For the fraction of a second it seemed she tottered there, on her knees, gazing directly at those who had taken her life. Then she fell backward, bending at the waist, with her legs doubled up beneath her. She lay prone, motionless, with her face turned towards the sky.

A non-commissioned officer, who accompanied a lieutenant, drew his revolver from the big, black holster strapped about his waist. Bending over, he placed the muzzle of the revolver almost – but not quite – against the left temple of the spy. He pulled the trigger, and the bullet tore into the brain of the woman.

Mata Hari was surely dead.

An American Journalist at the Storming of the Winter Palace, St Petersburg, 7 November 1917

John Reed

After the abdication of Tsar Nicholas II the Provisional Government tried to keep Russia in the war. But the Bolshevik programme of 'peace, land and bread' won popular support, and on 7 November a nearly bloodless Bolshevik coup seized government buildings, telegraph stations and other strategic points.

Like a black river, filling all the street, without song or cheer we poured through the Red Arch, where the man just ahead of me said in a low voice, 'Look out, comrades! Don't trust them. They will fire, surely!' In the open we began to run, stooping low and bunching together, and jammed up suddenly behind the pedestal of the Alexander Column . . .

After a few minutes huddling there, some hundreds of men, the army seemed reassured and without any orders suddenly began again to flow forward. By this time, in the light that streamed out of all the Winter Palace windows, I could see that the first two or three hundred men were Red Guards, with only a few scattered soldiers. Over the barricade of firewood we clambered, and leaping down inside gave a triumphant shout as we stumbled on a heap of rifles thrown down by the *yunkers* who had stood there. On both sides of the main gateway the doors stood wide open, light streamed out, and from the huge pile came not the slightest sound.

Carried along by the eager wave of men we were swept into the right-hand entrance, opening into a great bare vaulted room, the cellar of the east wing, from which issued a maze of corridors and staircases. A number of huge packing cases stood about, and upon these the Red Guards and soldiers fell furiously, battering them open with the butts of their rifles, and pulling out carpets, curtains, linen, porcelain, plates, glassware . . . One man went strutting around with a bronze clock perched on his shoulder; another found a plume of ostrich feathers, which he stuck in his hat. The looting was just beginning when somebody cried, 'Comrades! Don't take anything. This is the property of the People!' Immediately twenty voices were crying, 'Stop! Put everything back! Don't take anything! Property of the People!' Many hands dragged the spoilers down. Damask and tapestry were snatched from the arms of those who had them; two men took away the bronze clock. Roughly and hastily the things were crammed back in their cases, and self-appointed sentinels stood guard. It was all utterly spontaneous. Through corridors and up staircases the cry could be heard growing fainter and fainter in the distance, 'Revolutionary discipline! Property of the People . . .'

We crossed back over to the left entrance, in the west wing. There order was also being established. 'Clear the Palace!' bawled a Red Guard, sticking his head through an inner door. 'Come, comrades, let's show that we're not thieves and bandits. Everybody out of the Palace except the Commissars, until we get sentries posted.'

Two Red Guards, a soldier and an officer, stood with revolvers in their hands. Another soldier sat at a table behind them, with pen and paper. Shouts of 'All out! All out!' were heard far and near within, and the Army began to pour through the door, jostling, expostulating, arguing. As each man appeared he was seized by the self-appointed committee, who went through his pockets and looked under his coat. Everything that was plainly not his property was taken away, the man at the table noted it on his paper, and it was carried into a little room. The most amazing assortment of objects were thus confiscated; statuettes, bottles of ink, bedspreads worked with the Imperial monogram, candles, a small oil painting, desk blotters, gold-handled swords, cakes of soap, clothes of every description, blankets. One Red Guard carried three rifles, two of which he had taken away from *yunkers*; another had four portfolios bulging with written documents. The culprits either sullenly surrendered or pleaded like children. All talking at once the committee explained that stealing was not worthy of the people's champions; often those who had been caught turned around and began to help go through the rest of the comrades.

Yunkers came out in bunches of three or four. The committee seized upon them with an excess of zeal, accompanying the search with remarks like, 'Ah, Provocators! Kornilovists! Counter-revolutionists! Murderers of the People!' But there was no violence done, although the *yunkers* were terrified. They too had their pockets full of small plunder. It was carefully noted down by the scribe, and piled in the little room . . . The *yunkers* were disarmed. 'Now, will you take up arms against the People any more?' demanded clamouring voices.

'No,' answered the *yunkers*, one by one. Whereupon they were allowed to go free.

We asked if we might go inside. The committee was doubtful but the big Red Guard answered firmly that it was forbidden. 'Who are you anyway?' he asked. 'How do I know that you are not all Kerenskys?' (There were five of us, two women.)

'*Pazhal'st'*, *tovarishtchi!* Way, Comrades!' A soldier and a Red Guard appeared in the door, waving the crowd aside, and other guards with fixed bayonets. After them followed single file half-a-dozen men in civilian dress – the members of the Provisional Government. First came Kishkin, his face drawn and pale, then Rutenberg, looking sullenly at the floor; Terestchenko was next, glancing sharply around; he stared at us with cold fixity . . . They passed in silence; the victorious insurrectionists crowded to see, but there were only a few angry mutterings. It was only later that we learned how the people in the street wanted to lynch them, and shots were fired – but the sailors brought them safely to Peter-Paul . . .

In the meanwhile unrebuked we walked into the Palace. There was still a great deal of coming and going, of exploring new-found apartments in the vast edifice, of searching for hidden garrisons of *yunkers* which did not exist. We went upstairs and wandered through room after room. This part of the Palace had been entered also by other detachments from the side of the Neva. The paintings, statues, tapestries, and rugs of the great state apartments were unharmed; in the offices, however, every desk and cabinet had been ransacked, the papers scattered over the floor, and in the living rooms beds had been stripped of their coverings and wardrobes wrenched open. The most highly prized loot was clothing, which the working people needed. In a room where furniture was stored we came upon two soldiers ripping the elaborate Spanish leather upholstery from chairs. They explained it was to make boots with . . .

The old Palace servants in their blue and red and gold uniforms stood nervously about, from force of habit repeating, 'You can't go in there, *barin*! It is forbidden – ' We penetrated at length to the gold and malachite chamber with crimson brocade hangings where the Ministers had been in session all that day and night, and where the *shveitzari* had betrayed them to the Red Guards. The long table covered with green baize was just as they had left it, under arrest. Before each empty seat was pen, ink and paper; the papers were scribbled over with beginnings of plans of action, rough drafts of proclamations and manifestos. Most of these were scratched out, as their futility became evident, and the rest of the sheet covered with absent-minded geometrical designs, as the writers sat despondently listening while Minister after Minister proposed chimerical schemes. I took one of these scribbled pages, in the hand writing of Konovalov, which read, 'The Provisional Government appeals to all classes to support the Provisional Government – '

Breslau Prison, December 1917

Rosa Luxemburg

Pacifist and revolutionary socialist, Rosa Luxemburg was repeatedly imprisoned and eventually murdered by forces of the German Right on 15 January 1919.

Here I am lying in a dark cell upon a mattress hard as stone; the building has its usual churchyard quiet, so that one might as well be already entombed; through the window there falls across the bed a glint of light from the lamp which burns all night in front of the prison. At intervals I can hear faintly in the distance the noise of a passing train or close at hand the dry cough of the prison guard as in his heavy boots, he takes a few slow strides to stretch his limbs. The gride of the gravel beneath his feet has so hopeless a sound that all the weariness and futility of existence seems to be radiated thereby into the damp and gloomy night. I lie here alone and in silence, enveloped in the manifold black wrappings of darkness, tedium, unfreedom, and winter – and yet my heart beats with an immeasurable and incomprehensible inner joy, just as if I were moving in the brilliant sunshine across a flowery mead. And in the darkness I smile at life, as if I were the possessor of a charm which would enable me to transform all that is evil and tragical into serenity and happiness. But when I search my mind for the cause of this joy, I find there is no cause, and can only laugh at myself – I believe that the key to the riddle is simply life itself, this deep darkness of night is soft and beautiful as velvet, if only one looks at it in the right way. The gride of the damp gravel beneath the slow and heavy tread of the prison guard is likewise a lovely little song of life – for one who has ears to hear.

French Cavalry Charge, near Amiens, 26 March 1918

William Pressey

On the morning of the fifth day we had seen Uhlans on either side of us and had got out in a flaming hurry. Shells followed us as we had a hectic gallop through a village and dropped to a walk on going over a hill. Out of sight of the Germans over this hill we were walking along when we saw an unforgettable sight.

Coming towards us were a troop of French cavalry. I should say a hundred and fifty or two hundred strong. Gosh, but they looked splendid. I think word must have got to them about the German cavalry harassing us and they had come to put a stop to that. They could never have been told about the machine-guns. They laughed and waved their lances at us, shouting 'Le Bosch fini.' What a picture they made with sunlight gleaming on their lances. We slowed down as they trotted briskly past, and everyone was looking back at them.

Before reaching the top of the hill they opened out to about six feet between each horse and in a straight line. We hardly breathed. Over the top of the hill they charged, lances at the ready.

There was not a sound from us. Then, only a few seconds after they disappeared, the hellish noise of machine-guns broke out. We just looked at each other. The only words I heard spoken were 'Bloody hell . . .' That's what it must have been over that hill, for not one man came back. Several of their horses did, and trotted beside us, and were collected at our next stopping place.

The Death of a Brother, 15 June 1918

Vera Brittain

I had just announced to my father, as we sat over tea in the dining room, that I really must do up Edward's papers and take them to the post office before it closed for the weekend, when there came the sudden loud clattering at the front-door knocker that always meant a telegram.

For a moment I thought that my legs would not carry me, but they behaved quite normally as I got up and went to the door. I knew what was in the telegram — I had known for a week — but because the persistent hopefulness of the human heart refuses to allow intuitive certainty to persuade the reason of that which it knows, I opened and read it in a tearing anguish of suspense.

'Regret to inform you Captain E. H. Brittain M.C. killed in action Italy June 15th.'

'No answer,' I told the boy mechanically, and handed the telegram to my father, who had followed me into the hall. As we went back into the dining room I saw, as though I had never seen them before, the bowl of blue delphiniums on the table; their intense colour, vivid, ethereal, seemed too radiant for earthly flowers.

Then I remembered that we should have to go down to Purley and tell the news to my mother.

Late that evening, my uncle brought us all back to an empty flat. Edward's death and our sudden departure had offered the maid – at that time the amateur prostitute – an agreeable opportunity for a few hours' freedom of which she had taken immediate advantage. She had not even finished the household handkerchiefs, which I had washed that morning and intended to iron after tea; when I went into the kitchen I found them still hanging, stiff as boards, over the clothes-horse near the fire where I had left them to dry.

Long after the family had gone to bed and the world had grown silent, I crept into the dining room to be alone with Edward's portrait. Carefully closing the door, I turned on the light and looked at the pale, pictured face, so dignified, so steadfast, so tragically mature. He had been through so much – far, far more than those beloved friends who had died at an earlier stage of the interminable War, leaving him alone to mourn their loss. Fate might have allowed him the little, sorry compensation of survival, the chance to make his lovely music in honour of their memory. It seemed indeed the last irony that he should have been killed by the countrymen of Fritz Kreisler, the violinist whom of all others he had most greatly admired.

And suddenly, as I remembered all the dear afternoons and evenings when I had followed him on the piano as he played his violin, the sad, searching eyes of the portrait were more than I could bear, and falling on my knees before it I began to cry, 'Edward! Oh, Edward!' in dazed repetition, as though my persistent crying and calling would somehow bring him back.

Tsar Nicholas II and the Russian Imperial Family Shot in Ekaterinburg, 16 July 1918

Pavel Medvedev

The Provisional Government intended to send the royal family to England, but this was opposed by the Petrograd Soviet, and they were taken instead to Ekaterinburg (now Sverdlovsk) in the Urals. When White Russian forces approached this area, the local authorities were ordered to prevent a rescue.

In the evening of July 16th, between 7 and 8 p.m., when the time for my duty had just begun, Commandant Yurovsky [the head of the guard] ordered me to take all the Nagan revolvers from the guards and to bring them to him. I took twelve revolvers from the sentries as well as from some other of the guards, and brought them to the commandant's office. Yurovsky said to me, 'We must shoot *them all* tonight, so notify the guards not to be alarmed if they hear shots.' I understood, therefore, that Yurovsky had it in his mind to shoot the whole of the Tsar's family, as well as the doctor and the servants who lived with them, but I did not ask him where or by whom the decision had been made. I must tell you that in accordance with Yurovsky's order the boy who assisted the cook was transferred in the morning to the guardroom (in the Popov house). The lower floor of Ipatiev's house was occupied by the Letts from the Letts Commune, who had taken up their quarters there after Yurovsky was made commandant. They were ten in number. At about ten o'clock in the evening, in accordance with Yurovsky's order, I informed the guards not to be alarmed if they should hear firing. About midnight Yurovsky woke up the Tsar's family. I do not know if he told them the reason they had been awakened and where they were to be taken, but I positively affirm that it was Yurovsky who entered the rooms occupied by the Tsar's family. Yurovsky had not ordered me or Dobrynin to awaken the family. In about an hour the whole of the family, the doctor, the maid and the waiters got up, washed and dressed themselves. Just before Yurovsky went to awaken the family, two members of the Extraordinary Commission [of the Ekaterinburg Soviet] arrived at Ipatiev's house. Shortly after one o'clock a.m., the Tsar, the Tsaritsa, their four daughters, the maid, the doctor, the cook and the waiter left their rooms. The Tsar carried the heir in his arms. The Emperor and the heir were dressed in *gimnasterkas* [soldiers' shirts] and wore caps. The Empress and her daughters were dressed but their heads were uncovered. The Emperor, carrying the heir, preceded them. The Empress, her daughters and the others followed him. Yurovsky, his assistant and the two above-mentioned members of the Extraordinary Commission accompanied them. I was also present. During my presence none of the Tsar's family asked any questions. They did not weep or cry. Having descended the stairs to the first floor, we went out into the court, and from there by the second door (counting from the gate) we entered the ground floor of the house. When the room (which adjoins the store room with a sealed door) was reached, Yurovsky ordered chairs to be brought, and his assistant brought three chairs. One chair was given to the Emperor, one to the Empress, and the third to the heir. The Empress sat by the wall by the window, near the black pillar of the arch. Behind her stood three of her daughters (I knew their faces very well, because I had seen them every day when they walked in the garden, but I didn't know their names). The heir and the Emperor sat side by side almost in the middle of the room. Doctor Botkin stood behind the heir. The maid, a very tall woman, stood at the left of the door leading to the store room; by her side stood one of the Tsar's daughters (the fourth). Two servants stood against the wall on the left from the entrance of the room.

The maid carried a pillow. The Tsar's daughters also brought small pillows with them. One pillow was put on the Empress's chair; another on the heir's chair. It seemed as if all of them guessed their fate, but not one of them uttered a single sound. At this moment eleven men entered the room: Yurovsky, his assistant, two members of the Extraordinary Commission, and seven Letts. Yurovsky ordered me to leave, saying, 'Go on to the street, see if there is anybody there, and wait to see whether the shots have been heard.' I went out to the court, which was enclosed by a fence, but before I got to the street I heard the firing. I returned to the house immediately (only two or three minutes having elapsed) and upon entering the room where the execution had taken place, I saw that all the members of the Tsar's family were lying on the floor with many wounds in their bodies. The blood was running in streams. The doctor, the maid and two waiters had also been shot. When I entered the heir was still alive and moaned a little. Yurovsky went up and fired two or three more times at him. Then the heir was still.

Incident on the Advance to Damascus: Lawrence of Arabia Destroys a Turkish Column, 24 September 1918

T. E. Lawrence

The Arabs told us that the Turkish column – Jemal Pasha's lancer regiment – was already entering Tafas. When we got within sight, we found they had taken the village (from which sounded an occasional shot) and were halted about it. Small pyres of smoke were going up from between the houses. On the rising ground to this side, knee deep in the thistles, stood a remnant of old men, women and children, telling terrible stories of what had happened when the Turks rushed in an hour before.

We lay on watch, and saw the enemy force march away from their assembly ground behind the houses. They headed in good order toward Miskin, the lancers in front and rear, composite formations of infantry disposed in column with machine-gun support as flank guards, guns and a mass of transport in the centre. We opened fire on the head of their line when it showed itself beyond the houses. They turned two field guns upon us, for reply. The shrapnel was as usual over-fused, and passed safely above our heads.

Nuri came with Pisani. Before their ranks rode Auda abu Tayi, expectant, and Tallal, nearly frantic with the tales his people poured out of the sufferings of the village. The last Turks were now quitting it. We slipped down behind them to end Tallal's suspense, while our infantry took position and fired strongly with the Hotchkiss; Pisani advanced his half-battery among them; so that the French high explosive threw the rearguard into confusion.

The village lay stilly under its slow wreaths of white smoke, as we rode near, on our guard. Some grey heaps seemed to hide in the long grass, embracing the ground in the close way of corpses. We looked away from these, knowing they were dead; but from one a little figure tottered off, as if to escape us. It was a child, three or four years old, whose dirty smock was stained red over one shoulder and side, with blood from a large half-fibrous wound, perhaps a lance thrust, just where neck and body joined.

The child ran a few steps, then stood and cried to us in a tone of astonishing strength (all else being very silent), 'Don't hit me, Baba.' Abd el Aziz, choking out something – this was his village, and she might be of his family – flung himself off his camel, and stumbled, kneeling, in the grass beside the child. His suddenness frightened her, for she threw up her arms and tried to scream; but, instead, dropped in a little heap, while the blood rushed out again over her clothes; then, I think, she died.

We rode past the other bodies of men and women and four more dead babies, looking very soiled in the daylight, towards the village; whose loneliness we now knew meant death and horror. By the outskirts were low mud walls, sheepfolds, and on one something red and white. I looked close and saw the body of a woman folded across it, bottom upwards, nailed there by a saw bayonet whose haft stuck hideously into the air from between her naked legs. About her lay others, perhaps twenty in all, variously killed.

The Zaagi burst into wild peals of laughter, the more desolate for the warm sunshine and clear air of this upland afternoon. I said, 'The best of you bring me the most Turkish dead,' and we turned after the fading enemy, on our way shooting down those who had fallen out by the roadside and came imploring our pity. One wounded Turk, half naked, not able to stand, sat and wept to us. Abdulla turned away his camel's head, but the Zaagi, with curses, crossed his track and whipped three bullets from his automatic through the man's bare chest. The blood came out with his heart beats, throb, throb, throb, slower and slower.

Tallal had seen what we had seen. He gave one moan like a hurt animal; then rode to the upper ground and sat there a while on his mare, shivering and looking fixedly after the Turks. I moved near to speak to him, but Auda caught my rein and stayed me. Very slowly Tallal drew his headcloth about his face; and then he seemed suddenly to take hold of himself, for he dashed his stirrups into the mare's flanks and galloped headlong, bending low and swaying in the saddle, right at the main body of the enemy.

It was a long ride down a gentle slope and across a hollow. We sat there like stone while he rushed forward, the drumming of his hoofs unnaturally loud in our ears, for we had stopped shooting, and the Turks had stopped. Both armies waited for him; and he rocked on in the hushed evening till only a few lengths from the enemy. Then he sat up in the saddle and cried his war cry, 'Tallal, Tallal,' twice in a tremendous shout. Instantly their rifles and machine-guns crashed out, and he and his mare riddled through and through with bullets, fell dead among the lance points.

Auda looked very cold and grim. 'God give him mercy; we will take his price.' He shook his rein and moved slowly after the enemy. We called up the peasants, now drunk with fear and blood, and sent them from this side and that against the retreating column. The old lion of battle waked in Auda's heart, and made him again our natural, inevitable leader. By a skilful turn he drove the Turks into bad ground and split their formation into three parts.

The third part, the smallest, was mostly made up of German and Austrian machine-gunners grouped round three motor cars and a handful of mounted officers or troopers. They fought magnificently and repulsed us time and again despite our hardiness. The Arabs were fighting like devils, the sweat blurring their eyes, dust parching their throats; while the flame of cruelty and revenge which was burning in their bodies so twisted them that their hands could hardly shoot. By my order we took no prisoners, for the only time in our war.

At last we left this stern section behind, and pursued the faster two. They were in panic; and by sunset we had destroyed all but the smallest pieces of them, gaining as and by what they lost. Parties of peasants flowed in on our advance. At first there were five or six to a weapon: then one would win a bayonet, another a sword, a third a pistol. An hour later those who had been on foot would be on donkeys. Afterwards every man had a rifle and a captured horse. By nightfall the horses were laden, and the rich plain was scattered over with dead men and animals. In a madness born of the horror of Tafas we killed and killed, even blowing in the heads of the fallen and of the animals; as though their death and running blood could slake our agony.

Signing the Treaty of Versailles, 28 June 1919

Harold Nicolson

La journée de Versailles. Lunch early and leave the Majestic in a car with Headlam Morley. He is a historian, yet he dislikes historical occasions. Apart from that he is a sensitive person and does not rejoice in seeing great nations humbled. I, having none of such acquirements or decencies, am just excited.

There is no crowd at all until we reach Ville d'Avray. But there are poilus at every crossroad waving red flags and stopping all other traffic. When we reach Versailles the crowd thickens. The avenue up to the Château is lined with cavalry in steel-blue helmets. The pennants of their lances flutter red and white in the sun. In the Cour d'Honneur, from which the captured German cannon have tactfully been removed, are further troops. There are Generals, Pétain, Gouraud, Mangin. There are St Cyriens. Very military and orderly. Headlam Morley and I creep out of our car hurriedly. Feeling civilian and grubby. And wholly unimportant. We hurry through the door.

Magnificent upon the staircase stand the Gardes Républicains – two caryatides on every step – their sabres at the salute. This is a great ordeal, but there are other people climbing the stairs with us. Headlam and I have an eye-meet. His thin cigaretted fingers make a gesture of dismissal. He is not a militarist.

We enter the two anterooms, our feet softening on to the thickest of savonnerie carpets. They have ransacked the Garde Meubles for their finest pieces. Never, since the Grand Siècle, has Versailles been more ostentatious or more embossed . . .

We enter the Galerie des Glaces. It is divided into three sections. At the far end are the Press already thickly installed. In the middle there is a horseshoe table for the plenipotentiaries. In front of that, like a guillotine, is the table for the signatures. It is supposed to be raised on a dais but, if so, the dais can be but a few inches high. In the nearer distance are rows and rows of tabourets for the distinguished guests, the deputies, the senators and the members of the delegations. There must be seats for over a thousand persons. This robs the ceremony of all privilege and therefore of all dignity. It is like the Aeolian Hall.

Clemenceau is already seated under the heavy ceiling as we

arrive. 'Le roi', runs the scroll above him, 'gouverne par lui-même.' He looks small and yellow. A crunched homunculus.

Conversation clatters out among the mixed groups around us. It is, as always on such occasions, like water running into a tin bath. I have never been able to get other people to recognize that similarity. There was a tin bath in my house at Wellington: one turned it on when one had finished and ran upstairs shouting 'Baath ready' to one's successor: 'Right ho!' he would answer: and then would come the sound of water pouring into the tin bath below, while he hurried into his dressing-gown. It is exactly the sound of people talking in undertones in a closed room. But it is not an analogy which I can get others to accept.

People step over the Aubusson benches and escabeaux to talk to friends. Meanwhile the delegates arrive in little bunches and push up the central aisle slowly. Wilson and Lloyd George are among the last. They take their seats at the central table. The table is at last full. Clemenceau glances to right and left. People sit down upon their escabeaux but continue chattering. Clemenceau makes a sign to the ushers. They say 'Ssh! Ssh! Ssh!' People cease chattering and there is only the sound of occasional coughing and the dry rustle of programmes. The officials of the Protocol of the Foreign Office move up the aisle and say, 'Ssh! Ssh!' again. There is then an absolute hush, followed by a sharp military order. The Gardes Républicains at the doorway flash their swords into their scabbards with a loud click. 'Faîtes entrer les Allemands,' says Clemenceau in the ensuing silence. His voice is distant but harshly penetrating. A hush follows.

Through the door at the end appear two huissiers with silver chains. They march in single file. After them come four officers of France, Great Britain, America and Italy. And then, isolated and pitiable, come the two German delegates. Dr Müller, Dr Bell. The silence is terrifying. Their feet upon a strip of parquet between the savonnerie carpets echo hollow and duplicate. They keep their eyes fixed away from those two thousand staring eyes, fixed upon the ceiling. They are deathly pale. They do not appear as representatives of a brutal militarism. The one is thin and pink-eyelidded: the second fiddle in a Brunswick orchestra. The other is moon-faced and suffering: a privat-dozent. It is all most painful.

They are conducted to their chairs. Clemenceau at once breaks the silence. 'Messieurs,' he rasps, 'la séance est ouverte.' He adds a few ill-chosen words. 'We are here to sign a Treaty of Peace.' The Germans leap up anxiously when he has finished, since they know that they are the first to sign. William Martin, as if a theatre manager, motions them petulantly to sit down again. Mantoux translates Clemenceau's words into English. Then St Quentin advances towards the Germans and with the utmost dignity leads them to the little table on which the Treaty is expanded. There is general tension. They sign. There is a general relaxation. Conversation hums again in an undertone. The delegates stand up one by one and pass onwards to the queue which waits by the signature table. Meanwhile people buzz round the main table getting autographs. The single file of plenipotentiaries waiting to approach the table gets thicker. It goes quickly. The officials of the Quai d'Orsay stand round, indicating places to sign, indicating procedure, blotting with neat little pads.

Suddenly from outside comes the crash of guns thundering a salute. It announces to Paris that the second Treaty of Versailles has been signed by Dr Müller and Dr Bell. Through the few open windows comes the sound of distant crowds cheering hoarsely. And still the signature goes on.

We had been warned it might last three hours. Yet almost at once it seemed that the queue was getting thin. Only three, then two, and then one delegate remained to sign. His name had hardly been blotted before the huissiers began again their 'Ssh! Ssh!' cutting suddenly short the wide murmur which had again begun. There was a final hush. 'La séance est levée,' rasped Clemenceau. Not a word more or less.

We kept our seats while the Germans were conducted like prisoners from the dock, their eyes still fixed upon some distant point of the horizon.

Famine in Russia, October 1921

Philip Gibbs

*A drought in 1921, together with the disruption of food produc-
tion caused by the application of communist methods to the rural
economy, led to a famine in the Volga region in 1921–2, which
was the occasion of a major international relief effort headed by
Herbert Hoover.*

After four days in that train we came to Kazan which lay under a
heavy mantle of snow. It was now the capital of the Tartar
Republic – a province of Soviet Russia – and was at the head of
the richest grain-growing district of the Volga valley. Now there
was no grain because it had been burnt in its seed time by a
terrible drought, leaving the peasants without food because their
reserves had been taken up to feed the Red Army.

With deep snow on its roofs and lying thick on the ground so
that no passing footsteps sounded it was like a city in a Russian
fairy tale. Here in the old Tsarist days nobles had built villas and
laid out fine gardens for their pleasure in summer months. Now
those houses were filled with refugees from famine, dying of
hunger and disease, and across the snow came small children,
hand in hand, who had walked a long way from starving villages
where their parents were already dead. Like frozen birds many of
them died in the snow. There were forty homes here for abandoned or wandering children. I went into a number of them and
they were all alike in general character. In big, bare rooms the
children were naked and huddled together like little monkeys for
warmth. There was no other warmth as there was no fuel. Their
clothes had been burnt because of the lice which spread typhus
among them. There were no other clothes to replace their ragged
old sheepskins and woollen garments. Often it was too late to
check the epidemic of typhus and thousands died and now were
dying.

We went into the hospitals and they were dreadful. Because
there was no fuel the patients, stricken with typhus, dysentery,
and all kinds of diseases, lay together in unventilated wards. Many
of the beds had been burnt for fuel, and most of the inmates lay
on bare boards. Those who had beds lay together, two one way

and two the other. There were no medicines, no anaesthetics, no soap, no dressings . . .

There was ice on the Volga and we were the last boat to get through, having to break our way. I shall never forget that voyage – the flat mud banks of the great river lying white under snow, the Russian villages, deep in snow within their stockades, all with whitewashed churches with pear-shaped domes, the landing stages where little groups of gaunt hunger-stricken men and women waited to see us, and tell their tales, and beg for help. Now and then a man would come on board and our interpreter would question him. Always he told of the famine which was threatening 25 million people with death in the broad valley of the Volga.

We went into some of those villages and saw tragic things. There was no food in the marketplaces and money was useless, even if there were any money. At one stage of the journey we found a *troika* – a sledge with three horses – waiting for us. It had been ordered by the Commune of the district who had been notified by Moscow. The driver was excited by our presence and drove his *troika* like a Roman chariot at a great pace, with his long whip curling above the horses' heads. They seemed to be the only horses in the district. The others were dead and their skeletons lay on the roads, their flesh having been eaten. The villages were as quiet as death. No one stirred from the little wooden houses, though now and again we saw faces at the windows – pallid faces with dark eyes staring at us. In one village I remember we had as our guide a tall, middle-aged peasant who had blue eyes and a straw-coloured beard. When he spoke of the famine in all those villages hereabouts he struck his breast and tears came into his eyes. He led us into timbered houses where Russian families were hibernating and waiting for death. In some of them they had no food of any kind. There was one family I saw who left an indelible mark on my mind. The father and mother were lying on the floor when we entered and were almost too weak to rise. Some young children were on a bed above the stove, dying of hunger. A boy of eighteen lay back in a wooden settle against the window sill in a kind of coma. These people had nothing to eat – nothing at all.

In other houses they were still keeping themselves alive by a kind of brownish powder made of leaves ground up and mixed with the husks of grain. Others were eating some stuff which looked like lead.

It was a clay of some kind, dug from a hillside named Bitarjisk, and had some nutritive quality, though for young children it was harmful, making their stomachs swell. Everywhere we went in these villages peasant women, weeping quietly, showed us their naked children with distended stomachs, the sign of starvation at its last stage. From other cottages they came to where we stood, crossing themselves at the doorways in the old Russian way and then lamenting. Only once did we meet with a wild desperation which made the women fierce and frightening. They seemed to think we had brought food and they came shrieking and clawing at us like starving animals, as indeed they were! Mostly they were quiet, even in their weeping, and we went into homes where the little ones looked like fairy-tale children but with the wolf outside the door waiting for them.

The Execution of Henri D. ('Bluebeard') Landru, Murderer of Ten Women, 25 February 1922

Webb Miller

On the night of 24 February, together with half-a-dozen French reporters, I caught the electric train to Versailles. We went to the courthouse, obtained crudely mimeographed green *laissez-passers* for the execution and retired to the Hôtel des Réservoirs with five bottles of cognac to await dawn.

At 4 a.m. word came that M. Deibler, the famous executioner who performed all the executions throughout France, had arrived with his apparatus. Anatole Deibler, shy, wistful, goat-bearded, had performed more than 300 executions. His salary was 18,000 francs per year (a little over $1000 at the 1936 rate of exchange). He suffered from a weak heart and could not walk upstairs, but this did not seem to interfere with his gruesome vocation. He lived in a small house near Versailles under the name of M. Anatole, consorted very little with his neighbours, and led a retiring existence. He kept the guillotine in a shed outside his house. When performing an execution he wore white gloves and a long white 'duster'.

We hurried to the prison. Four hundred troops had drawn

cordons at each end of the street and permitted only the possessors of the little green mimeographed tickets to pass. According to the French law, executions must occur in the open street in front of the prison door. On the damp, slippery cobblestones beside the streetcar tracks workmen were rapidly erecting the guillotine a dozen feet outside the towering gate of Versailles prison. It was still quite dark. The only light came from the workmen's old-fashioned lanterns with flickering candles and the few electric street lights. The workmen bolted the grisly machine together and adjusted its balance with a carpenter's level. Deibler hauled the heavy knife to the top of the uprights.

Nearly one hundred officials and newspapermen gathered in a circle around the guillotine; I stood about fifteen feet away. News arrived from inside the prison that Landru, whose long black beard had been cut previously, asked that he be shaved.

'It will please the ladies,' he said to his gaolers.

His lawyer and a priest went into his cell. He refused the traditional cigarette and glass of rum always offered just before executions.

Landru wore a shirt from which the neck had been cut away, and a pair of cheap dark trousers. That was all – no shoes or socks. He would walk to the guillotine barefooted.

As his arms were strapped behind him his lawyer whispered, 'Courage, Landru.' 'Thanks, Maître, I've always had that,' he replied calmly.

Just as the first streaks of the chilly February dawn appeared, a large closed van drawn by horses arrived and backed up within a few feet of the right side of the guillotine. Deibler's assistants, wearing long smocks, pulled two wicker baskets from the van. They placed the small round basket carefully in front of the machine where the head would fall. Two assistants placed another basket about the size and shape of a coffin close beside the guillotine. Into that the headless body would roll.

The cordon of troops halted a streetcar full of workmen on their way to work. They decided to open the cordon to permit the car to proceed, and it slowly rumbled past within a few feet of the grim machine. Staring faces filled the windows.

The guillotine underwent a final test. Deibler raised the lunette, the half-moon-shaped wooden block which was to clamp down upon Landru's neck. Then he lowered it, and the heavy knife shot down from the top of the uprights with a crash which shook the machine. The lunette and knife were raised again. All was ready.

Suddenly the huge wooden gates of the prison swung open. The spectators became silent and tense. Three figures appeared, walking rapidly. On each side a gaoler held Landru by his arms, which were strapped behind him. They supported and pulled him forward as fast as they could walk. His bare feet pattered on the cold cobblestones, and his knees seemed not to be functioning. His face was pale and waxen, and as he caught sight of the ghastly machine, he went livid.

The two gaolers hastily pushed Landru face foremost against the upright board of the machine. It collapsed, and his body crumpled with it as they shoved him forward under the wooden block, which dropped down and clamped his neck beneath the suspended knife. In a split second the knife flicked down, and the head fell with a thud into the small basket. As an assistant lifted the hinged board and rolled the headless body into the big wicker basket, a hideous spurt of blood gushed out.

An attendant standing in front of the machine seized the basket containing the head, rolled it like a cabbage into the larger basket, and helped shove it hastily into the waiting van. The van doors slammed, and the horses were whipped into a gallop.

When Landru first appeared in the prison courtyard I had glanced at my wrist watch. Now I looked again. Only twenty-six seconds had elapsed.

German Inflation, 19 September 1922

Ernest Hemingway

During the immediate post-war years the value of the German mark deteriorated, largely as a result of reparation payments. In 1922 the exchange rate fell from 162 marks to the US dollar to 7000. By November 1923 it was down to 4200 billion marks to the dollar.

Kehl, Germany: The boy in a Strasburg motor agency where we went to make some inquiries about crossing the frontier, said, 'Oh yes. It is easy to get over into Germany. All you have to do is go across the bridge.'

'Don't you need a visa?' I said.

'No. Just a permit stamp to go from the French.' He took his passport out of his pocket and showed the back covered with rubber stamps. 'See? I live there now because it is so much cheaper. It's the way to make money.'

It is all right.

It is a three-mile streetcar ride from the centre of Strasburg out to the Rhine and when you get to the end of the line the car stops and everyone piles out to herd into a long picket-fenced pen that leads to the bridge. A French soldier with a fixed bayonet loafs back and forth across the road and watches the girls in the passport pen from under his steel-blue helmet. There is an ugly brick custom house at the left of the bridge and a wooden shed at the right where the French official sits behind a counter and stamps passports.

The Rhine is swift, yellow and muddy, runs between low, green banks, and swirls and sucks at the concrete abutments of the long, iron bridge. At the other end of the bridge you see the ugly little town of Kehl looking like some dreary section of Dundas [Toronto].

If you are a French citizen with a French passport the man back of the counter simply stamps your passport 'sortie Pont de Kehl' and you go across the bridge into occupied Germany. If you are a citizen of some other of the allied countries the official looks at you suspiciously, asks you where you are from, what you are going to Kehl for, how long you are going to stay, and then stamps your passport with the same sortie. If you should happen to be a citizen of Kehl who has been in Strasburg on business and is returning to dinner – and as Kehl's interests are bound up in Strasburg's as all suburbs are to the city they are attached to, you would be bound to have to go to Strasburg on business if you had any kind of business at all – you are held in line for fifteen to twenty minutes, your name is looked up in a card index to see if you have ever spoken against the French regime, your pedigree taken, questions put to you and finally you too are given the same old sortie. Everyone can cross the bridge but the French make it very nasty for the Germans.

Once across the muddy Rhine you are in Germany, and the German end of the bridge is guarded by a couple of the meekest and most discouraged-looking German soldiers you have ever seen. Two French soldiers with fixed bayonets walk up and down and the two German soldiers, unarmed, lean against a wall and look on. The French soldiers are in full equipment and steel helmets, but the

Germans wear the old loose tunics and high peaked, peacetime caps.

I asked a Frenchman the functions and duties of the German guard.

'They stand there,' he answered.

There were no marks to be had in Strasburg, the mounting exchange had cleaned the bankers out days ago, so we changed some French money in the railway station at Kehl. For 10 francs I received 670 marks. Ten francs amounted to about 90 cents in Canadian money. That 90 cents lasted Mrs Hemingway and me for a day of heavy spending and at the end of the day we had 120 marks left!

Our first purchase was from a fruit stand beside the main street of Kehl where an old woman was selling apples, peaches and plums. We picked out five very good-looking apples and gave the old woman a 50 mark note. She gave us back 38 marks in change. A very nice-looking, white-bearded old gentleman saw us buy the apples and raised his hat.

'Pardon me, sir,' he said, rather timidly, in German, 'how much were the apples?'

I counted the change and told him 12 marks.

He smiled and shook his head. 'I can't pay it. It is too much.'

He went up the street walking very much as white-bearded old gentlemen of the old regime walk in all countries, but he had looked very longingly at the apples. I wish I had offered him some. Twelve marks, on that day, amounted to a little under 2 cents. The old man, whose life's savings were probably, as most of the non-profiteer classes are, invested in German pre-war and war bonds, could not afford a 12 mark expenditure. He is a type of the people whose incomes do not increase with the falling purchasing value of the mark and the krone.

With marks at 800 to the dollar, or 8 to a cent, we priced articles in the windows of the different Kehl shops. Peas were 18 marks a pound, beans 16 marks; a pound of Kaiser coffee, there are still many 'Kaiser' brands in the German republic, could be had for 34 marks. Gersten coffee, which is not coffee at all but roasted grain, sold for 14 marks a pound. Flypaper was 150 marks a package. A scythe blade cost 150 marks, too, or 18¾ cents! Beer was 10 marks a stein or 1¼ cents.

Kehl's best hotel, which is a very well turned-out place, served a five-course table d'hôte meal for 120 marks, which amounts to 15 cents in our money. The same meal could not be duplicated in Strasburg, three miles away, for a dollar.

Because of the customs regulations, which are very strict on persons returning from Germany, the French cannot come over to Kehl and buy up all the cheap goods they would like to. But they can come over and eat. It is a sight every afternoon to see the mob that storms the German pastry shops and tea places. The Germans make very good pastries, wonderful pastries, in fact, that, at the present tumbling mark rate, the French of Strasburg can buy for a less amount apiece than the smallest French coin, the one sou piece. This miracle of exchange makes a swinish spectacle where the youth of the town of Strasburg crowd into the German pastry shop to eat themselves sick and gorge on fluffy, cream-filled slices of German cake at 5 marks the slice. The contents of a pastry shop are swept clear in half an hour.

In a pastry shop we visited, a man in an apron, wearing blue glasses, appeared to be the proprietor. He was assisted by a typical 'boche'-looking German with close-cropped head. The place was jammed with French people of all ages and descriptions, all gorging cakes, while a young girl in a pink dress, silk stockings, with a pretty, weak face and pearl ear-rings in her ears took as many of their orders for fruit and vanilla ices as she could fill.

She didn't seem to care very much whether she filled the orders or not. There were soldiers in town and she kept going over to look out of the window.

The proprietor and his helper were surly and didn't seem particularly happy when all the cakes were sold. The mark was falling faster than they could bake.

Meanwhile out in the street a funny little train jolted by, carrying the workmen with their dinner-pails home to the outskirts of the town, profiteers' motor cars tore by raising a cloud of dust that settled over the trees and the fronts of all the buildings, and inside the pastry shop young French hoodlums swallowed their last cakes and French mothers wiped the sticky mouths of their children. It gave you a new aspect on exchange.

As the last of the afternoon tea-ers and pastry-eaters went Strasburg-wards across the bridge the first of the exchange pirates coming over to raid Kehl for cheap dinners began to arrive. The two streams passed each other on the bridge and the two disconsolate-looking German soldiers looked on. As the boy in the motor agency said, 'It's the way to make money.'

British India: Civil Disobedience, 21 May 1930

Webb Miller

Gandhi began a protest against the Salt Tax as part of his Civil Disobedience campaign. He was arrested on 5 May 1930, but his followers, led by Imam Sahib, marched on the salt deposits at Dharsana. Webb Miller sent his report to the New Freeman.

Dungri consisted of a little huddle of native huts on the dusty plain. There were no means of transportation. I could find nobody who spoke English. By repeatedly pronouncing the word 'Dharsana' and pointing questioningly around the horizon, I got directions and set off across country on foot through cactus hedges, millet fields, and inch-deep dust, inquiring my way by signs.

After plodding about six miles across country lugging a pack of sandwiches and two quart bottles of water under a sun which was already blazing hot, inquiring from every native I met, I reached the assembling place of the Gandhi followers. Several long, open, thatched sheds were surrounded by high cactus thickets. The sheds were literally swarming and buzzed like a beehive with some 2500 Congress or Gandhi men dressed in the regulation uniform of rough homespun cotton *dhotis* and triangular Gandhi caps, somewhat like American overseas soldiers' hats. They chattered excitedly and when I arrived hundreds surrounded me, with evidences of hostility at first. After they learned my identity, I was warmly welcomed by young college-educated, English-speaking men and escorted to Mme Naidu. The famous Indian poetess, stocky, swarthy, strong-featured, bare-legged, dressed in rough, dark homespun robe and sandals, welcomed me. She explained that she was busy martialling her forces for the demonstration against the salt pans and would talk with me more at length later. She was educated in England and spoke English fluently.

Mme Naidu called for prayer before the march started and the entire assemblage knelt. She exhorted them, 'Gandhi's body is in gaol but his soul is with you. India's prestige is in your hands. You must not use any violence under any circumstances. You will be beaten but you must not resist; you must not even raise a hand to ward off blows.' Wild, shrill cheers terminated her speech.

Slowly and in silence the throng commenced the half-mile march to the salt deposits. A few carried ropes for lassoing the barbed-wire stockade around the salt pans. About a score who were assigned to act as stretcher-bearers wore crude, hand-painted red crosses pinned to their breasts; their stretchers consisted of blankets. Manilal Gandhi, second son of Gandhi, walked among the foremost of the marchers. As the throng drew near the salt pans they commenced chanting the revolutionary slogan, *Inquilab zindabad*, intoning the two words over and over.

The salt deposits were surrounded by ditches filled with water and guarded by 400 native Surat police in khaki shorts and brown turbans. Half-a-dozen British officials commanded them. The police carried *lathis* – five-foot clubs tipped with steel. Inside the stockade twenty-five native riflemen were drawn up.

In complete silence the Gandhi men drew up and halted a hundred yards from the stockade. A picked column advanced from the crowd, waded the ditches, and approached the barbed-wire stockade, which the Surat police surrounded, holding their clubs at the ready. Police officials ordered the marchers to disperse under a recently imposed regulation which prohibited gatherings of more than five persons in any one place. The column silently ignored the warning and slowly walked forward. I stayed with the main body about a hundred yards from the stockade.

Suddenly, at a word of command, scores of native police rushed upon the advancing marchers and rained blows on their heads with their steel-shod *lathis*. Not one of the marchers even raised an arm to fend off the blows. They went down like ten-pins. From where I stood I heard the sickening whacks of the clubs on unprotected skulls. The waiting crowd of watchers groaned and sucked in their breaths in sympathetic pain at every blow.

Those struck down fell sprawling, unconscious or writhing in pain with fractured skulls or broken shoulders. In two or three minutes the ground was quilted with bodies. Great patches of blood widened on their white clothes. The survivors without breaking ranks silently and doggedly marched on until struck down. When every one of the first column had been knocked down stretcher-bearers rushed up unmolested by the police and carried off the injured to a thatched hut which had been arranged as a temporary hospital.

Then another column formed while the leaders pleaded with them to retain their self-control. They marched slowly toward the police. Although every one knew that within a few minutes he would be beaten down, perhaps killed, I could detect no signs of wavering or fear. They marched steadily with heads up, without the encouragement of music or cheering or any possibility that they might escape serious injury or death. The police rushed out and methodically and mechanically beat down the second column. There was no fight, no struggle; the marchers simply walked forward until struck down. There were no outcries, only groans after they fell. There were not enough stretcher-bearers to carry off the wounded; I saw eighteen injured being carried off simultaneously, while forty-two still lay bleeding on the ground awaiting stretcher-bearers. The blankets used as stretchers were sodden with blood . . .

In the middle of the morning V. J. Patel arrived. He had been leading the Swaraj movement since Gandhi's arrest, and had just resigned as President of the Indian Legislative Assembly in protest against the British. Scores surrounded him, knelt, and kissed his feet. He was a venerable gentleman of about sixty with white flowing beard and moustache, dressed in the usual undyed, coarse homespun smock. Sitting on the ground under a mango tree, Patel said, 'All hope of reconciling India with the British Empire is lost for ever. I can understand any government's taking people into custody and punishing them for breaches of the law, but I cannot understand how any government that calls itself civilized could deal as savagely and brutally with non-violent, unresisting men as the British have this morning.'

By eleven the heat reached 116 degrees in the shade and the activities of the Gandhi volunteers subsided. I went back to the temporary hospital to examine the wounded. They lay in rows on the bare ground in the shade of an open, palm-thatched shed. I counted 320 injured, many still insensible with fractured skulls, others writhing in agony from kicks in the testicles and stomach. The Gandhi men had been able to gather only a few native doctors, who were doing the best they could with the inadequate facilities. Scores of the injured had received no treatment for hours and two had died. The demonstration was finished for the day on account of the heat.

I was the only foreign correspondent who had witnessed the

amazing scene – a classic example of *satyagraha* or non-violent civil disobedience.

Hunger Marchers, 27 October 1932

Wal Hannington

The hunger marchers were organized by the National Unemployed Workers' Movement. Their aim was to meet, from all parts of the country, in London and present a petition against the means test at the House of Commons.

Next morning, 27th October, the general public of London, emerging into the streets, found that special constables had taken over all the normal duties of the policemen on patrol and on traffic duty. This was a clear indication of the elaborate preparations for struggle which the police had made. By mid-day approximately 100,000 London workers were moving towards Hyde Park from all parts of London, to give the greatest welcome to the hunger marchers that had ever been seen in Hyde Park. By two o'clock Hyde Park and the streets around Marble Arch were black with the multitude of workers who had arrived and were now awaiting the arrival of the hunger marchers. It is estimated that 5000 police and special constables were gathered round the park, with many thousands more mobilized in the neighbourhood in readiness for action.

The press had announced that morning that all leave had been stopped for the Coldstream Guards in Wellington barracks, and that they were being held in readiness in case of trouble. As the various contingents of marchers began to enter the park at 2.30 there were signs of tremendous enthusiasm. London's warmest welcome, shouted from 100,000 throats in Hyde Park, was the working-class reply to the impudent campaign of lies by the capitalist press against the marchers.

As the last contingent of marchers entered the park gates, trouble broke out with the police. It started with the special constables; not being used to their task, they lost their heads, and, as the crowds swept forward on to the space where the meetings were to be held, the specials drew their truncheons in an effort to control the sea of surging humanity. This incensed the workers; they felt particularly bitter towards the specials, whom they had dubbed 'blackleg cops'. The workers turned on the special constables and put them to flight, but the fighting which they had been responsible for starting continued throughout the whole afternoon, whilst speakers from the marchers were addressing huge gatherings on the green.

The workers kept the police back from the meetings; several times mounted police charged forward, only to be repulsed by thousands of workers who tore up railings and used them as weapons and barricades for the protection of their meetings. Many mounted men were dragged from their horses. From the streets the fighting extended into the park and back again into the streets, where repeated mounted police charges at full speed failed to dislodge the workers. The foot police were on several occasions surrounded by strong forces of workers, and terrific fights ensued. Many workers and police were injured. Inside the park one could hear the roar of the crowd as they fought tenaciously around the Marble Arch and along Oxford Street. At one juncture a plain-clothes detective stepped forward to speak to a chief inspector; as he did so a zealous special constable struck him down with a terrific blow on the head with a staff. He was about to kick him as he lay on the ground, but was prevented from doing so by the officer in uniform, who stepped forward to reprimand him for the foolish mistake which he had made.

Bodyline Bowling, 13–19 January 1933

W. H. Ferguson

Although Douglas Jardine [the English captain] showed his hand, to some extent, in the second Test match at Melbourne at the turn of the year, the actual eruption of the volcano occurred during the third Test at Adelaide from 13th to 19th January. I sensed the preparations for assault on Australia when everyone – bar those on official business – was banned from the ground during the MCC pre-match practices.

This was destined to be an historic and sensational match, one of the most unpleasant exhibitions – from many aspects – it has been my misfortune to witness. I have no doubt in my mind that the Australian cricketers were terrified by Harold Larwood and his leg theory bowling, an attitude of mind fully justified by the events of the match.

One batsman after another suffered physically as Larwood relentlessly set about the job allocated to him by Jardine; Bill Ponsford, who frequently turned his back on the ball, had dozens of bruises to emphasize the folly of such attempted evasive action. Bill Woodfull, never very quick on his feet, suffered even more, and I was in full sympathy with his wife who feared for Woodfull's safety. It came as no surprise when, after receiving a severe blow on the chest from a Larwood delivery, Woodfull had to be taken to the dressing room, a very sick man.

When Bert Oldfield, always a popular figure with spectators, had to be carried to the pavilion, knocked unconscious with a fast, rising ball, the indignation of spectators was at boiling point. Maurice Tate, who was not playing for England, told me, 'Bill, I'm getting out of here. Somebody is going to get seriously hurt, and the people will start a riot.' I felt sure some hotheads in the crowd would jump the rails and try to assault the English cricketers, but, thank Heaven, it did not come to that.

'Plum' Warner, in an effort to do the right thing, looked into the Australian dressing room which, by this time, resembled a casualty clearing station, and expressed his regret for the injuries caused by the tourists' fast bowling. He received a snub which made front page news all over the world, when Woodfull told him, 'I don't want to speak to you, Mr Warner. There are two teams out there and one is playing cricket. If these tactics are persevered with, it may be better if I do not play the game. Good afternoon.'

The Reichstag Fire, 27 February 1933

D. Sefton Delmer

A Dutchman, van der Lubbe, confessed, at his trial, that he had started the Reichstag (parliament building) fire, but it is widely believed to have been organized by the Nazis, who used it as an excuse for suppressing political opposition and seizing dictatorial powers.

'This is a God-given signal! If this fire, as I believe, turns out to be the handiwork of Communists, then there is nothing that shall stop us now crushing out this murder pest with an iron fist.'

Adolf Hitler, Fascist Chancellor of Germany, made this dramatic declaration in my presence tonight in the hall of the burning Reichstag building.

The fire broke out at 9.45 tonight in the Assembly Hall of the Reichstag.

It had been laid in five different corners and there is no doubt whatever that it was the handiwork of incendiaries.

One of the incendiaries, a man aged thirty, was arrested by the police as he came rushing out of the building, clad only in shoes and trousers, without shirt or coat, despite the icy cold in Berlin tonight.

Five minutes after the fire had broken out I was outside the Reichstag watching the flames licking their way up the great dome into the tower.

A cordon had been flung round the building and no one was allowed to pass it.

After about twenty minutes of fascinated watching I suddenly saw the famous black motor car of Adolf Hitler slide past, followed by another car containing his personal bodyguard.

I rushed after them and was just in time to attach myself to the fringe of Hitler's party as they entered the Reichstag.

Never have I seen Hitler with such a grim and determined expression. His eyes, always a little protuberant, were almost bulging out of his head.

Captain Goering, his right-hand man, who is the Prussian Minister of the Interior, and responsible for all police affairs, joined us in the lobby. He had a very flushed and excited face.

'This is undoubtedly the work of Communists, Herr Chancellor,' he said.

'A number of Communist deputies were present here in the Reichstag twenty minutes before the fire broke out. We have succeeded in arresting one of the incendiaries.'

'Who is he?' Dr Goebbels, the propaganda chief of the Nazi Party, threw in.

'We do not know yet,' Captain Goering answered, with an ominously determined look around his thin, sensitive mouth. 'But we shall squeeze it out of him, have no doubt, doctor.'

We went into a room. 'Here you can see for yourself, Herr Chancellor, the way they started the fire,' said Captain Goering, pointing out the charred remains of some beautiful oak panelling.

'They hung cloths soaked in petrol over the furniture here and set it alight.'

We strode across another lobby filled with smoke. The police barred the way. 'The candelabra may crash any moment, Herr Chancellor,' said a captain of the police, with his arms outstretched.

By a detour we next reached a part of the building which was actually in flames. Firemen were pouring water into the red mass.

Hitler watched them for a few moments, a savage fury blazing from his pale blue eyes.

Then we came upon Herr von Papen, urbane and debonair as ever.

Hitler stretched out his hand and uttered the threat against the Communists which I have already quoted. He then turned to Captain Goering. 'Are all the other public buildings safe?' he questioned.

'I have taken every precaution,' answered Captain Goering. 'The police are in the highest state of alarm, and every public building has been specially garrisoned. We are waiting for anything.'

It was then that Hitler turned to me. 'God grant,' he said, 'that this is the work of the Communists. You are witnessing the beginning of a great new epoch in German history. This fire is the beginning.'

And then something touched the rhetorical spring in his brain.

'You see this flaming building,' he said, sweeping his hand dramatically around him. 'If this Communist spirit got hold of Europe for but two months it would be all aflame like this building.'

By 12.30 the fire had been got under control. Two Press rooms were still alight, but there was no danger of the fire spreading.

Although the glass of the dome has burst and crashed to the ground the dome still stands.

So far it has not been possible to disentangle the charred debris and see whether the bodies of any incendiaries, who may have been trapped in the building, are among it.

At the Prussian Ministry of the Interior a special meeting was called late tonight by Captain Goering to discuss measures to be taken as a consequence of the fire.

The entire district from the Brandenburg Gate, on the west, to the River Spree, on the east, is isolated tonight by numerous cordons of police.

The Burning Ghats, Benares, India, December 1933

Patrick Balfour

The women's sarees – peacock blue, crimson, canary yellow, orange, olive green – shone gaily in the sunshine, which was not yet bright enough to drain all colour from the scene. It was pleasant to watch this Aryan zeal for cleanliness, this delight in a bathe before breakfast. Only on close inspection was the true nature of the bathing-party evident, did automatic, ritualistic movements and continual chantings testify to a religious rather than a disinterestedly hygienic motive.

Through stagnant water, thick with scum and rotting flowers, we drifted towards the burning ghats, where a coil of smoke rose into the air from a mass of ashes no longer recognizable as a body. One pyre, neatly stacked in a rectangular pile, had just been lit, and the corpse, swathed in white, protruded from the middle. An old man, surrounded with marigolds, sat cross-legged on the step above. Men were supporting him and rubbing him with oil and sand. He submitted limply to their ministrations, staring, wide-eyed, towards the sun.

'Why are they massaging him like that?' I asked the guide.
'Because he is dead.'
And then I saw them unfold him from his limp position and carry

him towards the stack of wood. Yet he looked no more dead than many of the living around him. They put him face downwards on the pyre, turned his shaved head towards the river, piled wood on top of him and set it alight with brands of straw, pouring on him butter and flour and rice and sandalwood.

The ceremony was performed with despatch and a good deal of chat, while uninterested onlookers talked among themselves. When I drifted back, some ten minutes later, the head was a charred bone, and a cow was placidly munching the marigold wreaths.

The Arrest of Osip Mandelstam, 13 May 1934

Nadezhda Mandelstam

The circumstances surrounding the death of Osip Mandelstam, greatest Russian poet of the modern period, are still uncertain. According to one version he died in East Siberia on the way to a concentration camp. Anna Akhmatova, the poet, was staying with the Mandelstams at the time of the arrest described here.

The day dragged on with excruciating slowness. In the evening the translator David Brodski turned up and then just wouldn't leave. There wasn't a bit to eat in the house and M. went around to the neighbours to try and get something for Akhmatova's supper. We hoped that Brodski might now get bored and leave, but no, he shot after M. and was still with him when he returned with the solitary egg he had managed to scrounge. Sitting down again in his chair, Brodski continued to recite the lines he liked best from his favourite poets, Sluchevski and Polonski (there was nothing he didn't know about both Russian and French poetry). He just went on and on, quoting and reminiscing, and it was only after midnight that we realized why he was being such a nuisance . . .

Suddenly, at about one o'clock in the morning, there was a sharp, unbearably explicit knock on the door. 'They've come for Osip,' I said, and went to open the door.

Some men in civilian overcoats were standing outside – there seemed to be a lot of them. For a split second I had a tiny flicker of hope that this still wasn't it – my eye had not made out the uniforms under the covert-cloth topcoats. In fact, topcoats of this kind were also a sort of uniform – though they were intended as a disguise, like the old pea-green coats of the Tsarist *okhrana*. But this I did not know then. All hope vanished as soon as the uninvited guests stepped inside.

I had expected them to say, 'How do you do?' or 'Is this Mandelstam's apartment?' or something else of the kind that any visitor says in order to be let in by the person who opens the door. But the night visitors of our times do not stand on such ceremony – like secret police agents the world over, I suppose.

Without a word or a moment's hesitation, but with consummate skill and speed, they came in past me (not pushing, however) and the apartment was suddenly full of people already checking our identity papers, running their hands over our hips with a precise, well-practised movement, and feeling our pockets to make sure we had no concealed weapons.

M. came out of the large room. 'Have you come for me?' he asked. One of the agents, a short man, looked at him with what could have been a faint smile and said, 'Your papers.' M. took them out of his pocket, and after checking them, the agent handed him a warrant. M. read it and nodded.

In the language of the secret police this was what was known as a 'night operation' . . .

After checking our papers, presenting their warrants and making sure there would be no resistance, they began to search the apartment. Brodski slumped into his chair and sat there motionless, like a huge wooden sculpture of some savage tribe. He puffed and wheezed with an angry, hurt expression on his face. When I chanced at one point to speak to him – asking him, I think to get some books from the shelves for M. to take with him – he answered rudely, 'Let M. get them himself,' and again began to wheeze. Toward morning, when we were at last permitted to walk freely around the apartment and the tired Chekists no longer even looked searchingly at us as we did so, Brodski suddenly roused himself, held up his hand like a schoolboy and asked permission to go to the toilet. The agent directing the search looked at him with contempt. 'You can go home,' he said. 'What?' Brodski said in astonishment. 'Home,' the man repeated and turned his back. The secret police despised their civilian helpers. Brodski had no doubt been ordered to sit with us that evening in case we tried to destroy any manuscripts when we heard the knock on the door.

The Rattenbury Case, May–June 1935

James Agate

Wednesday, 29 May. The *Daily Express* asked me to do an impression of the Rattenbury Trial at the Old Bailey. The facts were very simple and hardly disputed. Mrs Rattenbury, aged thirty-eight, wife of an architect aged sixty-seven, had been the mistress of her eighteen-year-old chauffeur named Stoner. Somebody had hit the husband over the head with a mallet, both of them having at one time or another taken the blame on themselves.

It was all very like the three French major novelists. The way in which the woman debauched the boy so that he slept with her every night with her six-year-old son in the room, and the husband who had his own bedroom remaining cynically indifferent – all this was pure Balzac. In the box Mrs Rattenbury looked and talked exactly as I have always imagined Emma Bovary looked and talked. Pure Flaubert. And last there was that part of her evidence in which she described how, trying to bring her husband round, she first accidentally trod on his false teeth and then tried to put them back into his mouth so that he could speak to her. This was pure Zola. The sordidness of the whole thing was relieved by one thing and one only. This was when Counsel asked Mrs Rattenbury what her first thought had been when her lover got into bed that night and told her what he had done. She replied, 'My first thought was to protect him.' This is the kind of thing which Balzac would have called sublime, and it is odd that, so far as I saw, not a single newspaper reported it . . .

Friday, 31 May. Mrs Rattenbury acquitted and Stoner condemned to death. The second must not happen. If I had been on the jury I would have stuck out for a verdict of manslaughter, bad though that would have been in law, because there is no certainty that the recommendation to mercy made in this case, will be given effect to . . .

Wednesday, 5 June. As we are setting off in the car the newspapers came out with the placard: MRS RATTENBURY STABBED AND DROWNED. [Mrs Rattenbury stabbed herself six times on the bank of a river and toppled in, drowning herself.] Reggie Arkell said this was the most dramatic thing he had seen in the streets since TITANIC

SINKING. The two things in this kind which have shocked me most have been the arrest of Crippen, about which I read on the pier at Llandudno – I can still point out the exact plank on which I stood – and the newspaper placard announcing the death of Marie Lloyd. I remember how this rooted me to the pavement in Tottenham Court Road.

The Italian Campaign in Abyssinia: Retreat of the Emperor's Army to Korem, 4–5 April 1936

Colonel Konovaloff

Mussolini invaded Abyssinia (Ethiopia) on 3 October 1935. The native troops were ill-armed and barefoot, and the Italians, using modern armaments and mustard gas, inflicted heavy casualities. This account of the flight of the Ethiopian Army after its unsuccessful attack on the Italians at Mai Chow on 31 March is by Colonel Konovaloff, a White Russian military adviser with the Emperor's forces.

At this same hour something happened on the front which the Ethiopians had abandoned. The explosions of the enemy shells, though less frequent, sounded very near. Everybody knew how critically placed we were.

It was impossible to find a single man ready to obey an order or even in his proper place. Soldiers drifted about in every direction and in disorderly crowds: the mountain was full of them. The Emperor returned to his observation point after a late lunch, but there was a heavy mist and one could distinguish little. Before nightfall a new council. A little later they began to examine the objects which filled the cave to see what could be taken away; much opening of trunks and cases.

Near nightfall the Emperor began to distribute in person the things that he could not take with him: cartridges, oddments of clothing, liquor, preserved foods, supplies of all sorts. The cave filled up with soldiers who wished to profit from the occasion. When the Emperor wished to leave the cave he could force a passage only with the greatest difficulty. Beatings, shouts, gesticulations, and at last the mob left the place with their booty.

At 9.30 we left Aia and took the road for Korem.

Behind us they exploded all the artillery and rifle ammunition, the tins of petrol and drums of oil, which destroyed along with them all that remained of the piles of striped shirts and black satin capes with which we hoped the draw the Azebu Galla to our side.

The field radio station was abandoned with the rest.

The descent from our mountain was terrible, so dark was the night.

Every minute the road was jammed. When the Ethiopians march the main object of each man is to pass all the others. This mob of people trying to thread its way through donkeys, mules and hundreds of other Ethiopians created an incredible disorder.

We took the whole night to cover the ten kilometres or so which separated us from Lake Ashangi. I had lost sight of the Emperor and the sons of Ras Kassa with whom I had travelled before, and was marching now with a group of soldiers. It was only at dawn that two of the Emperor's pages joined me. They too had been separated in the crowd.

We hurried. At every moment the aeroplanes might appear.

These last days they had continually bombarded the shelterless borders of Lake Ashangi and the two passes to north and south of it, full of baggage trains and soldiers. After a moment's halt I decided to go on to Korem: my companions did not continue with me.

It was seven o'clock in the morning when the first aeroplane was seen. Bombs rained upon our troops in retreat. Other aeroplanes appeared. When I had crossed the pass and come down into the valley the bombardment was let loose in all ferocity.

Fourteen planes took turns to hurl their bombs upon the unbroken flood of humanity which surged towards Korem. I had to travel rather to the left of the crowd.

I shall never forget the picture that I saw.

The wide valley, which during the season of rains is inundated in part, lay level under the blazing African sun. To its side the blue surface of the lake was lightly ruffled by the breeze. Along the road the weary people dragged themselves, scattering for a moment in panic or massing together in groups. Four, six, eight bombs burst one after the other. They fell some distance from the road and hit nobody . . .

The people quicken pace. Here is another aeroplane which seems to be choosing its victims as it flies just over their heads. One explosion . . . then another which raises a jet of earth clods, sand and stones.

People are hit this time. Everything round me disperses. I turn round and see someone dying on the ground. A form that slightly moves.

Fear pushes the survivors upon their road without attending to the wretch who cannot follow them, for he has lost his legs.

At the same moment our allies the Azebu Galla fire on us from the hilltops where their villages lie. When they see stragglers they kill them and strip the bleeding bodies of rifles, cartridges and clothes.

Before us there is a corner of hell which none of us can avoid. On one side of the road is the lake, on the other are the mountains. The pass is narrow, and the human flood finds it hard to press forward and through.

Everybody knows that in the bush and behind the rocks hide the treacherous Azebu, on the watch. A hail of bombs burst all over the pass wounding animals and men.

Poor little Ethiopian donkeys! . . . how often have I seen them on the road, their jaws smashed to pieces, their eyes blown from their sockets, their stomachs opened by a bomb.

We crossed the dangerous pass. Blot after dark blot along our road. These were stains of blood dried quickly by the lively sun: they showed us the way.

We hurried on over bodies sprawled and tumbled. Once more I found myself in a wide open place where I tried to keep my distance from the crowd.

Behind a turn in the road a bomb has just burst. I see the Ethiopian in front of me bending over an extended body. 'Ato Gabre Mariam?' he said. 'What has happened?'

'Pomp, bakon madanit' ('Bomb, please medicine'), answers the wounded man, turning his eyes in supplication to me. And I do not want to be left behind. See us, me and the Ethiopian following me, running on along the road.

As I go, I see again a face now no more than a pulp of bleeding flesh, over which a young boy hangs sobbing, trying his best to help the wounded. Others are falling around us . . . we run on and on . . . and at last we are near the caves of Korem which will shelter us from the Azebu bullets and the aeroplanes.

On a range of hills, covered with bush, there are *tukuls* and the characteristic small properties of the Ethiopians, surrounded by palisades. Farther off on a small mountain there is a larger property kept more tidily. It belongs to the local *shum*. I run down the hill and on towards the slope where the caves are dug.

At my feet, until lost to view, spreads the valley inhabited by the terrible Azebu Galla. It is time I reached my refuge – two planes are already flying over me . . .

Abyssinia: An American Journalist with the Fascist Armoured Column Approaching Addis Ababa, 18 April 1936

Herbert Matthews

The climb to Alagi Pass was another cause for marvel at an engineering skill and physical stamina which could have carved such a road out of a steep mountainside that a mule would strain to climb. As we rose a panorama began to unfold behind us, as if someone were turning back the pages on all those journeys I had taken in seven months of campaigning. Near the top I stood up and turned back for a last look. Off to the east I could see where the plateau dipped down to Dankalia; and there was the Agamè, where Mariotti still chased the elusive Kassa Sebat; and the Tigrè, and Enderta, the Tembien, the Scirè and far off to the west, Ras Dascian, keeping its immemorial watch over that fierce and wonderful land . . .

Until noon we had made excellent progress, but as we were making another long ascent our progress was blocked by a jam which we thought contained a few dozen cars. Actually, we were in a traffic snarl that involved 800 trucks, stretching over twenty-five miles and lasting no less than twenty-three hours! For there we stayed, immovable, until eleven the next morning. The truck containing Tacle and our tents and bedding was far in the rear, which meant that we had to sleep in the Fiat, and it was, indeed, a very strange night.

We were nowhere in Abyssinia, high up on a mountainside from which an immense panorama could be sensed without being seen.

The enormous mass of tropical stars came out in all their spectacular finery. Fires sprang up, one by one, in an interminable line behind us that seemed to stretch down toward infinite depths, and for long we heard the comforting bustle and murmur of fellow human beings, preparing as we were to pass a night of romance and intense discomfort.

Major Branca proved again his inexhaustible ingenuity by having his operators set up a radio receiver, and he soon had us tuned in with Rome, London and Berlin. We felt like listeners in Mars capturing echoes of another world. It seemed incredible that there ever could be any connection between us and Europe from where those strains of jazz and plaintive Neapolitan songs came as we sat shivering in the cold night air during that pause on an historic journey.

Someone switched the dial over from Rome to London. It was the news broadcast, and it resounded clearly. It had been reported, it seems, that Dessye was occupied by the Italians [it had been occupied on 15 April] but the Ethiopian Government in Addis Ababa denied it, so all listeners were cautioned to reserve their judgement. It was true, however, that the Abyssinian position seemed 'rather difficult'. Then came an account of a battle which had taken place, it appeared, just north of Korem where a large force of Ethiopians had gallantly attacked the Italian army, and presumably halted their advance toward the south.

We did some quick figuring. There was no doubt of it. The location of the fighting was exactly where we were, and without having the vaguest notion of it, there we sat, in the midst of a sanguinary battle, on the way towards a city which the Italians had not captured yet! Oh, the folly of it! The Italians roared with laughter, but as a newspaperman I felt rather ashamed for my profession. And that unctuous voice with its pseudo 'Oxford accent', half feminine, half masculine, was inexpressibly irritating. Poor England!

The Spanish Civil War: Carlist Forces Drive Back the Basque Frente Popular near Irun, 26 August 1936

G. L. Steer

A night battle in forest is a magnificent sight to see. The unpleasant details of war are sponged away by night. No tired men, no wounded in sweat, no dead lying heavy on the dry uncomfortable grass. You are saved the view of the broken ammunition cases, the discarded tins and piled filth of the temporary camp. Quickly trowelled trenches do not gash the fern banks and the roads and fields are not pitted with ugly irregular shell-holes under a pall of dust. War is idealized into a symphony of blue and yellow lights against a dull background of explosions: bullets and shells take the part of strings and portentous wind in an untiring orchestra.

It is ethereal, war by night. Over there, where Zubelzu woods look in profile up to Erlaitz, the dark forest glitters with thousand upon thousand tinsel flashes, level spurts of fairy flame that illumine the tree boles like stiff upright threads. At the centre of Zubelzu, where a sable dome of hill cuts the light and starry night sky, tinsel sparkles back. Between, mortars discharge like red reflecting ornaments and their shells explode like candles lighting yellow. Tinsel, hangings, candles, glitter, the dark background: what is this but a giant Christmas tree alight, now hiding, now revealing from its foliage the decorations of our childhood, surfaces that catch and splinter fire into its prettiest particles, scarlets and electric blues and golden rays too fragile to be touched.

Charming illusion to me, who sit wrapped in pyjamas and in an infant wonder, gazing across the river that spins under the moon. And I hear the harmless crackle of this tinfoil game, like hangings that rub with metallic sharpness against the branches of the shaken Christmas tree when presents are cut down; and the louder explosions – those are crackers pulled round the festive candles of Zubelzu.

No killing and maiming, thirst, hunger and pain to be picked out through curious field-glasses. Only the prettiness of war, under the moon and against the sober foil of mountain and pinewood.

The Spanish Civil War: Guernica Destroyed by German Planes, 26 April 1937

Noel Monks

I passed through Guernica at about 3.30 p.m. The time is approximate, based on the fact that I left Bilbao at 2.30. Guernica was busy. It was market day. We passed through the town and took a road that Anton said would take us close to Marquina, where, as far as I knew, the front was. The front was there, all right, but Marquina was not. It had been smashed flat by bombers.

We were about eighteen miles east of Guernica when Anton pulled to the side of the road, jammed on the brakes and started shouting. He pointed wildly ahead, and my heart shot into my mouth when I looked. Over the tops of some hills appeared a flock of planes. A dozen or so bombers were flying high. But down much lower, seeming just to skim the treetops were six Heinkel 52 fighters. The bombers flew on towards Guernica, but the Heinkels, out for random plunder, spotted our car, and, wheeling like a flock of homing pigeons, they lined up the road – and our car.

Anton and I flung ourselves into a bomb hole, twenty yards to the side of the road. It was half filled with water, and we sprawled in mud. We half knelt, half stood, with our heads buried in the muddy side of the crater.

After one good look at the Heinkels, I didn't look up again until they had gone. That seemed hours later, but it was probably less than twenty minutes. The planes made several runs along the road. Machine-gun bullets plopped into the mud ahead, behind, all around us. I began to shiver from sheer fright. Only the day before Steer, an old hand now, had 'briefed' me about being strafed. 'Lie still and as flat as you can. But don't get up and start running, or you'll be bowled over for certain.'

When the Heinkels departed, out of ammunition I presumed, Anton and I ran back to our car. Nearby a military car was burning fiercely. All we could do was drag two riddled bodies to the side of the road. I was trembling all over now, in the grip of the first real fear I'd ever experienced . . . Then suddenly the quaking passed and I felt exhilarated. These were the days in foreign reporting when personal experiences were copy, for there hadn't been a war for eighteen years, long enough for those who went through the last one to forget, and for a generation and a half who knew nothing of war to be interested. We used to call them 'I' stories, and when the Spanish War ended in 1939 we were as heartily sick of writing them as the public must have been of reading them.

At the foot of the hills leading to Guernica we turned off the main road and took another back to Bilbao. Over to our left, in the direction of Guernica, we could hear the crump of bombs. I thought the Germans had located reinforcements moving up from Santander to stem the retreat. We drove on to Bilbao.

At the Presidencia, Steer and Holme were writing dispatches. They asked me to join them at dinner at Steer's hotel . . .

We'd eaten our first course of beans and were waiting for our bully beef when a government official, tears streaming down his face, burst into the dismal dining room crying, 'Guernica is destroyed. The Germans bombed and bombed and bombed.'

The time was about 9.30 p.m. Captain Roberts banged a huge fist on the table and said, 'Bloody swine.' Five minutes later I was in one of Mendiguren's limousines speeding towards Guernica. We were still a good ten miles away when I saw the reflection of Guernica's flames in the sky. As we drew nearer, on both sides of the road, men, women and children were sitting, dazed. I saw a priest in one group. I stopped the car and went up to him. 'What happened, Father?' I asked. His face was blackened, his clothes in tatters. He couldn't talk. He just pointed to the flames, still about four miles away, then whispered, '*Aviones . . . bombas . . . mucho, mucho.*'

In the good 'I' tradition of the day, I was the first correspondent to reach Guernica, and was immediately pressed into service by some Basque soldiers collecting charred bodies that the flames had passed over. Some of the soldiers were sobbing like children. There were flames and smoke and grit, and the smell of burning human flesh was nauseating. Houses were collapsing into the inferno.

In the Plaza, surrounded almost by a wall of fire, were about a hundred refugees. They were wailing and weeping and rocking to and fro. One middle-aged man spoke English. He told me, 'At four, before the market closed, many aeroplanes came. They dropped bombs. Some came low and shot bullets into the streets. Father Aronategui was wonderful. He prayed with the people in the Plaza while the bombs fell.' The man had no idea who I was, as far as I know. He was telling me what had happened to Guernica.

Most of Guernica's streets began or ended at the Plaza. It was impossible to go down many of them, because they were walls of flame. Debris was piled high. I could see shadowy forms, some large, some just ashes. I moved round to the back of the Plaza among survivors. They had the same story to tell, aeroplanes, bullets, bombs, fire.

Within twenty-four hours, when the grim story was told to the world, Franco was going to brand these shocked, homeless people as liars. So-called British experts were going to come to Guernica, weeks afterwards, when the smell of burnt human flesh had been replaced by petrol dumped here and there among the ruins by Mola's men, and deliver pompous judgements: 'Guernica was set on fire wilfully by the Reds.'

The Spanish Civil War: Wounded by a Fascist Sniper, near Huesca, 20 May 1937

George Orwell

I had been about ten days at the front when it happened. The whole experience of being hit by a bullet is very interesting and I think it is worth describing in detail.

It was at the corner of the parapet, at five o'clock in the morning. This was always a dangerous time, because we had the dawn at our backs, and if you stuck your head above the parapet it was clearly outlined against the sky. I was talking to the sentries preparatory to changing the guard. Suddenly, in the very middle of saying something, I felt – it is very hard to describe what I felt, though I remember it with the utmost vividness.

Roughly speaking it was the sensation of being *at the centre* of an explosion. There seemed to be a loud bang and a blinding flash of light all round me, and I felt a tremendous shock – no pain, only a violent shock, such as you get from an electric terminal; with it a sense of utter weakness, a feeling of being stricken and shrivelled up to nothing. The sandbags in front of me receded into immense distance. I fancy you would feel much the same if you were struck by lightning. I knew immediately that I was hit, but because of the seeming bang and flash I thought it was a rifle nearby that had gone off accidentally and shot me. All this happened in a space of time much less than a second. The next moment my knees crumpled up and I was falling, my head hitting the ground with a violent bang which, to my relief, did not hurt. I had a numb, dazed feeling, a consciousness of being very badly hurt, but no pain in the ordinary sense.

The American sentry I had been talking to had started forward. 'Gosh! Are you hit?' People gathered round. There was the usual fuss — 'Lift him up! Where's he hit? Get his shirt open!' etc., etc. The American called for a knife to cut my shirt open. I knew that there was one in my pocket and tried to get it out, but discovered that my right arm was paralysed. Not being in pain, I felt a vague satisfaction. This ought to please my wife, I thought; she had always wanted me to be wounded, which would save me from being killed when the great battle came. It was only now that it occurred to me to wonder where I was hit, and how badly; I could feel nothing, but I was conscious that the bullet had struck me somewhere in the front of my body. When I tried to speak I found that I had no voice, only a faint squeak, but at the second attempt I managed to ask where I was hit. In the throat, they said, Harry Webb, our stretcher-bearer, had brought a bandage and one of the little bottles of alcohol they gave us for field-dressings. As they lifted me up a lot of blood poured out of my mouth, and I heard a Spaniard behind me say that the bullet had gone clear through my neck. I felt the alcohol, which at ordinary times would sting like the devil, splash on to the wound as a pleasant coolness.

They laid me down again while somebody fetched a stretcher. As soon as I knew that the bullet had gone clean through my neck I took it for granted that I was done for. I had never heard of a man or an animal getting a bullet through the middle of the neck and surviving it. The blood was dribbling out of the corner of my mouth. 'The artery's gone,' I thought. I wondered how long you last when your carotid artery is cut; not many minutes, presumably. Everything was very blurry. There must have been about two minutes during which I assumed that I was killed. And that too was interesting — I mean it is interesting to know what your thoughts would be at such a time. My first thought, conventionally enough, was for my wife. My second was a violent resentment at having to leave this world which, when all is said and done, suits me so well. I had time to feel this very vividly. The stupid mischance infuriated me. The meaninglessness of it! To be bumped off, not even in battle, but in this stale corner of the trenches, thanks to a moment's carelessness! I thought, too, of the man who had shot me – wondered what he was like, whether he was a Spaniard or a foreigner, whether he knew he had got me, and so forth. I could not feel any resentment against him. I reflected that as he was a Fascist I would have killed him if I could, but that if he had been taken prisoner and brought before me at this moment I would merely have congratulated him on his good shooting. It may be, though, that if you were really dying your thoughts would be quite different.

They had just got me on to the stretcher when my paralysed right arm came to life and began hurting damnably. At the time I imagined that I must have broken it in falling; but the pain reassured me, for I knew that your sensations do not become more acute when you are dying. I began to feel more normal and to be sorry for the four poor devils who were sweating and slithering with the stretcher on their shoulders. It was a mile and a half to the ambulance, and vile going, over lumpy, slippery tracks. I knew what a sweat it was, having helped to carry a wounded man down a day or two earlier. The leaves of the silver poplars which, in places, fringed our trenches brushed against my face; I thought what a good thing it was to be alive in a world where silver poplars grow. But all the while the pain in my arm was diabolical, making me swear and then try not to swear, because every time I breathed too hard the blood bubbled out of my mouth.

The Louis–Schmeling Fight, 22 June 1938

Bob Considine

Schmeling became World Heavyweight Champion by defeating Jack Sharkey on a foul in 1930. He knocked out Joe Louis in the twelfth round on 19 June 1936 in New York. Louis won the world title in 1937 and retained it until March 1949, when he retired.

Listen to this, buddy, for it comes from a guy whose palms are still wet, whose throat is still dry, and whose jaw is still agape from the utter shock of watching Joe Louis knock out Max Schmeling.

It was a shocking thing, that knockout – short, sharp, merciless, complete. Louis was like this:

He was a big lean copper spring, tightened and retightened through weeks of training until he was one pregnant package of coiled venom.

Schmeling hit that spring. He hit it with a whistling right-hand punch in the first minute of the fight – and the spring, tormented with tension, suddenly burst with one brazen spang of activity. Hard brown arms, propelling two unerring fists, blurred beneath the hot white candelabra of the ring lights. And Schmeling was in the path of them, a man caught and mangled in the whirring claws of a mad and feverish machine.

The mob, biggest and most prosperous ever to see a fight in a ball yard, knew that here was the end before the thing had really started. It knew, so it stood up and howled one long shriek. People who had paid as much as $100 for their chairs didn't use them – except perhaps to stand on, the better to let the sight burn forever in their memories.

There were four steps to Schmeling's knockout. A few seconds after he landed his only punch of the fight, Louis caught him with a lethal little left hook that drove him into the ropes so that his right arm was hooked over the top strand, like a drunk hanging to a fence. Louis swarmed over him and hit with everything he had – until Referee Donovan pushed him away and counted one.

Schmeling staggered away from the ropes, dazed and sick. He looked drunkenly toward his corner, and before he had turned his head back Louis was on him again, first with a left and then that awe-provoking right that made a crunching sound when it hit the German's jaw. Max fell down, hurt and giddy, for a count of three.

He clawed his way up as if the night air were as thick as black water, and Louis – his nostrils like the mouth of a double-barrelled shotgun – took a quiet lead and let him have both barrels.

Max fell almost lightly, bereft of his senses, his fingers touching the canvas like a comical stew-bum doing his morning exercises, knees bent and the tongue lolling in his head.

He got up long enough to be knocked down again, this time with his dark unshaven face pushed in the sharp gravel of the resin.

Louis jumped away lightly, a bright and pleased look in his eyes, and as he did the white towel of surrender which Louis' handlers had refused to use two years ago tonight came sailing into the ring in a soggy mess. It was thrown by Max Machon, oblivious to the fact that fights cannot end this way in New York.

The referee snatched it off the floor and flung it backwards. It hit the ropes and hung there, limp as Schmeling. Donovan counted up to five over Max, sensed the futility of it all, and stopped the fight.

The big crowd began to rustle restlessly toward the exits, many only now accepting Louis as champion of the world. There were no eyes for Schmeling, sprawled on his stool in his corner.

He got up eventually, his dirty grey-and-black robe over his shoulders, and wormed through the happy little crowd that hovered around Louis. And he put his arm around the Negro and smiled. They both smiled and could afford to – for Louis had made around $200,000 a minute and Schmeling $100,000 a minute.

But once he crawled down in the belly of the big stadium, Schmeling realized the implications of his defeat. He, who won the title on a partly phony foul, and beat Louis two years ago with the aid of a crushing punch after the bell had sounded, now said Louis had fouled him. That would read better in Germany, whence earlier in the day had come a cable from Hitler, calling on him to win.

It was a low, sneaking trick, but a rather typical last word from Schmeling.

The Spanish Civil War: Nationalist Planes Bomb Barcelona, September 1938

Marcel Junod

As the Republicans fell back before Franco's Nationalist forces, the Republican Government moved from Valencia to Barcelona, which was suffering from acute food shortage. The author, Junod, became Director-General of the Red Cross.

Air warfare was now added to the horrors of famine, the arrests and the despair of a whole people. The capital of Catalonia became a special target for the bombing planes and their bombs fell at hazard on the houses and in the streets.

I remember in particular one morning in September. I saw the planes coming. As usual they emerged from behind the hill of Montjuich and made their way towards the town. I jumped down the stairs two at a time. Below the Spanish Red Cross officials were getting the ambulance ready. It was not long before the call came. Bombs had fallen on a school in the old quarter near the Generalidad.

I jumped into a car with ambulance attendants. When we arrived we found that the roof of the school and the upper storeys had collapsed burying over a hundred children in the ruins. We set to work desperately to open up the debris. At the same time we had to be careful because still-living children might be under the rubble.

We managed to extricate only ten complete bodies. All the others had been blown to pieces. It was atrocious. I saw one of the attendants recover a small blond head. Others picked up what might have been the feet of little angels. Not a single child who had been in the school was still alive.

The Second World War: The Evacuation of Children from London, 1 September 1939

Hilde Marchant

It was not until Friday morning, September 1st, that I really took the sharp, agonized breath of war. That day it began, in a slum in London.

The office had told me to cover the evacuation of some of London's schoolchildren. There had been great preparations for the scheme – preparations that raised strong criticism. Evacuation would split the British home, divide child and parent, break that domestic background that was our strength.

I went to a block of working-class flats at the back of Gray's Inn Road and in the early morning saw a tiny, frail, Cockney child walking across to school. The child had a big, brown-paper parcel in her hand and was dragging it along. But as she turned I saw a brown box banging against her thin legs. It bumped up and down at every step, slung by a thin string over her shoulder.

It was Florence Morecambe, an English schoolchild, with a gas mask instead of a satchel over her shoulder.

I went along with Florence to her school. It was a big Council school and the classrooms were filled with children, parcels, gas masks. The desks and blackboards were piled up in a heap in one corridor. They were not going to school for lessons. They were going on a holiday. The children were excited and happy because their parents had told them they were going away to the country. Many of them, like my little Florence, had never seen green fields. Their playground was the tarmac or a sandpit in the concrete square at the back.

I watched the schoolteachers calling out their names and tying luggage labels in their coats, checking their parcels to see there were warm and clean clothes. On the gates of the school were two fat policemen. They were letting the children through but gently asking the parents not to come farther. They might disturb the children. So mothers and fathers were saying goodbye, straightening the girls' hair, getting the boys to blow their noses, and lightly and quickly kissing them. The parents stood outside while the children went to be registered in their classrooms. There was quite a long wait before this small army got its orders through from the LCC [London County Council] to move off. In the meantime I sat in the school playground, watching these thin, wiry little Cockneys playing their rough-and-push games on the faded netball pitch. It was disturbing, for through the high grille their mothers pressed their faces, trying to see the one child that resembled them. Every now and then the policeman would call out a child's name and a mother who had forgotten a bar of chocolate or a toothbrush had a last chance to tell a child to be good, to write and to straighten her hat.

Labelled and lined up, the children began to move out of the school. I followed Florence, her live tiny face bobbing about, white among so many navy-blue school caps. She was chattering away to an older schoolgirl, wanting to know what the country was like, where they were going, what games they would play on the grass.

On one side of Gray's Inn Road this ragged crocodile moved towards the tube station. On the other, were mothers who were waving and running along to see the last of their children. The police had asked them not to follow, but they could not resist.

The children scrambled down into the tube.

Blitzkrieg: German Breakthrough on the Meuse, 15 May 1940

Erwin Rommel

The Maginot Line, an elaborate system of fortresses along the French–German frontier, was outflanked by the Germans in May 1940. By the evening of 12 May the Germans were across the Franco-Belgian frontier and overlooking the Meuse, in a sector where only the French 2nd and 9th Armies, without anti-tank guns or anti-aircraft artillery, faced them. Rommel was commanding 7th Panzer Division.

The way to the west was now open. The moon was up and for the time being we could expect no real darkness. I had already given orders, in the plan for the breakthrough, for the leading tanks to scatter the road and verges with machine and anti-tank gunfire at intervals during the drive to Avesnes, which I hoped would prevent the enemy from laying mines. The rest of the Panzer Regiment was to follow close behind the leading tanks and be ready at any time to fire salvoes to either flank. The mass of the division had instructions to follow up the Panzer Regiment lorry-borne.

The tanks now rolled in a long column through the line of fortifications and on towards the first houses, which had been set alight by our fire. In the moonlight we could see the men of 7th Motor-Cycle Battalion moving forward on foot beside us. Occasionally an enemy machine-gun or anti-tank gun fired, but none of their shots came anywhere near us. Our artillery was dropping heavy harassing fire on villages and the road far ahead of the regiment. Gradually the speed increased. Before long we were 500–1000–2000–3000 yards into the fortified zone. Engines roared, tank tracks clanked and clattered. Whether or not the enemy was firing was impossible to tell in the ear-splitting noise. We crossed the railway line a mile or so south-west of Solre le Château, and then swung north to the main road which was soon reached. Then off along the road and past the first houses.

The people in the houses were rudely awoken by the din of our tanks, the clatter and roar of tracks and engines. Troops lay bivouacked beside the road, military vehicles stood parked in farmyards and in some places on the road itself. Civilians and

French troops, their faces distorted with terror, lay huddled in the ditches, alongside hedges and in every hollow beside the road. We passed refugee columns, the carts abandoned by their owners, who had fled in panic into the fields. On we went, at a steady speed, towards our objective. Every so often a quick glance at the map by a shaded light and a short wireless message to Divisional HQ to report the position and thus the success of 25th Panzer Regiment. Every so often a look out of the hatch to assure myself that there was still no resistance and that contact was being maintained to the rear. The flat countryside lay spread out around us under the cold light of the moon. We were through the Maginot Line! It was hardly conceivable. Twenty-two years before we had stood for four and a half years before this selfsame enemy and had won victory after victory and yet finally lost the war. And now we had broken through the renowned Maginot Line and were driving deep into enemy territory. It was not just a beautiful dream. It was reality.

Dunkirk: The Beaches, 1 June 1940

John Charles Austin

Evacuation of the British Expeditionary Force from Dunkirk began on 26 May. By 4 June, when the operation ended, 198,000 British and 140,000 French and Belgian troops had been saved.

Eventually we arrived at the spot on this side of the last canal separating us from the sea, where we had to abandon the vehicles. They were smashed up in the darkness and pushed into the canal. The men formed up by the roadside and the roll was called for the last time. A weird scene, the Troop sergeant-majors calling out the names of the gunners in loud whispers and ticking them off on their lists by torchlight as the answers came back out of the darkness, from nowhere it seemed.

'All present and correct, sir.'

And once more the fifty of us started off, this time on foot, formed up in threes, the Major and I walking at the head of the column. To our great joy we discovered that the bridge spanning the canal had not been smashed. Once over it, and another obstacle between us and the Unknown had been passed. We continued towards Malo-les-Bains, crossing the railway, and marching through the ruined street of Rosendaal whose skeleton walls stood around us like the ruins of some bygone civilization. The only sound was the crunching of the broken glass under our feet, as if we were marching over hard ice crystals on a winter's day. Mysterious shadows flitted about the streets, in and out of broken doorways, and disappearing silently round corners. They were stray inhabitants who had been cut off by the swift march of events and were living in cellars. And a few looters. And, probably, a few spies. The German gunfire was now incessant, the flash of the explosions continually lighting up the scene for a second or two on every side of us.

Now we were no longer alone. We began to meet little batches of our infantry marching in the same direction. Often as we approached we would be hailed out of the darkness:

'Is that A Company, King's Own Scottish Borderers. . . ?' Or the name of some other unit would be shouted. These were bits of the rearguard coming back, and marching still in good formation down to the beaches.

The road became very narrow, and adding to the difficulties of getting along, the troops were harassed by an incessant hooting from behind, which after a time got on everybody's nerves more than the shellfire. Finally, we halted to discover what the fuss was about. A crowd of panic-stricken French poilus were trying to drive their lorries in the darkness right through our marching infantry, knocking them to right and left off the road into the ditches. Angry words passed. There seemed great likelihood that a fight would take place. Fortunately, at the last moment the French drivers thought better of it, and fell in behind the troops. It was high time, too. We were just in the mood to shoot if necessary. They followed behind us at a marching pace for some time till they turned off down another road.

We were now in the region of the dunes, which rose like humps of a deeper darkness. And these in their turn were dotted with the still-blacker shapes of abandoned vehicles, half sunk in the sand, fantastic twisted shapes of burned-out skeletons, and crazy-looking wreckage that had been heaped up in extraordinary piles by the explosions of bombs. All these black shapes were silhouetted against the angry red glare in the sky, which reflected down on us the agony of burning Dunkirk.

Slowly we picked our way between the wreckage, sinking ankle-deep in the loose sand, until we reached the gaunt skeletons of what had once been the houses on the promenade. The whole front was one long continuous line of blazing buildings, a high wall of fire, roaring and darting in tongues of flame, with the smoke pouring upwards and disappearing in the blackness of the sky above the rooftops. Out seawards the darkness was as thick and smooth as black velvet, except for now and again when the shape of a sunken destroyer or paddle-steamer made a slight thickening on its impenetrable surface. Facing us, the great black wall of the Mole stretched from the beach far out into sea, the end of it almost invisible to us. The Mole had an astounding, terrifying background of giant flames leaping a hundred feet into the air from blazing oil tanks. At the shore end of the Mole stood an obelisk, and the high explosive shells burst around it with monotonous regularity.

Along the promenade, in parties of fifty, the remnants of practically all the last regiments were wearily trudging along. There was no singing, and very little talk. Everyone was far too exhausted to waste breath. Occasionally out of the darkness came a sudden shout:

'A Company, Green Howards . . .'

'C Company, East Yorks . . .'

These shouts came either from stragglers trying to find lost units, or guides on the look-out for the parties they were to lead on to the Mole for evacuation.

The tide was out. Over the wide stretch of sand could be dimly discerned little oblong masses of soldiers, moving in platoons and orderly groups down towards the edge of the sea. Now and again you would hear a shout:

'Alf, where are you. . . ?'

'Let's hear from you, Bill . . .'

'Over this way, George . . .'

It was none too easy to keep contact with one's friends in the darkness, and amid so many little masses of moving men, all looking very much alike. If you stopped for a few seconds to look behind the chances were you attached yourself to some entirely different unit.

From the margin of the sea, at fairly wide intervals, three long thin black lines protruded into the water, conveying the effect of low wooden breakwaters. These were lines of men, standing in pairs behind one another far out into the water, waiting in queues till boats arrived to transport them, a score or so at a time, to the steamers and warships that were filling up with the last survivors. The queues stood there, fixed and almost as regular as if ruled. No bunching, no pushing, nothing like the mix-up to be seen at the turnstiles when a crowd is going into a football match. Much more orderly, even, than a waiting theatre queue.

About this time, afraid that some of our own men might be trailing off, I began shouting, '2004th Field Regiment . . . 2004th Field Regiment . . .' We were also having difficulty in finding our report centre.

'I wonder where this blasted report centre is,' said the Major. 'Give another shout. If they hear us they can shout back instructions and tell us what to do.'

So from this point I went along shouting. But the report centre failed to materialize, and soon we decided that hanging about any longer on the promenade looking for it might prove disastrous. Heavy shells commenced crashing into the tops of the ruined buildings along the promenade, bringing down heaps of brick and masonry almost on our heads.

'It'll be healthier on the beach,' said the Major.

A group of dead and dying soldiers on the path in front of us quickened our desire to quit the promenade. Stepping over bodies we marched down the slope on to the dark beach. Dunkirk front was now a lurid study in red and black; flames, smoke, and the night itself all mingling together to compose a frightful panorama of death and destruction. Red and black, all the time, except for an occasional flash of white low in the sky miles away to the left and right where big shells from coastal defence guns at Calais and Nieuport were being hurled into the town.

Down on the beach you immediately felt yourself surrounded by a deadly evil atmosphere. A horrible stench of blood and mutilated flesh pervaded the place. There was no escape from it. Not a breath of air was blowing to dissipate the appalling odour that arose from the dead bodies that had been lying on the sand, in some cases for several days. We might have been walking through a slaughter-house on a hot day. The darkness, which hid some of the sights of horror from our eyes, seemed to thicken this dreadful stench. It created the impression that death was hovering around, very near at hand.

We set our faces in the direction of the sea, quickening our pace to pass through the belt of this nauseating miasma as soon as possible.

'Water ... Water ...' groaned a voice from the ground just in front of us.

It was a wounded infantryman. He had been hit so badly that there was no hope for him. Our water bottles had long been empty, but by carefully draining them all into one we managed to collect a mouthful or two. A sergeant knelt down beside the dying man and held the bottle to his lips. Then we proceeded on our way, leaving the bottle with the last few drains in it near the poor fellow's hand so that he could moisten his lips from time to time.

Dogfight over the Channel, 3 September 1940

Richard Hillary

September 3 dawned dark and overcast, with a slight breeze ruffling the waters of the Estuary. Hornchurch aerodrome, twelve miles east of London, wore its usual morning pallor of yellow fog, lending an added air of grimness to the dimly silhouetted Spitfires around the boundary. From time to time a balloon would poke its head grotesquely through the mist as though looking for possible victims before falling back like some tired monster.

We came out on to the tarmac at about eight o'clock. During the night our machines had been moved from the Dispersal Point over to the hangars. All the machine tools, oil, and general equipment had been left on the far side of the aerodrome. I was worried. We had been bombed a short time before, and my plane had been fitted out with a new cockpit hood. This hood unfortunately would not slide open along its groove; and with a depleted ground staff and no tools, I began to fear it never would. Unless it did open, I shouldn't be able to bale out in a hurry if I had to. Miraculously, 'Uncle George' Denholm, our Squadron Leader, produced three men with a heavy file and lubricating oil, and the corporal fitter and I set upon the hood in a fury of haste. We took it turn by turn, filing and oiling, oiling and filing, until at last the hood began to move. But agonizingly slowly: by ten o'clock, when the mist had cleared and the sun was blazing out of a clear sky, the hood was still sticking firmly halfway along the groove; at 10.15, what I had feared for the last hour happened. Down the loudspeaker came the emotionless voice of the controller: '603 Squadron take off and patrol base; you will receive further orders in the air: 603 Squadron take off as quickly as you can, please.' As I pressed the starter and the engine roared into life, the corporal stepped back and crossed his fingers significantly. I felt the usual sick feeling in the pit of the stomach, as though I were about to row a race, and then I was too busy getting into position to feel anything.

Uncle George and the leading section took off in a cloud of dust; Brian Carbury looked across and put up his thumbs. I nodded and opened up, to take off for the last time from Hornchurch. I was flying No. 3 in Brian's section, with Stapme Stapleton on the right: the third section consisted of only two machines, so that our Squadron strength was eight. We headed south-east, climbing all out on a steady course. At about 12,000 feet we came up through the clouds: I looked down and saw them spread out below me like layers of whipped cream. The sun was brilliant and made it difficult to see even the next plane when turning. I was peering anxiously ahead, for the controller had given us warning of at least fifty enemy fighters approaching very high. When we did first sight them, nobody shouted, as I think we all saw them at the same moment. They must have been 500 to 1000 feet above us and coming straight on like a swarm of locusts. I remember cursing and going automatically into line astern: the next moment we were in among them and it was each man for himself. As soon as they saw us they spread out and dived, and the next ten minutes was a blur of twisting machines and tracer bullets. One Messerschmitt went down in a sheet of flame on my right, and a Spitfire hurtled past in a half-roll; I was weaving and turning in a desperate attempt to gain height, with the machine practically hanging on the air-screw. Then, just below me and to my left, I saw what I had been praying for – a Messerschmitt climbing and away from the sun. I closed in to 200 yards, and from slightly to one side gave him a two-second burst: fabric ripped off the wing and black smoke poured from the engine, but he did not go down. Like a fool, I did not break away, but put in another three-second burst. Red flames shot upwards and he spiralled out of sight. At that moment, I felt a terrific explosion which knocked the control stick from my hand, and the whole machine quivered like a stricken animal. In a second, the cockpit was a mass of flames: instinctively, I reached up to open the hood. It would not move. I tore off my straps and managed to force it back; but this took time, and when I dropped back into the seat and reached for the stick in an effort to turn the plane on its back, the heat was so intense that I could feel myself going. I remember a second of sharp agony, remember thinking, 'So this is it!' and putting both hands to my eyes. Then I passed out.

When I regained consciousness I was free of the machine and falling rapidly. I pulled the rip-cord of my parachute and checked my descent with a jerk. Looking down, I saw that my left trouser leg was burnt off, that I was going to fall into the sea, and that the English coast was deplorably far away. About twenty feet above the water, I attempted to undo my parachute, failed, and flopped into the sea with it billowing round me. I was told later that the machine went into a spin at about 25,000 feet and that at 10,000 feet I fell out – unconscious. This may well have been so, for I discovered later a large cut on the top of my head, presumably collected while bumping round inside.

The water was not unwarm and I was pleasantly surprised to find that my life-jacket kept me afloat. I looked at my watch: it was not there. Then, for the first time, I noticed how burnt my hands were: down to the wrist, the skin was dead white and hung in shreds: I felt faintly sick from the smell of burnt flesh. By closing one eye I could see my lips, jutting out like motor tires. The side of my parachute harness was cutting into me particularly painfully, so that I guessed my right hip was burnt. I made a further attempt to undo the harness, but owing to the pain of my hands, soon desisted. Instead, I lay back and reviewed my position: I was a long way from land; my hands were burnt, and so, judging from the pain of the sun, was my face; it was unlikely that anyone on shore had seen me come down and even more unlikely that a ship would come by; I could float for possibly four hours in my Mae West. I began to feel that I had perhaps been premature in considering myself lucky to have escaped from the machine. After about half an hour my teeth started chattering, and to quiet them I kept up a regular tuneless chant, varying it from time to time with calls for help. There can be few more futile pastimes than yelling for help alone in the North Sea, with a solitary seagull for company, yet it gave me a certain melancholy satisfaction, for I had once written a short story in which the hero (falling from a liner) had done just this. It was rejected.

The water now seemed much colder and I noticed with surprise that the sun had gone in though my face was still burning. I looked down at my hands, and not seeing them, realized that I had gone blind. So I was going to die. It came to me like that – I was going to die, and I was not afraid. This realization came as a surprise. The manner of my approaching death appalled and horrified me, but the actual vision of death left me unafraid: I felt only a profound curiosity and a sense of satisfaction that within a few minutes or a few hours I was to learn the great answer. I decided that it should be in a few minutes. I had no qualms about hastening my end and, reaching up, I managed to unscrew the valve of my Mae West. The air escaped in a rush and my head went under water. It is said by people who have all but died in the sea that drowning is a pleasant death. I did not find it so. I swallowed a large quantity of water before my head came up again, but derived little satisfaction from it. I tried again, to find that I could not get my face under. I was so enmeshed in my parachute that I could not move. For the next ten minutes, I tore my hands to ribbons on the spring-release catch. It was stuck fast. I lay back exhausted, and then I started to laugh. By this time I was probably not entirely normal and I doubt if my laughter was wholly sane, but there was something irresistibly comical in my grand gesture of suicide being so simply thwarted.

Goethe once wrote that no one, unless he had led the full life and realized himself completely, had the right to take his own life. Providence seemed determined that I should not incur the great man's displeasure.

It is often said that a dying man relives his whole life in one rapid kaleidoscope. I merely thought gloomily of the Squadron returning, of my mother at home, and of the few people who would miss me. Outside my family, I could count them on the fingers of one hand. What did gratify me enormously was to find that I indulged in no frantic abasements or prayers to the Almighty. It is an old jibe of God-fearing people that the irreligious always change their tune when about to die: I was pleased to think that I was proving them wrong. Because I seemed to be in for an indeterminate period of waiting, I began to feel a terrible loneliness and sought for some means to take my mind off my plight. I took it for granted that I must soon become delirious, and I attempted to hasten the process:

I encouraged my mind to wander vaguely and aimlessly, with the result that I did experience a certain peace. But when I forced myself to think of something concrete, I found that I was still only too lucid. I went on shuttling between the two with varying success until I was picked up. I remember as in a dream hearing somebody shout: it seemed so far away and quite unconnected with me.

Then willing arms were dragging me over the side; my parachute was taken off (and with such ease!); a brandy flask was pushed between my swollen lips; a voice said, 'OK, Joe, it's one of ours and still kicking'; and I was safe. I was neither relieved nor angry; I was past caring.

It was to the Margate lifeboat that I owed my rescue. Watchers on the coast had seen me come down, and for three hours they had been searching for me. Owing to wrong directions, they were just giving up and turning back for land when ironically enough one of them saw my parachute. They were then fifteen miles east of Margate.

While in the water I had been numb and had felt very little pain. Now that I began to thaw out, the agony was such that I could have cried out. The good fellows made me as comfortable as possible, put up some sort of awning to keep the sun from my face, and phoned through for a doctor. It seemed to me to take an eternity to reach shore. I was put into an ambulance and driven rapidly to hospital. Through all this I was quite conscious, though unable to see. At the hospital they cut off my uniform, I gave the requisite information to a nurse about my next of kin, and then, to my infinite relief, felt a hypodermic syringe pushed into my arm.

London Docks Bombed, 7 September 1940

Desmond Flower

Foiled in their attempt to destroy the RAF, the Germans turned their attention to London. The raid on the Surrey Docks, on the evening of 7 September, was the start of the London Blitz.

Suddenly we were gaping upwards. The brilliant sky was criss-crossed from horizon to horizon by innumerable vapour trails. The sight was a completely novel one. We watched, fascinated, and all work stopped. The little silver stars sparkling at the heads of the vapour trails turned east. This display looked so insubstantial and harmless; even beautiful. Then, with a dull roar which made the ground across London shake as one stood upon it, the first sticks of bombs hit the docks. Leisurely, enormous mushrooms of black and brown smoke shot with crimson climbed into the sunlit sky. There they hung and slowly expanded, for there was no wind, and the great fires below fed more smoke into them as the hours passed.

On Friday and Saturday morning the sky grew darker and darker as the oily smoke rose and spread in heavy, immobile columns, shutting out the sun . . .

Now we were nearer to the docks. The columns of smoke merged and became a monstrous curtain which blocked the sky; only the billows within it and the sudden shafts of flame which shot up hundreds of feet made one realize that it was a living thing and not just the backdrop of some nightmare opera. There were fire hoses along the side of the road, climbing over one another like a helping of macaroni, with those sad little fountains spraying out from the leaks, as they always seem to do from all fire hoses. Every two or three minutes we would pull into the gutter as a fire bell broke out stridently behind us and an engine in unfamiliar livery tore past at full tilt: chocolate or green or blue, with gold lettering – City of Birmingham Fire Brigade, or Sheffield, or Bournemouth. The feeling was something you had never experienced before – the excitement and dash of fire engines arriving to help from so far away, and the oily, evil smell of fire and destruction, with its lazy, insolent rhythm.

The Blitz: Chelsea, 14 September 1940

Frances Faviell

The Church of the Holy Redeemer is a massive building and I had been there several times to see the shelter in the crypt because some of our refugees liked the idea of this shelter so much that they wanted to change to it. It was very close to Cheyne Hospital and when, at first, two of them did go there, I had gone to see that they were all right; but we persuaded them that it was too far and that their own was just as safe. It was a popular shelter – perhaps because, like the refugees, others felt that nowhere would they be safer than under the protection of the Church – and at the time the bomb fell it was crowded.

The bomb was recorded by one of us telephonists in the Control Centre at 18.35. The message said that there was fire and casualties trapped in Holy Redeemer Church in Upper Cheyne Row. Requests followed in rapid succession for ambulances, blankets to cover the dead, fire services, and reports came in that there were many casualties.

The bomb had struck the church at an angle through a window in a most extraordinary way and had penetrated the floor and burst among the shelterers, mostly women and small children. Here George Thorpe, whom we knew as 'Bert', lost his life with those women and children whom he had visited to reassure them – as he always did, although he was not the shelter warden. He knew that they were apt to become nervous and needed moral support in the heavy raids and he used to drop in there to boost up their courage and cheer them up. He had just despatched Jo Oakman on duty and gone there when the bomb fell. The bomb exploded right amongst the shelterers. A woman who was in the shelter told me about it when I visited her afterwards in St Luke's Hospital. She was badly injured and said that the scene resembled a massacre – in fact, she compared it to an engraving she had seen of the massacre of the women and children of Cawnpore in the Indian Mutiny, with bodies, limbs, blood, and flesh mingled with little hats, coats, and shoes and all the small necessities which people took to the shelters with them. She said that people were literally blown to pieces and the mess was appalling. She herself was behind a pillar or buttress which protected her somewhat; and there was a pile of bodies between her and the explosion for it was still daylight – no one had gone to their bunks.

Jo and Len Lansdell were quickly at the scene, followed by all the ARP Services. They could not get into the crypt at first because the body of a very heavy woman barred the only entrance. The explosion had set fire to the great heaps of coke stored there for heating the church and the smoke from it made it difficult to see. Jo and Len Lansdell immediately set to work with stirrup pumps to try to extinguish it before the whole place became a crematorium. The body of Bert lay there face downwards. Jo, who had spoken to him only a few minutes before the bomb fell, turned him over. She said afterwards that she wished so much that she hadn't, so that she could have remembered him as he had been when he had sent her on duty. His equipment, which was taken back to his post, was described to me as being bright red with blood – as was everything which had been in that crypt.

The work of the ARP Services that night was magnificent – by nine o'clock in the evening the casualties were all extricated and were laid in the grounds of the church with the Home Guard in charge, and wonderful work was done by Dr Castillo and Fr Fali, of Tarapore. In our FAP we had numbers of casualties again, including some rare and interesting fractures which Dr Graham Kerr commented on for the instruction of us VADs. To watch her at work, deft, neat, cheerful, and competent, was a lesson in itself.

After a heavy raid with many casualties such as this one there was a task for which we were sometimes detailed from our FAP and to which both our Commandants disliked having to send us. This was to help piece the bodies together in preparation for burial. The bodies – or rather the pieces – were in temporary mortuaries. It was a grim task and Betty Compton felt that we were too young and inexperienced for such a terrible undertaking – but someone had to do it and we were sent in pairs when it became absolutely necessary. Betty asked me if I would go as I had studied anatomy at the Slade. The first time I went my partner was a girl I did not know very well called Sheila. It *was* grim, although it was all made as businesslike and rapid as possible. We had somehow to form a body for burial so that the relatives (without seeing it) could imagine that their loved one was more or less intact for that purpose. But it was a very difficult task – there were so many pieces missing and, as one of the mortuary attendants said, 'Proper jigsaw puzzle, ain't it, miss?' The stench was the worst thing about it – that, and having to realize that these frightful pieces of flesh had once been living, breathing people. We went out to smoke a cigarette when we simply could not go on – and some busybody saw Sheila smoking and reported her for smoking when in uniform and on duty. Betty Compton, who invariably supported her VADs, was most indignant about this, as indeed she was about us having to perform such a task at all. I thought myself that butchers should have done it.

After the first violent revulsion I set my mind on it as a detached systematic task. It became a grim and ghastly satisfaction when a body was fairly constructed – but if one was too lavish in making one body almost whole then another one would have sad gaps. There were always odd members which did not seem to fit and there were too many legs. Unless we kept a very firm grip on ourselves nausea was inevitable. The only way for me to stand it was to imagine that I was back in the anatomy class again – but there the legs and arms on which we studied muscles had been carefully preserved in spirit and were difficult to associate with the human body at all. I think that this task dispelled for me the idea that human life is valuable – it could be blown to pieces by blast – just as dust was blown by wind.

Spoil in North Africa: Italian Defeat at Nibeiwa, 12 December 1940

Alan Moorehead

Wavell, in a week's fighting against the Italians, recovered 400 square miles of territory and took 30,000 prisoners, recapturing Sidi Barrani on 11 December.

Clinging closely to the tracks the heavy infantry tanks had made, we came at last into Nibeiwa itself. Here and there before the breaches in the walls a dead man lay spreadeagled on the ground, or collapsed grotesquely at the entrance of his dugout under a gathering cloud of flies. Some sixty or seventy mules and donkeys, recovered now from their shock at the noise of battle, nosed mournfully and hopelessly among the debris in search of fodder and water. Finding none, they would lift their heads and bray pathetically into the heavy dust-laden air. Italian light tanks were grouped at the spot on the western wall where they had huddled for a last stand and there surrendered. Others had bolted inside the fort itself and were turned this way and that, indicating how they had sought at the last moment for some formation to meet the attack. Maletti's body covered with a beribboned tunic still lay sprawled on the threshold of his tent, his beard stained with sand and sweat.

Sand was blowing now out of the immense ruts cut up by the tanks, and, walking through it, we went from one tent to another, from one dugout by subterranean passage into the next. Extraordinary things met us wherever we turned. Officers' beds laid out with clean sheets, chests of drawers filled with linen and abundance of fine clothing of every kind. Uniforms heavy with gold lace and decked with the medals and colours of the parade ground hung upon hangers in company with polished jackboots richly spurred and pale blue sashes and belts finished with great tassels and feathered and embroidered hats and caps. An Indian came running to us through the camp with one of those silver and gilt belts – a gaudy shining thing that the Fascists sling around their shoulders on parade. We came on great blue cavalry cloaks that swathed a man to the ankles, and dressing-tables in the officers' tents were strewn with scents and silver-mounted brushes and small arms made delicately in the romantic northern arsenals of Italy.

We sat down on the open sand and ate from stores of bottled cherries and greengages; great tins of frozen hams and anchovies; bread that had been baked somehow here in the desert; and wines from Frascati and Falerno and Chianti, red and white, and Lacrimae Christi from the slopes of Vesuvius above Naples. There were wooden casks of a sweet, heady, fruity brandy, and jars of liqueurs of other kinds wrapped carefully in envelopes of straw. For water the Italians took bottles of Recoaro minerals – the very best in Italy – and these, like everything else, had been carted out to them in hundreds of cases across a thousand miles of sea and desert by ship and car and mule team.

Bomb Disposal: Llandaff, January 1941

John Miller

Travelling about the country on mining assignments, one was often asked for advice on unidentified objects which were found lying about after raids and were suspected of being dangerous. I had never seen a Molotov Bread Basket [an arrangement for dropping clusters of fire bombs from an aeroplane] and was glad of the chance to add to my knowledge, so we stepped into a police car and drove off to Llandaff. The policeman ushered us into the front garden of a small semi-detached villa, one of a delightful little circle, with white walls and green tiled roofs. Under the porch, a baby was asleep in a pram.

The policeman waved his hands towards the rosebed which edged the path. There, at full length, almost entirely buried in the soil, was lying one of the largest types of magnetic mines, badly damaged and in an exceedingly dangerous condition.

We had everybody out from all the houses at once.

Unfortunately, the fuse was underneath the mine and I had to make one of the cold-blooded calculations which are so common on these occasions. The houses, though charming, were worth perhaps £1500 each and if they were completely destroyed no harm would be done to the war effort. The mine, I could see, was a standard type and was not likely to yield any secrets. In other words, it was a case, in the jargon of the Service, where 'damage could be accepted'.

It would be possible to request one of my officers to dig a hole under the mine, crawl in, and work on it from underneath. Alternatively, I could call up a boiler and a steam hose, and request my friend to stand over the mine and dissolve the explosive filling with steam, till so little was left that if it did go up nobody would lose anything but a few windows. But either method was so dangerous that it would only have been justified if the mine had been lying in a vital spot, a power house, an important telephone exchange, a water works, or something of that sort. I decided to trust to luck and an ordinary municipal steamroller.

It is a cardinal principle of mining that you should carry out every possible process from a distance of 200 yards, under cover. Certain operations have to be performed actually straddling the mine, and these cannot be avoided, but there is a surprising amount that can be done at the end of a 200-yard line. My plan of action was to make fast one end of a wire cable to a projection on the mine and the other to a steamroller, and then very gently back the roller down the hill, heave the mine out of its hole and expose the fuse for attention. The joy about these operations is that everybody is keen to help, everybody wants the mine cleared, and I have never asked in vain for any piece of apparatus which was needed, however bizarre. The answer was always 'Yes'. A steamroller was immediately produced; there was an excellent driver in charge, who grasped perfectly what he had to do and quite understood that there must be absolutely no jerk at any stage of the proceedings. We made fast the wire, took cover in a position from which we could watch and signalled the driver to let his roller slide slowly down the hill. The wire took the strain sweetly, the huge bulk of the mine heaved slowly up out of the rosebed; when suddenly there was an appalling explosion.

When the dust subsided, there was practically nothing left of the circle of houses. The curious thing was that the people were angry. They said that the thing had been lying there a week and if we had only left it alone, they would never have lost their property.

German Airborne Invasion of Crete, 20 May 1941

Baron Van der Heydte

By 11 May all mainland Greece and all the Greek Aegean Islands except Crete were under German occupation. After German airborne landings at Maleme, Rethimnon and Iraklion, the battle for Crete lasted a week before General Freyberg, Allied Commander-in-Chief, was forced to evacuate the island.

I was roused by my adjutant and started awake, still drowsy, to hear a roar of engines growing louder and louder, as if coming from a great distance. It took me a moment or two to remember where I was and what lay before me.

'We are nearing Crete, sir.'

I got up and moved towards the open door, beside which the dispatcher, whose duty it was to see that all final preparations for the jump were ready, was seated. Our plane was poised steady in the air, almost as though motionless. Looking out, beyond the silver-grey wing with its black cross marking, I could see our target – still small, like a cliff rising out of the glittering sea to meet us – the island of Crete.

Slowly, infinitely slowly, like the last drops wrung from a drying well, the minutes passed. Again and again I glanced stealthily at my wrist watch. There is nothing so awful, so exhausting, as this waiting for the moment of a jump. In vain I tried to compel myself to be calm and patient. A strange unrest had also gripped most of those who were flying with me ... Scarcely able to bear it any longer, I stepped once again to the open door. We were just flying over the beaches. The thin strip of surf, which looked from above like a glinting white ribbon, separated the blue waters from the yellow-green of the shore. The mountains reared up before us, and the planes approaching them looked like giant birds trying to reach their eyries in the rocks.

We were still flying inland as if to run against a dark mountainside. It seemed almost as though we could touch the steep slopes upon which trees and solitary buildings appeared like toys. Then our left wing dipped and we swung away from the mountain and the plane started to circle; but soon we straightened out again, and at that moment there came the pilot's order, 'Prepare to jump!'

Everyone rose and started to fasten his hook to the static line which ran down the centre of the body of the plane. And while we stood there, securing our hooks, we noticed that we were losing height, and the pressure of air became hard, almost painful, to the ear.

Next came the order, 'Ready to jump!'

In two strides I was at the door, my men pressing close behind me, and grasped the supports on either side of it. The slipstream clutched at my cheeks, and I felt as though they were fluttering like small flags in the wind.

Suddenly, a lot of little white clouds appeared from nowhere and stood poised in the air about us. They looked harmless enough, like puffs of cotton-wool, for the roar of the plane's engines had drowned the sound of the ack-ack shells' detonation.

Below me was the village of Alikianou. I could see people in the streets staring up at us, others running away and disappearing into doorways. The shadows of our planes swept like ghostly hands over the sun-drenched white houses, while behind the village there gleamed a large mirror – the reservoir – with single coloured parachutes, like autumn leaves, drifting down towards it.

Our plane slowed down. The moment had come.

'Go!'

I pushed with hands and feet, throwing my arms forward as if trying to clutch the black cross on the wing. And then the slipstream caught me, and I was swirling through space with the air roaring in my ears.

Syria: British Forces Meet Resistance from the Vichy French, June 1941

Alan Moorehead

Lest Syria should fall under Axis control, British and Free French forces intervened there from Palestine on 8 June 1941, opposed by General Dentz, a nominee of the Vichy Government of France. After stiff fighting, Dentz was obliged to sign an armistice at Acre on 14 July.

We lived in a Jewish hotel high up Mount Carmel at Haifa – a lovely place overgrown with pines and flower gardens. Looking down from here – the very place where Elijah saw the cloud no bigger than a man's hand and beheld below him on the site of Haifa the priests of the temple of Baal – one had a panorama of the whole sweep of coastline around to Syria. Across the plains of Armageddon came the French and Axis bombers to raid the fleet in the port of Haifa at our feet.

In the night we stood on our balconies and saw the heavens open with tracer shells, flaming onions and the flowering bursts of the Navy's ack-ack fire. Sometimes in the moonlight you caught the silver outline of a bomb going down, and, knowing it was not headed in your direction, you watched fascinated for the explosion in the sea or along the shore directly beneath. Sometimes a raider, misjudging the sharpness of Carmel's slopes, would all but brush the pine trees above our heads and we would hear the pilot open his throttle for the next dive on the port. It was the nearest thing to being in one of the attacking machines oneself, and Mount Carmel must assuredly have been the world's best air-raid grandstand.

Over this chain of hills where the Carmelite Order had been founded and David and Jonathan had their last quarrel, the Jews had built big modern hotels and restaurants among the trees. Here every afternoon and evening the people came from the hot town below to listen nostalgically to *Lieder* from Germany and hot rhythm from America, and to dance under the trees. It was possible, if you wanted, to attend a tea dance on the mountain and afterwards drive down to the front in Syria for an hour or two in the evening. Returning at dusk, you would be in time for dinner in a German beer hall in the town and a night club on the mountain.

Each morning from my bedroom window I could see the fleet steaming out along the Syrian coast, and soon the noise of shelling would come sweeping across Armageddon into my window as the breakfast coffee came in.

The road through Acre into Syria was almost perfect, and the coast itself dissolved into rolling hills and plantations of wheat and olives and bananas reaching down to a yellow beach and a soft and warm green-blue sea. Usually before going up to the forward positions we would strip on the beach and swim for half an hour and drink the bottles of Carmel Hock we had brought from Haifa. It was still not too hot, and always the snow sat pleasantly on the mountains inland.

It was not quite so idyllic as all that for the soldiers at the front. They were being opposed by tough Algerians and Foreign Legionaries, and more and more Dewoitine fighters and Glen Martin bombers were arriving from French North Africa by way of Italy and Rhodes to bomb and strafe the British positions.

Pearl Harbor, 7 December 1941

A Veteran Reminisces

John Garcia

Japan's surprise attack on the US Pacific Fleet, at anchor at its naval base on Oahu Island, Hawaii, destroyed 14 ships and 150 aircraft, killed over 2000 men, and brought America into the war.

I was sixteen years old, employed as a pipe fitter apprentice at Pearl Harbor Navy Yard. On December 7, 1941, oh, around 8.00 a.m., my grandmother woke me. She informed me that the Japanese were bombing Pearl Harbor. I said, 'They're just practising.' She said, no, it was real and the announcer is requesting that all Pearl Harbor workers report to work. I went out on the porch and I could see the anti-aircraft fire up in the sky. I just said, 'Oh boy.'

I was four miles away. I got out on my motor-cycle and it took me five, ten minutes to get there. It was a mess.

I was working on the USS *Shaw*. It was on a floating dry dock. It was in flames. I started to go down into the pipe fitter's shop to get my toolbox when another wave of Japanese came in. I got under a set of concrete steps at the dry dock where the battleship *Pennsylvania* was. An officer came by and asked me to go into the *Pennsylvania* and try to get the fires out. A bomb had penetrated the marine deck, and that was three decks below. Under that was the magazines: ammunition, powder, shells. I said, 'There ain't no way I'm gonna go down there.' It could blow up any minute. I was young and sixteen, not stupid, not at sixty-two cents an hour. (Laughs.)

A week later, they brought me before a navy court. It was determined that I was not service personnel and could not be ordered. There was no martial law at the time. Because I was sixteen and had gone into the water, the whole thing was dropped.

I was asked by some other officer to go into the water and get sailors out that had been blown off the ships. Some were unconscious, some were dead. So I spent the rest of the day swimming inside the harbour, along with some other Hawaiians. I brought out I don't know how many bodies and how many were alive and how many dead. Another man would put them into ambulances and they'd be gone. We worked all day at that . . .

The following morning, I went with my tools to the *West Virginia*. It had turned turtle, totally upside down. We found a number of men inside. The *Arizona* was a total washout. Also the *Utah*. There were men in there, too. We spent about a month cutting the superstructure of the *West Virginia*, tilting it back on its hull. About three hundred men we cut out of there were still alive by the eighteenth day. It took two weeks to get all the fires out. We worked around the clock for three days. There was so much excitement and confusion. Some of our sailors were shooting five-inch guns at the Japanese planes. You just cannot down a plane with a five-inch shell. They were landing in Honolulu, the unexploded naval shells. They have a ten-mile range. They hurt and killed a lot of people in the city.

When I came back after the third day, they told me that a shell had hit the house of my girl. We had been going together for, oh, about three years. Her house was a few blocks from my place. At the time, they said it was a Japanese bomb. Later we learned it was an American shell. She was killed. She was preparing for church at the time.

The Japanese Bomb Manila, 8 December 1941

Carlos P. Romulo

On 8 December Taiwan-based Japanese bombers struck Clark and Iba airfields in the Philippines, destroying over half of the US Army's Far East aircraft. Manila fell to the Japanese on 2 January 1942.

We hadn't long to wait after Pearl Harbor.

The next day I stood on the balcony of the *Herald* building and saw the first enemy planes cut down through the skies like great aerial bolos.

Fifty-four Japanese sky monsters, flashing silver in the bright noonday, were flying in two magnificently formed Vs.

Above the scream of the sirens the church bells solemnly announced the noon hour.

Unprotected and unprepared, Manila lay under the enemy planes – a city of ancient nunneries and chromium-fronted night clubs, of skyscrapers towering over nipa shacks, of antiquity and modernity, of East and West.

I heard the *Herald* staff clattering out of the building into Muralla Calle, where citizens in the customary spotless white were being herded by the police under the moss-covered old Spanish wall. Women clustered under the acacia trees in the park. I found myself grinning – a few of them had opened their umbrellas for additional protection!

Half-a-dozen bearded Fathers came out of the College of San Juan de Letran next door, looked up and saw the planes, and, gathering up their white robes, rushed back into the building.

The capital had stopped moving. Trams were frozen in their tracks. Cars and carromatas, drawn by skinny ponies, were pulled obediently against the kerbs. There were no signs of panic – everyone was watching the planes.

We had been expecting the raiders since yesterday's news of Pearl Harbor. Within a few hours of that attack other Japanese planes had vomited destruction over Davao, in the south, Aparri, in the north, Camp John Hay in Baguio, Clark Field, and the Iba landing field. They were certain to bomb Manila, the capital of the Philippines.

Something pressed between my feet. It was Cola, the office cat, her feline instincts alarmed by the sirens. Their screaming stopped, and in their place we heard the throbbing of the planes.

Japanese Air and Submarine Attack Sinks HMS *Prince of Wales* and HMS *Repulse*, Singapore, 10 December 1941

From a Reporter on Board Repulse

Cecil Brown

Two months after this naval disaster, Singapore fell to the Japanese, 15 February 1942.

The torpedo strikes the ship about twenty yards astern of my position. It feels as though the ship has crashed into dock. I am thrown four feet across the deck but I keep my feet. Almost immediately, it seems, the ship lists.

The command roars out of the loudspeaker: 'Blow up your lifebelts!'

I take down mine from the shelf. It is a blue-serge affair with a rubber bladder inside. I tie one of the cords around my waist and start to bring another cord up around the neck. Just as I start to tie it the command comes: 'All possible men to starboard.'

But a Japanese plane invalidates that command. Instantly there's another crash to starboard. Incredibly quickly, the *Repulse* is listing to port, and I haven't started to blow up my lifebelt.

I finish tying the cord around my neck. My camera I hang outside the airless lifebelt. Gallagher already has his belt on and is puffing into the rubber tube to inflate it. The effort makes his strong, fair face redder than usual . . .

Captain Tennant's voice is coming over the ship's loudspeaker, a cool voice: 'All hands on deck. Prepare to abandon ship.' There is a pause for just an instant, then: 'God be with you.'

There is no alarm, no confusion, no panic. We on the flag deck move toward a companionway leading to the quarterdeck. Abrahams, the Admiralty photographer, Gallagher and I are together. The coolness of everyone is incredible. There is no pushing, but no pausing either. One youngster seems in a great hurry. He tries to edge his way into the line at the top of the companionway to get down faster to the quarterdeck.

A young sub-lieutenant taps him on the shoulder and says quietly, 'Now, now, we are all going the same way, too.'

The youngster immediately gets hold of himself . . .

The *Repulse* is going down.

The torpedo-smashed *Prince of Wales*, still a half to three-quarters of a mile ahead, is low in the water, half shrouded in smoke, a destroyer by her side.

Japanese bombers are still winging around like vultures, still attacking the *Wales*. A few of those shot down are bright splotches of burning orange on the blue South China Sea.

Men are tossing overboard rafts, lifebelts, benches, pieces of wood, anything that will float. Standing at the edge of the ship, I see one man (Midshipman Peter Gillis, an eighteen-year-old Australian from Sydney) dive from the Air Defence control tower at the top of the main mast. He dives 170 feet and starts to swim away.

Men are jumping into the sea from the four or five defence control towers that segment the main mast like a series of ledges. One man misses his distance, dives, hits the side of the *Repulse*, breaks every bone in his body and crumples into the sea like a sack of wet cement. Another misses his direction and dives from one of the towers straight down the smokestack.

Men are running all along the deck of the ship to get further astern. The ship is lower in the water at the stern and their jump therefore will be shorter. Twelve Royal Marines run back too far, jump into the water and are sucked into the propeller.

The screws of the *Repulse* are still turning. There are five or six hundred heads bobbing in the water. The men are being swept astern because the *Repulse* is still making way and there's a strong tide here, too.

On all sides of me men are flinging themselves over the side. I sit down on the edge of the *Repulse* and take off my shoes. I am very fond of those shoes. A Chinese made them for me just a few days ago in Singapore. They are soft, with a buckle, and they fit well. I carefully place them together and put them down as you do at the foot of your bed before going to sleep.

I have no vision of what is ahead, no concrete thoughts of how to save myself. It is necessarily every man for himself. As I sit there, it suddenly comes to me, the overwhelming, dogmatic conviction. I actually speak the words: 'Cecil, you are never going to get out of this.'

I see one man jump and land directly on another man. I say to myself, 'When I jump I don't want to hurt anyone.'

Down below is a mess of oil and debris, and I don't want to jump into that either. I feel my mind getting numb. I look across to the *Wales*. Its guns are flashing and the flames are belching through the greyish-black smoke.

My mind cannot absorb what my eyes see. It is impossible to believe that these two beautiful, powerful, invulnerable ships are going down. But they are. There's no doubt of that.

Men are sliding down the hull of the *Repulse*. Extending around the edge of the ship is a three-inch bulge of steel. The men hit that bulge, shoot off into space and into the water. I say to myself, 'I don't want to go down that way. That must hurt their backsides something terrible.'

About eight feet to my left there is a gaping hole in the side of the *Repulse*. It is about thirty feet across, with the plates twisted and torn. The hull of the *Repulse* has been ripped open as though a giant had torn apart a tin can. I see an officer dive over the side, dive into the hole underneath the line, dive back inside the ship.

I half turn to look back on the crazy-angled deck of the ship. The padre is beside one of the pom-poms, administering the final rites to a gunner dying beside his gun. The padre seems totally unconcerned by the fact that the *Repulse* is going down at any moment . . .

The jump is about twenty feet. The water is warm; it is not water, but thick oil. My first action is to look at my stopwatch. It is smashed at 12.35, one hour and twenty minutes after the first Japanese bomb came through 12,000 feet to crash into the catapult deck of the *Repulse*.

It doesn't occur to me to swim away from the ship until I see others striking out. Then I realize how difficult it is. The oil soaks into my clothes weighting them and I think underwater demons are tugging at me, trying to drag me down. The airless lifebelt, absorbing oil too, tightens and tautens the preserver cords around my neck. I say to myself, 'I'm going to choke to death, I'm going to choke to death.'

Next to confined places, all my life, I've been afraid of choking to death. This is the first moment of fear.

I have a ring on my left hand which Martha bought for me on the Ponte Vecchio in Florence when we were on our honeymoon. It is rather loose on my finger. With oil on my hands, I'm afraid I will lose it. I clench my fist so that it won't slip off.

I start swimming away with the left hand clenched. With my right hand I make one stroke, tug at the cord around my neck in a futile effort to loosen it, then make another stroke to get away from the ship.

That ring helps save my life. Something like it must have helped save the lives of hundreds of men. Your minds fastens itself on silly, unimportant matters, absorbing your thoughts and stifling the natural instinct of man to panic in the face of death.

I see a life preserver eighteen inches long and four inches thick. It is like a long sausage and I tuck it to me. A small piece of wood appears inviting and I take that too. A barrel comes near, but I reject that because the oil prevents me getting a grip on it. All around me men are swimming, men with blood streaking down their oil-covered faces.

The oil burns in my eyes as though someone is jabbing hot pokers into the eyes. That oil in the eyes is the worst thing. I've swallowed a bit of oil already, and it's beginning to sicken me.

Fifty feet from the ship, hardly swimming at all now, I see the bow of the *Repulse* swing straight into the air like a church steeple. Its red underplates stand out as stark and as gruesome as the blood on the faces of the men around me. Then the tug and draw of the suction of 32,000 tons of steel sliding to the bottom hits me. Something powerful, almost irresistible, snaps at my feet. It feels as though someone were trying to pull my legs out by the hip sockets. But I am more fortunate than some others. They are closer to the ship. They are sucked back.

When the *Repulse* goes down it sends over a huge wave, a wave of oil. I happen to have my mouth open and I take aboard considerable oil. That makes me terribly sick at the stomach.

Auschwitz: The Gas Chambers, 25 December 1941
A Survivor is Questioned

Sophia Litwinska

Auschwitz, largest of the Nazi extermination camps, was located near the Polish town of Oswiecim. Himmler established the first camp on 27 April 1940; this was supplemented in October 1941 by Auschwitz II or Birkenau, outside the nearby village of Brzezinka, where the SS developed a huge extermination complex. Estimates of the numbers who died at Auschwitz vary from 1 million to 2.5 million.

What happened on the day before Christmas day?   There was a big selection in Block No. 4, the hospital block. Over 3000 Jewish women had to parade in this selection, which was under the charge of Hoessler. We had to leave our beds very quickly and stand quite naked to attention in front of him and the doctors, Enna and Keonig. All those who could not leave their beds had their numbers taken, and it was clear to us that they were condemned to death. Those whose bodies were not very nice looking or were too thin, or whom those gentlemen disliked for some reason or other, had their numbers taken, and it was clear what that meant. My number also was taken. We stayed in Block No. 4 for a night and the next day were taken to Block No. 18. About half-past five in the evening trucks arrived and we were loaded into them, quite naked like animals, and were driven to the crematorium.

When you reached the crematorium what happened there?   The whole truck was tipped over in the way they do it sometimes with potatoes or coal loads, and we were led into a room which gave me the impression of a shower-bath. There were towels hanging round, and sprays, and even mirrors. I cannot say how many were in the room altogether, because I was so terrified, nor do I know if the doors were closed. People were in tears; people were shouting at each other; people were hitting each other. There were healthy people, strong people, weak people and sick people, and suddenly I saw fumes coming in through a very small window at the top. I had to cough very violently, tears were streaming from my eyes, and I had a sort of feeling in my throat as if I would be asphyxiated. I could not even look at the others because each of us concentrated on what happened to herself.

What was the next thing you remember? At that moment I heard my name called. I had not the strength to answer it, but raised my arm. Then I felt someone take me and throw me out from that room. Hoessler put a blanket round me and took me on a motor-cycle to the hospital, where I stayed six weeks. As the result of the gas I had still, quite frequently, headaches and heart trouble, and whenever I went into the fresh air my eyes were filled with tears. I was subsequently taken to the political department and apparently I had been taken out of the gas chamber because I had come from a prison in Lublin, which seemed to make a difference, and, apart from that, my husband was a Polish officer.

Dachau: The Medical Experiments, 1941–5

Dr Franz Blaha

The first Nazi concentration camp in Germany, established on 10 March 1933, about 12 miles north of Munich, Dachau became the model for all the SS-organized camps. It was the first and most important camp at which medical experiments were carried out. Seven of the doctors from Dachau were sentenced to death at Nuremberg.

I, Franz Blaha, being duly sworn, depose and state as follows:

I studied medicine in Prague, Vienna, Strasburg and Paris and received my diploma in 1920. From 1920 to 1926 I was a clinical assistant. In 1926 I became chief physician of the Iglau Hospital in Moravia, Czechoslovakia. I held this position until 1939, when the Germans entered Czechoslovakia, and I was seized as a hostage and held a prisoner for co-operating with the Czech Government. I was sent as a prisoner to the Dachau Concentration Camp in April 1941, and remained there until the liberation of the camp in April 1945. Until July 1941, I worked in a Punishment Company. After that I was sent to the hospital and subjected to the experiments in typhoid being conducted by Dr Mürmelstadt. After that I was to be made the subject of an experimental operation, and only succeeded in avoiding this by admitting that I was a physician. If this had been known before I would have suffered, because intellectuals were treated very harshly in the Punishment Company. In October 1941, I was sent to work in the herb plantation, and later in the laboratory for processing herbs. In June 1942, I was taken into the hospital as a surgeon. Shortly afterwards I was directed to conduct a stomach operation on twenty healthy prisoners. Because I would not do this I was put in the autopsy room, where I stayed until April 1945. While there I performed approximately 7000 autopsies. In all, 12,000 autopsies were performed under my direction.

From mid-1941 to the end of 1942 some 500 operations on healthy prisoners were performed. These were for the instruction of the SS medical students and doctors and included operations on the stomach, gall bladder, spleen and throat. These were performed by students and doctors of only two years' training, although they were very dangerous and difficult. Ordinarily they would not have been done except by surgeons with at least four years' surgical practice. Many prisoners died on the operating table and many others from later complications. I performed autopsies on all of these bodies. The doctors who supervised these operations were Lang, Mürmelstadt, Wolter, Ramsauer and Kahr. Standartenführer Dr Lolling frequently witnessed these operations.

During my time at Dachau I was familiar with many kinds of medical experiments carried on there with human victims. These persons were never volunteers but were forced to submit to such acts. Malaria experiments on about 1200 people were conducted by Dr Klaus Schilling between 1941 and 1945. Schilling was personally asked by Himmler to conduct these experiments. The victims were either bitten by mosquitoes or given injections of malaria sporozoites taken from mosquitoes. Different kinds of treatment were applied, including quinine, pyrifer, neosalvarsan, antipyrin, pyramidon and a drug called 2516 Behring. I performed autopsies on bodies of people who died from these malaria experiments. Thirty to forty died from the malaria itself. Three hundred to four hundred died later from diseases which proved fatal because of the physical condition resulting from the malaria attacks. In addition there were deaths resulting from poisoning due to overdoses of neosalvarsan and pyramidon. Dr Schilling was present at the time of my autopsies on the bodies of his patients.

In 1942 and 1943 experiments on human beings were conducted by Dr Sigismund Rascher to determine the effects of changing air pressure. As many as twenty-five persons were put at one time into a specially constructed van in which pressure could be increased or decreased as required. The purpose was to find out the effects of high altitude and of rapid parachute descents on human beings. Through a window in the van I have seen the people lying on the floor of the van. Most of the prisoners who were made use of died as a result of these experiments, from internal haemorrhages of the lungs or brain. The rest coughed blood when taken out. It was my job to take the bodies out and to send the internal organs to Munich for study as soon as they were found to be dead. About 400 to 500 prisoners were experimented on. Those not dead were sent to invalid blocks and liquidated shortly afterwards. Only a few escaped.

Rascher also conducted experiments on the effect of cold water on human beings. This was done to find a way for reviving aviators who had fallen into the ocean. The subject was placed in ice-cold water and kept there until he was unconscious. Blood was taken from his neck and tested each time his body temperature dropped one degree. This drop was determined by a rectal thermometer. Urine was also periodically tested. Some men lasted as long as 24 to 36 hours. The lowest body temperature reached was 19 degrees C., but most men died at 25 degrees C., or 26 degrees C. When the men were removed from the ice water attempts were made to revive them by artificial warmth from the sun, from hot water, from electrotherapy or by animal warmth. For this last experiment prostitutes were used and the body of the unconscious man was placed between the bodies of two women. Himmler was present at one such experiment. I could see him from one of the windows in the street between the blocks. I have personally been present at some of these cold-water experiments when Rascher was absent, and I have seen notes and diagrams on them in Rascher's laboratory. About 300 persons were used in these experiments. The majority died. Of those who lived many became mentally deranged. Those not killed were sent to invalid blocks and were killed, just as were the victims of the air-pressure experiments. I only know two who survived – a Yugoslav and a Pole, both of whom have become mental cases . . .

It was common practice to remove the skin from dead prisoners. I was commanded to do this on many occasions. Dr Rascher and Dr Wolter in particular asked for this human skin from human backs and chests. It was chemically treated and placed in the sun to dry. After that it was cut into various sizes for use as saddles, riding breeches, gloves, house slippers and ladies' handbags. Tattooed skin was especially valued by SS men. Russians, Poles and other inmates were used in this way, but it was forbidden to cut out the skin of a German. This skin had to be from healthy prisoners and free from defects. Sometimes we did not have enough bodies with good skin and Rascher would say, 'All right, you will get the bodies.' The next day we would receive twenty or thirty bodies of young people. They would have been shot in the neck or struck on the head so that the skin would be uninjured. Also we frequently got requests for the skulls or skeletons of prisoners. In those cases we boiled the skull or the body. Then the soft parts were removed and the bones were bleached and dried and reassembled. In the case of skulls it was important to have a good set of teeth. When we got an order for skulls from Oranienburg the SS men would say, 'We will try to get you some with good teeth.' So it was dangerous to have a good skin or good teeth.

Transports arrived frequently in Dachau from Studthof, Belsen, Auschwitz, Mauthausen and other camps. Many of these were ten to fourteen days on the way without water or food. On one transport which arrived in November 1942, I found evidence of cannibalism. The living persons had eaten the flesh from the dead bodies. Another transport arrived from Compiègne in France. Professor Limousin of Clermont-Ferrand, who was later my assistant, told me that there had been 2000 persons on this transport when it started. There was food available but no water. Eight hundred died on the way and were thrown out. When it arrived after twelve days more than 500 persons were dead on the train. Of the remainder, most died shortly after arrival. I investigated this transport because the International Red Cross complained, and the SS men wanted a report that the deaths had been caused by fighting and rioting on the way. I dissected a number of bodies and found that they had died from suffocation and lack of water; it was midsummer and 120 people had been packed into each car . . .

Many executions by gas or shooting or injections took place in the camp itself. The gas chamber was completed in 1944, and I was called by Dr Rascher to examine the first victims. Of the eight or nine persons in the chamber there were three still alive, and the remainder appeared to be dead. Their eyes were red and their faces were swollen. Many prisoners were later killed in this way. Afterwards they were removed to the crematorium, where I had to examine their teeth for gold. Teeth containing gold were extracted. Many prisoners who were sick were killed by injections while in hospital. Some prisoners killed in the hospital came through to the autopsy room with no name or number on the tag which was usually tied to their big toe. Instead the tag said: 'Do not dissect.'

I performed autopsies on some of these and found that they were perfectly healthy, but had died from injections. Sometimes prisoners were killed only because they had dysentery or vomited, and gave the nurses too much trouble. Mental patients were liquidated by being led to the gas chamber and injected there or shot. Shooting was a common method of execution. Prisoners would be shot just outside the crematorium and carried in. I have seen people pushed into the ovens while they were still breathing and making sounds, although if they were too much alive they were usually hit on the head first.

The Fall of Kuala Lumpur: The City Awaits the Japanese, 11 January 1942

Ian Morrison

By the end of January 1942, the Japanese had occupied all Malaya except Singapore Island.

The scene that met one's eyes in the city was fantastic. Civil authority had broken down. The European officials and residents had all evacuated. The white police officers had gone and most of the Indian and Malay constables had returned to their homes in the surrounding villages. There was looting in progress such as I have never seen before. Most of the big foreign department stores had already been whistled clean since the white personnel had gone. There was now a general sack of all shops and premises going on. The milling crowds in the street were composed chiefly of Tamils, who were the poorest section of the population and therefore perhaps had the greater inducement to loot, but there was also a good sprinkling of Chinese and Malays. The streets were knee-deep in boxes and cardboard cartons and paper. Looters could be seen carrying every imaginable prize away with them. Here was one man with a Singer sewing-machine over his shoulder, there a Chinese with a long roll of linoleum tied on to the back of his bicycle, here two Tamils with a great sack of rice suspended from a pole, there a young Tamil struggling along with a great box of the best Norwegian sardines. Radios, rolls of cloth, tins of preserved foods, furniture, telephones, carpets, golf-clubs, there was every conceivable object being fiercely fought for and taken away. One man had even brought an ox-cart into town and was loading it up in the main street outside Whiteaways. The most striking sight I saw was a young Tamil coolie, naked except for a green loincloth, who had had tremendous luck. He had found a long cylindrical tin, three inches in diameter and a foot long, well wrapped up. What could it contain? Obviously a tin like this could only contain some rare and luxurious Western delicacy. He sat on the kerbstone turning the tin round in his hand. He wished that he could read that Western language so that he might know what the tin contained. Should he open it now or should he wait until he got home? Curiosity got the better of him and he decided to open the tin. Carefully he peeled off the paper and took off the lid. Three white Slazenger tennis-balls rolled slowly out, bounced on the pavement and then trickled into the gutter where they soon lost their speckless whiteness . . .

We went up to the Residency to see if the Resident was still there. It was a large spacious white house in park-like grounds filled with flowering trees, surrounded at a distance by other official residences. The place was deserted. The flag was down. There seemed to be no one within miles. The big house was empty. It reminded me somehow of the *Marie Céleste*, that ship which was found in the South Atlantic sailing under full sail but without anyone on board and nothing to show what had happened. In the Residency a half-finished whisky and soda stood on the small table by the sofa in the drawing room. Upstairs a woman's dress, half ironed, lay on the ironing table in one of the bedrooms. Two dispatches addressed to the Governor, typed out but unsigned, lay on the desk upstairs. In the offices on the ground floor the files were intact. The staff appeared to have downed pens in the middle of whatever they were doing and made off. A lorry, still in good order, was parked at the side of the building. Cases of beautiful silver ornaments, daggers of superb native workmanship, the presentations, doubtless, of Malay princes, lay in glass cases in the hall. The official portraits of the King and Queen smiled down from the walls.

Those beautiful houses on the outskirts of Kuala Lumpur, those spacious mansions, with their lovely tropical gardens, where bougainvillaea and canna and hibiscus and many other flowering shrubs and creepers were in full bloom, were absolutely deserted, save perhaps for an old Chinese servant on the back premises or some dog whose master had not been able to take him south.

The Sinking of the *Tanjong Penang*, 19 February 1942
The Report of a British Nursing Sister

Anon.

The Tanjong Penang *carried 250 women and children, including eight nursing sisters, all of them refugees from Singapore. It was sunk by a Japanese destroyer.*

We settled down to sleep on deck for the night, when suddenly a searchlight shone on us, and without any warning a shot was fired, and then another, both hitting the ship. When they stopped shelling I found myself beside Sister Le Blanc Smith. People were lying dead and wounded all around us, but there was little we could do for the ship was sinking rapidly.

We both stepped into the water, and presently managed to pick up a small raft. Then we came across some other people with a raft. We joined them together. During the night we picked up more people; in the end there were sixteen of us holding on to the two rafts – including six children, two being under one year old.

We lost one or two the next morning; they just could not hold on, despite our attempts to bring them back. Sister Le Blanc died that afternoon, after being terribly brave. Two more also drifted away. What with the tropical sun beating on us, and at other times terrible storms, and no food or water, it was not very pleasant.

On the second day the children went mad, and we had a difficult time with them. We lost them all.

That night I found myself alone with one other woman, so we got rid of our raft and just used the small one. We could see small islands in the distance, so next day we tried with our hands to paddle towards them, but the current was against us and we just had to go round in a circle. That afternoon the other woman went off the raft, leaving me quite alone.

I was picked up on the fourth evening, February 21st, by a Japanese cruiser, and taken to Muntock on the island of Bangka.

Leningrad: during the Blockade, April–July 1942

Aleksandr A. Fadeyev

German forces had occupied the outskirts of Leningrad by September 1941. In the 900-day siege that followed 1 million people died, from scurvy and starvation, as well as air and artillery bombardment, and the effects of the bitter winter of 1941–2.

All my life I shall preserve the memory of that evening towards the end of April 1942, when our plane, escorted by fighters, flew very low over Lake Ladoga and beneath us, on the ice, which was cracked and fissured, with surging tides of water in between, stretched the road, the only road, which throughout the winter had linked Leningrad with the rest of the country. The people of Leningrad called it The Road of Life. It had already been torn to shreds – virtually obliterated – and in places was a mere flood of water. The plane flew straight towards the misty, crimson, diffuse globe of the sun, which caught the tops of the pines and firs along the entire length of the lake shore behind us in the tender glow of spring . . .

The people of Leningrad, above all the women of Leningrad, can be proud that, in the conditions of the blockade, they saved the children. A considerable proportion of the child population had been evacuated from Leningrad – I am not referring to them. I refer rather to the small children of Leningrad who sustained all the burdens and privations of their own city.

A wide network of kindergartens was set up in Leningrad to which the starving city gave up the best of what it had. During a period of three months I visited many of these kindergartens in Leningrad. Still more frequently, however, seated on a bench somewhere in one of the city's squares or in the park at Lesny, I spent hours, unobserved by the children, watching their games and listening to their conversation. In April, when I first saw the Leningrad children, they had already emerged from the most difficult period of their lives, but the hard experience of the winter was still imprinted on their faces and was still reflected in their games. It was reflected in the way many of the children played all by themselves; in the way that, even in their collective games, they played in silence, with grave faces. I saw the faces of children which expressed so grown-up a seriousness, children's eyes which reflected such thoughtfulness and sorrow, that those faces and eyes told one more than could be gathered from all the stories of the horrors of famine . . .

All the gardens, squares, open spaces, courtyards were given up to allotments; green things flourished everywhere. Wherever wild flowers had begun to grow, along the footpaths, in gardens and cemeteries, you could see the bent figures of women picking what was edible among them − dandelions, sorrel, nettles, goosefoot grass. Passing along the Champ de Mars, which was now laid out in allotments, I saw that the lower branches of the lime trees had been stripped as far as a hand could reach.

But you could recognize the people of Leningrad more than anything else by the way they kept the squares and gardens along the whole length of the Nevsky Prospect. As before the war, they were laid out not in allotments but in the most elegant flowerbeds. And at the crossroads you could already buy flowers from Leningrad's conservatories.

The rich, spreading green and the dazzling sunlit views of the waters of the Neva, of the Fontanka and Moika canals − this extraordinary mingling of water and green foliage blotted out in bright colours almost all the traces of destruction in the city. It was beautiful again. In the evenings groups of women and young people made their way back on foot or by tram from the ploughed fields and allotments in the suburbs, carrying armfuls of vegetables and bouquets of flowers.

Over Leningrad descended the white nights. You could stand for hours on the Troitsky Bridge when on a white night the moon rose over the Summer Garden, and below, along the Neva, motionless and beautiful in the lilac mist, rose the great colonnades of the old Bourse, the Winter Palace, the Admiralty.

And day and night the windows of Leningrad's dwellings were flung wide open. The sounds of wireless music or of gramophone records descended into the street. Wandering along a quiet shady street you would hear, from somewhere inside a wide-flung window, a girl carefully attacking her piano exercises and from time to time the severe voice of the piano teacher. And it was comforting, walking at night along the Neva, to see between the wings of the Kazan Cathedral the huge silver fish of a barrage balloon faintly stirring on its rigging and capable at a moment's notice of rising to the sky.

Five Fatal Minutes: Japanese Carriers Crippled, Battle of Midway, 4 June 1942

Mitsuo Fuchida

Approaching the Pacific island of Midway, the Japanese fleet was attacked, on 3 June, by US air and sea forces. In the four-day battle, regarded as the turning-point in the war in the Pacific, the Japanese lost all four of their heavy aircraft carriers and most of their best-trained naval pilots.

Preparations for a counter-strike against the enemy had continued on board our four carriers, throughout the enemy torpedo attacks. One after another, planes were hoisted from the hangar and quickly arranged on the flight deck. There was no time to lose. At 10.20 Admiral Nagumo gave the order to launch when ready. On *Akagi*'s flight deck all planes were in position with engines warming up. The big ship began turning into the wind. Within five minutes all her planes would be launched.

Five minutes! Who would have dreamed that the tide of battle would shift completely in that brief interval of time?

Visibility was good. Clouds were gathering at about 3000 metres, however, and though there were occasional breaks, they afforded good concealment for approaching enemy planes. At 10.24 the order to start launching came from the bridge by voice-tube. The Air Officer flapped a white flag, and the first Zero fighter gathered speed and whizzed off the deck. At that instant a lookout screamed, 'Hell-divers!' I looked up to see three black enemy planes plummeting toward our ship. Some of our machine-guns managed to fire a few frantic bursts at them, but it was too late. The plump silhouettes of the American 'Dauntless' dive bombers quickly grew larger, and then a number of black objects suddenly floated eerily from their wings. Bombs! Down they came straight toward me! I fell intuitively to the deck and crawled behind a command post mantelet.

The terrifying scream of the dive bombers reached me first, followed by the crashing explosion of a direct hit. There was a blinding flash and then a second explosion, much louder than the first. I was shaken by a weird blast of warm air. There was still another shock, but less severe, apparently a near miss. Then followed a startling quiet as the barking of guns suddenly ceased. I got up and looked at the sky. The enemy planes were already gone from sight.

The attackers had got in unimpeded because our fighters, which had engaged the preceding wave of torpedo planes only a few moments earlier, had not yet had time to regain altitude. Consequently, it may be said that the American dive-bombers' success was made possible by the earlier martyrdom of their torpedo planes. Also, our carriers had no time to evade because clouds hid the enemy's approach until he dived down to the attack. We had been caught flatfooted in the most vulnerable condition possible – decks loaded with planes armed and fuelled for an attack.

Looking about, I was horrified at the destruction that had been wrought in a matter of seconds. There was a huge hole in the flight deck just behind the amidship elevator. The elevator itself, twisted like molten glass, was drooping into the hangar. Deck plates reeled upward in grotesque configurations. Planes stood tail up, belching livid flame and jet-black smoke. Reluctant tears streamed down my cheeks as I watched the fires spread, and I was terrified at the prospect of induced explosions which would surely doom the ship. I heard Masuda yelling, 'Inside! Get inside! Everybody who isn't working! Get inside!'

Unable to help, I staggered down a ladder and into the ready room. It was already jammed with badly burned victims from the hangar deck. A new explosion was followed quickly by several more, each causing the bridge structure to tremble. Smoke from the burning hangar gushed through passageways and into the bridge and ready room, forcing us to seek other refuge. Climbing back to the bridge I could see that *Kaga* and *Soryu* had also been hit and were giving off heavy columns of black smoke. The scene was horrible to behold.

Akagi had taken two direct hits, one on the after rim of the amidship elevator, the other on the rear guard on the port side of the flight deck. Normally, neither would have been fatal to the giant carrier, but induced explosions of fuel and munitions devastated whole sections of the ship, shaking the bridge and filling the air with deadly splinters. As fire spread among the planes lined up wing to wing on the after flight deck, their torpedoes began to explode, making it impossible to bring the fires under control. The entire hangar area was a blazing inferno, and the flames moved swiftly toward the bridge.

Dieppe Raid, 19 August 1942

Ross Munro

Designed to test the strength of the German coastal defences, and also to alleviate Stalin's impatience at the Allied failure to establish a second front in Europe, the Dieppe raid was a costly blunder. The ill-supported force of 6000 Canadians was launched against near-impregnable fortifications. More than 3000 were lost.

We were about seven or eight miles from Dieppe when the first alarm shook us. To our left there was a streak of tracer bullets – light blue and white dots in the night – and the angry clatter of automatic guns. This wasn't according to plan and everyone in that boat of ours tightened up like a drum. We kept our heads down behind the steel bulwark of our little craft, but it was so crowded there that even to crouch was crowding someone beside you. I sat on a cartful of 3-inch mortar bombs. More tracer bullets swept across ahead of us and some pinged off our steel sides. A big sailor by my side rigged his Lewis gun through a slit at the stern of our boat and answered with a few short bursts. A blob in the night that was an enemy ship – an armed trawler or more likely an E-boat – was less than two hundred yards away. It was firing at half-a-dozen craft including ours, which was in the lead at that time. From other directions came more German tracer. There might have been four ships intercepting us.

There wasn't much we could do. There isn't any armament on these assault craft to engage in a naval action against E-boats or trawlers. Our support craft didn't seem to be about at that particular time. It looked as if we were going to be cut up piecemeal by this interception; our flotilla already had been broken up from the close pattern of two columns we had held before the attack.

I blew up my lifebelt a little more. A few more blasts of tracer whistled past and then there was a great flash and a bang of gunfire behind us. In the flash we could see one of our destroyers speeding up wide open to our assistance. It fired a dozen rounds at the enemy ships and they turned and disappeared towards the French coast. They probably went right into Dieppe harbour and spread the word that British landing craft were heading in.

Our coxswain tried to take us in to one section of the beach and it proved the wrong spot. Before he grounded he swung the craft out again and we fumbled through the smoke to the small strip of sand which was the Puits beach. The smoke was spotty and the last thirty yards was in the clear. Geysers from artillery shells or mortar bombs shot up in our path. Miraculously we weren't hit by any of them. The din of the German ack-ack guns and machine-guns on the cliff was so deafening you could not hear the man next to you shout.

The men in our boat crouched low, their faces tense and grim. They were awed by this unexpected blast of German fire, and it was their initiation to frightful battle noises. They gripped their weapons more tightly and waited for the ramp of our craft to go down.

We bumped on the beach and down went the ramp and out poured the first infantrymen. They plunged into about two feet of water and machine-gun bullets laced into them. Bodies piled up on the ramp. Some staggered to the beach and fell. Bullets were splattering into the boat itself, wounding and killing our men.

I was near the stern and to one side. Looking out the open bow over the bodies on the ramp, I saw the slope leading a short way up to a stone wall littered with Royals casualties. There must have been sixty or seventy of them, lying sprawled on the green grass and the brown earth. They had been cut down before they had a chance to fire a shot.

A dozen Canadians were running along the edge of the cliff towards the stone wall. They carried their weapons and some were firing as they ran. But some had no helmets, some were already wounded, their uniforms torn and bloody. One by one they were cut down and rolled down the slope to the sea.

I don't know how long we were nosed down on that beach. It may have been five minutes. It may have been twenty. On no other front have I witnessed such a carnage. It was brutal and terrible and shocked you almost to insensibility to see the piles of dead and feel the hopelessness of the attack at this point.

There was one young lad crouching six feet away from me. He had made several vain attempts to rush down the ramp to the beach but each time a hail of fire had driven him back. He had been wounded in the arm but was determined to try again. He lunged forward and a streak of red-white tracer slashed through his stomach.

I'll never forget his anguished cry as he collapsed on the blood-soaked deck: 'Christ, we gotta beat them; we gotta beat them!' He was dead in a few minutes.

For the rest of that morning one lost all sense of time and developments in the frantic events of the battle. Although the Puits landing had obviously failed and the headland to the east of Dieppe would still be held by the Germans, I felt that the main attack by three infantry battalions and the tanks had possibly fared better on the beach in front of the town.

Landing craft were moving along the coast in relays and the destroyers were going in perilously close to hit the headlands with shellfire. I clambered from one landing craft to another to try to learn what was going on. Several times we were bombed too closely by long, black German planes that sailed right through our flak and our fighter cover.

Smoke was laid by destroyers and our planes along the sea and on the beach. Finally the landing craft in which I was at the time, with some naval ratings, touched down on the sloping pebble main beach which ran about sixty yards at that point to a high sea wall and the Esplanade, with the town beyond.

Smoke was everywhere and under its cover several of our ratings ran on to the beach and picked up two casualties by the barbed wire on the beach, lugging them back to the boat. I floundered through the loose shale to the sea wall. There was heavy machine-gun fire down the beach towards the Casino. A group of men crouched twenty yards away under the shelter of the sea wall.

The tobacco factory was blazing fiercely. For a moment there was no firing. It was one of those brief lulls you get in any battle. I thought our infantry were thick in the town but the Esplanade looked far too bare and empty.

There was no beach organization as there should have been. Some dead lay by the wall and on the shale. The attack here had not gone as planned either. A string of mortar bombs whanged on the Esplanade. The naval ratings waved and I lunged back to the boat as the beach battle opened up again. In choking smoke we pulled back to the boat pool.

Nazi Extermination of the Jews in the Ukraine, October 1942

Hermann Graebe

On 5th October 1942, when I visited the building office at Dubno, my foreman told me that in the vicinity of the site Jews from Dubno had been shot in three large pits, each about thirty metres long and three metres deep. About 1500 persons had been killed daily. All of the 5000 Jews who had still been living in Dubno before the pogrom were to be liquidated. As the shooting had taken place in his presence, he was still much upset. Thereupon I drove to the site, accompanied by my foreman, and saw near it great mounds of earth, about thirty metres long and two metres high. Several trucks stood in front of the mounds. Armed Ukrainian militia drove the people off the trucks under the supervision of an SS man. The militia men acted as guards on the trucks and drove them to and from the pit. All these people had the regulation yellow patches on the front and back of their clothes and thus could be recognized as Jews. My foreman and I went directly to the pits. Nobody bothered us. Now I heard rifle shots in quick succession from behind one of the earth mounds. The people who had got off the trucks – men, women and children of all ages – had to undress upon the orders of an SS man, who carried a riding or dog whip. They had to put down their clothes in fixed places, sorted according to shoes, top clothing and underclothing. I saw a heap of shoes of about 800 to 1000 pairs, great piles of underlinen and clothing. Without screaming or weeping these people undressed, stood around in family groups, kissed each other, said farewells, and waited for a sign from another SS man, who stood near the pit, also with a whip in his hand. During the fifteen minutes that I stood near I heard no complaint or plea for mercy. I watched a family of about eight persons, a man and a woman, both about fifty, with their children aged about one, eight and ten, and two grown-up daughters of about twenty to twenty-four. An old woman with snow-white hair was holding the one-year-old child in her arms and singing to it and tickling it. The child was cooing with delight. The couple were looking on with tears in their eyes. The father was holding the hand of a boy about ten years old and speaking to him softly, the boy was fighting his tears. The father pointed to the sky, stroked his head and seemed to explain something to him. At that moment the SS man at the pit shouted something to his comrade. The latter counted about twenty persons and instructed them to go behind the earth mound. Among them was the family which I have mentioned. I well remember a girl, slim and with black hair, who as she passed close to me, pointed to herself and said, 'Twenty-three'. I walked around the mound and found myself confronted by a tremendous grave. People were closely wedged together and lying on top of each other so that only their heads were visible. Nearly all had blood running over their shoulders from their heads. Some of the people shot were still moving. Some were lifting their arms and turning their heads to show that they were still alive. The pit was already two-thirds full. I estimated that it already contained about 1000 people. I looked for the man who did the shooting. He was an SS man, who sat at the edge of the narrow end of the pit, his feet dangling into the pit. He had a tommy-gun on his knees and was smoking a cigarette. The people, completely naked, went down some steps which were cut in the clay wall of the pit and clambered over the heads of the people lying there, to the place to which the SS man directed them. They laid down in front of the dead or injured people; some caressed those who were still alive and spoke to them in a low voice. Then I heard a series of shots. I looked into the pit and saw that the bodies were twitching or the heads lying motionless on top of the bodies which lay before them. Blood was running away from their necks. I was surprised that I was not ordered away but I saw that there were two or three postmen in uniform near by. The next batch was approaching already. They went down into the pit, lined themselves up against the previous victims and were shot. When I walked back round the mound I noticed another truckload of people which had just arrived. This time it included sick and infirm persons. An old, very thin woman with terribly thin legs was undressed by others who were already naked, while two people held her up. The woman appeared to be paralysed. The naked people carried the woman around the mound. I left with my foreman and drove in my car back to Dubno.

On the morning of the next day, when I again visited the site, I saw about thirty naked people lying near the pit – about thirty to fifty metres away from it. Some of them were still alive; they looked straight in front of them with a fixed stare and seemed to notice neither the chilliness of the morning nor the workers of my firm who stood around. A girl of about twenty spoke to me and asked me to give her clothes and help her escape. At that moment we heard a fast car approach and I noticed that it was an SS detail. I moved away to my site. Ten minutes later we heard shots from the vicinity of the pit. The Jews still alive had been ordered to throw the corpses into the pit, then they had themselves to lie down in this to be shot in the neck.

El Alamein: The End of the Africa Corps, 4 November 1942

General Bayerlein

Montgomery launched his attack at El Alamein on 23 October. After a week's fighting the Germans had only 90 tanks left – the British, 800. On 3 November, however, Hitler forbade retreat.

On the morning of November 4th the remnants of the German Africa Corps, together with the 90th Light Division, held a thin front line on either side of the wide sand dune called Tel el Mampsra: though only some twelve feet high, this dune was a commanding feature. To the south was the equally weakened Italian armoured corps. Towards dawn I reported to General Ritter von Thoma, the commander of the Africa Corps, that I was about to set off for the area south of El Daba, where I was to establish a rear command post. For the first time Thoma was wearing a proper uniform, with his general's insignia, orders and decorations, which hitherto in the desert he had never bothered to put on. He now said to me:

'Bayerlein, Hitler's order [not to withdraw] is a piece of unparalleled madness. I can't go along with this any longer. Go to the El Daba command post. I shall stay here and personally take charge of the defence of Tel el Mampsra.'

I could see that Thoma was utterly disheartened and foresaw no good. His ADC, Lieutenant Hartdegen, remained with the General: he had a wireless transmitter. The General put on his greatcoat and picked up a small canvas bag. I wondered whether the General intended to die. Then I left Tel el Mampsra and drove to the rear.

It was eight o'clock before the British attacked, after approximately one hour's artillery preparation. Their main effort was directed against Tel el Mampsra. By committing all its forces the Africa Corps was able to hold attacks by two hundred British tanks.

At eleven o'clock Lieutenant Hartdegen appeared at my command post and said, 'General von Thoma has sent me back, with the radio transmitter. He doesn't need it any more. All our tanks, anti-tank guns and ack-ack have been destroyed on Tel el Mampsra. I don't know what has happened to the general.'

I immediately climbed into a small armoured reconnaissance car and drove off eastwards. Suddenly a hail of armour-piercing shot was whistling all about me. In the noontime haze I could see countless black monsters far away in front. They were Montgomery's tanks, the 10th Hussars. I jumped out of the armoured car and beneath the burning midday sun ran as fast as I could towards Tel el Mampsra. It was a place of death, of burning tanks and smashed flak guns, without a living soul. But then, about two hundred yards away from the sandhole in which I was lying, I saw a man standing erect beside a burning tank, apparently impervious to the intense fire which criss-crossed about him. It was General von Thoma. The British Shermans which were closing up on Tel el Mampsra had halted in a wide half-circle. What should I do? The General would probably regard it as cowardice on my part were I not to go forward and join him. But to run through the curtain of fire which lay between General von Thoma and myself would have been to court certain death. I thought for moment or two. Then the British tanks began to move forward once again. There was now no fire being put down on Tel el Mampsra. Thoma stood there, rigid and motionless as a pillar of salt, with his canvas bag still in his hand. A Bren carrier was driving straight towards him, with two Shermans just behind. The British soldiers signalled to Thoma. At the same time one hundred and fifty fighting vehicles poured across Tel el Mampsra like a flood.

I ran off westwards as fast as my legs could carry me. My car had vanished. After a while I met a staff car which took me to the command post at El Daba. There I found Rommel. I told him what I had seen. Huge dust clouds were now visible both south-east and south of the command post. The Italian tanks of the 20th Corps were fighting their last, desperate battle with some hundred heavy British tanks that had punched into the Italians' open right flank. After putting up a brave resistance, the Italian corps was annihilated.

The Africa Corps signals officer brought Rommel a decoded message, from the 10th Hussars to Montgomery, which our people had intercepted. It read: 'We have just captured a General named Ritter von Thoma.'

An English Poet in the Western Desert, December 1942

Keith Douglas

Douglas survived the North African campaign, but was killed in Normandy.

We began to creep forward, swinging west again to face the enemy. As we advanced, I remembered how we had sat so long during my first action within a stone's throw of enemy infantry, and I began to look very carefully at the trenches we passed. About two hundred yards from the German derelicts, which were now furiously belching inky smoke, I looked down into the face of a man lying hunched up in a pit. His expression of agony seemed so acute and urgent, his stare so wild and despairing, that for a moment I thought him alive. He was like a cleverly posed waxwork, for his position suggested a paroxysm, an orgasm of pain. He seemed to move and writhe. But he was stiff. The dust which powdered his face like an actor's lay on his wide open eyes, whose stare held my gaze like the Ancient Mariner's. He had tried to cover his wounds with towels against the flies. His haversack lay open, from which he had taken towels and dressings. His water bottle lay tilted with the cork out. Towels and haversack were dark with dried blood, darker still with a great concourse of flies. This picture, as they say, told a story. It filled me with useless pity . . .

The men with me were walking along bent double as though searching the ground. I said to them, 'It's no good ducking down. If you're going to be hit you'll be hit. Run across the open ground. Run.' They began to trot reluctantly, and I ran ahead. Presently I saw two men crawling on the ground, wriggling forward very slowly in a kind of embrace.

As I came up to them I recognized one of them as Robin, the RHA Observation Officer whose aid I had been asking earlier in the day: I recognized first his fleece-lined suede waistcoat and polished brass shoulder titles and then his face, strained and tired with pain. His left foot was smashed to pulp, mingled with the remainder of a boot. But as I spoke to Robin saying, 'Have you got a tourniquet, Robin?' and he answered apologetically, 'I'm afraid I haven't, Peter,' I looked at the second man. Only his clothes distinguished him as a human being, and they were badly charred. His face had gone: in place of it was a huge yellow vegetable. The eyes blinked in it, eyes without lashes, and a grotesque huge mouth dribbled and moaned like a child exhausted with crying.

Robin's mangled leg was not bleeding: a paste of blood and sand, or congealed slabs of blood, covered it. I thought it would be better left as it was than bandaged, now that the air had closed it. 'I'll go on back,' I said, 'and get hold of something to pick you up, a scout car or something. Stay here.' I ran on. Before I had gone a hundred yards I was ashamed: my own mind accused me of running to escape, rather than running for help. But I hurried on, determined to silence these accusations by getting a vehicle of some kind and bringing it back, in the face of the enemy if necessary. I knew that if only I could gain the cover of the ridge and stop to think, and if I could find where the regiment had gone, I should be able to reorganize myself and go back.

Stalingrad: December 1942
A German Infantryman's View

Benno Zieser

The Soviet counter-attack, launched on 19 November 1942, threatened to encircle the Germans outside Stalingrad. Early in January 1943 Kleist's 1st Panzer Army began its retreat westward to Rostov. The 6th German Army, under Paulus, surrendered on 2 February 1943. Shortage of winter clothing greatly increased the death rate among German troops. Trainloads of winter clothing were halted short of the front because the German High Command feared that issuing it would encourage the soldiers to think they would not take Stalingrad before the winter.

Then one night the great freeze-up began, and winter was with us, the second grim winter in that accursed country. Like a black cloak the frost folded over the land. A supplies truck came round and brought us greatcoats, gloves and caps with ear-flaps. Despite this issue, we froze miserably in our funk-holes. In the morning we would be numb with cold, our rifles and guns completely coated with thick hoar-frost. As it left our mouths our breath was as dense as cigarette smoke and immediately solidified over the side-flaps of our caps its glittering crystals of ice. When shells came over, each detonation rang out with a new, hard resonance and the clods of earth which were thrown high were like lumps of granite . . .

The truth was slowly borne in on us, as, dragging all they had with them, the remnants of defeated division after division fell back from all sides, before the on-pressing enemy, crowding and cramming into the heart of the cauldron. Gradually the columns of converging transport blocked all roads. On the road guns were blown up, and weapons of all kinds, tanks included, which had come to a standstill for want of fuel. Fully laden lorries, bogged in the snow, went up in flames. Munition dumps were sprung. Vast supplies of provisions and clothing had to become huge fireworks, not to fall into enemy hands. Installations erected at enormous effort were wiped out wholesale. The country for miles around was strewn with smaller equipment – tin hats, gasmasks in cases, groundsheets, cooking utensils, ammo pouches, trenching tools, even rifles, machine-pistols and grenades. All of this stuff had been thrown away because it had become a mere hindrance, or because the men who carried it had become the wounded in their endless columns, with blood-soaked bandages and tattered uniforms, summoning the last vestiges of their strength merely to drag themselves on through the snow. Or else the equipment had belonged to the countless men now rigid and dead, of whom nobody took any more notice than we did of all that abandoned material.

Completely cut off, the men in field grey just slouched on, invariably filthy and invariably louse-ridden, their weary shoulders sagging, from one defence position to another. The icy winds of those great white wastes which stretched for ever beyond us to the east lashed a million crystals of razor-like snow into their unshaven faces, skin now loose-stretched over bone, so utter was the exhaustion, so utter the starvation. It burned the skin to crumpled leather, it lashed tears from the sunken eyes which from over-fatigue could scarce be kept open, it penetrated through all uniforms and rags to the very marrow of our bones. And whenever any individual could do no more, when even the onward-driving lash of fear of death ceased to have meaning, then like an engine which had used its last drop of fuel the debilitated body ran down and came to a standstill. Soon a kindly shroud of snow covered the object and only the toe of a jackboot or an arm frozen to stone could remind you that what was now an elongated white hummock had quite recently been a human being.

Stalingrad: A War Correspondent Goes in after the German Capitulation, 4 February 1943

Alexander Werth

We set out at 3 p.m. on our fifty-mile trek from General Malinin's headquarters to Stalingrad. Our army driver said we would make it in four to five hours; it took us nearer thirteen.

There were half-a-dozen of us in a wretched van, without any seats or benches, sitting or half lying on bags or pieces of luggage. Every hour it became colder and colder. To add to our misery the back door of the van had no glass in it; it was almost as cold as driving in an open car.

It was a pity not to travel through this battle area during the day, but it couldn't be helped. Even so, I remember that night as one of my strangest experiences during the whole war. For one thing, I had never known such cold in all my life.

In the morning it had been only minus 20°, and then it was minus 30°, then minus 35°, then minus 40° and finally minus 44°. One has to experience 44° of frost to know what it means. Your breath catches. If you breathe on your glove, a thin film of ice immediately forms on it. We couldn't eat anything, because all our food – bread, sausage and eggs – had turned into stone. Even wearing *valenki* and two pairs of woollen socks, you had to move your toes all the time to keep the circulation going. Without *valenki* frostbite would have been certain, and the Germans had no *valenki*. To keep your hands in good condition, you had to clap them half the time or play imaginary scales. Once I took out a pencil to write down a few words: the first word was all right, the second was written by a drunk, the last two were the scrawl of a paralytic; quickly I blew on my purple fingers and put them back in the fur-lined glove.

And as you sit there in the van all huddled up and feeling fairly comfortable, you cannot bear to move, except your fingers and toes, and give your nose an occasional rub; a kind of mental and physical inertia comes over you; you feel almost doped. And yet you have to be on the alert all the time. For instance, I suddenly found the frost nibbling at my knees: it had got the right idea of attacking the tiny area between the end of my additional underwear and the beginning of the *valenki*! . . . Your only real ally, apart from clothes, on such occasions is the vodka bottle. And, bless it, it didn't freeze, and even a frequent small sip made a big difference. One could see what it must be like to fight in such conditions. For the last stage of the Battle of Stalingrad had been fought in weather only a little milder than it was on that February night.

The nearer we got to Stalingrad, the more bewildering was the traffic on the snow-bound road. This area, in which the battle had raged only so very recently, was now hundreds of miles from the front, and all the forces in Stalingrad were now being moved – towards Rostov and the Donets. About midnight we got stuck in a traffic jam. And what a spectacle that road presented – if one could still call it a road! For what was the original road and what was part of the adjoining steppe that had been taken in by this traffic — most of it moving west, but also some moving east — was not easy to determine. Between the two streams of traffic, there was now an irregular wall of snow that had been thrown up there by wheels and hoofs. Weird-looking figures were regulating the traffic — soldiers in long white camouflage cloaks and pointed white hoods; horses, horses and still more horses, blowing steam and with ice round their nostrils, were wading through the deep snow, pulling guns and gun-carriages and large covered wagons; and hundreds of lorries with their headlights full on. To the side of the road an enormous bonfire was burning, filling the air with clouds of black smoke that ate into your eyes; and shadow-like figures danced round the bonfire warming themselves; then others would light a plank at the bonfire, and start a little bonfire of their own, till the whole edge of the road was a series of small bonfires. Fire! How happy it made people on a night like this! Soldiers jumped off their lorries to get a few seconds of warmth, and have the dirty black smoke blow in their faces; then they would run after their lorry and jump on again.

Such was the endless procession coming out of Stalingrad: lorries, and horse sleighs and guns, and covered wagons, and even camels pulling sleighs — several of them stepping sedately through the deep snow as though it were sand. Every conceivable means of transport was being used. Thousands of soldiers were marching, or rather walking in large irregular crowds, to the west, through this cold deadly night. But they were cheerful and strangely happy, and they kept shouting about Stalingrad and the job they had done. Westward, westward!

German Rout in the Korsun Salient, Central Ukraine, 17 February 1943

By a Russian Officer

Major Kampov

All that evening the Germans had been in a kind of hysterical condition. The few remaining cows in the village were slaughtered and eaten with a sort of cannibal frenzy. When a barrel of pickled cabbage was discovered in one hut, it led to wild scrambles. Altogether they had been very short of food ever since the encirclement; with the German army in constant retreat, they didn't have large stores anywhere near the front line. So these troops at Korsun had been living mostly by looting the local population; they had done so even before the encirclement.

They had also had a lot to drink that night, but the fires started by the U-2s and then the bombing and the shelling sobered them up. Driven out of their warm huts they had to abandon Shanderovka. They flocked into the ravines near the village, and then took the desperate decision to break through early in the morning. They had almost no tanks left – they had all been lost and abandoned during the previous days' fighting, and what few tanks they still had now had no petrol. In the last few days the area where they were concentrated was so small that transport planes could no longer bring them anything. Even before, few of the transport planes reached them, and sometimes the cargoes of food and petrol and munitions were dropped on our lines.

So that morning they formed themselves into two marching columns of about 14,000 each, and they marched in this way to Lysianka where the two ravines met. Lysianka was beyond our front line, inside the 'corridor'. The German divisions on the other side were trying to batter their way eastward, but now the 'corridor' was so wide that they hadn't much chance.

They were a strange sight, these two German columns that tried to break out of the encirclement. Each of them was like an enormous mob. The spearhead and the flanks were formed by the SS men of the Wallonia Brigade and the Viking Division in their pearl-grey uniforms. They were in a relatively good state of physique. Then, inside the triangle, marched the rabble of the ordinary German infantry, very much more down at heel. Right in the middle of this, a small select nucleus was formed by the officers. These also looked relatively well fed. So they moved westward along two parallel ravines. They had started out soon after 4 a.m., while it was still completely dark. We knew the direction from which they were coming. We had prepared five lines – two lines of infantry, then a line of artillery, and then two more lines where the tanks and cavalry lay in wait . . . We let them pass through the first three lines without firing a shot. The Germans, believing that they had dodged us and had now broken through all our defences, burst into frantic jubilant screaming, firing their pistols and tommy-guns into the air as they marched on. They had now emerged from the ravines and reached open country.

Then it happened. It was about six o'clock in the morning. Our tanks and our cavalry suddenly appeared and rushed straight into the thick of the two columns. What happened then is hard to describe. The Germans ran in all directions. And for the next four hours our tanks raced up and down the plain crushing them by the hundred. Our cavalry, competing with the tanks, chased them through the ravines where it was hard for tanks to pursue them. Most of the time the tanks were not using their guns lest they hit their own cavalry. Hundreds and hundreds of cavalry were hacking at them with their sabres, and massacred the Fritzes as no one had ever been massacred by cavalry before. There was no time to take prisoners. It was a kind of carnage that nothing could stop till it was all over. In a small area over 20,000 Germans were killed. I had been in Stalingrad; but never had I seen such concentrated slaughter as in the fields and ravines of that small bit of country. By 9 a.m. it was all over. Eight thousand prisoners surrendered that day. Nearly all of them had run a long distance away from the main scene of the slaughter; they had been hiding in woods and ravines.

The Execution of an Allied Intelligence Officer by the Japanese, New Guinea, 29 March 1943

By a Japanese Eye Witness

Anon.

All four of us – Kurokawa, Nishiguchi, Yawate and myself – assembled in front of Headquarters at 1500 hrs ... The 'Tai' commander Komai, who came to the observation post today, told us personally that in accordance with the compassionate sentiments of Japanese *Bushido*, he was going to kill the prisoner himself, with his favourite sword. So we gathered to observe this. After we had waited a little more than ten minutes, the truck came along.

The prisoner who is at the side of the guard house is given his last drink of water. The surgeon, Major Komai, and Headquarters Platoon Commander come out of the Officers' Mess, wearing their military swords. The time has come. The prisoner with his arms bound and his long hair now cropped short totters forward. He probably suspects what is afoot but he is more composed than I thought he would be. Without more ado, he is put on the truck and we set out for our destination.

I have a seat next to the surgeon. About ten guards ride with us. To the pleasant rumble of the engine, we run swiftly along the road in the growing twilight. The glowing sun has set behind the western hills. Gigantic clouds rise before us and dusk is falling all around. It will not be long now. As I picture the scene we are about to witness, my heart beats faster.

I glance at the prisoner. He has probably resigned himself to his fate. As though saying farewell to the world, he looks about as he sits in the truck, at the hills, the sea, and seems in deep thought. I feel a surge of pity and turn my eyes away. The truck runs along the seashore now. We have left the Navy guard sector behind us and now come into the Army sector. Here and there we see sentries in the grassy fields and I thank them in my heart for their toil, as we drive on; they must have 'got it' in the bombing the night before last; there were great gaping holes by the side of the road, full of water from the rain. In a little over twenty minutes, we arrive at our destination and all get off.

Major Komai stands up and says to the prisoner, 'We are going to kill you.' When he tells the prisoner that in accordance with Japanese *Bushido* he would be killed with a Japanese sword and that he would have two or three minutes' grace, he listens with bowed head. He says a few words in a low voice. He is an officer, probably a flight lieutenant. Apparently, he wants to be killed with one stroke of the sword. I hear him say the word 'one'; the Major's face becomes tense as he replies, 'Yes.'

Now the time has come and the prisoner is made to kneel on the bank of a bomb crater, filled with water. He is apparently resigned. The precaution is taken of surrounding him with guards with fixed bayonets, but he remains calm. He even stretches his neck out. He is a very brave man indeed. When I put myself in the prisoner's place and think that in one minute it will be goodbye to this world, although the daily bombings have filled me with hate, ordinary human feelings make me pity him.

The Major has drawn his favourite sword. It is the famous *masamune* sword which he has shown us at the observation station.

It glitters in the light and sends a cold shiver down my spine. He taps the prisoner's neck lightly with the back of the blade, then raises it above his head with both arms and brings it down with a powerful sweep. I had been standing with muscles tensed but in that moment I closed my eyes.

A hissing sound – it must be the sound of spurting blood, spurting from the arteries: the body falls forward. It is amazing – he has killed him with one stroke.

The onlookers crowd forward. The head, detached from the trunk, rolls forward in front of it. The dark blood gushes out. It is all over. The head is dead white, like a doll. The savageness which I felt only a little while ago is gone, and now I feel nothing but the true compassion of Japanese *Bushido*.

A corporal laughs: 'Well – he will be entering Nirvana now.' A seaman of the medical unit takes the surgeon's sword and, intent on paying off old scores, turns the headless body over on its back and cuts the abdomen open with one clean stroke. They are thick-skinned, these *keto* [hairy foreigner – term of opprobrium for a white man]; even the skin of their bellies is thick. Not a drop of blood comes out of the body. It is pushed into the crater at once and buried.

Now the wind blows mournfully and I see the scene again in my mind's eye. We get on the truck again and start back. It is dark now. We get off in front of Headquarters. I say goodbye to the Major and climb up the hill with Technician Kurokawa. This will be something to remember all my life. If I ever get back alive, it will make a good story to tell; so I have written it down.

Luftwaffe Pilot: Tunisia, 7 April 1943

Alan Moorehead

A Messerschmitt, with silver wings, was only fifteen or twenty feet above our heads and as it roared on down the road the Bofors gun fire into its belly. For half a minute the machine continued straight onwards. It rose slightly, executed a graceful half-circle in the sky and then slithered down to a belly-landing among the wild flowers.

We jumped back into the car and drove a couple of miles to the river where we judged the plane had fallen. From many directions troops who had seen the incident were running through the shoulder-high wheat which was dotted with red poppies and sweet mustard and tall white lilies. In a few minutes we found the Messerschmitt. It had landed practically unharmed on the soft wheat, but the pilot had vanished. I clambered into the cockpit and felt the joystick and the trigger; it was still warm from the pilot's hand, still warm from the grip with which he had fired his guns at us along the road, a minute or two before.

On the bank of the river an Arab peasant was gesticulating and shouting and everyone ran across to the direction in which he was pointing. They found the pilot hiding in a dung heap under a lip in the bank and he made no effort to resist. He lay there until the pursuers found him and then he got up slowly with his hands above his head and walked toward his machine with a pistol pressed in his back.

He was a strikingly good-looking boy, not more than twenty-three or four, with fair hair and clear blue eyes, and he wore flying boots and overalls but no cap. The soldiers searched him and took from his pockets his revolver and his belt of bullets and a leather wallet. As they searched the German fumbled for a cigarette and made motions for someone to light it for him. He did this mechanically and without attempting to speak, and the hand which held the cigarette was shaking badly. Someone lit the cigarette and for some reason I could not understand the man with the pistol motioned the pilot to a place in the wheat about twenty yards from the fallen plane. Then quite accidentally everyone stepped back from the pilot at the same time and he was left alone standing in the wild flowers.

You could see very clearly what he was thinking. He was thinking, 'They are going to shoot me now. This is the end. The one with the pistol will fire at my body.' He stiffened and the hand holding the cigarette was tensed and shivering. Little globes of sweat came out in a line on his forehead and he looked straight ahead.

All this took only a moment and then, in the same involuntary way, the British troops moved toward him again and motioned him to march with them back toward the road.

The pilot did not comprehend for a moment. Then he relaxed and drew deeply on his cigarette, and it was again quite clear that he was saying to himself in a spasm of half-understood relief, 'It's all right. They are not going to shoot me.' Then we all walked back to the road. We felt pleased that the matter had ended so well and that punishment had come so quickly to the enemy who had fired at us on the road; but this actual physical contact with the pilot, his shock and his fear, suddenly made one conscious that we were fighting human beings and not just machines and hilltops and guns. Nearly always the battle to us was a mechanical thing and the enemy a sort of abstract evil in the distance. But now, having captured a human being from that dark continent which was the enemy's line, one wanted to talk to the pilot and argue with him and tell him he was wrong.

Hamburg, 27 July, 1943

Else Wendel

On the Tuesday night, 27 July, the bombers came back. In that raid over 45,000 people in Hamburg died. Mama and her friends went down into their cellar. The air warden stored sand and water and piled up tools ready for any digging that might be necessary.

It was the worst raid Mama had ever known. For hours they huddled there, with bombs crashing nearer, and the ceaseless rumblings of falling masonry. Then there was the loudest crash of all. The air warden ran out. He came back, his face grey. 'Leave the cellar at once!' he called. 'A phosphorus bomb has fallen at the entrance door. Quick, all of you . . .'

An indescribable panic started. Mothers grabbed children and rushed madly away. People fell over each other and Mama was separated from her friends. She didn't see them again. Out in the street people just rushed blindly away from the bomb, thinking of nothing else. An old man came near Mama, who was now standing dazed and alone. 'Come with me,' he said. She picked up her suitcase and followed him. It was unbearably hot in the street.

'I can't go through this. There's a cellar there not burning, I shall go down there,' she told him.

'Don't be a fool,' he said. 'All the houses here will catch fire soon, it's only a matter of time.'

A woman with two children joined them. 'Come on,' said the old man. 'This looks the clearest way.'

There were walls of flame round them now. Suddenly into the square came a fire engine drawn by two startled horses. They swerved aside, and one of the terrified children rushed down a side street. The mother followed, leaving her boy behind. As the first child reached a burning house, some blazing wood fell near her, setting her clothes alight. The mother threw herself on top of the child to try and smother the flames, but as she did so the whole top floor of the house opposite crashed down on the two of them.

The old man grabbed the boy's hand firmly. 'You come with us,' he ordered.

'I'll wait for my mummy,' said the boy.

'No,' said the old man, trying to make his voice sound harsh. 'It's getting too hot here. We will wait for your mummy farther away from the fire.'

Mama intervened quickly. 'We will find the best way out, and then come back and fetch your mummy.'

'All right,' said the little boy.

They went the same way as the horses, thinking the animals' instinct might have led them to safety. The boy fell down but got up, then fell down again.

'We can't go on like this,' said the man, pulling them towards a cellar. 'There's water here, pour it over your coats, and we'll put them over our heads and try that way.'

Up in the square again, the man took a hasty glance round and then grabbed the boy's hand. 'Now – come this way,' he told them. Mama grabbed her suitcase. 'Put it down,' shouted the old man. 'Save yourself, you can't bring that as well.'

But Mama would not let go. She took the boy's hand in her left hand and the case in her right. Out in the square it was like a furnace. Sweat poured down her body as they began to run. The smoke seeped through the wet coats and began to choke them. Only for a few yards could she carry the suitcase, then she dropped it and left it without another thought. The little boy ran between them, taking steps twice as fast as their own. He fell again and again, but was hauled to his feet. Were they still on the track of the horses? They didn't know, for every moment or two they had to turn to avoid burning wood and pylons which hurtled down from the houses around. Bodies were still burning in the road. Sometimes they stumbled against them. But on they went, with the little boy's feet running tap, tap, tap between them. A dog was howling madly somewhere. It sounded more pathetic and lost than they themselves. At last they came to a small green place, and ran to the centre of it and fell on their faces, the little boy between them. They fell asleep like exhausted animals, but only for a few minutes. The old man woke first.

'Wake up,' he said, shaking them both. 'The fire is catching up with us.'

Mama opened her eyes. They were lying in a small field, and the houses on one side were now alight; worse than alight; some kind of explosive material was there as well, it seemed. A great flame was shooting straight out towards them. A flame as high as the houses and nearly as wide as the whole street. As she stared in fascination the giant flame jerked back and then shot forward towards them again.

'My God, what is it?' she said.

'It's a fire-storm,' the old man answered.

'The beginning of one. Quick, come along, there's no time to lose. In a minute there will be dozens of flames like that and they'll reach us; quick, come on, we must run. I think there's a small stream on the other side of this field.'

Mama got up and bent over the boy. 'Poor little thing, what a shame to wake him.' She shook him gently. 'Get up! We must run again.'

The child did not stir. The man bent down and pulled him to his feet. 'Come on, boy,' he said. The child swayed and fell again. The man sank to his knees beside the child and took his hands.

'Oh, no!' he said in a shocked voice. 'No, it can't be. My God, he's dead!' The tears began to pour down his blackened face. He bent down lower over the little figure and began to whisper to it.

'You were a good little boy, a very brave little boy,' he said, stroking the child's face with a woman's tenderness. 'As long as Hamburg has boys as brave as you she won't die.' He kissed the child's face very gently. 'Sleep well, little boy,' he whispered. 'Sleep well; you got a kinder death than your mummy and sister. They were burnt alive like rats.'

Mama became nervous; another tongue of flame shot out from the side street. The roaring of the flames became stronger. The old man seemed quite oblivious now of their danger.

'Come on,' she called out. 'The boy is dead. We can't help him any more. Come on, we must go on.'

The old man did not look up. 'No,' he said. 'You go on by yourself. I shall die with this little boy.'

Mama yelled through the roaring wind. 'You're crazy! Come on!' The old man did not answer. He kissed the child's forehead again.

In despair Mama grabbed the man in her arms and tried to pull him away. Sparks were now beginning to reach their coats. Suddenly a hot gust of wind blew their coats off their backs, sending them blazing through the air. This brought the man to life again. He jumped up and started to run. As they raced across the field, the flames crept behind them. Once they fell and then got up and ran on. The field seemed wider and wider as they raced towards the stream, but at last they reached it. Unable to say another word, they both fell on the banks and slept, or perhaps they fainted first and slept afterwards.

US Marines Land on Tarawa, 20 November 1943

Robert Sherrod

The successful assault on the Japanese defences on Tarawa in the Gilbert Islands cost the US Marines 3300 in killed and wounded.

Another young Marine walked briskly along the beach. He grinned at a pal who was sitting next to me. Again there was a shot. The Marine spun all the way around and fell to the ground, dead. From where he lay, a few feet away, he looked up at us. Because he had been shot squarely through the temple his eyes bulged out wide, as in horrible surprise at what had happened to him, though it was impossible that he could ever have known what hit him.

'Somebody go get the son-of-a-bitch,' yelled Major Crowe. 'He's right back of us here, just waiting for somebody to pass by.' That Jap sniper, we knew from the crack of his rifle, was very close.

A Marine jumped over the sea wall and began throwing blocks of fused TNT into a coconut-log pillbox about fifteen feet back of the sea wall against which we sat. Two more Marines scaled the sea wall, one of them carrying a twin-cylindered tank strapped to his shoulders, the other holding the nozzle of the flame-thrower. As another charge of TNT boomed inside the pillbox, causing smoke and dust to billow out, a khaki-clad figure ran out the side entrance. The flame-thrower, waiting for him, caught him in its withering stream of intense fire. As soon as it touched him, the Jap flared up like a piece of celluloid. He was dead instantly but the bullets in his cartridge belt exploded for a full sixty seconds after he had been charred almost to nothingness.

A Birthday: Japanese Prison Camp, Kuching, Borneo, 5 April 1944

Agnes Newton Keith

George and his parents survived their internment, and were liberated in August 1945.

On April 5th George was four years old. It was his second birthday in prison camp. Harry [George's father] was in the guardhouse. George had no present from him.

At midday, Lilah and I got out the box of Red Cross food. We opened everything and divided each item into thirty-four sections. It required mathematical precision, but we did it. Every child then brought a bowl or plate to us, and watched with shining eyes.

We filled each plate with little mounds of salmon, sardine, butter, Spam, ham, jelly, meat, prunes, chocolate, cheese, and we had made a milk pudding with milk and rice, which we added. Then we called for cups, and distributed coffee with sugar. And all mothers were rewarded for being mothers, with cigarettes.

Each child took his plate, said 'Thank you' politely, said 'Happy Birthday' to George, and scurried home. Each face was pale with excitement. This was not fun or pleasure. This was tense, terrible, earnest participation in Paradise.

I had wondered beforehand if I was wrong in not saving the foodstuff for George, to feed to him over a period of time. But when I saw those faces I knew I was right.

George's melting gratification in having something to give, his pride in being a benefactor, made him swell all day long before my eyes, until by night-time he was twice-normal. How I loved him then!

Cassino: The Final Attack; 2nd Battalion Lancashire Fusiliers Advance, 16 May 1944

Fred Majdalany

Cassino, a key point in the German line blocking the Allied advance on Rome, was the scene of three savage battles. On 15 February Allied air attack demolished the Benedictine monastery (founded by St Benedict in 592), wrongly believed to be occupied by the Germans. Outflanked by the British, Monte Cassino eventually fell to a Polish corps of the 8th Army on 18 May.

07.10 hours. Time to get ready. The shouts of the sergeant-majors. Jokes and curses. The Infantry heaving on to their backs and shoulders their complicated equipment, their weapons and the picks and shovels they have to carry too, so that they can quickly dig in on their objective. The individuals resolving themselves into sections and platoons and companies. Jokes and curses.

'Able ready to move, sir.'

'Baker ready to move, sir.'

'Charlie ready to move, sir.'

'Dog ready to move, sir.'

The column moved off along the track we'd taken the previous night. It was Tuesday morning. It was the fifth day of the offensive. In England the headlines were announcing that the Gustav Line was smashed except for Cassino and Monastery Hill. 'Except' was the operative word. That was our job now. To break through and cut off Cassino and the Monastery.

On the stroke of nine there was an earth-shaking roar behind us as 400 guns opened fire almost as one. With a hoarse, exultant scream 400 shells sped low over our heads to tear into the ground less than 500 yards in front, bursting with a mighty antiphonal crash that echoed the challenge of the guns. It was Wagnerian.

From then on the din was continuous and simultaneous: the thunder of the guns, the hugely amplified staccato of the shellbursts close in front, and the vicious overhead scream that linked them with a frenzied counterpoint. And sometimes the scream became a whinny, and sometimes a kind of red-hot sighing, but most of the time it was just a scream – a great, angry, baleful scream. The fury of it was elemental, yet precise. It was a controlled cyclone. It was splendid to hear, as the moment of actual combat approached.

The makers of films like to represent this scene with shots of soldiers crouching dramatically in readiness, and close-ups of tense, grim faces. Whereas the striking thing about such moments is the matter-of-factness and casualness of the average soldier. It is true that hearts are apt to be thumping fairly hard, and everyone is thinking, 'Oh, Christ!' But you don't in fact look grim and intense. For one thing you would look slightly foolish if you did. For another you have too many things to do.

The two leading companies were due to advance exactly eight minutes after the barrage opened. So those eight minutes were spent doing such ordinary things as tying up boot laces, helping each other with their equipment, urinating, giving weapons a final check, testing wireless sets to make certain they were still netted, eating a bar of chocolate. The officers were giving last-minute instructions, marshalling their men into battle formations, or having a final check-up with the tank commanders with whom they were going to work.

Those who were not in the leading companies were digging like fiends, for they knew that the temporary calm would be quickly shattered as soon as the tanks and the leading infantry were seen emerging from it.

Meanwhile the barrage thundered on, and to its noise was added the roar of the Shermans' engines. A great bank of dust and smoke welled slowly up from the area the shells were pounding, so that you couldn't see the bursts any more. The spluttering of the twenty-five-pounders rippled up and down the breadth of the gun lines faster than bullets from a machine-gun, so numerous were they.

At eight minutes past nine they moved. Geoff led his company round the right end, Mark led his round the left end of the bank which concealed us from the enemy in front. Then the Shermans clattered forward, with a crescendo of engine roar that made even shouted conversation impossible. The battle was on.

Geoff and Mark were to reach the start line in ten minutes, at which time the barrage was due to move forward 200 yards. Geoff and Mark would edge up as close to it as possible – perhaps within 150 yards, and they'd wait until it moved on again, and then, following quickly in its wake, their bayonets and Brens would swiftly mop up any stunned remnants that survived. And while they were doing this the protective Shermans would blast with shells and machine-guns any more distant enemy post that sought to interfere.

Then the barrage would move forward another 200 yards. The process would be repeated until the first objective had been secured – farm areas in each case. Then Kevin, who would soon be setting off, would pass his company through Geoff's and assault the final objective the code word for which was 'Snowdrop'. When Kevin wirelessed 'Snowdrop' the day's work would be largely done. Highway Six would be only 2000 yards away.

Today was crucial. Today would decide whether it was to be a breakthrough or a stabilized slogging match here in the flat entrance to the Liri Valley, with our great concentrations of men and material at the mercy of the Monastery observation post.

The Boche reacted quickly. Within a few minutes of our barrage opening up the shells started coming back. The scream of their shells vied with the scream of ours. Salvo after salvo began to rain down on the farms and the groves to our rear, where our supporting echelons were massed ready to follow in the wake of the assault. The sun's rays, growing warmer every minute, cleared the last of the morning mist. The Monastery seemed to shed the haze as a boxer sheds his dressing-gown before stepping into the ring for the last round. Towering in stark majesty above the plain, where the whole of our force was stretched out for it to behold. This was the supreme moment – the final reckoning with the Monastery.

D-Day Minus One: US Paratroops Leave for France, 5 June 1944

General Matthew B. Ridgway

I looked at my watch. It was 10 p.m., 5 June 1944. D-Day minus 1. For men of the 82nd Airborne Division, twelve hours before H-Hour, the battle for Normandy had begun.

We flew in a V of Vs, like a gigantic spearhead without a shaft. England was on double daylight-saving time, and it was still full light, but eastward, over the Channel, the skies were darkening. Two hours later night had fallen, and below us we could see glints of yellow flame from the German anti-aircraft guns on the Channel

Islands. We watched them curiously and without fear, as a high-flying duck may watch a hunter, knowing that we were too high and far away for their fire to reach us. In the plane the men sat quietly, deep in their own thoughts. They joked a little and broke, now and then, into ribald laughter. Nervousness and tension, and the cold that blasted through the open door, had its effect upon us all. Now and then a paratrooper would rise, lumber heavily to the little bathroom in the tail of the plane, find he could not push through the narrow doorway in his bulky gear, and come back, mumbling his profane opinion of the designers of the C-47 airplane. Soon the crew chief passed a bucket around, but this did not entirely solve our problem. A man strapped and buckled into full combat gear finds it extremely difficult to reach certain essential portions of his anatomy, and his efforts are not made easier by the fact that his comrades are watching him, jeering derisively and offering gratuitous advice.

Wing to wing, the big planes snuggled close in their tight formation, we crossed to the coast of France. I was sitting straight across the aisle from the doorless exit. Even at fifteen hundred feet I could tell the Channel was rough, for we passed over a small patrol craft – one of the check points for our navigators – and the light it displayed for us was bobbing like a cork in a millrace. No lights showed on the land, but in the pale glow of a rising moon, I could clearly see each farm and field below. And I remember thinking how peaceful the land looked, each house and hedgerow, path and little stream bathed in the silver of the moonlight. And I felt that if it were not for the noise of the engines we could hear the farm dogs baying, and the sound of the barnyard roosters crowing.

D-Day, 6 June 1944
A German Private's View

Anon.

On that night of 6 June none of us expected the invasion any more. There was a strong wind, thick cloud cover, and the enemy aircraft had not bothered us more that day than usual. But then – in the night – the air was full of innumerable planes. We thought, 'What are they demolishing tonight?' But then it started. I was at the wireless set myself. One message followed the other. 'Parachutists landed here – gliders reported there,' and finally 'Landing craft approaching.' Some of our guns fired as best they could. In the morning a huge naval force was sighted – that was the last report our advanced observation posts could send us, before they were overwhelmed. And it was the last report we received about the situation. It was no longer possible to get an idea of what was happening. Wireless communications were jammed, the cables cut and our officers had lost grasp of the situation. Infantrymen who were streaming back told us that their positions on the coast had been overrun or that the few 'bunkers' in our sector had either been shot up or blown to pieces.

Right in the middle of all this turmoil I got orders to go with my car for a reconnaissance towards the coast. With a few infantrymen I reported to a lieutenant. His orders were to retake a village nearby. While he was still talking to me to explain the position, a British tank came rolling towards us from behind, from a direction in which we had not even suspected the presence of the enemy. The enemy tank immediately opened fire on us. Resistance was out of the question. I saw how a group of Polish infantrymen went over to the enemy – carrying their machine-guns and waving their arms. The officer and myself hid in the brush. When we tried to get through to our lines in the evening British paratroops caught us.

At first I was rather depressed, of course. I, an old soldier, a prisoner of war after a few hours of invasion. But when I saw the material behind the enemy front, I could only say, 'Old man, how lucky you have been!'

And when the sun rose the next morning, I saw the invasion fleet lying off the shore. Ship beside ship. And without a break, troops, weapons, tanks, munitions and vehicles were being unloaded in a steady stream.

The Germans Meet a New Foe, 7 June 1944
By a Staff Officer, 17SS Panzer Grenadier Division

Anon.

On 7 June our division received orders to leave the marshalling area in Thouars and to move to the invasion front in Normandy. Everyone was in a good and eager mood to see action again – happy that the pre-invasion spell of uncertainty and waiting was snapped at last.

Our motorized columns were coiling along the road towards the invasion beaches. Then something happened that left us in a daze. Spurts of fire flicked along the column and splashes of dust staccatoed the road. Everyone was piling out of the vehicles and scuttling for the neighbouring fields. Several vehicles were already in flames. This attack ceased as suddenly as it had crashed upon us fifteen minutes before. The men started drifting back to the column again, pale and shaky and wondering how they had survived this fiery rain of bullets. This had been our first experience with the *Jabos* [fighter bombers]. The march column was now completely disrupted and every man was on his own, to pull out of this blazing column as best he could. And it was none too soon, because an hour later the whole thing started all over again, only much worse this time. When this attack was over, the length of the road was strewn with splintered anti-tank guns (the pride of our division), flaming motors and charred implements of war.

The march was called off and all vehicles that were left were hidden in the dense bushes or in barns. No one dared show himself out in the open any more. Now the men started looking at each other. This was different from what we thought it would be like. It had been our first experience with our new foe – the American.

During the next few days we found out how seriously he was going about his business. Although now we only travelled at nights and along secondary roads rimmed with hedges and bushes, we encountered innumerable wrecks giving toothless testimony that some motorists had not benefited from the bitter experience we had had.

D-Day Plus One: A British Paratroop Seeks Directions, 7 June 1944

James G. Bramwell

A dog barked at my approach. From the corner of my eye I could see a stealthy figure flit from behind a haystack into the shadow of the barn. There was no answer to my first knock. The household was obviously fast asleep. I knocked louder, and this time I heard a scurrying on the stairs and a sudden clamour of French voices. Footsteps approached the door, withdrew, hesitated, then approached again. The door opened.

On the way I had been searching for suitable words with which to introduce ourselves – some calming, yet elegant, phrase worthy of the French gift of expression and of their infallible flair for the dramatic moment. But at the sight of the motherly, middle-aged peasant the gulf of the years disappeared, and I might have been back in 1939, an English tourist on a walking tour dropping in to ask for a glass of cider and some camembert.

'*Excusez-nous, Madame. Nous sommes des parachutistes anglais faisant partie du Débarquement Allié.*'

There was a moment of scrutiny, then the woman folded me in her arms. The tears streamed down her face, and in between kisses she was shouting for her husband, for lamps, for wine. In a moment, I was carried by the torrent of welcome into the warm, candle-lit kitchen. Bottles of cognac and Calvados appeared on the table, children came clattering down the wooden stairs, and we found ourselves – an evil-looking group of camouflaged cut-throats – surrounded and overwhelmed by the pent-up emotions of four years. The farmer and his wife wanted us to stay and drink, to laugh and cry and shake hands over and over again. They wanted to touch us, to tell us all about the Occupation, and to share with us their implacable hatred of the Boche. It seemed that the moment so long awaited could not be allowed to be spoilt by realities, till every drop of emotion was exhausted. I was nearly as much affected as they were. Warmed by the fiery trickle of Calvados, I rose to this – certainly one of the greatest occasions of my life – so completely that I forgot all about the Drop, all about the marshes and the Battery. It was the sight of my companions, bewildered by all this emotion and talk, automatically drinking glass after glass, that suddenly reminded me of what we had come for. I began politely to insist on answers to questions which had already been brushed aside more than once: Where were we? How far away were the nearest Germans? Once more the questions were ignored. '*Ah, mon Dieu, ne nous quittez pas maintenant! Ah, les pauvres malheureux! Ils sont tous mouillés!*'

It was moving and exasperating. At last I managed to get what we wanted – a pocket compass and a promise of escort to the hard road through the marshes to Varaville. Hodge and I went our way, leaving the sten-gunners, overcome by their first taste of French hospitality, to sleep it off in the hayloft.

Buzz Bombs: An Eight-Year-Old's Recollections, June 1944

Lionel King

About 8000 V1 pilotless flying bombs were launched against Britain between June and September 1944.

On the night of 12 June the first of Hitler's V1s fell on London and the South East. News spread in from the Kent and Sussex coasts of aircraft with 'jet nozzles', 'fire exhausts' and odd engine sounds. Over Kent some of these craft had suddenly stopped and fallen with a devastating explosion to follow. Bombing of course was familiar to our family. We had moved from West Ham earlier in the war. I'd spent endless nights in the dugout in the garden unable to sleep because of Nanny's snoring. Now it was happening in the daytime too.

The first came over one afternoon. Our windows and doors were open in those fine June days and the drone of the approaching flying bomb was quite unmistakable. It gave us little warning. Ten seconds and the engine cut out directly overhead. There was an oddly resounding explosion about half a mile away.

The Boy Foot, as my mother called him, cycled up there and reported back: 'King Edward Road – there's debris everywhere. Fire brigade and wardens are there, still digging 'em out. I saw it coming. I was up on the roof.' I was envious of his roof. You could have seen anything from there.

'Where's King Edward Road, Mum?' asked Doug.

'By the County Ground. It's where Mr Gibbons lives – you know, he's in the Home Guard with Dad.'

Next day we took to the shelter when we heard the drone. Again the engine cut out, again seemingly over the house. Then it spluttered into life again. Doug and I laughed out loud. It was all rather a joke. Mum told us to duck. The droning engine had stopped. Eight second wait. A disappointing, unspectacular bang.

'I'll find out where it dropped when I go up the shops in a minute,' said Mum. 'Don't open the door to any knocks.' Later she told us it had fallen on a railway siding behind the dust destructor. Three old railway trucks were destroyed, a railwayman had told her.

Soon so many V1s were coming over the authorities gave up air-raid warnings. They would have been sounding the siren all the time. When a bomb announced its approach, Doug and I dived for the shelter, not forgetting to grab our cat Jimmy if he was in sight. Sometimes Mum was out shopping and we went to the shelter alone. We were never worried or afraid. It was all over in ten seconds anyway.

One such afternoon a V1 fell further up the road. We jumped out of the shelter and saw a huge mushroom of dust and rubble rising above the rooftops. You could see individual bricks and planks of wood sailing up into the clear sky. It looked after a few seconds like a ragged umbrella. The traffic picked up again in the road. We ran through the house to the front door. Droves of people were rushing up the road, some on bicycles, many in great distress, towards the scene. Many we knew by sight.

'There goes that man from the oil shop,' exclaimed Doug. We'd never seen him this side of the counter before. The dust cloud had settled now. The first ambulances were pulling up at the Rest Centre at the church opposite. Scruffy-looking people, some shaking, were being helped in. Mum appeared. 'Back into the house!' she barked. 'Nanny will be home from work soon. She'll tell you all about it.'

Nanny came in later. The buzz bomb had fallen by her factory. 'Mrs Lea has copped it. It fell on her house in Lea Hall Road. It's in a state round there. When it exploded the foreman told her she could go round and see if her place was all right. I went with her. We went through it two or three minutes after it happened . . .' The incident was not without humour for Doug and me. 'A spotter on Jenkins's roof saw it coming. He just threw himself over the edge. It's eighty feet off the ground.'

The Russian Summer Offensive, July 1944

Alexander Werth

In Moscow today all hearts are filled with joy. Every night, sometimes once, sometimes twice, sometimes even three times, a familiar deep male voice, speaking like a man giving orders to soldiers, announces a new major victory, and then ten minutes later guns booms and thousands of coloured rockets light up the night and the summer sky. It is always much the same spectacle, but it remains equally thrilling. The new places now being captured by the Russians are in distant Lithuania or in western Byelo-Russia. And every night, in millions of Russian houses, little paper flags and pieces of coloured string and red pencils mark off more large slices of Soviet territory liberated from the enemy.

The present débâcle is the biggest disaster the Germans have suffered since Stalingrad. Their casualties are mounting up and are approaching the half-million mark. Division after division has been encircled and wiped out, hundreds of thousands killed and about a hundred thousand taken prisoner. The score of the generals captured is about twenty-five.

Of these hundred thousand or more prisoners, fifty-seven thousand were paraded through the streets of Moscow with their generals at their head. They had been concentrated on the race course for a couple of days; they were given plenty of food and drink and even a concert of music. Then they were taken to the railway stations in a number of groups, ten or fifteen thousand in each. The wide sunny avenues of the outer ring of Moscow's boulevards, with their ten- or twelve-storey blocks of flats, were lined with hundreds of thousands of people who had come to see the Fritzes. It was a bright, almost cheerful-looking crowd: girls in light, usually white summer dresses, young fellows in white open-necked shirts and light trousers, and everywhere children swarming about, many of them perched on lamp-posts or on top of cars and stationary trolley-buses. Many of them had got on to the roofs of the smaller houses. Moscow was looking its brightest and sunniest, and in its wide, modern avenues there was not the slightest sign of bomb damage. When the Germans were thinking of their own capital it must have annoyed them considerably.

The Moscow crowd was remarkably disciplined. They watched these Germans walk, or rather shuffle past, in their dirty green-grey uniforms – this green-grey mould which, as somebody remarked, had rotted away half of European Russia and was still rotting a great part of Europe. Most of the Germans shuffled along with a hang-dog look. Others, the younger ones, seemed surprised and startled at the sight of Moscow, which they had imagined would look quite different. They were startled at the clean, cheerful, and well-fed appearance of the crowds on either side of the street. A few of the Germans glared. The Moscow people looked on quietly without booing or hissing, and only a few youngsters could be heard shouting, 'Hey, look at the Fritzes, look at their ugly snouts.' But people only exchanged remarks in soft voices. I heard a little girl perched on her mother's shoulder say, 'Mummy, are these the people who killed Daddy?' And the mother hugged the child and wept.

The Bombing of Caen, 7 July 1944

Desmond Flower

The operation began on the evening of 7 July when 600 Lancasters and Halifaxes bombed the defensive positions immediately north of Caen just before twilight. This was the first time that heavy bombers had been used in direct support of an infantry attack, and to the twelve SS (Hitler Jugend) and sixteen GAF Divisions who received the full weight it must have come as a terrible shock. To those of us who watched from the ground in safety there was a sinister yet inspiring majesty about the scene. The earth was already in the shadow of night, and the sky itself was that electric blue which follows a day of cloudless heat. But the long line of bombers stretching back towards England as far as we could see was still in sunlight, and their metal twinkled like fairy lights against the darkening sky. The pathfinders dropped their markers over the target and wheeled away to the right. The flares they used were a kind of golden rain which dropped slowly in widening cascades like a shower of jewels reluctant to obey the force of gravity. Soon the sky was dotted with puffs of flak, like a giant net through the meshes of which the bombers flew on apparently undisturbed. In fact they must have been rocked by the explosions and torn by a million fragments, but from below they seemed to take no notice. Next there was a mushroom of black smoke from the target area, shot with red and yellow flames, which climbed into the sky as slowly as the flares had seemed to descend. Over it the bombers still streamed in, and I remember only one which banked away, stricken, to seek a landing place.

The Nazi Extermination Camp, Maidanek, 23 July 1944

Alexander Werth

On the outskirts of Lublin, Poland, Maidanek was converted into an extermination camp for Jews in 1942. According to some estimates, about 1.5 million died there. At first victims were disposed of in mass shootings; later, gas chambers using Zyklon-B were built. After the rebellion at Sobibor extermination camp in November 1943, the prisoners at Maidanek were killed, and the SS tried to obliterate traces of the massacre.

My first reaction to Maidanek was a feeling of surprise. I had imagined something horrible and sinister beyond words. It was nothing like that. It looked singularly harmless from outside. 'Is *that* it?' was my first reaction when we stopped at what looked like a large workers' settlement. Behind us was the many-towered skyline of Lublin. There was much dust on the road, and the grass was a dull, greenish-grey colour. The camp was separated from the road by a couple of barbed-wire fences, but these did not look particularly sinister, and might have been put up outside any military or semi-military establishment. The place was large; like a whole town of barracks painted a pleasant soft green. There were many people around – soldiers and civilians. A Polish sentry opened the barbed-wire gate to let our cars enter the central avenue, with large green barracks on either side. And then we stopped outside a large barrack marked *Bad und Desinfektion II*. 'This', somebody said, 'is where large numbers of those arriving at the camp were brought in.'

The inside of this barrack was made of concrete, and water taps came out of the wall, and around the room there were benches where the clothes were put down and *afterwards* collected. So this was the place into which they were driven. Or perhaps they were politely invited to 'Step this way, please?' Did any of them suspect, while washing themselves after a long journey, what would happen a few minutes later? Anyway, after the washing was over, they were asked to go into the next room; at this point even the most unsuspecting must have begun to wonder. For the 'next room' was a series of large square concrete structures, each about one-quarter of the size of the bath-house, and, unlike it, had no windows. The naked people (men one time, women another time, children the next) were driven or forced from the bath-house into these dark concrete boxes – about five yards square – and then, with 200 or 250 people packed into each box – and it was completely dark there, except for a small skylight in the ceiling and the spyhole in the door – the process of gassing began. First some hot air was pumped in from the ceiling and then the pretty pale-blue crystals of Zyklon were showered down on the people, and in the hot wet air they rapidly evaporated. In anything from two to ten minutes everybody was dead ... There were six concrete boxes – gas chambers – side by side. 'Nearly 2000 people could be disposed of here simultaneously,' one of the guides said.

But what thoughts passed through these people's minds during those first few minutes while the crystals were falling; could anyone still believe that this humiliating process of being packed into a box and standing there naked, rubbing backs with other naked people, had anything to do with disinfection?

At first it was all very hard to take in, without an effort of the imagination. There were a number of very dull-looking concrete structures which, if their doors had been wider, might anywhere else have been mistaken for a row of nice little garages. But the doors – the doors! They were heavy steel doors, and each had a heavy steel bolt. And in the middle of the door was a spyhole, a circle, three inches in diameter composed of about a hundred small holes. Could the people in their death agony see the SS-man's eye as he watched them? Anyway, the SS-man had nothing to fear: his eye was well protected by a steel netting over the spyhole. And, like the proud maker of reliable safes, the maker of the door had put his name round the spyhole: 'Auert, Berlin'. Then a touch of blue on the floor caught my eye. It was very faint, but still legible. In blue chalk someone had scribbled the word *vergast* and had drawn crudely above it a skull and crossbones. I had never seen this word before, but it obviously meant 'gassed' – and not merely 'gassed' but, with that eloquent little prefix *ver*, 'gassed out'. That's this job finished, and now for the next lot. The blue chalk came into motion when there was nothing but a heap of naked corpses inside. But what cries, what curses, what prayers perhaps, had been uttered inside that gas chamber only a few minutes before? Yet the concrete walls were thick, and Herr Auert had done a wonderful job, so probably no one could hear anything from outside. And even if they did, the people in the camp knew what it was all about.

It was here, outside *Bad und Desinfektion II*, in the side-lane leading into the central avenue, that the corpses were loaded into lorries, covered with tarpaulins, and carted to the crematorium at the other end of the camp, about half a mile away. Between the two there were dozens of barracks, painted the same soft green. Some had notice boards outside, others had not. Thus, there was an *Effekten Kammer* and a *Frauen-Bekleidungskammer*; here the victims' luggage and the women's clothes were sorted out, before they were sent to the central Lublin warehouse, and then on to Germany.

At the other end of the camp, there were enormous mounds of white ashes; but as you looked closer, you found that they were not perfect ashes: for they had among them masses of small human bones: collar bones, finger bones, and bits of skulls, and even a small femur, which can only have been that of a child. And, beyond these mounds there was a sloping plain, on which there grew acres and acres of cabbages. They were large luxuriant cabbages, covered with a layer of white dust. As I heard somebody explaining: 'Layer of manure, then layer of ashes, that's the way it was done . . . These cabbages are all grown on human ashes . . . The SS-men used to cart most of the ashes to their model farm, some distance away. A well-run farm; the SS-men liked to eat these overgrown cabbages, and the prisoners ate these cabbages, too, although they knew that they would almost certainly be turned into cabbages themselves before long . . .'

The Chopin Warehouse was like a vast, five-storey department store, part of the grandiose Maidanek Murder Factory. Here the possessions of hundreds of thousands of murdered people were sorted and classified and packed for export to Germany. In one big room there were thousands of trunks and suitcases, some still with carefully written-out labels; there was a room marked *Herrenschuhe* and another marked *Damenschuhe*; here were thousands of pairs of shoes, all of much better quality than those seen in the big dump near the camp. Then there was a long corridor with thousands of women's dresses, and another with thousands of overcoats. Another room had large wooden shelves all along it, through the centre and along the walls; it was like being in a Woolworth store: here were piled up hundreds of safety razors, and shaving brushes, and thousands of pen-knives and pencils. In the next room were piled up children's toys: teddy-bears, and celluloid dolls and tin automobiles by the hundred, and simple jigsaw puzzles, and an American-made Mickey Mouse . . . And so on, and so on. In a junk heap I even found a manuscript of a Violin Sonata, Op. 15, by somebody called Ernst J. Weil of Prague. What hideous story was behind this?

American Break-Out in Normandy, 24–25 July 1944

General Bayerlein

After establishing the Normandy bridgehead, and taking Saint-Lô on 18 July, the Americans broke through the German defences at Avranches on 31 July. This account is by the general commanding the Panzer division that opposed them.

By about 23 July, US troops had gained suitable jump-off positions for their offensive and had taken Saint-Lô. Panzer Lehr Division held a 6000-yard sector west of the town and, by allocating only weak reserves, had formed a defence zone of 4000 yards in depth. The fifty or sixty tanks and self-propelled anti-tank guns still remaining to the division were deployed in static positions as armoured anti-tank guns and the Panzer Grenadiers were well dug in on their field positions.

On 24 July, 400 American bombers attacked our sector, but without doing much damage. My AA battalion even managed to shoot down ten of their aircraft. The expected ground attack did not come.

But on the next day, there followed one of the heaviest blows delivered by the Allied air forces in a tactical role during the whole of the war. I learnt later from American sources that on 25 July a force consisting of 1600 Flying Fortresses and other bombers had bombed the Panzer Lehr's sector from nine in the morning until around midday. Units holding the front were almost completely wiped out, despite, in many cases, the best possible equipment of tanks, anti-tank guns and self-propelled guns. Back and forth the bomb carpets were laid, artillery positions were wiped out, tanks overturned and buried, infantry positions flattened and all roads and tracks destroyed. By midday the entire area resembled a moon landscape, with the bomb craters touching rim to rim, and there was no longer any hope of getting out any of our weapons. All signal communications had been cut and no command was possible. The shock effect on the troops was indescribable. Several of the men went mad and rushed dementedly round in the open until they were cut down by splinters. Simultaneous with the storm from the air, innumerable guns of the US artillery poured drum-fire into our field positions.

Birkenau Camp, August 1944
The Evidence of a Romanian Jewish Doctor

Dr Charles Sigismund Bendel

The huge Birkenau extermination complex was established in October 1941, not far from the extermination camp at Auschwitz. Dr Josef Mengele (b. 1911), who was appointed chief doctor at Auschwitz by Himmler and supervised the medical experiments on inmates, escaped to South America after the war.

Dr Mengele gave me the honour to attach me to the crematorium. The men who worked there were called Sonderkommando, a Special Kommando numbering 900. They were all deported people

. . . At first I lived in the camp with the other prisoners, but later on in the crematorium itself. The first time I started work there was in August 1944. No one was gassed on that occasion, but 150 political prisoners, Russians and Poles, were led one by one to the graves and there they were shot. Two days later, when I was attached to the day group, I saw a gas chamber in action. On that occasion it was the ghetto at Lodz — 80,000 people were gassed.

Would you describe just what happened that day?

I came at seven o'clock in the morning with the others and saw white smoke still rising from the trenches, which indicated that a whole transport had been liquidated or finished off during the night. In Crematorium No. 4 the result which was achieved by burning was apparently not sufficient. The work was not going on quickly enough, so behind the crematorium they dug three large trenches 12 metres long and 6 metres wide. After a bit it was found that the results achieved even in these three big trenches were not quick enough, so in the middle of these big trenches they built two canals through which the human fat or grease should seep so that work could be continued in a quicker way. The capacity of these trenches was almost fantastic. Crematorium No. 4 was able to burn 1000 people during the day, but this system of trenches was able to deal with the same number in one hour.

Will you describe the day's work?

At eleven o'clock in the morning the chief of the Political Department arrived on his motor-cycle to tell us, as always, that a new transport had arrived. The trenches which I described before had to be prepared. They had to be cleaned out. Wood had to be put in and petrol sprayed over so that it would burn quicker. About twelve o'clock the new transport arrived, consisting of some 800 to 1000 people. These people had to undress themselves in the court of the crematorium and were promised a bath and hot coffee afterwards. They were given orders to put their things on one side and all the valuables on the other. Then they entered a big hall and were told to wait until the gas arrived. Five or ten minutes later the gas arrived, and the strongest insult to a doctor and to the idea of the Red Cross was that it came in a Red Cross ambulance. Then the door was opened and the people were crowded into the gas chambers which gave the impression that the roof was falling on their heads, as it was so low. With blows from different kinds of sticks they were forced to go in and stay there, because when they realized that they were going to their death they tried to come out again. Finally, they succeeded in locking the doors. One heard cries and shouts and they started to fight against each other, knocking on the walls. This went on for two minutes and then there was complete silence. Five minutes later the doors were opened, but it was quite impossible to go in for another twenty minutes. Then the Special Kommandos started work. When the doors were opened a crowd of bodies fell out because they were compressed so much. They were quite contracted, and it was almost impossible to separate one from the other. One got the impression that they fought terribly against death. Anybody who has ever seen a gas chamber filled to the height of one and half metres with corpses will never forget it. At this moment the proper work of the Sonderkommandos starts. They have to drag out the bodies which are still warm and covered with blood, but before they are thrown into the ditches they have still to pass through the hands of the barber and the dentist, because the barber cuts the hair off and the dentist has to take out all the teeth. Now it is proper hell which is starting. The Sonderkommando tries to work as fast as possible. They drag the corpses by their wrists in furious haste. People who had human faces before, I cannot recognize again. They are like devils. A barrister from Salonica, an electrical engineer from Budapest – they are no longer human beings because, even during the work, blows from sticks and rubber truncheons are being showered over them. During the time this is going on they continue to shoot people in front of these ditches, people who could not be got into the gas chambers because they were overcrowded. After an hour and a half the whole work has been done and a new transport has been dealt with in Crematorium No. 4.

The Fall of Aachen, 17 October 1944

George Mucha

Aachen, city of Charlemagne, was the first large German city to be taken by the Allies. This account is by a Czech war correspondent.

I have just returned to Brussels after four days of street fighting in Aachen. I have seen the city of German Emperors being wiped out after it had refused the offer of honourable surrender, and I found its people crushed to desperation by a double misery, by our onslaught and by the cruelties of their Nazi masters. When I first approached Aachen, the town was burning. From an American observation post just above the city I could see immense columns of smoke rising to the sky where some sixty Allied dive-bombers were freely forming up for attack and diving unmolested on their objective. As the bombs came down, red jets of flame spouted up among the houses which stood there silent without a sign of life. It was an eerie sight, no enemy guns, no movements in the streets, only the incessant rumbling of explosions. And then we went in. On both sides of the deserted streets stood empty carcasses of burnt-out houses; glass, debris and tree branches were strewn on the pavements, and almost in every street a building was burning like a huge torch.

We arrived at a huge concrete surface shelter. These shelters are ugly, gloomy constructions with many floors above and below the ground, where hundreds of civilians were hiding for the last five weeks in darkness and stench. Army officers and the police had the entrance blocked, and no one was allowed to leave the place. In the meantime, Gestapo and soldiers were looting the town, grabbing in mad lust the property of their own people, although they had no hope to carry it away. The Army refused to open the shelter. For several hours it was besieged by American soldiers, then a German officer offered to surrender, if he was allowed to take away all his things, plus his batman.

Lieutenant Walker, a young Company Commander, made no effort to accept such a ridiculous offer and threatened to use flame-throwers. That helped. The doors opened and out came the drabbest, filthiest inhabitants of the underworld I have ever seen, as people came stumbling out into the light, dazed, then catching a breath of fresh air, and finally starting to jabber, push, scream and curse. Some precipitated themselves to me, brandishing their fists. 'Where have you been so long?' they shouted. 'Why didn't you deliver us sooner from those devils?' It was a stunning sight. These were the people of the first German town occupied by the Allies. And they were weeping with hysterical joy amidst the smouldering ruins of their homes. 'We have been praying every day for you to come,' said a woman with a pale, thin face. 'You can't imagine what we have had to suffer from them.' And then came the insults. Bloodhound, bandit, gangster. All this was the beloved Führer. There is no one who can hate and curse so thoroughly as the Germans, and these people were all green with hate of the Nazis. It was no trick. I certainly would not be cheated.

It was the breakdown of a nation after having played for five years on the wrong cards. Maybe it was the rage of a gangster, let down by his gang-leader, but it was a hatred you find only in civil wars.

The Bombing of Dresden, 14 February 1945

Margaret Freyer

Dresden, noted as one of the world's most beautiful cities — 'Florence on the Elbe' — was almost completely destroyed during 13–14 February 1945 by 800 British and US aircraft.

I stood by the entrance and waited until no flames came licking in, then I quickly slipped through and out into the street. I had my suitcase in one hand and was wearing a white fur coat which by now was anything but white. I also wore boots and long trousers. Those boots had been a lucky choice, it turned out.

Because of the flying sparks and the fire-storm I couldn't see anything at first. A witches' cauldron was waiting for me out there: no street, only rubble nearly a metre high, glass, girders, stones, craters. I tried to get rid of the sparks by constantly patting them off my coat. It was useless. I stopped doing it, stumbled, and someone behind me called out, 'Take your coat off, it's started to burn.' In the pervading extreme heat I hadn't even noticed. I took off the coat and dropped it.

Next to me a woman was screaming continually, 'My den's burning down, my den's burning down,' and dancing in the street. As I go on, I can still hear her screaming but I don't see her again. I run, I stumble, anywhere. I don't even know where I am any more. I've lost all sense of direction because all I can see is three steps ahead.

Suddenly I fall into a big hole – a bomb crater, about six metres wide and two metres deep, and I end up down there lying on top of three women. I shake them by their clothes and start to scream at them, telling them they must get out of here – but they don't move any more. I believe I was severely shocked by this incident; I seemed to have lost all emotional feeling. Quickly, I climbed across the women, pulled my suitcase after me, and crawled on all fours out of the crater.

To my left I suddenly see a woman. I can see her to this day and shall never forget it. She carries a bundle in her arms. It is a baby. She runs, she falls, and the child flies in an arc into the fire. It's only my eyes which take this in; I myself feel nothing. The woman remains lying on the ground, completely still. Why? What for? I don't know, I just stumble on. The fire-storm is incredible, there are calls for help and screams from somewhere but all around is one single inferno. I hold another wet handkerchief in front of my mouth, my hands and my face are burning; it feels as if the skin is hanging down in strips.

On my right I see a big, burnt-out shop where lots of people are standing. I join them, but think, 'No, I can't stay here either, this place is completely surrounded by fire.' I leave all these people behind, and stumble on. Where to? But every time towards those places where it is dark, in case there is no fire there. I have no conception of what the street actually looked like. But it is especially from those dark patches that the people come who wring their hands and cry the same thing over and over again: 'You can't carry on there, we've just come from there, everything is burning there!' Wherever and to whomsoever I turn, always that same answer.

In front of me is something that might be a street, filled with a hellish rain of sparks which look like enormous rings of fire when they hit the ground. I have no choice. I must go through. I press another wet handkerchief to my mouth and almost get through, but I fall and am convinced that I cannot go on. It's hot. Hot! My hands are burning like fire. I just drop my suitcase, I am past caring, and too weak. At least, there's nothing to lug around with me any more.

I stumbled on towards where it was dark. Suddenly, I saw people again, right in front of me. They scream and gesticulate with their hands, and then – to my utter horror and amazement – I see how one after the other they simply seem to let themselves drop to the ground. I had a feeling that they were being shot, but my mind could not understand what was really happening. Today I know that these unfortunate people were the victims of lack of oxygen. They fainted and then burnt to cinders. I fall then, stumbling over a fallen woman and as I lie right next to her I see how her clothes are burning away. Insane fear grips me and from then on I repeat one simple sentence to myself continuously: 'I don't want to burn to death – no, no burning – I don't want to burn!' Once more I fall down and feel that I am not going to be able to get up again, but the fear of being burnt pulls me to my feet. Crawling, stumbling, my last handkerchief pressed to my mouth ... I do not know how many people I fell over. I knew only one feeling: that I must not burn.

Then my handkerchiefs are all finished – it's dreadfully hot – I can't go on and I remain lying on the ground. Suddenly a soldier appears in front of me. I wave, and wave again. He comes over to me and I whisper into his ear (my voice has almost gone), 'Please take me with you, I don't want to burn.' But that soldier was much too weak himself to lift me to my feet. He laid my two arms crosswise over my breast and stumbled on across me. I followed him with my eyes until he disappears somewhere in the darkness.

I try once more to get up on my feet, but I can only manage to crawl forward on all fours. I can still feel my body, I know I'm still alive. Suddenly, I'm standing up, but there's something wrong, everything seems so far away and I can't hear or see properly any more. As I found out later, like all the others, I was suffering from lack of oxygen. I must have stumbled forwards roughly ten paces when I all at once inhaled fresh air. There's a breeze! I take another breath, inhale deeply, and my senses clear. In front of me is a broken tree. As I rush towards it, I know that I have been saved, but am unaware that the park is the Bürgerwiese.

I walk on a little and discover a car. I'm pleased and decide to spend the night in it. The car is full of suitcases and boxes but I find enough room on the rear seats to squeeze in. Another stroke of good luck for me is that the car's windows are all broken and I have to keep awake putting out the sparks which drifted in. I don't know how long I sat there, when a hand suddenly descended on my shoulder and a man's voice said, 'Hello! you must get out of there.' I got such a fright, because obviously someone was determined to force me away from my safe hiding place. I said, with great fear in my voice, 'Please, allow me to stay here, I'll give you all the money I've got on me.' (If I think about this now it almost sounds like a joke.) But the answer I got was 'No, I don't want your money. The car is on fire.'

Good God! I leapt out immediately and could see that indeed all four tyres were burning. I hadn't noticed because of the tremendous heat.

Now I looked at the man and recognized him as the soldier who had put my arms across my chest. When I asked him, he confirmed it. Then he started to weep. He continued to stroke my back, mumbling words about bravery, Russian campaign . . . but this here, this is hell. I don't grasp his meaning and offer him a cigarette.

We walk on a little way and discover two crouching figures. They were two men, one a railwayman who was crying because (in the smoke and debris) he could not find the way to his home. The other was a civilian who had escaped from a cellar together with sixty people, but had had to leave his wife and children behind, due to some dreadful circumstances. All three men were crying now but I just stood there, incapable of a single tear. It was as if I was watching a film. We spent half the night together, sitting on the ground too exhausted even to carry on a conversation. The continuous explosions didn't bother us, but the hollow cries for help which came continuously from all directions were gruesome. Towards six o'clock in the morning, we parted.

I spent all the daylight hours which followed in the town searching for my fiancé. I looked for him amongst the dead, because hardly any living beings were to be seen anywhere. What I saw is so horrific that I shall hardly be able to describe it. Dead, dead, dead everywhere. Some completely black like charcoal. Others completely untouched, lying as if they were asleep. Women in aprons, women with children sitting in the trams as if they had just nodded off. Many women, many young girls, many small children, soldiers who were only identifiable as such by the metal buckles on their belts, almost all of them naked. Some clinging to each other in groups as if they were clawing at each other.

From some of the debris poked arms, heads, legs, shattered skulls. The static water tanks were filled up to the top with dead human beings, with large pieces of masonry lying on top of that again. Most people looked as if they had been inflated, with large yellow and brown stains on their bodies. People whose clothes were still glowing . . . I think I was incapable of absorbing the meaning of this cruelty any more, for there were also so many little babies, terribly mutilated; and all the people lying so close together that it looked as if someone had put them down there, street by street, deliberately.

I then went through the Grosser Garten and there is one thing I did realize. I was aware that I had constantly to brush hands away from me, hands which belonged to people who wanted me to take them with me, hands which clung to me. But I was much too weak to lift anyone up. My mind took all this in vaguely, as if seen through a veil. In fact, I was in such a state that I did not realize that there was a third attack on Dresden. Late that afternoon I collapsed in the Ostra-Allee, where two men took me to a friend who lived on the outskirts of the city.

I asked for a mirror and did not recognize myself any more. My face was a mass of blisters and so were my hands. My eyes were narrow slits and puffed up, my whole body was covered in little black, pitted marks. I cannot understand to this day how I contracted these marks, because I was wearing a pair of long trousers and a jacket. Possibly the fire-sparks ate their way through my clothing.

US Troops Advance into Germany, March 1945

Lester Atwell

The Germans, letting go the Rhine, fell back in retreat, leaving roadblocks and detachments of men to engage us in delaying actions. Sometimes during the following week, the enemy dug in to make a desperate stand only to have large numbers of its men throw down their arms and stream towards us in surrender. After a disorganized rout, collapse and retreat, more roadblocks were thrown up and the wounded German Army fell back still farther.

One of the delaying actions made by the Germans, though of short duration and of obvious uselessness, stands out as one of the more ghastly episodes of the war. We were advancing down a road in convoy when a German tank drove out of a grove of trees, fired point-blank, killed two of our men, and then retreated from sight again. The convoy halted and two of our rifle companies went forward and surrounded the little grove that contained, they discovered, a platoon of German soldiers in deep foxholes. The German tanks kept swivelling and firing, and after a while four of our own tanks came up. Each from a different direction sprayed the tiny stretch of woods with long streams of flaming gasoline. Within a few seconds the place became an inferno, and the shrieks and screams of the Germans could be heard through the high curtains of fire. A few, in flames, tried to crawl through, but they were mowed down by our machine-guns. Within a half-hour we went on, and all that was left of the little wood was a deep bed of glowing golden coals, hideous to see and to think about in the spring sunlight.

Italian Partisans Assist the Allied Advance, near Trieste, 13 April 1945

Geoffrey Cox

At the new area a group of partisans with red scarves were waiting. They had been stopped by our own troops down by the river bank as suspicious characters. Enthusiastically (they were not yet disillusioned) they explained that they wanted to help. They had been told that there were several Germans hiding in this area. One, they said, was patently an officer. Gold braid had been seen on his shoulders. Could they not carry on with the search?

It took only five minutes to get their papers checked and to set them loose. At the same time we put part of the Headquarters Defence Platoon out on the same quest. 'Any prisoners you can get will be valuable,' I told the bearded partisan leader. He grinned. '*Si, si. Prigionieri*,' he said.

Half an hour later there were shots down by the river bank. An hour later the partisans were back. They had found the Germans, three of them. One was certainly an officer. Where was he? Ah, he had tried to escape. A very foolish fellow. '*Molto stupido, molto stupido.*' But here were his documents. And they handed over a blood-stained bundle.

I opened the top pay-book. Hauptmann. So he was an officer all right. An anti-tank gunner. Two passport photographs fell out of the book. The face on them might well have come from a stock propaganda shot of the stern SS-man. Here were those deep-set eyes, that hard thin mouth, that cheek crossed with duelling scars, that sleek yellow hair, that square German head of the ideal Nazi type. Every detail in the book bore out the picture. The man had been in the SS from the early days of Hitlerism; his list of decorations filled a whole page at the back. 'Medal for the Einmarsch into Austria; Medal for the Einmarsch into Czecho-slovakia; Medal for the Polish campaign; Iron Cross Second Class in France. Served with the infantry in Russia; Transferred to the anti-tank gunners at the end of 1943; Iron Cross First Class in the Crimea for destroying two *feindlicher Panzer Kampfwagen*. The medal of the Iron Cross, its ribbon stained crimson brown above its red, black and white, lay amongst the papers.

The Hauptmann's book was full of photographs of Storm Troops and of soldiers, of sisters in white blouses and dark skirts, of a heavy-built father with close-cropped hair, of other young officers with the same relentless faces. This was the type Hitler had loosed on Europe, brave, desperate, efficient. And now he had come to his end in an Italian field, shot down by an Italian farmer's boy with a Sten gun, shot in the back, I learned later, as he crouched in hiding.

The End of the War for a British POW: Stalag IIID, Berlin, 14–29 April 1945

Norman Norris

We were paraded to march but, owing to the intense air activity, the *Kommandant* did not give the order until the early hours of the morning. As the gates were flung open for the last time for us to march through, numbers of local civilians, mostly women, were waiting, imploring us to take them with us. One woman flung her arms around George Hamlet's neck, kissing him and pleading to be allowed to go with him. However, not one offer was taken up and we marched away from the huts and the barbed wire. Even the camp guards marching with us were glad to be marching westwards. With the advancing Russian soldiers discovering the hell-like conditions their compatriots were being kept in, it was little wonder that it was into British or American hands they wished to fall.

In the morning of 16 April we reached Potsdam. It had been raided the night before and there was chaos everywhere, with numbers of German soldiers hopelessly drunk. But as we marched through all this destruction, tough SS troops were erecting barricades in a desperate attempt to stem the Russian advance. Terror and panic could be seen amongst the civilian population. Our guards spread rumours that the Russians would murder us as well as the Germans if they overran us . . .

Eventually we reached a small village named Senzke, but there was something sinister about this place. It was packed with German troops, with a high proportion of officers. It appeared it was being used as a HQ and even our guards were not happy about remaining there so we marched on and rested under some trees. An hour later Russian aircraft came over to strafe the village and, without any opposition, dived backwards and forwards as if enjoying themselves. Our few remaining guards were just as perplexed as we where to go next, when we had a stroke of luck. A French prisoner of war appeared and, after a battle of languages, finally made us understand that if we followed him he would take us to a representative of the Red Cross.

Within a short while we came to a magnificent country mansion with a number of cottages scattered about. It seemed to be a small community on its own, farming the land and rich in dairy produce. The house itself was luxurious. Huge chandeliers hung in the main hall and many animal heads adorned the walls. On the upper floor at the top of the stairs stood a huge stuffed gorilla. A Baroness lived here, with her daughter, and she gave us a cold reception. Later we found that the daughter's husband was an officer in the SS and was fighting on the eastern front.

The Baroness allowed us to use the barn to sleep in, but told our guards that we could only have potatoes to eat. How we eyed the chickens running loose, the pigs in their sties, above all the cows standing ready to be milked in their immaculate stalls. Arrogant to the end, the Baroness must have known that it was only a matter of time when we would take all that we needed.

The German farm overseer wore the traditional jackboots and attempted to carry out the Baroness's wishes, but with the gunfire of the advancing Russian troops getting nearer each day he was unsure of himself. Amongst the farm workers were a number of Polish men and women and two Russian prisoners of war. After a while we made contact with the Red Cross representative, who was using this place as his HQ. He was a Swiss national and seemed a furtive type. We eyed him with suspicion, he seemed much too concerned with the Baroness. However, he did issue us some Red Cross food and cigarettes, which helped save the situation, though we noted that the Baroness was also smoking fairly heavily.

After a couple of days we woke to find that all our remaining guards had left in the night except one, who must have been at least sixty and just did not know what to do. In the end he sought our advice. Seeing that the old boy was getting on, and that he had given us no trouble in the past, the advice was unanimous. 'Get rid of your uniform, dad, and bugger off home.' Thanking us profusely, he disappeared across the fields.

We were now in a rather tricky position, sandwiched between the Germans and the advancing Russians, and, with the gunfire getting nearer, looked around for more protection. Exploring the farm buildings we discovered a plant for extracting alcohol from potatoes. Underneath lay vaults which were strongly built of brick and we decided we would take our chance there. We discovered we had made a wise choice when in one corner we found chairs and bedding that the farm overseer had moved down for his family.

As the Russians drew nearer, shells and mortars began to fall in and around the farm. German anti-tank gunners, dug in to resist the Russian armoured attacks, drew terrific fire. The two Russian prisoners of war, who had now joined us in the vaults, said they would contact the Russian advance troops when they arrived. Having them with us was a real stroke of luck.

Gunfire, coupled with the heavy explosions of mortars, now became intense. The Russians were pouring heavy fire on the area. Long lines of German troops could be seen running across the fields, their boots and uniforms covered with mud, as they tried to escape the withering fire. Some came running through the farm itself, with hunted looks in their eyes as they struggled to run even faster through the sea of mud. Two Polish prisoners of war, who were watching the fighting from the yard, were killed by one exploding mortar shell, mutilated beyond all recognition. A Polish girl running across the yard received severe leg wounds and was carried down into the vaults, where Cliff Kirkpatrick gave all the help he could.

Two British POWs attempting to get a better view were also hit. One had his face entirely skinned from a mortar blast. But the real tragedy, as far as we British were concerned, happened a little later. With the advance of Russian tanks on the outskirts of the farm a German anti-tank gun still continued to fire. The Russians now poured a withering fire at this last remaining gun crew, completely eliminating them. Unfortunately our Sergeant Major with another man was sheltering in a house near the gun site. A heavy tank shell went right through the walls, decapitating them both. It was indeed a tragedy after four years of imprisonment to be killed within minutes of freedom.

The ground now seemed to shake with the weight of advancing armour. Then at last we saw the first Russian tank lumber into the farmyard. Our two Russian prisoners of war ran across to it, shouting and waving their arms. We saw the tank commander emerge from the turret, jump down and engage them in conversation. Within a short time we were all shaking hands and hugging each other. As other tank crews arrived they too received the same treatment. And so, on 29 April 1945, we were free at last.

To soften up the German opposition for a further advance, the Russians now employed a remarkable weapon, the 'Katusha', or 'Stalin Organ'. This was a mobile rocket ramp which fired off amazing numbers of projectiles. They put a long line of them across the fields, wheel to wheel, and at the drop of a hand poured what seemed to be an endless rain of fire into the retreating Germans. While they were still retreating, we wrapped the bodies of our two dead comrades in sacks and, with heavy hearts, buried them in the private garden of the mansion.

Now that the Russians had taken over, the Baroness took orders instead of giving them. We no longer had to be satisfied with just potatoes. Within a short time chickens were being boiled and pigs were being slaughtered. And for the first time in four years we had fresh milk in abundance. The farm overseer tried to protest, but was ordered to keep quiet. Jim and I decided to look over his house. As a good Nazi, he no doubt had luxuries to show for it. We were rooting round in his bedroom when we heard him clumping upstairs. Seeing us calmly going through the drawers in his dressing table, he bellowed at us to get out. Taking no notice, Jim went over to the sideboard and found it locked. After a struggle to get it open, he turned to the German and asked for the key. '*Schweinrei!*' he spat at Jim. At that moment heavy footsteps sounded on the stairs.

The door slowly opened and into the room strode a Russian soldier, standing at least six foot tall and with his fur hat looking enormous. On either hip he sported an outsize pistol. Seeing Jim and I he gave a smile, but the smile vanished when his gaze fixed on the German. He could speak a little German and we managed to explain that we wanted the sideboard open. Drawing one of his pistols he pointed it at the German's head. Never have I seen a key produced and drawers opened so quickly.

Inside the sideboard we found a huge stock of cigarettes, cigars and pipe tobacco. He must have been a good Nazi considering how scarce these commodities were in Germany. By now his wife, hearing the commotion upstairs, had joined us. After removing the entire stock of tobacco, we began sharing it out with our Russian key producer. At first he refused to accept any, saying we had found it so it belonged to us, but we insisted on stuffing his pockets with part of the loot. As a parting gesture he said that, if the German had caused us any trouble, he would take him downstairs and shoot him. On hearing this both the German and his wife nearly collapsed with fright, but Jim and I declined our friend's offer and went downstairs with him, where we walked away to seek another treasure.

It was not long after this that the cry 'FIRE!' rang out. With almost incredible speed flames were racing through the Baroness's mansion. Hungry flames licked at the fine furniture and priceless relics and soon the whole house was burning fiercely. As the staircase collapsed the gorilla standing at the head of the stairs, like the Roman centurion at Pompeii, slowly toppled forward and plunged head first into the inferno below.

How the fire had started was a mystery. Our guess was that the Baroness had destroyed the mansion rather than let it be taken over by the Russian forces. Within a short while nothing remained but the charred shell of a once magnificent building.

Lüneburg, 20 April 1945
Recollection of a British Tank Officer

Desmond Flower

For us there were ten days of rest in an ancient, attractive and undamaged town. Here we changed the tracks of the M.10s for the last time. Lüneburg was one of the main hospital towns in Germany, and the doctors of the Wehrmacht had remained in strength to help their patients. It was strange to wander round this lovely old city and meet on every street corner one's hated enemy; unarmed and engaged on the world-embracing task of ministering to the sick and wounded, they seemed harmless enough. But the dark side of the moon glowed in its sinister horror all too close to us. Our own Commanding Officer, Lieutenant-Colonel Taylor, was away at Belsen, taking over the camp from Kramer with one of the Oxford Hussar batteries for guards. In Lüneburg, across the street from our billets which were a row of comfortable upper middle-class modern houses near to the centre of the town, lay a small hospital made up of wooden huts. In these huts lay a mass of Russian slave labour – men and women operatives of a factory which not long before had been attacked by the RAF. As the bombs fell many of the operatives had left their machines and run for cover across the open space surrounding the factory. There they were an easy target for the SS troopers who, with a warped pleasure which only Himmler could explain, shot them down; those who stayed in the factory were buried, dead or alive, beneath the debris. When the attack was over such of the wounded as could be got out without much trouble were assembled in these huts, twenty-five yards away from 146 Battery HQ, which was established in a house the owner of which was always wandering in to see if we had scratched the paint.

The nearest building to us was the morgue, in which were laid the Russians who died of their injuries; some of the naked bodies laid out in heaps on the slabs had been there a long time. In the huts a doctor came once a day, and there was one German nurse who, even had she wished, could have done but little. The Russians lay gaunt-eyed, too weak to move, in tumbled grey things which had once been bedclothes, bathed in their own sweat and the pus of their untended wounds. Our men took them food, cigarettes and sweets, and many saw for the first time what it meant to be conquered by the Germans. My own servant, dear Mullins from Bermuda, came back moved beyond words; as he went about his duties after his visit of mercy he muttered, 'They kissed my hand; they kissed my hand.'

Belsen: 24 April 1945

Patrick Gordon-Walker

The Nazi concentration camp at Belsen, near Celle, did not have gas chambers, but an estimated 37,000 prisoners died there from starvation, disease and overwork. It was the first camp to be liberated by the Allies, on 15 April 1945. The Commandant, Josef Kramer, notorious for his cruelty, was hanged by the British on 17 November 1945.

I went to Belsen. It was a vast area surrounded by barbed wire. The whole thing was being guarded by Hungarian guards. They had been in the German Army and are now immediately and without hesitation serving us. They are saving us a large number of men for the time being. Outside the camp, which is amidst bushes, pines, and heather, all fairly recently planted, were great notices in red letters: DANGER — TYPHUS.

We drove into what turned out to be a great training camp, a sort of Aberdeen, where we found the officers and men of the Oxfordshire Yeomanry. They began to tell us about the concentration camp.

It lies south of the training area and is behind its own barbed wire. The Wehrmacht is not allowed near it. It was entirely guarded by SS-men and women. This is what I discovered about the release of the camp that happened about the fifteenth. I got this story from Derek Sington, political officer, and from officers and men of Oxfordshire Yeomanry.

Typhus broke out in the camp, and a truce was arranged so that we could take the camp over. The Germans originally had proposed that we should bypass the camp. In the meanwhile, thousands and thousands of people would have died and been shot. We refused these terms, and demanded the withdrawal of the Germans and the disarmament of the SS guards. Some dozen SS-men and women were left behind under the command of Higher Sturmführer Kramer, who had been at Auschwitz. Apparently they had been told all sorts of fairy tales about the troops, that they could go on guarding, and that we would let them free and so forth.

We had only a handful of men so far, and the SS stayed there that night. The first night of liberty, many hundreds of people died of joy.

Next day some men of the Yeomanry arrived. The people crowded around them kissing their hands and feet – and dying from weakness. Corpses in every state of decay were lying around, piled up on top of each other in heaps. There were corpses in the compound in flocks. People were falling dead all around, people who were walking skeletons. One woman came up to a soldier who was guarding the milk store and doling the milk out to children, and begged for milk for her baby. The man took the baby and saw that it had been dead for days, black in the face and shrivelled up. The woman went on begging for milk. So he poured some on the dead lips. The mother then started to croon with joy and carried the baby off in triumph. She stumbled and fell dead in a few yards. I have this story and some others on records spoken by the men who saw them.

On the sixteenth, Kramer and the SS were arrested. Kramer was taken off and kept in the icebox with some stinking fish of the officers' home. He is now going back to the rear. The rest, men and women, were kept under guard to save them from the inmates. The men were set to work shovelling up the corpses into lorries.

About 35,000 corpses were reckoned, more actually than the living. Of the living, there were about 30,000.

The SS-men were driven and pushed along and made to ride on top of the loaded corpses and then shovel them into their great mass open graves. They were so tired that they fell exhausted amongst the corpses. Jeering crowds collected around them, and they had to be kept under strong guard.

Two men committed suicide in their cells. Two jumped off the lorry and tried to run away and get lost in the crowd. They were shot down. One jumped into a concrete pool of water and was riddled with bullets. The other was brought to the ground, with a shot in the belly.

The SS-women were made to cook and carry heavy loads. One of them tried to commit suicide. The inmates said that they were more cruel and brutal than the men. They are all young, in their twenties. One SS-woman tried to hide, disguised as a prisoner. She was denounced and arrested.

The camp was so full because people had been brought here from east and west. Some people were brought from Nordhausen, a five-day journey, without food. Many had marched for two or three days. There was no food at all in the camp, a few piles of roots – amidst the piles of dead bodies. Some of the dead bodies were of people so hungry that though the roots were guarded by SS-men they had tried to storm them and had been shot down then and there. There was no water, nothing but these roots and some boiled stinking carrots, enough for a few hundred people.

Men and women had fought for these raw, uncooked roots. Dead bodies, black and blue and bloated, and skeletons had been used as pillows by sick people. The day after we took over, seven block leaders, mostly Poles, were murdered by the inmates. Some were still beating the people. We arrested one woman who had beaten another woman with a board. She quite frankly admitted the offence. We are arresting these people.

An enormous buried dump of personal jewellery and belongings was discovered in suitcases. When I went to the camp five days after its liberation, there were still bodies all around. I saw about a thousand.

In one place, hundreds had been shovelled into a mass grave by bulldozers; in another, Hungarian soldiers were putting corpses into a grave that was sixty feet by sixty feet and thirty feet deep. It was almost half full.

Other and similar pits were being dug. Five thousand people had died since we got into the camp. People died before my eyes, scarcely human, moaning skeletons, many of them gone mad. Bodies were just piled up. Many had gashed wounds and bullet marks and terrible sores. One Englishman, who had lived in Ostend, was picked up half dead. It was found that he had a great bullet wound in his back. He could just speak. He had no idea when he had been shot. He must have been lying half unconscious when some SS-man shot him as he was crawling about. This was quite common. I walked about the camp. Everywhere was the smell and odour of death. After a few hours you get used to it and don't notice it any more. People have typhus and dysentery.

In one compound I went, I saw women standing up quite naked, washing among themselves. Near by were piles of corpses. Other women suffering from dysentery were defecating in the open and then staggering back, half dead, to their blocks. Some were lying groaning on the ground. One had reverted to the absolute primitive.

A great job has been done in getting water into the camp. It has been pumped in from the outside and carried by hoses all over the camp with frequent outlet points. There are taps of fresh clean water everywhere. Carts with water move around.

The Royal Army Service Corps has also done a good job in getting food in.

I went into the typhus ward, packed thick with people lying in dirty rags of blankets on the floor, groaning and moaning. By the door sat an English Tommy talking to the people and cheering them up. They couldn't understand what he said, and he was continually ladling milk out of a caldron. I collected together some women who could speak English and German and began to make records. An amazing thing is the number who managed to keep themselves clean and neat. All of them said that in a day or two more, they would have gone under from hunger and weakness.

There are three main classes in the camp: the healthy, who have managed to keep themselves decent, but nearly all of these had typhus; then there were the sick, who were more or less cared for by their friends; then there was the vast underworld that had lost all self-respect, crawling around in rags, living in abominable squalor, defecating in the compound, often mad or half mad. By the other prisoners they are called Mussulmen. It is these who are still dying like flies. They can hardly walk on their legs. Thousands still of these cannot be saved, and if they were, they would be in lunatic asylums for the short remainder of their pitiful lives.

There were a very large number of girls in the camp, mostly Jewesses from Auschwitz. They have to be healthy to survive. Over and over again I was told the same story. The parades at which people were picked out arbitrarily for the gas chambers and the crematorium, where many were burnt alive. Only a person in perfect health survived. Life and death was a question of pure chance.

Rich Jews arrived with their belongings and were able to keep some. There were soap and perfume and fountain pens and watches. All amidst the chance of sudden, arbitrary death, amidst work commandos from which the people returned to this tomb so dead beat that they were sure to be picked for the gas chamber at the next parade, amidst the most horrible death, filth, and squalor that could be imagined.

People at Auschwitz were saved by being moved away to work in towns like Hamburg and were then moved back to Belsen as we advanced. At Auschwitz every woman had her hair shaven absolutely bald.

I met pretty young girls whose hair was one inch long. They all had their numbers tattooed on their left arm, a mark of honour they will wear all their lives.

One of the most extraordinary things was the women and men – there were only a few – who had kept themselves decent and clean.

On the first day many had on powder and lipstick. It seems that the SS stores had been located and looted and boots and clothes had been found. Hundreds of people came up to me with letters, which I have taken and am sending back to London to be posted all over the world. Many have lost all their relatives. 'My father and mother were burned. My sister was burned.' This is what you hear all the time. The British Army is doing what it can. Units are voluntarily giving up blankets. Fifty thousand arrived while I was there and they are being laundered. Sweets and chocolate and rations have been voluntarily given.

Then we went to the children's hut. The floors had been piled with corpses there had been no time to move. We collected a chorus of Russian girls from twelve to fourteen and Dutch boys and girls from nine to fifteen. They sang songs. The Russian children were very impressive. Clean and quite big children, they had been looked after magnificently amidst starvation. They sang the songs they remembered from before captivity. They looked happy now. The Dutch children had been in camp a long time and were very skinny and pale. We stood with our backs to the corpses, out in the open amidst the pines and the birch trees near the wire fence running around the camp.

Men were hung for hours at a time, suspended by their arms, hands tied behind their back, in Belsen. Beatings in workshops were continuous, and there were many deaths there. Just before I left the camp a crematorium was discovered. A story of Auschwitz was told to me by Helen – and her last name, she didn't remember. She was a Czechoslovak.

When women were given the chance to go and work elsewhere in the work zones like Hamburg, mothers with children were, in fact, given the choice between their lives and their children's. Children could not be taken along. Many preferred to stay with their children and face certain death. Some decided to leave their children. But it got around amongst the six-year-old children that if they were left there they would at once be gassed. There were terrible scenes between children and their mothers. One child was so angry that though the mother changed her mind and stayed and died, the child would not talk to her.

That night when I got back at about eleven o'clock very exhausted, I saw the Jewish padre again and talked to him as he was going to bed. Suddenly, he broke down completely and sobbed.

The next morning I left this hell-hole, this camp. As I left, I had myself deloused and my recording truck as well. To you at home, this is one camp. There are many more. This is what you are fighting. None of this is propaganda. This is the plain and simple truth.

The Fall of Berlin, 1 May 1945
A German Citizen's Report

Claus Fuhrmann

By 25 April the Russians had encircled Berlin and joined up with the Americans on the Elbe. Having ordered the German 12th Army to relieve Berlin, Hitler committed suicide on 30 April.

Panic had reached its peak in the city. Hordes of soldiers stationed in Berlin deserted and were shot on the spot or hanged on the nearest tree. A few clad only in underclothes were dangling on a tree quite near our house. On their chests they had placards reading: 'We betrayed the Führer.' The Werewolf pasted leaflets on the houses: 'Dirty cowards and defeatists/We've got them all on our lists!'

The SS went into underground stations, picked out among the sheltering crowds a few men whose faces they did not like, and shot them then and there.

The scourge of our district was a small one-legged Hauptschar-führer of the SS, who stumped through the street on crutches, a machine pistol at the ready, followed by his men. Anyone he didn't like the look of he instantly shot. The gang went down cellars at random and dragged all the men outside, giving them rifles and ordering them straight to the front. Anyone who hesitated was shot.

The front was a few streets away. At the street corner diagonally opposite our house Walloon Waffen SS had taken up position; wild, desperate men who had nothing to lose and who fought to their last round of ammunition. Armed Hitler Youth were lying next to men of the Vlassov White Russian Army.

The continual air attacks of the last months had worn down our morale; but now, as the first shells whistled over our heads, the terrible pressure began to give way. It could not take much longer now, whatever the Walloon and French Waffen SS or the fanatic Hitler Youth with their 2-cm. anti-aircraft guns could do. The end was coming and all we had to do was to try to survive this final stage.

But that was by no means simple. Everything had run out. The only water was in the cellar of a house several streets away. To get bread one had to join a queue of hundreds, grotesquely adorned with steel helmets, outside the baker's shop at 3 a.m. At 5 a.m. the Russians started and continued uninterruptedly until 9 or 10. The crowded mass outside the baker's shop pressed closely against the walls, but no one moved from his place. Often the hours of queuing had been spent in vain; bread was sold out before one reached the shop. Later one could buy bread only if one brought half a bucket of water.

Russian low-flying wooden biplanes machine-gunned people as they stood apathetically in their queues and took a terrible toll of the waiting crowds. In every street dead bodies were left lying where they had fallen.

At the last moment the shopkeepers, who had been jealously

hoarding their stocks, not knowing how much longer they would be allowed to, now began to sell them. Too late! For a small packet of coffee, half a pound of sausages, thousands laid down their lives. A salvo of the heavy calibre shells tore to pieces hundreds of women who were waiting in the market hall. Dead and wounded alike were flung on wheelbarrows and carted away; the surviving women continued to wait, patient, resigned, sullen, until they had finished their miserable shopping.

The pincers began to narrow on the capital. Air raids ceased; the front lines were too loose now for aircraft to distinguish between friend and foe. Slowly but surely the T.52 tanks moved forward through Prenzlauer Allee, through Schonhauser Allee, through Kaiserstrasse. The artillery bombardment poured on the city from three sides in unbroken intensity. Above it, one could hear sharply close and distinct, the rattling of machine-guns and the whine of bullets.

Now it was impossible to leave the cellar. And now the bickering and quarrelling stopped and we were suddenly all of one accord. Almost all the men had revolvers; we squatted in the farthest corner of the cellar in order to avoid being seen by patrolling SS, and were firmly determined to make short shrift of any Volkssturm men who might try to defend our house.

Under the direction of a master mason who had been a soldier in Russia for two years we 'organized' our supplies. We made a roster for parties of two or three to go out and get water and bread. We procured steel helmets; under artillery fire we heaped up mountains of rubble outside the cellar walls in order to safeguard against shells from tanks.

The Nazis became very quiet. No one took the Wehrmacht communiqué seriously now, although Radio Berlin went on broadcasting it until 24 April. A tiny sheet of paper, the last newspaper of the Goebbels press, *Der Panzerbär* [the tank bear] announced Goering's deposition and the removal of the 'government' seat to Flensburg.

We left the cellar at longer and longer intervals and often we could not tell whether it was night or day. The Russians drew nearer; they advanced through the underground railway tunnels, armed with flame-throwers; their advance snipers had taken up positions quite near us; and their shots ricocheted off the houses opposite. Exhausted German soldiers would stumble in and beg for water – they were practically children; I remember one with a pale, quivering face who said, 'We shall do it all right; we'll make our way to the north west yet.' But his eyes belied his words and he looked at me despairingly. What he wanted to say was, 'Hide me, give me shelter. I've had enough of it.' I should have liked to help him; but neither of us dared to speak. Each might have shot the other as a 'defeatist'.

An old man who had lived in our house had been hit by a shell splinter a few days ago and had bled to death. His corpse lay near the entrance and had already began to smell. We threw him on a cart and took him to a burnt-out school building where there was a notice: 'Collection point for Weinmeisterstrasse corpses.' We left him there; one of us took the opportunity of helping himself to a dead policeman's boots.

The first women were fleeing from the northern parts of the city and some of them sought shelter in our cellar, sobbing that the Russians were looting all the houses, abducting the men and raping all the women and girls. I got angry, shouted I had had enough of Goebbels' silly propaganda, the time for that was past. If that was all they had to do, let them go elsewhere.

Whilst the city lay under savage artillery and rifle fire the citizens now took to looting the shops. The last soldiers withdrew farther and farther away. Somewhere in the ruins of the burning city SS-men and Hitler Youth were holding out fanatically. The crowds burst into cellars and storehouses. While bullets were whistling through the air they scrambled for a tin of fish or a pouch of tobacco.

On the morning of 1 May our flat was hit by a 21-cm. shell and almost entirely destroyed. On the same day water carriers reported that they had seen Russian soldiers. They could not be located exactly; they were engaged in house-to-house fighting which was moving very slowly. The artillery had been silent for some time when at noon on 2 May rifle fire too ceased in our district. We climbed out of our cellar.

From the street corner Russian infantry were slowly coming forward, wearing steel helmets with hand grenades in their belts and boots. The SS had vanished. The Hitler Youth had surrendered.

Bunny rushed and threw her arms round a short slit-eyed Siberian soldier who seemed more than a little surprised. I at once went off with two buckets to fetch water, but I did not get beyond the first street corner. All men were stopped there, formed into a column and marched off towards the east.

A short distance behind Alexanderplatz everything was in a state of utter turmoil and confusion. Russian nurses armed with machine-pistols were handing out loaves of bread to the German population. I took advantage of this turmoil to disappear and got back home safely. God knows where the others went.

After the first wave of combatant troops there followed reserves and supply troops who 'liberated' us in the true Russian manner. At our street corner I saw two Russian soldiers assaulting a crying elderly woman and then raping her in full view of the stunned crowd. I ran home as fast as I could. Bunny was all right so far. We had barricaded the one remaining room of our flat with rubble and charred beams in such a manner that no one outside could suspect that anyone lived there.

Every shop in the district was looted. As I hurried to the market I was met by groups of people who were laden with sacks and boxes. Vast food reserves belonging to the armed forces had been stored there. The Russians had forced the doors open and let the Germans in.

The cellars, which were completely blacked out, now became the scene of an incredible spectacle. The starving people flung themselves like beasts over one another, shouting, pushing and struggling to lay their hands on whatever they could. I caught hold of two buckets of sugar, a few boxes of preserves, sixty packages of tobacco and a small sack of coffee which I quickly took back home before returning for more.

The second raid was also successful. I found noodles, tins of butter and a large tin of sardines. But now things were getting out of hand. In order not to be trampled down themselves the Russians fired at random into the crowds with machine-pistols, killing several.

I cannot remember how I extricated myself from this screaming, shouting chaos; all I remember is that even here in this utter confusion, Russian soldiers were raping women in one of the corners.

Bunny had meanwhile made me promise not to try to interfere if anything were to happen to her. There were stories in our district of men being shot trying to protect their wives. In the afternoon two Russians entered our flat, while Bunny was sitting on the bed with the child. They looked her over for some time; evidently they were not very impressed with her. We had not washed for a fortnight, and I had expressly warned Bunny not to make herself tidy, for I thought the dirtier and more neglected she looked the safer.

But the two gentlemen did not seem to have a very high standard as far as cleanliness was concerned. With the usual words, 'Frau komm!' spoken in a menacing voice, one of them went towards her. I was about to interfere; but the other shouted 'Stoi' and jammed his machine-pistol in my chest. In my despair I shouted 'Run away, quick'; but that was, of course, impossible. I saw her quietly lay the baby aside, then she said, 'Please don't look, darling.' I turned to the wall.

When the first Russian had had enough they changed places. The second was chattering in Russian all the time. At last it was over. The man patted me on the shoulder: 'Nix Angst! Russki Soldat gut!'

Kamikaze Attack, 9 May 1945

Michael Moynihan

Kamikaze ('divine wind') attacks sank 34 ships between October 1944 and the end of the war, and at Okinawa inflicted the heaviest losses ever suffered by the US Navy in a single battle. The planes were usually ordinary service aircraft, loaded with bombs and extra fuel tanks, which would explode on impact. A piloted, rocket-powered missile was also deployed, from which the pilot had no means of escape.

Out of a clear evening sky Japanese Kamikazes swooped for the second time in five days on heavy units of the British Pacific Fleet . . . The first two to penetrate the fighter and flak screen made for the same ship, an aircraft carrier. Both hit the flight deck and both by some lucky chance plunged from there into the sea, blazing wrecks. A Kamikaze attack is unlike anything one has known in the Western war. At the back of one's mind continually is the thought of the pilots, fanatical, cold-blooded, whose last ambition is that death might also be glory. They wear, we are told, some kind of ceremonial uniform.

Of the death dive of a third Kamikaze I had a breath-taking view from the Admiral's bridge. Its approach was signalled as usual by the gun flashes of battleship, carrier, cruiser, destroyer, and the growing rash of smoke puffs against the clear sky. The Zeke was flying low and we could see it now speeding on level course across the Fleet, ringed round, pursued, by the bursting shells. It seemed to bear a charmed life, cutting unscathed through the murderous hail of flak. Less than a mile from us we saw it turn aft of another carrier. It was approaching its kill. The air all around was smudged and clamorous with the bursting shells, joined now by the sharper points of pom-poms firing from the carrier's decks.

The Jap climbed suddenly and dived. It was all a matter of seconds. He came up the centre of the flight deck, accurate as a homing plane, and abruptly all was lost in a confusion of smoke and flame. The whole superstructure of the ship vanished behind billows of jet-black smoke shot through by flames as the tanks of aircraft ranged on the deck exploded.

It seemed at the time that the ship was doomed, that nothing could survive that inferno. But within half an hour the flames were extinguished and the smoke had drifted and dispersed in the sunlight. Through glasses we could see the armour-plated deck of the carrier swarming with activity. The island was blackened and a hole gaped at its base, but the damage seemed negligible for all that chaos of smoke and flame. When a few weeks ago this carrier was hit by a Kamikaze, planes were taking off again within seven minutes.

Nagasaki, 9 August 1945

William T. Laurence

Dropped three days after the Hiroshima bomb, the atomic bomb on Nagasaki killed about 35,000 people and devastated 1.8 square miles.

We are on our way to bomb the mainland of Japan. Our flying contingent consists of three specially designed B-29 Superforts, and two of these carry no bombs. But our lead plane is on its way with another atomic bomb, the second in three days, concentrating in its active substance an explosive energy equivalent to 20,000 and, under favourable conditions, 40,000 tons of TNT.

We have several chosen targets. One of these is the great industrial and shipping centre of Nagasaki, on the western shore of Kyushu, one of the main islands of the Japanese homeland.

I watched the assembly of this man-made meteor during the past two days and was among the small group of scientists and Army and Navy representatives privileged to be present at the ritual of its loading in the Superfort last night, against a background of threatening black skies torn open at intervals by great lightning flashes.

It is a thing of beauty to behold, this 'gadget'. Into its design went millions of man-hours of what is without doubt the most concentrated intellectual effort in history. Never before had so much brain power been focused on a single problem.

This atomic bomb is different from the bomb used three days ago with such devastating results on Hiroshima.

I saw the atomic substance before it was placed inside the bomb. By itself it is not at all dangerous to handle. It is only under certain conditions, produced in the bomb assembly, that it can be made to yield up its energy, and even then it gives only a small fraction of its total contents – a fraction, however, large enough to produce the greatest explosion on earth.

The briefing at midnight revealed the extreme care and the tremendous amount of preparation that had been made to take care of every detail of the mission, to make certain that the atomic bomb fully served the purpose for which it was intended. Each target in turn was shown in detailed maps and in aerial photographs. Every detail of the course was rehearsed – navigation, altitude, weather, where to land in emergencies. It came out that the Navy had submarines and rescue craft, known as Dumbos and Superdumbos, stationed at various strategic points in the vicinity of the targets, ready to rescue the fliers in case they were forced to bail out.

The briefing period ended with a moving prayer by the chaplain. We then proceeded to the mess hall for the traditional early-morning breakfast before departure on a bombing mission.

A convoy of trucks took us to the supply building for the special equipment carried on combat missions. This included the Mae West, a parachute, a lifeboat, an oxygen mask, a flak suit, and a survival vest. We still had a few hours before take-off time, but we all went to the flying field and stood around in little groups or sat in jeeps talking rather casually about our mission to the Empire, as the Japanese home islands are known hereabouts.

In command of our mission is Major Charles W. Sweeney, twenty-five, of 124 Hamilton Avenue, North Quincy, Massachusetts. His flagship, carrying the atomic bomb, is named *The Great Artiste*, but the name does not appear on the body of the great silver ship, with its unusually long, four-bladed, orange-tipped propellers. Instead, it carries the number 77, and someone remarks that it was 'Red' Grange's winning number on the grid-iron.

We took off at 3.50 this morning and headed north-west on a straight line for the Empire. The night was cloudy and threatening, with only a few stars here and there breaking through the overcast. The weather report had predicted storms ahead part of the way but clear sailing for the final and climactic stages of our odyssey.

We were about an hour away from our base when the storm broke. Our great ship took some heavy dips through the abysmal darkness around us, but it took these dips much more gracefully than a large commercial air liner, producing a sensation more in the nature of a glide than a 'bump', like a great ocean liner riding the waves except that in this case the air waves were much higher and the rhythmic tempo of the glide was much faster.

I noticed a strange eerie light coming through the window high above the navigator's cabin, and as I peered through the dark all around us I saw a startling phenomenon. The whirling giant propellers had somehow become great luminous disks of blue flame. The same luminous blue flame appeared on the Plexiglas windows in the nose of the ship, and on the tips of the giant wings. It looked as though we were riding the whirlwind through space on a chariot of blue fire.

It was, I surmised, a surcharge of static electricity that had accumulated on the tips of the propellers and on the di-electric material of the plastic windows. One's thoughts dwelt anxiously on the precious cargo in the invisible ship ahead of us. Was there any likelihood of danger that this heavy electric tension in the atmosphere all about us might set it off?

I expressed my fears to Captain Bock, who seemed nonchalant and unperturbed at the controls. He quickly reassured me.

'It is a familiar phenomenon seen often on ships. I have seen it many times on bombing missions. It is known as St Elmo's fire.'

On we went through the night. We soon rode out the storm and our ship was once again sailing on a smooth course straight ahead, on a direct line to the Empire.

Our altimeter showed that we were travelling through space at a height of 17,000 feet. The thermometer registered an outside temperature of 33 degrees below zero Centigrade, about 30 below Fahrenheit. Inside our pressurized cabin the temperature was that of a comfortable air-conditioned room and a pressure corresponding to an altitude of 8000 feet. Captain Bock cautioned me, however, to keep my oxygen mask handy in case of emergency. This, he explained, might mean either something going wrong with the pressure equipment inside the ship or a hole through the cabin by flak.

The first signs of dawn came shortly after five o'clock. Sergeant Curry, of Hoopeston, Illinois, who had been listening steadily on his earphones for radio reports, while maintaining a strict radio silence himself, greeted it by rising to his feet and gazing out the window.

'It's good to see the day,' he told me. 'I get a feeling of claustrophobia hemmed in in this cabin at night.'

He is a typical American youth, looking even younger than his twenty years. It takes no mind-reader to read his thoughts.

'It's a long way from Hoopeston,' I find myself remarking.

'Yep,' he replies, as he busies himself decoding a message from outer space.

'Think this atomic bomb will end the war?' he asked hopefully.

'There is a very good chance that this one may do the trick,' I assured him, 'but if not, then the next one or two surely will. Its power is such that no nation can stand up against it very long.' This was not my own view. I had heard it expressed all around a few hours earlier, before we took off. To anyone who had seen this man-made fireball in action, as I had less than a month ago in the desert of New Mexico, this view did not sound over-optimistic.

By 5.50 it was really light outside. We had lost our lead ship, but Lieutenant Godfrey, our navigator, informs me that we had arranged for that contingency. We have an assembly point in the sky above the little island of Yakushima, south-east of Kyushu, at 9.10. We are to circle there and wait for the rest of our formation.

Our genial bombardier, Lieutenant Levy, comes over to invite me to take his front-row seat in the transparent nose of the ship, and I accept eagerly. From that vantage point in space, 17,000 feet above the Pacific, one gets a view of hundreds of miles on all sides, horizontally and vertically. At that height the vast ocean below and the sky above seem to merge into one great sphere.

I was on the inside of that firmament, riding above the giant mountains of white cumulus clouds, letting myself be suspended in infinite space. One hears the whirl of the motors behind one, but it soon becomes insignificant against the immensity all around and is before long swallowed by it. There comes a point where space also swallows time and one lives through eternal moments filled with an oppressive loneliness, as though all life had suddenly vanished from the earth and you are the only one left, a lone survivor travelling endlessly through interplanetary space.

My mind soon returns to the mission I am on. Somewhere beyond these vast mountains of white clouds ahead of me there lies Japan, the land of our enemy. In about four hours from now one of its cities, making weapons of war for use against us, will be wiped off the map by the greatest weapon ever made by man. In one tenth of a millionth of a second, a fraction of time immeasurable by any clock, a whirlwind from the skies will pulverize thousands of its buildings and tens of thousands of its inhabitants.

But at this moment no one yet knows which one of the several cities chosen as targets is to be annihilated. The final choice lies with destiny. The winds over Japan will make the decision. If they carry heavy clouds over our primary target, that city will be saved, at least for the time being. None of its inhabitants will ever know that the wind of a benevolent destiny had passed over their heads. But that same wind will doom another city.

Our weather planes ahead or us are on their way to find out where the wind blows. Half an hour before target time we will know what the winds have decided.

Does one feel any pity or compassion for the poor devils about to die? Not when one thinks of Pearl Harbor and of the Death March on Bataan.

Captain Bock informs me that we are about to start our climb to bombing altitude.

He manipulates a few knobs on his control panel to the right of him, and I alternately watch the white clouds and ocean below me and the altimeter on the bombardier's panel. We reached our altitude at nine o'clock. We were then over Japanese waters, close to their mainland. Lieutenant Godfrey motioned to me to look through his radarscope. Before me was the outline of our assembly point. We shall soon meet our lead ship and proceed to the final stage of our journey.

We reached Yakushima at 9.12 and there, about 4000 feet ahead of us, was *The Great Artiste* with its precious load. I saw Lieutenant Godfrey and Sergeant Curry strap on their parachutes and I decided to do likewise.

We started circling. We saw little towns on the coastline, heedless of our presence. We kept on circling, waiting for the third ship in our formation.

It was 9.56 when we began heading for the coastline. Our weather scouts had sent us code messages, deciphered by Sergeant Curry, informing us that both the primary target as well as the secondary were clearly visible.

The winds of destiny seemed to favour certain Japanese cities that must remain nameless. We circled about them again and again and found no opening in the thick umbrella of clouds that covered them. Destiny chose Nagasaki as the ultimate target.

We had been circling for some time when we noticed black puffs of smoke coming through the white clouds directly at us. There were fifteen bursts of flak in rapid succession, all too low. Captain Bock changed his course. There soon followed eight more bursts of flak, right up to our altitude, but by this time we were too far to the left.

We flew southward down the channel and at 11.33 crossed the coastline and headed straight for Nagasaki, about one hundred miles to the west. Here again we circled until we found an opening in the clouds. It was 12.01 and the goal of our mission had arrived.

We heard the prearranged signal on our radio, put on our arc-welder's glasses, and watched tensely the manoeuvrings of the strike ship about half a mile in front of us.

'There she goes!' someone said.

Out of the belly of *The Great Artiste* what looked like a black object went downward.

Captain Bock swung around to get out of range; but even though we were turning away in the opposite direction, and despite the fact that it was broad daylight in our cabin, all of us became aware of a giant flash that broke through the dark barrier of our arc-welder's lenses and flooded our cabin with intense light.

We removed our glasses after the first flash, but the light still lingered on, a bluish-green light that illuminated the entire sky all around. A tremendous blast wave struck our ship and made it tremble from nose to tail. This was followed by four more blasts in rapid succession, each resounding like the boom of cannon fire hitting our plane from all directions.

Observers in the tail of our ship saw a giant ball of fire rise as though from the bowels of the earth, belching forth enormous white smoke rings. Next they saw a giant pillar of purple fire, 10,000 feet high, shooting skyward with enormous speed.

By the time our ship had made another turn in the direction of the atomic explosion the pillar of purple fire had reached the level of our altitude. Only about 45 seconds had passed. Awe-struck, we watched it shoot upward like a meteor coming from the earth instead of from outer space, becoming ever more alive as it climbed skyward through the white clouds. It was no longer smoke, or dust, or even a cloud of fire. It was a living thing, a new species of being, born right before our incredulous eyes.

At one stage of its evolution, covering millions of years in terms of seconds, the entity assumed the form of a giant square totem pole, with its base about three miles long, tapering off to about a mile at the top. Its bottom was brown, its centre was amber, its top white. But it was a living totem pole, carved with many grotesque masks grimacing at the earth.

Then, just when it appeared as though the thing had settled down into a state of permanence, there came shooting out of the top a giant mushroom that increased the height of the pillar to a total of 45,000 feet. The mushroom top was even more alive than the pillar, seething and boiling in a white fury of creamy foam, sizzling upward and then descending earthward, a thousand Old Faithful geysers rolled into one.

It kept struggling in an elemental fury, like a creature in the act of breaking the bonds that held it down. In a few seconds it had freed itself from its gigantic stem and floated upward with tremendous speed, its momentum carrying it into the stratosphere to a height of about 60,000 feet.

But no sooner did this happen when another mushroom, smaller in size than the first one, began emerging out of the pillar. It was as though the decapitated monster was growing a new head.

As the first mushroom floated off into the blue it changed its

638

shape into a flowerlike form, its giant petals curving downward, creamy white outside, rose-coloured inside. It still retained that shape when we last gazed at it from a distance of about 200 miles. The boiling pillar of many colours could also be seen at that distance, a giant mountain of jumbled rainbows, in travail. Much living substance had gone into those rainbows. The quivering top of the pillar was protruding to a great height through the white clouds, giving the appearance of a monstrous prehistoric creature with a ruff around its neck, a fleecy ruff extending in all directions, as far as the eye could see.

Visiting Hiroshima, 9 September 1945

Marcel Junod

The atomic bomb on Hiroshima killed between 70,000 and 80,000 people and injured more than 70,000 others.

The bare cone of Fujiyama was just visible on the horizon as we flew over the 'inland sea' which lay beneath us like a lavender-blue carpet picked out in green and yellow with its numerous promontories and wooded islands . . .

Towards midday a huge white patch appeared on the ground below us. This chalky desert, looking almost like ivory in the sun, surrounded by a crumble of twisted ironwork and ash heaps, was all that remained of Hiroshima . . .

The journalist described the main official buildings of the town, which were built of reinforced concrete and dominated a sea of low-roofed Japanese houses extending over six miles to the wooded hills I could see in the distance.

'The town was not much damaged,' he explained. 'It had suffered very little from the bombing. There were only two minor raids, one on March 19th last by a squadron of American naval planes, and one on April 30th by a Flying Fortress.

'On August 6th there wasn't a cloud in the sky above Hiroshima, and a mild, hardly perceptible wind blew from the south. Visibility was almost perfect for ten or twelve miles.

'At nine minutes past seven in the morning an air-raid warning sounded and four American B-29 planes appeared. To the north of the town two of them turned and made off to the south and disappeared in the direction of the Shoho Sea. The other two, after having circled the neighbourhood of Shukai, flew off at high speed southwards in the direction of the Bingo Sea.

'At 7.31 the all-clear was given. Feeling themselves in safety people came out of their shelters and went about their affairs and the work of the day began.

'Suddenly a glaring whitish pinkish light appeared in the sky accompanied by an unnatural tremor which was followed almost immediately by a wave of suffocating heat and a wind which swept away everything in its path.

'Within a few seconds the thousands of people in the streets and the gardens in the centre of the town were scorched by a wave of searing heat. Many were killed instantly, others lay writhing on the ground screaming in agony from the intolerable pain of their burns. Everything standing upright in the way of the blast, walls, houses, factories and other buildings, was annihilated and the debris spun round in a whirlwind and was carried up into the air. Trams were picked up and tossed aside as though they had neither weight nor solidity. Trains were flung off the rails as though they were toys. Horses, dogs and cattle suffered the same fate as human beings. Every living thing was petrified in an attitude of indescribable suffering. Even the vegetation did not escape. Trees went up in flames, the rice plants lost their greenness, the grass burned on the ground like dry straw.

'Beyond the zone of utter death in which nothing remained alive houses collapsed in a whirl of beams, bricks and girders. Up to about three miles from the centre of the explosion lightly built houses were flattened as though they had been built of cardboard. Those who were inside were either killed or wounded. Those who managed to extricate themselves by some miracle found themselves surrounded by a ring of fire. And the few who succeeded in making their way to safety generally died twenty or thirty days later from the delayed effects of the deadly gamma rays. Some of the reinforced concrete or stone buildings remained standing but their interiors were completely gutted by the blast.

'About half an hour after the explosion whilst the sky all around Hiroshima was still cloudless a fine rain began to fall on the town and went on for about five minutes. It was caused by the sudden rise of over-heated air to a great height, where it condensed and fell back as rain. Then a violent wind rose and the fires extended with terrible rapidity, because most Japanese houses are built only of timber and straw.

'By the evening the fire began to die down and then it went out. There was nothing left to burn. Hiroshima had ceased to exist.'

The Japanese broke off and then pronounced one word with indescribable but restrained emotion: 'Look.'

We were then rather less than four miles away from the Aioi Bridge, which was immediately beneath the explosion, but already the roofs of the houses around us had lost their tiles and the grass was yellow along the roadside. At three miles from the centre of the devastation the houses were already destroyed, their roofs had fallen in and the beams jutted out from the wreckage of their walls. But so far it was only the usual spectacle presented by towns damaged by ordinary high explosives.

About two and a half miles from the centre of the town all the buildings had been burnt out and destroyed. Only traces of the foundations and piles of debris and rusty charred ironwork were left. This zone was like the devastated areas of Tokyo, Osaka and Kobé after the mass fall of incendiaries.

At three-quarters of a mile from the centre of the explosion nothing at all was left. Everything had disappeared. It was a stony waste littered with debris and twisted girders. The incandescent breath of the fire had swept away every obstacle and all that remained upright were one or two fragments of stone walls and a few stoves which had remained incongruously on their base.

We got out of the car and made our way slowly through the ruins into the centre of the dead city. Absolute silence reigned in the whole necropolis.

The Execution of Nazi War Criminals, 16 October 1946

Kingsbury Smith

On 1 October 1946, the International Military Tribunal at Nuremberg delivered its verdicts, after 216 court sessions. Of the original twenty-four defendants, twelve (including Martin Bormann, tried in absentia) were sentenced to death by hanging. The author of this account, Kingsbury Smith of the International News Service, was chosen by lot to represent the American press at the executions.

Hermann Wilhelm Goering cheated the gallows of Allied justice by committing suicide in his prison cell shortly before the ten other condemned Nazi leaders were hanged in Nuremberg gaol. He swallowed cyanide he had concealed in a copper cartridge shell, while lying on a cot in his cell.

The one-time Number Two man in the Nazi hierarchy was dead two hours before he was scheduled to have been dropped through the trapdoor of a gallows erected in a small, brightly lighted gymnasium in the gaol yard, 35 yards from the cell block where he spent his last days of ignominy.

Joachim von Ribbentrop, foreign minister in the ill-starred regime of Adolf Hitler, took Goering's place as first to the scaffold.

Last to depart this life in a total span of just about two hours was Arthur Seyss-Inquart, former *Gauleiter* of Holland and Austria.

In between these two once-powerful leaders, the gallows claimed, in the order named, Field Marshal Wilhelm Keitel; Ernst Kaltenbrunner, once head of the Nazis' security police; Alfred Rosenberg, arch-priest of Nazi culture in foreign lands; Hans Frank, *Gauleiter* of Poland; Wilhelm Frick, Nazi minister of the interior; Fritz Sauckel, boss of slave labour; Colonel General Alfred Jodl; and Julius Streicher, who bossed the anti-Semitism drive of the Hitler Reich.

As they went to the gallows, most of the ten endeavoured to show bravery. Some were defiant and some were resigned and some begged the Almighty for mercy.

All except Rosenberg made brief, last-minute statements on the scaffold. But the only one to make any reference to Hitler or the Nazi ideology in his final moments was Julius Streicher.

Three black-painted wooden scaffolds stood inside the gymnasium, a room approximately 33 feet wide by 80 feet long with plaster walls in which cracks showed. The gymnasium had been used only three days before by the American security guards for a basketball game. Two gallows were used alternately. The third was a spare for use if needed. The men were hanged one at a time, but to get the executions over with quickly, the military police would bring in a man while the prisoner who preceded him still was dangling at the end of the rope.

The ten once great men in Hitler's Reich that was to have lasted for a thousand years walked up thirteen wooden steps to a platform eight feet high which also was eight feet square.

Ropes were suspended from a crossbeam supported on two posts. A new one was used for each man.

When the trap was sprung, the victim dropped from sight in the interior of the scaffolding. The bottom of it was boarded up with wood on three sides and shielded by a dark canvas curtain on the fourth, so that no one saw the death struggles of the men dangling with broken necks.

Von Ribbentrop entered the execution chamber at 1.11 a.m. Nuremberg time.

He was stopped immediately inside the door by two Army sergeants who closed in on each side of him and held his arms, while another sergeant who had followed him in removed manacles from his hands and replace them with a leather strap.

It was planned originally to permit the condemned men to walk from their cells to the execution chamber with their hands free, but all were manacled immediately following Goering's suicide.

Von Ribbentrop was able to maintain his apparent stoicism to the last. He walked steadily toward the scaffold between his two guards, but he did not answer at first when an officer standing at the foot of the gallows went through the formality of asking his name. When the query was repeated he almost shouted, 'Joachim von Ribbentrop!' and then mounted the steps without any sign of hesitation.

When he was turned around on the platform to face the witnesses, he seemed to clench his teeth and raise his head with the old arrogance. When asked whether he had any final message he said, 'God protect Germany,' in German, and then added, 'May I say something else?'

The interpreter nodded and the former diplomatic wizard of Nazidom spoke his last words in loud, firm tones: 'My last wish is that Germany realize its entity and that an understanding be reached between the East and the West. I wish peace to the world.'

As the black hood was placed in position on his head, Von Ribbentrop looked straight ahead.

Then the hangman adjusted the rope, pulled the lever, and Von Ribbentrop slipped away to his fate.

Field Marshal Keitel, who was immediately behind Von Ribbentrop in the order of executions, was the first military leader to be executed under the new concept of international law – the principle that professional soldiers cannot escape punishment for waging aggressive wars and permitting crimes against humanity with the claim they were dutifully carrying out orders of superiors.

Keitel entered the chamber two minutes after the trap had dropped beneath Von Ribbentrop, while the latter still was at the end of his rope. But Von Ribbentrop's body was concealed inside the first scaffold; all that could be seen was the taut rope.

Keitel did not appear as tense as Von Ribbentrop. He held his head high while his hands were being tied and walked erect toward the gallows with a military bearing. When asked his name he responded loudly and mounted the gallows as he might have mounted a reviewing stand to take a salute from German armies.

He certainly did not appear to need the help of guards who walked alongside, holding his arms. When he turned around atop the platform he looked over the crowd with the iron-jawed haughtiness of a proud Prussian officer. His last words, uttered in a full, clear voice, were translated as 'I call on God Almighty to have mercy on the German people. More than 2 million German soldiers went to their death for the fatherland before me. I follow now my sons – all for Germany.'

After his black-booted, uniformed body plunged through the trap, witnesses agreed Keitel had showed more courage on the scaffold than in the courtroom, where he had tried to shift his guilt upon the ghost of Hitler, claiming that all was the Führer's fault and that he merely carried out orders and had no responsibility.

With both Von Ribbentrop and Keitel hanging at the end of their ropes there was a pause in the proceedings. The American colonel directing the executions asked the American general representing the United States on the Allied Control Commission if those present could smoke. An affirmative answer brought cigarettes into the hands of almost every one of the thirty-odd persons present. Officers and GIs walked around nervously or spoke a few words to one another in hushed voices while Allied correspondents scribbled furiously their notes on this historic though ghastly event.

In a few minutes an American army doctor accompanied by a Russian army doctor and both carrying stethoscopes walked to the first scaffold, lifted the curtain and disappeared within.

They emerged at 1.30 a.m. and spoke to an American colonel. The colonel swung around and facing official witnesses snapped to attention to say, 'The man is dead.'

Two GIs quickly appeared with a stretcher which was carried up and lifted into the interior of the scaffold. The hangman mounted the gallows steps, took a large commando-type knife out of a sheath strapped to his side and cut the rope.

Von Ribbentrop's limp body with the black hood still over his head was removed to the far end of the room and placed behind a black canvas curtain. This all had taken less than ten minutes.

The directing colonel turned to the witnesses and said, 'Cigarettes out, please, gentlemen.' Another colonel went out the door and over to the condemned block to fetch the next man. This was Ernst Kaltenbrunner. He entered the execution chamber at 1.36 a.m., wearing a sweater beneath his blue double-breasted coat. With his lean haggard face furrowed by old duelling scars, this terrible successor to Reinhard Heydrich had a frightening look as he glanced around the room.

He wet his lips apparently in nervousness as he turned to mount the gallows, but he walked steadily. He answered his name in a calm, low voice. When he turned around on the gallows platform he first faced a United States Army Roman Catholic chaplain wearing a Franciscan habit. When Kaltenbrunner was invited to make a last statement, he said, 'I have loved my German people and my fatherland with a warm heart. I have done my duty by the laws of my people and I am sorry my people were led this time by men who were not soldiers and that crimes were committed of which I had no knowledge.'

This was the man, one of whose agents – a man named Rudolf Hoess – confessed at a trial that under Kaltenbrunner's orders he gassed 3 million human beings at the Auschwitz concentration camp!

As the black hood was raised over his head Kaltenbrunner, still speaking in a low voice, used a German phrase which translated means, 'Germany, good luck.'

His trap was sprung at 1.39 a.m.

Field Marshal Keitel was pronounced dead at 1.44 a.m. and three minutes later guards had removed his body. The scaffold was made ready for Alfred Rosenberg.

Rosenberg was dull and sunken-cheeked as he looked around the court. His complexion was pasty-brown, but he did not appear nervous and walked with a steady step to and up the gallows.

Apart from giving his name and replying 'no' to a question as to whether he had anything to say, he did not utter a word. Despite his avowed atheism he was accompanied by a Protestant chaplain who followed him to the gallows and stood beside him praying.

Rosenberg looked at the chaplain once, expressionless. Ninety seconds after he was swinging from the end of a hangman's rope. His was the swiftest execution of the ten.

There was a brief lull in the proceedings until Kaltenbrunner was pronounced dead at 1.52 a.m.

Hans Frank was next in the parade of death. He was the only one of the condemned to enter the chamber with a smile on his countenance.

Although nervous and swallowing frequently, this man, who was converted to Roman Catholicism after his arrest, gave the appearance of being relieved at the prospect of atoning for his evil deeds.

He answered to his name quietly and when asked for any last statement, he replied in a low voice that was almost a whisper, 'I am thankful for the kind treatment during my captivity and I ask God to accept me with mercy.'

Frank closed his eyes and swallowed as the black hood went over his head.

The sixth man to leave his prison cell and walk with handcuffed wrists to the death house was 69-year-old Wilhelm Frick. He entered the execution chamber at 2.05 a.m., six minutes after Rosenberg had been pronounced dead. He seemed the least steady of any so far and stumbled on the thirteenth step of the gallows. His only words were, 'Long live eternal Germany,' before he was hooded and dropped through the trap.

Julius Streicher made his melodramatic appearance at 2.12 a.m.

While his manacles were being removed and his hands bound, this ugly, dwarfish little man, wearing a threadbare suit and a well-worn bluish shirt buttoned to the neck but without a tie (he was notorious during his days of power for his flashy dress), glanced at the three wooden scaffolds rising up menacingly in front of him. Then he glared around the room, his eyes resting momentarily upon the small group of witnesses. By this time, his hands were tied securely behind his back. Two guards, one on each arm, directed him to Number One gallows on the left of the entrance. He walked steadily the six feet to the first wooden step but his face was twitching.

As the guards stopped him at the bottom of the steps for identification formality he uttered his piercing scream: 'Heil Hitler!'

The shriek sent a shiver down my back.

As its echo died away an American colonel standing by the steps said sharply, 'Ask the man his name.' In response to the interpreter's query Streicher shouted, 'You know my name well.'

The interpreter repeated his request and the condemned man yelled, 'Julius Streicher.'

As he reached the platform, Streicher cried out, 'Now it goes to God.' He was pushed the last two steps to the mortal spot beneath the hangman's rope. The rope was being held back against a wooden rail by the hangman.

Streicher was swung around to face the witnesses and glared at them. Suddenly he screamed, '*Purim Fest 1946*.' [Purim is a Jewish holiday celebrated in the spring, commemorating the execution of Haman, ancient persecutor of the Jews described in the Old Testament.]

The American officer standing at the scaffold said, 'Ask the man if he has any last words.'

When the interpreter had translated, Streicher shouted, 'The Bolsheviks will hang you one day.'

When the black hood was raised over his head, Streicher said, 'I am with God.'

As it was being adjusted, Streicher's muffled voice could be heard to say, 'Adele, my dear wife.'

At that instant the trap opened with a loud bang. He went down kicking. When the rope snapped taut with the body swinging wildly, groans could be heard from within the concealed interior of the scaffold. Finally, the hangman, who had descended from the gallows platform, lifted the black canvas curtain and went inside. Something happened that put a stop to the groans and brought the rope to a standstill. After it was over I was not in a mood to ask what he did, but I assume that he grabbed the swinging body and pulled down on it. We were all of the opinion that Streicher had strangled.

Then, following removal of the corpse of Frick, who had been pronounced dead at 2.20 a.m., Fritz Sauckel was brought face to face with his doom.

Wearing a sweater with no coat and looking wild-eyed, Sauckel proved to be the most defiant of any except Streicher.

Here was the man who put millions into bondage on a scale unknown since the pre-Christian era. Gazing around the room from the gallows platform he suddenly screamed, 'I am dying innocent. The sentence is wrong. God protect Germany and make Germany great again. Long live Germany! God protect my family.'

The trap was sprung at 2.26 a.m. and, as in the case of Streicher, there was a loud groan from the gallows pit as the noose snapped tightly under the weight of his body.

Ninth in the procession of death was Alfred Jodl. With the black coat-collar of his Wehrmacht uniform half turned up at the back as though hurriedly put on, Jodl entered the dismal death house with obvious signs of nervousness. He wet his lips constantly and his features were drawn and haggard as he walked, not nearly so steady as Keitel, up the gallows steps. Yet his voice was calm when he uttered his last six words on earth: 'My greetings to you, my Germany.'

At 2.34 a.m. Jodl plunged into the black hole of the scaffold. He and Sauckel hung together until the latter was pronounced dead six minutes later and removed.

The Czechoslovak-born Seyss-Inquart, whom Hitler had made ruler of Holland and Austria, was the last actor to make his appearance in this unparalleled scene. He entered the chamber at 2.38½ a.m., wearing glasses which made his face an easily remembered caricature.

He looked around with noticeable signs of unsteadiness as he limped on his left clubfoot to the gallows. He mounted the steps slowly, with guards helping him.

When he spoke his last words his voice was low but intense. He said, 'I hope that this execution is the last act of the tragedy of the

Second World War and that the lesson taken from this world war will be that peace and understanding should exist between peoples. I believe in Germany.'

He dropped to death at 2.45 a.m.

With the bodies of Jodl and Seyss-Inquart still hanging, awaiting formal pronouncement of death, the gymnasium doors opened again and guards entered carrying Goering's body on a stretcher.

He had succeeded in wrecking plans of the Allied Control Council to have him lead the parade of condemned Nazi chieftains to their death. But the council's representatives were determined that Goering at least would take his place as a dead man beneath the shadow of the scaffold.

The guards carrying the stretcher set it down between the first and second gallows. Goering's big bare feet stuck out from under the bottom end of a khaki-coloured United States Army blanket. One blue-silk-clad arm was hanging over the side.

The colonel in charge of the proceedings ordered the blanket removed so that witnesses and Allied correspondents could see for themselves that Goering was definitely dead. The Army did not want any legend to develop that Goering had managed to escape.

As the blanket came off it revealed Goering clad in black silk pyjamas with a blue jacket shirt over them, and this was soaking wet, apparently the result of efforts by prison doctors to revive him.

The face of this twentieth-century freebooting political racketeer was still contorted with the pain of his last agonizing moments and his final gesture of defiance.

They covered him up quickly and this Nazi warlord, who like a character out of the days of the Borgias, had wallowed in blood and beauty, passed behind a canvas curtain into the black pages of history.

Revenge Killing, Arabia, November 1946

Wilfred Thesiger

The author, Wilfred Thesiger, lived with the Bedu of Southern Arabia, before the discovery of oil changed the region and destroyed the old way of life.

We left Shisur on 9 November in the chill of dawn; the sun was resting on the desert's rim, a red ball without heat. We walked as usual till it grew warm, the camels striding in front of us, a moving mass of legs and necks. Then one by one, as the inclination took us, we climbed up their shoulders and settled in our seats for the long hours which lay ahead. The Arabs sang, 'the full-throated roaring of the tribes'; the shuffling camels quickened their pace, thrusting forward across the level ground, for we had left the hills behind us and were on the steppes which border on the Sands. We noticed the stale tracks of oryx, saw gazelle bounding stiff-legged across the plain, and flushed occasional hares from withered salt bushes in shallow watercourses . . .

Bin Mautlauq spoke of the raid in which young Sahail was killed. He and fourteen companions had surprised a small herd of Saar camels. The herdsman had fired two shots at them before escaping on the fastest of his camels, and one of these shots had hit Sahail in the chest. Bakhit held his dying son in his arms as they rode back across the plain with the seven captured camels. It was late in the morning when Sahail was wounded, and he lived till nearly sunset, begging for water which they had not got. They rode all night to escape from inevitable pursuit. At sunrise they saw some goats, and a small Saar encampment under a tree in a shallow valley. A woman was churning butter in a skin, and a boy and a girl were milking the goats. Some small children sat under the tree. The boy saw them first and tried to escape but they cornered him against a low cliff. He was about fourteen years old, a little younger than Sahail, and he was unarmed. When they surrounded him he put his thumbs in his mouth as a sign of surrender, and asked for mercy. No one answered him. Bakhit slipped down off his camel, drew his dagger, and drove it into the boy's ribs. The boy collapsed at his feet, moaning, 'Oh my father! Oh my father!' and Bakhit stood over him till he died. He then climbed back into his saddle, his grief a little soothed by the murder which he had just committed. As Bin Mautlauq spoke, staring across the level plain with his hot, rather bloodshot eyes, I pictured the scene with horrible distinctness. The small, long-haired figure, in white loincloth, crumpled on the ground, the spreading pool of blood, the avid clustering flies, the frantic wailing of the dark-clad women, the terrified children, the shrill insistent screaming of a small baby.

Grand National, 29 March 1947

John Hislop

Faced by food and fuel shortages, the post-war public sought relief in sport. The Home Secretary decreed that the 1947 Grand National should by run on a Saturday, so as not to disrupt the working week.

There were fifty-seven of us lined up at the start, like sardines in a tin. Kami's position was about one-third of the way from the inside, between Rearmament and Some Chicken. As usual, there was much restiveness and scrimmaging, with the starter shouting, 'Keep off the tapes!'

Then the gate went up and we jumped off, most of us as eagerly as if we had only five furlongs to go. Taking into consideration the heavy going after the morning's rain, the initial pace of the field as a whole was such that no horse could hope both to maintain it and complete the course.

Kami was squeezed when the field 'broke', but settled into a swinging stride, which was not fast enough to keep anywhere near the solid wall of leaders, and we found ourselves going over the first fence well behind but clear of any interference.

Kami jumped it perfectly, in the style of a real Aintree horse, standing well back and landing without 'pitching'.

There were two or three other horses lying in the same area as Kami, with a loose horse or two in the vicinity. I went rather a long way round, towards the outside – for two reasons. In the first place the going there was less churned up. Second, I wanted Kami to be completely clear of any bumps or other mishap which would have put a horse of such frail build 'on the floor'.

He was still jumping perfectly. In fact, Kami never put a foot wrong all the way. His swinging, even gait gave me the greatest confidence and the consistency of his jumping – every fence measured off long before he got to it – made me feel certain that wherever he finished he would complete the course.

As we turned into the country for the last circuit, Kami gradually began to overtake the field. Jumping Becher's for the second time, our hopes of a possible victory became something more than the ambition of every steeplechase rider. There were, I suppose, some six or eight horses – that is, with their riders still on board – in front of me, but most of them were tiring, and as I passed them at least one rider threw me a word of encouragement that means so much in a race of this kind. 'Well done, Johnny, keep going,' someone said. As we crossed the road with only two more fences to jump I could see Prince Regent in front of me visibly tiring, and, still a good way ahead, the green jacket of Lough Conn and the green and blue of the eventual winner, of whose identity I was as ignorant as, I suppose, were the majority of spectators.

Coming into the last fence but one, there were two loose horses in front of me, and, on the inside, Prince Regent. I realized then that I had no hope of winning, as Kami was tiring; the heavy going had taken toll of his delicate frame and only his courage and innate stamina kept him going. But he jumped the fence perfectly, and went on towards the last with, I think, Prince Regent about level with us, but very tired.

We landed safely with the long stretch to the winning post spread out before us, both tired, but with Prince Regent beaten for sure. I got out my whip and kept swinging it without ever hitting Kami, and he answered nobly, gradually overhauling Mr Rank's gallant horse to take us into third place.

And so the placed jockeys rode back to the three unsaddling enclosures appointed for first, second, and third. Ahead of me went the winner, Caughoo, between two mounted policemen, surrounded by a crowd including the owner, trainer, and friends, all running alongside to pat the winning mount and to congratulate his rider.

As for me, my feeling is of three-fold gratitude – to the horse for his courage and the way he carried me; to Tom Mason, the trainer, for Kami's wonderful condition; and to the gods for the luck which followed our journey.

Stalingrad, 1949

John Steinbeck

Across the street was the repaired Intourist Hotel where we were to stay. We were given two large rooms. Our windows looked out on acres of rubble, broken brick and concrete and pulverized plaster, and in the wreckage the strange dark weeds that always seem to grow in destroyed places. During the time we were in Stalingrad we grew more and more fascinated with this expanse of ruin, for it was not deserted. Underneath the rubble were cellars and holes, and in these holes many people lived. Stalingrad was a large city, and it had had apartment houses and many flats, and now has none except the new ones on the outskirts, and its population has to live some place. It lives in the cellars of the buildings where the apartments once were. We would watch out of the window of our room, and from behind a slightly larger pile of rubble would suddenly appear a girl, going to work in the morning, putting the last little touches to her hair with a comb. She would be dressed neatly, in clean clothes, and she would swing out through the weeds on her way to work. How they could do it we have no idea. How they could live underground and still keep clean, and proud, and feminine. Housewives came out of other holes and went away to market, their heads covered with white headcloths, and market baskets on their arms. It was a strange and heroic travesty on modern living.

There was one rather terrifying exception. Directly behind the hotel, and in a place overlooked by our windows, there was a little garbage pile, where melon rinds, bones, potato peels, and such things were thrown out. And a few yards farther on, there was a little hummock, like the entrance to a gopher hole. And every morning, early, out of this hole a young girl crawled. She had long legs and bare feet, and her arms were thin and stringy, and her hair was matted and filthy. She was covered with years of dirt, so that she looked very brown. And when she raised her face, it was one of the most beautiful faces we have ever seen. Her eyes were crafty, like the eyes of a fox, but they were not human. The face was well developed and not moronic. Somewhere in the terror of the fighting in the city, something had snapped, and she had retired to some comfort of forgetfulness. She squatted on her hams and ate watermelon rinds and sucked the bones of other people's soup. She usually stayed there for about two hours before she got her stomach full. And then she went out in the weeds, and lay down, and went to sleep in the sun. Her face was of a chiselled loveliness, and on her long legs she moved with the grace of a wild animal. The other people who lived in the cellars of the lot rarely spoke to her. But one morning I saw a woman come out of another hole and give her half a loaf of bread. And the girl clutched at it almost snarlingly and held it against her chest. She looked like a half-wild dog at the woman who had given her the bread, and watched her suspiciously until she had gone back into her own cellar, and then she turned and buried her face in the slab of black bread, and like an animal she looked over the bread, her eyes twitching back and forth. And as she gnawed at the bread, one side of her ragged filthy shawl slipped away from her dirty young breast, and her hand automatically brought the shawl back and covered her breast, and patted it in place with a heart-breaking feminine gesture.

We wondered how many there might be like this, minds that could not tolerate living in the twentieth century any more, that had retired not to the hills, but into the ancient hills of the human past, into the old wilderness of pleasure and pain, and self-preservation. It was a face to dream about for a long time.

Trafalgar Square Incident, 23 September 1950

Kingsley Martin

Last Sunday afternoon two small seven-year-olds, a boy and a girl, decided, very sensibly, to bathe in the fountains of Trafalgar Square. Happily and uninhibited, they undressed near a bench occupied by three grown-ups, whose faces expressed: 'This is nothing to do with us.' Once undressed, the children dashed joyously to the fountains, bathed in the spray with shrieks of delight, jumped on to the side of the basin and dangled their toes in the blue water; then, still laughing, they rushed back to the bench, dried themselves with their underclothes, and then dashed back again to the water.

They were still having a wonderful time – and so were the

passers-by – when the Law descended. It was a smiling young policeman who came ambling round the Square and walked across to the children. A friend who was near by did not hear what the policeman said, but he helped the boy to adjust his braces, and then fastened the buttons of the girl's dress. 'Got children of his own, I dare say,' said a bystander. The children walked away, rather crestfallen, towards the main road. Turning suddenly, they saw the policeman following them. Instead of running away, they came back towards him, and he, taking a hand in each of his, guided them safely across the traffic. A more eloquent plea for a children's Lido could hardly be made; nor will anyone ever frighten those two little ones with the nursery warning: 'I'll tell a policeman.'

The Korean War: Civilian Casualty near Namchanjan, 17 October 1950

Reginald Thompson

The Korean War began in June 1950 when the Communist North Koreans, prompted by the Soviet Union, attacked South Korea across the 38th Parallel. The United Nations joined the war on the side of South Korea; the People's Republic of China aided North Korea. After about 5 million people had been killed the war ended on 27 July 1953 with an armistice that stabilized the existing boundary between North and South.

We were up with the Argylls. The road ran through rice fields without cover, and a bridge led over a deep gully with the road winding on round a bend of a hill, down to Hungso-ri. But first a tragedy of war. There was the crack of carbines, a burst or two of automatic fire, somewhere away to the right, and a peasant woman crumpled into the ditch by the roadside with her two babes crawling upon her. I photographed her as she lay there, peaceful, seeming only to sleep. But dead. One babe sat on her belly, small hands reaching up to her face, stroking, pulling at her lips, growing frantic, inconsolable, its screams agonizing, as it knew, as it tried to suckle the warm still heavy breasts, to wake the dead. The other child sat in a kind of torpor of dejection at his dead mother's feet.

Someone tried to divert the young child with an apple. Nothing could stem this infant grief. It smote us all down, reminding us of the unforgettable meaning of war. A medical truck had been ordered up, and a corporal took the children in his arms to the beginning of their orphan lives, and the woman was alone in the ditch.

The Korean War: The American Retreat from the Chongchon River, 27–28 November 1950

Reginald Thompson

After MacArthur's amphibious landing at Inchon, which cut the North Korean supply lines, the Americans advanced northwards, crossing the 38th Parallel despite Chinese warnings that this would force them to intervene. On 25 November 1950, 180,000 Chinese 'volunteers' entered the war, and by 15 December Allied troops had been driven back to the 38th Parallel.

It was a game of blind man's buff in these wild rugged irregular hills in which the enemy moved freely, easily eluding the groping arms of the Americans by day, and swooping down upon them, blind in the night, with devastating fury and magnificent discipline. Not a shot was fired by the Chinese until they were within thirty yards of the target.

Meanwhile the Americans were road-bound with their immense weight of useless weapons. The guns were rolling back. The great columns had gone into reverse. For a hundred miles the huge vehicles crammed the narrowing road lanes nose to tail. Back across the Chongchon the 25th Division were coming over the fordings while Colonel Stevens threw his rearguard round the Pakchon bridgehead and the road through to Sinanju. But there were few enemy hampering him; only the sense of terrific urgency before the torrent might burst these slender human dams and envelop the whole Eighth Army.

The smoke rising from ten thousand fires blotted out the moon and threw the stricken figures of the toiling refugees into silhouette, like some ancient frieze, an endless repetition of characters, the human story, plodding on.

There was no rest or sleep by night. Within five seconds of wild bugle calls the attacks came in, seven men out of each ten literally draped with percussion grenades on sticks, and the remaining three with automatic weapons. The lead battalion across the river was hit on the night of the 27th, and as it tried to withdraw across the Chongchon the Chinese were already waiting on the banks with machine-guns sited in the American rear. A bazooka brewed up an American tank, and in the lurid glare of the blazing tank the battalion struggled through, the remaining tanks carrying men across the frozen river. The jeeps had frozen solid to the ground, the men struggled in the shallows at the fording point with their unwieldy shoe paks freezing in great blocks to their feet. And all the time the enemy machine-guns rasped their leaden terror through the night.

The second in command was no sooner across the river than he turned back with a tank to rescue more of his men under a hail of fire. A grenade exploded on his tin hat, but by a miracle the dazed man struggled to his feet, collected ten of his comrades, regained the tank and got back. Others bore wounded on their backs.

From a military point of view it was a disaster. There was never any question of staying and meeting these attacks, of regaining the lost ground by day – for it was deserted – and even pushing forward. Only trained and disciplined troops could do that. These men acted and behaved as heroically as men may hope to behave, but their attitude when attacked was always, quite openly: 'Let's get the hell out of here!' And they did. Often it would have paid them to stay, but this would have meant hard training, good officers and NCOs, a fire plan, strict discipline, and these things they had not got.

It was curious that in the day we could move back over the eerie wilderness of the night. It was like moving in a land of shadows and ghosts and dead. It was a terrible prospect to stand in the midst of the burning hills which rise in cones and ridges from the bleak banks of the Chongchon in a desolate grandeur, and it is as though an ocean had been frozen, petrified suddenly, in the midst of storm, a wild riot of hills.

'We're like the meat in a sandwich,' said a young GI, 'and the Chinks are the bread.' There was a quietness and humour in the Americans I had not known before. You could see here quite clearly the great gash in the middle of the whole race where the middle class would have been. At the top there were these first-class colonels, and at the bottom these first-class people. But all the people from whom officers, civil servants, and all the rest of the educated men of background and integrity are drawn just were not there.

'Seems like the Chinese don't want us on that Yalu River,' remarked a sergeant, as he led a weary section back to find some transport. He said it without a trace of bitterness. It was 'OK with him'. They could have it. And they all knew that the Korean war was ended.

The Korean War: Padre Blaisdell and the Refugee Children, Seoul, December 1950

René Cutforth

At dawn Padre Blaisdell dressed himself in the little icy room at the top of the orphanage in Seoul. He put on his parka and an extra sweater, for the Siberian wind was fluting in the corners of the big grey barrack of the school which he had shamed the Government into lending him. The water in his basin was solid ice. His fifty-fourth and last Dawn Patrol was going to be an exceptionally unpleasant one.

His boots clicked along the stone flags in the freezing passages which led to the main door. The truck was waiting, and on the snow-covered gravel in the yellow-grey light of sunrise the two Korean nurses stood as usual, ready for duty – pig-tailed adolescents, their moon faces as passive and kindly as cows'.

They climbed into the truck and gave the driver his instructions. Down University Street and along the tram lines to the portentous South Gate, six tiled roofs high and solid as a fort; along Black Market Alley and down towards the river through the silent city where the first groups of refugees were only now beginning to stir, gathering their wraps and bundles about them for the day's trek.

By the time he reached Riverside Road the padre had passed through the normal first stage of reaction to the wind, that daily renewed indignation that so much malice could exist: he was content now in his open vehicle to lie back and admire the effortless skill of the wind's razor as it slashed him to the bone.

There's a dingy alley off Riverside Street, narrow, and strewn with trodden straw and refuse which would stink if the cold allowed it life enough. This alley leads to the arches of the railway bridge across the Han River. At the entrance to the alley, one of Seoul's slum-dwellers, a woman, tired, dilapidated and old at twenty-eight, stood waiting for the truck. She was a unit in the padre's intelligence corps, and when she had given her information to the nurses, she received 500 won – one shilling. She had risen at dawn and waited half an hour in the wind for this fee.

The truck's wheels crackled over the frozen ordure in the alley, passed from it down a sandy track and halted at the second arch of the bridge; it was boarded up on the far side, and in front of the boarding lay a pile of filthy rice sacks, clotted with dirt and stiff as boards. The padre removed the top four layers of the pile and revealed a terrible sight.

It was a child, practically naked and covered with filth. It lay in a pile of its own excrement in a sort of nest it had scratched out among the rice sacks. Hardly able to raise itself on an elbow, it still had energy enough to draw back cracked lips from bleeding gums and snarl and spit at the padre like an angry kitten. Its neck was not much thicker than a broom handle and it had the enormous pot-belly of starvation. With its inadequate neck and huge goggle eyes, it looked like some frightful fledgling disturbed in the nest.

Gingerly handling this appalling object, which continued weakly to scratch and bite, though it uttered no sound, the padre advanced with it in his arms towards the truck. There, the Korean nurses wrapped it in blankets and contrived to get it to swallow a little warm milk which they poured from a vacuum flask. Then the padre gave the truck driver another address, and the Dawn Patrol moved off to another assignation.

At eleven o'clock that morning, when the padre returned to the orphanage, his truck was full.

'They are the real victims of the war,' the padre said in his careful, diffident, colourless voice. 'Nine-tenths of them were lost or abandoned in the refugee columns. No one will take them in unless they are relations, and we have 800 of these children at the orphanage. Usually they recover in quite a short time, but the bad cases tend to become very silent children, even when they have grown sturdy again. They don't care to mix with the others. I have a little boy who has said nothing for three months now but "Yes" and "No".'

Rabbiting, 3 November 1952

Joe Ackerley

J. R. Ackerley (1896–1967), author of My Dog Tulip, *was for many years a celebrated literary editor of the* Listener.

Victor and I took little Bernard, aged ten?, for a walk rabbiting. He is the son of an embezzler, serving some years in prison, a curious child with enormous blue eyes, rather uncanny. He begged to be taken. He was in warlike attire – Indian trousers made of sacking, gum boots and a metal rod which he said was a gun. We had not gone far when Tripp, the hotel dog, located a rabbit in a bramble clump and killed it. He took some time to kill it, owing to the thickness of the undergrowth in which they both were, so that he could not get at the rabbit properly. He is said not to be good at killing things anyway. Quick though he is to catch them. So the rabbit squealed and squealed.

The effect on Bernard was most interesting. He almost had hysterics. He was quite overwrought. 'No. No. Oh, look, look. Let me. Let me. There it is. Oh, stop it, stop it' – all that kind of exclamation; he tried to rush into the bush, jumped about, began to cry, pulled himself together, and every now and then looked into my face, gave a sort of smile, and then darted back to the bush again. All within a minute. Victor was very good with him. He commanded him firmly to behave, said he would send him home if he misbehaved, and pulling the still-alive though bleeding rabbit out of the bush, dispatched it with a single blow of his hand. Then he told Bernard that he must not be so silly, rabbits were vermin and had to be killed and that if he wanted to come hunting he must get used to it. Bernard recovered and wanted and was allowed to carry the corpse, but every now and then as we walked he remarked, 'I heard it squeal. I heard it squeal.' Later on, since it was awkward for him to carry it by its legs in his hand, we decided to tie my dog's lead to it so that he could sling it over his shoulder. Before doing this, Victor held the rabbit by its ears and shook it, so that the contents of its bowels and bladder fell out. Then he tied my lead round its legs. He pulled the knot tight. 'Not so tight! Not so tight!' cried poor little Bernard, thinking for a moment still that the rabbit was being hurt. Then he appeared to forget and became a mighty hunter, pretending to shoot more rabbits and birds with his metal rod.

Of course it was disgusting, say what one may about vermin, and I disliked it too, but life has inured me to its horrors. The episode will obviously be remembered by Bernard all his life. (Though he had wanted to come out hunting rabbits, he has always wanted a pet rabbit for his own.) Whether it will affect his life, and if so for good or ill, who can tell. It was certainly a frightful shock to him.

And vermin! How arrogant people are. Does the earth belong to them? Do not the rabbits think *them* vermin too, so to speak. And are they, in fact, not a greater menace to the whole living world than the rabbits themselves?

The Conquest of Everest, 29 May 1953

James (Jan) Morris

The successful 1953 Everest expedition was led by Sir John Hunt and approached the 29,002-feet-high peak from Nepal. Previous climbers had approached from Tibet.

The masters of Everest, Hillary and Tensing, returned to this camp (22,000 ft) from the South Col yesterday afternoon in a blaze of sunshine and triumphant emotion, bringing their news with them.

It was a significantly beautiful day among the snows of the upper Western Cwm. All was crisp and sparkling, with the awful block of Nuptse only faintly shining with the curious greasy sheen of the melting surface snow. From the ridge of Lhotse a spiral of snow powder was driven upwards by the wind like a genie from a bottle. From down the Cwm came from time to time a sudden thrilling high-pitched whistle as a boulder screamed down from the heights. Everest itself, its rock ridge graceless against a blue sky, was as hard and enigmatical as ever.

It was a day for great news. Here in the camp on the north side of the Cwm there was already yesterday morning a tension, nerve-racking and yet deliciously exciting. At 9 a.m. on the previous day, 29 May, the two summit climbers had been seen by their support group, Gregory, Lowe, and a Sherpa, already crossing the South Summit at about 28,500 feet, and going strongly up the final ridge.

The weather had been perfect, the gales of the preceding days which had so ravaged Camp VII on the South Col had died down. Hillary and Tensing were known to be two of the most powerful climbers in the world, and were using the well-tested open-circuit oxygen equipment. Reports brought down from the South Summit by Bourdillon and Evans, who had reached it on 26 May in the expedition's first assault, seemed to show that the unknown final ridge was not impassable, though undoubtedly difficult.

Because of these several encouraging factors, hopes at Camp IV were dangerously high, and the feeling of taut nerves and suppressed wild convictions was immeasurably strengthened when, just before lunch, five tiny figures were seen making their way across the traverse at the top of the face of Lhotse. They could only be the summit team and their supporters from the South Col. They were moving fast, and in three hours they would be in the Cwm. The camp was now alive with stinging expectation. Here in the camp Colonel Hunt sat on a wooden packing case, physically immobile, his waterproof hat jammed hard over his head, his face white with plastered glacier cream. Four or five of the climbers vacantly fingered newspapers in the big pyramid tent. One man sat outside with binoculars reporting the progress of the descending party.

'They must be getting to Camp VI,' the watchers said. 'They are hidden behind that serac [ice-pinnacle] with the vertical crack in it – you know the one.' 'Two of them are sitting down; now they are up again.' 'Only another hour to wait. What are the odds?' At last, soon after 1.30, just as the radio was announcing the reported failure of the assault, the party emerged above a rise in the ground 300 yards or so above the camp, their blue windproof jackets sharp and cheerful against the glistening snow. Hillary and Tensing were leading. All at once it was through the camp by the magic wireless of excitement that Everest had been climbed.

There was a sudden rush up the snow slope in the sunshine to meet the assault party. Hillary, looking extraordinarily fresh, raised his ice axe in greeting. Tensing slipped sideways in the snow and smiled, and in a trice they were surrounded. Hands were wrung ecstatically, photographs taken, there was the whirr of the ciné camera, and laughter interrupted congratulations.

Hillary and Tensing, by now old climbing colleagues, posed with arms interlocked, Hillary's face aglow but controlled, Tensing's split with a brilliant smile of pleasure. As the group moved down the hill into the camp a band of Sherpas came diffidently forward to pay tribute to the greatest climber of them all. Like a modest monarch, Tensing received their greeting. Some bent their bodies forward, their hands clasped as in prayer. Some shook hands lightly and delicately, the fingers scarcely touching. One veteran, his pigtail flowing, bowed to touch Tensing's hand with his forehead.

'We so far forgot ourselves,' wrote an English climber of an earlier generation, 'as to shake hands on the summit.' This expedition so far forgot itself that everywhere one fancied that sunglasses were steaming embarrassingly: and suddenly, as if spontaneously, each climber, Hillary and Tensing the first of them, turned to Colonel Hunt, reflective in the background, and shook his hand in recognition of the truth that in a team venture of great happiness and success his has been the friendly hand which inexorably as it seems has led the expedition to success.

In the pyramid tent, over an omelette served on an aluminium plate, Hillary told the story of the final climb . . . It was at 11.30 a.m., 29 May 1953, that they stepped at last on to the snow-covered final eminence of Everest.

Hillary describes this as 'a symmetrical, beautiful snow-cone summit' — very different from the harsh rock ridge which is all that can be seen from below. The view was not spectacular. They were too high for good landscape, and all below looked flat and monotonous.

To the north the route to the summit on which pre-war Everest expeditions pinned their hopes looked in its upper reaches prohibitively steep. Tensing spent the fifteen minutes on the summit eating mint cake and taking photographs, for which purpose Hillary removed his oxygen mask without ill effects. Tensing produced a string of miscellaneous flags and held them high, while Hillary photographed them. They included the Union Jack, the Nepal flag, and that of the United Nations. Tensing, who is a devout Buddhist, also laid on the ground in offering some sweets, bars of chocolate, and packets of biscuits.

The Intelligent Bull, Sanlúcar de Barrameda, Spain, Spring 1957

Norman Lewis

The first picador was carried off to the infirmary with concussion, a limp and broken figure on a board; while the others, refusing to play their part, clattered out of the ring – an almost unheard-of action – receiving, to my surprise, the public's full support. Most of the two or three thousand spectators were on their feet waving their handkerchiefs in the direction of the president's box and demanding the bull's withdrawal. The bull itself, monstrous, watchful, and terribly intact, had placed itself in front of the *burladero*, behind which Cardeño and his three *peons* had crowded wearing the kind of expression that one might expect to see on the faces of men mounting the scaffold. Occasionally one of the *peons* would dart out and lap a forlorn cape, and the bull would chase him back, groping after him round the corner of the *burladero* with its horn, without violence, like a man scooping unhopefully with blunt finger after a whelk withdrawn into the depths of its shell. The crowd was on its feet all the time producing a great inarticulate roaring of mass protest, and the bullfight had come to a standstill. A bull cannot properly be fought by a man armed only with a sword until it has been pic-ed and has pranced about a great deal, tiring itself in its efforts to free itself from the *banderillas* clinging to the hide of its neck. The sun-cured old herdsman at my side wanted to tell all his neighbours, some of whom were mere townspeople, just how bad this bull was. 'I knew the first moment I set eyes on him in the corral. I said someone's been having a game with that brute, and they've no right to put him in the ring with Christians ... Don't you fight him sonny,' he yelled to Cardeño. 'You're within your rights in refusing to go out there and have that devil carve you up.' That was the attitude of the crowd as a whole, and it rather surprised me. They were sympathetic to the bullfighters' predicament. They did not want the fight to go on on these terms, and when the four men edged out from behind the *burladero* and the bull charged them and they threw their capes in its face and ran for their lives, the girls screamed and the men cursed them angrily for the risks they were taking. The crowd hated this bull. Bullfight regulars, as well as most writers on the subject, are addicts of the pathetic fallacy. Bulls that are straightforward, predictable, and therefore easy to fight, are 'noble', 'frank', 'simple', 'brave'. They are described as 'co-operating loyally' in the neat fifteen-minute routine which is at once the purpose, climax and culmination of their existences, and they often receive an ovation from an appreciative audience as the trio of horses drag them, legs in air, from the ring. No one in a Spanish audience has any affection for the one bull in a thousand that possesses that extra grain of intelligence. The ideal bull is a character like the British Grenadier, or the Chinese warrior of the last century, who is supposed to have carried a lamp when attacking at night, to give the enemy a sporting chance.

In the next day's newspaper report this bull was amazingly classified as 'tame', although it was the most aggressive animal I have ever seen in my life. When any human being appeared in the line of its vision it was on him like a famished tiger, but tameness apparently was the professional name for the un-bull-like quality of calculation which caused this bull not only to reject the cape in favour of the man but to attempt to cut off a man's flight by changing the direction of its charge. This sinister and misplaced intelligence provoked many furious reactions. I was seated in the *barrera* – the first row of seats behind the passageway. Just below me a Press photographer was working with a Leica fitted with a long-focus lens, and this man, carried away by his passion, leaned over the barrier fence and struck the bull on the snout with his valuable camera. A spectator, producing a pistol, clambered down into the passageway, where he was arrested and carried off by plain-clothes policemen and bull-ring servants. The authorities' quandary was acute, because the regulations as laid down prevented their dismissing a bull on any other grounds than its physical inability to fight in a proper manner, or the matador's failure to kill it within fifteen minutes of the time when he takes his sword and goes to face it. But physically this bull was in tremendous shape, and although half an hour had passed, the third episode of the fight, sometimes referred to in Spanish as 'the Luck of Death', had not yet begun.

The outcome of this alarming farce was inevitably an anticlimax, but it taught me something I had never understood before: that bullfighters – at least some of them – can be brave in a quite extraordinary way. Black *banderillas* had been sent for. They are *banderillas* of the ordinary kind, wrapped in black paper, and their use imposes a kind of rare public degradation on the bull like the stripping of an officer's badges of rank and decorations before his dishonourable discharge for cowardice in the face of the enemy. The *peons*, scampering from behind cover, managed to place two of the six *banderillas*, one man hurling them like enormous untidy darts into the bull's shoulders while another distracted its attention with his cape. After that, Cardeño, shrugging off the pleadings of the crowd, took the sword and *muleta* – the red square of cloth stretched over wooden supports that replaces the cape when the last phase of the drama begins – and walked towards the bull followed by his three obviously terrified *peons*. Although Cardeño had been standing in the shade for the last ten minutes, his forehead and cheeks were shining with sweat and his mouth was open like a runner's after a hard race. No one in this crowd wanted to see Cardeño killed. They wanted this unnatural monster of a bull disposed of by any means, fair or foul, but the rules of the bull ring provided no solution for this kind of emergency. These was no recognized way out but for Cardeño to take the sword and *muleta* and try to stay alive for fifteen minutes, after which time the regulations permit the president to order the steers to be driven into the ring to take out a bull which cannot be killed.

Cardeño showed his bravery by actually fighting the bull. Perhaps he could not afford to damage his reputation by leaving this bull unkilled, however excusable the circumstances might have made such a course. With the unnerving shrieks of the crowd at his back he went out, sighted along the sword, lunged, and somehow escaped the thrusting horns. It was not good bullfighting. This was clear even to an outsider. Good bullfighting, as a spectacle, is a succession of sculptural groupings of man and beast, composed, held, and re-formed, with the appearance almost of leisure, and contains nothing of the graceless and ungainly skirmishing that was all that the circumstances permitted Cardeño to offer. Once the sword struck on the frontal bone of the bull's skull, and another time Cardeño blunted its point on the boss of the horns. Several times it stuck an inch or two in the muscles of the bull's neck, and the bull shrugged it out, sending it flying high into the air. The thing lasted probably half an hour, and, contrary to the rules, the steers were not sent for – either because the president was determined to save Cardeño's face, even at the risk of his life, or because there were no steers ready as there should have been. In the end the too-intelligent bull keeled over, weakened by the innumerable pinpricks that it had probably hardly felt. It received the *coup de grâce* and was dragged away, to a general groan of execration. Cardeño, who seemed suddenly to have aged, was given a triumphant tour of the ring by an audience very pleased to see him alive.

Stoning to Death, Jeddah, February 1958

R. M. Macoll

The unending procession of brand new giant American cars nosed slowly along the dusty street.

The shop windows near by were crammed with glittering goods – refrigerators and air-conditioners from America, cameras from Germany, electrical fittings from Italy.

Round the corner plasterers were hard at work putting the finishing touches to a twelve-storey modernistic office building, one of scores that are being rushed to a finish all over the bursting, bustling seaport of Jeddah.

But the big and silent crowd had eyes for none of this.

A prince, a nephew of the king, sat stern-faced on a chair. Before him was a strip of carpet. From a lorry a man was led forward by two khaki-clad policemen. He was in his late twenties and was completely composed.

His hands were chained together behind him and he walked awkwardly because of the chains festooned about his ankles.

Arrived at the edge of the carpet he knelt and was told by the police to keep his eyes fixed on the prince's face.

At his side an official unrolled a scroll and started to read aloud the man's misdeeds and the punishment decreed by the court. The crowd was now utterly hushed.

Suddenly the line of police parted and the executioner appeared, sword in hand. He approached the victim from behind and on tiptoe. As the reading stopped the executioner bent and touched the kneeling man lightly on the back with his finger.

Instinctively the man started, and in so doing raised his head. On the instant, with a swift and expert blow, the executioner decapitated him.

A long, slow sigh came from the onlookers.

Now a woman was dragged forward. She and the man had together murdered her former husband. She, too, was under thirty, and slender.

The recital of her crime too was read out as she knelt, and then the executioner stepped forward with a wooden stave and dealt a hundred blows with all his strength upon her shoulder.

As the flogging ended the woman sagged over on her side.

Next, a lorry loaded with rocks and stones was backed up and its cargo deposited in a pile. At a signal from the prince the crowd leaped on the stones and started pelting the woman to death.

It was difficult to determine how she was facing her last and awful ordeal, since she was veiled in Muslim fashion and her mouth was gagged to muffle her cries.

Had this scene been taking place in the middle of the desert it would have been grim enough, but that it should have been enacted in the heart of modern Jeddah's business neighbourhood lent it a dismally macabre quality.

The sun shone down from a glorious blue sky. A familiar American soft-drink advertisement showed its gentle blandishments. 'Come to the Middle East,' pleaded an air lines travel poster in a nearby window. 'Savour its romance, its colour, its quaint traditions . . .'

The crowd were no longer silent. The men snarled and shouted as they flung their stones, their faces transformed into masks of sadism.

The execution of the man? Well, let us not forget that it was as recently as 1936 that the French held their last public execution. And the beheading was at least humanely and quickly carried out.

But the doing to death of the woman is something which the handful of horrified Europeans in the crowd will not quickly forget.

It took just over an hour before the doctor in attendance, who halted the stoning periodically to feel the victim's pulse, announced her dead.

This double execution took place just the other day.

The Vietnam War: South Vietnamese Casualty, 1965

Gavin Young

The Vietnam War (1955–75) escalated rapidly during 1965. Control of South Vietnam by Communist guerrillas seemed imminent: in response, 18,000 American troops had been sent to the country by the end of the year.

In 1965, before the American forces landed *en masse* in Vietnam, the Vietnamese Army seemed to be heading for total destruction; it was losing a battalion or two every week, most of them in engagements very close to Saigon. One day I travelled from Saigon to the riverside township of My To, south of the capital, in a bus crowded with Vietnamese civilians and soldiers; bundles of shopping and chickens cluttered the floor under the seats.

We crossed bridges fortified with sandbags and barbed wire, and sometimes soldiers stopped the driver and peered in at the passengers. Two laughing Vietnamese behind me leaned over my shoulder: 'Aren't you frightened of VC? Maybe Vietcong come on bus.'

A day later, with my Leitz binoculars strapped around my neck, I was walking in a single file of Vietnamese soldiers along the narrow banks that divided the paddy fields of the Mekong delta. The column was part of a larger force scraped together to clear the Vietcong out of an area of several square miles of trees, paddies, water buffaloes and hamlets. Sometimes we heard a propeller-driven aircraft overhead, and the deep voice of artillery.

On the wider tracks it was possible to break the single file, and I walked beside the young Vietnamese soldier who had been in front of me. He looked like a child playing soldier; his helmet was absurdly big, his American carbine too long and heavy. His dull-green battledress revealed the amazing slightness of his body. Small dark crescents of sweat stained his armpits and the small of his back. He pointed at my suede boots and said admiringly, 'Shoes you number one.'

'I give them to you.'

'Oh, no. You very big. Small, me.' After a pause he looked up at me again. 'Home America?'

'England.'

'Home me Nha Trang. You see Nha Trang?'

I hadn't, up to then; I got to know it later, a small and beautiful city on the South China Sea. It has fine beaches, and in those days a French restaurant served fresh lobsters.

'So much fishing in Nha Trang,' the soldier said, smiling.

I hadn't met many Vietnamese at that time, and I looked at him with interest. Where the fine line of his oriental cheekbones swept down to the rosebud mouth there was no hint of hair. He couldn't have been much over nineteen.

It began to rain, and the dark stain on my new friend's back quickly widened as water dripped from his helmet. He turned his carbine upside down on his shoulder so that the rain wouldn't run down the barrel, then he put a hand on my sleeve and smiled up at me.

'You number one friend. Come Nha Trang, OK?'

'I come Nha Trang.'

A sergeant waved impatiently and laid a finger on his lips. In silence now, except for the drumming of the rain and an occasional clink of metal or a cough, we approached a tree line. When the shell burst, my impression was that a small volcano had sprung out of the ground, not that something had fallen from the sky. I felt a tremendous shudder through the soles of my boots, and then the blast threw me to the ground.

I lay there waiting for other shells, but it was not an ambush or even a sustained harassment. Another shell roared much further away, and then heavy silence fell. My heart thumped and my hands shook. Then I heard a human sound quite close, half sob, half gasp. A helmet lay on the ground like an abandoned seashell, and near it was my friend from Nha Trang, clasping his stomach with one hand, pushing feebly at the ground with the other, trying to get up. I went over and stopped him.

I put my left hand around his shoulder and made him lean back across my knees, but I didn't know what to do next. His eyes were closed, and the rain poured through his hair and down his face and neck. There was a terrible smell. I opened his sodden shirt and saw below his breast-bone a dark, shining mess – ripped clothing stained black with rain, blood, bile and whatever else comes out of bellies torn open by metal splinters.

His eyelids flickered open and he frowned. 'Hurt, me,' he said faintly.

He was dying. He fumbled for my right hand – in a futile way, I had been trying to wipe the rain from his face – and pressed it to the warm, liquid mess. I didn't feel the least disgust. I had an idea that between us we might hold him together.

'Hurt, me,' he whispered again. At the inner corner of the delicate half-moon fold of his eyelid a drop of water had lodged. Rain? A tear?

Soon people came and carefully carried him away, limp, with his head lolling back as if a hinge in his neck had snapped.

I was left with my hands and clothes stinking of an abattoir. The strap of the binoculars around my neck had snapped, so that the glasses were slippery with blood and bile. Something seemed to have got into the lenses, for later, however much I wiped them, blobs and blotches remained that had not been there before.

The Vietnam War: A Reporter with the Vietcong, near Hanoi, 10 December 1965

James Cameron

Relentless US bombing of North Vietnam was a feature of the Vietnam War.

Through the daylight hours nothing moves on the roads of North Vietnam, not a car nor a truck. It must look from the air as though the country had no wheeled transport at all. That, of course, is the idea, it is the roads and bridges that are being bombed; it is no longer safe after sunrise to be anywhere near either.

In the paddies the farmers are reaping their third harvest of the year, which has been particularly abundant. They move among the rice with their sickles, bowed under a shawl of foliage, the camouflage that gives everyone a faintly carnival air, like so many Jacks-in-the-Green.

At the corners of the paddies stand what look like sheaves of corn and are stacks of rifles. The roads stretch long and empty, leading from nowhere to nowhere.

Then the sun goes down and everything starts to move.

At dust the roads become alive. The engines are started and the convoys grind away through the darkness behind the pinpoints of masked headlamps. There are miles of them, heavy Russian-built trucks, anti-aircraft batteries, all deeply buried under piles of branches and leaves; processions of huge green haystacks. North Vietnam by day is abandoned; by night it thuds and grinds with movement. It is a fatiguing routine: working by day and moving by night.

In this fashion I drove down to what is called the 'fighting areas' in the central province of Thanh Hoa. It was a wildly theatrical landscape: a plain studded with strange little precipitous mountains, as though a shower of meteorites had fallen; it was like riding, in a Soviet-made Jeep through the middle of a Chinese watercolour . . .

The great showplace of Thanh Hoa is the famous Ham Rong bridge. It has been attacked more than 100 times, by at least 1000 aircraft; it is scarred and pitted and twisted and the area around is a terrible mess, but the bridge still carries the road and the railroad. It lies between two very steep hills, and must be extremely difficult to hit; it would need a very steep and oblique bombing run . . .

At the village of Nanh Ngang, hard by the bridge, I was presented to Miss Nguyen Thi Hang, who is a Labour Hero and a People's Hero, and is clearly adjusted to a measure of local celebrity as the nation's Resistance pin-up. She once led a delegation to Moscow.

She is a pert, trim young woman in her late twenties, dressed in the regulation white blouse and broad black trousers; she is pretty, as some 99.9 per cent. of all Vietnamese girls are pretty. To have her photograph taken was clearly no great novelty for her.

Miss Hang commands the women's corps of the Nanh Ngang militia, and she put them through their paces for me – a mock alert, a covey of most nubile little girls popping into foxholes and pointing their rifles at the sky, with Miss Hang gesturing upwards, exactly as in her pictures.

It all seemed so palpably make-believe – this vital bridge defended by a chorus of sweet little girls; I felt awkward and rueful.

And then, in the middle of the performance, as I walked back from the river to the village – the alarm went in all truth, and the war game was real after all, in the sighing howl of jets overhead, the thud of ack-ack, and for all I know, for I could not be sure, a tiny volley from Miss Hang's young ladies in the foxholes.

The aeroplanes were not after us this time, but streaking

homeward south. The village took cover philosophically, but by the time the children were herded into the earth dugouts, the flight was, doubtless, miles away.

There were several such raids while I moved about the country, and it is fair to try to analyse one's reaction. It is not easy. What supervened, I think, was not the emotion of fear (for I was in no particular danger) nor high-minded horror – there was somehow a sense of outrage against civility: what an *impertinence*, one felt, what arrogance, what an offence against manners. These people in North Vietnam are agreeable, shy people, and very poor. Will this sort of thing blow Communism out of their heads?

The Vietnam War: Winning Hearts and Minds, Tuylon, South Vietnam, 23 August 1967

John Pilger

In mid-1966 the US inaugurated 'pacification' campaigns, isolating villages to protect them from guerrillas, and spraying vast areas to defoliate trees that might provide cover for the Vietcong.

When Sergeant Melvin Murrell and his company of United States Marines drop by helicopter into the village of Tuylon, west of Danang, with orders to sell 'the basic liberties as outlined on page 233 of the Pacification Programme Handbook' and at the same time win the hearts and minds of the people (see same handbook, page 86 under WHAM) they see no one: not a child or a chicken. The population has watched them come out of the sky, and most of them have retired to the paddies or stand silent in the shadows of their houses.

'Come on out, we're your friends,' Sergeant Murrell shouts through a loud-hailer, in English.

'Come on out, everybody, we got rice and candy and tooth-brushes to give you,' he coos in the hot silence.

'Listen, either you gooks come out from wherever you are or we're going to come in there and get you,' he jokes, as soldiers at war are given to joke.

So the people of Tuylon come out from wherever they are and queue to receive packets of bulk supplies of US 'miracle rice', Uncle

Ben's brand, and Hershey chocolate bars and 7000 toothbrushes, which come in four colours, and comics for the children – *Superman*, etc.– and in a separate, almost touching little ceremony, the district chief is presented with four yellow, portable, battery-operated flush lavatories.

'If these are right for your requirements,' says Sergeant Murrell, 'there will be more where they came from.' And when it is all over and the children cheer on cue, Sergeant Murrell notes in his log of the day: 'At first, they did not appear to understand that we had come to help them. However, they were persuaded otherwise, and at this time they are secured and on our side. I believe they respect our posture of strength and humanity. I believe the colonel will be pleased.'

The Marines with whom I have come to Tuylon are called a CAC unit, which stands for Combined Action Company, which means their role is both military and civil. First, a CAC unit moves into a village and 'protects' it – whether or not the villagers have asked to be protected – with trenches and booby traps and barbed wire. Then they declare the village 'friendly' and set about selling 'the basic liberties as outlined on page 233 of the Pacification Programme Handbook' to old men and young men, women and children.

There is, however, a problem. The United States Marines would rather fight the Vietnamese than sell them the basic liberties and win their hearts and minds. 'I'll say this for these people,' says Murrell, 'they do what they're told. I guess it's like I always say: whoever's got the guns calls the tune.'

Tuylon, one week later:

Colonel Richard Trueball has arrived. 'Well, slap my mouth, it sure is good to see you, sir!' says Sergeant Murrell.

'How is everything here, Murrell? How is the hygiene pro-gramme coming along? Toothbrushes, toilets cause an impact?'

'Yes indeedie, sir. Toothbrushes went down a dandy but as for gettin' them to go to the bathroom and all that – well, I'm afraid these people been doin' it other ways for thousands of years and they seem to like it that way.'

The colonel thinks.

'Never say die, Murrell. I'll send you in a portable shower unit on Thursday.'

'Yes, *sir!*'

The Vietnam War: C Company, US 11th Infantry Brigade Pacify My Lai, 16 March 1968

Time Magazine Correspondent

News of the My Lai massacre did not break until November 1969. US Army investigation of the incident had begun in September 1968. Lieutenant William Calley was court-martialled for the murder of 109 Vietnamese civilians.

West, a squad leader in a platoon commanded by Lieutenant Jeffrey La Cross, followed Calley's platoon into My Lai. 'Everyone was shooting,' he said. 'Some of the huts were torched. Some of the *yanigans* [young soldiers] were shooting kids.' In the confusion, he claims, it was hard to tell 'mama-sans from papa-sans', since both wore black pyjamas and conical hats. He and his squad helped round up the women and children. When one of his men protested that 'I can't shoot these people', West told him to turn a group over to Captain Medina. On the way out of the village, West recalls seeing a ditch filled with dead and dying civilians. His platoon also passed a crying Vietnamese boy, wounded in both a leg and an arm. West heard a GI ask, 'What about him?' Then he heard a shot and the boy fell. 'The kid didn't do anything,' said West, 'He didn't have a weapon' . . .

Another soldier in the group following Calley's was SP4 Varnado Simpson, twenty-two. 'Everyone who went into the village had in mind to kill,' he says. 'We had lost a lot of buddies and it was a VC stronghold. We considered them either VC or helping the VC.' His platoon approached from the left flank. 'As I came up on the village there was a woman, a man and a child running away from it towards some huts. So I told them in their language to stop, and they didn't, and I had orders to shoot them down and I did this. This is what I did. I shot them, the lady and the little boy. He was about two years old.'

A detailed account came from Paul David Meadlo, twenty-two, a member of Calley's platoon . . . Meadlo says his group ran through My Lai, herding men, women, children and babies into the centre of the village – 'like a little island'.

'Lieutenant Calley came over and said, "You know what to do with them, don't you?" And I said, "Yes." And he left and came back about ten minutes later, and said, "How come you ain't killed them yet?" And I told him that I didn't think he wanted us to kill them, that he just wanted us to guard them. He said, "No, I want them dead." So he started shooting them. And he told me to start shooting. I poured about four clips [68 shots] into them. I might have killed ten or fifteen of them.

'So we started to gather more people, and we had about seven or eight, and we put them in the hootch [hut] and then we dropped a hand grenade in there with them. And then they had about seventy to seventy-five people all gathered up by a ravine, so we threw ours in with them and Lieutenant Calley told me, "Meadlo, we got another job to do." And so he walked over to the people, and he started pushing them off and started shooting. We just pushed them all off and just started using automatics on them.'

According to SP5 Jay Roberts, the rampaging GIs were not interested solely in killing, although that seemed foremost in their minds. Roberts told *Life*, 'Just outside the village there was this big pile of bodies. This really tiny kid – he had only a shirt on, nothing else – he came over to the pile and held the hand of one of the dead. One of the GIs behind me dropped into a kneeling position thirty metres from this kid and killed him with a single shot.' Roberts also watched while troops accosted a group of women, including a teenage girl. The girl was about thirteen, wearing black pyjamas: 'A GI grabbed the girl and with the help of others started stripping her,' Roberts related. 'Let's see what she's made of,' a soldier said. 'VC boom-boom,' another said, telling the thirteen-year-old girl that she was a whore for the Vietcong. 'I'm horny,' said a third. As they were stripping the girl, with bodies and burning huts all around them, the girl's mother tried to help her, scratching and clawing at the soldiers.

Continued Roberts: 'Another Vietnamese woman, afraid for her own safety, tried to stop the woman from objecting. One soldier kicked the mother, and another slapped her up a bit. Haeberle [the photographer] jumped in to take a picture of the group of women. The picture shows the thirteen-year-old girl hiding behind her mother, trying to button the top of her pyjamas. When they noticed Ron, they left off and turned away as if everything was normal. Then a soldier asked, "Well, what'll we do with 'em?" "Kill 'em," another answered. I heard an M60 go off, a light machine-gun, and when we turned all of them and the kids with them were dead.'

The First Men on the Moon, 21 July 1969

Neil Armstrong and Edwin E. Aldrin

Apollo II, carrying Neil Armstrong, Lieutenant-Colonel Michael Collins, and Colonel Edwin Aldrin, was launched on 16 July. At 03.56 BST on 21 July Armstrong stepped off the ladder of lunar landing vehicle Eagle on to the Moon.

NEIL ARMSTRONG: The most dramatic recollections I had were the sights themselves. Of all the spectacular views we had, the most impressive to me was on the way to the Moon, when we flew through its shadow. We were still thousands of miles away, but close enough, so that the Moon almost filled our circular window. It was eclipsing the Sun, from our position, and the corona of the Sun was visible around the limb of the Moon as a gigantic lens-shaped or saucer-shaped light, stretching out to several lunar diameters. It was magnificent, but the Moon was even more so. We were in its shadow, so there was no part of it illuminated by the Sun. It was illuminated only by earthshine. It made the Moon appear blue-grey, and the entire scene looked decidedly three-dimensional.

I was really aware, visually aware, that the Moon was in fact a sphere not a disc. It seemed almost as if it were showing us its roundness, its similarity in shape to our Earth, in a sort of welcome. I was sure that it would be a hospitable host. It had been awaiting its first visitors for a long time . . .

[*After touchdown*] The sky is black, you know. It's a very dark sky. But it still seemed more like daylight than darkness as we looked out the window. It's a peculiar thing, but the surface looked very warm and inviting. It was the sort of situation in which you felt like going out there in nothing but a swimming suit to get a little sun. From the cockpit, the surface seemed to be tan. It's hard to account for that, because later when I held this material in my hand, it wasn't tan at all. It was black, grey and so on. It's some kind of lighting effect, but out the window the surface looks much more like light desert sand than black sand . . .

EDWIN E. ALDRIN [*on the moon*]: The blue colour of my boot has completely disappeared now into this – still don't know exactly what colour to describe this other than greyish-cocoa colour. It appears to be covering most of the lighter part of my boot . . . very fine particles . . .

[*Later*] The Moon was a very natural and pleasant environment in which to work. It had many of the advantages of zero gravity, but it was in a sense less *lonesome* than Zero G, where you always have to pay attention to securing attachment points to give you some means of leverage. In one-sixth gravity, on the Moon, you had a distinct feeling of being *somewhere* . . . As we deployed our experiments on the surface we had to jettison things like lanyards, retaining fasteners, etc., and some of these we tossed away. The objects would go away with a slow, lazy motion. If anyone tried to throw a baseball back and forth in that atmosphere he would have difficulty, at first, acclimatizing himself to that slow, lazy trajectory; but I believe he could adapt to it quite readily . . .

Odour is very subjective, but to me there was a distinct smell to the lunar material – pungent, like gunpowder or spent cap-pistol caps. We carted a fair amount of lunar dust back inside the vehicle with us, either on our suits and boots or on the conveyor system we used to get boxes and equipment back inside. We did notice the odour right away.

Veterans' March, Washington DC, 25 April 1971

John Pilger

The US invasion of Cambodia in 1970, to destroy Vietcong bases, intensified anti-Vietnam War demonstrations around the world. The war did not end until April 1975, when the South Vietnamese Government surrendered and Saigon fell without a struggle.

'The truth is out! Mickey Mouse is dead! The good guys are really the bad guys in disguise!' The speaker is William Wyman, from New York City. He is nineteen and has no legs. He sits in a wheelchair on the steps of the United States Congress, in the midst of a crowd of 300,000, the greatest demonstration America has ever seen. He has on green combat fatigues and the jacket is torn where he has ripped away the medals and the ribbons he has been given in exchange for his legs, and along with hundreds of other veterans of the war in Vietnam, he has hurled them on the Capitol steps and described them as shit; and now to those who form a ring of pity around him, he says, 'Before I lost these legs, I killed and killed! We all did! Jesus, don't grieve for *me*!'

All week the veterans have been in Washington. Never before in this country have young soldiers marched in protest against the war they themselves have fought and which is still going on. They have stopped Mr and Mrs America in the street and told them about the gore and what they did, which they describe as atrocities. They have marched, or tried to march, a battalion of shuffling stick figures, to the Department of Defence, where they have tried to give themselves up, only to be told by a bemused one-star general, 'Sorry, we don't take American prisoners here.'

Dale Grenada, a former quartermaster on a destroyer, shouting through a loud-hailer, describes to rush-hour shoppers how he helped to raze a Vietnamese village: 'Listen to this, friends . . . the whole village was burning but the spotter planes reported people fleeing across the open fields, so we switched to fragmented shells and began to chop the people up. Then we began firing phosphorus shells and watched them burn.'

The veterans' presence in Washington today is deeply confusing to the American mood. A police sergeant on duty at the Capitol says, 'Hell, I'd throw in my badge before I touch these guys.' A businessman, who was just passing by, now fussily clears a path for Bill Loivie, who has spent two years in military hospitals and will always need crutches. An old couple, he in red baseball cap, she in blue rinse, have come up from Georgia to see Washington in the spring and now they march with a woman who lost a son over there. Even a party of enormous ladies from the Daughters of the American Revolution, an organization that would gleefully detonate the world tomorrow and which happened to be meeting in Washington today, stand transfixed and almost crying, almost, as the carnage passes them by, including Jack Saul from California wearing a grotesque mask of Richard Nixon smiling. And when someone asks Jack, jokingly, what he himself looks like, he takes it off and reveals a face that looks as though he has just finished pouring acid on it. 'Peace,' he says.

'It was the Christians': The Massacre at Chatila, 16–17 September 1982

Robert Fisk

Israeli forces had invaded Southern Lebanon on 6 June, and the PLO forces were evacuated to Syria at the end of August under American supervision. The Israelis then gave the Lebanese militia the run of the Palestinian refugee camps at Chabra and Chatila. Major Haddad was a cashiered Lebanese army officer.

They were everywhere, in the road, in laneways, in backyards and broken rooms, beneath crumpled masonry and across the top of garbage tips. The murderers – the Christian militiamen whom Israel had let into the camp to 'flush out terrorists' fourteen hours before – had only just left. In some cases the blood was still wet on the ground. When we had seen a hundred bodies, we stopped counting.

Even twenty-four hours after the massacre of the Palestinians at Chatila had ended, no one was sure how many had been killed there. Down every alleyway there were corpses – women, young men, babies and grandparents – lying together in lazy and terrible profusion where they had been knifed or machine-gunned to death.

Each corridor through the rubble produced more bodies. The patients at a Palestine hospital simply disappeared after gunmen ordered the doctors to leave. There were signs of hastily dug mass graves. Perhaps a thousand people were butchered here, perhaps half that number again.

The full story of what happened in Chatila on Friday night and Saturday morning may never be known, for most of the witnesses are either dead or would never wish to reveal their guilt.

What is quite certain is that at six o'clock on Friday night, truckloads of gunmen in the uniform – and wearing the badges – of the right-wing Christian Phalange militia and Major Saad Haddad's renegade army from Southern Lebanon were seen by reporters entering the southern gate of the camp.

There were bonfires inside and the sound of heavy gunfire. Israeli troops and armour were standing round the perimeter of the camp and made no attempt to stop the gunmen – who have been their allies since their invasion of Lebanon – going in.

A spokesman for the Israeli foreign ministry was to say later that the militias had been sent into Chatila to hunt down some of the 2000 Palestinian 'terrorists' whom the Israelis alleged were still in the camp. Correspondents were forbidden to enter.

What we found inside the camps at ten o'clock next morning did not quite beggar description, although it would perhaps be easier to retell in a work of fiction or in the cold prose of a medical report.

But the details should be told for – this being Lebanon – the facts will change over the coming weeks as militias and armies and governments blame each other for the horrors committed upon the Palestinian civilians.

Just inside the southern gates of the camp, there used to be a number of single-storey concrete-walled houses. When we walked across the muddy entrance of Chatila, we found that these buildings had all been dynamited to the ground. There were cartridge cases across the main road and clouds of flies swarmed across the rubble. Down a laneway to our right, not more than fifty yards from the entrance, there lay a pile of corpses.

There were more than a dozen of them, young men whose arms and legs had become entangled with each other in the agony of death. All had been shot at point-blank range through the right or left cheek, the bullet tearing away a line of flesh up to the ear and entering the brain. Some had vivid crimson scars down the left side of their throats. One had been castrated. Their eyes were open, and the flies had only begun to gather. The youngest was perhaps only twelve or thirteen years old.

On the other side of the main road, up a track through the rubble, we found the bodies of five women and several children. The women were middle-aged, and their corpses lay draped over a pile of rubble. One lay on her back, her dress torn open, and the head of a little girl emerging from behind her. The girl had short, dark curly hair and her eyes were staring at us and there was a frown on her face. She was dead.

Another child lay on the roadway like a discarded flower, her white dress stained with mud and dust. She could have been no more than three years old. The back of her head had been blown away by a bullet fired into her brain. One of the women also held a tiny baby to her body. The bullet that had passed through her breast had killed the baby too.

To the right of us there was what appeared to be a small

barricade of concrete and mud. But as we approached it we found a human elbow visible on the surface. A large stone turned out to be part of a torso. It was as if the bodies had been bulldozed to the side of the laneway, as indeed they had. A bulldozer – its driver's seat empty – stood guiltily just down the road.

Beyond this rampart of earth and bodies there was a pile of what might have been sacks in front of a low redstone wall. We had to cross the barricade to reach it and tried hard not to step on the bodies buried beneath.

Below the low wall a line of young men and boys lay prostrated. They had been shot in the back against the wall in a ritual execution, and they lay, at once pathetic and terrible, where they had fallen. The execution wall and its huddle of corpses was somehow reminiscent of something seen before, and only after-wards did we realize how similar it all was to those old photographs of executions in Occupied Europe during the Second World War. There may have been twelve or twenty bodies there. Some lay beneath others . . .

It was always the same. I found a small undamaged house with a brown metal gate leading to a small courtyard. Something instinctive made me push it open. The murderers had just left. On the ground there lay a young woman. She lay on her back as if she was sunbathing in the heat and the blood running from her back was still wet. She lay, feet together, arms outspread, as if she had seen her saviour in her last moments. Her face was peaceful, eyes closed, almost like a madonna. Only the small hole in her chest and the stain across the yard told of her death . . .

There had been fighting inside the camp. The road was slippery with cartridge cases and ammunition clips near the Sabra mosque and some of the equipment was of the Soviet type used by the Palestinians.

There have clearly been guerrillas here. In the middle of this part of the road, however, there lay – incredibly – a perfectly carved scale-model wooden Kalashnikov rifle, its barrel snapped in two. It had been a toy . . .

Across Chatila came the disembodied voice of an Israeli officer broadcasting through a Tannoy from atop an armoured personnel carrier. 'Stay off the streets,' he shouted. 'We are only looking for terrorists. Stay off the streets. We will shoot.'

An hour later, at Galerie Semaan – far from Chatila – someone did open fire at the soldiers and I threw myself into a ditch beside an Israeli Major. The Israelis fired shoals of bullets into a ruined building beside the road, blowing pieces of it into the air like confetti. The Major and I lay huddled in our ditch for fifteen minutes. He asked about Chatila and I told him all I had seen.

Then he said, 'I tell you this. The Haddad men were supposed to go in with us. We had to shoot two of them yesterday. We killed one and wounded another. Two more we took away. They were doing a bad thing. That is all I will tell you.' Was this at Chatila? I asked. Had he been there himself? He would say no more.

Then his young radio operator, who had been lying behind us in the mud, crawled up next to me. He was a young man. He pointed to his chest. 'We Israelis don't do that sort of thing,' he said. 'It was the Christians.'

The Fall of President Marcos, Manila, Philippines, 24–25 February 1986

James Fenton

Faced with mass popular protest and revolt in the army, Marcos left Malacañang Palace in a US Air Force H-3 helicopter on the evening of Tuesday, 25 February. James Fenton's account starts on 24 February, when he hurried to the palace following a report that Marcos had abdicated. The second part describes his return to the palace on the evening of the President's flight. Imelda is Marcos's wife. Camp Crame was a centre of the Army's revolt.

Something very odd was happening. Where the vegetable garden had been (it had been planted on Imelda's instructions, as part of some pet scheme), they were now laying a lawn. And the sculpture garden too – all the concrete statues were being smashed and carried away. The workers watched us as we passed. There were tanks by the next gate, and the security check was still in operation. 'It's extraordinary, isn't it,' someone said, 'the way they keep going on as if nothing had happened. That platform – they must have been told to put it up for the inauguration. Now Marcos has gone and they're still putting it up.'

As we came through security, a voice began to speak over the public address. It was giving instructions to the military to confine itself to the use of small arms in dealing with attacks. It was outlining Marcos's supposed policy of the whole election campaign – Maximum Tolerance.

'Whose voice is that?' I asked.

'It's Marcos. It must be a recording.'

We ran up the grand staircase and turned right into the ante-room. And there sat Marcos himself, with Imelda and the family all around him, and three or four generals to the right. They had chosen the ante-room rather than the main hall, for there were only a few journalists and cameramen, and yesterday's great array of military men was nowhere to be seen. I looked very closely at Marcos and thought: it isn't him. It looked like ectoplasm. Like the Mighty Mekon. It was talking in a precise and legalistic way, which contrived to sound both lucid and utterly nonsensical. It had its left hand under the table, and I watched the hand for a while to see whether it was being deliberately concealed. But it wasn't . . .

General Ver was quivering and in an evident panic. I wondered whether his gums had swollen. He stepped forward and asked for permission to bomb Camp Crame. There were two government F-5 jets circling over it, he said. (Just outside the palace someone had told me that the crowd at Camp Crame appeared to think that these jets were on their side, for they cheered every time the aircraft came over.) Marcos told Ver they were not to be used. Ver's panic increased.

'The Air Force, sir, is ready to attack were the civilians to leave the vicinity of Camp Crame immediately, Mr President. That's why I came here on your orders so we can immediately strike them. We have to immobilize the helicopters that they got.' (Marcos had sent helicopter gunships against the camp, but the pilots had come out waving white flags and joined the rebels.)

Marcos broke in with tired impatience, as if this had been going on all through the night and he was sick and tired of Ver. 'My order is not to attack. No, no, no. Hold on; not to attack.'

Ver was going wild. 'Our negotiations and our prior dialogue have not succeeded, Mr President.'

Marcos: 'All I can say is that we may have to reach the point we may have to employ heavy weapons, but you will use the small weapons in hand or shoulder weapons in the meantime.'

Ver said: 'Our attack forces are being delayed.'

The *Christian Science Monitor*, at my elbow, said: 'This is absurd. It's a Mutt-and-Jeff act.'

Ver said: 'There are many civilians near our troops, and we cannot keep on withdrawing. We cannot withdraw all the time, Mr President.'

All this was being broadcast live on Channel Four, which Marcos could see on a monitor. Ver finally saluted, stepped backwards and left with the other officers. I forget who they were, just as Marcos, when he introduced them to us, had forgotten all their names and needed prompting. Now the family withdrew as well.

An incident then occurred whose significance I didn't appreciate at the time. The television began to emit white noise. A soldier stepped forward and fiddled with the knobs. The other channels were working, but Channel Four had been knocked off the air. The rebels had taken the government station, which Marcos must have realized. But he hardly batted an eyelid. It was as if the incident were some trival disturbance, as if the television were simply on the blink . . .

I turned back and walked down the centre of the road to Malacañang, my feet crunching broken glass and stones. I asked a policeman whether he thought it safe to proceed. Yes, he said, there were a few Marcos men hiding in the side streets, but the fighting had all stopped. A child came running past me and called out, 'Hey Joe, what's the problem?' but didn't wait for an answer.

As I came within view of the palace I saw that people were climbing over the railings, and just as I caught up with them a gate flew open. Everyone was pouring in and making straight for the old Budget Office. It suddenly occurred to me that very few of them knew where the palace itself was. Documents were flying out of the office and the crowd was making whoopee. I began to run . . .

Bing was just behind me, looking seraphically happy, with his cameras bobbing round his neck. We pushed our way through to a kind of hall, where an armed civilian told us we could go no further. The journalists crowded round him, pleading to be allowed a look. The man had been sent by the rebel troops. He had given his word of honour, he said. He couldn't let anybody past. But it was all, I'm afraid, too exciting. One of the Filipino photographers just walked past the guard, then another followed, then Bing went past; and finally I was the only one left.

I thought: oh well, he hasn't shot them, he won't shoot me. I scuttled past him in that way people do when they expect to be kicked up the backside. 'Hey, man, stop,' said the guard, but as he followed me round the corner we both saw he had been standing in the wrong place: the people in the crowd had come round another way and were now going through boxes and packing-cases to see what they could find. There were no takers for the Evian water. But everything else was disappearing. I caught up with Bing, who was looking through the remains of a box of monogrammed towels. We realized they had Imelda's initials. There were a couple left. They were irresistible.

I couldn't believe I would be able to find the actual Marcos apartments, and I knew there was no point in asking. We went up some servants' stairs, at the foot of which I remember seeing an opened crate with two large green jade plates. They were so large as to be vulgar. On the first floor a door opened, and we found ourselves in the great hall where the press conferences had been held. This was the one bit of the palace the crowd would recognize, as it had so often watched Marcos being televised from here. People ran and sat on his throne and began giving mock press conferences, issuing orders in his deep voice, falling about with laughter or just gaping at the splendour of the room. It was all fully lit. Nobody had bothered, as they left, to turn out the lights.

I remembered that the first time I had been here, the day after the election, Imelda had slipped in and sat at the side. She must have come from that direction. I went to investigate.

And now, for a short while, I was away from the crowd with just one other person, a shy and absolutely thunderstruck Filipino. We had found our way, we realized, into the Marcoses' private rooms. There was a library, and my companion gazed in wonder at the leather-bound volumes while I admired the collection of art books all carefully catalogued and with their numbers on the spines. This was the reference library for Imelda's worldwide collection of treasures. She must have thumbed through them thinking: *I'd like one of them*, or *I've got a couple of them in New York*, or *That's in our London house*. And then there was the Blue Drawing Room with its twin portraits of the Marcoses, where I simply remember standing with my companion and saying, 'It's beautiful, isn't it.' It wasn't that it *was* beautiful. It looked as if it had been purchased at Harrods. It was just that, after all the crowds and riots, we had landed up in this peaceful, luxurious den. My companion had never seen anything like it. He didn't take anything. He hardly dared touch the furnishings and trinkets. We both simply could not believe that we were there and the Marcoses weren't.

I wish I could remember it all better. For instance, it seemed to me that in every room I saw, practically on every available surface, there was a signed photograph of Nancy Reagan. But this can hardly be literally true. It just felt as if there was a lot of Nancy in evidence.

Another of the rooms had a grand piano. I sat down.

'Can you play?' said my companion.

'A little,' I exaggerated. I can play Bach's Prelude in C, and this is what I proceeded to do, but my companion had obviously hoped for something more racy.

A soldier came in, carrying a rifle. 'Please co-operate,' he said. The soldier looked just as overawed by the place as we were. We co-operated.

When I returned down the service stairs, I noticed that the green jade plates were gone, but there was still some Evian water to be had. I was very thirsty, as it happened. But the revolution had asked me to co-operate. So I did.

Outside, the awe had communicated itself to several members of the crowd. They stood by the fountain looking down at the coloured lights beneath the water, not saying anything. I went to the parapet and looked across the river. I thought: somebody's still fighting; there are still some loyal troops. Then I thought: that's crazy – they can't have started fighting now. I realized that I was back in Saigon yet again. *There* indeed there had been fighting on the other side of the river. But here it was fireworks. The whole city was celebrating.

Sources

Ackerley, J. R., *My Sister and Myself: the Diaries of J. R. Ackerley*, Francis King (ed.), Hutchinson, 1982

Acosta, José de, *Natural and Moral History of the Indies*, 1590, trans. in *Purchas His Pilgrimes*, 1625

Agate, James, *The Selective Ego*, Tim Beaumont (ed.), Harrap, 1976

Anon. ('The Arrest of the Catholic Priest Edmund Campion and his Associates'), George Elliot, in Arber, *English Garner*, 1877

Anon. ('D-Day, 6 June 1944'), in Henning Krabbe (ed.), *Voices from Britain: Broadcast History 1939–45*, Allen & Unwin, 1947

Anon. ('Death of a Climbing Boy, 29 March 1813'), *Minutes of Evidence Taken Before the Parliamentary Committee on Employment of Boys in Sweeping of Chimnies*, 23 June 1817

Anon. ('The Execution of an Allied Intelligence Officer by the Japanese, New Guinea, 29 March 1943'), in Major-General Charles A. Willoughby and John Chamberlain, *MacArthur, 1941–1951: Victory in the Pacific*, McGraw-Hill, 1956

Anon. ('The Execution of Archbishop Cranmer'), in Strype, *Memorials of Archbishop Cranmer*, 1854

Anon. ('The Germans Meet a New Foe, 7 June 1944'), in Milton Shulman, *Defeat in the West*, Secker & Warburg, 1947

Anon. ('The Indian Mutiny: Scene of the Massacre of British Women and Children at Cawnpore, 21 July 1857'), *Annual Register*, 1857

Anon. ('The Sinking of the *Tanjong Penang*, 19 February 1942'), in Ian Hay, *A Hundred Years of Army Nursing*, Cassell, 1953

Arbuthnot, Mrs, *The Journal of Mrs Arbuthnot*, Francis Bamford and the Duke of Wellington (eds.), Macmillan, 1950

Armstrong, Neil, and Edwin E. Aldrin, *First on the Moon: A Voyage with Neil Armstrong, Michael Collins, Edwin E. Aldrin Jr.*, written with Gene Farmer and Dora Jane Hamblin, Michael Joseph, 1970

Atwell, Lester, *Private*, New York, Matson, 1958

Austin, John Charles, *Return Via Dunkirk, By 'Gun Buster'*, Hodder and Stoughton, 1940

Badcock, Midshipman, in E. Fraser, *Sailors Whom Nelson Led*, 1913

Baker, Geoffrey le, *Chronicle*, trans. Edith Rickert, in Rickert (comp.), Clair C. Olson and Martin M. Crow (eds.), *Chaucer's World*, Oxford University Press, 1948

688

Balfour, Patrick, *Grand Tour*, London, John Long, 1934

Bamford, Samuel, *Passages in the Life of a Radical*, H. Dunckley (ed.), 1893

Bayerlein, General, ('American Break-Out in Normandy, 24–25 July 1944'), in B. H. Liddell Hart (ed.), *The Rommel Papers*, Collins, 1953

Bayerlein, General, ('El Alamein: The End of the Africa Corps, 4 November 1942'), in W. Richardson and S. Freidin (eds.), C. Fitzgibbon (trans.), *The Fatal Decisions*, Michael Joseph, 1956

Beatty, Dr William, *Despatches and Letters of Nelson*, Nicolas (ed.), 1845

Behâ-ed-Din, from T. A. Archer (sel. and arr.), *The Crusade of Richard I, 1189–92*, 1888

Bendel, Dr Charles Sigismund, in Raymond Phillips (ed.), *The Trial of Joseph Kramer*, Hodge, 1949

Bennett, Arnold, *Journals*, Newman Flower (ed.), Cassell, 1932

Bentley, Elizabeth, in *Report of Parliamentary Committee on the Bill to Regulate the Labour of Children in Mills and Factories*, 1832

Bion, John, *An Account of the Torments the French Protestants Endure Aboard the Galleys*, 1708

Bishop, Mrs D. H., *New York Times*, 19 April 1912

Blaha, Dr Franz, in *Trial of the Major German War Criminals, Proceedings of the International Military Tribunal at Nuremberg*, HMSO, 1946

Blakeney, Robert, *A Boy in the Peninsular War*, Julian Sturgis (ed.), 1899

Blériot, Louis, in Leslie Bailey, *Scrapbook 1900–1914*, Frederick Muller, 1957

Boswell, James, *Life of Johnson*, third edition, 1799

Bradford, William, *A Relation of the English Plantation at Plymouth*, 1622

Bramwell, James G., in James Byron, *The Unfinished Man*, Chatto & Windus, 1957

Bride, Harold, *New York Times*, 19 April 1912

Brittain, Vera, *Testament of Youth*, Gollancz, 1933

Brontë, Charlotte, in Clement Shorter, *The Brontës' Life and Letters*, 1907

Brown, Cecil, *Suez to Singapore*, New York, Random House, 1942

Brown, Lieutenant George, in E. Fraser, *Sailors Whom Nelson Led*, 1913

Bruce, James, *Travels to Discover the Sources of the Nile*, 1790

Buchan, Anna, *Olivia in India*, Hodder & Stoughton, 1913

Burney, Fanny, *Selected Letters and Journals*, Joyce Hemlow (ed.), Oxford University Press, 1986

Burritt, Elihu, *A Journal of a Visit to Skibbereen and its Neighbourhood*, 1847

Caesar, Julius, *Gallic War*, from Caesar, *The Conquest of Gaul*, trans. S. A. Handford, Penguin, 1951

Calendar of Coroner's Rolls, quoted in Edith Rickert (comp.), Clair C. Olson and Martin M. Crow (eds.), *Chaucer's World*, Oxford University Press, 1948

Cameron, James, *What a Way to Run the Tribe*, Macmillan, 1968

Carleton, Sir Dudley, in H. Ellis, *Original Letters*, 1824–46

Case, Adelaide, *Day by Day at Lucknow*, 1858

Cellini, Benvenuto, *Life*, trans. J. Aldington Symons, 1887

Chaney, Bert, in Michael Moynihan (ed.), *People at War 1914–1918*, David & Charles, 1973

Chateaubriand, François-René de, *Memoirs*, trans. Robert Baldick, London, Hamish Hamilton, 1961

Churchill, Winston, *My Early Life*, Heinemann, 1930

City of London Letter-books, from H. T. Riley (sel. and trans.), *Memorials of London Life AD 1276–1419*, 1868

Cleveland Herald, in J. Cutler Andrews, *The North Reports the Civil War*, 1955

Coleridge, Samuel Taylor, *Letters*, E. L. Griggs (ed.), Oxford University Press, 1956–71

Colonie, M. de la, *The Chronicles of an Old Campaigner*, trans. W. C. Horsley, 1904

Considine, Bob, International News Service, 22 June 1938

Coryate, Thomas, *Observations on Constantinople*, 1625

Cotton, Sergeant-Major Edward, *A Voice from Waterloo*, 1847

Cox, Geoffrey, *The Road to Trieste*, Heinemann, 1947

Crabbe, George, in *The Life of George Crabbe by his Son*, 1834

Crane, Stephen, 'War Memories', in *The Anglo-Saxon Review*, December 1898

Creelman, James, *On the Great Highway*, 1901

Cromwell, Oliver, in Carlyle, *Cromwell's Letters and Speeches*, 1845

Cutforth, René, *Korean Reporter*, Allan Wingate, 1952

Darwin, Charles, *Journal of the Voyage of HMS Beagle*, 1839

Davies, W. H., *The Autobiography of a Supertramp*, A. C. Fifield, 1908

Davis, Richard Harding, ('The Graeco-Turkish War: The Siege of Prevesa, 18 April 1897') *A Year from a Correspondent's Notebook*, 1898

Davis, Richard Harding, ('The German Army Marches through Brussels, 21 August 1914') *News Chronicle*, 23 August 1914

Delmer, D. Sefton, *Daily Express*, 28 February 1933

Denbigh, Cissy, Countess of, in Winefride Elwes, *The Feilding Album*, Geoffrey Bles, 1950

Dickens, Charles, *Pictures from Italy*, 1846

Douglas, Keith, *Alamein to Zem Zem*, Desmond Graham (ed.), Oxford University Press, 1979

Dumas, Alexandre, *Adventures in the Caucasus*, trans. A. E. Murch, Peter Owen, 1962

Eber, Nandor, *The Times*, London, June 1860

Edgeworth de Firmont, Henry Essex, in J. M. Thompson, *English Witnesses of the French Revolution*, Blackwell, 1938

Eldred, John, in Arber, *English Garner*, 1877

Ellis, Lieutenant, in E. Fraser, *Sailors Whom Nelson Led*, 1913

Evelyn, John, *Diary*, E. S. de Beer (ed.), Oxford University Press, 1959

Fadeyev, Aleksandr A., *Leningrad in the Days of the Blockade*, trans. R. D. Charques, Hutchinson, 1946

Fadlan, Ibn, from A. S. Cook, 'Ibn Fadlan's Account of Scandinavian Merchants on the Volga in 922', *Journal of English and Germanic Philology*, 1923

Faviell, Frances, *A Chelsea Concerto*, Cassell, 1959

Fenton, James, 'The Snap Revolution', *Granta 18*, Granta Publications/ Penguin Books, 1986

Ferguson, W. H., *Mr Cricket: The Autobiography of W. H. Ferguson*, as told to David R. Jack, Nicholas Kaye, 1957

Fielding, Henry, *Journal of a Voyage to Lisbon*, 1755

Fioravanti, Cristoforo, trans. in *Purchas His Pilgrimes*, 1625

Fisk, Robert, *The Times*, 20 September 1982

Flaubert, Gustave, *Flaubert in Egypt*, trans. Francis Steegmuller, The Bodley Head, 1972

Fleetwood, William, in H. Ellis, *Original Letters*, 1824–46

Fletcher, Giles, *Of the Russe Commonwealth*, 1591

Flower, Desmond, ('The Bombing of Caen, 7 July 1944': 'Lüneburg, 20 April 1945'), *History of the Argyll and Sutherland Highlanders, 1939–1945*, Nelson, 1950

Flower, Desmond, ('London Docks Bombed, 7 September 1940'), in Desmond Flower and James Reeves (eds.), *The War 1939–1945*, Cassell, 1960

Forbes, Archibald, ('The Suppression of the Paris Commune, 23–24 May 1871'), *Daily News*, 26 May 1871

Forbes, Archibald, ('The Paris Commune: The Finale, 29 May 1871'), *Memorials of War and Peace*, 1894

Fox, George, *Journal*, Norman Penney (ed.), Cambridge University Press, 1924

Francis, Ernest, in Michael Moynihan (ed.), *People at War 1914–1918*, David & Charles, 1973

Freyer, Margaret, in Alexander McKee, *Dresden, 1945: The Devil's Tinderbox*, Granada, 1982

Froissart, Sir John, *Chronicles of England, France and Spain*, trans. Lord Berners, 1523–5

Fry, Elizabeth, *Memoirs of the Life of Elizabeth Fry Edited by her Two Daughters*, 1847

Fuchida, Mitsuo, *Midway: The Battle that Doomed Japan*, with Masataka Okumiya, Hutchinson, 1957

Fuhrmann, Claus, in Louis Hagen, *Follow My Leader*, Allan Wingate, 1951

Gapon, Father, *The Story of My Life*, 1905

Garcia, John, in Studs Terkel, *The Good War: An Oral History of World War II*, Hamish Hamilton, 1985

Gardner, James Anthony, *Recollections*, Sir R. Vesey (ed.), 1906

Gascoigne, George, *The Spoyle of Antwerpe*, 1576

Gauguin, Paul, *Noa Noa: Voyage to Tahiti*, trans. Jonathan Griffin, Bruno Cassirer, 1961

Gerard, John, *The Autobiography of an Elizabethan*, trans. Philip Caraman, Longmans, 1951

Gibbs, Philip, ('The Siege of Sidney Street, 3 January 1911'), *Adventures in Journalism*, Heinemann, 1923

Gibbs, Philip, ('Famine in Russia, October 1921'), *The Pageant of the Years*, Heinemann, 1946

Gordon-Walker, Patrick, broadcast to the USA, 1945

Graebe, Hermann, in *The Trial of German Major War Criminals*, HMSO, 1949

Graves, Robert, *Goodbye to All That*, Cassell, 1929

Gray, Thomas, *Correspondence*, Toynbee and Whibley (eds.), Oxford University Press, 1935

Greenhalgh, John, in H. Ellis, *Original Letters*, 1824–46

Greville, Charles, *Leaves from the Greville Diary*, Philip Morrell (ed.), 1929

Grim, Edward, from W. H. Hutton (ed.), *St Thomas of Canterbury 1118–1220*, 1889

Hannington, Wal, *Unemployed Struggles, 1919–1936*, Lawrence & Wishart, 1977

Harris, Rifleman, from Sir John Kincaid, *Recollections of Rifleman Harris* in *Adventures in the Rifle Brigade*, 1830

Harvey, Dr Elwood, in Harriet Beecher Stowe, *A Key to Uncle Tom's Cabin*, 1853

Havelock, General, *Annual Register*, 1857

Haydon, B. R., *Autobiography and Journals*, 1847

Hemingway, Ernest, in William White (ed.), *By-Line: Ernest Hemingway*, Collins, 1967

Herodian, *Histories*, trans. in B. K. Workman, *They Saw It Happen in Classical Times*, Blackwell, 1964

Hervey, Lord, *Memoirs of the Reign of King George II*, Romney Sedgwick (ed.), William Kimber, 1952

Hillary, Richard, *The Last Enemy*, Macmillan, 1942

Hislop, John, *Observer*, 30 March 1947

Holwell, J. Z., in *Annual Register*, 1758

Hoste, William, *Memoirs and Letters*, 1833

Howe, Samuel Gridley, Letter to Charles Sumner, in Harriet Beecher Stowe, *A Key to Uncle Tom's Cabin*, 1853

Hudson, W. H., *Afoot in England*, 1909

Hugo, Victor, *The History of a Crime*, trans. T. H. Joyce and Arthur Locker, 1886

Hurault, André, Sieur de Maisse, *Journal of an Embassy from Henry IV to Queen Elizabeth, 1597*, trans. G. B. Harrison and R. A. Jones, Nonesuch Press, 1931

Ingilby, Lieutenant W. B., in H. T. Siborne (ed.), *Waterloo Letters*, 1891

Jevtic, Borijove, *New York World*, 29 June 1924

Josephus, *The Jewish Wars*, in *Works*, Loeb Classical Library, 1926–81

Junod, Marcel, *Warrior Without Weapons*, Cape, 1951

Kampov, Major, in Alexander Werth, *Russia at War*, Barry and Rockcliff, 1964

Kay-Shuttleworth, James, in Frank Smith, *The Life and Work of Sir James Kay-Shuttleworth*, 1923

Keith, Agnes Newton, *Three Came Home*, Michael Joseph, 1955

Kemble, Frances Ann, *Some Recollections of a Girlhood*, 1878

Kendall, Captain H. G., in Leslie Bailey, *Scrapbook 1900–1914*, Frederick Muller, 1957

Kincaid, Captain J., *Adventures in the Rifle Brigade*, 1830

King, Lionel, in Michael Moynihan (ed.), *People at War*, David and Charles, 1974

King-Wilson, Norman, in Michael Moynihan (ed.), *People at War 1914–1918*, David & Charles, 1973

Knighton, Henry, *Chronicles*, trans. Edith Rickert, in Rickert (comp.), Clair C. Olson and Martin M. Crow (eds.), *Chaucer's World*, Oxford University Press, 1948

Kokoschka, Oskar, *My Life*, trans. David Britt, Thames and Hudson, 1974

Konovaloff, Colonel, in G. L. Steer, *Caesar in Abyssinia*, Hodder and Stoughton, 1936

Kurnakov, Sergyei N., *Savage Squadrons*, Boston, Hale, Cushman and Flint, 1935

Las Casas, Bartolomé de, *Brief Report on the Destruction of the Indians, 1542*, trans. in *Purchas His Pilgrimes*, 1625

Laurence, William T., *New York Times*, 9 September 1945

Lawrence, D. H., *Twilight in Italy*, Heinemann, 1916

Lawrence, T. E., *Revolt in the Desert*, 1927

Leo, John, *A Geographical Historie of Africa*, 1600

Lewis, Norman, *The Changing Sky*, Cape, 1959 (under new title *A View of the World*, Eland, 1986)

Lichtenberg, Georg Christoph, *Lichtenberg's Visits to England as Described in his Diaries*, M. L. Mare and W. H. Quarrell (trans.), 1938

Linschoten, John Huyghen Van, *Discourse of Voyages into the East and West Indies*, 1598

Litwinska, Sophia, in Raymond Phillips (ed.), *The Trial of Joseph Kramer*, Hodge, 1949

London, Jack, *Collier's Weekly*, 5 May 1906

London, John, Roger Townshend, Richard Layton and Geoffrey Chamber, in H. Ellis, *Original Letters*, 1824–46

Lunardi, Vincent, *An Account of the First Aerial Voyage in England*, 1784

Luxemburg, Rosa, *Letters from Prison*, trans. Eden and Cedar Paul, Allen & Unwin 1921

Lytton, Constance, *Prisons and Prisoners*, 1914

Macoll, R. M., *Daily Express*, 11 February 1958

MacDonagh, Michael, *In London During the Great War*, Eyre and Spottiswoode, 1935

MacGahan, J. A., *The Turkish Atrocities in Bulgaria*, 1876

Majdalany, Fred, *The Monastery*, The Bodley Head, 1945

Mandelstam, Nadezhda, *Hope Against Hope*, trans. Max Hayward, Collins and Harvill Press, 1971

Marchant, Hilde, *Women and Children Last*, Gollancz, 1941

Marconi, Guglielmo, in Leslie Bailey, *Scrapbook 1900–1914*, Frederick Muller, 1957

Martin, Kingsley, *Critic's London Diary, From the New Statesman, 1931–1956*, Secker and Warburg, 1960

Matthews, Herbert, *Eyewitness in Abyssinia*, Secker and Warburg, 1937

Mayhew, Henry, *London Labour and the London Poor*, 1851

Medvedev, Pavel, in Robert Wilton, *The Last Days of the Romanovs*, 1920

Méneval, Baron Claude François de, *Memoirs to Serve for the History of Napoleon I*, trans. R. H. Sherard, 1894

Mercer, Field Captain A. C., in H. T. Siborne (ed.), *Waterloo Letters*, 1891

Meryon, Charles Lewis, *Travels of Lady Hester Stanhope*, 1846

Miller, John, *Saints and Parachutes*, Constable, 1951

Miller, Webb, *I Found No Peace*, Victor Gollancz, 1937

Millingen, J. G., in J. M. Thompson, *English Witnesses of the French Revolution*, Oxford, Blackwell, 1938

Monks, Noel, *Eyewitness*, Frederick Muller, 1955

Montagu, Lady Mary Wortley, *Letters*, Robert Halsband (ed.), Oxford University Press, 1965

Moorehead, Alan, *African Trilogy*, Hamish Hamilton, 1944

Moritz, Carl Philipp, *Travels in England in 1782*, P. E. Matheson (ed.), 1924

Morris, James, *The Times*, 8 June 1953

Morrison, Ian, *Malayan Postscript*, London, Faber, 1942

Moryson, Fynes, *Itinerary*, 1617

Moynihan, Michael, in Moynihan (ed.), *People at War*, David & Charles, 1974

Mucha, George, in Henning Krabbe (ed.), *Voices from Britain: Broadcast History 1939–45*, Allen and Unwin, 1947

Munro, H. H. ('Saki'), *The Square Egg*, 1924

Munro, Ross, *Gauntlet to Overlord*, Canada, Macmillan, 1945

Napier, Sir Charles, in W. F. Butler, *Sir Charles Napier*, 1890

Neilly, J. E., *Besieged with Baden-Powell*, 1900

Nichol, John, in E. Fraser, *Sailors Whom Nelson Led*, 1913

Nichols, George, *The Story of the Great March*, 1865

Nicolson, Harold, *Peacemaking 1919*, Constable, 1933

Norris, Norman, in Michael Moynihan (ed.), *People at War*, David & Charles, 1974

Orwell, George, *Homage to Catalonia*, Secker & Warburg, Harcourt Brace Jovanovich Inc., 1937

Pepys, Samuel, *Diary*, Robert Latham and William Matthews (eds.), vol. VII, G. Bell & Sons, 1970–83

Perry, Commodore Matthew C., *The Japan Expedition 1852–1854: The Personal Journal of Commodore Matthew C. Perry*, Roger Pineau (ed.), Washington, Smithsonian Institution Press, 1968

Phillips, Miles, in Hakluyt, *Voyages*, 1589

Pilger, John, *The Last Day*, London, Syndication International, 1975

Plato, *Phaedo*, trans. H. N. Fowler, Loeb, 1914

Pliny the Younger, *Letters*, trans. Betty Radice, Penguin Classics, 1963, 1969

Polo, Marco, *The Travels of Marco Polo*, trans. Ronald Latham, Penguin, 1958

Powell, Captain H. W., in H. T. Siborne, *Waterloo Letters*, 1891

Pressey, William, in Michael Moynihan (ed.), *People at War 1914–1918*, David & Charles, 1973

Priscus, in Dindorf (ed.), *Historici Graeci Minores*, trans. B. K. Workman, in *They Saw It Happen in Classical Times*, Oxford, Blackwell, 1964

Reed, John, *Ten Days That Shook the World*, Lawrence & Wishart, 1926

Ridgway, General Matthew B., *Soldier*, Harper and Bros, 1956

Roe, Sir Thomas, *Journal*, in *Purchas His Pilgrimes*, 1625

Rogers, Woodes, *A Cruising Voyage Round the World*, 1712

Rommel, Erwin, in B. H. Liddell Hart (ed.), *The Rommel Papers*, Collins, 1953

Romulo, Carlos P., *I Saw the Fall of the Philippines*, Harrap, 1943

Russell, William Howard, *The Times*, London, 14 November 1854

Sala, George Augustus, *Daily Telegraph*, London, 12 September 1859

Sanderson, John, *Personal Voyages*, in *Purchas His Pilgrimes*, 1625

Saussure, César de, *A Foreign View of England*, trans. Madame Van Muyden, 1902

Schnirdel, Hulderike, trans. in *Purchas His Pilgrimes*, 1625

Scot, Edmund, *A Discourse on Java*, 1606

Scott, Captain, in L. Huxley, *Scott's Last Expedition*, 1913

Senior, Harry, *New York Times*, 19 April 1912

Shaw, George Bernard, *Collected Letters, 1911–1925*, vol. III, Dan H.

Lawrence (ed.), Max Reinhardt, 1985
Shelvocke, George, A Voyage Round the World, 1726
Sherrod, Robert, Tarawa: Story of a Battle, Duell, Sloan & Pearce, 1944
Sitwell, Osbert, Great Morning, Macmillan, 1948
Smith, Elias, New York Tribune, March 1865
Smith, Kingsbury, in Clark Kinnaird (ed.), It Happened in 1946, 1947
Spears, Brigadier General E. L., Liaison 1914, London, Heinemann, 1930
Spiegel, Adolf K. G. E. von, U-Boat 202, trans. Barry Domvile, 1919
Stanley, H. M., New York Herald, 10 August 1872
Steer, G. L., The Tree of Gernika, Hodder and Stoughton, 1938
Steevens, George W., Daily Mail, London, 29 April 1898
Steinbeck, John, A Russian Journal, Heinemann, 1949
Stevenson, Robert Louis, Across the Plains, 1883
Stewart, Colonel William, Despatches and Letters of Nelson, Nicolas (ed.), 1845
Stukeley, William, Itinerarium Curiosum, 1776
Tacitus, The Annals of Imperial Rome, trans. Michael Grant, Penguin, 1956, 1959, 1971
Taine, Hippolyte, Notes on England, trans. N. F. Rae, 1872
Tavernier, Jean-Baptiste, Travels in India, V. Ball (trans. and ed.), 1889
Terry, Edward, A Voyage to East India, 1655
Thesiger, Wilfred, Arabian Sands, Longmans, 1959
Thompson, Leonard, in Ronald Blythe, Akenfield, 1969
Thompson, Reginald, Cry Korea, London, MacDonald, 1951
Thucydides, History, trans. C. F. Smith, Loeb, 1919
Time Magazine, 5 December 1969
Trelawny, Edward John, The Last Days of Shelley and Byron, 1858
Tristan, Flora, The London Journal of Flora Tristan, trans. Jean Hawkes, Virago, 1982
Twain, Mark, The Innocents Abroad, 1869
Twiss, Richard, A Trip to Paris, 1792
Uffenbach, Zacharias Conrad Von, Travels, W. H. Quarrell and Margaret Mare (trans. and ed.), Faber, 1934
Valbourg, Misson de, Mr Misson's Memoirs & Observations in England, trans. J. Ozell, 1719
Van der Heydte, Baron, Daedalus Returned, trans. W. S. Moss, Hutchinson, 1958
Vaughan, Edwin Campion, Some Desperate Glory, Frederick Warne, 1981
Veer, Gerrit de, The Three Voyages of Barents, 1598
Vega, Garcilaso de la, History of Peru, trans. in Purchas His Pilgrimes, 1625
Vespucci, Amerigo, from J. Pohl, Amerigo Vespucci: Pilot Major, Columbia University Press, 1944
Victoria, Queen, Journal of our Life in the Highlands, Smith, Elder & Co., 1868

Wales, Henry G., International News Service, 19 October 1917

Walker, Reverend John M. S., in Michael Moynihan (ed.), *People at War 1914–1918*, David & Charles, 1973

Walker, Richard, in George Anson, *A Voyage Round the World in the Years 1740–44*, 1748

Walpole, Horace, *Correspondence*, Oxford University Press, W. S. Lewis (ed.), 1937–83

Walpole, Hugh, in Rupert Hart-Davis, *Hugh Walpole: A Biography*, Macmillan, 1952

Wavrin, Jehan de, *Chronicles, 1399–1422*, trans. Sir W. Hardy and E. Hardy, 1887

Wendel, Else, *Hausfrau at War*, Odhams Press, 1947

Werth, Alexander, ('The Russian Summer Offensive, July 1944'), in Henning Krabbe (ed.), *Voices from Britain: Broadcast History 1939–45*, Allen & Unwin, 1947

Werth, Alexander, ('Stalingrad: A War Correspondent Goes in after the German Capitulation, 4 February 1943': 'The Nazi Extermination Camp, Maidanek, 23 July 1944'), *Russia at War*, Barry and Rockcliff, 1964

Wesley, John, *Journal*, Everyman's Library, 1906

Whitbourne, Richard, *Discourse and Discovery of Newfoundland*, 1622

Whitman, Walt, *Memoranda During the War*, 1875

Wilkinson, Samuel, *New York Times*, 6 July 1863

William of Newburgh, from J. Stevenson (ed.), *Church Historians of England*, 1856

Winchester, Lieutenant R., in H. T. Siborne (ed.), *Waterloo Letters*, 1891

Woodforde, James, *Diary of a Country Parson*, John Beresford (ed.), Oxford University Press, 1924

Wordsworth, Dorothy, *Journals*, Mary Moorman (ed.), Oxford University Press, 1958

Wynkfielde, Robert, in H. Ellis, *Original Letters*, 1824–46

Xenophon, *The Persian Expedition*, trans. Rex Warner, Penguin Classics, 1949

Young, Arthur, in J. M. Thompson, *English Witnesses of the French Revolution*, Oxford, Blackwell, 1938

Young, Gavin, *Slow Boats to China*, Hutchinson, 1981

Zieser, Benno, *In Their Shallow Graves*, trans. Alec Brown, Elek Books, 1956

Acknowledgements

Thanks are due to the following for permission to reprint extracts from the titles listed:

Academy Chicago Press for *Flaubert in Egypt*, trans. Francis Steegmuller (1979); Basil Blackwell Ltd for *Histories* by Herodian, trans. B. K. Workman in *They Saw It Happen in Classical Times* (1964), *Historici Graeci Minores* by Priscus, ed. Dindorf, trans. B. K. Workman as above (1964), *English Witnesses of the French Revolution* by J. M. Thompson (1938); Jonathan Cape Ltd for *Warrior Without Weapons* by Marcel Junod, trans. Edward Fitzgerald (1951); Bruno Cassirer Ltd for *Noa Noa: Voyage to Tahiti* by Paul Gauguin, trans. Jonathan Griffin (1961); Collins Publishers and Scribners (USA) for *By-Line: Ernest Hemingway*, ed. William White (1967); Collins Publishers and Atheneum Publishers (USA) for *Hope Against Hope* by Nadezhda Mandelstam, trans. Max Hayward (1971); Collins Publishers and Harcourt Brace Jovanovich Inc. (USA) for *The Rommel Papers*, © 1953 by B. H. Liddell Hart, renewed 1981 by Lady Kathleen Liddell Hart, Fritz Beyerlein-Dittmar and Manfred Rommel; Columbia University Press for *Chaucer's World*, trans. Edith Rickert (1948); Constable & Co. Ltd for *Saints and Parachutes* by John Miller (1951); Curtis Brown Ltd for *My Early Life* by Winston S. Churchill, © the Estate of Sir Winston Churchill (1930); Mrs Sheila Cutforth for *Korean Reporter* by Rene Cutforth (Allan Wingate, 1952); David & Charles Ltd for *People at War 1914–1918*, ed. Michael Moynihan (1973); Eland Books for *A View of the World* (formerly *The Changing Sky*) by Norman Lewis (1986); Faber & Faber Ltd for *Malayan Postscript* by Ian Morrison (1942); the excerpt from *Testament of Youth* by Vera Brittain is included with the permission of her literary executors and Victor Gollancz Ltd; Hamish Hamilton Ltd for *Chateaubriand's Memoirs* trans. Robert Baldick; Harrap Ltd and A. D. Peters (USA) for *The Selective Ego* by James Agate, ed. Tim Beaumont (1976); Harrap Ltd and Harold Matson Company Inc. for *I Saw the Fall of the Philippines* by Carlos P. Romulo (1943); A. M. Heath & Co. Ltd for *The Monastery* by Fred Majdalany, © the Estate of Fred Majdalany (1945); Sir Rupert Hart-Davis for *Hugh Walpole: A Biography* by Rupert Hart-Davis (1952); William Heinemann Ltd and Viking Penguin Inc. (USA) for *A Russian Journal* by John Steinbeck (1949); David Higham Associates Ltd for *Akenfield* by Ronald

Blythe (1969), *The Unfinished Man* by James Byron (1957), *The Road To Trieste* by Geoffrey Cox (1947), *Great Morning* by Osbert Sitwell (1948), *Return Via Dunkirk* by John Austin (1940); Mrs W. J. Kenyon-Jones and Hodder & Stoughton (USA) for *Caesar in Abyssinia* by G. L. Steer (1936); Mrs W. J. Kenyon-Jones for *The Tree of Gernika* by G. L. Steer (1938); Lawrence & Wishart Ltd for *Unemployed Struggles, 1919–1936* by Wal Hannington (1977); London Express News and Feature Services for 'Stoning to Death, Jeddah 1958' by R. M. Macoll, *Daily Express* 11 February 1958, 'The Reichstag Fire' by D. Sefton Delmer, *Daily Express* 28 February 1933; Macdonald & Co. Ltd for *Cry Korea* by Reginald Thompson (1951); Frances McElwaine for *The Pageant of the Years* by Philip Gibbs (1946); McGraw-Hill Book Company for *MacArthur, 1941– 1951: Victory in the Pacific* by Willoughby & Chamberlain (1956); Macmillan & Co. Ltd for *The Last Enemy* by Richard Hillary (1942), *The Journal of Mrs Arbuthnot*, ed. Bamford & the Duke of Wellington (1950), *What a Way to Run the Tribe* by James Cameron (1968); Macmillan Publishing Co. Inc., New York for *Journals* by Arnold Bennett, ed. Newman Flower, *The War 1939–45*, ed. Desmond Flower and James Reeves (1960), *A Chelsea Concerto* by Frances Faviell (1959), *A Hundred Years of Army Nursing* by Ian Hay (1953); Harold Matson Company Inc. for *Private* by Lester Atwell (1958); Muller Blond & White Ltd for *Scrapbook 1900–1914* by Leslie Bailey (1957), *Eyewitness* by Noel Monks (1955); Thomas Nelson & Sons Ltd for *History of the Argyll and Sutherland Highlanders 1939–1945* by Desmond Flower (1950); *The New York Times* for 'Eyewitness account of dropping of A- Bomb on Nagasaki, 9 September 1945' by William L. Laurence; Nigel Nicolson for *Peacemaking 1919* by Harold Nicolson (1933); *The Observer* for 'Grand National' 30 March 1947 by John Hislop; The Estate of the late Sonia Brownell Orwell, Martin Secker & Warburg Ltd and Harcourt Brace Jovanovich Inc. for *Homage to Catalonia* by George Orwell (1937); Peter Owen Ltd for *Adventures in the Caucasus* by Alexandre Dumas, trans. A. E. Murch (1962); Oxford University Press for *Diary* by John Evelyn, ed. E. S. de Beer (1959), *Letters* by Lady Mary Wortley Montagu, ed. Robert Halsband (1965), *Journals* by Dorothy Wordsworth, ed. Mary Moorman (1958), *Fanny Burney: Selected Letters and Journals*, ed. Joyce Hemlow, *Alamein to Zem Zem* by Keith Douglas, ed. Desmond Graham (1979) © Marie J. Douglas 1966, 1979; Penguin Books Ltd for *The Persian Expedition* by Xenophon, trans. Rex Warner (1949) © Rex Warner, *The Conquest of Gaul* by Caesar, ed. S. A. Handford (Penguin Classics, 1951) © S. A. Handford, *The Annals of Imperial Rome* by Tacitus, trans. Michael Grant (Penguin Classics, 1956, 1959, 1971) © Michael Grant Publications Ltd, *The Jewish Wars* by Josephus, trans. G. A. Williamson (Penguin Classics, 1959, 1969), © G. A. Williamson, *The Letters of the Younger Pliny*, trans. Betty Radice (Penguin Classics, 1963, 1969) © Betty Radice, *The Travels*

Index of Names